BARRON'S

THE TRUSTED NAME IN TEST PREP

# Digital SAT® Study Guide Premium

## 2024

Brian W. Stewart, M.Ed.



*Committed to Educate the Nation*

NEW AGE

*Publishing Globally*

IN INDIA

NEW AGE INTERNATIONAL (P) LIMITED, PUBLISHERS

Bangalore • Chennai • Cochin • Guwahati • Hyderabad • Kolkata • Mumbai

Visit us at www.newagepublishers.com

## Dedication

Dedicated to Caitlin, Andrew, and Eloise—without your love and support, this book would not have been possible. I would like to thank my mom, my dad, Andy, Pam, Leah, Tiffany, Thapasvi, Sarah, and Bella. A special thank you to Michal Strawn for her invaluable help. I am grateful to all the support from my publisher, especially Jennifer Goodenough and Angela Tartaro.

Thanks so much to all of my students over the years—I have learned far more from you than you have learned from me.

**BARRON'S Digital SAT® Study Guide Premium** by Brian W. Stewart, M.Ed.

**Published by Kaplan** North America, LLC, d/b/a Barron's Educational Series
1515 W Cypress Creek Road
Fort Lauderdale, Florida 33309, USA

Originally Published in the ***United States of America.***



Indian Sub-Continent Edition: 2024 by **NEW AGE International (P) Ltd., Publishers**

This special low-priced edition is for sale in **TERRITORY: (SAARC) South Asian Association for Regional Cooperation (Afghanistan, Bangladesh, Bhutan, India, Maldives, Nepal, Pakistan** and **Sri Lanka**) only.



**BRANCHES**

- **Bangalore** 37/10, 8th Cross (Near Hanuman Temple), Azad Nagar, Chamarajpet, Bangalore- 560 018
  **Tel.:** (080) 26756823, **Mob.:** 9315905288, **E-mail: bangalore@newagepublishers.com**
- **Chennai** 26, Damodaran Street, T. Nagar, Chennai-600 017, **Tel.:** (044) 24353401, **Mob.:** 9315905309
  **E-mail: chennai@newagepublishers.com**
- **Cochin** CC-39/1016, Carrier Station Road, Ernakulam South, Cochin-682 016
  **Tel.:** (0484) 4051304, **Mob.:** 9315905289, **E-mail: cochin@newagepublishers.com**
- **Guwahati** Hemsen Complex, Mohd. Shah Road, Paltan Bazar, Near Starline Hotel
  Guwahati-781 008, **Tel.:** (0361) 2513881, **Mob.:** 9315905296, **E-mail: guwahati@newagepublishers.com**
- **Hyderabad** 105, 1st Floor, Madhiray Kaveri Tower, 3-2-19, Azam Jahi Road, Near Kumar Theater
  Nimboliadda Kachiguda, Hyderabad-500 027, **Tel.:** (040) 24652456, **Mob.:** 9315905326
  **E-mail: hyderabad@newagepublishers.com**
- **Kolkata** RDB Chambers (Formerly Lotus Cinema) 106A, 1st Floor, S N Banerjee Road
  Kolkata-700 014, **Tel.:** (033) 22273773, **Mob.:** 9315905319, **E-mail: kolkata@newagepublishers.com**
- **Mumbai** 142C, Victor House, Ground Floor, N.M. Joshi Marg, Lower Parel, Mumbai-400 013
  **Tel.:** (022) 24927869, 24915415, **Mob.:** 9315905282, **E-mail: mumbai@newagepublishers.com**
- **New Delhi** 22, Golden House, Daryaganj, New Delhi-110 002, **Tel.:** (011) 23262368, 23262370
  **Mob.:** 9315905300, **E-mail: sales@newagepublishers.com**

**C-23-10-13834**

Printed in India at Goyal Offset Works (P) Ltd., Sonipat, Haryana.

**NEW AGE INTERNATIONAL (P) LIMITED, PUBLISHERS**
7/30 A, Daryaganj, New Delhi - 110002
Visit us at **www.newagepublishers.com**
**(CIN: U74899DL1966PTC004618)**

# About the Author

Brian W. Stewart is the founder and president of BWS Education Consulting, Inc., a boutique tutoring and test preparation company based in Columbus, Ohio. Brian is a nationally recognized test preparation expert, having over 30,000 hours of direct instructional experience with a wide variety of learners from all over the world. He has achieved a perfect score on the SAT, helped hundreds of students reach their college admissions goals, and presented on best tutoring practices at national conferences.

Brian has used his experience and expertise to write several best-selling books with Barron's, including *Barron's ACT* and *Barron's Digital PSAT/NMSQT*. He is a former high school teacher and graduate of Princeton University (A.B.) and The Ohio State University (M.Ed.).

Brian resides in Columbus with his wife, two children, and an assortment of pets.

To learn more about Brian's online tutoring and group presentations, please visit www.bwseducationconsulting.com.

BWS EDUCATION CONSULTING
*a boutique educational experience*

# Table of Contents

## PART 4: WRITING



## PART 5: MATH



## PART 6: PRACTICE TESTS 1 AND 2



## PART 7: PRACTICE TEST 3: ADAPTIVE

# How to Use This Book

This book is designed to allow for highly targeted preparation for the new Digital SAT. Based on your previous official practice test scores or the Diagnostic Test in this book, review the strategies and content knowledge that are most relevant to your needs. There are hundreds of drills that range in difficulty from easy to challenging so that you can achieve the very best results for your personal situation.

## Diagnostic Test

First, take the Diagnostic Test to gain an understanding of your strengths and weaknesses. It is a complete test with answer explanations and a question-type analysis guide so you know what types of concepts need the most attention.

## Review and Practice

The Reading, Writing, and Math sections each have:

- Proven test-taking strategies that allow you to customize your approach
- Extensive review of key concepts, particularly grammar and math knowledge
- Practice questions fully aligned with the new Digital SAT content
- Plenty of practice drills for ambitious students

## Practice Tests

The final section of the book offers the opportunity to take three full-length practice tests that include all question types found on the actual SAT for the Reading and Writing and Math sections. The final practice test models the section-adaptive format of the new Digital SAT. Comprehensive answer explanations are provided for all questions. To maximize the material available for practice, there is no overlap of questions in the different adaptive modules.

## Online Practice

In addition to the Diagnostic Test and three practice tests within this book, there are also more than three tests' worth of practice questions (300 questions) in the online drills. You can target your weak areas since the drills are broken down by question type. All questions include answer explanations. Our online resources also include explanations to the most challenging official Digital SAT practice test questions.

## For Students

Every strategy and explanation is based on what I have found works best for students on the actual SAT. No matter your personal goals or background knowledge, you will find practice drills and test-taking strategies that are geared toward your situation. Look at the SAT as an opportunity to showcase all of your knowledge and skills for colleges.

## For Teachers

While many students will like working through this book independently, others will maximize their learning when they have a great teacher or tutor as their guide. Help your students work smarter instead of simply harder by utilizing the concept reviews and drills most appropriate for your students' needs. Also, you can coach your students on which test-taking strategies will be the best fit based on their past performance. I am hopeful that the skills students develop from using this book will help them not just with the SAT, but also with their academic coursework and future careers. If you have any suggestions for future editions, please reach out via the publisher.

Sincerely,
Brian W. Stewart

# PART 1
# Introduction to the Digital SAT

# Welcome to the Digital SAT

## Overview

The SAT is a standardized test administered in a digital format designed to assess your readiness for college-level work. Approximately 1,700,000 students take the exam each year, and most U.S. colleges and universities accept it for admissions consideration. Many schools also use the SAT to determine eligibility for scholarships. The SAT is one of many factors that colleges use to grant admission, along with evaluations of high school coursework, application essays, extracurricular involvement, and more. Beginning in 2023 for international students and 2024 for U.S. students, the SAT will be given in a digital, adaptive format. The longer paper-based version of the SAT will be retired.

## Frequently Asked Questions

### What Does It Mean That the SAT Is an "Adaptive" Test?

So that the Digital SAT test can take around two hours instead of around three hours, the SAT is now adaptive, meaning the test changes depending on how the individual test-taker is doing. The second modules of both the Reading and Writing section and the Math section will change in difficulty based on how a student did on the first modules of each section. Students who perform better on the first modules will have more challenging questions in the second modules, while students who do not perform as well will have easier questions in the second modules. If you move on to the more difficult second module of a section, be mindful that the pacing could be more challenging.

### What Is the Format of the Digital SAT?

The Digital SAT takes a little over two hours to complete, and is broken down as follows:

| SAT Module | Format |
|---|---|
| *Reading & Writing One* | 32 Minutes, 27 Questions, Standard Difficulty |
| *Reading & Writing Two* | 32 Minutes, 27 Questions, Adaptive Difficulty (easier or harder questions depending on how you did on the first Reading and Writing section) |
| **Break–10 Minutes** | |
| *Math One* | 35 Minutes, 22 Questions, Standard Difficulty |
| *Math Two* | 35 Minutes, 22 Questions, Adaptive Difficulty (easier or harder questions depending on how you did on the first Math section) |

### How Is the Digital SAT Scored?

- The SAT score is broken up into two halves:
  - Reading and Writing is scored from 200–800 points.
  - Math is scored from 200–800 points.

- The total SAT score is therefore between 400 and 1600 points, with 1600 being a perfect score and 1000 being approximately an average score.
  - There is no penalty for guessing, so be sure to answer every question, including fill-in questions in the Math section.

### How is the new Digital SAT different from the older paper-based SAT?

#### Test Length

| Old SAT | Digital SAT |
|---|---|
| ▪ About three hours long, including breaks and administration.<br>▪ 65 minutes for Reading<br>▪ 35 minutes Writing and Language<br>▪ 25 minutes for Non-Calculator Math<br>▪ 55 minutes for Calculator Math | ▪ A little over two hours long; assesses the same skills as the longer SAT by having an "adaptive" format.<br>▪ Less time needed for test administration because students can download the testing app ahead of time. |

#### Test Format

| Old SAT | Digital SAT |
|---|---|
| ▪ One test form for all students on a particular test day<br>▪ Paper test booklets with Scantron sheets for answers<br>▪ Can go back to questions within a section before time is called<br>▪ Students should bring their own watches and calculators—they are not provided.<br>▪ Can write on the test booklet<br>▪ Experimental questions (ones that don't count towards your score), if given, are in a section after the test. | ▪ Different test questions for different students.<br>▪ Taken on a laptop that students provide or that the test center makes available.<br>▪ Can still go back and review questions. Questions can be flagged.<br>▪ Countdown clock and calculator built into the program, although students can still bring a watch and calculator if they would like.<br>▪ Can write on provided scrap paper.<br>▪ A few experimental questions are incorporated into each test section. |

#### Reading and Writing

| Old SAT | Digital SAT |
|---|---|
| ▪ Reading passages are 500–750 words long and have 10–11 questions each.<br>▪ Reading genres include fiction, social science, historical documents, and natural science<br>▪ Writing and Language passages are about 450 words long and have 11 questions each. | ▪ Reading and Writing texts are no longer than 150 words. Each text has just one question accompanying it.<br>▪ Will have a greater variety of reading genres represented. Along with the current SAT reading genres, there will be humanities, drama, and poetry excerpts. |

#### Math

| Old SAT | Digital SAT |
|---|---|
| ▪ Non-Calculator and Calculator Sections<br>▪ Formula sheet provided at the beginning of the test section.<br>▪ Students need to bring their own calculators. | ▪ Calculator permitted throughout the test.<br>▪ Formula sheet and digital calculator available in the program.<br>▪ Word problems are typically more concise than they currently are. |

## Why Is the College Board Making This Change to the SAT?

- Adaptive tests have a long track record of success. The GRE and GMAT, both of which are used for graduate school admissions, are computer-based adaptive assessments. These tests are shorter than they would otherwise be since they adjust the difficulty of the questions based on student performance.
- Students have become more comfortable with computer-based assessments. With so many students learning remotely during the pandemic, digital learning has become far more common.
- The test should be easier to administer. Testing administrators will not have to secure test booklets. If schools want to offer the SAT during the school day, they will not have to take as much time away from the classroom and can offer the test to different groups of students on different days.
- Test security should be improved. Since students will have different test questions, it is far more difficult to cheat. Also, it will be far less likely that a test security breach will lead to score cancellations.

## How Do You Register for the Test? When Is It Offered?

Go to the College Board website and set up an account here:

*https://collegereadiness.collegeboard.org/sat/register*

The SAT is typically offered seven times throughout the year in the following months: March, May, June, August, October, November, and December. Check on the above website link for the most updated information on test dates. Many schools may also offer an in-school test date; check with your guidance counselor for more details. Given the more flexible nature of the Digital SAT, schools will have more freedom to offer the test on days that work well for schools' and students' schedules.

## What Is a Good SAT Score?

There is not a "passing" score on the SAT—a good score for you depends on your specific goals for college admissions. Look at this free College Board website for detailed information on typical scores for admitted students at schools throughout the United States:

*https://bigfuture.collegeboard.org/*

## Will Every Question on the SAT Count the Same Towards the Score?

The College Board is developing a scoring manual as they gather more data from test-takers that will employ the principles of Item Response Theory—this is a scoring approach that looks at how you perform on individual test questions in the context of that general category of test questions. Using this will allow the test-makers to better assess student proficiency using fewer questions. Under this approach to scoring, performance on certain questions may carry more weight than performance on others. What does this mean for you as a test taker? First, do your very best on each and every question. With fewer questions on the Digital SAT than on the previous paper SAT, each question has more of an impact on your score. Second, look at *collegeboard.org* closer to your actual SAT date to see the latest on how your test will be scored. For this book, we will rely on previous SAT test curves to give you our best estimate as to how your performance on your practice tests will roughly equate to scores on the actual SAT.

## Does the SAT Potentially Offer Accommodations?

For students whose test-taking is impacted by a documented disability, such as ADHD, dyslexia, or visual or motor impairments, the SAT may offer accommodations. The most typical accommodation is extended time, although some students may receive more specific accommodations like extended breaks.

One interesting potential accommodation with the Digital SAT is that you could be eligible to take the test in a paper-based, non-adaptive format. Should you take this paper-based, non-adaptive SAT, the test is longer: the Reading/Writing Modules each have 33 questions last 39 minutes, and the Math modules will each have 27 questions and last 43 minutes. Should you have this format for your test, you can download a longer non-adaptive practice test from the College Board.

If you have an IEP or 504 plan with your school, talk to your guidance counselor or school administrator about applying for accommodations on the SAT. Having an IEP or a 504 plan will not necessarily lead to having accommodations on the SAT, but it usually helps. Allow plenty of time to apply for accommodations—at least seven weeks. Go to this website for the latest details on requesting SAT accommodations:

*https://accommodations.collegeboard.org/*

## Does the SAT Offer Accommodations for English Language Learners?

Students who are actively enrolled in an English as a Second Language program at their school may be able to take the SAT with 50% extra time, translated test directions, and the use of a bilingual dictionary. This service is currently available on school-day SATs, but not on the national test dates on weekends. Go to this website for further information about SAT supports for English language learners:

*https://collegereadiness.collegeboard.org/educators/k-12/english-learner-supports*

## What Are the Similarities and Differences Between the SAT and ACT?

The SAT and ACT have many similarities:

- They both test English grammar.
- They both test high school math up through pre-calculus.
- They both test reading comprehension.
- They both assess students' ability to analyze graphs and charts.
- There is no guessing penalty on either test—be sure to answer every question.
- Colleges throughout the United States that use test scores in admissions (the vast majority of colleges) will accept results from either the SAT or ACT.

There are some important differences:

- The SAT is given in a digital, adaptive format; the ACT is given in a non-adaptive, typically paper-based format. The Digital SAT will be shorter than the ACT, with a little over half the testing time of the ACT. The ACT typically gives the same sets of questions to all students, and the questions will not change from section to section based on student performance.
- The SAT gives students more time to complete the same amount of material. For example, on the SAT math, you have about 95 seconds for each question, while on the ACT, you have about 60 seconds for each question. So, if you are more comfortable taking your time in completing the test, the SAT may be a better fit than the ACT. If you like a faster test with slightly more straight-forward questions, the ACT may be preferable.

- The SAT focuses more deeply on certain math topics, emphasizing algebra and data analysis. The ACT has a broader array of math topics, including things like matrices, logarithms, and hyperbolas.
- The ACT has a Science section, while the SAT tests scientific skills throughout the test. The final section of the ACT is a stand-alone science reasoning section, which assesses your skill in analyzing experiments, scientific research, and scientific theories. The SAT has questions on each section that will ask you to interpret graphs and charts.

## What Should I Do Right Before the SAT?

Immediately before the SAT, prioritize sleep and relaxation. You will do far better on the SAT if you are well rested and have a positive mindset. In the week before the test, try to get 8–9 hours of sleep a night. Since the SAT is very much a critical thinking test, the better rested you are, the better you will be able to read, problem solve, and edit. Some practice shortly before the test is perfectly fine to do, but make sure you are not staying up late and cramming.

## What Should I Bring with Me to the SAT?

- Admissions ticket
- Computer or tablet with the testing program already installed. You will be allowed to use your own computer or tablet for the Digital SAT—permitted options include a Windows laptop or tablet, a Mac laptop, an Ipad, or a school-managed Chromebook. Be sure to download the Bluebook testing program well in advance so that you can become familiar with the testing interface and will not have to download the program on test day. If you do not have a computer or tablet you wish to use, request in your test registration that the testing center provide you with a device. Your device needs to be charged such that it has at least three hours of battery life.
- Calculator with fresh batteries—most any graphing or scientific calculator is fine.
    - There is a Desmos calculator with graphing features given in the program, but most students will find it easier to use their own calculator.
    - Check to see if your calculator is approved here:

      *https://collegereadiness.collegeboard.org/sat/taking-the-test/calculator-policy*

- A snack and a drink to have during your breaks (don't have food/drink out on your desk)
- Do not have your cell phone with you during the duration of the test—you are welcome to use it after the test has concluded, but the proctors do not want to see phones used during the test or during breaks to prevent possible cheating.
- Pen or pencil. You can use your preferred pen or pencil to write on the provided scrap paper.
- Watches, paper, and highlighters are not needed. The test program gives you an annotation feature and a countdown timer that you can view or hide, and the testing site will provide you with scrap paper.

## Important Features of the Digital SAT User Interface

**Timer:** There is a timer at the top of the screen. You can hide it if you find it distracting or leave it up if you prefer. The timer will automatically display when 5 minutes remain on the module.

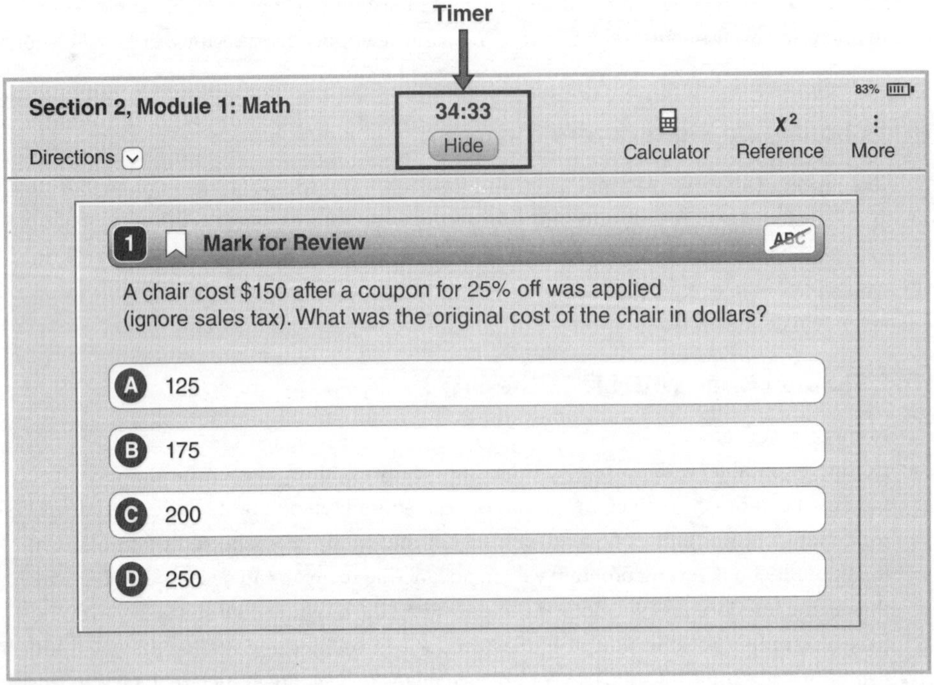


**Mark Question for Review:** There is a bookmark logo on which you can click to mark a question for review at the end of a module.

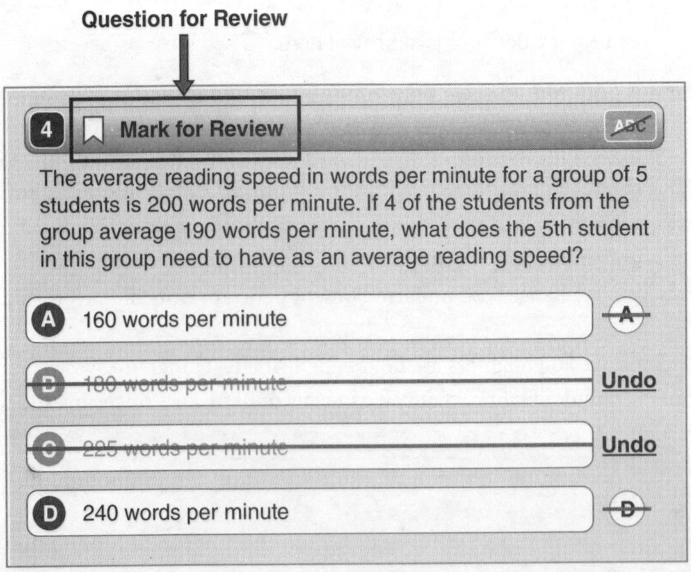

Before you submit your answers on the entire module, you will see a screen that shows you which questions you have answered, which you have left unanswered, and which you have marked for review. Go back to any of the marked questions you would like to check out again. Keep in mind that since there is no guessing penalty, you should be certain to answer all the questions.

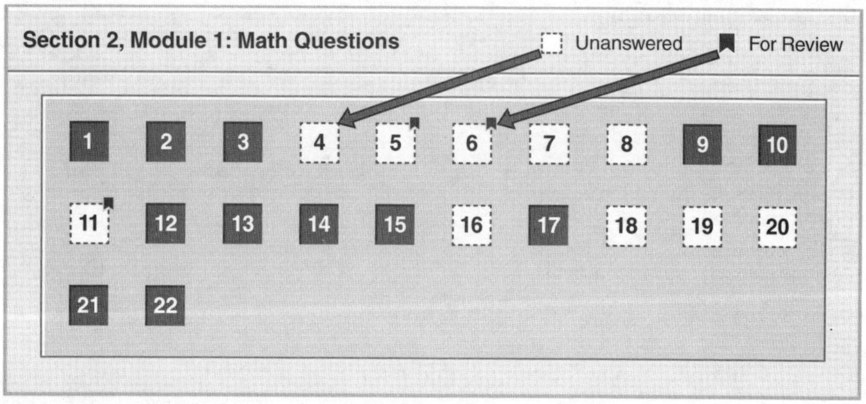


**Eliminate Answer Choices:** You can mark off answers you believe to be incorrect.

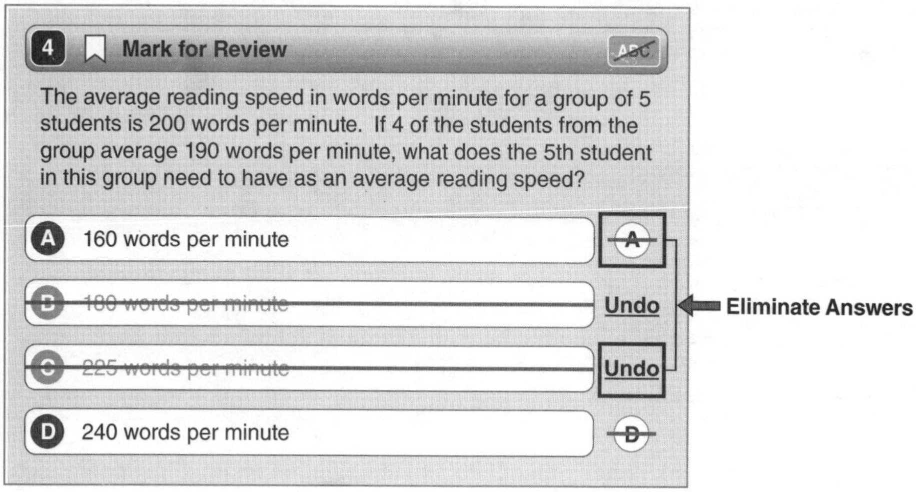

**Text Annotation:** You can highlight and make notes on the text and questions using the annotation tool.

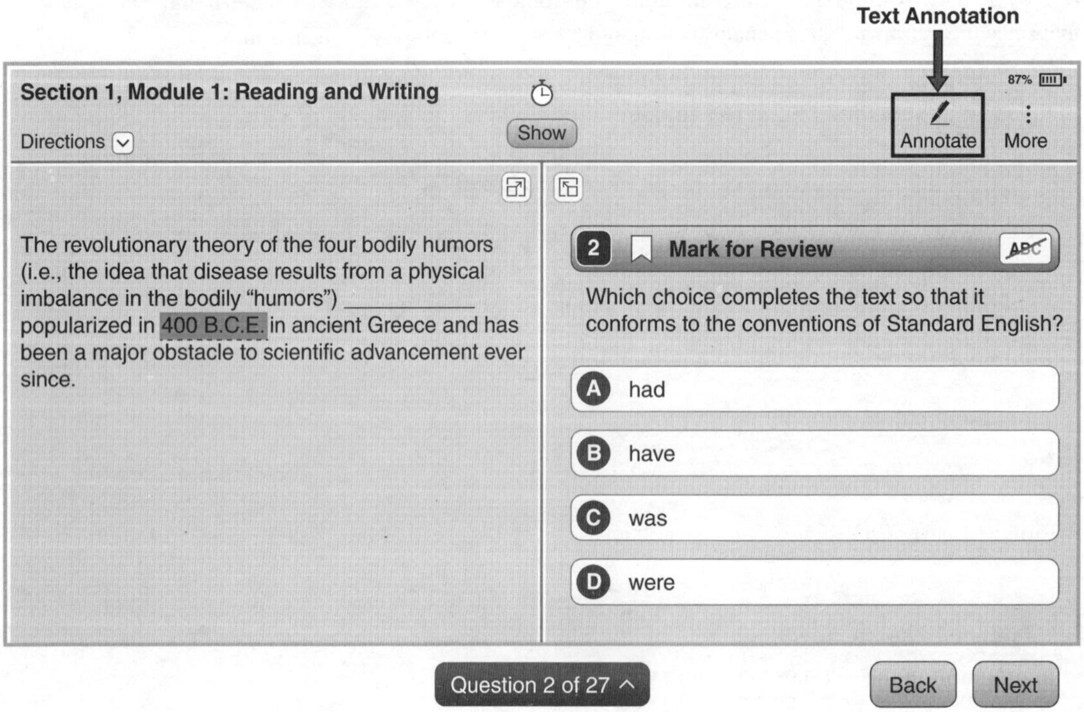

When you click on the "annotate" feature, you will be able to select text and make notes about what you have read.

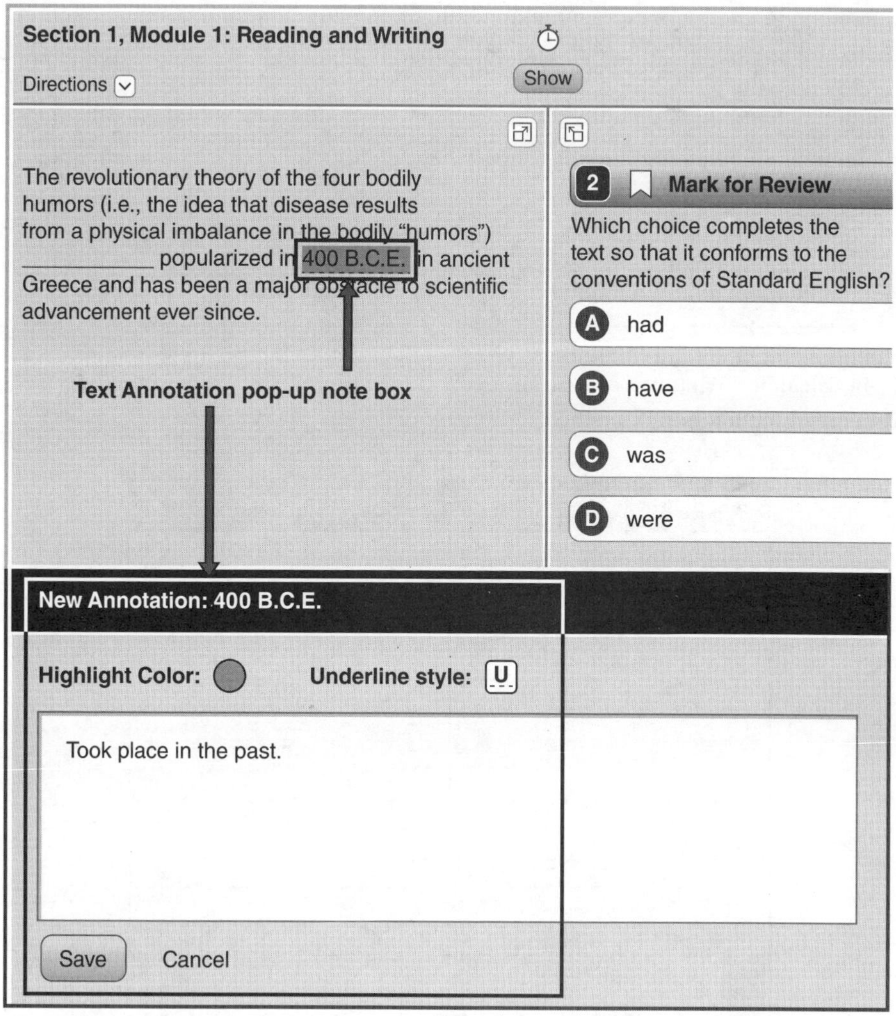


With the annotation feature closed, when you move the cursor over the selected text, your notes will appear above the selection.

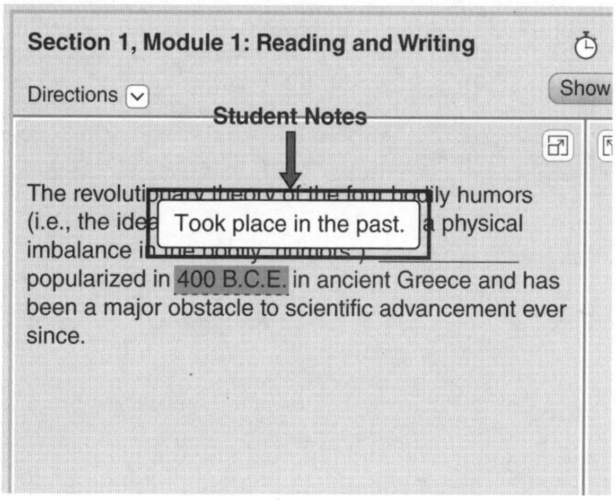

**Student-Produced Math Responses:** You can preview what your answer will look like before submitting your answer.

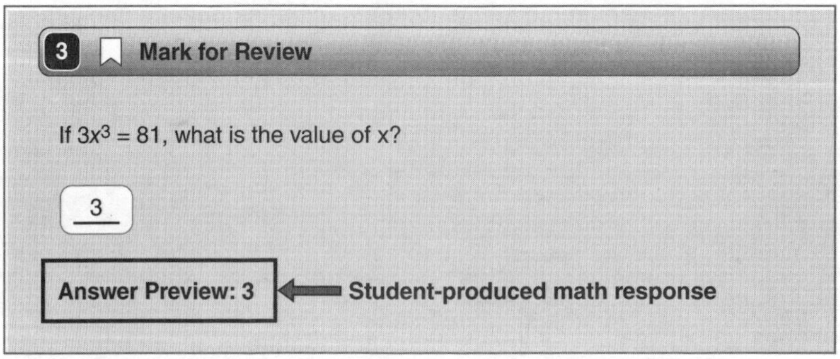


**Built-in Calculator:** While you can use an approved calculator of your own, you can also use the built-in calculator that uses Desmos.com™ technology.

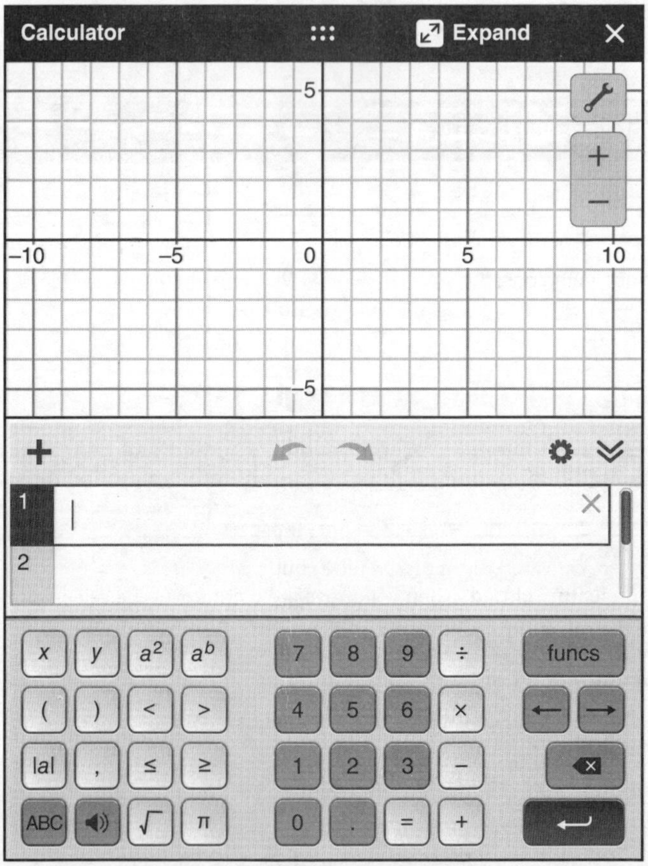

**Math Reference Sheet:** While in the math section, you can click to display the reference sheet any time you need to see one of the provided geometry or trigonometry formulas/facts.

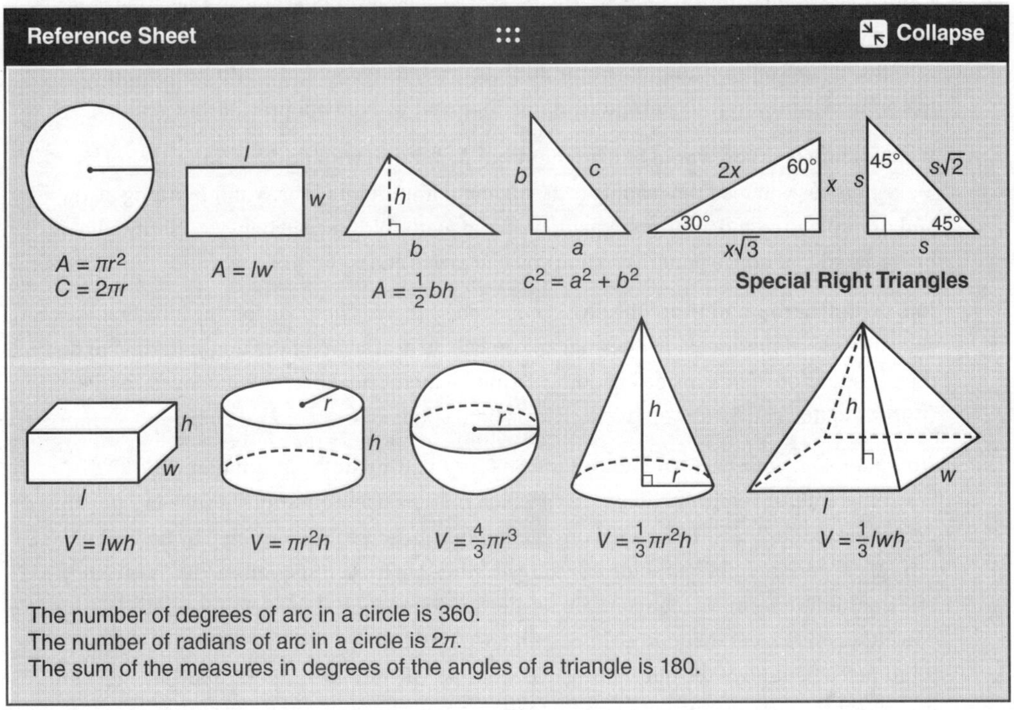


**Zooming In and Out:** You can make the text larger or smaller using the Zoom feature. Depending on the make of your computer, you can either use Control + and Control –, or Command + and Command –.

## General SAT Test-Taking Strategies

While there are plenty of strategies applicable to individual sections of the SAT, here are ten strategies that are important throughout the exam:

1. **Answer every question.** There is no penalty for guessing on the SAT, so be sure to enter an answer for every question. Even on the fill-in questions on the SAT Math, there is no penalty for guessing. Put down some number so you have at least a chance of earning credit.

2. **Become thoroughly familiar with the testing program features ahead of time.** Download the Bluebook testing app from *collegeboard.org* ahead of time and practice with the program. You do not want the actual test to be the first time you use the testing program. The Digital SAT will have several features to help you as you take your exam:

   - A clock you can use to see how much time remains on your testing module
   - A flagging feature to highlight questions you want to return to
   - A crossing-out feature so you can eliminate incorrect answers
   - A zoom feature you can use to read graphics and reading material more easily
   - An annotation feature to make notes as you read
   - A built-in graphing calculator you can use throughout the math program
     - It is based on the Desmos™ program that many students have previously used.
   - A reference sheet you can click on should you need a geometry or trigonometry formula

3. **Focus on understanding the question.** If a question asks for the circumference and you instead calculate the area, you will be incorrect. Take time to thoroughly understand what is being asked.

4. **Come back to questions if needed.** Do not look at skipping a question as a sign that you have given up. Instead, use it as an opportunity to let your subconscious mind process the question while you consider other questions. Flag the question and revisit it after some time has gone by, and you will likely notice something that you did not previously see.

5. **Write as much as you would like on the scrap paper and with the annotation feature.** Make notes as you read the reading texts, highlight important phrases in the writing texts, and draw pictures and write out equations in the math. Writing will help you clarify what is being asked and notice patterns so that you can arrive at a solution.

6. **Use the full amount of time.** The SAT is not a race—there is no prize for finishing first. Also, since the questions are often challenging, you will be best served by taking your time to do the questions once well instead of doing them repeatedly, making the same mistakes. Pace yourself so that you finish your work right as time is called.

7. **Do not look at your performance on the SAT as an all-or-nothing situation.** The SAT is very different from typical school tests in which missing a few questions results in a greatly decreased grade. The SAT is graded on a curve, so your score is determined by how other test-takers perform, not just some arbitrary number. On most tests, you can likely miss several questions to achieve the score you desire. So, do not look at the SAT as something where you either do great or do poorly—a score that isn't perfect can still be excellent. Also, keep in mind that a handful of the questions you encounter will be experimental and will not count towards your score; you will not be able to determine which questions these are, so don't worry about them.

8. **Try to figure things out.** Instead of looking at SAT problems as knowledge to be recalled, look at them as puzzles to be solved. Do not be intimidated by a problem that you do not immediately know how to solve—instead, patiently think your way through it. The SAT is a test of your skill in problem solving, not simply a test of memorized knowledge.

9. **Know that there will be one definite answer to each question.** The College Board goes to extraordinary lengths to be sure that test questions are fair and have a definitive answer. Each question is independently reviewed by several test developers or educators before it makes it onto an actual SAT.[1] In addition, each test question is pre-tested on hundreds of students to be sure it performs as expected prior to inclusion on a real SAT.[2] Given these checks, you can be assured that the questions are well crafted. Do not overthink the questions because you are looking for a trick. Instead, give the SAT the benefit of the doubt and if you do not see a correct answer, review the texts and the questions to be sure you did not miss anything.

10. **What works for one student may not work for another.** This book provides you with a variety of strategic tools—use whatever works best for your personal situation. Students differ in terms of how quickly they read, how much they comprehend, their knowledge of English grammar, how much math they have taken, and their competency with different types of math problems. Just because a strategy worked well for your friend does not necessarily mean it would work well for you. Use this book to fine-tune the strategies and review the content knowledge that just you need.

---

[1]https://collegereadiness.collegeboard.org/educators/higher-ed/test-validity-design/test-development
[2]https://collegereadiness.collegeboard.org/pdf/sat-suite-assessments-technical-manual.pdf

## Managing Test Anxiety

Like with other major performances—such as ones in music, athletics, or theater—it is natural to have some anxiety. While some anxiety may release adrenaline that helps sharpen your focus and improves your stamina, too much anxiety can be problematic. Here are some tips to help keep your anxiety under control:

### Make Your Practice as Realistic as Possible

Take a full-length practice test under timed conditions with the usual breaks. Become familiar with the testing app on your computer or tablet so there are no surprises on test day. Eat the same food and have the same drink you will have during your break. See how your body and your mind perform under realistic conditions, and then make any needed adjustments. By practicing like this before the actual test, you will both consciously and subconsciously know what to expect.

### Realize That SAT Results Are But One Part of a College Application

While test results are perhaps the easiest part of the application to quantify, they are one component in a holistic admissions process. If the other parts of your application are quite strong, the test results will be less important. If you have not done as well in school or have not had as many extracurricular opportunities, the SAT can give you an opportunity to showcase your college readiness.

### Start Early with Your Testing

Plan on taking the SAT after you have completed Algebra 2 so you have nearly all the math the test requires. If you take the test early, you will not feel like your entire college application is riding on your performance on a single day; instead, you will know that you will have multiple opportunities to retake the exam. Colleges routinely look at your best performance, and if your early performance is not all that great, it should not be an issue.

### You Will Likely Be Able to Superscore

More and more schools allow "superscoring," i.e., taking the best score from each of the two test sections over multiple test dates. For example, if you scored a 700 on the Reading and Writing and a 500 on the Math on a test in March, and then scored a 600 on the Reading and Writing and a 700 on the Math on a test in May, your superscore would be $700 + 700 = 1{,}400$. So, if one half of the test does not go as well, it is OK—you can focus on the more challenging half on the next test date. Colleges will accept results from both the older paper-based SAT and the newer digital SAT for admissions and superscoring purposes.

## Preparing for the Test

Use previous test results to help you target your preparation. Even if the results were from a paper-based test, they will align with the Digital SAT and will help you plan your preparation. If you have previously taken the PSAT or SAT, look at your scores on the College Board website:

*https://collegereadiness.collegeboard.org/*

If you have not previously taken the PSAT or SAT, take the Diagnostic Test at the beginning of this book to help you determine the areas that you most need to review. Each chapter in this book has extensive reviews and drills for each type of question or text selection you will face, so you can focus on the areas that need the most work. Including the Diagnostic Test, there are a total of four practice SAT tests along with hundreds of sample digital SAT questions. Practice full-length tests under timed conditions to develop your problem-solving skills and learn to manage your timing.

## Recommended Study Plans

*If you only have one day to prepare:*

- Review the general SAT strategies in this introductory chapter.
- Skim through an entire SAT practice test to become familiar with the directions, timing, and format.
- Try a few questions from each section.
- Do not stay up late to cram before the test—get a good night's sleep.

*If you have about a week to prepare:*

- Review any past PSAT or SAT test results to determine where you need to focus your preparation.
- Read the test-taking strategies in each of the book chapters so you have a clear plan for how to attack the exam.
- Study the specific review and drills that are most relevant given your strengths and weaknesses.
- Take a full-length timed practice test. Score it, review your answers, and analyze what you need to do better in terms of timing and strategy to do your best on the actual test.

*If you have a month or more to prepare:*

- Take the full-length Diagnostic Test
- Work through all of the book chapters to review important strategies and content. Pay especially close attention to the areas where you struggled in the diagnostic test.
- Take additional full-length practice SAT Tests and review the in-depth solutions for each question that you missed.

### The Bottom Line

With your preparation—it is not just practice that makes perfect... it is perfect practice that makes perfect. In particular:

- Actively assess where you need the most help and target your review accordingly. Do not skip over challenging sections to review and do not waste time reviewing concepts you already fully understand.
- Practice using the timing you will use on the actual test. Do not rush through a practice test just to get it done, only to find that you have made several careless errors. Pace yourself just as you would want to do on test day.

## Beyond the Book

The SAT assesses your fundamental academic skills and your readiness for college-level work. So, anything you can do to build your reading, writing, and mathematical problem-solving skills will help you perform better on the SAT.

- **Take rigorous courses, like Advanced Placement and International Baccalaureate classes.** The College Board administers the AP exam program, so there is considerable cross-over between the skills assessed on AP exams and the skills assessed on the SAT.
- **Read widely on your own.** Students who read for fun tend to find the reading comprehension section easier than students who look at reading as a boring chore. Go to your local library, talk to a librarian, and find a book or magazine that really interests you. Install an e-reader on your phone so that you can easily read when you have spare time.

- **Download the testing app from the College Board and practice the adaptive tests on it.** The online resources for this book include tips on how to best practice with the official adaptive digital SAT tests from College Board along with explanations to the most challenging questions found on those tests. With the tests and drills in this book along with the free material from College Board, you will have more than enough material to use to get ready for test day.

Let's get to work!

# PART 2
# Diagnostic Test

# Diagnostic Test

A full-length SAT diagnostic test is on the pages that follow. Allow a little over two hours of uninterrupted time to complete the entire test. Find a spot to take the test where you will not be distracted. You can take a ten-minute break after the two Reading and Writing modules and before the two Math modules.

Completing this diagnostic test will help you determine your SAT strengths and weaknesses.

Think about the following after you take the test.

- How are you with timing?
- Do you find certain types of reading questions to be challenging?
- Do particular reading texts and genres give you more difficulty than others?
- Do you need to review English grammar concepts?
- Do some types of writing questions give you more trouble than others?
- Do you need to review or learn some math concepts?
- What kinds of math questions are toughest for you?

After completing the test, review your answers with the "Diagnostic Test Analysis Guide" to determine what types of questions and concepts you most need to study.

Good luck!

## Overview

This SAT Practice Test is made up of a Reading and Writing section and a Math section.

**Note:** In this book, there is an answer sheet you can use to write down your letter choices and math answers. Feel free to use the sheet to record your answers or simply circle and write down your answers in the test as you go.

**Section 1:** Reading and Writing (54 Questions)

There are two 27-question modules in the Reading and Writing section.

**Section 2:** Math (44 Questions)

There are two 22-question modules in the Math section. You can use a calculator throughout the math section.

### Modules

The modules in each section are timed separately. You can review your answers in each module before time expires. When the time reaches zero, you will automatically move on to the next section. You are unable to return to a completed module.

### Directions

At the beginning of each section, there are directions for answering the questions.

# ANSWER SHEET
## Diagnostic Test

### Section 1, Module 1: Reading and Writing

1. ____
2. ____
3. ____
4. ____
5. ____
6. ____
7. ____
8. ____
9. ____
10. ____
11. ____
12. ____
13. ____
14. ____
15. ____
16. ____
17. ____
18. ____
19. ____
20. ____
21. ____
22. ____
23. ____
24. ____
25. ____
26. ____
27. ____

# ANSWER SHEET
## Diagnostic Test

### Section 1, Module 2: Reading and Writing

| | | |
|---|---|---|
| 1. ____ | 10. ____ | 19. ____ |
| 2. ____ | 11. ____ | 20. ____ |
| 3. ____ | 12. ____ | 21. ____ |
| 4. ____ | 13. ____ | 22. ____ |
| 5. ____ | 14. ____ | 23. ____ |
| 6. ____ | 15. ____ | 24. ____ |
| 7. ____ | 16. ____ | 25. ____ |
| 8. ____ | 17. ____ | 26. ____ |
| 9. ____ | 18. ____ | 27. ____ |

# ANSWER SHEET
## Diagnostic Test



### Section 2, Module 1: Math

| | | | |
|---|---|---|---|
| 1. | _____ | 12. | _____ |
| 2. | _____ | 13. | _____ |
| 3. | _____ | 14. | _____ |
| 4. | _____ | 15. | _____ |
| 5. | _____ | 16. | _____ |
| 6. | _____ | 17. | _____ |
| 7. | _____ | 18. | _____ |
| 8. | _____ | 19. | _____ |
| 9. | _____ | 20. | _____ |
| 10. | _____ | 21. | _____ |
| 11. | _____ | 22. | _____ |

# ANSWER SHEET
## Diagnostic Test

### Section 2, Module 2: Math

1. ____
2. ____
3. ____
4. ____
5. ____
6. ____
7. ____
8. ____
9. ____
10. ____
11. ____
12. ____
13. ____
14. ____
15. ____
16. ____
17. ____
18. ____
19. ____
20. ____
21. ____
22. ____

# Diagnostic Test

## Section 1, Module 1: Reading and Writing

32 MINUTES, 27 QUESTIONS

**DIRECTIONS**

You will be tested on a variety of important reading and writing skills. Each question has one or more passages, possibly including a graph or table. Carefully read each passage and question and choose the best answer to the question based on the passage(s).

Every question in this section is multiple-choice with four possible answers. Each question has only one best answer.

One of the most common ways that people can amass wealth is through ________ equity in their homes.

**1**

Which choice completes the text with the most logical and precise word or phrase?

Ⓐ assembling
Ⓑ manufacturing
Ⓒ building
Ⓓ fabricating

Modern day graffiti creates the same questions. Most people would agree that a quickly spray-painted tag is not art, but some graffiti is very elaborate, well planned, and objectively beautiful. Some graffiti ________ the value of an area by making it appear abandoned and unkempt.

**2**

Which choice completes the text with the most logical and precise word or phrase?

Ⓐ quiets
Ⓑ recedes
Ⓒ lowers
Ⓓ muffles

## 1 MODULE 1 1

While there certainly are many potential careers that students may find rewarding, students with a math and science ________ should give engineering serious consideration.

**3**

Which choice completes the text with the most logical and precise word or phrase?

Ⓐ aptitude
Ⓑ warmth
Ⓒ hankering
Ⓓ frenzy

Making something that is truly delicious for one's friends and family can be a formative experience that leads one to pursue a career as a chef. While not everybody can be a celebrity chef with millions of television fans, there are many ________ to a fulfilling career in the food services industry.

**4**

Which choice completes the text with the most logical and precise word or phrase?

Ⓐ boulevards
Ⓑ promenades
Ⓒ thoroughfares
Ⓓ avenues

One key reason *C. lecturlarius* (bedbugs) can be so difficult to remove is their physical properties. They are tiny brown bugs that live solely on the blood of other animals, so edible poison traps won't work the way they do for ants. In addition, they can live months without food, which makes starving them out nearly impossible, and they lay eggs that are ________ to regular pest control methods and stick in unreachable nooks and crannies.

**5**

Which choice completes the text with the most logical and precise word or phrase?

Ⓐ susceptible
Ⓑ prone
Ⓒ impervious
Ⓓ vulnerable

# 1 MODULE 1 1



The following text is from Georgia Douglas Johnson's 1920 poem "Calling Dreams."

The right to make my dreams come true,
I ask, nay, I demand of life;
Nor shall fate's deadly contraband
Impede my steps, nor countermand;
Too long my heart against the ground
Has beat the dusty years around;
And now at length I rise! I wake!
And stride into the morning break!

**6**

Which choice best states the main purpose of the text?

Ⓐ To express the inevitable frustration that comes when you cannot accomplish a goal
Ⓑ To show a more contemplative attitude towards acceptance of your fate
Ⓒ To present a personal narrative about the importance of travel to a richer life
Ⓓ To emphasize the need to not let anything stand in the way of achieving your dreams

The following is a portion of an address given by Senator Herbert H. Lehman at the annual membership meeting of the Urban League of Greater New York in June of 1956, as reported in the *Arizona Sun*.

The Urban League has furnished a framework within which men of good will of all races could work together to achieve steady advances toward the goal of adjustment, focusing their efforts on the neighborhood and the community. This organization has helped to show how vast are the ramifications of inter-group and inter-racial adjustment, what concrete and specific evils flow from discrimination and segregation, and what must and can be done about it. Some people, including some of the leaders of our government, act as though civil rights were a brand-new problem, which has just arisen and needs nothing so much as to be studied. And they indicate that just as soon as they finish studying it, they will probably do something about it. <u>And, of course, that may take a long time.</u>

**7**

Which choice best describes the function of the underlined sentence in the text as a whole?

Ⓐ To show how those who oppose the advancement of civil rights will inevitably resort to personal attacks
Ⓑ To emphasize the need for increased funding for socially active causes
Ⓒ To assert that opponents of civil rights progress will likely use excessive delay to achieve their aims
Ⓓ To argue that the goal of public policy is to promote social justice

The following text is from Upton Sinclair's 1906 novel *The Jungle.*

And then there was Marija Berczynskas, who, fired with jealousy by the success of Jurgis, had set out upon her own responsibility to get a place. Marija had nothing to take with her save her two brawny arms and the word "job," laboriously learned; but with these she had marched about Packingtown all day, entering every door where there were signs of activity. Out of some she had been ordered with curses; but Marija was not afraid of man or devil, and asked everyone she saw—visitors and strangers, or work-people like herself, and once or twice even high and lofty office personages, who stared at her as if they thought she was crazy. In the end, however, she had reaped her reward.

**8**

According to the text, Marija most likely has what level of proficiency in the English language?

Ⓐ Totally fluent
Ⓑ Mostly fluent
Ⓒ Somewhat proficient
Ⓓ Very limited

The following passage is from *A Portrait of the Artist as a Young Man* by James Joyce, published in 1916. Stephen Dedalus, Joyce's protagonist, yearns to be an artist but was raised and educated to join the clergy. Below he contemplates the diverging paths before him after a priest warns him of the permanence of his intended holy position.

The Reverend Stephen Dedalus, S.J.

His name in that new life leaped into characters before his eyes and to it there followed a mental sensation of an undefined face or colour of a face. The colour faded and became strong like a changing glow of pallid brick red. Was it the raw reddish glow he had so often seen on wintry mornings on the shaven gills of the priests? The face was eyeless and sour-favoured and devout, shot with pink tinges of suffocated anger. Was it not a mental spectre of the face of one of the Jesuits whom some of the boys called Lantern Jaws and others Foxy Campbell?

**9**

According to the text, how would the narrator most likely characterize how most priests in this story would handle their emotions?

Ⓐ By repressing them
Ⓑ By celebrating them
Ⓒ By eliminating them
Ⓓ By expressing them

# 1 MODULE 1 1



**Text 1**

In her essay, "The Realities of Love at First Sight," Fisher explains how we evaluate an individual within three minutes of meeting them based on their physical attributes, voice, and words. First, we decide if they are attractive, then we evaluate their clothing and stature, before moving on to the sound and tone of their voice. Lastly, we consider what they actually say. She concludes that we choose partners whose biological chemicals complement our own.

**Text 2**

*Psychology Today* renders love a three-step scientific process. First, a release of the hormone dopamine causes "feel good" emotions. In this stage, we feel attracted to an individual and associate them with feelings of intense joy. Next, our neurotransmitters—norepinephrine and phenylethylamine—lead to focused attention on the object of our attraction. Lastly, our brain reward system is activated, sending chemical messages that elevate mood and make an addiction-like urge to be with that person.

**10**

How does the analysis of the love process in Text 2 differ from the one in Text 1?

Ⓐ It cites the role that chemicals might play.
Ⓑ It focuses on the actual chemistry of the process.
Ⓒ It has just two concrete steps.
Ⓓ It emphasizes the essential importance of human decision making.

Microplastics are microscopic particles of plastic that tend to accumulate toxins and are in some cases toxic themselves. Unfortunately, microplastics tend to end up being eaten by various organisms. The primary reason for this problem is that in recent years, approximately 380 million tons of plastic are produced annually. Plastic is not biodegradable, which means that once it enters the environment it can take several hundred years to degrade. In fact, if all the plastic that was produced between 1950 and 1960 had been disposed of in the ocean, ________

**11**

Which insertion at the end of the text, if true, would best support the author's claim?

Ⓐ nearly all of it would remain.
Ⓑ about half of it would remain.
Ⓒ about one-third of it would remain.
Ⓓ almost none of it would remain.

# 1 MODULE 1 1

*The Souls of Black Folk* is a 1903 literary work by American author W. E. B. Du Bois. One cultural aspect on which Du Bois focuses in this work is the prevalence of "sorrow songs" in African American culture, i.e., musical compositions that evoke the suffering of slaves. In this work, Du Bois strongly suggests that American creativity is focused on energetic inventiveness: ________________

**12**

Which quotation from *The Souls of Black Folk* most effectively illustrates the claim?

Ⓐ "Out of [the slave songs] rose for me morning, noon, and night, bursts of wonderful melody, full of the voices of my brothers and sisters, full of the voices of the past."

Ⓑ "Little of beauty has America given the world save the rude grandeur God himself stamped on her bosom; the human spirit in this new world has expressed itself in vigor and ingenuity rather than in beauty."

Ⓒ "Some [slave songs], like "Near the lake where drooped the willow," passed into current airs and their source was forgotten; others were caricatured on the 'minstrel' stage and their memory died away."

Ⓓ "[Slave songs] are the music of an unhappy people, of the children of disappointment; they tell of death and suffering and unvoiced longing toward a truer world, of misty wanderings and hidden ways."

# 1 MODULE 1 1



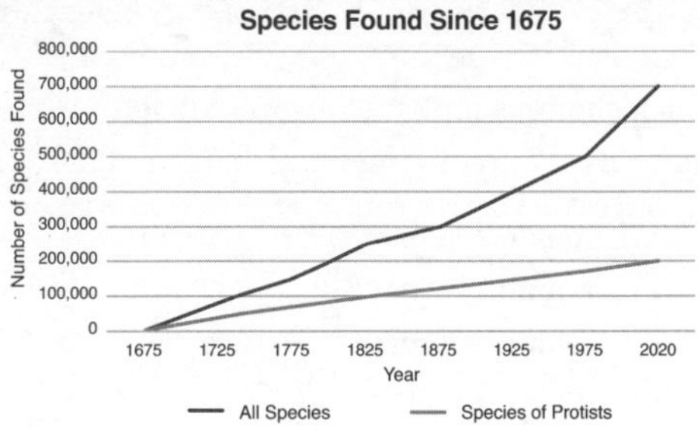


Through the improvement of technology and microscopy techniques, the differences between prokaryotes and eukaryotes were discovered. Protists previously fell under the category of prokaryotes, which were originally classified as anucleate organisms and unicellular. Technological advances led to the understanding that protists are eukaryotic organisms even though most protists do remain unicellular. Since 1675, scientists ___________

**13**

Which choice most effectively uses data from the graph to complete the example?

Ⓐ have found far more species of protists than other animal species.

Ⓑ conducted experiments on over 100,000 species of protists in laboratory environments.

Ⓒ have discovered approximately 200,000 new species of protists.

Ⓓ analyzed a total of 900,000 plant and protist species in their quest to find new life forms.

Ernst Haeckel was a German zoologist, naturalist, philosopher, physician, and about every about other type of scientist. He lived from 1834–1919. He was a contemporary of Charles Darwin and helped popularize *On the Origin of Species* in Germany. Contrary to Darwin and what we know now, Haeckel believed humans originated in Asia, not Africa. An accomplished artist, he created illustrations of animals and sea creatures with the same color and detail as the ornithological illustrations of James Audubon. Even though Americans aren't as familiar with Haeckel as they are with Darwin or Audubon, Haeckel ___________

**14**

Which choice most logically completes the text?

Ⓐ is a historical figure who is worth studying.

Ⓑ continues to write intriguing articles in the present day.

Ⓒ should be consigned to the dustbin of history.

Ⓓ was truly a literary pioneer and poetic innovator.

## 1 MODULE 1 1

In considering the following __________ be well to bear in mind that records of the bird migration in this locality have been made each year for the past thirty-one years.

**15**

Which choice completes the text so that it conforms to the conventions of Standard English?

Ⓐ remarks: it may
Ⓑ remarks; it may
Ⓒ remarks, it may
Ⓓ remarks it may

We hear about water every day. More than 70% of __________ surface is covered with water. Water is a requirement for terrestrial life. Water makes up most of our bodies.

**16**

Which choice completes the text so that it conforms to the conventions of Standard English?

Ⓐ our planets
Ⓑ their planets
Ⓒ our planet's
Ⓓ their planets'

It is believed that __________ on as near the actual date of their arrival as it would ordinarily be possible to obtain them.

**17**

Which choice completes the text so that it conforms to the conventions of Standard English?

Ⓐ the great majority of species: were recorded
Ⓑ the great majority of species were recorded
Ⓒ the great majority of species, were recorded
Ⓓ the great majority of species; were recorded

Schrödinger, a father of quantum mechanics himself, surely understood the uses of quantum superposition but also sought to bring attention to __________ shortcomings.

**18**

Which choice completes the text so that it conforms to the conventions of Standard English?

Ⓐ its
Ⓑ it's
Ⓒ their
Ⓓ there

# MODULE 1



General Douglas MacArthur and President Harry __________ both American leaders in the late 1940s and early 1950s in the aftermath of the Allied victory during World War II.

**19**

Which choice completes the text so that it conforms to the conventions of Standard English?

Ⓐ Truman; Great Men, by all accounts—were
Ⓑ Truman—Great Men, by all accounts, were
Ⓒ Truman: Great Men, by all accounts—were
Ⓓ Truman—Great Men, by all accounts—were

Two of the primary positions "between" nurse and doctor __________ those of nurse practitioner and physician assistant. You can think of a nurse practitioner as a more advanced nurse and a physician assistant as a more restricted doctor.

**20**

Which choice completes the text so that it conforms to the conventions of Standard English?

Ⓐ are
Ⓑ is
Ⓒ has
Ⓓ was

Over time, when the town began to adopt more mainstream customs with respect to family dynamics, the rate of cardiovascular disease __________.

**21**

Which choice completes the text so that it conforms to the conventions of Standard English?

Ⓐ rise
Ⓑ risen
Ⓒ rose
Ⓓ rised

## 1 MODULE 1 1

Henrik Ibsen and August Strindberg are truly giants of playwriting. The hallmarks of modern theater in their present incarnation—from stark realism to surreal expressionism—__________

**22**

Which choice completes the text so that it conforms to the conventions of Standard English?

Ⓐ from the two mens' works directly derive.
Ⓑ from the works of these two men directly derive.
Ⓒ derive directly from the works of these two men.
Ⓓ come directly from this.

Music is a combination of specific sound waves started and stopped at specific times. Some waves align nicely with one another or contrast nicely with one another, __________ others are neither regularly contrasting nor matching.

**23**

Which choice completes the text with the most logical transition?

Ⓐ while
Ⓑ because
Ⓒ since
Ⓓ so

Specific engineering disciplines focus on particular types of physical problems. __________ aerospace engineering is mostly concerned with optimizing the performance of airplanes, while civil engineering is mostly concerned with improving physical structures and public works.

**24**

Which choice completes the text with the most logical transition?

Ⓐ However,
Ⓑ In addition,
Ⓒ For instance,
Ⓓ Surprisingly,

In the past few years, more than one horribly botched painting has made the news when it was delivered back to the owner looking nothing like the original. __________ the art restorer working on the painting is not both topnotch and very well trained in artistic techniques from the time-period of the piece, the results of a restoration attempt can be disastrous.

**25**

Which choice completes the text with the most logical transition?

Ⓐ If
Ⓑ While
Ⓒ Because
Ⓓ Since

While researching a topic, a student has taken the following notes:

- Robert Frost is one of the most popular poets in modern day.
- His poems centered around philosophical and social issues, questioning common assumptions with ironic writing.
- One of his most famous poems is "The Road Not Taken."
- It encourages readers to take the path less traveled by the world or by peers.
- Another one of Frost's poems is "Nothing Gold Can Stay."
- This poem reflects on the fleeting nature of beauty and life.

**26**

The student wants to introduce Robert Frost to an audience unfamiliar with his work. Which choice most effectively uses relevant information from the notes to accomplish this goal?

Ⓐ "The Road Not Taken" considers taking the path less traveled by others.

Ⓑ Robert Frost is a famous modern poet whose work encourages critical thinking.

Ⓒ Analysis of beauty and life are common themes in many modern-day poems by Robert Frost and others.

Ⓓ Irony is a useful poetic device to convey one's skepticism about worldly assumptions.

While researching a topic, a student has taken the following notes:

- Flying squirrels are the most numerous squirrels in Ohio, yet they are the least frequently observed.
- Flying squirrels are nocturnal.
- Flying squirrels do not actually fly; loose skin extends from wrist to ankle and allows them to glide between trees.
- Flying squirrels prefer to live in forests and not in suburbs.
- Habitat loss is one of the greatest threats facing flying squirrels.

**27**

The student wants to correct a likely misconception about flying squirrels. Which choice most effectively uses relevant information from the notes to accomplish this goal?

Ⓐ Flying squirrels can usually be observed at night as opposed to the day.

Ⓑ Despite their name, flying squirrels glide rather than fly.

Ⓒ While hunting poses a threat to flying squirrels, habitat loss is ultimately the greater danger.

Ⓓ Even though flying squirrels are scarce in Ohio, they can still be easily seen.

## Section 1, Module 2: Reading and Writing

32 MINUTES, 27 QUESTIONS

**DIRECTIONS**

You will be tested on a variety of important reading and writing skills. Each question has one or more passages, possibly including a graph or table. Carefully read each passage and question and choose the best answer to the question based on the passage(s).

Every question in this section is multiple-choice with four possible answers. Each question has only one best answer.

---

The vacation had the opposite effect on Jim. He despised the upcoming days and was depressed at the thought of his recent break-up. Although he marched into work 15 minutes early on Monday morning, he was feeling very ___________.

**1**

Which choice completes the text with the most logical and precise word or phrase?

Ⓐ energetic
Ⓑ dispirited
Ⓒ invigorated
Ⓓ rejuvenated

---

An education is usually thought to have intrinsic ___________ rather than extrinsic. That is, its worth comes from the love of knowledge rather than something monetary. However, with the rising cost of tuition, one could maybe argue that there is a fiscal price related to education.

**2**

Which choice completes the text with the most logical and precise word or phrase?

Ⓐ value
Ⓑ price
Ⓒ principles
Ⓓ standard

---

The night sky erupted with great displays of sound and light. Every couple of minutes, from dusk till late, the loud, explosive sounds would shake the sky and some unsuspecting and innocent below. It is not lightning or anything ___________; rather, it is meant to be a symbol of patriotism. It was a week before the Fourth of July, a day meant to celebrate the United States and those who defend it, and the fireworks had already begun.

**3**

Which choice completes the text with the most logical and precise word or phrase?

Ⓐ considerate
Ⓑ nefarious
Ⓒ congenial
Ⓓ duplicitous

## MODULE 2

Though Friedel and Crafts discovered a new chemical reaction, this reaction technique was virtually useless to the scientific community because it lacked selectivity. Selectivity causes a reaction to favor one product over another potential product of the reaction. Without selectivity, it is impossible for chemists to __________ the products of their reaction. Not being able to separate one product from another makes a reaction useless because even a small alteration in a molecule can result in adverse effects.

**4**

Which choice completes the text with the most logical and precise word or phrase?

Ⓐ create
Ⓑ demonstrate
Ⓒ reciprocate
Ⓓ isolate

As anyone who has watched a bag of instant popcorn expand knows, the tray inside of a microwave oven rotates as the food cooks. This rotation has the interesting effect of increasing the kinetic energy of the food's polar molecules, as they too must constantly rotate to remain aligned with the field. As they do so, these molecules rub and grind against their neighbors, converting their kinetic energy into intermolecular friction, and thus evolving heat. In fact, the motion of molecules is so directly related to internal heat that one can calculate a material's exact temperature by averaging the kinetic energy of the atoms and molecules that comprise it.

**5**

As used in the text, what does the word "evolving" most nearly mean?

Ⓐ Advancing
Ⓑ Reproducing
Ⓒ Selecting
Ⓓ Generating

## 1 MODULE 2 1

Advocates of the presidential model posit that it is more democratic than the parliamentary system because the people themselves choose their executive. They contend that the fixed terms even allow for some stability that the parliamentary organization does not allow. Likewise, a further benefit lies in the separation of powers subject to checks and balances, in which the executive and legislative bodies can monitor one another and assure that power is not centralized. Yet, critics of the system assert that the president's national status affords tendencies toward authoritarianism. Furthermore, as a rule, deadlocks or stalemates are much more common within a system that often has executive and legislative bodies under the control of different parties. Cynics therefore suggest that the presidential model is privy to discord and inefficiency—not to mention, presidents are difficult to remove when thought to be unfit.

**6**

Which choice best states the main purpose of the text?

Ⓐ It explores the pros and cons of the presidential model.
Ⓑ It compares the presidential and parliamentary models.
Ⓒ It highlights the superior aspects of the presidential model.
Ⓓ It gives specific examples of countries that practice presidential politics.

Some people simply believe that few, if any, other civilizations outside those on Earth exist. The Rare Earth Hypothesis suggests that Earth is unique, and so, therefore, is intelligent life. Others theorize that intelligent life has a tendency of destroying itself quickly; they hypothesize that self-annihilation occurs before contact can be made. On the other hand, many postulate that extraterrestrial intelligence (ETI) does exist, but we see no evidence for a variety of reasons. Perhaps we are too far apart in space or time; perhaps humans, a relatively new species, haven't searched long enough or maybe we aren't listening properly; what if our distant neighbors are using different frequencies?

**7**

Which choice best describes the function of the final sentence in the overall structure of the text?

Ⓐ It explains why the author is quite pessimistic about the possibility of finding ETI.
Ⓑ It offers suggestions that have not likely been considered by scientists.
Ⓒ It gives a recommended course of action to solve a scientific problem.
Ⓓ It elaborates on possible reasons why we have not found evidence of ETI.

# MODULE 2



The following text is from Carl Sandburg's 1916 poem "Theme in Yellow."

I spot the hills
With yellow balls in autumn.
I light the prairie cornfields
Orange and tawny gold clusters
And I am called pumpkins.
On the last of October
When dusk is fallen
Children join hands
And circle round me
Singing ghost songs
And love to the harvest moon;
I am a jack-o'-lantern
With terrible teeth
And the children know
I am fooling.

**8**

The narrator of the poem is best described as which of the following?

Ⓐ A child
Ⓑ A pumpkin
Ⓒ A ghost
Ⓓ A season

1 MODULE 2 1

A historian writes an article suggesting that a shortcoming of the Iroquois Great League governmental structure was a decision-making process that led to paralysis.

**9**

Which quotation from the article would best illustrate this claim?

Ⓐ "The Great League of Peace and Power maintained Iroquois peace from the 15th century until the American Revolution."

Ⓑ "The Iroquois council could not decide unanimously which side to choose. With no consensus, each nation made its own decision. The League split."

Ⓒ "Despite being scattered, the Iroquois survived. Today in New York State, a strong Iroquois Reservation remains."

Ⓓ "These Iroquois are strongly independent and demand sovereignty. Despite this, they are also American citizens. On the reservations, traditions live on, as does the spirit of the Great League."

A biologist analyzes the relationship between Midwestern bird species and the honeysuckle fruit. They find that the organisms have developed a mutualist relationship: native species of birds throughout the Midwest rely on honeysuckle fruit as a staple food source in the fall, while honeysuckle benefits in being spread to new regions when its seeds are eaten and subsequently dispersed by the birds.

**10**

Which of the following situations would be most resemble the relationship discussed in the text?

Ⓐ Large whale species consume krill at higher latitudes.

Ⓑ The male gorilla does not help with infants but does help defend against predators.

Ⓒ Oxpecker birds eat predatory insects off the backs of zebras.

Ⓓ Humans consume the eggs of organically raised chickens.

Occupational therapists work with clients to help them better perform their daily tasks. An occupational therapist examines what aspect of occupational therapy will most likely lead to positive client outcomes, replacing dysfunctional occupations (activities) and replacing them with functional ones. The therapist hypothesizes that a collaborative relationship between the occupational therapist and patient will minimize occupational dysfunction.

**11**

Which of the following, if true, would most directly support the therapist's hypothesis?

Ⓐ Other occupations, like substance abuse, lead to occupational dysfunction. These dysfunctional occupations are not productive and can be detrimental to health and wellness.

Ⓑ Behaviors, habits, and performance patterns are changed when dysfunctional occupation is reduced or extinguished and replaced with meaningful, psychologically rewarding functional occupation.

Ⓒ Changing dysfunctional occupation and replacing it with functional occupation is challenging for the client; through therapeutic use of self, the occupational therapist can establish the necessary trust and rapport.

Ⓓ Self-regulation strategies include personal awareness of stressors, stress management, and using occupation to reduce stress.

**Human Influenza Outbreaks**

| Name | Year | Subtype | Reservoir | Geography | Estimated Cases | Estimated Fatality Rate (%) |
|---|---|---|---|---|---|---|
| Russian Flu | 1889 | Unknown | Unknown | Global | 6.6 million | 0.15 |
| Spanish Flu | 1918 | N1H1 | Humans, pigs, birds | Global | 500 million | 2.0 |
| Asian Flu | 1957 | N2H2 | Birds | Global | 9.5 million | 0.12 |
| Hong Kong Flu | 1968 | N3H2 | Pigs | Global | 8 million | <0.1 |
| Avian Flu | 2005 | H5N1 | Birds | Asia | 840 | 60 |
| Swine Flue | 2009 | H1N1 | Humans, pigs, birds | Global | 89 million | 2.5 |
| N/A | 2013 | H7N9 | Birds | China | 220 | 25 |

Epidemic illnesses can cause significant loss of human life. A virologist attempts to determine what characteristics of flu viruses will result in the greatest human mortality. The virologist hypothesizes that if a flu virus has too high a fatality rate, its victims will die off before they can transmit the virus to other humans, ultimately resulting in relatively few cases.

**12**

Which of the viruses in the table would most effectively be used to support the virologist's hypothesis?

Ⓐ H5N1 and H7N9
Ⓑ H1N1 and H2N2
Ⓒ H3N2 and H1N1
Ⓓ H3N2 and H2N2

# 1 MODULE 2 1



**Fatal passenger vehicle crash involvements per 100 million miles traveled by driver age and gender, 2017**

| | Male | | | Female | | | Total* | | |
|---|---|---|---|---|---|---|---|---|---|
| Age | Crash Involvements | Miles | Rate | Crash Involvements | Miles | Rate | Crash Involvements | Miles | Rate |
| 16-19 | 2,003 | 31,732,691,896 | 6.3 | 959 | 30,677,731,652 | 3.1 | 2,963 | 62,410,423,548 | 4.7 |
| 20-29 | 7,119 | 187,497,565,846 | 3.8 | 3,225 | 198,148,511,278 | 1.6 | 10,346 | 385,646,077,124 | 2.7 |
| 30-59 | 12,958 | 785,270,175,131 | 1.7 | 6,162 | 558,224,868,022 | 1.1 | 19,124 | 1,343,495,043,154 | 1.4 |
| 60-69 | 2,929 | 207,918,951,320 | 1.4 | 1,354 | 136,711,746,704 | 1.0 | 4,283 | 344,630,698,024 | 1.2 |
| ≥70 | 3,034 | 401,684,593,355 | 2.9 | 1,488 | 66,739,614,422 | 2.2 | 4,522 | 171,424,207,778 | 2.6 |
| Total* | 28,053 | 1,317,103,977,548 | 2.1 | 13,191 | 990,502,472,079 | 1.3 | 41,277 | 2,307,606,449,627 | 1.8 |

*Total includes other and/or unknowns

Graph source: *www.iihs.org/topics/fatality-statistics/detail/gender*

A researcher who specializes in analyzing the aftermath of car wrecks determines that car crash dummies are almost always designed to represent the male skeletal and muscular anatomy. The researcher thinks that car manufacturers as well as consumers should demand that the National Highway Traffic Safety Administration develop dummies that represent not just men and women, but a variety of sizes of men and women as well as a variety of sizes of children. The researcher argues that the government should prioritize diverse demographic representation among crash test dummies to gather the most helpful information for consumers.

**13**

Which statement would best utilize the information in the table to provide an argument against the researcher's position?

Ⓐ Given the higher crash rate of male drivers as compared to female drivers, it is understandable that car manufacturers may prioritize male crash test dummies.

Ⓑ Since drivers over 70 years of age are over twice as likely to get in vehicle crashes as those in their 60s, increased regulations about the maximum driver age should be implemented.

Ⓒ Teenage drivers are far more likely to get in car accidents than those in other age groups, so the age to earn a driver's license should be increased.

Ⓓ Female drivers represent the majority of miles driven in a given year, so it is critical that there be a higher priority on their safety.

## 1 MODULE 2 1

English chemist John Newlands proposed a "law of octaves" that was based, shockingly, on the standard musical scale, and which suggested that the periodicity of the elements follows a similar eight "note" pattern. Though his contemporaries heavily criticized Newlands, the idea was eventually vindicated by the octet theory of chemical bonding, which ______

**14**

Which choice most logically completes the text?

Ⓐ demonstrated the need for additional research to confirm his hypothesis.

Ⓑ confirmed the significance of the eight-element series in chemical behavior.

Ⓒ approached the problem of chemical classification differently from Newlands.

Ⓓ served to disprove his interesting yet ultimately inaccurate theory.

---

Bacteria is adapting and changing in response to our attempts to quash it and is consequently becoming more of a threat than ever before. Doctors and patients should be cautious and should ensure that antibiotics are truly necessary before contributing to this issue. Fewer antibiotics prescribed will mean less of a chance for *C. diff* for each individual patient and a greater chance that antibiotics will ______

**15**

Which choice most logically completes the text?

Ⓐ remain effective for the people who genuinely need them.

Ⓑ develop increased resistance to bacterial modification.

Ⓒ contribute to the outbreak of endemic illnesses.

Ⓓ become increasingly recommended for a host of illnesses.

---

______ that live in the eastern region of Australia and in Tasmania. Platypuses typically live in bodies of freshwater like rivers, wetlands, billabongs, and estuaries; however, they have been known to live in brackish—a combination of fresh and salt water—estuaries as well.

**16**

Which choice completes the text so that it conforms to the conventions of Standard English?

Ⓐ *Ornithorhynchus anatinus* also known as platypuses are semi-aquatic mammals

Ⓑ *Ornithorhynchus anatinus*, also known as platypuses are semi-aquatic mammals

Ⓒ *Ornithorhynchus anatinus*—also known as platypuses, are semi-aquatic mammals

Ⓓ *Ornithorhynchus anatinus*, also known as platypuses, are semi-aquatic mammals

1 MODULE 2 1



The bystander effect is a psychological phenomenon that prevents people from helping those in need. The psychology behind this phenomenon is actually fairly simple. __________ In a crowded place such as a stadium, people may think "I couldn't get there in time," or, "there are so many people who are closer to the scene of distress."

**17**

Which choice completes the text so that it conforms to the conventions of Standard English?

Ⓐ When several people observe a situation that calls for intervention, the responsibility to help feels less pressing since it is diffused among all the observers.
Ⓑ When several people observe a situation that calls for intervention: the responsibility to help feels less pressing since it is diffused among all the observers.
Ⓒ When several people observe a situation that calls for intervention: the responsibility to help feels less pressing, since it is diffused among all the observers.
Ⓓ When several people observe a situation that calls for intervention—the responsibility to help feels—less pressing since it is diffused among all the observers.

Scientists speculate that the even though the evolutionary purpose of the toxins in ergot fungus was to discourage animals from eating it, humans were unable to prevent its consumption. __________ harvested en masse and was only rarely sorted to remove ergot fungus.

**18**

Which choice completes the text so that it conforms to the conventions of Standard English?

Ⓐ Rye, like other grains, was
Ⓑ Rye, like other grains was
Ⓒ Rye—like other grains—were
Ⓓ Rye—like other grains, was

# 1 MODULE 2 1

States can best be characterized by their natural idiosyncrasies. Florida has its powdered sugar beaches; Nebraska, its butterscotch ________

**19**

Which choice completes the text so that it conforms to the conventions of Standard English?

Ⓐ cornfields; and Arizona it's majestic Grand Canyon.
Ⓑ cornfields: Arizona its majestic Grand Canyon.
Ⓒ cornfields; and Arizona, its majestic Grand Canyon.
Ⓓ cornfields, and Arizona, it's majestic Grand Canyon.

While hiking has always been known to be a good form of exercise, current research ________ that its added mental benefits have a significant impact on the physical health of those who hike.

**20**

Which choice completes the text so that it conforms to the conventions of Standard English?

Ⓐ suggest
Ⓑ suggests
Ⓒ had suggested
Ⓓ has suggesting

When visiting museums, most people take for granted the rooms upon rooms of historic paintings, often hundreds of years old, that ________ carefully preserved for the public's view.

**21**

Which choice completes the text so that it conforms to the conventions of Standard English?

Ⓐ is
Ⓑ are
Ⓒ has
Ⓓ was

Servals are medium-sized, gold-colored cats covered in darker patterns of stripes and spots. Having a lighter-colored coat with a darker pattern ________ more difficult to spot them.

**22**

Which choice completes the text so that it conforms to the conventions of Standard English?

Ⓐ make them
Ⓑ makes them
Ⓒ makes it
Ⓓ make it

# 1 MODULE 2 1



The Y-Bridge (named for its distinctive Y-shape) was designed to span the confluence of the Muskingum and Licking rivers. __________ it crosses both rivers, Ripley's Believe It Or Not once claimed that the Y-Bridge was the only bridge in the world where it was possible to cross and still end up on the same side of the river, and Amelia Earhart once called Zanesville "the most recognizable city in the country" because of the bridge.

**23**

Which choice completes the text with the most logical transition?

Ⓐ For
Ⓑ Because
Ⓒ While
Ⓓ When

Chronic traumatic encephalopathy (CTE) is a progressive neurodegenerative brain disease that is largely difficult to diagnose and treat. Indeed, __________ accurate diagnosis can only be done by looking at portions of the brain under a microscope, a true CTE diagnosis can't be made until an autopsy is done on a deceased sufferer.

**24**

Which choice completes the text with the most logical transition?

Ⓐ since
Ⓑ and
Ⓒ also
Ⓓ in fact

While researching a topic, a student has taken the following notes:

- Ballet traces its history to the Italian Renaissance in the 15th century.
- Catherine de Medici, a native Italian, was queen consort of France in the mid-1500s.
- Catherine de Medici enjoyed ballet, introduced it to the French court, and sponsored large and detailed performances.
- The French court continued to value ballet and King Louis XIV even performed in ballets.
- The world's first ballet school, Académie Royale de Danse, was founded in France in 1661 with the support of King Louis XIV.
- The ballet school introduced the five positions all ballet students still learn today.

**25**

The student wants to make a generalization about the early sponsors of ballet. Which choice most effectively uses relevant information from the notes to accomplish this goal?

Ⓐ Catherine de Medici was one of the greatest ballet enthusiasts of all time.
Ⓑ Some of the same ballet moves that originated in the 1600s are still used today.
Ⓒ French and Italian royals were significant backers of ballet dance performance.
Ⓓ Both male and female dancers have been skilled ballet dancers throughout history.

While researching a topic, a student has taken the following notes:

- There are two types of hearing loss: conductive and sensorineural.
- Conductive hearing loss happens when sounds cannot get through, or conduct, to the inner ear.
- Conductive hearing loss can have many causes and sometimes it's a simple cause, such a blockage in the ear canal.
- Sensorineural hearing loss happens when structures in the inner ear are damaged.
- Sensorineural hearing loss also has many causes—two common causes are aging and exposure to loud noises.

**26**

The student wants to recommend specific measures that people can take to avoid hearing loss. Which choice most effectively uses relevant information from the notes to accomplish this goal?

Ⓐ Conductive hearing loss can result from the blockage of sound in the inner ear.

Ⓑ To prevent hearing loss, avoid putting objects inside your ear, and cover your ears at loud rock concerts.

Ⓒ Older people are more susceptible to sensorineural hearing loss since this sort of loss becomes exacerbated with the passage of time.

Ⓓ Much like with blindness, hearing loss can often be prevented by taking precautionary steps.

While researching a topic, a student has taken the following notes:

- Effective Altruism is an emerging form of charity that evaluates causes through a framework of data and evidence.
- To be a good candidate for Effective Altruism, a problem must be solvable.
- Effective Altruism seeks to use charity money in the most efficient way to do the most good.
- This results in Effective Altruism targeting specific causes that may have previously been overlooked by charitable endeavors.
- Some causes that have benefited from Effective Altruism include the nearing eradication of Guinea worm disease, the treatment of diabetic eye disease in Bangladesh, and cash incentives for completing routine childhood vaccines in Nigeria.

**27**

The student wants to suggest a charitable cause that would be a good candidate for the approach of Effective Altruism. Which choice most effectively uses relevant information from the notes to accomplish this goal?

Ⓐ Marching in a local parade to encourage the world to seek out peaceful resolutions to warfare.

Ⓑ Encouraging museum donors to purchase an additional sculpture for the largest wing of the museum.

Ⓒ Earning a graduate degree in statistics so that one can more readily evaluate the costs and benefits of certain governmental actions.

Ⓓ Raising money to remove poisonous lead-based paints from school facilities in an impoverished city.

## Section 2, Module 1: Math

35 MINUTES, 22 QUESTIONS

**DIRECTIONS**

- All expressions and variables use real numbers.
- All figures are drawn to scale.
- Every figure lies in a plane.
- The domain of given functions is the set of all real numbers for which the corresponding value of the function is real.

For **multiple-choice questions**, solve the problem and pick the correct answer from the provided choices. Each multiple-choice question has only one correct answer.

For **student-produced response questions,** solve each problem and enter your answer following these guidelines:

- If you find **more than one correct answer,** enter just one answer.
- You can enter up to five characters for a **positive** answer and up to six characters (this includes the negative sign) for a **negative** answer.
- If your answer is a **fraction** that does not fit in the given space, enter the decimal equivalent instead.
- If your answer is a **decimal** that does not fit in the given space, enter it by stopping at or rounding up at the fourth digit.
- If your answer is a **mixed number** (like $4\frac{1}{2}$), enter it as an improper fraction (9/2) or its decimal equivalent (4.5).
- Do not enter **symbols** like a comma, dollar sign, or percent sign.

## Examples

| Answer | Acceptable Entries | Unacceptable Entries That Will Receive Zero Credit |
|---|---|---|
| 4.5 | 4.5<br>4.50<br>9/2 | $4\frac{1}{2}$<br>41/2 |
| $\frac{8}{9}$ | 8/9<br>.8888<br>.8889<br>0.888<br>0.889 | 0.88<br>.88<br>.89<br>0.89 |
| $-\frac{1}{9}$ | −1/9<br>−.1111<br>−0.111 | −.11<br>−0.11 |

**REFERENCE** ∨

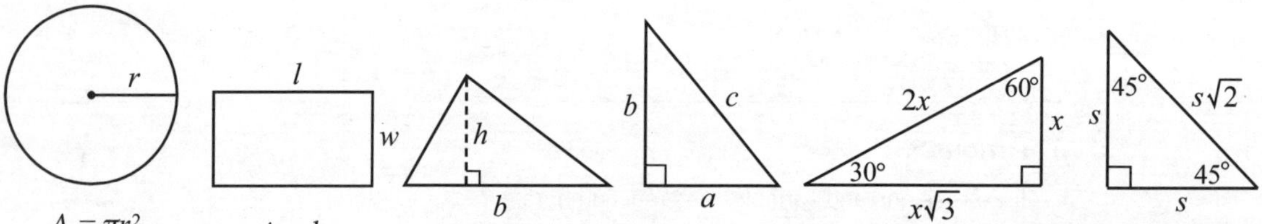


$A = \pi r^2$
$C = 2\pi r$

$A = lw$

$A = \frac{1}{2}bh$

$c^2 = a^2 + b^2$

Special Right Triangles

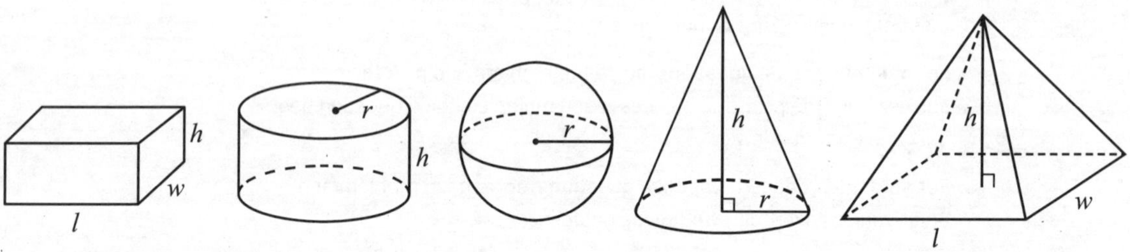


$V = lwh$

$V = \pi r^2 h$

$V = \frac{4}{3}\pi r^3$

$V = \frac{1}{3}\pi r^2 h$

$V = \frac{1}{3}lwh$

The number of degrees of arc in a circle is 360.
The number of radians of arc in a circle is $2\pi$.
The sum of the measures in degrees of the angles of a triangle is 180.

# 2 MODULE 1 2



**1**

$$\frac{6}{7} \times \frac{14}{3} = ?$$

Ⓐ $\frac{1}{3}$
Ⓑ 4
Ⓒ $\frac{27}{4}$
Ⓓ 9

**2**

If $\frac{2}{3}x - 1 = \frac{1}{6}x + 4$, what is the value of $x$?

**3**

The graph of a line in the $x$-$y$ plane is totally vertical and has a negative $x$-intercept. Which of the following could represent a line with these conditions?

Ⓐ $x = -5$
Ⓑ $y = -4$
Ⓒ $y = -x - 2$
Ⓓ $x = -4y$

**4**

If $\frac{x}{4} = 6$, what is $\frac{x}{8}$?

Ⓐ 3
Ⓑ 4
Ⓒ 8
Ⓓ 12

**5**

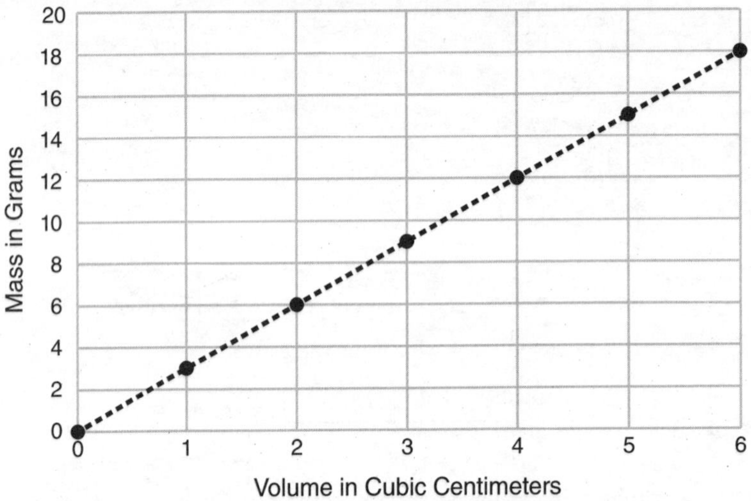


What equation represents the relationship between mass, $m$, and volume, $v$, in the above graph?

Ⓐ $v = 3m$
Ⓑ $m = 3v$
Ⓒ $m = 6v$
Ⓓ $v = m + 2$

**6**

What is the median of this set of numbers?

$$\{2, 5, 7, 9, 12, 16\}$$

Ⓐ 7
Ⓑ 8
Ⓒ 8.5
Ⓓ 9

**7**

There are 3 teaspoons in a tablespoon and 16 tablespoons in a cup. How much of a cup or cups would there be in 12 teaspoons?

Ⓐ $\frac{1}{12}$ cup
Ⓑ $\frac{1}{4}$ cup
Ⓒ 2 cups
Ⓓ 6 cups

**8**

The total calories for a particular salad are 1,100. The salad consists of only cheese, vegetables, and dressing. If the total caloric value of the cheese and vegetables is 650, and each packet of dressing used on the salad has 75 calories, how many packets of dressing were used on the salad?

______

**9**

If $\frac{x^2}{6} = \frac{x}{2}$, what is the value of $x$?

______

**10**

Suppose the price of a product is typically $p$ dollars. If a 30% discount is applied to the price, what is the discounted price in terms of $p$?

Ⓐ $0.03p$
Ⓑ $0.3p$
Ⓒ $0.7p$
Ⓓ $1.3p$

**11**

The equation for gravitational force, $F_g$, is the following:

$$F_g = G\frac{m_1 m_2}{r^2}$$

$G$ is the gravitational constant, $m_1$ and $m_2$ are the masses of objects, and $r$ is the distance between the objects.

How would the gravitational force between two objects change if the distance between the objects doubles while all other quantities remain the same?

Ⓐ It would be twice the original force.
Ⓑ It would be four times the original force.
Ⓒ It would be $\frac{1}{2}$ of the original force.
Ⓓ It would be $\frac{1}{4}$ of the original force.

**12**

**Pet Owners Who Have Only One Pet**

| | Dog | Cat | Total |
|---|---|---|---|
| Male | 60 | 40 | 100 |
| Female | 50 | 38 | 88 |
| Total | 110 | 78 | 188 |

If there were a randomly selected pet owner from the table above, what is the probability that they would be a male cat owner?

Ⓐ $\frac{40}{188}$
Ⓑ $\frac{40}{100}$
Ⓒ $\frac{60}{188}$
Ⓓ $\frac{40}{78}$

# 2 MODULE 1 2



**13**

A restaurant charges \$5 for a cheeseburger and \$4 for a hamburger. If Connor wants to buy at least 2 of each sandwich and spend a total of between \$20–\$30 (inclusive) on sandwiches, what is a possible value for the number of cheeseburgers Connor purchased?

________

**14**

What is $y$ in terms of $x$ in the following inequality?

$$12 < -4x + 6y$$

Ⓐ $3 + 2x > y$
Ⓑ $6x - 2 < y$
Ⓒ $\frac{1}{2}x + 3 > y$
Ⓓ $2 + \frac{2}{3}x < y$

**15**

A particular line is graphed in the $xy$-plane and uses only real numbers. The line has a positive slope and a positive $y$-intercept. Which of these points could be on the line?

Ⓐ $(-4, 5)$
Ⓑ $(2, 0)$
Ⓒ $(3, -6)$
Ⓓ $(0, -1)$

**16**

Triangle $ABC$ has a right angle $B$. If side $AB$ has a length of 7 units and side $BC$ has a length of 24 units, what is the length in units of side $AC$?

________

**17**

The function $f$ is expressed as $f(x) = k$ for all values of $x$, and $k$ is a constant real number. Which of the following must be true?

I. $f(x)$ forms a line.

II. $f(x)$ has a slope of zero.

III. $f(x)$ has a range from $-\infty$ to $+\infty$.

Ⓐ I only
Ⓑ II only
Ⓒ Only I and II
Ⓓ Only II and III

**18**

In a right rectangular prism, the smallest edge is 2 cm long. The next greatest edge is twice the length of the smallest edge, and the greatest edge is 3 times the length of the smallest edge. What is the surface area of the prism?

Ⓐ 6 sq cm.
Ⓑ 24 sq cm.
Ⓒ 64 sq cm.
Ⓓ 88 sq cm.

**19**

Kamini wants to make money from recycling aluminum cans and glass bottles. Her local government pays her \$0.10 per can and \$0.16 for each bottle. If she wants to earn a total of at least \$100 and has collected a total of 600 cans, what is the minimum number of bottles she would need to collect to reach her goal?

Ⓐ 250
Ⓑ 270
Ⓒ 300
Ⓓ 420

**20**

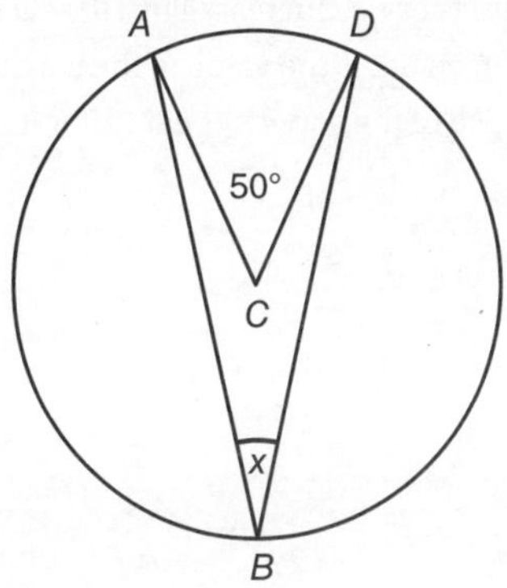


What is the measure in degrees of $\angle X$ given that *AB*, *AC*, *CD*, and *DB* are straight lines and *C* is the center of the circle?

**21**

Jane is watering her garden and spends 5 minutes watering each tree and 2 minutes watering each shrub. If she can spend no more than 30 minutes watering her garden, which inequality represents the number of *T* trees and *S* shrubs she can water given these constraints?

Ⓐ $5T + 2S \geq 30$
Ⓑ $5T + 2S \leq 30$
Ⓒ $5 \times T \times S \leq 30$
Ⓓ $5 > 30 \times T \times S$

2 MODULE 1 2

22

The price of a video streaming service increases by 15% each year. If the price, $P$, of the service begins at $v$ dollars, what is the value of the constant $c$ in the following function that models the price of the service $t$ years after it begins?

$$P = vc^t$$

Ⓐ 0.15
Ⓑ 0.85
Ⓒ 1.15
Ⓓ 1.55

## Section 2, Module 2: Math

35 MINUTES, 22 QUESTIONS

---

**DIRECTIONS**

- All expressions and variables use real numbers.
- All figures are drawn to scale.
- Every figure lies in a plane.
- The domain of given functions is the set of all real numbers for which the corresponding value of the function is real.

For **multiple-choice questions**, solve the problem and pick the correct answer from the provided choices. Each multiple-choice question has only one correct answer.

For **student-produced response questions,** solve each problem and enter your answer following these guidelines:

- If you find **more than one correct answer,** enter just one answer.
- You can enter up to five characters for a **positive** answer and up to six characters (this includes the negative sign) for a **negative** answer.
- If your answer is a **fraction** that does not fit in the given space, enter the decimal equivalent instead.
- If your answer is a **decimal** that does not fit in the given space, enter it by stopping at or rounding up at the fourth digit.
- If your answer is a **mixed number** (like $4\frac{1}{2}$), enter it as an improper fraction (9/2) or its decimal equivalent (4.5).
- Do not enter **symbols** like a comma, dollar sign, or percent sign.

---

## Examples

| Answer | Acceptable Entries | Unacceptable Entries That Will Receive Zero Credit |
|---|---|---|
| 4.5 | 4.5<br>4.50<br>9/2 | $4\frac{1}{2}$<br>41/2 |
| $\frac{8}{9}$ | 8/9<br>.8888<br>.8889<br>0.888<br>0.889 | 0.88<br>.88<br>.89<br>0.89 |
| $-\frac{1}{9}$ | −1/9<br>−.1111<br>−0.111 | −.11<br>−0.11 |

**REFERENCE ∨**

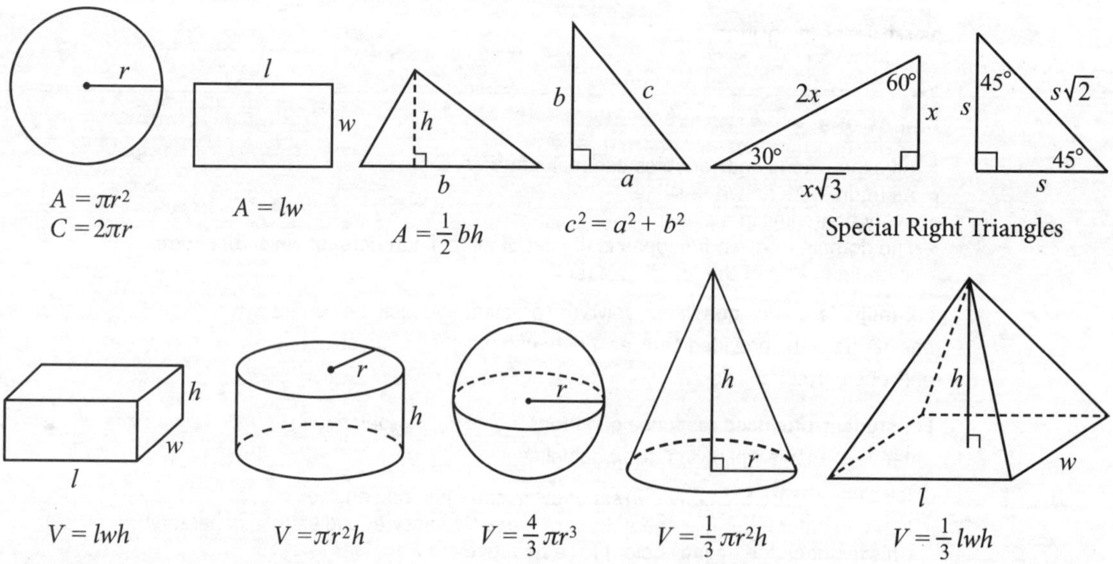


The number of degrees of arc in a circle is 360.
The number of radians of arc in a circle is $2\pi$.
The sum of the measures in degrees of the angles of a triangle is 180.

# 2 MODULE 2 2



**1**

Density equals mass divided by volume. If density is graphed as a line with mass corresponding to the *y* value and the volume corresponding to the *x* value, what aspect of the function corresponds to the density of the substance?

Ⓐ slope
Ⓑ *y*-intercept
Ⓒ *x*-intercept
Ⓓ domain

**2**

What is the sum of the following polynomials?

$$5x^3 - x + 4 \quad \text{and} \quad 6x^3 + x^2 - 3$$

Ⓐ $30x^6 + x^3 - x + 1$
Ⓑ $30x^3 + 2x^2 + x - 1$
Ⓒ $11x^3 + x^2 - x + 1$
Ⓓ $11x^3 - x^2 + x - 1$

**3**

Which of the following is equivalent to $8^{\left(\frac{1}{3}\right)}$?

Ⓐ 0
Ⓑ 1
Ⓒ 2
Ⓓ 6

**4**

$$2x - 3y = 7$$
$$6x + ky = 21$$

For what value of the constant *k* will the above system of equations have infinitely many solutions?

Ⓐ $-9$
Ⓑ $-7$
Ⓒ 2
Ⓓ 13

## 2 MODULE 2 2

**5**

What is the $y$-intercept of the graph of the function $y = 2^x - 3$ ?

Ⓐ $-3$
Ⓑ $-2$
Ⓒ $0$
Ⓓ $1$

**6**

Which of the following is an equivalent form of $z = x - y$ ?

Ⓐ $z = (\sqrt{x} - \sqrt{y})(\sqrt{x} - \sqrt{y})$
Ⓑ $z = (\sqrt{x} - \sqrt{y})(\sqrt{x} + \sqrt{y})$
Ⓒ $z = (\sqrt{x} + \sqrt{y})(\sqrt{x} + \sqrt{y})$
Ⓓ $z = \frac{(\sqrt{x} + \sqrt{y})}{(\sqrt{x} - \sqrt{y})}$

**7**

If $x + 3 = y$ and $xy = 40$, what is the sum of $x$ and $y$, given that both $x$ and $y$ are positive?

Ⓐ 5
Ⓑ 8
Ⓒ 13
Ⓓ 15

# 2 MODULE 2 2

**8**

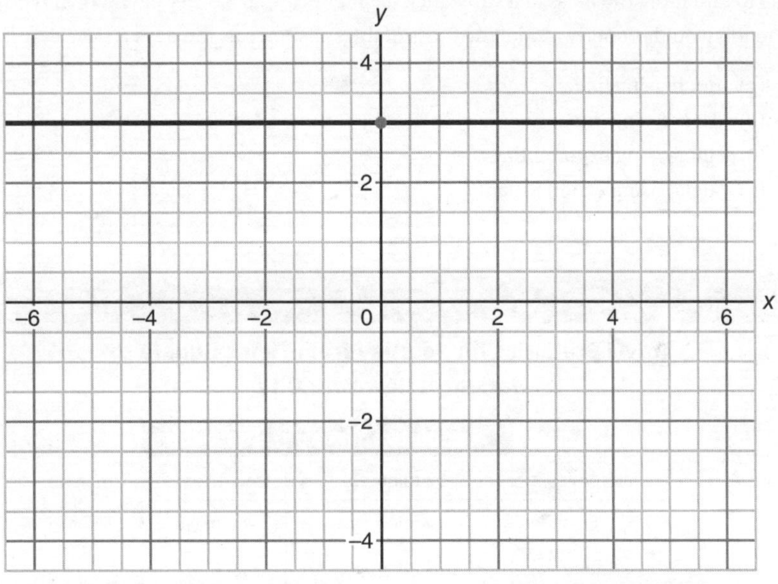


The graph of the above line is portrayed by which of the following equations?

Ⓐ $y = 3$

Ⓑ $y = \frac{1}{3}x$

Ⓒ $y = 3x$

Ⓓ $y = x + 3$

**9**

$$2a - 3b = 5$$
$$3a - 2b = 10$$

The solution to the above system of equations is $(a, b)$. What is the value of $a - b$?

__________

## 2 MODULE 2 2

**10**

Due to radiation, the mass of a substance decreases by 0.5% every day. Which type of function would properly model the mass of the substance as the days go by?

Ⓐ increasing linear
Ⓑ decreasing linear
Ⓒ increasing exponential
Ⓓ decreasing exponential

**11**

**Travel Statistics on Journey from Times Square to Harlem in New York City**

| | Estimated Time | Distance |
|---|---|---|
| **Subway** | 17 minutes | 5 miles |
| **Car** | 19 minutes | 4.9 miles |
| **Walk** | 93 minutes | 4.6 miles |
| **Bicycle** | 33 minutes | 5.7 miles |

If Sarah took the subway from Times Square to Harlem, what was her speed in miles per hour, to the nearest tenth?

Ⓐ 0.7 mph
Ⓑ 3.4 mph
Ⓒ 17.6 mph
Ⓓ 204.0 mph

**12**

If $x + y = 7$ and $x - y = 3$, what is the value of $3x^2 - 3y^2$?

# 2 MODULE 2 2



**13**

Water from the ocean has 3.5% salt, and water from the Dead Sea has 33.7% salt. If someone has 10 gallons of ocean water, how many gallons of water from the Dead Sea (measured to the nearest hundredth of a gallon) need to be added so that the solution has 10% salt?

__________

**14**

Which of the following is a solution for $x$ in the equation $4x = 2 - 3x^2$?

Ⓐ $\frac{-3+\sqrt{10}}{4}$

Ⓑ $\frac{2-\sqrt{5}}{3}$

Ⓒ $\frac{\sqrt{3}}{4}$

Ⓓ $\frac{-2-\sqrt{10}}{3}$

**15**

A function $g(x)$ has values given in the table below:

| $x$ | $g(x)$ |
|---|---|
| –3 | –1 |
| –2 | 0 |
| –1 | 2 |
| 0 | 1 |
| 1 | 0 |
| 2 | 3 |

Which of the following would be a factor of $g(x)$?

Ⓐ $(x-1)(x+2)$
Ⓑ $(x-2)(x+3)$
Ⓒ $(x+1)(x-2)$
Ⓓ $(x+2)(x-2)$

# 2 MODULE 2 2

**16**

Students at a university were surveyed as to whether they wanted a new library for the university. Out of the 100 students surveyed, 40% said they wanted a new library. What is justifiable based on this information?

Ⓐ Of the 100 students surveyed, 40 wanted a new library.
Ⓑ 40% of all people in the university community want a new library.
Ⓒ Exactly 40 students at the university want a new library.
Ⓓ No more than 40 university students want a new library.

**17**

A circle has the equation $(x - a)^2 + (y - b)^2 = 9$, in which $a$ and $b$ are positive constants. What must the values of $a$ and $b$ be in order for all the $x$ and $y$ coordinates of the circle to be greater than zero?

Ⓐ $a < 9$ and $b > 9$
Ⓑ $a > \sqrt{3}$ and $b > \sqrt{3}$
Ⓒ $a > 6$ and $b < 6$
Ⓓ $a > 3$ and $b > 3$

**18**

$$v_e = \sqrt{\frac{2GM}{r}}$$

The escape velocity for a given spherical body, like a planet or a star, is given by the above formula, in which $G$ is the gravitational constant, $r$ is the distance from the center of the body's mass to the object, and $m$ is the mass of the spherical body. What is $M$ in terms of the other variables?

Ⓐ $M = \frac{(v_e)G}{2r}$
Ⓑ $M = \frac{2G}{(v_e)^2 r}$
Ⓒ $M = \frac{(v_e)^2 r}{2G}$
Ⓓ $M = \frac{2r\sqrt{v_e}}{G}$

# 2 MODULE 2 2



**19**

A sphere has a volume of 8 cubic feet. What is the volume in cubic feet of a sphere with twice the radius of the original one?

______

**20**

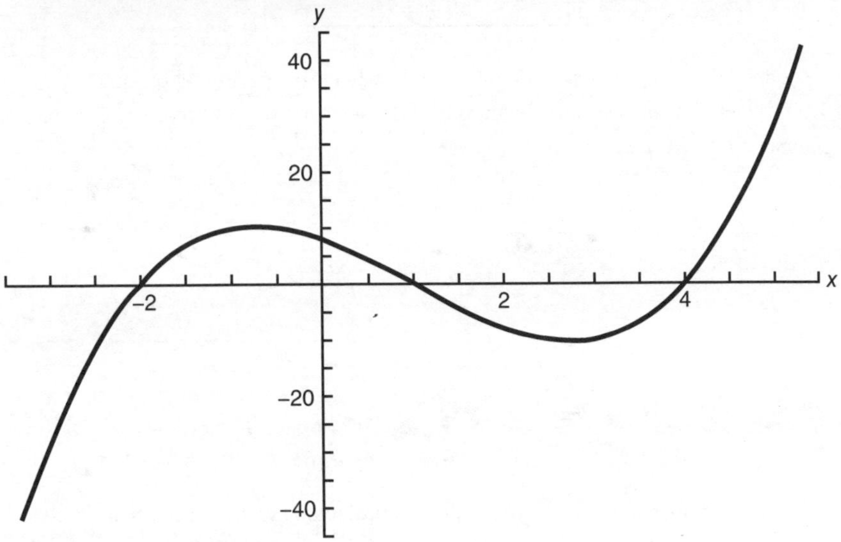


Which equation would portray the function graphed above?

Ⓐ $y = (x - 2)(x + 4)(x - 1)$
Ⓑ $y = (x - 4)(x + 2)(x - 1)$
Ⓒ $y = (x - 4)(x - 2)$
Ⓓ $y = (x + 1)(x + 2)$

## 2 MODULE 2 2

**21**

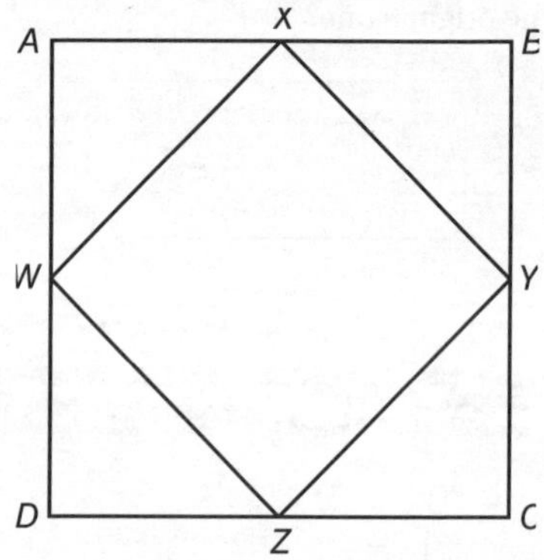


If square *ABCD* has an area of 36 square units, what is the perimeter of square *WXYZ* given that each vertex of square *WXYZ* bisects the side of square *ABCD* that it intersects?

Ⓐ 6
Ⓑ $6\sqrt{3}$
Ⓒ 12
Ⓓ $12\sqrt{2}$

**22**

$$h(t) = -16t^2 + 16t + 10$$

The function above portrays the height, $h$, of a projectile $t$ seconds after being thrown. Which of the following would be the time in seconds at which the height of the projectile is at its maximum value?

# ANSWER KEY
## Diagnostic Test



### Section 1

#### Reading and Writing Module 1

| | | |
|---|---|---|
| 1. **C** | 10. **B** | 19. **D** |
| 2. **C** | 11. **A** | 20. **A** |
| 3. **A** | 12. **B** | 21. **C** |
| 4. **D** | 13. **C** | 22. **C** |
| 5. **C** | 14. **A** | 23. **A** |
| 6. **D** | 15. **C** | 24. **C** |
| 7. **C** | 16. **C** | 25. **A** |
| 8. **D** | 17. **B** | 26. **B** |
| 9. **A** | 18. **A** | 27. **B** |

#### Reading and Writing Module 2

| | | |
|---|---|---|
| 1. **B** | 10. **C** | 19. **C** |
| 2. **A** | 11. **C** | 20. **B** |
| 3. **B** | 12. **A** | 21. **B** |
| 4. **D** | 13. **A** | 22. **C** |
| 5. **D** | 14. **B** | 23. **B** |
| 6. **A** | 15. **A** | 24. **A** |
| 7. **D** | 16. **D** | 25. **C** |
| 8. **B** | 17. **A** | 26. **B** |
| 9. **B** | 18. **A** | 27. **D** |

# ANSWER KEY
## Diagnostic Test

### Section 2

#### Math Module 1

1. **B**
2. **10**
3. **A**
4. **A**
5. **B**
6. **B**
7. **B**
8. **6**
9. **3**
10. **C**
11. **D**
12. **A**
13. **2, 3, or 4**
14. **D**
15. **A**
16. **25**
17. **C**
18. **D**
19. **A**
20. **25**
21. **B**
22. **C**

#### Math Module 2

1. **A**
2. **C**
3. **C**
4. **A**
5. **B**
6. **B**
7. **C**
8. **A**
9. **3**
10. **D**
11. **C**
12. **63**
13. **2.74**
14. **D**
15. **A**
16. **A**
17. **D**
18. **C**
19. **64**
20. **B**
21. **D**
22. **0.5 or $\frac{1}{2}$**

## Digital SAT Scoring Chart

This will give you an approximation of the score you would earn on the Digital SAT.[1] Tally the number of correct answers from the Reading and Writing section (out of 54) and the Math section (out of 44). Take the total for each of these and find the corresponding section score in the tables below.

| Number of Correct Reading and Writing Questions (Out of 54) | Reading and Writing Test Score (Out of 800) |
|---|---|
| 0 | 200 |
| 1 | 210 |
| 2 | 220 |
| 3 | 230 |
| 4 | 240 |
| 5 | 250 |
| 6 | 260 |
| 7 | 270 |
| 8 | 280 |
| 9 | 290 |
| 10 | 300 |
| 11 | 310 |
| 12 | 330 |
| 13 | 340 |
| 14 | 350 |
| 15 | 360 |
| 16 | 380 |
| 17 | 390 |
| 18 | 400 |
| 19 | 410 |
| 20 | 430 |
| 21 | 440 |
| 22 | 460 |
| 23 | 470 |
| 24 | 490 |
| 25 | 500 |
| 26 | 510 |
| 27 | 520 |
| 28 | 530 |
| 29 | 540 |
| 30 | 550 |
| 31 | 560 |
| 32 | 570 |
| 33 | 580 |
| 34 | 590 |
| 35 | 600 |
| 36 | 610 |
| 37 | 620 |
| 38 | 630 |
| 39 | 640 |
| 40 | 650 |
| 41 | 660 |
| 42 | 670 |
| 43 | 680 |
| 44 | 690 |
| 45 | 700 |
| 46 | 710 |
| 47 | 720 |
| 48 | 730 |
| 49 | 740 |
| 50 | 750 |
| 51 | 760 |
| 52 | 770 |
| 53 | 790 |
| 54 | 800 |

[1]Keep in mind that some of the questions on an actual SAT test will be research questions that will not count towards your actual score. For the sake of simplicity, we are including possible research questions in your calculation.

| Number of Correct Math Questions (Out of 44) | Math Section Score (Out of 800) | Number of Correct Math Questions (Out of 44) | Math Section Score (Out of 800) |
|---|---|---|---|
| 0 | 200 | 23 | 520 |
| 1 | 220 | 24 | 530 |
| 2 | 230 | 25 | 540 |
| 3 | 240 | 26 | 550 |
| 4 | 250 | 27 | 560 |
| 5 | 280 | 28 | 570 |
| 6 | 300 | 29 | 580 |
| 7 | 320 | 30 | 590 |
| 8 | 340 | 31 | 600 |
| 9 | 350 | 32 | 610 |
| 10 | 360 | 33 | 620 |
| 11 | 380 | 34 | 630 |
| 12 | 390 | 35 | 650 |
| 13 | 400 | 36 | 660 |
| 14 | 410 | 37 | 680 |
| 15 | 430 | 38 | 690 |
| 16 | 440 | 39 | 700 |
| 17 | 450 | 40 | 720 |
| 18 | 460 | 41 | 750 |
| 19 | 480 | 42 | 770 |
| 20 | 490 | 43 | 790 |
| 21 | 500 | 44 | 800 |
| 22 | 510 | | |

Add the Reading and Writing section score and the Math section score to find your total SAT test score:

____________ Reading and Writing Section Score +

____________ Math Section Score =

____________ **Total SAT Test Score (between 400 and 1600)**

Approximate your testing percentiles (1st to 99th) using this chart:[2]

| Total Score | Section Score | Total Percentile | Reading and Writing Percentile | Math Percentile |
|---|---|---|---|---|
| 1600 | 800 | 99+ | 99+ | 99 |
| 1500 | 750 | 98 | 98 | 96 |
| 1400 | 700 | 94 | 94 | 91 |
| 1300 | 650 | 86 | 86 | 84 |
| 1200 | 600 | 74 | 73 | 75 |
| 1100 | 550 | 59 | 57 | 61 |
| 1000 | 500 | 41 | 40 | 42 |
| 900 | 450 | 25 | 24 | 27 |
| 800 | 400 | 11 | 11 | 15 |
| 700 | 350 | 3 | 3 | 5 |
| 600 | 300 | 1 | 1 | 1 |
| 500 | 250 | 1 | 1 | 1 |
| 400 | 200 | 1 | 1 | 1 |

[2] Scoring Data based on information at *collegeboard.org*

## Test Analysis

Use this guide to determine which skills you should focus on when you review the chapters. As you go through the test, circle the questions you missed. This will let you easily identify the areas in which you need to improve. The test questions that correspond to different skills are organized below.

### Reading and Writing Module 1

Reading: Words in Context: 1, 2, 3, 4, 5
Reading: Structure and Purpose: 6, 7
Reading: Central Ideas and Details: 8, 9
Reading: Cross-Text Connections: 10
Reading: Textual Evidence: 11, 12
Reading: Quantitative Evidence: 13
Reading: Inferences: 14
Writing: Number and Tense: 18, 20, 21
Writing: Punctuation: 15, 16, 17, 19
Writing: Sentence Structure and Organization: 22
Writing: Transitions: 23, 24, 25
Writing: Rhetorical Synthesis: 26, 27

### Reading and Writing Module 2

Reading: Words in Context: 1, 2, 3, 4, 5
Reading: Structure and Purpose: 6, 7
Reading: Central Ideas and Details: 8
Reading: Textual Evidence: 9, 10, 11
Reading: Quantitative Evidence: 12, 13
Reading: Inferences: 14, 15
Writing: Punctuation: 16, 17, 18, 19
Writing: Number and Tense: 20, 21, 22
Writing: Transitions: 23, 24
Writing: Rhetorical Synthesis: 25, 26, 27

### Math Module 1

Algebra: 1, 2, 3, 4, 5, 14, 15, 17
Problem Solving and Data Analysis: 6, 7, 12
Advanced Math: 8, 9, 10, 11, 13, 19, 21, 22
Geometry and Trigonometry: 16, 18, 20

### Math Module 2

Algebra: 1, 2, 4, 6, 7, 8, 9
Problem Solving and Data Analysis: 10, 11, 13, 16
Advanced Math: 3, 5, 12, 14, 15, 18, 20, 22
Geometry and Trigonometry: 17, 19, 21

## Diagnostic Self-Assessment

Check any areas you feel you need to work on.

### Reading

- Reading timing
- Overthinking Reading questions
- Not sure how to think through Reading questions
- Careless errors on Reading questions
- Other issues?

### Writing

- Writing timing
- Writing grammar review
- Overthinking Writing questions
- Not sure how to think through Writing questions
- Careless errors on Writing questions
- Other issues?

### Math

- Math timing
- Math formula and concept review
- Overthinking Math questions
- Not sure how to think through Math questions
- Careless errors on Math questions
- Other issues?

### General

- Test anxiety and testing mindset issues?

# Answer Explanations

## Section 1, Module 1: Reading and Writing

1. **(C)** "Building" is the most appropriate word in this context to describe the process of accumulating wealth. The other words are all more associated with the physical construction of items and are not used to describe the wealth creation process.

2. **(C)** "Lowers" would be the most appropriate word to describe the monetary value of a neighborhood changing. "Quiets" and "muffles" are typically used with sounds, and "recedes" with erosion or physically moving away from something.

3. **(A)** "Aptitude" refers to natural skill or ability, so this would make sense given the reference to math and science. Choice (B) does not make sense in referring to math and science abilities, and choices (C) and (D) are overly casual given the more formal tone of the text.

4. **(D)** "Avenues" can mean potential "paths" that one could take to becoming a culinary professional—it does not have to mean a literal road. The other options are commonly used to refer to actual roads and do not have the potential double meaning that "avenue" has.

5. **(C)** The eggs are unable to be affected by regular pest control methods, making "impervious" the most appropriate option. The other options would all mean that the eggs could actually be affected by these pest control methods.

6. **(D)** The poem uses language to convey that "fate" will not "impede my steps," and that the narrator will "rise" and "stride" to show a sense of resolution. Thus, choice (D) makes the most sense. It is not choice (A) because the narrator is taking action instead of giving in to frustration. It is not (B) because the narrator is overcoming obstacles instead of merely accepting them. It is not (C) because the narrator is using travel metaphorically instead of literally.

7. **(C)** The text states that government leaders will take too long to analyze civil rights problems, declaring that they need to be studied thoroughly, and that only then can some course of action be taken. Therefore, the author suggests that opponents of civil rights progress will use excessive delay to achieve their aims. There is no mention of personal attacks in this text, making choice (A) incorrect. And choices (B) and (D) are incorrect because they are goals that those in favor of civil rights progress would likely seek, not goals of those opposed to civil rights progress.

8. **(D)** The text mentions that Marija knew only the word "job," and even this word was very difficult for her to learn. Her English fluency, therefore, is "very limited."

9. **(A)** The text gives blunt language as to how the narrator understands priests in the story: "eyeless" and "sour-favoured" individuals with "suffocated anger." So, he would describe them as repressing emotions, not celebrating or expressing them. Choice (C) doesn't work because the narrator thinks the anger is still present, just suffocated. Choices (B) and (D) convey the opposite of the intended meaning.

10. **(B)** Text 1 focuses on the thought process involved in determining interpersonal attraction while only briefly mentioning biological chemicals. Text 2, on the other hand, describes the actual chemistry of the attraction process far more in-depth, mentioning the specific neurotransmitters involved and the brain's chemical messaging. Therefore, choice (B) makes the most sense. It is not (A) because Text 1 does cite the role of chemicals, although it does

not go into detail. It is not (C) because there are three steps mentioned in Text 2. It is not (D) because this would describe Text 1 instead of Text 2.

11. **(A)** The passage states that because plastic is not biodegradable, it can take several hundred years to degrade. Thus, if the plastic from a few decades ago had been disposed of in the ocean, it is most likely that "nearly all of it would remain." The other options would suggest a greater degree of plastic biodegradability.

12. **(B)** This selection remarks on America's general contribution to the world and gives evidence of what Du Bois sees as its attention to "vigor" (strength and determination) and "ingenuity" (inventiveness and insight) over beauty. Choice (A) illustrates the impact the sorrow songs had on Du Bois. Choice (C) discusses how some songs were lost or forgotten. Choice (D) concludes Du Bois's ideas on the lasting effect and significance of the songs.

13. **(C)** The previous sentence ends by referring to protists, so it is logical that the final sentence of the text would continue this reference. Also, the graph shows that since 1675, approximately 200,000 species of protists have been discovered. It is not (A) because the line for "all species" is greater than that for just "protists," making it impossible to know how many animal species have been found. It is not (B) because there is no specific evidence in the graph as to the number of experiments conducted. It is not (D) because there is no specific evidence that the line for "all species" is composed of only protists and plants.

14. **(A)** The text refers to Haeckel in very positive terms, citing his many significant accomplishments. Therefore, it is logical to state that he is a historical figure who is worth studying. It is not (B) because Haeckel died in 1919 according to the text. It is not (C) because this is far too negative. It is not (D) because there is no evidence in the text about Haeckel's literary and poetic accomplishments, so it would not make sense to introduce them here.

15. **(C)** Use a comma to separate the introductory phrase from the complete sentence that follows. A semicolon or colon will not work, as in choices (A) and (B) since there is not a complete sentence beforehand. No comma whatsoever, as in (D), would not allow for a needed pause.

16. **(C)** To be consistent with the use of "we" in the previous sentence, you should use "our." You can therefore eliminate choices (B) and (D) since they use "their." You can also eliminate choice (A). It fails to show that the "planet" possesses the "surface" because it lacks an apostrophe followed by an "s." That leaves you with choice (C) as the correct answer. It properly uses "our" to be consistent with the previous sentence and "planet's" to demonstrate that the singular planet possesses the surface.

17. **(B)** Do not separate the subject "the great majority of species" from the verb "were recorded." The other options incorrectly separate the subject from the verb.

18. **(A)** We need a possessive to serve as a stand-in for "quantum superposition," which is a singular noun. "Its" is the best substitute for quantum superposition's. Choices (B) and (D) are not possessive, and choice (C) refers to multiple people or things: quantum superposition is one thing.

19. **(D)** "Great Men, by all accounts" is a parenthetical statement. If you remove it from the sentence, the clause still functions well. The general rule with parenthetical statements is that there can be either two commas or two dashes separating the statement from the rest of the sentence. Choice (B) is close, but it starts with a dash and concludes with a comma, which breaks with parallelism.

20. **(A)** "Are" is the only plural verb out of the options. A plural verb is necessary to match with the plural subject of "two of the primary positions." The other options are all singular verbs.

21. **(C)** "Rose" is the correct past tense version of the verb "rise," making its use consistent with the other past tense verb in the sentence, "began." "Rise" is present tense, "risen" is used in conjunction with "have" or "had," and "rised" is not the proper past tense conjugation for the irregular verb "to rise."

22. **(C)** Choices (A) and (B) have inverted word order, and choice (D) is too vague. Choice (C) puts the words in a logical sequence and uses precise wording.

23. **(A)** "While" is the only option that gives a contrast between the first part of the sentence that mentions the nice alignment or contrast of some musical waves and the second part of the sentence that mentions waves that do not align or contrast in a regular fashion. Choices (B), (C), and (D) show a cause-and-effect relationship.

24. **(C)** Choice (C) logically leads to the example that clarifies a type of engineering that deals with a particular type of physical problem. The other options would not lead into a clarifying example.

25. **(A)** "If" sets up a logical relationship between the two parts of the sentence: If the restorationist "art restorer" is not skilled, the result is that the restoration attempt can be a disaster. The other transitions would not set up this logical relationship. Even though "because" and "since" can express cause and effect, they would not work because they would show that this is a definitive situation rather than a possibility.

26. **(B)** The student wants to introduce Robert Frost to an audience unfamiliar with his work. Choice (B) provides a broad description of Frost's identity and overall style, making it the most effective answer. Choice (A) does not focus on Frost himself. Choice (C) refers to Frost only in passing. Choice (D) does not discuss Frost whatsoever.

27. **(B)** The third bullet implies that it is correcting a misconception by stating "flying squirrels do not actually fly." Thus, choice (B) does the best job out of these options in correcting this misconception. It is not (A) because there is no indication that this is a misconception. It is not (C) because there is no mention of hunting in the text. It is not (D) because the first bullet states that flying squirrels are "numerous."

## Section 1, Module 2: Reading and Writing

1. **(B)** Vacation is supposed to replenish and relax you, but it had an opposite result. Words like "despised" and "depressed" make it easy to guess at Jim's condition—he is feeling "dispirited." "Although" is a contrasting word, so how he feels must contradict his getting to work early and prepared. Choices (A), (C), and (D) are antonyms of what the writer is trying to convey.

2. **(A)** "Value" is synonymous with "worth," indicating that education has an intrinsic "value" or "worth." It is not "price" because this would be associated with something that can be bought or sold, not necessarily something that has worth for its own sake. "Principles" and "standard" would not be synonymous with "worth."

3. **(B)** The text expresses that the fireworks are not intended to be anything harmful, and the intention is instead for them to patriotic. Going along with the text, "nefarious" would make the most sense since it would convey something that would be ill-intentioned. It is not (A) or (C)

because these convey positive feelings. It is not (D) because this would be an apt description of someone's desire to deceive, but not an apt description of the mindset behind detonating fireworks.

4. **(D)** The text expresses that selectivity is needed for chemists to use the products of their reaction, and that the process allows them to separate one product from another. Put another way, the products of the reactions are "isolated," making choice (D) correct. The other options do not convey a separation of chemical products.

5. **(D)** "Evolving" is used to describe the process by which molecules gradually give off heat in the microwave, so "generating" would best capture this meaning. While the other options do give possible definitions of "evolving," they do not reflect the process of giving off heat.

6. **(A)** The text addresses the pros and cons of the presidential model, making (A) correct. Choice (B) is not accurate because the parliamentary model is not analyzed in any way like the presidential model. (C) is imprecise because it provides details of the text but does not encompass the perceived disadvantages as well as the benefits. Choice (D) is wrong because it doesn't give specific examples of countries following this system in the text.

7. **(D)** The text gives possible explanations for why we have not encountered ETI's even if they do exist. There is no evidence as to the author's opinion, as in (A). Choices (B) and (C) are incorrect because neither a recommendation nor suggestion is given in these lines.

8. **(B)** The poem explicitly states "I am called pumpkins," and uses pumpkin imagery like "orange" and "jack-o'-lantern" to convey the identity. The other options are briefly mentioned in passing, but do not have the same supporting evidence as pumpkin does.

9. **(B)** This option shows that the government was structured in such a way that it led to paralysis because the council could not come to a consensus and each nation went its own separate way with decision making. It is not (A) because this identifies a strength, not a shortcoming. It is not (C) or (D) because these choices look at the historical legacy of the Iroquois instead of analyzing their government.

10. **(C)** The text describes a "mutualist" relationship, in which the species help one another. This is most like the oxpecker birds' eating the predatory insects off the backs of zebras, since the oxpeckers are gaining food, and the zebras are being cleaned. Choices (A) and (D) involve relationships only beneficial to one of the species, and choice (B) does not establish a reciprocal relationship with another species.

11. **(C)** This option focuses on how the occupational therapist can establish trust and support, which would be associated with collaboration. Choice (A) focuses on dysfunctional occupations instead of on collaboration. Choice (B) focuses on the replacement of dysfunctional occupations with functional ones but does not highlight collaboration. Choice (D) focuses on what a patient can do on their own to minimize stress but does not integrate the occupational therapist in this process.

12. **(A)** H5N1 and H7N9 have the very highest fatality rates of any of the illnesses presented in the table. However, the case numbers for each of these viruses were only in the hundreds. Other less lethal illnesses in the table causes far greater numbers of infection. These two viruses would therefore provide the most effective support to the virologist's hypothesis that if the flu virus has too high a fatality rate, it will not ultimately cause many cases. The other options do not show such a relationship.

13. **(A)** We can see in the table that men have higher rates of crash involvement than women in every age range. It therefore might be argued that car safety engineers should focus on male safety more as males are the ones who more often need to be saved. This would be against what the researcher believes but could be supported with the data. This makes choice (A) the best option. The text does not discuss age-related safety, so choices (B) and (C) would be incorrect as they do not argue against the researcher. Choice (D) would support the researcher's position, not providing an argument against it, and is therefore incorrect.

14. **(B)** The earlier part of the sentence says that Newlands was "vindicated," which means he was proven correct. Choice (B) would demonstrate that his theory was indeed correct, since his theory suggested that the elements would follow an eight-element pattern. The other options would not demonstrate how Newlands was proven correct.

15. **(A)** The text advocates that doctors should not overprescribe antibiotics so that antibiotic-resistant bacteria will not form. By minimizing over-prescription, the antibiotics have a greater chance of remaining effective for those who most need them, aligning with choice (A). The other options represent outcomes that conflict with the ideas expressed in the text.

16. **(D)** Choice (D) correctly places commas around the parenthetical phrase that clarifies the scientific term. Choices (A) and (B) do not punctuate around the parenthetical phrase, while (C) uses inconsistent punctuation around the phrase.

17. **(A)** Choice (A) provides a comma between the dependent introductory clause and the independent clause that follows. Choice (B) does not have a complete sentence before the colon. Choice (C) does not have a complete sentence before the semicolon. Choice (D) unnecessarily uses a series of dashes to interrupt the phrasing of the sentence.

18. **(A)** Choice (A) uses a comma both before and after the parenthetical phrase like other grains, correctly setting this clarifying phrase aside. Choice (B) does not have a comma at the end of the phrase. Choice (C) incorrectly uses the plural verb "were." And choice (D) is inconsistent in the punctuation used before and after the parenthetical phrase.

19. **(C)** Notice the parallelism of listing: as each item in the list has a comma inside the item, it is proper to separate the items using semicolons. Choices (B) and (D) do not have the proper structure. Now notice the comma after each state in the previous items. Choice (A) omits that comma after "Arizona." Additionally, choice (A) makes use of "it's," meaning "it is," where the correct answer should use the possessive form "its."

20. **(B)** The subject that corresponds to the verb is the singular word "research." Choice (B) correctly uses the present tense and a singular verb. Choice (A) is plural, and choice (C) is not in the present tense. While "has" as used in choice (D) would indicate the present perfect tense, the word "suggesting" is the improper conjugation of "to suggest" in the present perfect form.

21. **(B)** "Are" is consistent with the plural subject "paintings" and matches the other verbs by being in the present tense. The other choices are all singular verbs.

22. **(C)** "Makes it" is most appropriate since the sentence is making the declaration that it is more difficult for the servals to be spotted. Also, "makes" is consistent with the singular "having a lighter-colored coat." Choices (A) and (D) do not match up numerically with the subject, and (B) would not work in terms of making a declaration.

23. **(B)** This transition refers to the relationship between the first and second clauses in this sentence, where the first clause is the cause, and the second clause is the effect. In essence,

"because" of clause one, then clause two. Choice (A) leaves the sentence disjointed and lacking fluidity. Choice (C) is used to introduce simultaneous (but often contradictory) clauses, while (D) is also generally a lead-in for two actions occurring at the same time.

24. **(A)** "Since" is the only option that provides the cause-and-effect transition needed between the fact that a microscopic analysis is needed to do a CTE diagnosis and the need to wait for such analysis until after a patient has died.

25. **(C)** Choice (C) is the only option that makes a generalization about the early sponsors of ballet. Based on the notes, these early sponsors were Italian and French queens and kings. Choices (A) and (B) are too specific, and choice (D) is a generalization about gender representation in ballet as opposed to the early ballet sponsors.

26. **(B)** The notes specifically suggest that causes of hearing loss could be the result of blockage in the ear canal or exposure to loud noises. Choice (B) gives examples of how someone could apply this specific advice to the real world. It is not (A) because this does not give a specific way that someone can avoid hearing loss. It is not (C) because this talks about the population more vulnerable to hearing loss. It is not (D) because it is too vague.

27. **(D)** The student wants to take the information from the notes and come up with a cause that would fit the goals of Effective Altruism. Based on the notes, a cause like this should be solvable, specific, data-driven, and efficient. Raising money to remove poisonous lead-based paints from school facilities in an impoverished city would align with these goals, since it is a problem that could be solved by removing the paint and is highly targeted on a clear objective. It is not (A) because this sort of goal is overly imprecise. It is not (B) because this is not an overlooked charitable cause since it can reasonably be inferred that the museum already has extensive facilities and art pieces. It is not (C) because this does not specify a cause but instead focuses on the training needed to evaluate a cause.

## Section 2, Module 1: Math

1. **(B)**

$$\frac{6}{7} \times \frac{14}{3} \rightarrow \text{Reduce the 6 and 3} \rightarrow$$

$$\frac{2}{7} \times \frac{14}{1} \rightarrow \text{Reduce the 14 and 7} \rightarrow$$

$$\frac{2}{1} \times \frac{2}{1} = \frac{4}{1} = 4$$

2. **(10)**

$$\frac{2}{3}x - 1 = \frac{1}{6}x + 4 \rightarrow$$

$$\frac{2}{3}x = \frac{1}{6}x + 5 \rightarrow$$

$$\frac{2}{3}x - \frac{1}{6}x = 5 \rightarrow$$

$$\frac{4}{6}x - \frac{1}{6}x = 5 \rightarrow$$

$$\frac{3}{6}x = 5 \rightarrow$$

$$\frac{1}{2}x = 5 \rightarrow x = 10$$

3. **(A)** For a line to be totally vertical, the line must have a constant value for $x$. $x = -5$ works because no matter what the value of $y$ would be, the value of $x$ will always be $-5$. Here is what $x = -5$ looks like when graphed:

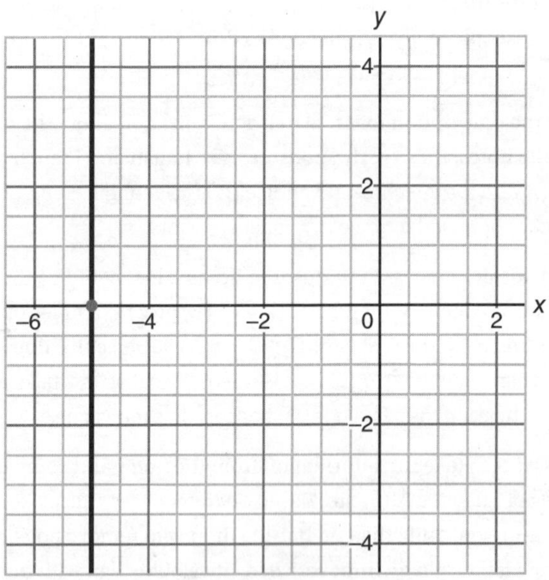


$y = -4$ represents a horizontal line, and the other options are neither horizontal nor vertical.

4. **(A)**

$$\frac{x}{4} = 6 \rightarrow x = 6 \times 4 \rightarrow x = 24$$

Now that we know $x = 24$, divide 24 by 8 to get the solution:

$$\frac{24}{8} = 3$$

5. **(B)** Put the equation in slope-intercept form: $y = mx + b$ The $y$-intercept is 0, and the slope is 3—calculate the slope either by visualizing the rise over the run, or by plugging in points to the slope formula. You can use the points (0, 0) and (2, 6):

$$slope = \frac{y_2 - y_1}{x_2 - x_1} = \frac{6 - 0}{2 - 0} = 3$$

The mass corresponds to the $y$ value and the $v$ corresponds to the $x$ value. So, the equation will then be $m = 3v$.

6. **(B)** The numbers are already in order from least to greatest. Since there is an even number of terms and the two middle terms are different from one another, take the average of the two middle terms, 7 and 9, to find the median of the set:

$$\frac{7 + 9}{2} = 8$$

7. **(B)** Convert from teaspoons, to tablespoons, and then to cups.

$$12 \text{ teaspoons} \times \frac{1 \text{ tablespoon}}{3 \text{ teaspoons}} \times \frac{1 \text{ cup}}{16 \text{ tablespoons}} \rightarrow$$

$$12 \cancel{\text{teaspoons}} \times \frac{1 \cancel{\text{tablespooon}}}{3 \cancel{\text{teaspoons}}} \times \frac{1 \text{ cup}}{16 \cancel{\text{tablespoons}}} = \frac{12}{3 \times 16} = \frac{12}{48} = \frac{1}{4} \text{cup}$$

8. **(6)** Subtract the calories of the cheese and vegetables from the total calories for the salad to find how many calories come from salad dressing:

$$1,100 - 650 = 450$$

Now, divide 450 by 75 to find the number of salad dressing packets used:

$$450 \div 75 = 6$$

So, 6 packets of salad dressing were used.

9. **(3)**

$$\frac{x^2}{6} = \frac{x}{2} \rightarrow \text{Divide both sides by } x \rightarrow$$

$$\frac{x}{6} = \frac{1}{2} \rightarrow x = \frac{6}{2} \rightarrow x = 3$$

10. **(C)** If there is a 30% discount, the new price of the product is 100% − 30% = 70% of the original price. Since the original price is $p$, take 70% of $p$. Move the decimal point on 70 to the left two spots, giving you 0.7. Then multiply it by $p$ for the solution: $0.7p$.

11. **(D)** Distance is represented by $r$ in the equation. Double the r to see how the overall force would change:

$$F_g = G\frac{m_1 m_2}{r^2} \rightarrow \text{Double the } r \rightarrow$$

$$F_g = G\frac{m_1 m_2}{(2r)^2} = G\frac{m_1 m_2}{4r^2}$$

So, the force would change such that it is of the original force.

12. **(A)** There are a total of 188 people in the table. Out of these 188, there are 40 male cat owners. So, divide 40 by 188 to get the probability that a randomly selected pet owner would be a male cat owner: $\frac{40}{188}$

13. **(2, 3, or 4)** Any one of these numbers would work as a solution. This is easiest to solve by plugging in some possible numbers. If Connor purchases 2 cheeseburgers for $10, he will need to purchase 3, 4, or 5 hamburgers to be within the $20–$30 range. If Connor purchases 3 cheeseburgers for $15, he will need to purchase 2, 3, or 4 hamburgers to be in the range. If he purchases 4 cheeseburgers for $20, he could purchase 2 hamburgers to be in the range. And if he purchases more than 4 cheeseburgers, he will fall outside the range since he must purchase at least 2 hamburgers.

14. **(D)**

$$12 < -4x + 6y \rightarrow$$

Divide everything by 2 to simplify:

$$6 < -2x + 3y \rightarrow$$

Get $y$ by itself $\rightarrow$

$$6 + 2x < 3y \rightarrow$$

Divide both sides by 3 $\rightarrow$

$$2 + \frac{2}{3}x < y$$

15. **(A)**

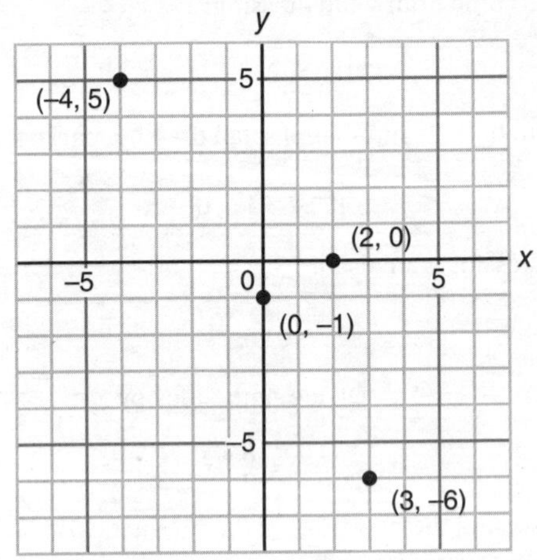


Given that the line has both a positive slope and a positive *y*-intercept, the line must be above the *x* axis for values of *x* greater than 0. So, choices (B), (C), and (D) will not work since they would fall on or underneath the *x*-axis for values of *x* greater than 0. Choice (A) would work because it is already above the *x*-axis even when it has a negative value for *x*. A line with the point (−4, 5) could continue with a positive slope to also have a positive *y*-intercept.

16. **(25)** The triangle can be drawn as follows:

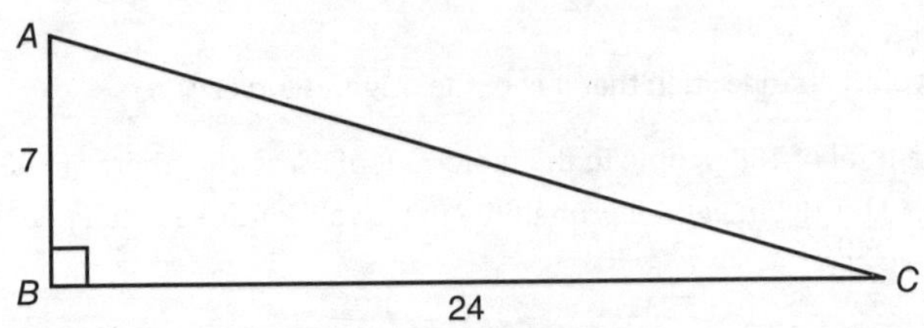


Solve for the unknown side by using the Pythagorean theorem:

$$a^2 + b^2 = c^2 \rightarrow$$

$$7^2 + 24^2 = 625 = c^2 \rightarrow$$

$$\sqrt{625} = 25 = c$$

So, the side $AC = 25$. Alternatively, you can recognize that this is a Pythagorean triple that you could have memorized: 7-24-25.

17. **(C)** Plug in a number for $k$ to visualize the situation. Suppose that $k$ is equal to 3. Then, the function would be $f(x) = 3$. The function would look like this:

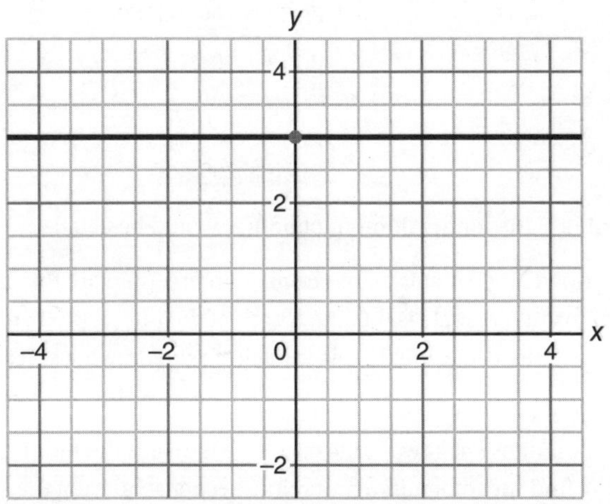


Condition 1 fits since the function is a line. Condition 2 fits since the function is flat and has a slope of zero. Condition 3 does not fit because the *domain* (corresponds to $x$ values) goes from positive to negative infinity, but the *range* (corresponds to $y$ values) is only 3. So, just conditions 1 and 2 will apply.

18. **(D)** The smallest edge is 2 cm, the next greatest edge will be 4 cm, and the greatest edge will be 6 cm. The prism will look like this:

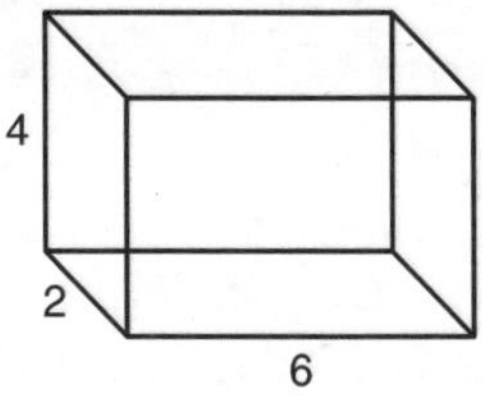


There are two sides with dimensions $2 \times 4$, two sides with dimensions $4 \times 6$, and two sides with dimensions $2 \times 6$. So, add these surfaces areas together to find the total surface area of the prism:

$$2(2 \times 4) + 2(4 \times 6) + 2(2 \times 6) =$$
$$2(8) + 2(24) + 2(12) =$$
$$16 + 48 + 24 = 88$$

19. **(A)** Use $a$ as the number of aluminum cans and $g$ as the number of glass bottles to create an inequality expressing that the total money made is at least \$100.

$$0.1a + 0.16g \geq 100$$

Then, substitute 600 in for *a*, since we know that she has collected 600 cans, and solve for *g*:

$$0.1(600) + 0.16g \geq 100 \rightarrow$$
$$60 + 0.16g \geq 100 \rightarrow$$
$$0.16g \geq 40 \rightarrow$$
$$g \geq \frac{40}{0.16} \rightarrow$$
$$g \geq 250$$

So, the least possible value for the number of bottles would be 250.

20. **(25)** $\angle X$ is an inscribed angle that is across from an intercepted arc that measures 50 degrees. The rule is that an inscribed angle is half the length of the intercepted arc, so take half of 50 to get 25 degrees. You could also estimate this value from the drawing since the figure is drawn to scale.

21. **(B)** The number of minutes spent watering each tree is 5, and the number of minutes water each shrub is 2. So, find the total number of minutes spent watering the sum of the plants by multiplying the number of each plants by the amount of time each plant type is watered:

$$5T + 2S$$

This total must be no more than 30 minutes, meaning it can be less than or equal to 30 minutes. Putting this all together, you have this expression:

$$5T + 2S \leq 30$$

22. **(C)** Use the formula for compound interest:

$A =$ Future Value
$P =$ Initial Value (Principal)
$r =$ Interest Rate Expressed as a Decimal ($r$ is positive if increasing, negative if decreasing)
$t =$ Time
$n =$ Number of Times Interest is Compounded over Time Period $t$

$$A = P\left(1 + \frac{r}{n}\right)^{nt}$$

Applying this formula to the problem, $v$ would be the initial value, and $t$ would be the number of years. The constant $c$ corresponds to the part in parentheses: $1 + \frac{r}{n}$. Since the price increases 15% each year, the number of times that it is compounded is just one. So, turn 15% into a decimal to determine what will equal:

$$1 + \frac{r}{n} \rightarrow 1 + \frac{0.15}{1} = 1.15$$

So, the constant $c$ will equal 1.15.

## Section 2, Module 2: Math

1. **(A)** Since the slope is defined as the change in *y* divided by the change in *x*, and since the mass corresponds to the *y* value and the *v* corresponds to the *x* value, the slope will equal the density of the substance.

2. **(C)**

$$(5x^3 - x + 4) + (6x^3 + x^2 - 3) =$$
$$(5x^3 + 6x^3) + x^2 - x + (4 - 3) =$$
$$11x^3 + x^2 - x + 1$$

3. **(C)** $8^{\left(\frac{1}{3}\right)} \rightarrow \sqrt[3]{8} = 2$

4. **(A)** For the equations to have infinitely many solutions, the two equations should be multiples of each other.

$$2x - 3y = 7$$
$$6x + ky = 21$$

The second equation is three times that of the first equation, since 21 is three times 7 and 6 is three times 2. So, *k* should be three times $-3$, which is $-9$.

5. **(B)** The *y*-intercept is the point at which the function intersects the *y*-axis—the value of *x* at this point must be 0. So, plug 0 in for *x* to the equation to solve for the *y*-intercept (keep in mind that a number to the zero power is equal to 1):

$$y = 2^x - 3 \rightarrow y = 2^0 - 3 \rightarrow 1 - 3 = -2$$

6. **(B)** Choice (B) is the only option that will eliminate terms when it is simplified, allowing it to look like $z = x - y$:

$$(\sqrt{x} - \sqrt{y})(\sqrt{x} + \sqrt{y}) \rightarrow \text{FOIL the expression} \rightarrow$$
$$(\sqrt{x})(\sqrt{x}) + (\sqrt{x})(\sqrt{y}) - (\sqrt{x})(\sqrt{y}) - (\sqrt{y})(\sqrt{y}) =$$
$$x + \cancel{(\sqrt{x})(\sqrt{y})} - \cancel{(\sqrt{x})(\sqrt{y})} - y =$$
$$x - y$$

You could also think about the above calculation as the difference of squares: after *FOILing* the expression, the outer and inner terms cancel, leaving you with just the first and last terms.

7. **(C)** Start by substituting $x + 3$ in for *y* to the second equation:

$$x(x + 3) = 40$$

Now, solve for *x*:

$$x(x + 3) = 40 \rightarrow$$
$$x^2 + 3x = 40 \rightarrow$$
$$x^2 + 3x - 40 = 0 \rightarrow$$
$$(x + 8)(x - 5) \rightarrow$$
$$x = -8 \text{ or } 5$$

Since the question states that both $x$ and $y$ must be positive, use 5 as the value of $x$. Then, plug 5 in to the first equation to solve for $y$:

$$x + 3 = y \rightarrow 5 + 3 = 8 = y$$

Now, find the sum of $x$ and $y$ by adding their values together:

$$8 + 5 = 13$$

8. **(A)** The line is horizontal, with every value of $x$ giving the same value of $y$: 3. So, the equation of the line is $y = 3$.

9. **(3)** Notice a pattern here—if you add the two equations together, you will be able to simplify the expression so that you can solve for $a - b$.

$$\begin{array}{r} 2a - 3b = 5 \\ + \quad \underline{3a - 2b = 10} \\ 5a - 5b = 15 \end{array}$$

Then, divide the whole equation by 5, and you will have the needed expression:

$$\frac{5a - 5b = 15}{5} \rightarrow a - b = 3$$

Thus, $a - b$ is equal to 3.

10. **(D)** You can eliminate choices (A) and (C) since the mass is going down. And you can eliminate choice (A) because the mass is not decreasing at a steady, linear rate. So, the answer is (D) because the mass is both decreasing and doing so at an exponential rate.

11. **(C)** Sarah traveled 5 miles for 17 minutes. So, convert 5 miles per 17 minutes to miles per hour:

$$\frac{5 \text{ miles}}{17 \cancel{\text{minutes}}} \times \frac{60 \cancel{\text{minutes}}}{1 \text{ hour}} = 17.6 \text{ miles/hour}$$

12. **(63)** Since $(x + y)(x - y) = x^2 - y^2$, substitute 7 and 3 in for these expressions and multiply the product by 3 to arrive at the answer:

$$3x^2 - 3y^2 = 3(x + y)(x - y) = 3(7)(3) = 63$$

13. **(2.74)** Set up an equation that uses $x$ as the number of gallons of Dead Sea water that would be needed to add to the 10 gallons of ocean water to get water with a percent of salt at 10%. The 3.35% is expressed as 0.035 and the 33.7% is expressed as 0.337 since you move the decimal point to the right two spots when calculating percentages. The $10 + x$ represents the total number of gallons.

$$0.035 \times 10 + 0.337x = .1(10 + x) \rightarrow$$

$$0.35 + 0.337x = 1 + 0.1x \rightarrow$$

$$0.337x = .65 + 0.1x \rightarrow$$

$$0.237x = 0.65 \rightarrow$$

$$x = \frac{0.65}{0.237} = 2.74$$

14. **(D)** Looking ahead to the format of the answers, it appears that the quadratic formula will be used to solve for this. Start by putting the equation in quadratic form:

$$4x = 2 - 3x^2 \rightarrow$$
$$3x^2 + 4x - 2 = 0$$

Now, use the quadratic equation to solve for $x$:

$$x = \frac{-b \pm \sqrt{b^2 - 4ac}}{2a} \rightarrow$$
$$3x^2 + 4x - 2 = 0 \rightarrow$$
$$a = 3,\ b = 4,\ c = -2$$
$$x = \frac{-4 \pm \sqrt{4^2 - 4(3)(-2)}}{2(3)} \rightarrow$$
$$x = \frac{-4 \pm \sqrt{16 + 24}}{6} \rightarrow$$
$$x = \frac{-4 \pm \sqrt{40}}{6} = \frac{-4 \pm \sqrt{4 \times 10}}{6} \rightarrow$$
$$x = \frac{-4 \pm 2\sqrt{10}}{6} = \frac{-2 \pm \sqrt{10}}{3}$$

Out of the two solutions, $\frac{-2 - \sqrt{10}}{3}$ is the only one given, making (D) correct.

15. **(A)** Factors of the function can be found at the $x$-intercepts. Look for the $x$ values where $g(x)$ is equal to 0: $-2$ and 1. Then, see which option would make it so that plugging these two numbers in would result in a value of 0. The only option is choice A. $(x - 1)(x + 2)$

16. **(A)** Since we do not know if the students who participated in the survey were randomly selected, we can only reasonably generalize as to the opinions of those who participated in the survey. So, we can justify the statement that out of the 100 students surveyed, 40 wanted a new library. It is not (B) because we cannot generalize as to the opinions of all university community members based on this non-randomized sample. And it is not (C) or (D) because these options confuse the sample percentage with the number of students.

17. **(D)** The radius of the circle will be 3 since the square root of 9 is 3. So, the values of $a$ and $b$ must each be greater than 3 so that all the coordinates of the circle will be greater than zero—this will place the circle in the first quadrant, as modeled in the graph below:

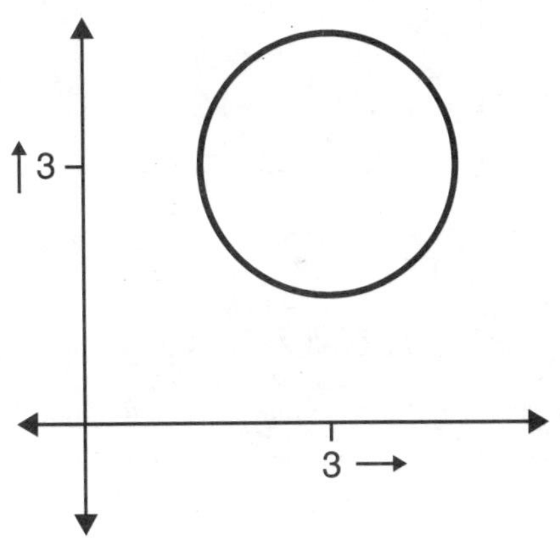

18. **(C)** Manipulate the equation so that $M$ is isolated.

$$v_e = \sqrt{\frac{2GM}{r}} \rightarrow \text{Square both sides} \rightarrow$$

$$(v_e)^2 = \frac{2GM}{r} \rightarrow \text{Get } M \text{ by itself} \rightarrow$$

$$\frac{(v_e)^2 r}{2G} = M$$

19. **(64)** Write an equation for the original sphere:

$$V = \frac{4}{3}\pi r^3 \rightarrow$$

$$8 = \frac{4}{3}\pi r^3$$

A sphere with a radius of twice this original one would have a radius of $2r$. Calculate the value of this new sphere in terms of $r$:

$$V = \frac{4}{3}\pi(2r)^3 = \frac{4}{3}\pi(8r)$$

So, the volume of the new sphere is 8 times the volume of the original sphere: $8 \times 8 = 64$ cubic feet.

20. **(B)** The graph of the function intersects the $x$-axis at $-2$, 1, and 4. So, see which equation would have those as zeros, i.e., plugging in these numbers would cause the value of the function to equal zero. The only one that has all three of these numbers as zeros is $y = (x - 4)(x + 2)(x - 1)$

21. **(D)** Since the area of the square is 36 square units, the length of each side will be the square root of 36: 6. Label the drawing to visualize the side lengths and notice that 45-45-90 triangles are inscribed in the larger square, since each side is bisected by a vertex of the inner square.

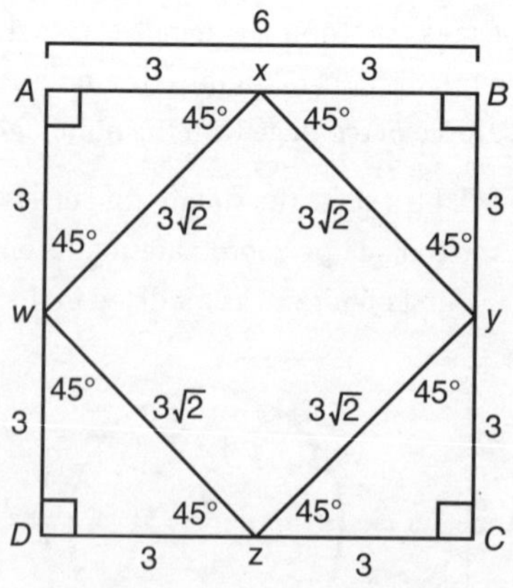


Add the four sides of square $WXYZ$ to find its perimeter:

$$3\sqrt{2} + 3\sqrt{2} + 3\sqrt{2} + 3\sqrt{2} = 12\sqrt{2}$$

22. **(0.5. or $\frac{1}{2}$)** Solve for the vertex of the parabola, since at that point the projectile will reach its maximum. Use the formula $\frac{-b}{2a}$ to find the time at which it will reach its maximum. The function $h(t) = -16t^2 + 16t + 10$ is already in quadratic form, so you can see the values needed for $a$ and for $b$. Use for $a$ and 16 for $b$:

$$\frac{-b}{2a} \rightarrow \frac{-(-16)}{2(16)} = \frac{16}{32} = \frac{1}{2}$$

# PART 3
# Reading

# Reading for the Digital SAT

## Overview of the SAT Reading Modules

The SAT Reading tests your ability to analyze reading passages, appropriately use vocabulary, and determine supporting evidence in a wide variety of texts: fiction, historical documents, poetry, natural science, social science, drama, and more. No matter your choice of college major or career, it will be important to be skilled in interpreting written material and graphics. While you will not need any specific background knowledge of the passage topics, the more widely and deeply you have read, the easier the SAT Reading questions will be for you.

### SAT Reading Structure

Here is the breakdown of the adaptive testing modules:

| SAT Reading and Writing Modules | |
|---|---|
| Reading and Writing One | 32 Minutes, 27 Questions, Standard Difficulty |
| Reading and Writing Two | 32 Minutes, 27 Questions, Adaptive Difficulty (easier or harder questions depending on how you did on the first Reading/Writing section) |

- Reading and Writing texts are no longer than 150 words.
- Each text has just one question accompanying it.
- The reading questions come first within each module, followed by the writing questions.
- Approximately 29 of the 54 total SAT Reading and Writing questions are reading ones.
- Out of these roughly 29 questions, the specific reading question types are likely to be in this order and allocated as follows (based on the released SAT tests from College Board):

| Question Type | Likely Percentage of Reading Questions | Example |
|---|---|---|
| Words in Context | 34% | Which choice completes the text with the most logical and precise word or phrase? |
| Structure and Purpose | 12% | Which choice best states the main purpose of the text? |
| Cross-Text Connections | 3% | Based on the texts, how would the researcher in Text 2 most likely describe the view of the theorists presented in Text 1? |
| Central Ideas and Details | 11% | Which choice best states the main idea of the text? |
| Quantitative Evidence | 11% | Which choice most effectively uses data from the table to complete the example? |
| Textual Evidence | 17% | Which quotation from the text most effectively illustrates the claim? |
| Inferences | 12% | Which choice most logically completes the text? |

- **Within each of the above question types, the difficulty of the questions will generally progress from easy to hard.** For example, the Words in Context questions will gradually become more difficult and then when you start the Structure and Purpose questions, the difficulty will again progress from easy to hard, and so on. This ordering of the questions is helpful for you as a test-taker, since you will get used to a particular question style before taking on the more difficult questions of that type.

## General SAT Reading Strategies

**1. Realize that the SAT is not the type of test you are used to.** If you approach the SAT Reading section in the same way you approach a school-based assignment that assesses text recall, you will have some major difficulty. Here are some fundamental differences in how you should tackle typical tests and the SAT Reading:

| Typical School-Based Reading Tests | SAT Reading |
|---|---|
| The tests are almost always **closed-book**, so you need to read and reread to be certain you remember everything that might be tested. | The SAT is **open-book**—you don't have to know anything ahead of time or memorize the text. You can go back to the text as often as you need. |
| Test questions are often about **specific facts**, so it is vital that you memorize details and definitions as you read. | Test questions are more often about **inference, purpose, and big ideas**, so focus on general paraphrasing instead of specific memorizing. |
| Occasionally, there are mistakes on a test with a **couple of right answers** to a question. It is easy for a question to be thrown out if there is an error. | SAT questions are very well written, and there will be **just one correct answer** to each question. The College Board does not want to throw out the results for hundreds of thousands of test-takers, so they invest tremendous resources into ensuring that the questions have answers that are 100% correct. |

If you have told yourself that you are "a bad test-taker," ask yourself . . . "Am I taking the SAT in the same way I take a school-based test?" If so, the problem is not with you but with your strategy.

**2. Do not rush.** A major shift in the Digital SAT is to make it an easier test to complete within the time constraints. Most test-takers will find that the SAT Reading questions are quite manageable to complete.

**3. Read at a steady pace, at about 100–120 words per minute.** 100–120 words per minute is approximately the pace at which most students talk, so reading in this way is very doable. There is no need to skim or speed-read.

**4. Take approximately 70 seconds on average for each question** in the Reading and Writing section.

**Use the countdown clock embedded in the testing program to manage your time.** You can have the countdown clock visible or hidden throughout the test, except for the last five minutes of the module when it will automatically display. You can hide the clock if you find it distracting or leave it open if you find it helpful.

You will likely do your best if you use the full amount of time to read the texts well and think through the questions carefully. There is no prize for finishing early. In fact, if you find yourself finishing the SAT Reading and Writing modules with time to spare, you may want to try reading the more challenging texts a couple of times before attempting the questions. Re-reading can be particularly helpful with texts like poetry where the meaning is often quite subtle.

If you do have difficulty finishing the SAT Reading and Writing, you can pick your battles by focusing on just those questions that come to you most easily (perhaps the words in context and inferences since they are typically shorter) and guessing on the questions you do not have time to attempt, since there is no guessing penalty.

**5. Come back to questions if needed.** You can flag questions in the testing program, making it easy to revisit the questions that you skipped. If you become stuck on a question, come back to it so that you can allow your subconscious mind to process the possibilities. Once you come back to the question with fresh eyes, you will often surprise yourself at how well you can think through it at that point.

If you know that the reading questions are more difficult for you than the grammar questions in the same testing module, you could do the grammar questions first and save the reading questions for later. You could also save some of the more challenging categories of reading questions to do later, since the questions progress in a predictable order. Recognize that you are in control of the order that you answer questions within the testing module, so answer them in the order that best suits you.

**6. You may want to read the question before reading each text.** Since each reading text has just one question that accompanies it, you may find it easier to focus on what you need to look for if you read the question before reading the text. This could be especially helpful on questions that ask you to focus on something more specific in the text: words in context, text structure and purpose, and textual evidence. On questions that involve determining the meaning of the passages in a more general way—central ideas and details, inferences, and cross-text connections—you may want to go ahead and read the passage before doing the questions. Starting with the questions before reaching each text can be especially helpful for students in these situations:

- Students who have a hard time focusing on the text may find previewing the questions helpful. They will get a sense of what things they should focus on while reading the passage.
- Students who overthink the reading because they want to memorize all the details also may want to review the question beforehand. Knowing what they will be asked about might help them relax while reading, enabling them to focus on the big picture instead of trying to remember every fact and figure.

**7. Focus on the overall meaning of the text(s) as you read.** You should be able to restate the "gist" of what you have read—don't worry about memorizing details from the passage. Before each text, there may be a brief summary of the author, text source, and authorship date that will give you some information about what you are about to read. Be sure to read this summary before reading the actual passage, as it will help you preview the general meaning of what follows. If any of the topics are unfamiliar or the passage language seems too lofty, don't be alarmed. If you carefully read the passages, you will have the information necessary to answer the questions well—the SAT makers do not expect you to be a master of all potential topics and potential writing styles.

**8. Read the text actively, not passively.** It is easy to let yourself become distracted or bored when reading a text, such that while your eyes may be moving across the page, your mind is somewhere else. Keep this from happening by doing the following:

- ***Ask questions about the text.*** The more you ask yourself questions as you read, the easier it will be to answer the question you are asked. Previewing the question before reading can help you if you struggle with generating your own questions as you read.

- ***Make connections to the text topic***. Just as you would try to find something in common with someone you just met to get to know them, see what experiences or knowledge you have that can relate to the topic.
- ***Make predictions about what may come next.*** Try to anticipate where a story or an argument is headed, then see if you are correct as you read further. Look at the introductory information about a text to make predictions before even starting. On comparative texts, consider the argument in the first text to make an educated guess about what the second text may argue before you read it.
- ***Catch yourself if you begin to lose focus.*** If you read the first couple of sentences and they didn't sink in, give the beginning another quick read. Don't allow yourself to get halfway through the text having no idea what is going on.
- ***Paraphrase the text.*** The more comfortable you are putting the message of the text in your own words as you read, the easier it will be for you to answer questions that ask you to paraphrase and analyze the selection.
- ***Make notations to stay engaged with the passage.*** You can annotate the text in the testing application, and you will likely have scrap paper available on which you can make notes. While you do not need to take detailed notes as you would if you were preparing for a big test in school, in which you would have to read lots of material over a longer period, some small notations and highlights may help you keep your focus.
- ***You will only need the information that is provided.*** While having background knowledge about the reading topic can be helpful, everything you need to understand the text is right in front of you. If you read it actively, you will be in excellent shape to answer the question.
- ***Take mini-breaks to maintain focus.*** Rather than rushing to the end of the Reading and Writing module, take a break every few questions to let your mind wander for a few seconds so you can maintain your attention throughout the test.

Think of active reading like active listening. In your school classes, you will get much more out of the teacher's lecture if you connect to what they are saying and ask questions about the topic. You will be much better prepared for the test if you are mentally active, not mentally passive, just mindlessly copying down notes while your mind is on other topics.

**9. Adjust how you read based on the type of text.** Fiction and poetry are structured very differently from non-fiction arguments. Change the way you approach each text to maximize comprehension.

| Type of Text | Types of Questions to Ask to Read Actively |
|---|---|
| Fiction | Which character is speaking right now? |
| | What is the sequence of events? Are there any flashbacks? |
| | What emotions are being expressed in the story? |
| Poetry | Who is the intended audience? |
| | Does any of the language have symbolic meaning? |
| | How does the author or narrator seem to be feeling? |
| Science (Social and Natural) | Is this an argumentative text, and if so, what is their argument? |
| | Is this a presentation of scientific findings? What is a summary of the main discoveries? |
| | Is the author considering objections? Am I avoiding confusing the author's position and the position of others? |
| | If there are graphs, how do they relate to what is presented in the passage? |

| Type of Text | Types of Questions to Ask to Read Actively |
|---|---|
| Historical Document | What type of document is this? A speech, a letter, an editorial, or a governmental document? |
| | What is the point of this document? Is it to present an argument, or highlight an issue? |
| | What are the cultural assumptions in the environment in which the document was written? Does the author suggest different views from modern ones about gender, ethnicity, and social class? |
| Text 1 and Text 2 | What is the thesis—the main argument—of each passage? What are they trying to show the reader or convince the reader to believe? |
| | What is similar about the texts? Do they share any assumptions in terms of facts or opinions? |
| | What is different about the texts? What would each author think about the other author's argument? |

**10. Fully understand every part of the question.** A careless mistake in reading a question will likely lead to a wrong answer. Instead of quickly reading through the question, and then having to reread it, read it one time well. This will ensure that you not miss wording critical to understanding what the question is asking, such as "hypothesis," "inferred," "main idea," and so forth. Since questions of a similar type come back-to-back, it is easier to get into a rhythm of thinking in a certain way for each cluster of questions. Even though the questions are rather predictable in their likely wording, since the SAT has the same types of questions over and over, be sure to take your time to understand what is being asked.

**11. Create an answer in your own words before looking at the choices.** On factual recall tests, checking out the answers before you have formulated an answer can help you narrow it down. With the critical thinking questions on the SAT, in contrast, you will often find yourself misled by persuasive but ultimately incorrect answers. Take control of the questions and don't let them control you. Try your best to come up with an idea of the answer before actually looking at the answer choices. When you do look at the answers, you can mark off each incorrect answer choice one-by-one using the testing application. Do not "jump" to an answer or eliminate an answer without patiently thinking through all the possibilities.

**12. Go back to the text as often as you need.** Most tests we take are closed-book—the SAT Reading is open-book. If you had an open-book test in school, you would surely use your textbook and notes to help you answer the questions. With so many SAT questions giving underlined sentences and key words, it makes sense to use the text whenever necessary.

**13. The answers will be 100% correct or totally wrong.** A single word can contaminate an answer, making it completely wrong. When you narrow the choices down to two options, don't just look for the "best" answer—look for the "flawless" answer. Try to quickly debate with yourself the correctness or incorrectness of each answer, knowing that there is one that is definitely correct, and three that are definitely wrong. The College Board has put a great deal of effort into creating the questions you will see on the SAT, so you can safely assume they will be of the very highest quality.

**14. Focus on meaning, not matching.** On ordinary school tests, we are often used to matching the choices with facts we recall from the assigned reading or the in-class lecture. On the SAT, the fact that an answer has wording that matches parts of the text is no guarantee that it is correct.

There is nothing wrong with picking an answer because it does have wording that is in the passage; just don't pick an answer only because it has matching wording. Be certain the overall meaning of an answer gives the correct idea.

**15. Don't worry about your performance while testing.** Since the Digital SAT is adaptive, the later sections will change in difficulty depending on your performance on earlier sections. It will do you no good to try to evaluate how difficult the later section questions are—you will waste time and energy that could be spent on figuring out the problems in front of you. Do your best to stay in the moment and not think back about how you performed on earlier sections. Moreover, be mindful that four of the Reading and Writing questions you encounter will be experimental and not scored—if a question seems a bit odd to you, do your best to answer it but don't dwell on it.

**16. Practice with the testing application ahead of time.** You will be able to download the software that you will use on the actual Digital SAT—go to *collegeboard.org* for the latest details on how to do so. You can practice with this program on your own computer or on one at a library or school. Familiarize yourself with the software interface—the timer, the question flagging feature, and the adaptive question style. The program will allow you to mark off answers you have eliminated and zoom in on the passages if you want to focus on part of the text. Since the passages are less than 150 words, you should have no difficulty seeing the entirety of the passage on the screen while you work through the question.

**17. Give every question your best shot.** With fewer questions on the Digital SAT, each question has a larger impact on your score. Given the adaptive nature of the Digital SAT, the questions you will be given on the later modules are designed to be of a difficulty appropriate for you. Be sure to give every question your very best effort—do not allow yourself to become frustrated and quickly guess the answer.

**18. When in doubt about your strategy, give the SAT the benefit of the doubt.** On poorly written tests, tricks and gimmicks can help you succeed—such shortcuts will not help you perform well on the new SAT. The SAT is an extraordinarily well-constructed assessment based on years of research. As a result, do not waste your time and energy while taking the SAT looking for flaws in the test. Instead, give the SAT Reading the benefit of the doubt and focus on how you can improve your reading comprehension and critical thinking skills.

## Improving Overall Reading Comprehension

In order to strengthen reading skills, it is imperative to read regularly outside of what you might be assigned for school. The type of reading materials you select is very important. It should be something that you enjoy learning about or reading so that you are motivated to continue even when it is difficult. The reading should be slightly more difficult than what you are used to in order to strengthen your mental abilities. Improving your reading comprehension is similar to lifting weights. If you never add more weight to the bar, you'll never get stronger. Reading is the same—if you never read difficult texts, your reading skills won't improve. On the other hand, texts that are just slightly above your comfort level will help improve your abilities so that difficult texts can feel manageable, just like easier texts are now.

Below are some resources that you can use to find reading materials that you enjoy. By using these resources, you will be able to find reading materials that both interest you and represent the type of material you may find on the SAT. After the heading for each resource is a summary of how you can best use it to improve your reading skills. Infinite reading possibilities may seem overwhelming, so if that ends up being the case, asking a librarian for help with be your best bet—they can assist you in developing a short list of books and readings that is tailored for you.

One final note: if you don't enjoy the topic you're reading about, if the book seems silly and the characters unbearable, or if you just don't care about the scientific study the article is covering, just stop. Put it down. Find something you're more interested in to read. In personal reading, there is no requirement to finish books you don't like. Forcing yourself to do so will only lead to you to dreading your daily reading time and to finding excuses to do literally anything else.

### Project Gutenberg

*https://www.gutenberg.org/*
This is an enormous online library full of books that are in the public domain (public domain means they're old enough that no one holds copyrights to them anymore—they can be freely used). There are thousands of classics stored there. On the main web page, there are options for various searches. The top 100 list and the bookshelves are very helpful. Top 100 will lead you to a list of books you've probably heard of before but never read. Bookshelves will allow you to explore by genre or topic—if there is a topic you're interested in, that would be a good place to start.

### Internet Archives

*https://archive.org/*
The Internet Archives contains more reading material than you could read in a lifetime! Its self-description is that it's "a non-profit library of millions of free books, movies, software, music, websites, and more." You'll want to focus on the books. It's easy to get lost on this website, so it might be simplest to stick with just the open library collection. From the main page, select "books" off the menu and then "open library" from there. At the top of the open library page, there will be options to browse by subject. You can also browse selections curated by librarians. Be careful on the Internet Archives—it's endless, and you can easily lose a whole afternoon that you meant to spend studying!

> The open library, at *openlibrary.org,* has a lot of textbooks. If you ever find yourself writing an essay and you left your textbook at school, it can be a lifesaver!

### Library of Congress Archives

*https://www.loc.gov/collections/*
The above link is to the Library of Congress digital collections. These are great for practice on historical reading and most other genres. For example, you can read a selection of papers by Abraham Lincoln, whose writings may be used on the SAT.

*http://www.read.gov/teens/*
This second link is to the Library of Congress's teen page. If browsing the online digital collection is overwhelming or maybe the content is too difficult for your reading level, the teen page has a lot of resources to help you find reading material that might be interesting to you. You can even email a librarian to ask for suggestions.

### Local Library Resources/Phone E-reader

Most communities have a local library—have you ever been to yours? It's full of reading materials and employs people who love reading and can help you find things you'll love reading too. Go ask your librarian for some help! Something a lot of people don't realize is that libraries have done a great job keeping up with the times. Many are part of online collaborations that allow patrons to check out just about any book in existence, and often, those books can be checked out via an app and read entirely on an e-reader or phone. This allows you to take your reading with you anywhere you go so that you can get your reading time in between practices, in waiting rooms, or while stuck in a traffic jam (while someone else is driving, of course).

### School Library

In addition to the local library, you likely also have a school library (which many schools now call a resource center). While school libraries are often small, they are in the building where you already spend dozens of hours each week and so are very accessible. They don't have just books and magazines, but also resources geared specifically to students your age. It is likely that there will also be a librarian there who spends a large portion of their work time keeping on top of what students like to read so that they can recommend specific literature that is geared to the interests of the students. Make friends with this person—they can be a huge help to students looking for interesting reading materials.

### Magazines

If you're interested in a specific hobby or area of study, magazines are a resource that are often forgotten. Trade publications and more serious magazines (*TIME*, *Scientific American*, *National Geographic*, and so on) are written at a fairly high level. If you're into robotics, see if you can subscribe to a robotics magazine—when it's delivered to your mailbox, it will remind you to read! You can also read magazines at your local library or often on their website, but the physical reminder is often nice.

### Audiobooks and Podcasts

It can be difficult to find time to sit down and read a good book. Audiobooks and podcasts are a great way to consume high quality media while doing something else, like driving in the car, or exercising. The website www.audible.com has many free audiobooks you can try, and your public library will have a variety of audiobooks you can borrow. Your reading comprehension will increase even if you are listening to someone else read the book but aren't physically reading the words yourself.

## Using This Book to Prepare for the SAT Reading Test?

Review and practice with the specific types of questions that are most challenging for you on the following pages:


- Words in Context (page 103)
- Structure and Purpose (page 112)
- Cross-Text Connections (page 119)
- Central Ideas and Details (page 124)
- Quantitative Evidence (page 132)
- Textual Evidence (page 150)
- Inferences (page 156)

Study further with **practice**, starting on page **162**, which focus on the types of questions that are most difficult for you.

Practice with **advanced drills**, starting on page **171**, which present the most challenging types of reading and questions you might encounter on the SAT.

Review the **Vocabulary Resources of 50 word roots and 250 SAT words**, starting on page **180,** to bolster your understanding of the most common challenging words you may come across on the SAT.

Practice with the full-length Reading and Writing tests, carefully watching your time management.

Good luck!

## Words in Context

### Sample Question Language:

- Which choice completes the text with the most logical and precise word or phrase?
- As used in the text, what does the word "compromise" most nearly mean?

### How Important Is Vocabulary Study to Success on the SAT Reading?

The SAT Reading primarily focuses on your ability to decipher the meaning of words in context. Does this mean you should no longer focus on memorizing word definitions? Not necessarily. If you do not have a strong baseline level of vocabulary—you frequently encounter words in the texts and questions that you do not know—some focused vocabulary memorization will be useful to you. Also, if English is not your native language, memorizing words that you will likely encounter on the SAT will help you improve your score. That is why there is a Vocabulary Resource at the end of this Reading chapter. It has 50 important word roots and definitions and examples for 250 common words you may find in SAT texts. Use these valuable tools to help you build your vocabulary so you no longer come across words in the texts and the questions you do not understand.

#### How can you succeed on Words in Context Questions?

- **Create a synonym of your own when asked to complete the text with a word or phrase.** Having an idea before reviewing the answer choices is like having a shopping list before going to the store—you will be more decisive and accurate in picking what you need.
- **If you do not know what a particular answer option means, do not immediately eliminate it as a possibility.** When presented with a choice between an option you know versus an option you do not know, you may typically choose the word you know, even if the option is not a good fit. Instead of this approach, realize that whatever the correct answer is will work 100%, so even if you do not know what a word means, do not eliminate it as a possibility. Instead, use the fact that if the other options only partially work, they are completely wrong.
    - Realize that a word may take on one of its alternative meanings. Words usually have several different possible definitions. Be mindful that the appropriate meaning for the word in question may be the third or fourth most common meaning instead of the first.
    - Try plugging in the options to the text to see what is most logical. If you are having trouble deciding on a word meaning solution, try taking the different options and substituting them for the word.

### Example

Measles is a highly contagious viral infection, which results, among other symptoms, in a rash and high fever. Measles is most dangerous to children under five years old, adults over 20 years old, and people with __________ immune systems. Complications from measles can result in hearing loss, intellectual disability, and respiratory and neurological conditions.

Which choice completes the text with the most logical and precise word or phrase?

(A) dynamic
(B) compromised
(C) evolved
(D) enhanced

### Answer Explanation

Start by reading the entire text carefully. Paraphrasing the text, we understand that measles is a dangerous illness and can result in serious complications. Since the text is discussing a disease, we can ask ourselves what description of an immune system would result in measles being a significant threat. Create a synonym in your own words; if someone had a "weak" or "vulnerable" immune system, having a measles infection would present a greater challenge than it would to people who have strong immune systems. Now, we can evaluate the choices. "Dynamic" is a positive word, indicating that the person would be full of energy—this does not fit the needed meaning. "Evolved" and "enhanced" are also positive words, showing that the immune system goes beyond the typical capabilities of what might be found in a human. "Compromised," choice (B), makes the most sense, since one of the definitions of "compromised" is "weakened." Although this is not the most typical definition of the word, it is a definition nonetheless—be flexible as you consider the possible meanings of the words.

## Practice Questions

1. I expect that people are so reluctant to register to become organ donors primarily because of the anonymity of the people one would be saving. When dealing with strangers, the whole concept is more abstract and __________, because you haven't seen the suffering of those you would help.

   Which choice completes the text with the most logical and precise word or phrase?

   (A) concrete
   (B) substantial
   (C) comprehensive
   (D) impersonal

2. Colony collapse disorder (CCD) is an issue that has, over the last ten years, caused a __________ amount of concern as to the feasibility of the continued bee population in North America. Fruit and vegetable crops are pollinated by bees. Should the bee population drop drastically, the availability of these healthy options would be dramatically reduced.

   Which choice completes the text with the most logical and precise word or phrase?

   (A) minimal
   (B) skeptical
   (C) grave
   (D) draconian

3. Teenagers spend a significant portion of their time on social media, and they don't know any differently. This cohort consists of the guinea pigs of one of the biggest communications revolutions of all time. As they grow and change, their brains can be studied to see how this constant __________ online social communication affects them.

   Which choice completes the text with the most logical and precise word or phrase?

   (A) admission to
   (B) dearth of
   (C) ignorance of
   (D) exposure to

4. *C. diff* is an often fairly __________ bacteria that is sometimes found in humans and can be picked up from the environment. In small amounts and balanced with other bacteria that keep it under control, *C. diff* can be carried by humans without serious repercussions to health.

   Which choice completes the text with the most logical and precise word or phrase?

   (A) deleterious
   (B) innocuous
   (C) subversive
   (D) organic

5. Poor sleep impacts many body systems. Of particular interest to adolescents, and their parents, is the __________ effect of poor sleep on academic performance. Lack of sleep makes it difficult to focus on lectures and classwork.

   Which choice completes the text with the most logical and precise word or phrase?

   (A) detrimental
   (B) benevolent
   (C) dishonest
   (D) dissenting

6. The following text is from Upton Sinclair's 1906 novel *The Jungle*.

   The stench was almost overpowering, but to Jurgis it was nothing. His whole soul was dancing with joy—he was at work at last! He was at work and earning money! All day long he was <u>figuring</u> to himself. He was paid the fabulous sum of seventeen and a half cents an hour; and as it proved a rush day and he worked until nearly seven o'clock in the evening, he went home to the family with the tidings that he had earned more than a dollar and a half in a single day!

   As used in the text, what does the word "figuring" most nearly mean?

   (A) Believing
   (B) Calculating
   (C) Assuming
   (D) Doubting

7. The following is an excerpt from Jane Austen's novel *Mansfield Park* (1814). The novel's protagonist, Fanny Price, returns home after many years of living with her wealthy relatives at Mansfield Park.

   The instinct of nature was soon satisfied, and Mrs. Price's attachment had no other source. Her heart and her time were already quite full; she had neither leisure nor affection to bestow on Fanny. Her daughters never had been much to her. She was fond of her sons, especially of William, but Betsey was the first of her girls whom she had ever much regarded. To her she was most injudiciously indulgent. William was her pride; Betsey her darling; and John, Richard, Sam, Tom, and Charles <u>occupied</u> all the rest of her maternal solicitude, alternately her worries and her comforts.

   As used in the text, what does the word "occupied" most nearly mean?

   (A) Stayed
   (B) Resided
   (C) Dwelled
   (D) Engaged

8. While Mr. Davis, the art teacher, approved of creativity, he couldn't ________ the students expressing themselves in the form of graffiti. Stylistically, he could appreciate the pieces, but he still considered them vandalism.

   Which choice completes the text with the most logical and precise word or phrase?

   (A) sanction
   (B) consent with
   (C) confirm that
   (D) boycott

9. The canoe was going too quickly toward the rapids. Yusef was ________ the shore to slow them down. While they hit the bank hard, it slowed the boat down enough that Yusef and his friend were able to jump out and pull the canoe off the water.

   Which choice completes the text with the most logical and precise word or phrase?

   (A) hitting off
   (B) counting on
   (C) swimming on
   (D) depositing

10. It is probable that humans have been cooking since not long after our ancestors harnessed the power of fire some several hundred thousand years ago. Since that time, the sophistication of our technology has increased exponentially, and the technology of cooking is no exception. Insofar as it pertains to heat, the nature of culinary innovation has fallen primarily into one of two categories common to many technology ________: speed and precision.

    Which choice completes the text with the most logical and precise word or phrase?

    (A) beliefs
    (B) arcs
    (C) hypotheses
    (D) motives

11. Much like Old Faithful at Yellowstone National Park—by far the most well-known of the American geysers—Halley's Comet is neither the most visually __________ nor the largest of its kind, but rather its renown derives from the dependable frequency with which it can be observed. Halley's Comet falls into a category called Great Comets, which are those comets that become bright enough during their passage near Earth to be observed by the naked eye.

    Which choice completes the text with the most logical and precise word or phrase?

    (A) brilliant
    (B) conceited
    (C) intellectual
    (D) august

12. There is one <u>linchpin</u> name, however, too frequently omitted from surveys of the early impressionist art movement. Eugène Boudin—a friend and contemporary of the Paris impressionists—never described himself as an innovator or revolutionary, and yet his work tremendously influenced the transmigration of impressionism from the walls of radical art galleries to those of homes and businesses throughout Europe.

    As used in the text, what does the word "linchpin" most nearly mean?

    (A) Artistic
    (B) Essential
    (C) Commercial
    (D) Improvisational

13. Depending on the severity and type of infection, a doctor may select a narrow or broad-spectrum bactericidal drug. Narrow-spectrum drugs are better for the patient as they only kill the microorganism causing the infection via a specific mechanism of action. This differs from broad-spectrum drugs as they kill the microorganism and any other cell with the same type of mechanism of action. This often causes __________ and unpleasant side effects for the patient, such as superinfections and a wipeout of the body's natural flora barrier.

    Which choice completes the text with the most logical and precise word or phrase?

    (A) severe
    (B) thoughtful
    (C) genuine
    (D) quiet

14. Not only does studying abroad help students to find their career path, but it also makes them more __________ to employers. Among the marketable benefits are language skills, an extensive network, cultural adaptability, self-reliance, open-mindedness, and an appreciation for diversity.

    Which choice completes the text with the most logical and precise word or phrase?

    (A) disparaging
    (B) appealing
    (C) introverted
    (D) monetarist

15. The staggering plurality of postmodern theater itself we must attribute, at least in part, to the initial fracturing of the modern drama in its __________ state, when refusing to yield to prevailing winds, Strindberg and Ibsen produced a cyclone.

    Which choice completes the text with the most logical and precise word?

    (A) outset
    (B) germinating
    (C) floral
    (D) germinal

16. Echolocation is the highly sophisticated sense of hearing in which sound waves bounce off objects and emit echoes that microbats use to detect obstacles. It is this __________ that allows the nocturnal microbat to sense where an object is, how big or small that object may be, and even how fast that object is moving.

    Which choice completes the text with the most logical and precise word?

    (A) object
    (B) material
    (C) phenomenon
    (D) thing

17. After degree completion, teachers need to acquire a teaching certificate, or a license to teach—most often, this licensing is achieved via teacher education programs where __________ teachers student-teach under more experienced instructors.

    Which choice completes the text with the most logical and precise word?

    (A) perspective
    (B) prospective
    (C) prospecting
    (D) previewing

18. The great dramatists of the 20th century—Arthur Miller, Tennessee Williams, John Osborne, and Harold Pinter—still owe an enormous creative debt to their 19th-century __________, most particularly to the two Scandinavian playwrights Henrik Ibsen and August Strindberg.

    Which choice completes the text with the most logical and precise word or phrase?

    (A) forebears
    (B) elders
    (C) seniors
    (D) historians

19. His is a household name, and he is most often thought of as a man unearthing the world's most __________ mysteries while napping under an apple tree. He is Sir Isaac Newton, an English physicist and mathematician responsible for the law of universal gravitation.

    Which choice completes the text with the most logical and precise word?

    (A) imminent
    (B) eminent
    (C) complimentary
    (D) complementary

20. Social media has also been connected to better company retention. Some technologically savvy employers have created company pages where staff can make announcements, share ideas, discuss problems, and congratulate one another on excellent work. The page becomes a __________ where colleagues can support one another, but also where the company itself can show appreciation.

    Which choice completes the text with the most logical and precise word?

    (A) space
    (B) dimension
    (C) clearing
    (D) separation

## Answer Explanations

1. **(D)** The text discusses the idea that people may be reluctant to consider donating organs to strangers with whom they don't have a connection. The most logical choice would therefore be "impersonal" since people may not see a personal connection to those who would benefit from the organ donation. Choices (A) and (B) are the opposite of what is needed, and (C) would include a large variety of ideas instead of the single one expressed.
2. **(C)** The text indicates that there is a possibility that the bee population could drastically drop, resulting in a need to convey a strong negative possibility, making "grave" the best option. Choices (A) and (B) are not sufficiently negative, while (D) is negative in a different way—"harshly authoritative"—which does not work in this context.
3. **(D)** The text states that teens are spending a significant portion of their time on social media, making it most logical to say that they have had "exposure to" online social communication. It is not (A) since they are not admitting anything. It is not (B) since "dearth" means a "lack" of something, which is the opposite of what is needed here. It is not (C) because the teens are clearly not ignorant of online social communication.
4. **(B)** The words are a bit more challenging on this question. "Deleterious" means "harmful," "innocuous" means "harmless," "subversive" means "rebellious," and "organic" means "related to life." Since the text states that this bacteria can be carried by humans without affecting their health, it can best be described as "harmless," making "innocuous" correct.
5. **(A)** The text goes on to emphasize the negative effects of a lack of sleep, such as the resulting difficulty with focus in school. Thus, the overall effect of poor sleep would be harmful, making "detrimental" the most logical insertion. "Benevolent" means "kind," "dishonest" means "lacking honesty," and "dissenting" means "disagreeing."

6. **(B)** When handling these vocabulary questions, insert each option into the sentence to determine which best fits the context. "All day long he was figuring to himself" means that he was counting the money he was making; he was "calculating" his earnings, as in choice (B). Insert "believing," "assuming," and "doubting" into the sentence; none of these choices provides a logical statement.

7. **(D)** "Engaged" accurately refers to Mrs. Price's absorption with her sons. It is appropriate to say they "engaged," or preoccupied, her attention. None of the other words fit; the sons neither "stay," "reside," nor "dwell" her worry or care.

8. **(A)** The teacher in the text wants his students to be creative but does not want to allow graffiti that he would consider to be vandalism. He therefore does not want to "permit" or "sanction" that activity. Choices (B) and (C) would show that he agrees with the student behavior, which is the opposite of what is needed. It is not (D) because to "boycott" would be to avoid participating in an action oneself—instead of being an actor himself, he is prohibiting others from taking action.

9. **(B)** Yusef is hoping that the shore would slow the canoe down so they can safely get out of the water—thus, "counting on" makes the most sense. The other options do not express this idea.

10. **(B)** The word "arc" in this context takes on a more unusual definition—"development." The text discusses some of the technological developments that have taken place with respect to cooking. The other options all have to do with mental states than with developments, making them incorrect.

11. **(A)** "Brilliant" in this context can mean "visually bright" or "radiant," making this an appropriate word to describe the look of a comet. The other options would not be appropriate to describe the physical characteristics of a comet.

12. **(B)** "Essential" is most fitting, since the text goes on to discuss Boudin's tremendous influence on the artistic scene, making a history of impressionism severely lacking without mentioning him. The other words do give descriptions that can be associated with impressionism, but they do not fit this context.

13. **(A)** In context, the use of severe "and unpleasant side effects" forms the most logical sentence—unpleasant side effects could be described as "intense" or "severe." Nonhuman side effects cannot be described as "thoughtful," "genuine," or "quiet."

14. **(B)** The text highlights how studying abroad can make students more marketable to potential employers; in other words, the students would be more "appealing." "Disparaging" means "insulting," "introverted" means "shy," and "monetarist" is associated with economic theory.

15. **(D)** "Germinal" indicates that it is in its earliest stage of development. "Outset," in choice (A), has the correct general meaning but is the wrong part of speech since it is a noun instead of an adjective. "Germinating" and "floral" refer to plant life.

16. **(C)** This word refers to "echolocation," which is best described as a "phenomenon" since it is a process that allows bats to navigate. The other options are all associated with physical items.

17. **(B)** "Prospective" means "preparing to do so in the future," which applies to teachers who are being trained since they are not yet licensed professionals. "Perspective" in choice (A) indicates a point of view. "Prospecting" in (C) indicates searching. "Previewing" in (D) does not apply to people in the process of learning their profession, although it could refer to what the trainees themselves will be doing with respect to professional skills.

18. **(A)** The sentence first mentions 20th-century dramatists and then states that they owe a great deal to those who preceded them in the 19th century, making "forebears" the most sensible option. "Elders" in (B) and "seniors" in (C) refer to older groups of people but without the connotation of paving the way for current generations. "Historians" in (D) refers to those who study history, not to those who are studied by historians.

19. **(B)** This question tests you on the meaning of some commonly confused words. "Eminent" means "noteworthy," which makes sense in reference to a famous concept like that of gravity. "Imminent," choice (A), means "about to happen." "Complimentary," choice (C), is associated with praise. "Complementary," choice (D), is associated with combining things together so they improve the quality of each other.

20. **(A)** "Space" in this context takes on one of its less common definitions—"free area." This word makes the most sense since social media is described as something that has helped employers retain staff by creating a sense of community. While the other options are possible definitions of "space," they do not make sense in this context.

## Structure and Purpose

### Sample Question Language:

- Which choice best states the main purpose of the text?
- Which choice best describes the function of the underlined sentence in the text as a whole?
- Which choice best describes the overall structure of the text?

### How Can You Succeed on Structure and Purpose Questions?

- **Understand the text in its entirety to fully grasp the purpose of different selections.** It is difficult to perform well on structure and purpose questions without reading the text in its entirety. If you do not comprehend the overall point of the text, it will be challenging to determine the significance of particular parts.
- **Distinguish between "purpose" and "summary."** Students often answer structure and purpose questions by summarizing the text instead of finding the purpose of the text. A summary tells you what the text is about, while purpose tells you why the text was written—these are two very different tasks.
- **Carefully consider the context before and after the selection.** When asked a question about the function of a sentence, carefully read the sentences before and after so that you have a better sense of what the function of the sentence would be. Look out for transitional words—words like "although," "however," "additionally," and "in fact"—to better understand the connection to the surrounding material.
- **If you are asked about the "main" purpose, be sure it is not overly specific.** It is easy to be trapped by choices on "main purpose" questions that do provide you with something that is true about the text, but don't capture the overall significance of the text. Make certain that you go for an answer that captures the "main purpose," not one that merely focuses on a small portion of the text.

### Example

This excerpt from "The American Forests" was part of John Muir's 1897 campaign to save the American wilderness. He would later be called the godfather of the American environmental movement.

Surely, then, it should not be wondered at that lovers of their country, bewailing its baldness, are now crying aloud, "Save what is left of the forests!" <u>Clearing has surely now gone far enough; soon timber will be scarce, and not a grove will be left to rest in or pray in.</u> The remnant protected will yield plenty of timber, a perennial harvest for every right use, without further diminution of its area, and will continue to cover the springs of the rivers that rise in the mountains and give irrigating waters to the dry valleys at their feet, prevent wasting floods and be a blessing to everybody forever.

Which choice best describes the function of the underlined sentence in the text as a whole?

(A) It advocates for the importance of nationalism, militarism, and expansionism.
(B) It underscores the need to emphasize environmentalism, scholarship, and piety.
(C) It makes appeals that focus on economics, leisure, and religion.
(D) It encourages a prioritization of justice, individualism, and truth.

### ✓ Answer Explanation

Let us start by reading the introductory information. This excerpt is from a text that advocates environmentalism and saving the American wilderness. It therefore comes as no surprise that the excerpt will align with these themes. Next, read the text in its entirety and paraphrase its argument. It starts by stating that people who love the country are now greatly saddened by the destruction of the forests. The underlined sentence states that the clearing of the forest needs to stop, since timber is not plentiful, and people will no longer have places to relax and worship. The text goes on to argue that the forest can be responsibly managed to provide ongoing supplies of timber and water for irrigation. So, the purpose of the sentence is to support the general argument that the forests need to be preserved by emphasizing the potential negative consequences that will happen if the forests continue to be destroyed. Now we can evaluate the different choices. It is not (A) because the sentence focuses on peaceful themes, not militaristic ones. It is not (B) because while there is a focus on environmentalism, there is not an emphasis on the need for scholarship. It is not (D) because the sentence does not discuss the theme of individualism—even a single flaw in an answer will make it incorrect. This leaves us with choice (C), which does work because it appeals to the reader by focusing on economics (the scarcity of timber), leisure (no grove in which to rest), and religion (no grove in which to pray).

## Practice Questions

1. When developing any new technology, we need to stop and give the proposal critical thought. What does this development contribute to society? How many people will benefit from this development? In what ways can this development be harmful? Maybe most importantly, why? Why should time and resources be dedicated to this project, when time and resources are limited, and potential projects are unlimited? But this responsibility shouldn't fall entirely upon the developer. We, as consumers, need to take a more active role as well. How does this technology help me? Does this technology do any harm? Why do I need this technology? Only once we've considered the relative benefits and costs of one project versus another can we begin to consider whether it's worth it.

   What choice best describes the overall structure of the text?

   (A) It presents both society-wide and individual consumer questions that should be asked about potential new technology development.
   (B) It provides a series of specific critiques about the increasing advancement of technology in the modern world.
   (C) It questions whether technological advances should be halted to return to the morals of a simpler era.
   (D) It suggests that instead of technology, alternative approaches to solving social problems of development and resource allocation should be embraced.

2. What does it mean to be a "cinephile" in the 2020s? In the mid-1990s, Susan Sontag famously argued that the globalization and hyper-industrialization of Hollywood had "killed" cinema as an art form in favor of its big, formulaic blockbusters. However, other critics argue that independent art cinema has simply moved outside of the Hollywood studio system, onto YouTube and other user-generated video platforms. Some critics even challenge the term "cinephilia" for its snobbish connotations and apolitical origins.

   What choice best describes the overall structure of the text?

   (A) It decries the decay of the modern film industry.
   (B) It criticizes the advent of user-generated videos in the place of major studio productions.
   (C) It provides different perspectives on the notion of cinephilia.
   (D) It suggests that other forms of entertainment will ultimately displace film.

3. The following is an excerpt from the fairy tale "The Mouse, the Bird, and the Sausage" by the Brothers Grimm, published in 1812.

   Once upon a time, a mouse, a bird, and a sausage entered into a partnership and set up house together. For a long time all went well; they lived in great comfort, and prospered so far as to be able to add considerably to their stores. <u>The bird's duty was to fly daily into the wood and bring in fuel; the mouse fetched the water, and the sausage saw to the cooking</u>.

   Which choice best describes the function of the underlined sentence in the text as a whole?

   (A) It describes the methods whereby each creature carried out its chores
   (B) It conveys the primary moral of the fable
   (C) It analyzes the individual differences in each creature's motivations
   (D) It outlines the daily obligations of the three creatures

4. <u>For the past fifty years it has been the conventional credence of ecologists and biologists alike that invasive, non-native plant species are, without exception, detrimental to the host ecosystem.</u> However, recent studies at Penn State University indicate that the eradication of invasive plants—specifically fruit-bearing shrubs—can do more harm than good for the native animal populations.

   Which choice best states the function of the underlined sentence in the text as a whole?

   (A) It establishes the narrator's scholarly authority in this field of study.
   (B) It states the principal argument of the author.
   (C) It summarizes a common understanding that is subsequently refuted.
   (D) It contrasts the work of ecologists with those of biologists.

5. While significant structural and functional differences exist between the various classes, a surfactant, simply put, describes any compound capable of reducing the surface tension between a liquid and one other substance. Surface tension, one will recall, refers to the tendency of liquid molecules to coalesce with one another, thus minimizing their collective surface area. This phenomenon is the physical principle underlying a familiar adage, "oil and water do not mix." Phrased more precisely, oils, which contain primarily nonpolar hydrocarbon bonds, are immiscible with aqueous solutions, meaning they will not spontaneously dissolve in water, which consists of highly polar hydrogen-oxygen bonds. Instead, oils will tend to form a film over polar solvents, while surface tension serves to stabilize this film at the oil-water interface.

   Which choice best describes the function of the underlined phrase in the text as a whole?

   (A) It explains the process in which two immiscible substances are emulsified.
   (B) It implies that most laypeople cannot understand the topic of this article.
   (C) It shows that substances that do not have triglycerides cannot undergo saponification.
   (D) It connects the esoteric analysis to a commonly understood phenomenon.

6. The following is the preface to *The White Slaves of England*, a book published in 1854 to decry the horrible working and living conditions among the poor working classes of England.

   Let her *miners*, her *operatives*, *the tenants of her workhouses*, her *naval service*, and the millions upon millions in the Emerald Isle and in farther India attest its fallacy. These are the legitimate results of the laws and institutions of Great Britain; and they reach and affect, in a greater or less degree, all her dependencies. Her *church and state*, and her *laws of entail and primogeniture*, are the principal sources of the evils under which her people groan; and until these are changed there is no just ground of hope for an improvement in their condition. The tendency of things is, indeed, to make matters still worse. The poor are every year becoming poorer, and more dependent upon those who feast upon their sufferings, while the wealth and power of the realm are annually concentrating in fewer hands and becoming more and more instruments of oppression. The picture is already sufficiently revolting.

   Which choice best states the main purpose of the italicized terms in the text?

   (A) It names those who approve of oppression.
   (B) It underscores the widespread presence of injustice.
   (C) It legitimizes the British policy toward social class.
   (D) It shows the diversity of various empowered groups.

7. Excerpt from *The Last Man*, a novel by Mary Shelley, published in 1826.

   My fortunes have been, from the beginning, an exemplification of the power that mutability may possess over the varied tenor of man's life. With regard to myself, this came almost by inheritance. My father was one of those men on whom nature had bestowed to prodigality the envied gifts of wit and imagination, and then left his bark of life to be impelled by these winds, without adding reason as the rudder, or judgment as the pilot for the voyage. His extraction was obscure; but circumstances brought him early into public notice, and his small paternal property was soon dissipated in the splendid scene of fashion and luxury in which he was an actor.

   Which choice best describes the function of the underlined sentence in the text as a whole?

   (A) It shows that the narrator shares many of his father's personality characteristics.
   (B) It demonstrates that the narrator received considerable financial resources to ensure a comfortable life.
   (C) It shows that the narrator has the same self-reliant and self-disciplined mindset as his ancestors.
   (D) It demonstrates how the narrator is rather fortunate in how the nature of chance seems to favor him.

8. *Thalassemia* describes a group of disorders in which either the α or β chain is quantitatively reduced. Depending on the mutation, these defects can present with a wide range of anemia-related symptoms, and are particularly prevalent throughout Africa, Southeast Asia, and the Mediterranean. This geographical distribution is anything but random. Many studies have demonstrated that the production of suboptimal hemoglobin confers a degree of protection against malaria, a potentially deadly infectious disease caused by members of the *Plasmodium* genus, which parasitize red blood cells. It follows, then, that whereas in many regions throughout the world thalassemia may merely constitute disease, in those where malaria is endemic, it represents a favorable evolutionary advantage.

   Which choice best states the main purpose of the text?

   (A) It links hemoglobin development to migration patterns.
   (B) It compares cultural characteristics to evolutionary traits.
   (C) It considers geographic particularities to evolutionary adaptation.
   (D) It connects environmental forces to medical innovations.

9. So why is it, with a rejuvenated effort to find evidence of extraterrestrial intelligence, the Search for Extraterrestrial Intelligence (SETI) has not found convincing evidence for alien life? Despite billions of dollars and years of research, SETI has nothing substantial to show for itself. In fact, the closest thing to ETI contact is the Wow! Signal: a strong narrowband radio signal detected in 1977 by Jerry R. Ehman of Ohio State University's Big Ear radio telescope project. Ehman was able to successfully observe the signal for a 72-second window, circling its non-natural waves and writing "Wow!" next to it—his enthusiasm led to its name, but not to any significant breakthrough. Since 1977, efforts to relocate the signal have failed again and again.

   Which choice best states the main purpose of the text?

   (A) It shows that there is decisive evidence in favor of alien life.
   (B) It argues that the search for extraterrestrial intelligence has been virtually fruitless.
   (C) It presents how scientists are redoubling their efforts to build on Ehman's discovery.
   (D) It observes how astronomers are notable for the enthusiasm with which they conduct their observations.

10. David Benson was a timid boy born to parents who had long since stopped worrying about having children. Willie and Louise had three grown girls, the youngest was nineteen and leaving to cosmetology school the year David was born. Louise had suspected an arsenal of health issues before realizing she was with child, and even then, she waited another three weeks to tell her unsuspecting husband.

    Which choice best describes the function of the underlined sentence in the text as a whole?

    (A) It demonstrates the age difference between David and his siblings.
    (B) It scientifically explains how David was genetically predisposed towards having a more introverted personality.
    (C) It gives a reason for why David went to live with a different family.
    (D) It gives insight into David's personality and his parents' state of mind.

## Answer Explanations

1. **(A)** Consider the overall way that the text is organized. It gives a series of questions that could be used to evaluate the pros and cons of new technological developments—this aligns with choice (A). It is not (B) because it does not critique technology in general but focuses on how one can evaluate a specific new technology. It is not (C) because the author does not advocate an end to the entirety of technological advancement. It is not (D) because the text does not focus on suggesting different approaches to solving social problems.

2. **(C)** Do not focus on the specific argument but on the overall organization of the text. The text starts by asking what it means to be a cinephile, i.e., someone who loves movies. The text proceeds to share different opinions about what it means to be a film-lover. Thus, choice (C) makes the most sense. It is not (A) because while the first perspective presented seems to take this position, the second perspective does not. It is not (B) because there is not a critique of user-generated videos. It is not (D) because it does not suggest that film will be displaced but does present the possibility that it could be changed in its presentation.

3. **(D)** In this sentence, the chores for the creatures are described, helping the reader better understand the story that follows. It is not (A) because the chores are simply named, and no discussion of the methods of carrying out the chores is given. It is not (B) because this gives us no preview of a moral of the story. It is not (C) because while differences in the chores are given, there is no discussion of the motivations of the creatures.

4. **(C)** The author immediately contradicts this statement in the following sentence. The general purpose of this sentence is to give a general summary of what many people think about this issue, and then to use the rest of the text to state that most people are incorrect on this topic. It is not (A) since this text only indirectly establishes the author's authority. It is not (B) because the primary position of the author comes in the sentence that follows. It is not (D) because ecologists and biologists agree according to this sentence.

5. **(D)** The phrase is provided as a relevant and recognizable example in a sea of very technical analysis. "Esoteric" means likely to be understood by only a specialized audience. Choices (A) and (C) involve concepts not referred to in this sentence. Choice (B) is incorrect because the example is used to extend understanding to laypeople rather than imply they cannot understand it.

6. **(B)** In this text, the narrator introduces the abuses found in 19th-century English society. The italicized selections can be reasonably inferred to be groups that could bear witness to the abuses. Since there are so many different groups that could highlight these abuses, it underscores the widespread presence of injustice in English society at the time. It is not (A) or (C) because the narrator is not suggesting these groups would approve or legitimize these practices. It is not (D) because while these groups were diverse, they were not empowered at the time.

7. **(A)** In this text, the narrator is not talking about an inheritance of money or items. Rather, he goes on in the text to describe his father as a means of informing the reader of the personality or situation he inherited. This makes choice (A) the best option. Choice (B) is incorrect as there is no evidence of a monetary inheritance. Choice (C) is incorrect as the father is not described as self-reliant or self-disciplined, so the author would not have inherited these traits. Choice (D) is incorrect as we are not led to believe that this inheritance makes the speaker fortunate.

8. **(C)** The text considers the geographical specificity of thalassemia disorders and explains that it is not coincidental but linked to evolution's defense against malaria, making (C) accurate. The distribution is not linked to migration as in (A) or related to cultural phenomena as in (B). Finally, (D) is incorrect because there is no connection made to medical innovation in the text.

9. **(B)** The text provides evidence for the claim that "SETI has nothing substantial to show for itself." These text shows how a 72-second anomaly in 1977 that was never relocated is the closest thing we have of evidence of outside life. Hence, (B) is correct. Choice (A) implies that this evidence proved alien existence, which is false. We have no evidence for (C); we only know that efforts have failed in the past. Choice (D) is incorrect because it assumes that the significance of this example is Ehman's "Wow!" rather than its feeble status as the closest we've come to proof.

10. **(D)** The underlined sentence provides an exposition that explains why David and his parents are the way they are, so (D) is the best choice. His siblings are not introduced until the following sentence, making (A) incorrect. (B) states that he is timid, but the lines do not offer a scientific explanation of the genetic reasons behind this. Moving in with a different family could refer to an outcome of David's personality and his parents' state of mind, rather than a cause, making (C) incorrect.

# Cross-Text Connections

## Sample Question Language

- Based on the texts, how would Goodenough and Strawn (Text 2) most likely respond to Tartaro's findings (Text 1)?
- Based on the texts, how would the sociologists and their colleagues (Text 1) most likely describe the approach of the researchers in Text 2?

## How Can You Succeed on Cross-Text Connections Questions?

- **Be clear on the main argument of each text.** Text 1 and Text 2 combinations are typically argumentative—each text will have a clear thesis that is presented and supported with examples. If you can put the main argument of each text in your own words, you will likely do well on these questions.
- **Do not confuse an author's viewpoint with the author's consideration of possible objections.** In argumentative essays, authors frequently present and analyze views with which they do not agree. After all, one of the best ways to convince someone of a position is to show why the opposite position is flawed. When you read the comparative texts, pay close attention if the author shifts to considering objections. Be mindful that not everything in a text may necessarily represent what its author believes.
- **Realize that the relationships between texts will often be more nuanced.** Instead of having clear pro and con arguments on a topic, the texts may have some similarities and very subtle differences. The texts could present somewhat different accounts of the same historical event; one text could provide an explanation for the events or phenomena described in the other text; one text could summarize a topic in a more general way, while the other text investigates the topic in a more specific way. Keep an open mind to determine the precise nature of the relationship between the texts.

### Example

**Text 1**

Through a combination of luck and perhaps cruelty, Beaumont's work has since led several scholarships, awards, and buildings to be named in his honor. Despite his unethical research methods, Beaumont's findings about the digestive tract have paved the way for further research in this field and have even led him to be called the Father of Gastric Physiology.

**Text 2**

Beaumont realized he could use St. Martin's unique wound to learn more about the mechanisms behind digestion—he just needed St. Martin to participate. Beaumont decided to ask St. Martin to sign a document, and St. Martin, being unable to read, had no idea he was signing away his rights. As he signed that document, St. Martin became a legally bound test-subject. In the over 200 subsequent experiments on St. Martin, Beaumont was able to gain an understanding of the human digestive system.

Based on the texts, the opinion of the author of Text 1 about the treatment of St. Martin in Text 2 would most likely be

(A) ambivalent.
(B) apathetic.
(C) flattering.
(D) antagonistic.

### Answer Explanation

You might find it most helpful to read the question first so that you have an idea of what you might focus on while you read the text. Paraphrasing the question, we need to understand the overall mindset of the author of Text 1 and understand how St. Martin is treated in Text 2. Text 1 acknowledges the merit of Beaumont's digestive research, but also mentions his possible "cruelty" and the "unethical" nature of his research methods. In Text 2 we learn that St. Martin unknowingly signed away his rights and became a digestive test subject. Without having St. Martin as a research subject, Beaumont would have been unlikely to learn as much as he did about the mechanisms of human digestion. Beaumont was only able to secure St. Martin as a research subject through unethical conduct. Given the positives and negatives of this situation, the author of Text 1 would most likely feel conflicted about St. Martin's treatment. Choice (A), "ambivalent," means feeling conflicted making (A) the correct answer. "Apathetic" would indicate no opinion at all, "flattering" is too positive, and "antagonistic" is too negative.

## Practice Questions

1. Text 1 is an adaptation from the newspaper *The Record-Union* on January 30, 1893. It records the events that occurred in Hawaii that led to the annexation of the island chain for the United States, including the resignation of Hawaii's last monarch, Queen Liliuokalani. Text 2 is an excerpt from the obituary of Queen Liliuokalani upon her death as recorded in *The Union Times* on November 15, 1917.

**Text 1**

The commissioners are here on their way to Washington, and simply state that their instructions are to get the consent of our government to annex the islands . . .
[Upon her abdication, Queen Liliuokalani stated:]
"I, Liliuokalani, by grace of God and under the Constitution of the Hawaiian Kingdom, Queen, do hereby solemnly protest against any and all acts done against myself and the constitutional government of the Hawaiian Kingdom by certain persons claiming to have established a provisional government of and for this Kingdom."

**Text 2**

The queen's bold attempt to deprive the white residents of any voice in the affairs of government led to prompt retaliatory measures. The businessmen of the community named a "committee of safety," which proceeded immediately with the formation of a provisional government and the reorganization of the volunteer military companies which had been disbanded in 1890 . . .

How do the two texts use quotation marks differently?

(A) Text 1 uses them to label a term, while Text 2 uses them to quote a historical figure.
(B) Text 1 uses them to quote a historical figure, while Text 2 uses them to label a term.
(C) Both texts use them to designate quotations from historical figures.
(D) Both texts use them to label terms.

2. **Text 1**

The great abundance of microplastics in marine and other environments is very detrimental to the ecosystem. In Japan, plastic-eating bacteria were discovered in a landfill. Since then, much research has been devoted to optimizing these bacteria so that they can eat plastic more quickly. It seems clear that plastic-eating bacteria are the most likely solution to our plastic crisis because the amount of plastic in the environment has built up to a point where it is already damaging the ecosystem.

**Text 2**

Right now, almost all of the plastics in the ocean are in macroscopic objects, but if they are broken down by plastic-eating bacteria, an explosion in the amount of microplastics in the ocean seems inevitable. This massive accumulation in microplastics could have an extremely detrimental effect on the ocean's ecosystem. Thus, plastic-eating bacteria must be carefully researched before these creatures are released into the ocean.

The relationship between the two texts is best summarized as

(A) Text 1 presents an approach to solving a problem, while Text 2 is skeptical of this approach.
(B) Text 1 considers and addresses each of the objections from Text 2.
(C) Text 1 and Text 2 largely agree on both the nature of a problem and its best solution.
(D) Text 1 dismisses a potential environmental issue, while Text 2 proposes a method to deal with the environmental issue.

3. **Text 1**

Not long before it was eradicated by vaccination, smallpox virus erased entire cultures on two continents, where fatality rates rose as high as 90%. For those who survived, it was a cause of permanent, often debilitating disfigurement. Prior to the HiB and DTaP vaccines, epiglottitis caused by *Haemophilus influenzae*, and diphtheria caused by *Corynebacterium diptheriae* were both exceedingly common causes of death in young children, largely because of their tendency to develop rapidly and obstruct the airway.

**Text 2**

Philosophically, medicine is premised on a balance between beneficence, and nonmaleficence. That is to say, for a medical intervention to be deemed ethical and appropriate, the risks of not treating an individual must always outweigh the risks inherent in the treatment itself. Risk accompanies every medical intervention, and vaccination is no exception.

Someone with the philosophy outlined in Text 2 would most likely have what response to the information presented in Text 1?

(A) While smallpox is clearly a case in which vaccination would be recommended, it is not clear that any intervention in the case of diphtheria would be needed.
(B) Children are an exception to the rule when it comes to whether medical interventions are needed in anticipation of savings someone's life.
(C) It would be ethically unwarranted to use experimental interventions to preemptively treat relatively mild illnesses.
(D) The use of the HiB and DTaP vaccines was clearly a case in which the risks of not treating individuals outweighed the risks of treating them.

4. The following is an excerpt adapted from Booker T. Washington's notable "Atlanta Exposition Speech" in 1895. The second is part of a 1903 response, titled "Of Mr. Booker T. Washington and Others," by W. E. B. Du Bois.

**Text 1**

Our greatest danger is, that in the great leap from slavery to freedom we may overlook the fact that the masses of us are to live by the productions of our hands, and fail to keep in mind that we shall prosper in proportion as we learn to dignify and glorify common labor and put brains and skill into the common occupations of life . . . It is at the bottom of life we must begin and not the top. Nor should we permit our grievances to overshadow our opportunities.

**Text 2**

Mr. Washington represents . . . the old attitude of adjustment and submission, but adjustment at such a peculiar time as to make his program unique . . . Mr. Washington's program naturally takes an economic cast, becoming a gospel of work and money to such an extent as apparently almost completely to overshadow the higher aims of life.

Based on the texts, what Washington would most likely define as African American "compromise," Du Bois would most likely define as

(A) treason.
(B) negotiation.
(C) obedience.
(D) persistence.

5. **Text 1**

Many historians find that general trends tend to repeat themselves if you look far enough back through the records of humanity. It truly can be said that there is nothing new under the sun. Perhaps this is simply a function of how long humans have been around, but perhaps it also says something about just how similar all humans are, even across thousands of years.

**Text 2**

Studying fashion history is a lot like listening to remixes of your favorite songs. As you examine textiles from around the world and through time, you'll see constantly that most "new" fashions are just old ideas remade. And so, the women's high-waisted shirts from the early 2000s weren't anything new or different: they were simply 18th-century empire-style gowns remixed for a new generation.

How would the historians of Text 1 most likely describe the high-waisted shirts from the early 2000s?

(A) They are an example of a trend that recurs.
(B) They demonstrate the modern revolution in fashion.
(C) History will look upon them as being in poor taste.
(D) They are altogether different from gowns in the 18th-century empire style.

## Answer Explanations

1. **(B)** Text 1 uses the quotation marks to quote Liliuokalani, while Text 2 uses them to label the term "committee of safety." Choice (A) is incorrect because it has the relationship backwards. And choices (C) and (D) are incorrect because the texts differ in how they use quotation marks.

2. **(A)** Text 1 presents plastic-eating bacteria as an approach to solving the problem of plastic pollution in the ocean, while Text 2 expresses skepticism of plastic-eating bacteria as a solution, arguing that using plastic-eating bacteria will be ineffective and lead to additional problems. It is not choice (B) because Text 1 does not consider and address each objection mentioned in Text 2. It is not (C) because while they both agree that plastic pollution is a problem, they disagree on a solution. It is not (D) because Text 1 underscores the environmental problem of plastic pollution and doesn't dismiss it; additionally, Text 2 does not present an approach to dealing with plastic pollution.

3. **(D)** The overall philosophy outlined in Text 2 is that medical practitioners must do a cost-benefit analysis to determine whether the possible benefits of a medical intervention outweigh the possible costs of the intervention. If the risks of not acting outweigh the risks of acting, the medical intervention should proceed. So, someone with this outlook would look at the vaccines described in Text 1 in a positive light, since people without vaccination for these diseases would be more susceptible to death. Therefore, choice (D) makes the most sense. It is not (B) because Text 2 does not make an exception for certain age groups. It is not (C) because this is not relevant to the main claim in Text 2. It is not (A) because both smallpox and diphtheria carry a risk of mortality as outlined by the text, making it likely that someone with the philosophy in Text 2 would recommend intervention.

4. **(C)** Text 1 expresses the idea that freed slaves should be patient in their quest to advance in society, taking advantage of the opportunities presented to them as they begin to advance up the economic ladder. Text 2, however, argues that the attitude in Text 2 is one of "submission" that overshadows the "higher aims of life" beyond making money. So, Du Bois, the author of Text 2, would most likely define the "compromise" in Text 1 as "obedience." While Du Bois has a negative attitude towards Washington's position, it is not so negative as to describe it as treasonous, as in (A). The relatively positive ideas in (B) and (D) would not align with the position in Text 2.

5. **(A)** Text 1 expresses the position that "there is nothing new under the sun" since historical patterns repeat. The historians with this position would look at the recurrence of an older fashion trend as an example of the tendency for historical events to recur. It is not (B) because the high-waisted shirts are not revolutionary but represent a recurrence of a trend. It is not (C) because the historians do not take a particular position as to fashion taste. It is not (D) because the gowns are like ones from the 18th-century empire style.

## Central Ideas and Details

### Sample Question Language:

- Which choice best states the main idea of the text?
- According to the text, why would a boat built for a freshwater lake be ill-fitted for a saltwater environment?
- According to the text, what is true about Jonathan?

### How Can You Succeed on Central Ideas and Details Questions?

- **Carefully read and thoroughly paraphrase the text before examining the answer choices.** While this is good advice on most all SAT Reading questions, it is particularly important on central ideas questions. The meaning will likely be based on the text as a whole rather than one small part of it, so understand the entirety of what is given. If the text is a more challenging genre, like poetry, you may want to re-read the text until it makes sense.
- **Be careful not to latch on to answers just because they mention specific parts from the text.** If you don't fully grasp the general meaning of the text, it will be easy to become trapped by answers that are partially right in citing specific language in the selection.
- **Be flexible as you evaluate choices.** There are nearly infinite ways that answers to big picture questions can be phrased, so do not eliminate choices too quickly—keep an open mind.

#### Example

The massacre at My Lai increased domestic opposition to U.S. involvement in the Vietnam War and helped mobilize an anti-war march of half a million people in December 1969 in Washington. Following the march, widespread campus protests resulted in the killing of four students by National Guardsmen in Ohio. By the early 1970s, American involvement in the war was winding down. Deployed soldiers were reported to be disillusioned, angry, frustrated, and using drugs as a coping mechanism. Domestically, the brutality of My Lai and the government's continued attempts to conceal it exacerbated anti-war sentiment. Direct U.S. military involvement in the Vietnam War ended in 1973.

Which choice best states the main idea of the text?

(A) The My Lai massacre was a tragic example of the death of college students fighting for their political beliefs.

(B) After their defeat in My Lai, National Guardsmen returned to the United States to quell a rebellion by half a million people.

(C) Anti-war sentiment led to the tragic outcome of the massacre of My Lai.

(D) Reaction to the My Lai massacre contributed to the eventual withdrawal of the United States from the Vietnam War.

### ✓ Answer Explanation

Thoroughly read the text and put its overall meaning in your own words. Be sure to avoid simply restating specific language and instead paraphrase the big picture. Overall, the text connects the My Lai massacre to anti-war sentiment, anti-war protests, and discouragement of deployed U.S. soldiers; the text ends by stating that U.S. involvement in Vietnam ended after these events. So, the My Lai massacre helped lead to feelings among the U.S. people that led to the U.S. withdrawal from Vietnam. The question asks us to state the main idea of the test, so when we evaluate the choices, we must be certain that our chosen answer gives us the big idea of the text, not just specific information. It is not (A) because there is no evidence in the text that the My Lai massacre had college students as the victims; moreover, this choice does not connect to the main idea of how the massacre affected U.S. attitudes towards the war. It is not (B) because while some of this specific language—"half a million" and "National Guardsmen"—is mentioned, there is no evidence that the guardsmen returned to the United States to quell a rebellion by 500,000 people. It is not (C) because the text focuses on the effects of the My Lai massacre, not its causes. Choice (D) is correct because the text connects the feelings that resulted from the My Lai massacre to the eventual withdrawal of the United States from the Vietnam War.

## Practice Questions

1. The text is adapted from the 1949 Geneva Conventions.

   Any breach of the law is bound to be committed by one or more individuals and it is normally they who must answer for their acts. Nevertheless, if the author of the act contrary to international law is an agent of the State, which is indubitably the capacity of members of the armed forces who take others prisoner or are responsible for guarding them, it is not his responsibility alone which is involved, but also that of the State, which must make good the damage and punish the offender. To the extent, however, that individual men and women acquire "international" rights and obligations as they do in connection with the laws and customs of war, so are they invested with the capacity of committing international offences, for which they personally may be held responsible, as well as the State to which they belong.

   According to the text, under the Geneva Conventions, who or what of the following could be held responsible for violation of the rules of war?

   (A) Only individuals
   (B) Only States
   (C) Both individuals and States
   (D) Only individuals in violation of the orders of their government

2. The following is an excerpt from Jane Austen's novel *Mansfield Park* (1814). The novel's protagonist, Fanny Price, returns home after many years of living with her wealthy relatives at Mansfield Park.

   Of her two sisters, Mrs. Price very much more resembled Lady Bertram than Mrs. Norris. She was a manager by necessity, without any of Mrs. Norris's inclination for it, or any of her activity. Her disposition was naturally easy and indolent, like Lady Bertram's; and a situation of similar affluence and do-nothingness would have been much more suited to her capacity than the exertions and self-denials of the one which her imprudent marriage had placed her in. She might have made just as good a woman of consequence as Lady Bertram, but Mrs. Norris would have been a more respectable mother of nine children on a small income.

   According to the text, Mrs. Norris is

   (A) more capable than Mrs. Price.
   (B) similar in personality to Mrs. Price.
   (C) more lethargic than Mrs. Price.
   (D) less respectable than Mrs. Price.

3. The trillion-dollar question is, when the ink dries, will the European Union be listed in the chapters of current events? Or will it be relegated to the annals of academia, its skeleton but a diplomatic case study of oil and water, its ashes little more than a Kennedy School lecture on the perils of collaboration between square pegs and round holes?

   What is the main concern of the text?

   (A) Will the countries of the European Union end their conflicts peacefully or by resorting to an expensive arms race?
   (B) Will the European Union become obsolete and only read about in textbooks as a lesson in things that are dysfunctional?
   (C) Will the Kennedy School give frequent lectures about the European Union and its success?
   (D) Will the European Union extend loans to their members to ensure future success and prosperity for all countries?

4. The following text is adapted from F. Scott Fitzgerald's 1920 novel *This Side of Paradise*. The novel opens with the following character introduction of Fitzgerald's semi-autobiographical protagonist, Amory Blaine.

   When Amory was five, he was already a delightful companion for her. He was an auburn-haired boy, with great, handsome eyes which he would grow up to in time, a facile imaginative mind, and a taste for fancy dress. From his fourth to his tenth year, he did the country with his mother in her father's private car, from Coronado, where his mother became so bored that she had a nervous breakdown in a fashionable hotel, down to Mexico City, where she took a mild, almost epidemic consumption...

   So, while more or less fortunate little rich boys were defying governesses on the beach at Newport or being spanked or tutored or read to from "Do and Dare," or "Frank on the Mississippi," Amory was biting acquiescent bell-boys in the Waldorf, outgrowing a natural repugnance to chamber music and symphonies, and deriving a highly specialized education from his mother.

   According to the text, Amory's upbringing and education can best be described as

   (A) demanding.
   (B) scholarly.
   (C) exhausting.
   (D) unique.

5. "I'm Nobody! Who Are You" is a poem by Emily Dickinson, published in 1890.

   I'm Nobody! Who are you?

   Are you - Nobody - too?

   Then there's a pair of us!

   Don't tell! they'd advertise - you know!

   How dreary - to be - Somebody!

   How public - like a Frog -

   To tell one's name - the livelong June -

   To an admiring Bog!

   Which choice best states the main idea of the text?

   (A) The public at large will recognize artists for their accomplishments.
   (B) Charitable giving is preferable to selfish accumulation of wealth.
   (C) It is better to be anonymous than to be famous.
   (D) Modern commercialism has impacted natural beauty.

6. The following is an adaptation from *The Three Stages of Clarinda Thorbald* by William T. Hamilton, Jr. In it, young Clarinda is waiting for the day of her wedding to arrive.

   Clarinda sat in an old chair and read a thesis upon love, and she found set forth in this thesis that without love the world would not go around. Further, without love life would be but dross and hideous calamity. She also found therein that men have died from love, and women have languished in torments when it was unrequited.

   According to the text, the message in the thesis that Clarinda reads can best be summarized as:

   (A) Love is not important to life since it leads to trivial distractions.
   (B) Love is essential to life; without it, life would be dreadfully dull.
   (C) Love takes hard work from both parties to be successful.
   (D) Love cannot be fully understood without a literary education.

7. The following is an excerpt from a letter by Mary Wollstonecraft. In it, she discusses a trip to Sweden and her observations of the Swedish servant class in the late 19th century.

   The population of Sweden has been estimated from two million and a half to three million; a small number for such an immense tract of country, of which only so much is cultivated—and that in the simplest manner—as is absolutely requisite to supply the necessaries of life; and near the seashore, whence herrings are easily procured, there scarcely appears a vestige of cultivation. The scattered huts that stand shivering on the naked rocks, braving the pitiless elements, are formed of logs of wood rudely hewn; and so little pains are taken with the craggy foundation that nothing like a pathway points out the door.

   According to the text, how does the author describe Sweden's relationship to its natural resources?

   (A) Overly exploiting them
   (B) Lacking in them
   (C) Not taking full advantage of them
   (D) Allowing foreigners to interfere with them

8. This is an adaptation of a letter written in April of 1775, shortly before the American Revolution, by John Adams under the pen name Novanglus. In it, he discusses the relationship between Great Britain and her colonies.

    There is no provision in the common law, in English precedents, in the English government or constitution, made for the case of the colonies. It is not a conquered, but a discovered country. It came not to the king by descent, but was explored by the settlers. It came not by marriage to the king, but was purchased by the settlers . . . It was not granted by the king of his grace, but was dearly, very dearly earned by the planters, in the labour, blood, and treasure which they expended to subdue it to cultivation. It stands upon no grounds then of law or policy, but what are found in the law of nature, and their express contracts in their charters, and their implied contracts in the commissions to governors and terms of settlement.

    According to the text, Adams most likely considered which of the following as most responsible for creating the colonies?

    (A) The British monarch
    (B) Foreign dominions
    (C) Settlers
    (D) The English government

9. The following text is adapted from William Shakespeare's 1609 poem "Sonnet 12," in which he addresses another person.

    When I do count the clock that tells the time,
    And see the brave day sunk in hideous night;
    When I behold the violet past prime,
    And sable curls, all silvered o'er with white;
    When lofty trees I see barren of leaves,
    Which erst from heat did canopy the herd,
    And summer's green all girded up in sheaves,
    Borne on the bier with white and bristly beard,
    Then of thy beauty do I question make,
    That thou among the wastes of time must go

    What is the main idea of the text?

    (A) Love for the person the narrator addresses endures just as much as the beautiful things found in nature.
    (B) The beauty of the person the narrator addresses is just as fleeting as natural beauty.
    (C) To attain true serenity, it is most helpful to mediate in a setting surrounded by beautiful living things.
    (D) When time goes by too quickly, one can seemingly slow time's passage through contemplation.

10. The following excerpt is from Mary Shelley's 1826 novel *The Last Man.*

    I am the native of a sea-surrounded nook, a cloud-enshadowed land, which, when the surface of the globe, with its shoreless ocean and trackless continents, presents itself to my mind, appears only as an inconsiderable speck in the immense whole; and yet, when balanced in the scale of mental power, far outweighed countries of larger extent and more numerous population. So true it is, that man's mind alone was the creator of all that was good or great to man, and that Nature herself was only his first minister. England, seated far north in the turbid sea, now visits my dreams in the semblance of a vast and well-manned ship, which mastered the winds and rode proudly over the waves.

    According to the text, England is a country that

    (A) is limited in its influence due to its unfavorable geography.
    (B) he has not personally visited, but dreams of with great frequency.
    (C) has exceeded what might be expected of it given its size and location.
    (D) has weather that made him determined to seek a more pleasant climate.

## Answer Explanations

1. **(C)** The text references the punitive liability of individuals if they were to commit war crimes and mentions that that same liability applies to states: "so are (individuals) invested with the capacity of committing international offences, for which they personally may be held responsible, as well as the State to which they belong." Thus, choice (C) is the correct answer.

2. **(A)** The text compares Mrs. Price to her sisters, indicating that Mrs. Price is more inclined to the idleness of Lady Bertram than the vigor of Mrs. Norris, so choice (A) is correct. Choice (B) falsely implies that Mrs. Price and Mrs. Norris are comparable, (C) suggests that Mrs. Price is the industrious one, and (D) wrongly indicates that Mrs. Price's negative qualities make her more respectful.

3. **(B)** The text poses the question of whether the European Union will survive. An appropriate paraphrasing can be found in choice (B). The text does not indicate an arms race as in (A). The concern is not actually whether lectures will be given about the European Union, but instead if it will become something purely historical, making (C) incorrect. Finally, the text does not focus on the possibility of loans for European Union members, making (D) incorrect.

4. **(D)** The text indicates that Amory's upbringing is unlike other "little rich boys" and that his education is "highly specialized," making choice (D) correct. Choices (A) and (C) are not supported since the text describes Amory's youth as one of advantage and leisure. While Amory was certainly educated, his knowledge came from atypical experiences rather than from the more conventional scholarly methods, making (B) incorrect.

5. **(C)** The poem starts by saying that one shouldn't tell anyone else about who they are, and then goes on to discuss how dreary it would be to be well-known. Hence, the main idea of the text is that it is better to be anonymous than famous. It is not (A) because the poem emphasizes how good or bad it is to be known, not whether the public will recognize the accomplishments of artists. It is not (B) because the focus of the poem is on fame, not distribution of wealth. It is not (D) because while nature is mentioned in passing—the frog and the bog—these are metaphorical references to how well-known someone might be.

6. **(B)** The text indicates that the thesis that Clarinda reads states that "without love, the world would not go around," and that "life would be but dross and hideous calamity." In other words, without love, life would be dull and disastrous. Choice (A) would be the opposite of the intended meaning; (C) may be true but is not suggested in this text; choice (D) is incorrect because while understanding literature may be helpful to better understanding love, given that Clarinda is reading a thesis, it is not suggested that it cannot be fully understood without a literary education.

7. **(C)** Wollstonecraft describes Sweden as cultivating only "so much" of the immense tract of its land, suggesting that Sweden is not taking full advantage of its natural resources. It is not choice (A), since she argues they are not using the resources as much as they could. It is not (B) because she mentions Sweden as having an immense tract of land. It is not (D) because she does not discuss foreign interference with the resources.

8. **(C)** In the text, Adams clearly states that in his view, the colonies came to be acquired through the diligence of the settlers, not from some other source. He states the colonies were "very dearly earned by the planters, in the labour, blood, and treasure which they expended to subdue it to cultivation." The other options would ascribe creation of the colonies to foreign sources, which the text does not support.

9. **(B)** The narrator alludes to various things that deteriorate in appearance as time goes by—violets, trees, the sun, for example. The narrator ends the excerpt by saying "Then of thy beauty do I question make / That thou among the wastes of time must go." In other words, the narrator is starting to question whether the person he is addressing will waste away like the objects observed from nature. This makes (B) correct, since "fleeting" means "temporary." It is not (A) because the narrator is highlighting the temporary nature of things, not their permanence. It is not (C) because the narrator does not indicate that being surrounded by natural beauty will curtail his negative thoughts. It is not (D) because the narrator emphasizes the inevitable decay of things instead of the power to slow the apparent passage of time.

10. **(C)** In the first part of the text, the speaker discusses the "sea-surrounded nook" on which he lives. Later in the paragraph, this "nook" is revealed to be England. All of the text is a discussion of England. In discussing England, the speaker says that it "appears only as an inconsiderable spec in the immense whole; and yet, when balanced in the scale of mental power, far outweighed countries of larger extent and more numerous population." In short, he is saying that while England is small, it is disproportionately powerful. This makes (C) the best choice. Choice (A) is incorrect because while the geography is unfavorable, its influence hasn't been limited. Choice (B) is incorrect because the speaker lives in England. Choice (D) is incorrect as we have no evidence that the speaker wants to move to a better climate.

## Quantitative Evidence

### Sample Question Language

- Which choice most effectively uses data from the table to complete the example?
- Which choice best describes data from the table that support the scientist's claim?
- Which choice best describes data from the graph that weakens the researcher's claim?

### How Can You Succeed on Quantitative Evidence Questions?

- **Take time to fully grasp the claim or conclusion in the text.** Read the entirety of the text, but read the last sentence especially closely as that is where the claim or conclusion is likely to be stated. Carefully review the key, labels, and headings of the graph. The graphs will come in a variety of forms—circle graphs, tables, and linear charts. Be patient as you familiarize yourself with the organization of the graph before you dive into the quantitative evidence questions. You likely will not need to fully understand every bit of data presented in the graph to answer the question; focus on the big picture.
- **Watch the scales on the axes.** Sometimes the least value in a graph will be at zero; other times, the least value may be at a higher number. Also, sometimes the spacing between numbers on the $x$-axis may be different from that on the $y$-axis. Avoid careless mistakes on the quantitative evidence questions by paying close attention to where the numbers begin and the separation between data points.
- **Limit yourself to the evidence provided.** Even if you have background knowledge on the data presented in the graph, base your analysis solely on the information provided. The SAT will not expect you to have specific knowledge on the information in the graphs; the test will provide you with the information you need to draw reasonable conclusions.
- **Use trends in the chart to make predictions.** If a question asks you to make a prediction for a scenario not pictured in the graph, use the trends evident in the data presented to make a reasonable prediction. See if the numbers are increasing or decreasing, and if they seem to be doing so in a linear or exponential way. The SAT will not try to "trick" you by having you make extremely precise predictions—the answers will be far enough apart from one another that you can make a good estimate to be correct.

### Quantitative Evidence Skill-Building Exercise

Before we dive into the actual Quantitative Evidence questions, let's begin with this exercise in graph interpretation. This drill will help you build the skills necessary to succeed on the Quantitative Evidence questions.

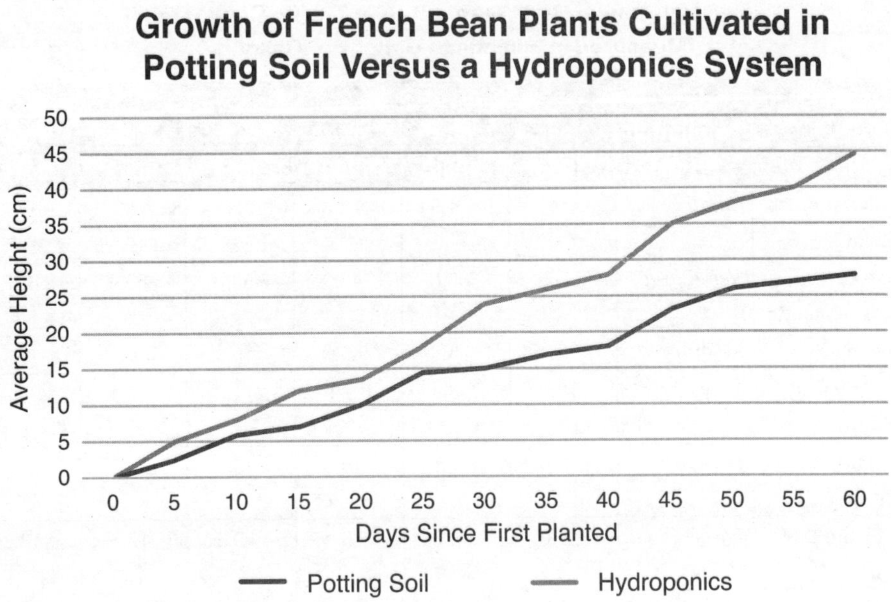


**Figure 1**

*Scientists monitored the growth of French bean plants over a period of two months. The average height of the French bean plants in potting soil versus a hydroponics system was charted over time.*

1. According to Figure 1, what was the average height of the French bean plants that were planted in the potting soil 30 days after being planted?

   (A) 12 cm
   (B) 15 cm
   (C) 26 cm
   (D) 30 cm

2. The information in Figure 1 most strongly suggests that

   (A) planting French bean plants in either hydroponics or in potting soil gives similar results.
   (B) planting French bean plants in either hydroponics or in potting soil negatively affects the plant growth.
   (C) planting French bean plants in hydroponics generally results in greater plant height than when French bean plants are planted in potting soil.
   (D) planting French bean plants in potting soil generally results in greater plant height than when French bean plants are planted in hydroponics.

3. Based on Figure 1, at the completion of the observation period, approximately how great a difference was there between the average French bean plant height from the potting soil group and the average French bean plant height from the hydroponics group?

   (A) 12 cm
   (B) 17 cm
   (C) 28 cm
   (D) 45 cm

**Average Annual Fuel Wasted Due to Traffic Congestion (Measured in Millions of Gallons of Gasoline)**

| City Name | City Population Profile | Year 1985 | Year 1990 | Year 1995 | Year 2000 | Year 2005 | Year 2010 |
|---|---|---|---|---|---|---|---|
| **Anchorage, Alaska** | *Small* | 0.9 | 1.5 | 2.3 | 3.2 | 3.7 | 4.0 |
| **Boston, Massachusetts** | *Very Large* | 29.5 | 38.6 | 43.9 | 59.0 | 65.4 | 67.3 |
| **Dayton, Ohio** | *Medium* | 2.4 | 3.5 | 5.0 | 6.8 | 7.2 | 7.1 |
| **Los Angeles, California** | *Very Large* | 119.9 | 148.3 | 182.9 | 211.6 | 242.1 | 238.4 |
| **Orlando, Florida** | *Large* | 3.6 | 7.1 | 10.5 | 15.9 | 21.3 | 21.9 |
| **Salt Lake City, Utah** | *Large* | 3.0 | 4.0 | 5.7 | 9.4 | 12.6 | 13.2 |

Source: *www.bts.gov/content/annual-wasted-fuel-due-congestion*

**Figure 2**

4. Based on Figure 2, between the years 1985 and 2010, the average annual fuel wasted due to traffic congestion in the very large cities in the table roughly

   (A) doubled.
   (B) tripled.
   (C) quadrupled.
   (D) quintupled.

5. Another city is added to Figure 2 and has an average annual fuel wasted due to traffic congestion in the year 2000 of 12 million gallons of gasoline. Based on the overall pattern in the figure, what it is the most likely population category of this city?

   (A) Small
   (B) Medium
   (C) Large
   (D) Very Large

6. An economist hypothesizes that during an economic downturn, some cities may see a decrease in their average annual fuel wasted due to traffic congestion. If that were the case, based on Figure 2, during which of the following years would the economist most likely conjecture that an economic downturn took place?

   (A) 1988
   (B) 1997
   (C) 2000
   (D) 2007

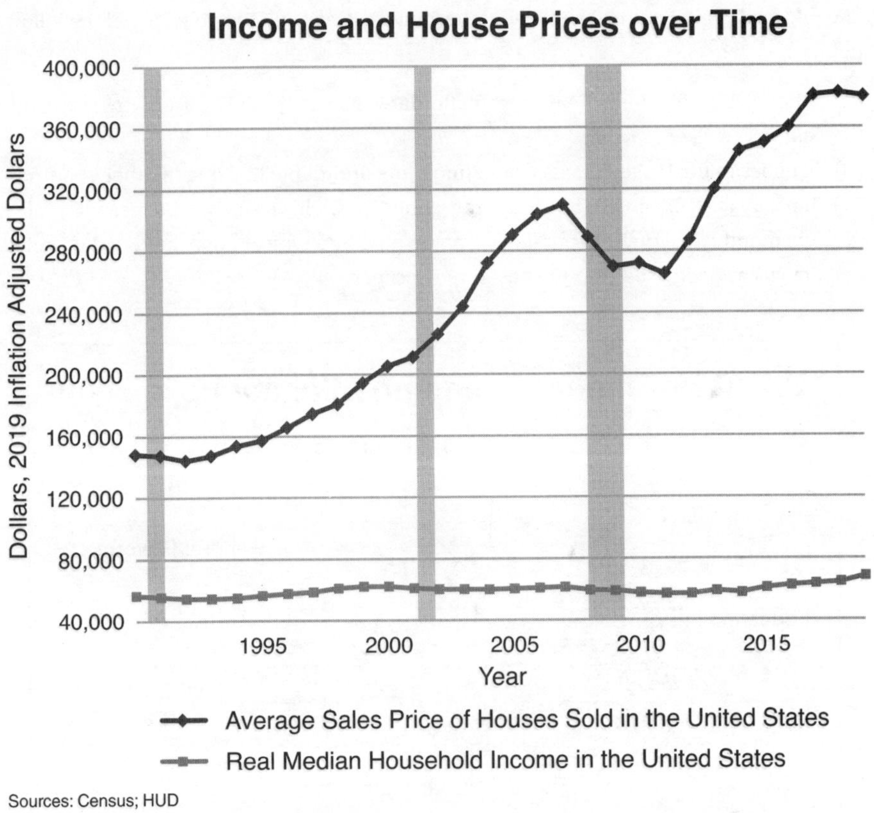


Data and table gathered from the St. Louis Federal Reserve: *https://fred.stlouisfed.org*
Note: Gray areas indicate economic recessions.

**Figure 3**

7. Which statement best generalizes the overall trend in Figure 3 in the real median household income in the United States over the time from 1995 to 2010?

 (A) It increases exponentially.
 (B) It decreases exponentially.
 (C) It stays relatively constant.
 (D) There is insufficient information to make a determination.

8. Which of the following is an accurate statement about the trend in Figure 3 in the average sales prices for homes in the United States before and after economic recessions?

 (A) They consistently decrease.
 (B) They consistently increase.
 (C) They remain the same.
 (D) They sometimes increase and sometimes decrease.

9. The information in Figure 3 would lend the greatest direct support to which of the following points of view?

   (A) A home has become increasingly unaffordable for the typical household in the United States.
   (B) Families in the United States would find more affordable housing in other countries.
   (C) The very least expensive houses in the United States have steadily increased in value.
   (D) The monthly payment to purchase a home paid by a typical household in the United States has decreased over the past three decades.

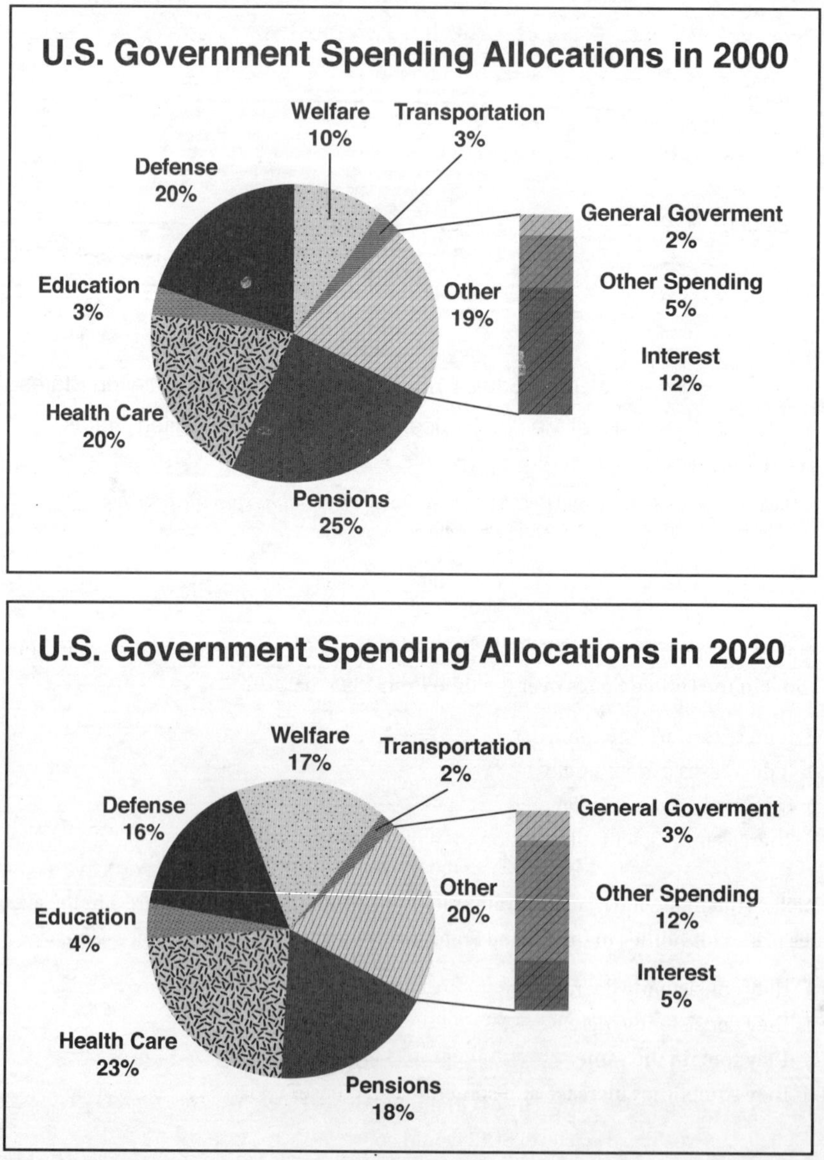


Source: *govinfo.gov*

**Figure 4**

10. According to Figure 4, which spending categories were the largest in 2000 and in 2020 respectively?

    (A) "Other" in both
    (B) Pensions, Health Care
    (C) Defense, Welfare
    (D) Health Care, Defense

11. Which of the following facts, if added to Figure 4, would give the reader a more precise understanding of spending categories of the United States government in the year 2020?

    (A) The budgets for each of the individual states
    (B) The total spending of the U.S. government in 2010
    (C) The popularity of the different U.S. political parties in 2020
    (D) What comprises the "other spending" category

12. Based on Figure 4, a U.S. Federal budget analyst in 2000 as compared to one in 2020 would be more likely to be concerned about overspending on which of the following categories?

    (A) Education
    (B) Interest
    (C) Health Care
    (D) Welfare

## Answer Explanations

1. **(B)** Follow the darker line that represents the potting soil, and find what the *y* value is when the *x* value is at 30—it is 15 cm.

2. **(C)** For all the days after the start of the study, the beans cultivated in the hydroponics system had an average height greater than the beans cultivated in the potting soil. Therefore, the graph most strongly suggests that planting French bean plants in hydroponics generally results in greater plant height than when French bean plants are planted in potting soil. It is not choice (A) because the results diverge, and it is not choice (B) because the plants do indeed grow, suggesting that there is not a negative impact from these environments.

3. **(B)** The graph provides 60 days of observations, so look at the final set of points on the far right side of the graph to compare. At 60 days, the hydroponics sample has an average height of 45, while the potting soil sample has an average height of 28. Subtract 28 from 45 to get 17 cm as the difference in height.

4. **(A)** The two very large cities in the table are Boston and Los Angeles. Their average annual fuel wasted due to traffic congestion roughly doubled between 1985 and 2010, with Boston's going from 29.5 to 67.3, and L.A.'s going from 119.9 to 238.4.

5. **(C)** In the year 2000, the large city of Orlando had 15.9, and the large city of Salt Lake City had 9.4. An unknown city with a level of 12 would come closest to the levels of these large cities.

6. **(D)** Between the years 2005 and 2010, the level in Dayton decreased from 7.2 to 7.1, and the level in Los Angeles decreased from 242.1 to 238.4. Since these are the only examples of a decrease in average annual fuel waste over a period of time, the economist would likely believe that during the interval of 2005–2010, an economic downturn took place. The only option that has a year within this interval is 2007.

7. **(C)** The real median household income is represented by the lower line, and in the interval between 1995 and 2010, it stays relatively constant.

8. **(D)** In the first and third economic recessions indicated in the graph, in the years 1991 and 2008, the average sale price of houses sold in the United States decreased. In the second economic recession in 2001, the average increased. Therefore, it would be accurate to say that the average sales prices for homes in the United States sometimes increase and sometimes decrease after recessions.

9. **(A)** In 1990, the average home price was approximately 150,000, while the average household income was around 55,000—the home price was about three times that of household income. By 2019, the home price was approximately 380,000, while household income was around 70,000—the home price was then about five times that of household income. Given the increase in the ratio over time, it would be reasonable to state that based on this data, a home has become increasingly unaffordable for the typical U.S. household. It is not choice (B) because there is nothing in the graph to compare home prices in the United States to those in other countries. It is not choice (C) because only the average sales prices of homes are presented—there is no breakdown into least expensive vs. most expensive homes. And it is not choice (D) because the amount a household must pay per month to buy a house is not presented; it is possible that factors other than the home price, such as interest rates and taxes, would affect the average monthly payment.

10. **(B)** "Respectively" is a word that sometimes comes up in questions, meaning that the descriptions apply in the order the items are mentioned—in this situation it means that the first adjective will apply to the first item, and the second adjective will apply to the second term. In the year 2000, pensions were the largest category at 25% of government spending. In the year 2020, health care was the largest category at 23% of government spending.

11. **(D)** In the 2020 graph, 12% of the overall government spending is labelled as "other." It would help the reader have a more precise understanding of spending categories in 2020 if a detailed breakdown of what comprised the "other" category were provided. It is not choice (A) because the graph provides information on the overall U.S. government spending, not on individual state spending. It is not choice (B) because while this would help a reader better understand the amount of money spent, it would not help clarify what the spending categories were. And it is not choice (C) because even with an understanding of the popularity of different political parties, there would not necessarily be clarity on the makeup of the government spending.

12. **(B)** In the year 2000, interest represented 12% of U.S. government spending, while in 2020, interest represented 5%. So, it would be reasonable to conclude that a federal budget analyst would be more concerned about overspending on interest in 2000 than in 2020. The other three categories all *increased* in their percentage of federal spending from 2000 to 2020, so it would be more likely that an analyst would be concerned about overspending in these categories in 2020, not in 2000.

## Quantitative Evidence Question

Now that we have warmed up with the previous exercise, let us do an example of what you will actually see on the SAT for this type of question.

### Example

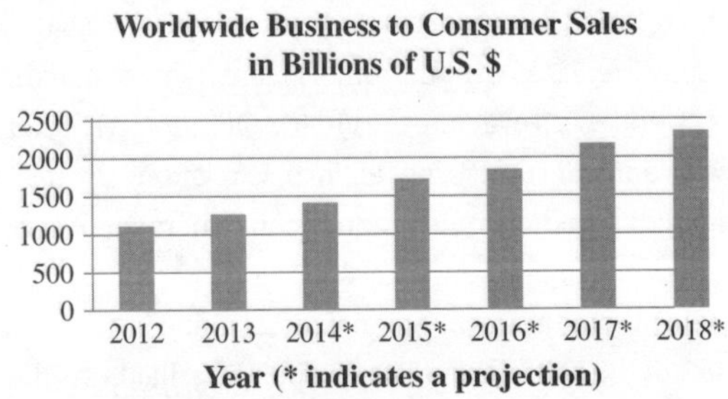

Source: Adapted from Statista.com

Through observations of foot traffic at local shopping malls over a five-year period between 2011 and 2016, a student concludes that most consumers are increasingly interested in shopping at in-person locations. The student argues that while consumers may be aware of the possibility of Internet shopping, they are not showing an increased interest in purchasing items using an Internet-based platform.

Which choice best describes data from the figures that would weaken the student's argument?

(A) The worldwide number of digital consumers and the worldwide business to consumer sales have an inverse relationship.

(B) Worldwide business to consumer sales and the number of digital consumers both consistently increased from 2011–2016.

(C) While consumers increasingly spent their money on Internet-based platforms between the years 2011–2016, consumers significantly curtailed the amount of money they spent at physical store locations.

(D) The amount of digital consumer spending leveled off in the years 2015 and 2016, demonstrating an increasing reluctance to embrace a new medium for shopping.

## ✓ Answer Explanation

Start by reading the text and the question. On quantitative evidence questions, the primary claim, conclusion, or hypothesis is typically stated in the final sentence of the text. So, while you should read the entirety of the text, be certain to read the final sentence of the text very carefully. The main argument expressed in the text is that while consumers are aware of Internet shopping, they are not actually purchasing items over the Internet. The question asks us to find data from the figures that would hurt the student's argument—in other words, we need data that shows that consumers are purchasing items over the Internet. Now, let's examine the figures to find evidence of this. Figure 1 shows that business to consumer sales consistently increased over this time. Figure 2 shows that the number of digital buyers increased over this period. Let's evaluate the choices. It is not (A) because there is a positive correlation between the sales and consumers, not an inverse relationship. It is not (C) because there is no information in the figures about how much money consumers spent at physical store locations. It is not (D) because the amount of digital consumer spending increased, not leveled off; also, this claim would support the author's argument rather than undermine it. The correct answer is choice (B) because it cites evidence about the increase in Internet spending that hurts the author's argument.

## Practice Questions

1.

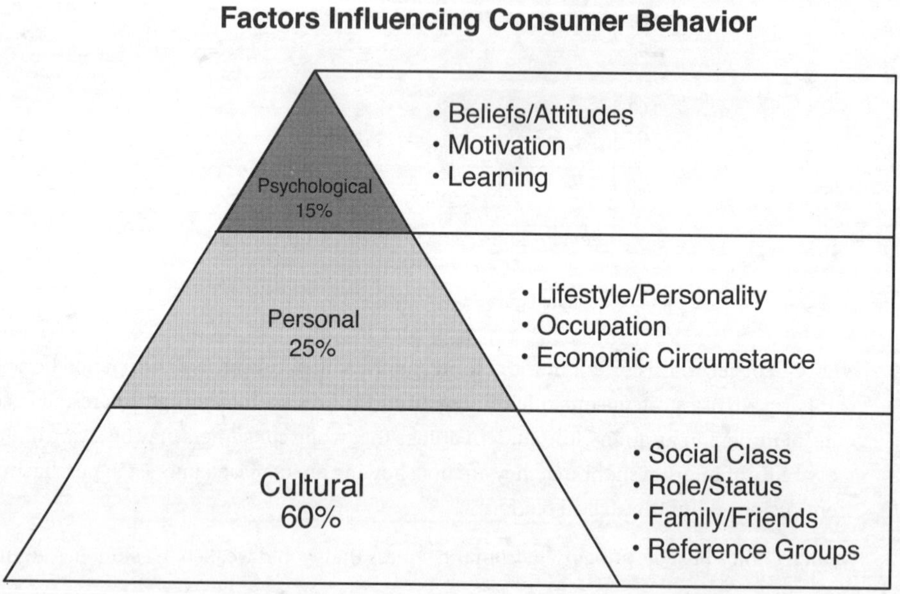


Market researchers have found that consumer behavior is influenced by many factors. Some factors, like motivation and learning, are based on concrete mental actions over which consumers feel they have a choice. While consumers may want to feel they are in control of their purchasing decisions, psychological factors are only about 15% of what influences their commercial behavior. Personal and cultural factors, largely outside of a consumer's psychological control, constitute a/an ________

Which choice most effectively uses information from the graph to complete the statement?

(A) mere 25% of what influences consumers.
(B) significant 60% of the factors affecting consumers.
(C) important component of what consumers learn.
(D) much larger 85% of what impacts consumer behavior.

2.

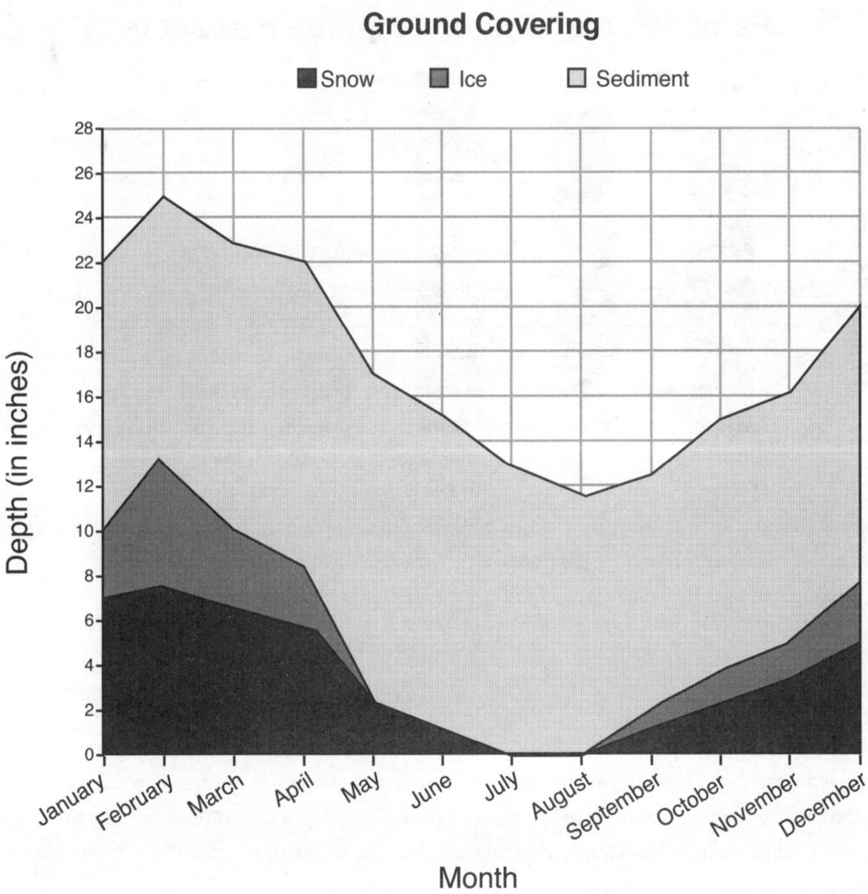


Depending on the time of year, different substances play a greater role in providing ground covering. In the winter months, ice and snow can together constitute nearly half of what covers the ground in a given area. In the summer, the ice and snow melt away, leaving virtually nothing but sediment on the ground. So, while the ice and snow will vary quite a bit from month to month, the amount of sediment on the ground __________

Which choice most effectively uses data from the graph to complete the example?

(A) remains roughly the same depth throughout the year.
(B) is thickest in February.
(C) is thinnest in August.
(D) increases in depth from August to December.

3.

*Scientists studied 164 families over a period of five years. During that time, the researchers recorded the families' perceptions of well-known stressors as positive or negative. The results of this study are summarized in th figure above.*

Some researchers argue that knowledge about the typical family perception of common stressors can be helpful to psychologists in anticipating what life events are most likely and least likely to cause patients stress. A college professor takes a different approach, arguing that some events are not consistently viewed as positive or negative by patients, making it more challenging for psychologists to predict how patients will perceive life events.

Which choice gives an example from the table that the college professor would most likely cite to support her argument?

(A) Birth of a new child
(B) Marriage
(C) Moving to a new home
(D) Job loss

4.

| Antibiotic | Year Discovered | Year Resistant Bacteria Discovered |
|---|---|---|
| Penicillin | 1941 | 1942 Penicillin-resistant *Staphylococcus aureus* |
| | | 1967 Penicillin-resistant *Streptococcus pneumoniae* |
| | | 1976 Penicillinase-producing *Neisseria gonorrhoeae* |
| Vancomycin | 1958 | 1988 Plasmid-mediated vancomycin-resistant *Enterococcus faecium* |
| | 2002 | Vancomycin-resistant *Staphylococcus aureus* |
| Amphotericin B | 1959 | 2016 Amphotericin B-resistant *Candida auris* |
| Methicillin | 1960 | 1960 Methicillin-resistant *Staphylococcus aureus* |
| Azithromycin | 1980 | 2011 Azithromycin-resistant *Neisseria gonorrhoeae* |
| Caspofungin | 2001 | 2004 Caspofungin-resistant *Candida* |
| Daptomycin | 2003 | 2004 Daptomycin-resistant methicillin-resistant *Staphylococcus aureus* |
| Ceftazidime-avibactam | 2015 | 2015 Ceftazidime-avibactam-resistant KPC-producing *Klebsiella pneumoniae* |

*Information in table sourced from https://www.cdc.gov/drugresistance/about.html*

It is critical that doctors not overprescribe antibiotics to patients. While it is difficult for a doctor to ignore the illness of the patient in their immediate care, they must consider that by prescribing antibiotics to those patients not in an acute situation, they might be contributing to the development of antibiotic-resistant bacteria. The increasing speed at which antibiotic-resistant bacteria develop after the discovery of a new antibiotic underscores the critical need for doctors to be prudent in their prescriptions.

Which choice best describes data from the table that supports the writer's argument?

(A) After all—penicillin had antibiotic-resistant bacteria discovered not once, not twice, but three times over the years.

(B) Impressively, biologists were able to craft an antibiotic that managed to avoid becoming antibiotic resistant for over five decades: Amphotericin B.

(C) Some antibiotics are simply not as effective as others; methicillin, for example, had an antibiotic-resistant strain of bacteria discovered in the very same year the antibiotic was created by scientists.

(D) While it took thirty years before an antibiotic-resistant bacteria for vancomycin to form, an antibiotic-resistant bacteria to the newer ceftazidime-avibactam developed in the same year the drug was introduced.

5.

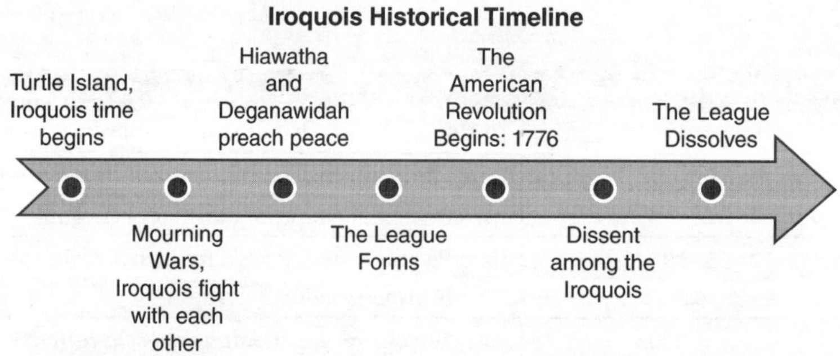


During the colonial era, when the Iroquois remained unified, they represented a major obstacle to the advancement of European settlers on the American continent. Once the Iroquois became disunited, however, they became a less formidable opponent to settlers, eventually leading to their conquest. The historical turning point from the period of Iroquois unity to disunity is typically seen as ________

Which choice most effectively uses data from the timeline to complete the example?

(A) Turtle Island
(B) Mourning Wars
(C) the American Revolution
(D) the Dissolution of the League

6.

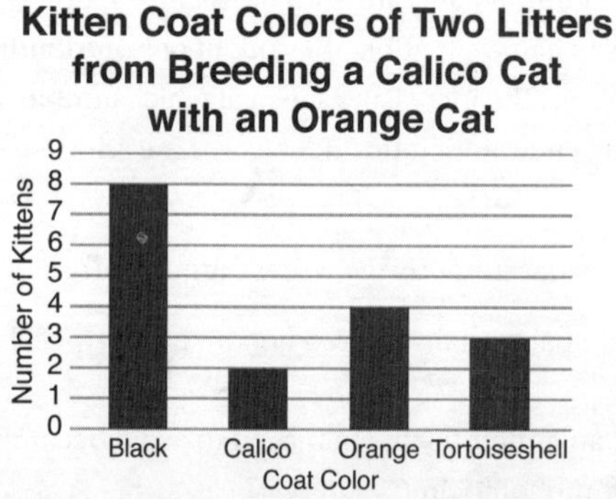


Tortoiseshell cats have a coat that contains a mixture of orange and black fur, while calico cats have orange, white, and black patches. Cats with these two coat variations have a lot in common, including the reason why they have both orange and black fur. Nearly all tortoiseshell and calico cats are female. This is because the gene that dictates whether the cat's fur is orange or black is located on the X chromosome. Since male cats have XY chromosomes, they will usually only have one allele coding for either orange fur or black fur. As indicated in a recent breeding study in which a calico cat was bred with an orange cat, with the results in the accompanying graph, it is most likely that these two groupings of cat coloration would have some male members: ________

Which choice most effectively uses data from the chart to complete the example?

(A) Calico and black
(B) Tortoiseshell and calico
(C) Orange and black
(D) Orange and tortoiseshell

7.

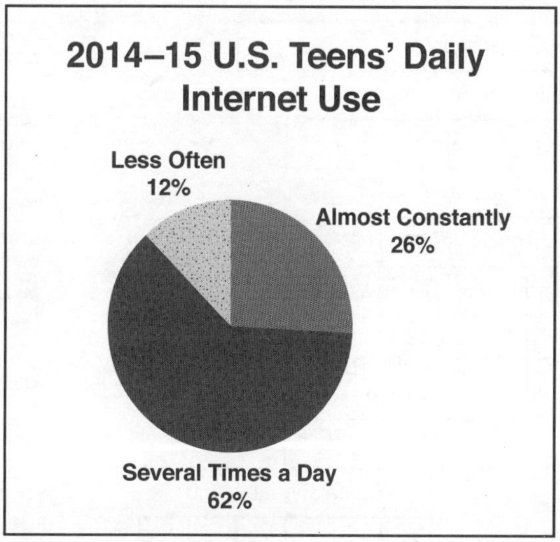


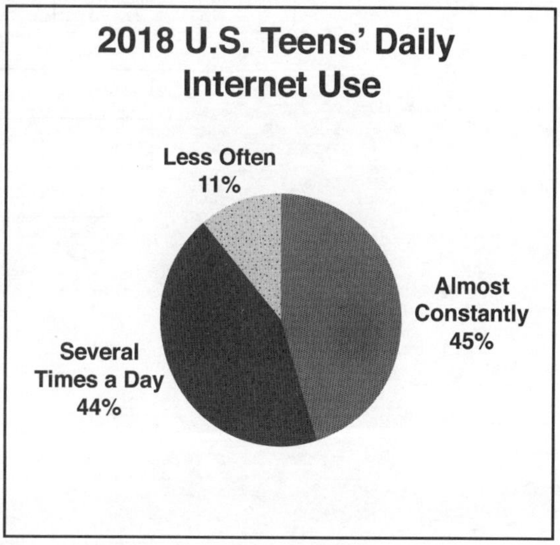


Adapted from *pewresearch.org.*

To investigate the popularity of web usage by high school students, a sociologist utilized a study from the 2010s that asked teens not just if they used the Internet, but how frequently they used the Internet daily. The sociologist concluded that between the years of 2014 and 2018, while there was not a significant change in those teens who chose to use the Internet, the frequency of their Internet use increased significantly.

Which choice best describes data from the graphs that support the sociologist's conclusion?

(A) The percentage of teens who reported using the Internet almost constantly increased from 26% to 45% between 2014 and 2018.

(B) Teens who reported using the Internet less often slightly decreased between 2014 and 2018, going down a full percentage point.

(C) The total percentage of teens who either use the Internet several times a day or almost constantly remained roughly the same between the years 2014 and 2018.

(D) The total number of teenage Internet users increased significantly between the years 2014 and 2018.

8.

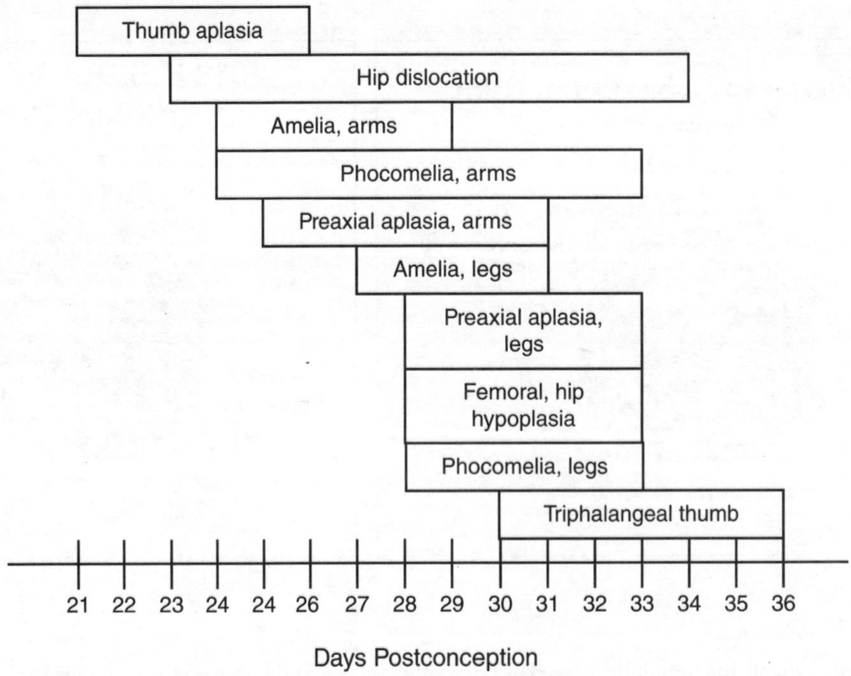


Critical exposure periods for thalidomide-associated developmental defects during human development. Source: *Thalidomide: The Tragedy of Birth Defects and the Effective Treatment of Disease,* by James Kim. Published in 2011.

Thalidomide was marketed toward pregnant women in the mid-1900s with promises to alleviate morning sickness. What the pharmaceutical company that marketed this drug and consumers did not know is that the reaction behind the making of this drug produced two products with remarkably similar structures. One structure was a sedative while the other was teratogenic, meaning it could disrupt the development of a fetus. The drug was banned from production after this fact was realized, but not before countless children around the world had been born with severe birth defects. In fact, if the drug had been administered at the following interval after conception, it could potentially cause multiple birth defects: ________

Which choice most effectively uses data from the chart to complete the example?

(A) days 21–23.

(B) days 24–26.

(C) days 27–31.

(D) days 32–35.

9. **Department of Housing Preservation and Development (HPD) Bedbug Complaints and Violations—FY 2004–2010**

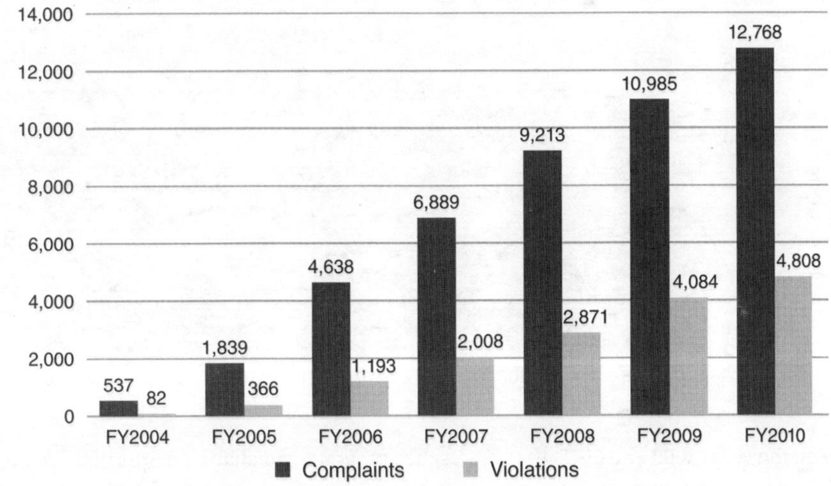


(Source: NYC Department of Housing Preservation and Development (HPD), 2010)

Bedbug infestations present a major threat to the safety and comfort of people living in major urban areas. Once bedbug infestations take hold, they are very difficult to stop. While bedbugs are a significant concern, sometimes residents take advantage of the fear of bedbugs to make unwarranted complaints. One government official concludes that there is little to no connection between bedbug complaints and actual bedbug violations.

Which choice best describes data from the chart that would weaken the government official's conclusion?

(A) While there were 12,768 bedbug complaints in 2010 in New York City, there were only 4,808 actual bedbug violations that year.

(B) The number of bedbug violations never rose above 5,000 in any given year between 2004 and 2010 in New York City.

(C) There is a direct correlation between bedbug complaints and bedbug violations in New York City between 2004 and 2010.

(D) In 2012, there were no recorded bedbug violations, demonstrating that a governmental policy to encourage bedbug complaints is unwarranted.

10.

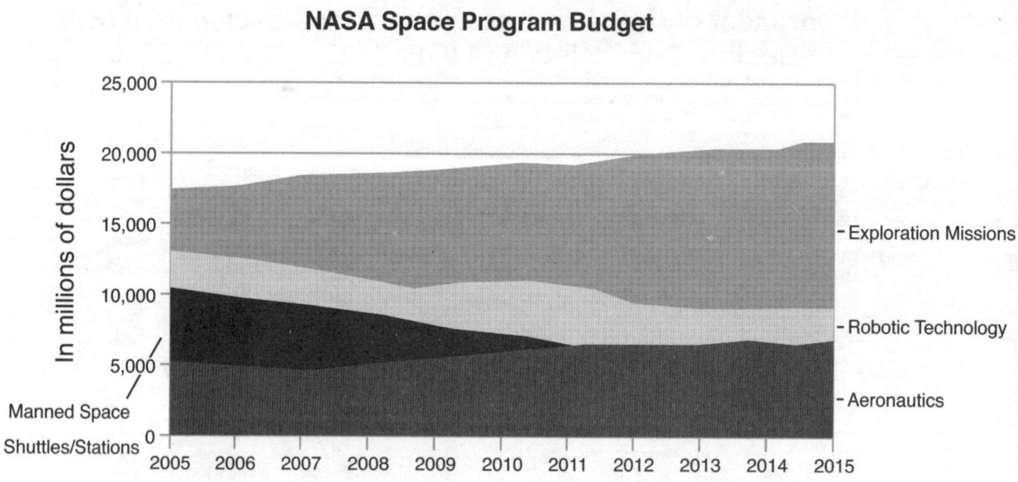


Between the years 2008 and 2015, the NASA space program had changing priorities. At the beginning of the time period, manned space missions were a significant component of the program budget, while towards the end of the time period, exploration missions took on a greater role. One thing that was constant, however, was growth in the overall NASA budget. One component of the budget consistently mirrored the changes in the overall NASA budget over this time period: __________

Which choice most effectively uses data from the chart to complete the statement?

(A) exploration missions.
(B) robotic technology.
(C) space shuttles/stations.
(D) aeronautics.

## Answer Explanations

1. **(D)** This is the only option that provides the accurate sum of the personal and cultural factors from the graph: 25% for personal, 60% for cultural, making a total of 85% for them both. Choices (A) and (B) do not provide the total sum, and (C) is too vague.

2. **(A)** The sediment curve fluctuates between 12 and 14 inches in thickness all year long, making (A) the correct choice. Choice (D) may be appealing, but be careful; the overall ground covering increases, but the amount of sediment stays pretty steady.

3. **(C)** The graph shows what percentage of people consider certain stressors to be positive or negative. The central bar on the graph is labeled "Moving to a New Home" and is split nearly in half. This tells us that about half of people find moving to be a positive stressor, while the other half find it to be a negative stressor. This would make it difficult to predict how any given person would feel about moving. The other stressors shown on the graph all have clear majorities, which would make it much easier to predict how a person would feel about that event. This example would then support the approach of the college professor, who argues that some events are not consistently viewed as positive or negative by patients, making (C) the best option and the other choices incorrect.

4. **(D)** The overall argument of the writer is that doctors need to be careful to not overprescribe antibiotics because antibiotic-resistant bacteria are developing increasingly quickly. Choice (D) uses data from the table to support this argument, since it points out that it took quite a while for antibiotic-resistant bacteria to form for an earlier antibiotic, but it is taking much less time for antibiotic-resistant bacteria to form for a newer antibiotic. Choice (A) is not relevant to the claim, (B) would contradict the author's claim, and (C) does not focus on how the effectiveness of antibiotics has changed over time.

5. **(C)** The example shows that there is a historical turning point from a period of unity to disunity. According to the timeline, the event prior to the American Revolution is the formation of the league, indicating unity. The event after the American Revolution is dissent among the Iroquois, showing that the American Revolution would have been the turning point from unity to disunity. The other options do not show this change.

6. **(C)** According to the text, most tortoiseshell and calico cats are female. Therefore, choices (A), (B), and (D) are unlikely since they all mention the tortoiseshell and/or the calico cats as being male. Choice (C) is correct because this grouping has just orange and black coloration, making it more likely that some of its members could be male. Further, the text states that male cats have "one allele coding for either orange fur or black fur," making (C) the most appealing option.

7. **(A)** The sociologist concludes that while teen participation in Internet use would remain relatively constant over this period, the amount of Internet usage by these teens would greatly increase. Choice (A) highlights the near doubling in the percentage of teens who used the Internet almost constantly, which would strongly support the sociologist's conclusion. It is not (B) because this does not focus on frequency of Internet use. Choice (C) would not provide evidence to show an increase in Internet usage. Choice (D) would contradict the sociologist's claim that the number of teens using the Internet remained fairly constant.

8. **(C)** Looking at the figure, we can see that exposure to thalidomide in days 27–31 could lead to nine different birth defects (excluding only thumb aplasia). Exposure in this range, therefore, would interfere with the most developmental processes. Choice (A) is incorrect as exposure in this range could only lead to thumb aplasia. (B) is incorrect as exposure in this range would only lead to five different defects. (D) is incorrect as exposure in this range would only lead to six possible birth defects.

9. **(C)** The conclusion of the government official is that there is little to no connection between bedbug complaints and actual bedbug violations. Since we are asked to determine what would weaken this conclusion, we must find something that shows the government official would be incorrect. Choice (C) does this effectively, since it states that the bedbug complaints and bedbug violations are directly correlated, showing a likely connection between the two statistics. The other options do not effectively demonstrate how there would indeed be a connection between complaints and violations, weakening the official's argument.

10. **(D)** The sum of the four curves will give the entire budget, so the budget went from about 18 million to 21 million. We can rule out (B) and (C) since these components show a decrease. Finally, the graph indicates that exploration missions doubled from about 5 million (18–13) to 10 million (21–11), which is not representative of the more gradual increase in the program budget. Aeronautics, on the other hand, went from about 5 to 8 million, and maintained about a third of the entire budget consistently, so it is closely mirrored with the budget itself.

## Textual Evidence

### Sample Question Language:

- Which finding, if true, would most directly undermine Smith's hypothesis?
- Which finding, if true, would most directly support the economists' hypothesis?
- Which quotation from the surveys best illustrates the researcher's claim?

### How Can You Succeed on Textual Evidence Questions?

- **Paraphrase the author's claim or hypothesis.** Having a clear idea of the author's position will ensure that you can identify further information that would support or undermine that argument. Imagine that you had to explain the author's thesis to a third party—if you can create a good summary of their position, you understand what you have read.
- **Give yourself time to make sense of the question.** Other SAT Reading questions, like ones that ask you to determine the best word given the context, are easily understood in a few seconds. On Textual Evidence questions, you may need to consider what sort of evidence could support an argument or undermine (hurt) an argument. These questions may take more time to fully grasp—do not rush through them.
- **Realize that the answer will not be "in" the passage.** Since Textual Evidence questions typically ask you to think about new information or different positions, do not try to "find" the answer in the wording of the text. Instead, focus on applying the big ideas of the text to different situations.

#### Example

Haitian Creole is a complex mixture of Western European, West African, Native American, and other languages. Europeans invaded Haiti in the 1500s, bringing enslaved Africans to Haiti to work alongside the native Arawak people. An anthropologist claims that Haitian Creole originated in the late 1600s and early 1700s when the number of native French workers, African slaves, and freed Africans were roughly the same, and linguistic interactions among the different groups were frequent.

Which finding, if true, would best support the anthropologist's claim?

(A) Historical documents demonstrating that European influence on the native populations in Haiti culminated in the 1800s rather than the 1700s.

(B) A survey of Haitian correspondence from the early 1600s shows no use of Creole, while a survey of Haitian correspondence from the late 1700s shows extensive use of Creole.

(C) Linguistic analysis that finds the similarities of Haitian Creole to the Creole languages of Louisiana and other areas in the Americas.

(D) Economic data that shows the increased productivity of freed slaves as compared to both enslaved native Arawak and enslaved West Africans.

### ✓ Answer Explanation

Carefully read the text and pay especially close attention to its final sentence, since that is typically where the claim will be stated. The text introduces Haitian Creole and briefly summarizes its history. The specific claim to evaluate is that Haitian Creole originated in the late 1600s and early 1700s because of the frequent interactions among different ethnic groups at the time. Think about what sort of evidence would support this claim—it would need to demonstrate that there was a fairly clear beginning to Haitian Creole during this time period. Now, let's consider the choices. It is not (A) because this would not align with the time period when the anthropologist claims the language was initiated. It is not (C) because this statement is not directly relevant to the claim. It is not (D) because this focuses on economics instead of linguistic history. Choice (B) is correct because a survey that showed this shift in correspondence, from not using to Haitian Creole to using it over this time period, would provide clear evidence supporting the anthropologist's claim.

## Practice Questions

1. The "red tide" in coastal Florida is a harmful algal bloom from microscopic algae that makes fish caught in affected areas unsafe to consume. Researchers claim that pollution from the fertilizer used on Floridian farms is the most significant cause of the red tide.

   Which finding, if true, would best support the researchers' claim?

   (A) The red tide intensity is positively correlated with the amount of fertilizer in the water.
   (B) In the state of Texas, researchers found less red tide than there is in Florida.
   (C) Some fish are more susceptible to fertilizer pollutants than others.
   (D) People who suffer from color blindness are less likely to perceive the effects of the red tide.

2. "The Convergence of the Twain" is an early 1900s poem by Thomas Hardy. The poem addresses the tragic loss of the ship *Titanic* in the year 1912. An English professor claims that in the poem, the speaker alludes to the luxury and opulence of the ship before its demise: ________.

   Which quotation from "The Convergence of the Twain" most effectively illustrates the claim?

   (A) "Steel chambers, late the pyres/Of her salamandrine fires"
   (B) "Jewels in joy designed/To ravish the sensuous mind"
   (C) "For her—so gaily great—/A Shape of Ice, for the time far and dissociate."
   (D) "Said "Now!" And each one hears,/And consummation comes, and jars two hemispheres."

3. A sociologist studies the influence of colors in business marketing. She notes that fast-food restaurants significantly rely on red and yellow coloration in their signs and logos. She claims that red and yellow colors subconsciously influence consumers to desire the food at the fast-food restaurants since they create positive feelings. This idea is known as the "ketchup-and-mustard" marketing theory, with red ketchup and yellow mustard associated with these colors.

   Which of the following, if true, would best support the sociologist's claim?

   (A) A phone survey of adults who self-selected as fast-food diners found that most diners preferred ketchup and mustard as condiments when ordering a sandwich.
   (B) A study of fast-food restaurant signs found that 45% of fast-food signs were in some combination of yellow and red, while 55% of fast-food signs were in a combination of other colors.
   (C) Fast-food restaurants that have red and yellow signage consistently had lower revenue per customer than restaurants that have signage featuring other colors.
   (D) A randomized survey of adults found that a statistically significant majority found red and yellow signs more likely to prompt their appetite than signs in other common colors.

4. "When I Consider How I Spend My Light" is a mid-1600s poem by John Milton. In the poem, Milton expresses his frustration with losing his sight, preventing him from carrying out his work. However, as a Puritan, he resolves that despite his unfortunate fate, he will still obey God: ________.

   Which quotation from "When I Consider How I Spend My Light" most effectively illustrates the claim?

   (A) When I consider how my light is spent/Ere half my days, in this dark world and wide,
   (B) And that one Talent which is death to hide/Lodged with me useless, though my Soul more bent
   (C) To serve therewith my Maker, and present/My true account, lest he returning chide;
   (D) God doth not need/Either man's work or his own gifts; who best/Bear his mild yoke, they serve him best.

5. *Ghosts* is an 1881 play by Henrik Ibsen. A drama critic claims that Ibsen uses the play to critique the societal emphasis on the accumulation of wealth instead of on ethical conduct: ________.

   Which quotation from *Ghosts* most effectively illustrates the claim?

   (A) "Oh, let me help you. That's it. Why, how wet it is! I will hang it up in the hall. Give me your umbrella, too; I will leave it open, so that it will dry."
   (B) "And the immorality of such a marriage! Simply for the sake of the money—! What sum was it that the girl had?"
   (C) "That was all very kindly done. The only thing I cannot justify was your bringing yourself to accept the money."
   (D) "So then Joanna and I decided that the money should go towards the child's bringing-up, and that's what became of it; and I can give a faithful account of every single penny of it."

6. Christopher Ries is an American glass artist from central Ohio who has produced some of the largest crystal sculptures ever made. In a paper for an art history class, a student claims that Ries made significant advances in art because he was able to utilize the capacities of industry in his process of artistic creation.

   Which of the following, if true, would best support the student's claim?

   (A) Ries had his artwork recognized by the Columbus Museum of Art for excellence by an artist native to the state of Ohio.
   (B) A particular sculpture by Ries causes the viewer to feel that they are looking at the emissions from a smokestack.
   (C) Ries became an artist-in-residence at a Pennsylvania factory where he had access to the finest glass sculpting material.
   (D) Art historians note the similarities in the biography of Ries to the biography of Francis Hayman, a British artist during the Industrial Revolution.

7. *The Importance of Being Earnest* is an 1885 play by Oscar Wilde. The play takes place in Victorian London, and surprised audiences of the time by avoiding discussion of the serious political and moral issues of the day. Instead, as a critic claims, the play turns social expectations upside down by emphasizing the need to treat trivial issues seriously: ________.

   Which quotation from *The Importance of Being Earnest* most effectively illustrates the claim?

   (A) "I am sick to death of cleverness. Everybody is clever nowadays. You can't go anywhere without meeting clever people. The thing has become an absolute public nuisance. I wish to goodness we had a few fools left."
   (B) "Oh, before the end of the week I shall have got rid of him. I'll say he died in Paris of apoplexy. Lots of people die of apoplexy, quite suddenly, don't they?"
   (C) "Your German grammar is on the table. Pray open it at page fifteen. We will repeat yesterday's lesson."
   (D) "Your guardian enjoys the best of health, and his gravity of demeanour is especially to be commended in one so comparatively young as he is. I know no one who has a higher sense of duty and responsibility."

8. Loyalty to a widespread approach kept Hill and Becquerel from further innovations in color photographic technology.

   Which quotation from a passage about this topic most effectively illustrates the claim?

   (A) We tend to think of color photography as a profoundly modern innovation, belonging to an era no earlier than the 1950s.
   (B) A new approach was required before color photography could emerge as a truly viable artistic and documentary medium.
   (C) Pioneers of color photography such as American minister Levi Hill and renowned French physicist A.E. Becquerel were hampered in their efforts by a fidelity to the then-popular daguerreotype method.
   (D) Color variants of this method—such as Hill's toilsome "heliochromy"—often took several days to develop and yielded only dim images with colors that faded rapidly when exposed to direct light.

9. As the immediate successor of textualis, the Schwabacher style strove for increased readability with significant reductions to capital embellishment, and a smoother, more curvaceous form invocative of handwriting. Though Schwabacher is sometimes associated with the Italian humanist writings of the early 16th century, it saw substantial use throughout all of Europe in the century thereafter and was only partially deposed by Fraktur in the late 1700s. Schwabacher continued to appear in printed texts as a secondary typeface into the 20th century.

   Which finding, if true, would most strongly support the author's claim about the popularity of Schwabacher style in the 1600s?

   (A) A survey of European documents in the 1600s showing the popularity of textualis
   (B) A consistency in the use of Schwabacher throughout European manuscripts in the 1600s
   (C) An emphasis on Schwabacher fonts in the religious texts in Asia and the Americas
   (D) Twentieth-century government documents that use Schwabacher style in official publications

10. The following is an adaptation of an excerpt from Vice President Al Gore's speech on August 17, 1997, which was the 125th anniversary of the founding of Yellowstone National Park and the National Park System.

   Despite the hundreds of millions of people who come here every year, not every American has been to Yellowstone, and not every American has seen its grandeur and its glory. But every American has a stake in this land because it is part of our heritage. It belongs to us all, and we have an obligation to ensure that it is here for us all, for the next 125 years.

   Which of the following statements would most undermine the argument made in the text?

   (A) Tourists indicate that they are primarily interested in enjoying the parklands with their younger relatives.
   (B) Some members of the Shoshone tribe considered the lands of Yellowstone their exclusive territory.
   (C) Legal action has prevented mining companies from excavating gold and other precious minerals from Yellowstone.
   (D) While some Americans have been able to visit Yellowstone, not every American has been able to see it.

## Answer Explanations

1. **(A)** This is the only option that draws a direct connection between the pollution from the fertilizer on the farms to the red tide. Choice (B) is irrelevant because it brings up information about a different state. Choice (C) does not focus on the red tide in general. Choice (D) deals with the perception of rather than the actuality of the red tide.

2. **(B)** We need an option that focuses on luxury and opulence—choice (B) effectively does this by referring to jewels and sensuous thoughts. The other options do not refer to luxury and opulence.

3. **(D)** The sociologist claims that red and yellow colors subconsciously influence consumers to desire the food at the fast-food restaurants since they create positive feelings. Choice (D) would best support this claim since it is a well-crafted survey with results that would demonstrate evidence for the claim. It is not (A) because it doesn't focus on the coloration of

signage. It is not (B) because this does not connect to subconscious consumer preferences. It is not (C) because it would show the opposite of what the sociologist claims, given the lower sales at restaurants with red and yellow signs.

4. **(D)** The claim is that the narrator will still obey God despite his unfortunate fate. Choice (D) states that those who bear God's mild yoke, or burden, will serve him best, giving the most effective illustration of this claim. Choices (A) and (B) do not focus on obedience, and choice (C) emphasizes the need for honesty instead of emphasizing obedience.
5. **(B)** The claim is that the Ibsen uses the play to critique the societal emphasis on the accumulation of wealth instead of on ethical conduct. Choice (B) shows how Ibsen would make such a critique, since this selection expresses surprise and outrage at the immorality of a marriage done solely for the sake of money. It is not choice (A) because the person is acting in a helpful manner by assisting someone with their umbrella. Choice (C) also emphasizes kind conduct. Choice (D) highlights the meticulous recordkeeping of the narrator.
6. **(C)** The claim is that Ries made significant advances in art because he was able to utilize the capacities of industry in his process of artistic creation. Choice (C) effectively accomplishes this goal, since Ries was able to use the finest glass sculpting material available at an industrial factory to make his art. The other options do not connect using industrial capacities to help with artistic creation.
7. **(A)** The critic claims that the play turns social expectations upside down by emphasizing the need to treat trivial issues seriously. Choice (A) demonstrates the need to treat trivial issues seriously by expressing weariness with cleverness and a wish that there were "a few fools left." It is not (B) because this addresses the serious issue of mortality. It is not (C) because the narrator has a serious tone that is focused on getting the lesson completed. It is not (D) because this emphasizes the more serious themes of duty and responsibility.
8. **(C)** The text states that loyalty to a common approach kept Hill and Becquerel from making further innovations. Choice (C) effectively illustrates this by stating that the two were "hampered in their efforts by fidelity" (loyalty) to a popular method. Choice (A) does not address the problems that the two encountered. Choice (B) is vague and does not connect to the two researchers. Choice (D) provides specific information but does not connect to the claim.
9. **(B)** The author claims that Schwabacher was substantially used throughout all of Europe in the 1600s, since this would be the century after the 16th century (the 16th century is the 1500s). So, choice (B) would strongly support this claim since it would demonstrate the widespread use and popularity of this form of writing. It is not (A) because this underscores the popularity of a different type of writing. It is not (C) because the author does not discuss the popularity of this style in Asia and the Americas. It is not (D) because this refers to the incorrect time period.
10. **(B)** The text states that these lands belong "to us all," indicating that the narrator believes that all Americans have some claim to this land. If there were members of the Shoshone who considered the lands of Yellowstone their exclusive territory, that would hurt the claim that the lands rightly belong to all Americans, thus undermining Gore's argument. It is not choice (A) because tourists wanting to visit national parks would support Gore's argument to preserve these lands for all. It is not (C) because it would support the idea that governmental intervention is necessary to preserve the lands from economic exploitation. And it is not (D) because Gore acknowledges that not every American has visited Yellowstone but responds by arguing that Yellowstone remains a part of our country's heritage.

## Inferences

### Sample Question Language:

- Which choice most logically completes the text?

### How Can You Succeed on Inference Questions?

Inference questions will ask you to determine what the author suggests or implies based on different selections of a passage. How can you do well on these questions?

- **Have a general feel of your answer before evaluating the choices.** There are plenty of ways you could state what could logically complete a short text. When creating your own answer on these types of questions, it is better to be broad and flexible than it is to be specific and rigid. Doing so will ensure that you are open-minded as you review the possible options.
- **Watch the transitions before the underlined portion.** There will often be a transitional word immediately before the underlined portion—be sure you pay attention to it since it will have an impact on how you answer.
- **Do not be overly literal.** Look for what the author may be saying indirectly—what is being suggested or implied? Especially watch out for overly literal interpretations when you read genres like fiction, poetry, and drama.
- **There will be a definite answer.** It is easy to dismiss an inference question as being just based on someone's opinion, making it a matter of luck to pick the correct option. This will not be the case on the SAT Reading—inference questions (along with all other test questions) will have a definite answer with a clear justification. If you are having difficulty formulating an answer on inference questions, give the test the benefit of the doubt instead of immediately assuming there must be a test question error.
- **Do not eliminate answers too quickly.** Since you are determining the best possibility for completing a text, you will be better served by keeping answer choices open as possibilities instead of crossing them off too quickly. Sometimes when you look at an answer choice a second time, you will more fully grasp its meaning and it will make more sense as a possibility.

**Example**

Microplastics are microscopic particles of plastic that tend to accumulate toxins and are in some cases toxic themselves. Unfortunately, microplastics tend to end up being eaten by various organisms. The primary reason for this problem is that in recent years, approximately 380 million tons of plastic are produced annually. Plastic is not biodegradable, which means that once it enters the environment it can take several hundred years to degrade. Some have proposed plastic-eating microorganisms as a revolutionary solution to this critical issue. Others are skeptical of the claims made about ________

Which choice most logically completes the text?

(A) whether a bacteria could have any role in harming the environment.
(B) the capacity of microbiologists to analyze bacteria in a laboratory setting.
(C) this bacteria's utility in consuming massive plastic deposits.
(D) the possibility of plastic extending the length it needs to biodegrade.

### ✓ Answer Explanation

Start by reading and paraphrasing the text so you have a clear idea of what it is about. The text outlines the problem that microplastics pose to the environment: millions of tons of plastic are produced, and microplastics are ingested by different organisms. Moreover, it takes hundreds of years for the plastic debris to disintegrate, causing a long-term negative impact on the environment. Towards the end of the text, the author notes that some have proposed using microorganisms to help consume plastic waste. In the final sentence, the author acknowledges the opposite view of those who are skeptical about this claim. So, it is most logical to complete the text with something that states what it is that the skeptics would question. It is not (A) because this would be the opposite meaning of what is needed here—if it had said "helping" instead of "harming," perhaps this would work. It is not (B) because the question is about whether microorganisms can help remove plastic, not about whether scientists can analyze bacteria in a lab. It is not (D) because there is no discussion of possibly modifying the span of time needed for plastic to degrade. Choice (C) is correct because this summarizes the claim about which the skeptics would have questions.

## Practice Questions

1. Companies like FedEx have grown to be an integral part of the American landscape. FedEx first specialized in overnight deliveries via aircraft and then grew into a full-service provider using a truck network in conjunction with air transport. "When it absolutely, positively has to be there overnight" is its mantra, and it basically provides certainty of service for a premium price that consumers are willing to bear. Therefore, ________

   Which choice most logically completes the text?

   (A) businesses that want to ship products will primarily utilize air transport instead of land transport.
   (B) customers who use overnight delivery services are primarily concerned with reliability.
   (C) other companies do not focus the reliability of their shipping process in their marketing initiatives.
   (D) people who want to use overnight delivery services put a premium on cost savings.

2. There is a natural tendency to confuse change with progress. This is perfectly understandable, especially considering that we went from inventing electricity to perfecting aviation to reaching the moon all in a time analogous to just a blink in the grand scheme of human history. Such prodigious leaps have left us hungry for more leaps, and there are benefits to restlessness, even if entropic; ________

   Which choice most logically completes the text?

   (A) systematic, focused research will lead to a successful result.
   (B) amateur researchers should be put on equal footing with academic researchers.
   (C) nearly all useful recent innovations have come as the result of chaotic creativity.
   (D) throw enough aimless darts in every direction and you'll find a bull's eye, even if by accident.

3. Many parents, as they lovingly tuck their children into bed, repeat a short rhyme that has been around for centuries: night-night, sleep tight, don't let the bedbugs bite! This phrase refers to a time when even the wealthy had to deal with the constant scourge of bedbugs and other pests that preyed on sleeping humans. With the advent of modern pesticides, bedbugs were, for a time, largely an issue of the past. However, in the past few years they have come back with a vengeance, __________

   Which choice most logically completes the text?

   (A) as modern science has successfully eradicated the threat of bedbugs.
   (B) once again plaguing people rich and poor and proving very difficult to eradicate.
   (C) given the lack of interest that modern city dwellers have in attaining a good night's rest.
   (D) since the anatomy of bedbugs are now better understood thanks to advances in technology.

4. Our nation's heroes are not the only ones who may experience the detrimental effects of fireworks. Furry companions also can be frightened by the loud blasts above for nights on end. Veterinary practices, animal shelters, and other animal organizations frequently send out reminders in the weeks leading up to the Fourth of July to protect our pets from running away out of fright. These may include reminders to microchip our pets, keep pets indoors, and take pets on walks early in the day in case they are too afraid to relieve themselves during the fireworks. Their efforts are not without reason. In fact, __________

   Which choice most logically completes the text?

   (A) many pets enjoy the spectacle of fireworks just as much as their human counterparts.
   (B) veterinarians recommend that pet owners should take their pets to firework displays.
   (C) days on which fireworks are displayed statistically have the same number of pet injuries as days on which fireworks are not displayed.
   (D) more pets run away on the night of the Fourth of July than any other night of the year.

5. Since the transition from alkylation to acylation for benzene reactions, chemists' abilities to safely modify benzene have expanded exponentially. What seemed revolutionary in the late 1800s is now part of undergraduate organic chemistry experiments in courses throughout universities worldwide. Benzene is no longer solely thought of as a carcinogenic and volatile compound. It now used in a variety of products including plastics, drugs, pesticides, detergents, etc. Its importance to modern chemistry, materials science and pharmaceuticals is therefore __________

   Which choice most logically completes the text?

   (A) unquestioned in the scientific community.
   (B) a subject of great debate among practicing chemists.
   (C) ridiculed by economists and politicians.
   (D) a matter on which the jury is still out.

6. Varroa mites are an issue for bee colonies for several reasons. The primary issue is that they attach themselves to the bodies of worker bees and feed on them. This can affect a bee's immune system, ability to flush out pesticides, and regulation of hormones. When the mite abandons the bee for a fresh host, it leaves behind an open wound which often leads to infection by one of the many bee viruses that the mites carry. The overall effect is that the bees are much weaker when mites are present. This weakness means that worker bees ________

   Which choice most logically completes the text?

   (A) become increasingly able to thrive given their auspicious circumstances.
   (B) are much less able to perform their crucial tasks as they try to maintain the colony.
   (C) are animals that live in colonies under the control of a queen bee that they protect.
   (D) will increase their overall capacity to benefit other members of the bee colony.

7. One of the primary effects of social media use that has already been observed in populations that utilize social media regularly is a decrease in mental health and self-esteem. As far back as 1998, a study showed that increased social media use correlated with decreased in-person interactions with their friends and family. This was hypothesized to lead to issues with symptoms of depression. As modern social media developed, this decrease in personal face-to-face interactions increased. In England a recent study by the National Institute of Health (NIH) found a significant correlation between social media usage and symptoms of depression in high school aged subjects. This correlation was not found among older social media users. Of course, correlation is not causation: ________

   Which choice most logically completes the text?

   (A) depression most likely comes because of using social media.
   (B) social media use is not associated with an increased likelihood of depression.
   (C) an increase in depression is associated with a decrease in social media use.
   (D) already depressed people could just tend to use social media more.

8. It's fair to say that the world in which we live is made up of chemicals, though the cultural emphasis in recent years on natural or "organic" products has somewhat demonized this notion. "Chemophobia," in fact, is a term that has emerged to describe the irrational fear of chemistry and chemical nomenclature. In general, individuals affected by chemophobia tend to view the precisely planned manipulation of molecular compounds with suspicion, and perceive products rendered by these means as both "unnatural" and inherently inferior to those derived through cruder avenues. In reality, ________

   Which choice most logically completes the text?

   (A) nothing could be more natural than the intricate, multistep reactions of organic chemistry.
   (B) artificial substances present a clear and present danger to the health and safety of humans.
   (C) psychology provides a more promising avenue for the improvement of wellbeing than does chemistry.
   (D) organic agriculture provides a safe alternative to commercial crops raised with chemical fertilizers.

9. The first way that many teachers approach classroom discipline is the "permissive" approach. To relate to the students, the teachers put up very few personal barriers. Positive outcomes in contrast with negative consequences are emphasized. What does the permissive classroom look like? Teachers let the students take control, asking for them to act properly rather than demanding it. Looking at their teachers as friends, the students do not look at them as authority figures. Students may like their teachers but will probably not respect them. Detentions are not an option, but extra credit for good behavior is abundant. Little actual learning can proceed in a classroom like this since __________

   Which choice most logically completes the text?

   (A) respect will be maintained.
   (B) chaos will reign.
   (C) punishment is freely meted out.
   (D) trust is encouraged.

10. Although the signaling pathway for light production in fireflies is complex enough, the methods by which different species regulate their luminescence are as various as the uses for luminescence that those species employ. As we have seen, fireflies tend to use their light to attract a mate, but females of one large species of firefly have been known to mimic the glow pattern of another, smaller variety, to attract males of the smaller species and eat them. Similarly, _________

    Which choice most logically completes the text?

    (A) Amazonian spiders craft nearly invisible webs that they use to trap their dinner.
    (B) bats use echolocation, a capacity akin to sonar, to locate food sources despite a dark environment.
    (C) the deep-sea dwelling anglerfish uses its glowing appendage to lure in unsuspecting prey.
    (D) humans who camp sometimes utilize global positioning systems in addition to their compasses should they become lost.

## Answer Explanations

1. **(B)** The text makes clear that customers who want overnight delivery are primarily concerned with "reliability." Customers are willing to pay "a premium price" for this "certainty," so it's reasonable to assume that reliability is most important. The other options do not connect to the primacy of reliability.

2. **(D)** The text implies that restlessness can be beneficial to scientific discovery—choice (D) expresses this idea by saying that if you try to throw enough darts around, you'll eventually get a bull's eye, i.e., a success. It is not (A) because "entropic" means "chaotic," which would not make sense with a systematic approach. It is not (B) because the focus is on the usefulness of restlessness, not on whether amateurs are going to be successful. It is not (C) because this is too extreme in this context, stating that "nearly all" innovations are coming from this type of thinking.

3. **(B)** Immediately before this, the author states that bedbugs have "come back with a vengeance." Choice (B) is the most logical option in that it states that people from all different walks of life are susceptible to bedbugs. It is not (A) because this is the opposite of what is

being argued. It is not (C) because there is no evidence that modern city dwellers no longer care about getting enough rest. It is not (D) because there is no evidence in the text about an increased understanding of the anatomy of bedbugs.

4. **(D)** The insertion here should elaborate on why the efforts to keep animals safe on the Fourth of July are not without reason. Choice (D) accomplishes this aim by stating that more pets run away on this night than any other. It is not (A) because the focus in the text is on the danger to pets, not on their entertainment. It is not (B) because this goes against the recommendations of pet organizations. It is not (C) because this would contradict the author's argument about the Fourth of July with its fireworks presenting a greater-than-average risk to animals.

5. **(A)** The text emphasizes how benzene went from something that was revolutionary in chemistry research to something that is used in a wide variety of important products. Thus, it is most logical to state that its importance is "unquestioned in the scientific community." It is not (B) or (D) because the debate about its importance has been settled. It is not (C) because with its widespread importance, benzene is certainly not ridiculed.

6. **(B)** The text presents the problems that varroa mites pose to bee colony vitality. Choice (B) expands on this by giving a concrete consequence of the impact that varroa mites will have on bees. It is not (A) or (D) because these would be positive outcomes. It is not (C) because this is merely a definition of what a bee is, instead of a statement about the impact that varroa mites have on bees.

7. **(D)** The previous part of the sentence, that "correlation is not causation," means that just because two things happen simultaneously, it cannot be concluded that one event is the cause of the other. Also, the previous part of the sentence sets up a transition from the previous material with the phrase "of course," indicating a contrast. Choice (D) is the most logical since it would show that social media is not necessarily the cause of depression; it may be something merely associated with people who are already depressed. It is not (A) because this is the opposite of what is needed. It is not (B) or (C) because these choices focus on the possibility of direct correlations instead of a lack of connection.

8. **(A)** The earlier part of the text refers to how those with chemophobia believe that manipulation of chemical compounds is inherently unnatural. This excerpt shows that this is not the case. In fact, manipulating things with organic chemistry is quite natural. It is not (B) because this would not provide a contrast. It is not (C) or (D) because these are irrelevant to what is being discussed—transformation of compounds.

9. **(B)** The text outlines the permissive approach to classroom discipline, in which students get to run the classroom, respect is lacking, and detentions are not possible. It would make sense to say that in a classroom like this in which little learning is taking place that "chaos will reign." The other options contradict the description of what a classroom managed in the permissive style will be like.

10. **(C)** We need to come up with a situation that is like the one outlined in the previous sentence. One species of firefly uses its glow to attract food. Similarly, in choice (C), the anglerfish uses its glow to lure prey. Choices (A) and (B) discuss how animals can find food, but they use different methods from what the firefly does. Choice (D) does not focus on food location.

# Additional Practice Exercises

*The problems in these exercises represent the variety of SAT Reading questions you could encounter. Take about ten minutes for each exercise.*

## Additional Practice Drill 1

1. Veterinary students will research, diagnose, and treat medical conditions of pets, livestock, and other animals. Some will __________ companion animals and work in private clinics and hospitals, while others will choose to work with farm animals or in research facilities.

   Which choice completes the text with the most logical and precise word or phrase?

   (A) specialize in
   (B) be hired by
   (C) despair about
   (D) become ill from

2. Relaxation strategies are used across disciplines to address a wide variety of diagnoses. These strategies are beneficial in managing anxious feelings and feelings of not being __________ Relaxation techniques are used to address stress and impulse management. Some approaches may include meditation, progressive muscle relaxation, yoga, deep breathing, progressive muscle relaxation, and personal mantras.

   Which choice completes the text with the most logical and precise word or phrase?

   (A) away from one another.
   (B) across the way.
   (C) in debt to someone.
   (D) in control of oneself.

3. In 1970, Norman Borlaug was awarded the Nobel Peace Prize and credited with saving over a billion people from starvation. In what is now called the Green Revolution, Borlaug led the research and development over a two-decade span beginning in the 1940's to dramatically increase agricultural production worldwide. He introduced the synthetic farming methods already common in the United States and Britain to a global market, focusing particularly on the developing world, and succeeded in hiking food production and saving lives. Borlaug's initiative calls for celebration.

   As used in the text, what does the word "common" most nearly mean?

   (A) Widespread
   (B) Lowly
   (C) Communal
   (D) Corporate

4. The following text is from Nathaniel Hawthorne's 1852 novel *The Blithedale Romance*.

   Happy the man that has such a man beside him when he comes to die! And unless a friend like Hollingsworth be at hand—as most probably there will not—he had better make up his mind to die alone. How many men, I wonder, does one meet with, in a lifetime, whom he would choose for his death-bed companion? At the crisis of my fever, I besought Hollingsworth to let nobody else enter the room, but continually to make me sensible of his own presence, by a grasp of the hand, a word, a prayer, if he thought good to utter it; and that then he should be the witness to how courageously I would encounter the worst.

   Which choice best states the main purpose of the text?

   (A) To recount a generally light-hearted anecdote for the reader
   (B) To describe a character for whom the narrator is quite grateful
   (C) To contemplate the meaning of life at the outset of a hopeful journey
   (D) To interrogate another character about his suitability for a position

5. **Text 1**

   When a couple gets married, a classic purchase is the diamond engagement ring. There are many different styles to choose from: round, princess, cushion, emerald, and marquise. A lot of thought is given to the specifications of the ring; given its significant cost, it is something for which the purchaser might save for quite some time. Often missed, however, is the story behind the diamond. The first use of diamond engagement rings was in Austria in 1477. Since then, these jewels have been sought after and shaped into glittering centerpieces atop gold bands.

   **Text 2**

   A new option has become available in the wedding industry—lab-created diamonds. These diamonds are not found naturally in the environment but created in a laboratory. What makes this option so appealing to buyers is that these artificially created diamonds are 50–60% less expensive than a naturally mined diamond. Because of this, the popularity for laboratory jewels has been skyrocketing.

   Based on the texts, how might the "couple" in Text 1 most likely respond to the notion of lab-created diamonds in Text 2?

   (A) By questioning the lack of statistical evidence in the text
   (B) By considering it as a possibility to save money for an important purchase
   (C) By dismissing the need to purchase an expensive symbol of love
   (D) By disputing the historical origins of a recent invention

6. Could robots soon be delivering your mail? Allow me to set the scene: you're coming home from school, walking toward your front door, and bam—a flying robot drops your oldest sister's just-ordered movie collection on your front porch. This is not as farfetched as it sounds. Today is the age of the drone, also known as the unmanned aerial vehicle (UAV), so __________

   Which choice most logically completes the text?

   (A) it is difficult to predict what the future holds.
   (B) it's only a matter of time before it becomes an everyday occurrence.
   (C) advances in technology will lead to revolutionary health care treatments.
   (D) nothing can replace the personal touch of a human delivering your order.

7. In the past, politicians have touted their "trickle down" policies as being in the best interest of everyday Americans. It was commonly thought that tax breaks and other assistance for companies and individuals at the top would lead the wealth to slowly move down to middle class and impoverished families. Many politicians still use the trickle-down argument when pushing for aid to large corporations and wealthy individuals. After all, it makes sense that a wealthy person who comes into money will spend that money and that money will end up in the hands of service people and other workers. Economists, however, have struggled to find evidence of such policies helping anyone but those at the top.

   Which statement, if true, would most directly support the claim of the "economists" mentioned in the last sentence?

   (A) An investigation of recent political rhetoric demonstrating the popularity of the "trickle down" argument.
   (B) Statistics showing an increase in poverty in towns that have had recent factory closures by major businesses.
   (C) A historical analysis showing increased economic stratification after tax breaks for the wealthy are implemented.
   (D) A survey of the economic beliefs of wealthy individuals that indicates a preference for "trickle down" political policies.

8. 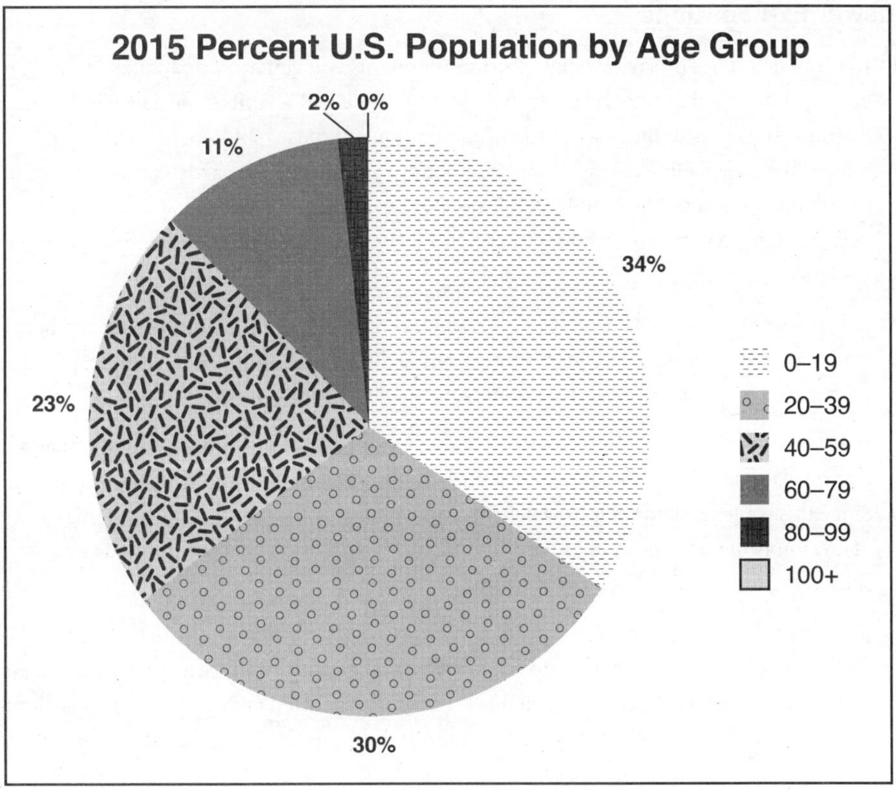


Source: *https://www.census.gov/en.html*

Despite significant advances in medicine, there has been a limited increase in human longevity. While there are certainly many octogenarians and nonagenarians, this is more the exception than the rule. Most of the population is younger, not older.

Which choice best describes data from the graph that supports the conclusion outlined in the text?

(A) The majority of the 2015 U.S. population was under 40 years of age.
(B) It is about three times as likely that a randomly selected U.S. citizen is in their 40s or 50s as it is that they would be in their 60s or 70s.
(C) Women represent a slight minority of the overall U.S. population.
(D) Significant numbers of Americans in 2015 were in their 80s and 90s.

## Answer Explanations

1. **(A)** The text starts by saying what veterinary students will generally do in their studies and careers. It then goes on to say what some will specifically do—thus, "specialize in" makes the most sense. (B) is illogical since the companion animals would not do the hiring. It is not (C) because feeling despair about companion animals for no particular reason would be unsuitable for a veterinary student. It is not (D) because it is unlikely that the students would become ill from companion animals, and this is inconsistent with the statement later in the sentence.

2. **(D)** The text highlights how relaxation strategies can help address impulse management, which goes along with being "in control of oneself." The other options have to do with interpersonal or physical interactions, not personal feeling management.

3. **(A)** The text refers to Borlaug's contribution to ending worldwide poverty and hunger, stating that he extended the farming methods "already common in the United States and Britain." Since this is referring to their prevalence, "widespread" is the correct choice. "Lowly" means of low importance. "Communal" and "corporate" would imply that the methods were literally shared among members of a community.

4. **(B)** The narrator describes how helpful a friend Hollingsworth has been to him in his time of illness—in other words, the narrator is describing a character for whom he is grateful, going with choice (B). It is not (A) because this is not a light-hearted anecdote; rather, it is about a serious topic. It is not (C) because the narrator is not trying to figure out the meaning of life. It is not (D) because the narrator is not intensively questioning another character.

5. **(B)** The "couple" in Text 1 is likely to want to purchase a diamond engagement ring when they become engaged to be married. Text 1 emphasizes that a diamond purchase is considered "classic," something about which "a lot of thought" will be devoted, and something for which the purchaser might save for a while. Therefore, it makes sense that for a major purchase, the couple might be interested in learning more about the lab-created diamonds mentioned in Text 2 so that they could explore it as a way of possibly saving money. It is not (A) because there is not a lack of statistical evidence in Text 2. It is not (C) because the importance of this purchase is emphasized. It is not (D) because there is no dispute about the historical origins of this technique—the likely dilemma is whether to purchase a naturally made or artificially created diamond.

6. **(B)** Earlier in the text it states that drone delivery is "not as farfetched as it sounds," so it is logical to complete the text by stating that it is only a matter of time before such deliveries become commonplace. It is not (A) because the narrator is indeed making a prediction. It is not (C) because the text is not focused on health care treatments. It is not (D) because this is not relevant to the claim that the passage is making.

7. **(C)** The economists claim that trickle-down economics will mainly benefit those at the top of the economic ladder. Therefore, a historical analysis that shows increased divides between rich and poor (i.e., stratification) after the implementation of tax breaks for the wealthy would help make this case. It is not (A) because the question is not about political popularity but about economic consequences. It is not (B) because factory closures are not directly attributable to the tax changes the economists are referencing. It is not (D) because a survey of wealthy individuals will not give clear evidence as to the society-wide merit of such policies.

8. **(A)** The text states that there has been a limited increase in human longevity, and that most of the population is younger, not older. Choice (A) provides evidence for this, showing that the U.S. population is primarily under 40 years of age. It is not (B) because this only focuses on Americans over 40 years of age. It is not (C) because there is no information about gender in the graph. It is not (D) because 2% could not reasonably be described as "significant numbers."

## Additional Practice Drill 2

1. Although open online courses have failed to transform higher education in the abrupt manner that many reformers predicted, the current push for discernible and accessible digital __________ from accredited institutions will be a turning point in education. This will result in students having the documentation necessary to demonstrate to potential employers that they have the skills needed to succeed in the workforce.

   Which choice completes the text with the most logical and precise word or phrase?

   (A) lessons
   (B) credentials
   (C) instruction
   (D) interaction

2. Inadequate sleep affects the nervous system through decreased ability for memory and learning. Lack of sleep __________ the endocrine system by, among other things, disrupting cortisol regulation and metabolism.

   Which choice completes the text with the most logical and precise word or phrase?

   (A) inspects
   (B) impacts
   (C) forbids
   (D) improves

3. An earthquake with a magnitude of 3.0–3.9 is called a "minor earthquake." These can usually be felt by most people, but very rarely cause any damage. Often, people end up attributing these small quakes to other causes like large trucks passing or large public transit vehicles. Earthquakes on the higher end of this range may cause <u>slight</u> shaking of household objects.

   As used in the text, what does the word "slight" most nearly mean?

   (A) Mild
   (B) Quick
   (C) Luminous
   (D) Irrelevant

4. At the forefront of my desire to spend a semester or two abroad is personal growth. The evidence is empirical: a survey by the Institute for the International Education of Students found that studying abroad was a defining moment in a young person's life that continues to impact them long after their domestic return. In fact, 98% of the 3,400 respondents allowed that their experience abroad had left them with a better understanding of themselves, their cultural values, and their biases. Increased tolerance, compassion, and confidence are a few of the advantages. The individual change that occurs when studying abroad is a dynamic that works from the inside out—you become a better human being and opportunity arises for a better world.

   What choice best describes the overall structure of the text?

   (A) A thesis followed by consideration of objections to the thesis
   (B) A statistical analysis of an educational dilemma coupled with a plan of action
   (C) A suggestion of a possible course of action along with self-reflection
   (D) A statement of a goal followed by supporting reasons for that goal

5. A classroom that fails to challenge a student's fundamental principles and create a hunger for lifetime learning fails altogether. Whether teaching the humanities or the sciences, the educator is the one who lays out a puzzle and pilots instances of profound, sublime enlightenment. A student lucky enough to study under a true teacher is never satisfied, but instead, is relentlessly looking for answers.

   What choice best describes the function of the underlined sentence in the text as a whole?

   (A) It emphasizes how an excellent teacher will inspire their students to be curious.
   (B) It provides a counterexample to the primary claim of the text.
   (C) It elaborates on the specific methods that a teacher can use to achieve a goal.
   (D) It portrays the likely career trajectory for a prospective educator.

6. **Text 1**

   For most of western history, head coverings in the forms of hats and scarves have been the norm. Only in the last 40 years have hats for everyday use gone out of style to the point where anything other than a baseball cap is considered odd or pretentious. No longer is it considered a sign of politeness or culture to cover one's head, and that convention is not coming back. Hat fashion is dead; hair fashion is here to stay.

   **Text 2**

   The recent decrease in hat wearing is merely a blip on the radar of fashion. Large-brimmed hats are common for beach wear, and the bucket hat is making a resurgence for both men and women. People like hats not just for warmth or sun protection, but also as a fashion statement. Hats may add an extra layer of fiddlyness to an outfit, but when done well they enhance the look exponentially. People are remembering this, and hats are coming back.

   How would the author of Text 2 most likely respond to the statement "Hat fashion is dead" in Text 1?

   (A) By wholeheartedly agreeing with it.
   (B) By moderately agreeing with it.
   (C) By strongly disagreeing with it.
   (D) By being indifferent to it.

7. It is safe to say no one posts any picture of themselves looking anything less than their best. They don't post about the boredom of their internship, their "staying-in" sweatpants, or the ramen noodles they eat most evenings for dinner. This creates a false online environment. People logging into Instagram after school each day see what appears to be all their friends and acquaintances living amazing and exciting lives. As they eat a frozen dinner and try to decide what to watch on Netflix, people scroll through engaging and perfect pictures and feel ________

Which choice most logically completes the text?

(A) satisfied that they can stay in touch with friends in other cities.
(B) worse about themselves and their seemingly inferior lives.
(C) personally fulfilled with the intellectual stimulation they find.
(D) a desire to improve their computer fluency through additional study.

8. **Estimated Percent Increase in Employment, 2012–2022**

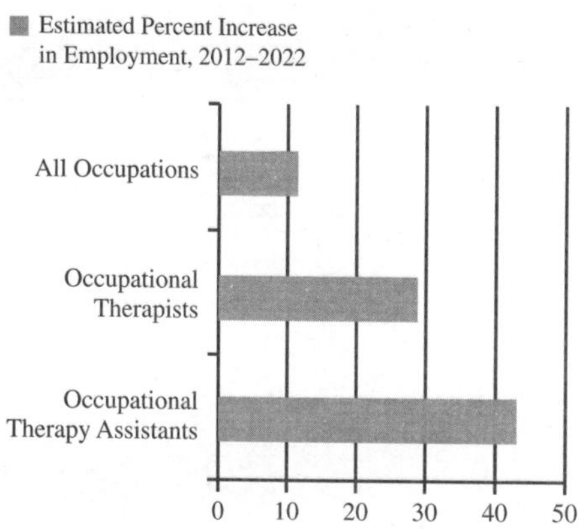


Adapted from the Bureau of Labor Statistics

Occupational therapy is a healthcare profession that uses holistic therapeutic practices to enable patients to regain their quality of life. The field of occupational therapy is growing, with significant gains in employment relative to employment in other potential careers.

Which choice best describes data from the graph that supports the conclusion expressed in the text?

(A) The Bureau of Labor Statistics projects that occupational therapy assistants saw increased career prospects when compared to occupational therapists; in fact, the difference between the two is approximately 14%.
(B) The Bureau of Labor Statistics estimates that there was an increase in employment for occupational therapists of 29% between 2012 and 2022, whereas the estimate for the increase in all jobs is 11%.
(C) The Bureau of Labor Statistics estimates that the employment for occupational therapists increased 43% between 2012 and 2022. The estimate for the increase in all jobs is 11%.
(D) The Bureau of Labor Statistics estimates that the employment for occupational therapists increased 11% between 2012 and 2022. The estimate for the increase in all jobs is 29%.

## Answer Explanations

1. **(B)** "Credentials" would be documentation that show someone's readiness for a particular career, making this the most logical option. While the other words could be helpful preparing students for the workforce, they will not necessarily result in usable documentation that employers can review.

2. **(B)** An appropriate synonym would be "affects" since the lack of sleep with affect the systems of the body. "Impacts" is most synonymous with this word. The other options do not align with "affects."

3. **(A)** "Mild" is an appropriate word since the text refers to "minor earthquakes." The other choices do not accurately depict a level of severity or magnitude.

4. **(D)** The narrator states their goal of wanting to spend a semester or two abroad; the narrator then goes on to provide specific reasons why this is a worthy goal. All of this aligns with choice (D). It is not (A) because the narrator does not focus on considering objections. It is not (B) because the narrator provides just one statistic—this cannot be considered a statistical analysis of a dilemma. It is not (C) because the narrator is not doing self-reflection but is convincing the reader of the worthiness of this goal.

5. **(A)** The text overall is focused on showing what makes for a good classroom environment, with this final sentence showing how students who learn under a "true teacher" will be perpetually curious. This goes along with choice (A). It is not (B) because it complements the text rather than contradicts it. It is not (C) because it makes a broad rather than a specific statement. It is not (D) because it does not get into career specifics.

6. **(C)** The author of Text 2 asserts that hats are making a comeback, so it is most logical to state that the author of Text 2 would strongly disagree with this statement. The other options do not capture the precise likely opinion.

7. **(C)** The narrator emphasizes how social media posting leads to a "false online environment" that makes it seem like other people are living amazing and exciting lives. This would logically lead to some people feeling worse about their own personal situations by comparison. It is not (A) because the users are not described as actively conversing with friends, but rather passively watching the activities of others. It is not (C) because there is no emphasis on personal fulfillment. It is not (D) because the use of social media is not described as academic in this context.

8. **(B)** Based on the first column at the top of the graph, all occupations experienced an 11% growth from 2012–2022, and based on the middle column of the graph, occupational therapists experienced a 29% increase in employment in the same period. The other options give incorrect information based on the graph.

## Advanced Drills

The following questions are designed to represent the most challenging sorts of questions you could encounter on the SAT Reading. Take about ten minutes for each exercise.

### Advanced Drill 1

1. Oils, which contain primarily nonpolar hydrocarbon bonds, are immiscible with aqueous solutions, meaning they will not spontaneously dissolve in water, which consists of highly polar hydrogen-oxygen bonds. Instead, oils will tend to form a film over polar solvents, while surface tension serves to stabilize this film at the oil-water interface. Because they are amphiphilic—meaning they possess both polar and nonpolar domains—surfactants may interact with both components of this interface and interfere with the electrochemical forces that maintain its <u>integrity</u>. Due to this unique property, surface tension lowering agents have found a host of applications in diverse commercial products, and are used as emulsifiers, foaming agents, and detergents.

   As used in the text, what does the word "integrity" most nearly mean?

   (A) Rectitude
   (B) Solidarity
   (C) Cohesion
   (D) Decadence

2. At the risk of oversimplifying, soaps are created by exposing triglycerides gathered from either plant or animal sources to a strong base in a process called saponification. The base hydrolyzes triglycerides to form glycerol and amphipathic free fatty acids. The glycerol, in turn, is removed, and the fatty acids are complexed with sodium. While the words "soap" and "detergent" are sometimes used interchangeably in common parlance, one should note that detergents are not synthesized by saponification.

   The author's overall description of soaps and detergents is that they are

   (A) commonly thought of as interchangeable but in fact having an important difference.
   (B) one and the same insofar as their chemical properties, such as molecular structure.
   (C) different with respect to their capacity to mix in emulsions.
   (D) major obstacles to the widespread acceptance of biosurfactants.

3. The following excerpt is from James Joyce's 1916 novel *A Portrait of the Artist as a Young Man*.

   > The snares of the world were its ways of sin. He would fall. He had not yet fallen but he would fall silently, in an instant. Not to fall was too hard, too hard; and he felt the silent lapse of his soul, as it would be at some instant to come, falling, falling, but not yet fallen, still unfallen, but about to fall.

   The tone of the text is best described as one of

   (A) resignation.
   (B) terror.
   (C) corruption.
   (D) decreasing.

4. The following excerpt is from *Meditations on First Philosophy*, by René Descartes, 1641, in which he muses about the nature of knowledge.

   But it may be said, perhaps, that, although the senses occasionally mislead us respecting minute objects, and such as are so far removed from us as to be beyond the reach of close observation, there are yet many other of their informations (presentations), of the truth of which it is manifestly impossible to doubt; as for example, that I am in this place, seated by the fire, clothed in a winter dressing gown, that I hold in my hands this piece of paper.

   The main purpose of the text is to illustrate Descartes' thinking about

   (A) the pitfalls of human perception.
   (B) the superiority of logical reasoning.
   (C) the importance of proper observational tools.
   (D) the spectrum of sensory certainty.

5. Within the red blood cell, hemoglobin exists as a four-subunit complex, or "tetramer," each subunit of which is made up of one "heme" metalloprotein, and one of several varieties of "globin." Comprised of iron and a carbon-nitrogen ring, heme is responsible for both the oxygen-binding capacity of hemoglobin, and for the red coloration of blood. Globin, meanwhile, refers to a folded chain of polypeptides, and it is the combination of these chains that imparts each type of hemoglobin with its unique characteristics.

   Based on the text, what makes the hemoglobin varieties distinct?

   (A) Whether there is a carbon-nitrogen ring
   (B) Whether there is a red coloration of the blood
   (C) Variation in the arrangement of metalloprotein chains
   (D) Variation in the arrangement of polypeptide chains

6. The following text is adapted from 1894 short story "The End of Books," by Octave Uzanne. In this story, a group of gentlemen gather after dinner to discuss what they think the future holds. Eventually they come to the topic of the future of books, and the following monologue is given by one of the group.

   I take my stand upon this incontestable fact, that the man of leisure becomes daily more reluctant to undergo fatigue, that he eagerly seeks for what he calls the comfortable, that is to say for every means of sparing himself the play and the waste of the organs. You will surely agree with me that reading, as we practice it today, soon brings on great weariness; for not only does it require of the brain a sustained attention which consumes a large proportion of the cerebral phosphates but it also forces our bodies into various fatiguing attitudes. If we are reading one of our great newspapers it constrains us to acquire a certain dexterity in the art of turning and folding the sheets; if we hold the paper wide open it is not long before the muscles of tension are overtaxed, and finally, if we address ourselves to the book, the necessity of cutting the leaves and turning them one after another, ends by producing an enervated condition very distressing in the long run.

   According to the text, the narrator considers a major issue with reading to be

   (A) its physical demands.
   (B) its dull subject matter.
   (C) its intellectual requirements.
   (D) its obscure language.

7. The following text is from John Cobden's 1854 book *The White Slaves of England*, published to decry the horrible working and living conditions among the poor working classes of England.

   Our plan has been to quote English authorities wherever possible. <u>Out of their own mouths shall they be condemned.</u> We have been much indebted to the publications of distinguished democrats of England, who have keenly felt the evils under which their country groans, and striven, with a hearty will, to remove them. They have the sympathies of civilized mankind with their cause. May their efforts soon be crowned with success, for the British masses and oppressed nations far away in the East will shout loud and long when the aristocracy is brought to the dust!

   Which choice best describes the function of the underlined sentence in the text as a whole?

   (A) It shares the heartfelt confessions of those who were formerly oppressors.
   (B) It considers the objections of those who dismiss democracy.
   (C) It expresses a desire to use the words of authorities against them.
   (D) It demonstrates the widespread acceptance of a point of view.

8. Scientists have demonstrated that most animal genes participate in alternative splicing to one extent or another; far from a mere biochemical curiosity, it is a vital biological strategy to maximize the economy of genetic material, which must be laboriously reproduced with each cell division, while maintaining an immense diversity in the protein-encoding capacity of a genome. In an extreme example, the genome of the insect species *Drosophila melanogaster* contains the large sum of about 15,000 genes. Yet, through alternative splicing, one single D melanogaster gene—known as DSCAM—has been shown to encode as many as 38,000 different proteins.

   Based on the text, which expression gives the most likely range of values for the total number of proteins in a *Drosophila melanogaster* genome?

   (A) Number of total proteins $= 15{,}000 + 38{,}000$
   (B) Number of total proteins $= 38{,}000 - 15{,}000$
   (C) Number of total proteins $\leq 38{,}000 \times 15{,}000$
   (D) Number of total proteins $> 38{,}000 / 15{,}000$

## Answer Explanations

1. **(C)** From the context, we understand that surfactants reduce surface tension and can interfere with the stability of an oil-water film. Therefore, if its properties allow a surfactant to interfere with forces that maintain integrity, we can assume the proper word choice is "cohesion," or "the act of sticking together." "Rectitude" refers to another meaning of integrity, like "virtue." "Decadence" is, then, the opposite of "rectitude." "Solidarity," while a tempting choice, usually refers to unity among a group of individuals.

2. **(A)** The author makes sure to differentiate soaps and detergents even though they "are sometimes used interchangeably." Choices (B) and (C) give misleading information that doesn't account for the text's explanation that they are neither identical in structure nor in creation. Choice (D) is incorrect because this is not referred to in the text.

3. **(A)** At the conclusion of the text, the narrator yields to his fate. He is "still unfallen, but about to fall," so the best description of this tone would be resignation. "Terror" is too strong. "Corruption," although related to sin, is not depictive of the narrator's tone. "Decreasing" would be used improperly here since the tone is not lessening in size or strength.

4. **(D)** The text refers to Descartes' acknowledgement that there are some truths that are "manifestly impossible to doubt." As examples, Descartes presents sensory observations like his location, clothing, and current activities as occurrences of knowledge that he cannot refute. So, (D) is correct. He is emphasizing the certainties of human perception, rather than the pitfalls. Additionally, he is not referring to "logical reasoning" or "tools" but merely to fundamental senses.

5. **(D)** The text states that a combination of polypeptide chains accounts for the varieties of hemoglobin. Choices (A) and (B) refer to characteristics of the heme that each type of hemoglobin has in common. Choice (C) is imprecise because metalloprotein refers to collective heme, not to the distinct chains associated with the globin.

6. **(A)** Throughout this text, the author underscores the physical demands of reading in the printed form—needing to have "dexterity" to turn and fold the sheets and to hold the paper wide open. The author suggests that a "man of leisure" will be more and more unwilling to undergo fatigue and would therefore be open to a less physically demanding type of media. So, it is reasonable to infer that the physical demands of reading are what the author considers to be a major issue. Choices (B), (C), and (D) all could represent shortcomings of reading, but they are not mentioned in this text.

7. **(C)** In the previous sentence, the narrator says that the plan "has been to quote English authorities wherever possible," indicating a desire to use the words of authorities against them. It is not choice (A) because there would be no need to condemn those who confessed in a heartfelt way. It is not (B) because the narrator is not trying to consider the objections of authorities, but to trap them in their contradictions. And it is not (D) because the narrator understands that English authorities likely have very different points of view from those whom they oppress.

8. **(C)** We can find the number of proteins by multiplying how many genes there are by how many proteins they code for. The last sentence tells us that this particular gene—that codes for 38,000 proteins—is "an extreme example." Therefore, if the genome has about 15,000 genes, it is highly unlikely that they all encode for that many proteins. Hence, we can assume that the total number of proteins is less than 15,000 multiplied by 38,000. In fact, even if the genes were all similarly extreme, (C) would still be correct because the total proteins would be equal to 15,000 multiplied by 38,000.

### Advanced Drill 2

1. Agricultural and biological engineers develop medicines, create better ways of growing and protecting our food supply, and, along with environmental engineers, help to create a cleaner, safer environment in which to breathe, grow food, and have safe drinking water. Even if you have not met such an engineer before, they have set an example of how to be good <u>stewards</u> of our resources, and we have all benefitted from what they have done for us.

   As used in the text, what does the word "stewards" most nearly mean?

   (A) Attendants
   (B) Curators
   (C) Assistants
   (D) Guardians

2. The following text is adapted from Nathaniel Hawthorne's 1852 novel *The Blithedale Romance.* Mr. Coverdale, an idealistic young man, who has recently moved onto a utopian communal farm, is recovering from a fever. He is attended first by Hollingsworth, a philanthropist, and second by Zenobia, a beautiful wealthy resident of the farm.

   All other members of the Community showed me kindness according to the full measure of their capacity. Zenobia brought me my gruel, every day, made by her own hands; and whenever I seemed inclined to converse, would sit by my bedside, and talk with so much vivacity as to add several gratuitous throbs to my pulse. Her poor little stories and tracts never half did justice to her intellect. It was only the lack of a fitter avenue that drove her to seek development in literature. She was made (among a thousand other things that she might have been) for a stump-oratress. I recognized no severe culture in Zenobia; her mind was full of weeds. It startled me, sometimes, in my state of moral as well as bodily faint-heartedness, to observe the hardihood of her philosophy.

   In the narrator's view, what was the major factor that drove Zenobia into her primary intellectual pursuit?

   (A) Significant natural talent.
   (B) Her desire to shock her contemporaries.
   (C) Religious zeal.
   (D) A scarcity of opportunities.

3. The more compact and less delicate color camera designed by German photographer Adolf Miethe simply included a rotating filter disc, which allowed three photographs to be taken in rapid succession. From 1909 to 1915, Miethe's design was used by his Russian protégé, Sergei Prokudin-Gorsky, in a project appointed to him by Czar Nicholas II to document visually the history, culture and modernization of the Russian Empire. His extensive and compelling work in the Russian provinces constitutes the first major series of color photojournalism. However, whenever a moving object was included in the frame—particularly water—the shortcomings of Miethe's design became obvious. The consecutive of exposure of plates, however swift, would always leave some room for visual conflict between the three images.

   Based on the text, it can be logically concluded that a Miethe-designed camera could most successfully photograph a river under what weather conditions?

   (A) At high noon on a summer day with a light breeze
   (B) On a rainy, blustery day with mild flooding
   (C) On a freezing, windless day
   (D) Any form of water with equally low quality

4. Text 1 is adapted from Walt Whitman's 1860 poem "I Hear America Singing." Text 2 is adapted from Langston Hughes's 1925 poem "I, Too."

   **Text 1**

   I hear America singing, the varied carols I hear,

   Those of mechanics, each one singing his as it should be blithe and strong,

   The carpenter singing his as he measures his plank or beam,

   The mason singing his as he makes ready for work, or leaves off work,

The boatman singing what belongs to him in his boat, the deckhand singing on the steamboat deck,

The shoemaker singing as he sits on his bench, the hatter singing as he stands,

The wood-cutter's song, the ploughboy's on his way in the morning, or at noon intermission or at sundown,

The delicious singing of the mother, or of the young wife at work, or of the girl sewing or washing,

Each singing what belongs to him or her and to none else,

The day what belongs to the day—at night the party of young fellows, robust, friendly,

Singing with open mouths their strong melodious songs.

**Text 2**

I, too, sing America.

I am the darker brother.

They send me to eat in the kitchen

When company comes,

But I laugh,

And eat well,

And grow strong.

Tomorrow,

I'll be at the table

When company comes.

Nobody'll dare

Say to me,

"Eat in the kitchen,"

Then.

Besides,

They'll see how beautiful I am

And be ashamed—

I, too, am America.

What best describes the different themes of Text 1 and Text 2 respectively?

(A) Career advancement and artistic awareness
(B) Individual creation and racial inclusion
(C) Musical talent and gustatory sensibility
(D) Present day and distant past

5. Mites do not necessarily mean the end of bees. These mites are slow to spread in nature, and North America is a big place. However, because of commercial farming practices, there is a major concern that mites and their associated viruses could soon infect most colonies in North America. Most bees, despite what people think, do not just stay in one area. In fact, most hives do not stay in one area. They travel the country. Beekeepers in today's agricultural setting rent out their bees to massive farms. One great example is the almond orchards in California. Natural bees in the area are not populous enough to pollinate the thousands and thousands of almond trees. So, apiarists (beekeepers) __________.

   Which choice most logically completes the text?

   (A) notify governmental authorities when bee populations become overly burdensome on the environment.
   (B) aid bees in their migratory journey away from the California orchards.
   (C) rent hives out to the almond farms for a few months each year to get the job done.
   (D) attain professional credentials through vocational agricultural programs.

6. The following text is from Harriet Beecher Stowe's 1852 novel *Uncle Tom's Cabin.*

   The prayer-meeting at Uncle Tom's Cabin had been protracted to a very late hour, and Tom and his worthy helpmeet were not yet asleep, when between twelve and one there was a light tap on the windowpane.

   "Good Lord! what's that?" said Aunt Chloe, starting up. "My sakes alive, if it aint Lizzy! Get on your clothes, old man, quick. I'm gwine to open the door."

   And suiting the action to the word, the door flew open, and the light of the candle which Tom had hastily lighted, fell on the face of Eliza. "I'm running away, Uncle Tom and Aunt Chloe—carrying off my child. Master sold him."

   Which choice best states the function of the underlined sentence in the text as a whole?

   (A) To show that Eliza feared unwanted detection
   (B) To demonstrate that Eliza respected nightly rituals
   (C) To highlight how Chloe was hesitant to share bad news
   (D) To express how Chloe understood her misdeeds

7. Eugène Boudin was a 19th-century French landscape painter who famously painted while outdoors. Which quotation from an article describing these paintings gives the best evidence that Boudin's painting was characterized by subjects from a variety of socioeconomic classes?

   (A) "Though these works brought him very little financial profit, it is known that he was exceptionally fond of them."
   (B) "Having worked as a bay fisherman in his youth, it has been claimed that Boudin was perhaps somewhat ashamed of his reputation as painter."
   (C) "These works provide us with a compelling contrast to paintings by other artists of the languorous, well-to-do beach-goers."
   (D) "Together they provide a rare, panoptical insight into the full social spectrum of French life by the sea in the mid-to-late 19th century."

8.

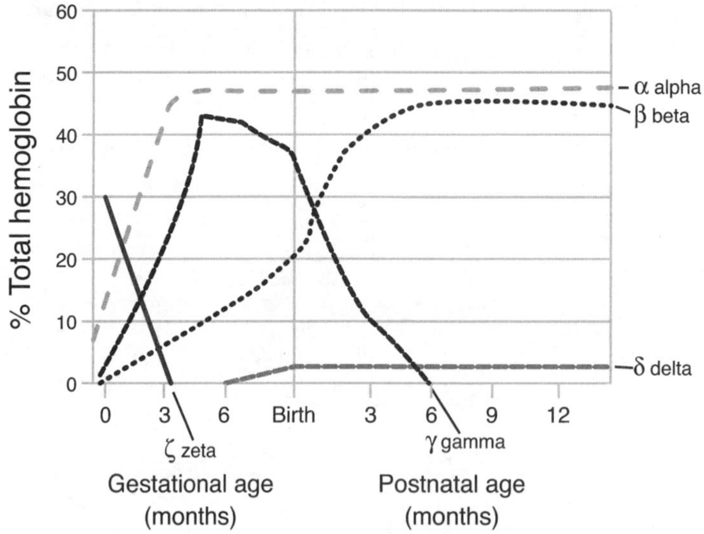


A neonatal medical scientist claims that an examination of percentages of globin chains can give doctors a relatively clear idea of the age of both fetuses and children. The scientist claims that particular globin makeups will often correspond to particular ages.

Based on the graph, a rough measurement of which of the following globin chains would give the clearest indication that a child was born two months premature?

(A) Alpha
(B) Beta
(C) Gamma
(D) Zeta

## Answer Explanations

1. **(D)** The text states that engineers have exemplified "how to be good stewards of our resources." Before this statement, the author discusses how agricultural, biological, and environmental engineers have helped to create a cleaner, safer, and all-around higher quality environment for us. Hence, guardian, or "protector" is the closest meaning. Curators are keepers of museums. Finally, both attendants and assistants indicate helpers, so they are too tepid for this context.

2. **(D)** The text indicates that Coverdale believes that Zenobia pursued literature because there was a lack of a "fitter avenue" and that her literary works did not do justice to her intellect. So, her primary intellectual pursuit of literature was primarily a result of a lack of opportunities. Choices (A) and (B) both give characteristics that would apply to her mindset but would not hold her back. And while she has passion and zeal for her beliefs, there is no evidence that her zeal is religious in nature; even if it were, this would not hold her back from her goals.

3. **(C)** The second to the last sentence suggests that the major shortcoming of Miethe's design was its inability to photograph properly moving objects because it needed a more expanded exposure time. If an object were relatively stable, as objects would likely be on a freezing, windless day, Miethe's design would be more successful. Choices (A) and (B) would not work due to the presence of wind, and choice (D) would not work because frozen water would be more clearly photographed than moving water.

4. **(B)** The first poem focuses on how individuals create things through their various professions, doing so in a harmonious fashion. The second poem emphasizes the need to include people of color in America. So, the different themes of the texts are individual creation and racial inclusion, respectively. It is not (A) because Text 1 is not addressing the need for career advancement. It is not (C) because there is not a focus on taste and sensation in Text 2. It is not (D) because Text 2 is written from a present-day perspective, not one from the distant past.

5. **(C)** The text draws attention to the fact that bees and their hives can be moved from place to place and that there are not sufficient natural bees to pollinate the almond orchards in California. Therefore, it would be logical for beekeepers to help solve this problem by renting out their hives to the almond farms to help with pollination. It is not (A) because the previous sentence says that there is a lack of bees. It is not (B) because it wouldn't make sense for the beekeepers to help bees move away from an area where they are needed. It is not (D) because this does not relate to the need for their specific services to solve the almond pollination problem.

6. **(A)** It is safe to assume that the "light tap" is indicative of Eliza's discretion, as she must be very secretive about her plans to run away. So, it is fitting to say that she is trying to avoid detection as in choice (A). Choice (C) is incorrect because we know she risked visiting Tom specifically to share the news. Choice (B) wrongly assumes her caution is related to offending Tom and Chloe by visiting them so late. Finally, (D) inaccurately assumes she is worried more about breaking the law than about being caught.

7. **(D)** By referring to "the full social spectrum of French life," Choice (D) gives the best evidence that Boudin's painting was characterized by subjects from a variety of socioeconomic classes. The other options do not indicate that the subjects of his paintings would be from a variety of different social and economic classes.

8. **(B)** To find the clearest indication that a child was born two months premature, we would want to determine the level of a particular hemoglobin protein that had an easily measurable and unique value at 7 months of gestation—beta is approximately 20% at this point, and this is the only time that it meets the level. It is not (A) because the alpha maintains its 7-month percent for some time. It is not (C) because gamma is at its 7-month percent both at 7 months and at 5 months. It is not (D) because zeta ceases to be a factor after 3 and half months of gestation.

# Vocabulary Resources

## 50 Common Word Roots

Efficiently build your SAT vocabulary by studying these fifty common word roots and their definitions as well as common SAT words that incorporate these word roots.

### › Root: *Ab*

**Definition:** away

**SAT Words:**

- **abrogate** (deny, repeal (make it go away))
- **abstain** (do away with)

### › Root: *Ambi*

**Definition:** both

**SAT Words:**

- **ambidextrous** (able to use both hands)
- **ambivalent** (undecided; could go "both" ways)

### › Root: *Ambul*

**Definition:** move or walk

**SAT Words:**

- **ambulate** (walk around)
- **somnambulate** (walk while sleeping)

### › Root: *Ami*

**Definition:** love

**SAT Words:**

- **amiable** (pleasant and friendly)
- **amicable** (done in a friendly way)
- **amity** (friendship)

### › Root: *Contra*

**Definition:** against

**SAT Words:**

- **contradict** (claim the opposite of another statement)
- **contraposition** (opposition)

### › Root: *Cred*

**Definition:** believe

**SAT Words:**

- **credible** (believable)
- **credulous** (overly eager to believe something, gullible)
- **incredulous** (unwilling to believe)

### › Root: *Crypt*

**Definition:** hidden

**SAT Words:**

- **cryptic** (having a mysterious meaning)
- **decrypt** (decode a secret message)
- **encrypt** (convert something into a secret code)

### › Root: *Cycl*

**Definition:** circle or ring

**SAT Words:**

- **cycloid** (circular)
- **cyclone** (circular storm)
- **cyclotron** (a circular machine that physicists use to accelerate particles)

### › Root: *Dem*

**Definition:** people

**SAT Words:**

- **demagogue** (a leader who appeals to popular prejudice instead of rationality)
- **democracy** (a government elected by the people)
- **demography** (the study of human population statistics)

### › Root: *Derm*

**Definition:** skin

**SAT Words:**

- **dermatology** (a branch of medicine that is associated with the treatment of skin)
- **hypodermic** (related to the parts beneath the skin)
- **intradermal** (between the layers of the skin)

### › Root: *Dict*

**Definition:** speak

**SAT Words:**

- **edict** (an order from an authority figure)
- **indict** (to formally accuse someone of a crime)
- **malediction** (a curse)

### › Root: *Domin*

**Definition:** master

**SAT Words:**

- **dominant** (most powerful)
- **domineering** (controlling and overbearing)
- **dominion** (area of control)

### › Root: *Dur*

**Definition:** hard

**SAT Words:**

- **durable** (able to withstand damage)
- **endurance** (capacity to last)
- **obdurate** (stubborn)

### › Root: *Ego*

**Definition:** I, self

**SAT Words:**

- **alter ego** (second version of oneself)
- **egomaniacal** (obsessed with oneself)
- **egotistical** (self-centered)

### › Root: *Esth*

**Definition:** feeling

**SAT Words:**

- **aesthetic** (associated with an appreciation for beauty)
- **anesthetic** (something that reduces painful sensations)

### › Root: *Extra*

**Definition:** outside

**SAT Words:**

- **extralegal** (outside of the law)
- **extraneous** (outside of what is needed)
- **extrapolate** (to make a prediction based on past data and experiences)

### › Root: *Fid*

**Definition:** faith

**SAT Words:**

- **confidant** (a person in whom you have faith and trust)
- **fidelity** (being faithful, loyal)
- **perfidy** (being faithless, disloyal)

### › Root: *Flect*

**Definition:** bend

**SAT Words:**

- **deflect** (to divert something)
- **genuflect** (to bend on your knee to show respect)
- **inflection** (to make your voice rise and fall (to "bend" your voice))

### › Root: *Flor*

**Definition:** flower

**SAT Words:**

- **efflorescence** (blossoming)
- **florid** (flowery)

### › Root: *Fract/Frag*

**Definition:** break

**SAT Words:**

- **fracture** (to break)
- **fragile** (breakable)
- **refract** (to alter waves on a straight path)

### › Root: *Fug*

**Definition:** run away

**SAT Words:**

- **(fleeting)**
- **refugee** (a person forced to leave his or her home)
- **subterfuge** (evasion, deceit)

### › Root: *Gen*

**Definition:** birth, production

**SAT Words:**

- **genesis** (creation)
- **genteel** (well-bred, refined)
- **progeny** (descendants)

### › Root: *Gram*

**Definition:** something written

**SAT Words:**

- **epigram** (a witty saying)
- **monogram** (a decorative design made of two or more letters)
- **phonogram** (a symbol that represents a spoken sound)

### › Root: *Graph*

**Definition:** to write

**SAT Words:**

- **bibliography** (a list of scholarly sources)
- **cosmography** (a description of the universe)
- **typography** (the style of printed material)

### › Root: *Grat*

**Definition:** pleasing

**SAT Words:**

- **gratify** (to give satisfaction)
- **gratuitous** (done freely, often unwarranted)
- **ingratiate** (to gain favor by helping someone)

### › Root: *Gress*

**Definition: to** step, to go

**SAT Words:**

- **digress** (to go away from the main topic)
- **egress** (exit)
- **transgress** (to violate a law)

### › Root: *Hetero*

**Definition:** different

**SAT Words:**

- **heterodox** (nonconformist)
- **heterogeneous** (diverse)
- **heteromorphic** (having different forms)

### › Root: *Homo*

**Definition:** same

**SAT Words:**

- **homogeneous** (of the same type)
- **homologous** (similar, especially biologically)
- **homophone** (words with the same pronunciation but different meanings (e.g., "son" and "sun"))

### › Root: *Idio*

**Definition:** peculiar, distinct

**SAT Words:**

- **idiom** (an expression that is distinct to native speakers of a language)
- **idiosyncrasy** (a peculiar characteristic of an individual)

### › Root: *Judi*

**Definition:** judge, lawyer

**SAT Words:**

- **adjudicate** (to make a judgment)
- **judicial** (concerning the administration of justice)
- **judicious** (possessing sound judgment)

### › Root: *Ling*

**Definition:** language

**SAT Words:**

- **linguist** (a person who studies languages)
- **linguistics** (the study of languages)

### › Root: *Loqu*

**Definition:** speak

**SAT Words:**

- **colloquial** (used in informal conversation)
- **eloquent** (able to express oneself well)
- **loquacious** (talkative)

### › Root: *Magn*

**Definition:** large, great

**SAT Words:**

- **magnanimous** (greatly noble in spirit)
- **magnate** (a greatly influential person)
- **magnitude** (greatness, size)

### › Root: *Mal*

**Definition:** bad

**SAT Words:**

- **malcontent** (a difficult person)
- **malevolent** (showing evil intent)
- **malign** (evil)

### › Root: *Mut*

**Definition:** change

**SAT Words:**

- **immutable** (unchangeable)
- **permutation** (a change in the arrangement of a set of items)
- **transmute** (to change in form)

### › Root: *Ob*

**Definition:** against

**SAT Words:**

- **obdurate** (stubborn)
- **obtrusive** (unpleasantly noticeable)

### › Root: *Phil*

**Definition:** love

**SAT Words:**

- **philanthropist** (a person who loves to help others, usually by donating money)
- **philosophy** (the study of knowledge (love of wisdom); a way of thinking)
- **technophile** (a person who loves advanced technology)

### › Root: *Plac*

**Definition:** calm

**SAT Words:**

- **complacent** (unconcerned; self-satisfied)
- **placate** (to make someone less angry)
- **placid** (calm, peaceful)

### › Root: *Re*

**Definition:** back, again

**SAT Words:**

- **relegate** (downgrade, lower)
- **remunerate** (to pay back for services)
- **renege** (to go back on a promise)

### › Root: *Sagac*

**Definition:** wise

**SAT Words:**

- **sagacious** (having wisdom, good judgment)
- **sagacity** (wisdom)

### › Root: *Sang*

**Definition:** having to do with blood

**SAT Words:**

- **sanguinary** (bloody or bloodthirsty)
- **sanguine** (cheerful and optimistic (being red-faced with hope rather than blue with despair))

### › Root: *Sequ*

**Definition:** follow

**SAT Words:**

- **consequently** (as a result)
- **obsequious** (excessively obedient)
- **subsequent** (following in time)

### › Root: *Somn*

**Definition:** sleep

**SAT Words:**

- **insomnia** (an inability to sleep)
- **somnambulate** (sleepwalk)
- **somnolent** (sleepy)

### › Root: *Tac/Tic*

**Definition:** be silent

**SAT Words:**

- **reticent** (reluctant to speak)
- **tacit** (unspoken)
- **taciturn** (uncommuicative)

### › Root: *Troph*

**Definition:** feed, grow

**SAT Words:**

- **autotroph** (an organism that makes its own food)
- **heterotroph** (an organism that obtains its food from sources outside of itself)

### › Root: *Ultim*

**Definition:** last

**SAT Words:**

- **penultimate** (second to last)
- **ultimate** (last)
- **ultimatum** (a final demand)

### › Root: *Vener*

**Definition:** respectful

**SAT Words:**

- **venerable** (worthy of respect)
- **venerate** (to show respect)
- **veneration** (great respect)

### › Root: *Vit*

**Definition:** life

**SAT Word:**

- **vitality** (life force, energy)

### › Root: *Voc*

**Definition:** voice

**SAT Words:**

- **advocate** (to voice support)
- **invocation** (the act of summoning divine help)
- **vociferous** (loudly and repeatedly expressive)

### › Root: *Vol*

**Definition:** fly, wish

**SAT Words:**

- **benevolent** (wishing kindness)
- **volition** (using one's ability to choose)
- **voluntary** (freely chosen)

## 250 Words Important to the SAT Reading

Review these frequently found SAT vocabulary words to help you perform your best on the words-in-context questions and to fully understand the reading passages.

**Abject**—Abject is often used to describe negative things and heighten the negativity. You might see loneliness, poverty, or sadness described as being abject. It describes the highest level of loneliness, poverty, or sadness a person could reach.

Example sentence: Having lost his wife to the bubonic plague, the young man fell into abject sadness that did not lift until life provided him with a new companion some 25 years later.

**Abode**—Put simply, an abode is a place where people live. It could be anything from a house, to a cave, to an apartment, to a van. If humans take shelter there, it can be called an abode.

Example sentence: "Welcome to my humble abode," said the nomad, as he lifted a flap to allow me entrance to his colorfully furnished canvas home.

**Abstract**—When something is abstract, it isn't concrete or tangible. It might exist as an idea only (the concept of gravity is abstract), or it might be something that you can touch but that represents ideas or feelings (like abstract art, which is art that does not depict real items).

Example sentence: She soon realized that while they often had long talks about the future, they were not concrete discussions. Rather, he discussed the future abstractly, as something he couldn't really see.

**Acknowledge**—To acknowledge someone or something is to notice it and make sure it knows that it has been noticed. If a student raises her hand during a lecture, a teacher may nod toward the student to acknowledge the student. That is, the head nod says, "I see you have your hand raised. Just a moment while I finish up my thought."

Example sentence: After training longer and harder than any of his teammates, the new tennis player was proud to receive the "most improved" award as an acknowledgement of all his hard work.

**Adapt**—To adapt is to change to fit the situation. If a fish is switched to a new tank, it may need a few days to adapt before going back to its more normal patterns of existence.

Example sentence: The sudden change of rules was very upsetting for the mock trial team, but soon they were hard at work adapting their strategy in order to best take advantage of the new situation.

**Admonition**—An admonition is the noun form of the word admonish. Therefore, an admonition is the scolding you might receive if you have done something wrong.

Example sentence: Having been caught with her hand in the cookie jar, the little girl hung her head and waited for the admonition she was sure she would receive from her parent.

**Affluent**—To be affluent is to be very well off financially.

Example sentence: Having grown up in an affluent home, John Smith was well accustomed to all the luxuries and sophistication of upper-class life.

**Agitate**—To agitate means to work up or disturb. The big post that is sometimes in the middle of a clothes washing machine is called an agitator because it helps work the soap into a lather. You might also agitate a human or animal by annoying them or frustrating them until they become all worked up.

Example sentence: As the baby's cries grew louder and louder, the other theatergoers became more and more agitated until someone was finally so fed up that he asked the parents to take the baby outside.

**Aggrandize**—If you notice the word *grand* in aggrandize, it may help you remember how this word is used. Generally, to aggrandize something is to make it grander; oftentimes people mentally aggrandize and think of things as grander than they really are.

Example sentence: Since they lived in different states, the young couple had spent a lot of time apart. When they finally saw each other again, they realized that they had each aggrandized the other, and were disappointed in the real person in front of them.

**Aggregate**—When discussing the aggregate (as a noun), you're talking about the whole, not the parts.

Aggregate can also be a verb in which you build up the parts to create a whole.

Example sentence: I've been very busy at work since my superior asked that I aggregate all the available data on consumer habits and present it as a complete report to the CEO.

**Alternation**—Alternating is simply taking turns. For example, you and your sibling might alternate doing the dishes so that no one has to do them two nights in a row. Alternation, then, is simply the noun form of the verb alternate.

Example sentence: The alternation of quarterbacks from one play to the next confused the opposing team and caused them to misread several plays, leading to our team scoring a touchdown.

**Amicable**—To be amicable with other people means to get along with them. It is a warm word often used to describe friendly, but not overly friendly, relationships with coworkers, neighbors, and other acquaintances.

Example sentence: After the hubbub from the move settled down, the roommates forged an amicable relationship. While never becoming close friends, they were more than happy to bring in the other's mail and to live in relative peace and harmony.

**Analogous**—When two things are analogous to each other, they can be compared to one another. Often, this comparison will help clarify something about one of the things being compared. Think of the word analogy when thinking about what analogous means.

Example sentence: Finding my missing phone was analogous to trying to find a needle in a haystack—it was pretty hopeless.

**Analogy**—An analogy is a comparison between two items using *like* or *as*.

Example analogy: The young boy's jealousy grew inside him like a little green monster, waiting to escape.

**Anomaly**—An anomaly is something strange or out of the usual pattern of things. If, for example, a very kind and sweet classmate lost their temper just one time, you might call that occurrence an anomaly.

Example sentence: The scientist assured the worried townspeople that the strange lights at night were merely a meteorological anomaly and not the signals of arriving aliens.

**Antipathy**—If you were to hate someone's guts, you might say you felt antipathy toward them. It is a very negative feeling toward another person or thing.

Example sentence: While he loved his wife very much, he felt nothing but antipathy toward his in-laws, which put a definite strain on their marriage.

**Apparition**—Apparition sounds like the word appear. An apparition is something that suddenly appears. Oftentimes, ghosts and other supernatural phenomena will be described as being apparitions.

Example sentence: The youth quaked as they heard a strange sound; they should have never broken into the abandoned house, which was full of apparitions.

**Arbitrary**—This word can usually be replaced with the word random.

Example sentence: The seating chart had previously been arbitrary, but the teacher had to be more deliberate in assigning seats during the second quarter so as to prevent cheating.

**Ascertain**—To ascertain something is to find it out or confirm it. For example, the police may hold a person for a certain amount of time while they try to ascertain the details of the crime committed.

Example sentence: The town waited with bated breath as the counters worked to ascertain the winner of the mayoral election.

**Aspire**—If someone were to tell you to "aspire to higher things," it might be interpreted as "dream big." Aspiring means working toward a lofty goal.

Example sentence: Though I'm only a yellow belt at the moment, I aspire to be a black belt in a few years.

**Autocratic**—An autocrat is someone in charge who has all the power. The czars in Russia, for example, were autocrats. There was no governmental power outside of them. Autocratic, then, is the adjectival form of autocrat—it can be used to describe someone who is acting like an autocrat.

Example sentence: Mrs. Nafziger is a very strict teacher and is quite autocratic in the way she runs her history classes.

**Automated**—Think about the word automatic. Automated means something has been changed to make it now automatic where as previously it was not. For example, a dishwasher would automate the dishwashing process.

Example sentence: The factory workers were very concerned about losing their jobs as more and more tasks around the plant were automated.

**Beget**—When you beget something, it means you take steps to bring that thing into existence. It can also refer to an action that leads to something. You might say that if you pass around a petition to bring chicken nuggets back to the cafeteria, you are trying to beget change. (Don't mess this word up with the similar-sounding word baguette, which is a long, thin loaf of French bread).

Example sentence: Planting seeds in the spring is the only way to beget a harvest in the fall.

**Benevolent**—To be benevolent is to be kind. Quite often, this word is used to describe elderly people who are willing to give away all they have and charities that work to better people's lives by giving.

Example sentence: When hard times hit the community, many people turned to the benevolent philanthropist who live just outside of town. It was well known that he would help everyone he could.

**Bestow**—To bestow something is to give it to someone. This is often use when giving titles and other honors.

Example sentence: After his heroic actions on the battlefield left him with grave injuries, the government bestowed upon the soldier the Purple Heart medal.

25

**Biological**—Biology is the study of life; biological is describing something related to the study of life or related to life itself. For example, if you are infected with bacteria, you could call how your body reacts a biological response.

Example sentence: When I broke my leg, my doctor explained the biological process my body would go through to bring about healing; it was really neat to learn!

**Calibrate**—To calibrate something is to adjust it so that it runs the way it should. This is especially applicable to machines that have readouts. If your car's speedometer tells you that you're going 30 miles per hour when you're really going 55 miles per hour, then you need to have your speedometer calibrated.

Example sentence: The old oven was in bad shape. When we set it to 350, it only reached 200. We called a repair person to calibrate the dial, and that fixed the problem.

**Calisthenics**—Calisthenics are a type of exercise that rely on body weight. They include push-ups, sit-ups, jumping jacks, and other simple movements that require no equipment.

Example sentence: While the elderly man was far past the point in life where he could lift heavy weights, he still stuck to the daily calisthenics routine that he had in the Army some 50 years earlier.

**Capacity**—The capacity of something is a measure of its ability. A room has a maximum capacity, which says how many people can be in that room. A car may have the capacity to go 150 miles per hour. A person could have the capacity to handle a difficult situation.

Example sentence: What the president was asking the man to do was far beyond his capacity; he would need to request backup.

**Celestial**—When something is celestial, it has to do with outer space.

Example sentence: When studying astronomy, it is helpful to have a celestial map for reference.

**Censure**—To censure someone is to give them a formal reprimand. Quite often, governments hand out censures to their members for having done something wrong, but not necessarily illegal.

Example sentence: The young representative received a censure after his foolish and dangerous antics were published by a respectable newspaper.

**Circulation**—Circulation is quite often thought of in relation to blood moving through the body, but it can refer to anything moving back and forth or around in a predictable pattern.

Example sentence: The circulation of rumors can be quite detrimental to a person's reputation.

**Coerce**—To coerce someone is to get them to do something by threat of force.

Example sentence: When asking nicely fails to work, bad people often turn to coercion to get what they want.

**Cognition**—Cognition is the ability to understand something. When people get older and develop dementia, quite often their cognition is negatively impacted.

Example sentence: Getting plenty of sleep is instrumental in increasing one's cognition.

**Colloquial**—The word colloquial almost always describes language. Colloquial language is everyday language. In English, for example, you probably use a lot of colloquial language with your friends, but likely speak a bit more properly to teachers and other adults.

Example sentence: When my turn came to speak to the foreign dignitary, I did my best to speak formally and avoid using colloquial language.

**Commercial**—Commercial has to do with the buying and selling of goods. For example, if you begin a commercial enterprise, you are likely setting out to go into business to buy, sell, create, or distribute goods.

Example sentence: Many companies now use overnight delivery to get their commercial goods to the customers who have ordered them.

**Complementary**—When something is complementary, it goes well with the thing around it.

Example sentence: Milk and cookies are complementary foods that I greatly enjoy eating simultaneously.

**Complimentary**—Something that is provided free of charge. Also, a compliment is a nice thing to say about someone.

Example sentence: Compliments about your excellent work cost the teacher nothing—they are complimentary.

**Conflate**—Oftentimes, we are warned not to conflate things. This means we need to keep the two things separate and not assume that they are the same idea. For example, in history class you may conflate the feminist movement and the suffragette movement. While they have some similarities, they aren't the same thing.

Example sentence: Be careful not to conflate infatuation and love. That is a surefire way to end up with a broken heart.

**Conjure**—To conjure is to bring something up. When telling a scary story, you may conjure up images that are terrifying to the listeners.

Example sentence: If a small child demands candy when you have none, you might reply, "I'm afraid I can't conjure up sweets out of thin air just because you want them."

**Consensus**—When everyone agrees, there is a consensus.

Example sentence: In government, rarely is there a consensus. Rather, there are a multitude of opinions vying to be heard.

**Consequence**—Consequences are the results of an action taken. There can be positive consequences, but more often this word is used to indicate a negative result or a punishment for negative actions.

Example sentence: If you fail to show up at practice, the consequence is that you don't get to play.

**Conservator**—A conservator is a person whose job it is to conserve or preserve something. This word could also be used to just mean a general guardian.

Example sentence: The art collection had a marvelous conservator who did all she could to ensure that the art would be enjoyed for many generations to come.

**Constitution**—We are likely all familiar with the governmental term constitution. But this word can also apply to someone's bodily health or how something is put together. Any of those three meanings could pop up on the SAT.

Example sentences: Since the constitution of the carriage was not very sturdy, a delegate was involved in an accident on his way to the Constitutional Convention. Luckily, the delegate had a strong personal constitution, and he recovered easily in just a few days.

**Contingent**—When something is contingent, it is relying on other factors to come to be. An outdoor field trip, for example, might be contingent on the weather.

Example sentence: I am planning on traveling to the capital to watch the soccer team play for the state title. That is contingent, of course, on us winning this last playoff game.

**Conventional**—When something is conventional, it follows the traditional rules that are set up. For example, a bride wearing white is very conventional while a bride wearing bright red would be unconventional.

Example sentence: My family tends to be very conventional at Thanksgiving. We always eat a turkey with stuffing, mashed potatoes, and a few side dishes, and then we have pumpkin pie for dessert.

**Convey**—To convey something is to get it across. You could convey a tin of cookies safely from your grandmother to your mother. If you are an effective public speaker, you can convey ideas from your mind to the minds of others.

Example sentence: Try as he might, the student teacher continually failed to convey his expectations to the class. This resulted in a rather disorderly classroom experience.

**Convoke**—Generally, the word convoke means to call a meeting.

Example sentence: Convoke the leaders of the nations; we must come together or we shall surely perish.

**Convulsion**—To convulse is a physical movement. Think of a person having a seizure—all of their muscles are convulsing. They are therefore having convulsions.

Example sentence: The audience stared in amazement as the snake charmer's snake exited the basket, its body racked with convulsions as it heard the mesmerizing music.

**Cooperatively**—You likely know the word cooperate. Cooperatively just means working in a cooperative manner.

Example sentence: During times of international crisis, it is best for governments to work cooperatively with one another.

50

**Cultivate**—To cultivate something is to bring it up or to try to make it grow or exist. Farmers cultivate crops. Your teachers try to cultivate in you a love of learning.

Example sentence: Holidays like the 4th of July, Labor Day, and Memorial Day all have a side effect of cultivating a sense of patriotism in the population.

**Dawdle**—To dawdle is to lag behind.

Example sentence: "Don't dawdle or you'll miss the school bus," the grandfather called, as he turned around to see what was taking his grandchild so long.

**Decipher**—To decipher something is to figure it out. A spy might decipher a special code, for instance.

Example sentence: The store clerk looked puzzled as he tried to decipher why the customer in front of him was so upset.

**Deficient**—When something is deficient, it isn't enough; it is lacking something. In the winter, people are often vitamin D deficient due to spending too much time indoors.

Example sentence: The young man, while highly educated, had no work ethic. Due to this deficiency, he was nearly unemployable.

**Degrade**—To degrade is to break something down slowly over time.

Example sentence: While the engine was still sound, the body of the car had degraded to the point where it was no longer safe to drive.

**Demur**—To demur is to politely say no to something or avoid it.

Example sentence: When offered a second helping of food, the man politely demurred since he already felt full.

**Desolation**—Desolation is total abandonment, emptiness, and destruction. Desolation occurs when everything of value and everything alive is destroyed.

Example sentence: War seemed more imminent each day, and families quickly began fleeing the city, worried at what seemed to be the certain desolation to come.

**Despoil**—Despoil is related to the phrase *the spoils of war*. The spoils of war are the things that invaders would take from the inhabitants upon victory. Pretty much anything of worth would be looted or plundered. To despoil is the act of taking away anything of value.

Example sentence: The greedy criminals broke into the historic mansion to despoil it.

**Deter**—To deter someone is to stop them from doing something.

Example sentence: The would-be bank robbers were deterred when they saw that security had been increased dramatically.

**Disenfranchise**—To disenfranchise is to take away someone's right to vote, or prevent them from using it.

Example sentence: For most of human history, women were disenfranchised.

**Disparity**—A disparity is an inequality or a difference between two things. For instance, there may be a disparity between the posted rules in a classroom and the rules that are actually enforced.

Example sentence: Small children are quick to point out any disparity between the dessert they receive and the dessert their brother or sister receives.

**Disseminate**—To disseminate is to pass out or to ensure the spread of something (quite often information).

Example sentence: At the end of the security meeting, the participants were asked not to disseminate the knowledge that they had acquired, since doing so could put people in harm's way.

**Dissimilar**—Things that are dissimilar are not the same (not similar).

Example sentence: While they had grown up in the same house, at the same time, with the same parents, the twins were quite dissimilar.

**Diverge**—When two things move apart, they diverge. (This is the opposite of when two things come together, which is when they converge.)

Example sentence: Quite often, when students graduate, they diverge from their friends and move on with life.

**Doctrine**—A doctrine is a sincerely held belief, often of the religious variety, but also political or other beliefs as well.

Example sentence: Some people do not stand for the pledge as it goes against their religious doctrine—this is their right under the First Amendment.

**Doldrums**—The word doldrums is often used to describe a time in which nothing happens. It is also used in sailing to describe an area of water that is not moving in which a sail boat would be trapped. Doldrums are never a good thing and can sometimes even be used to describe depression, boredom, and other negative mental states.

Example sentence: After his breakup, he entered a period of doldrums which lasted for several weeks.

**Domestic**—When something is described as domestic, it is related to the home. If someone hires domestic help, they are likely hiring someone to help take care of their house or something in it. It could be a gardener, maid, or cook.

Example sentence: Compared to the other families of 1900, their marriage was unconventional, with her working and bringing home a paycheck while he stayed home and attended to domestic matters.

**Dominion**—Dominion is control or authority over someone or something.

Example sentence: The king frequently exercised his dominion over the serfs to extract more and more work from them in less and less time.

**Dubious**—To be dubious is to be doubtful and uncertain.

Example sentence: While my friend was eager to explore the cave, I was much more dubious about doing so.

**Earnest**—When someone is earnest, they are showing that they are serious. They really believe what they are saying and they find it important that you understand that.

Example sentence: The young man spoke earnestly as he told her of his feelings and tried to convince her to accept his proposal.

**Eddy**—An eddy is when water or air moves swiftly in a circular motion.

Example sentence: The boat, caught in a persistent eddy, appeared to be lost forever.

**Effectual**—The word effectual means that the desired result has been achieved through that action.

Example sentence: I have found that asking for help is far more effectual than simply waiting for someone to offer.

**Efficacy**—The efficacy of something is how effective that thing is.

Example sentence: The efficacy of the treatment came into question when the wound became infected instead of healing.

**Efficient**—When something is efficient, it is done in the most direct way possible using the least amount of time and resources to get the best result.

Example sentence: Jennifer completed her errands quite efficiently and was back at home just an hour after she had left.

**Embellish**—To embellish is to add details or flair to something—either verbally or physically.

Example sentence: The seamstress told embellished tales of her youth while embellishing the wedding dress with thousands of tiny pearl beads.

75

**Emit**—Emit means to give off.

Example sentence: After having been sprayed by a skunk, the puppy emitted a horrid smell for several days to come.

**Empathize**—When you empathize with someone, you feel what they're feeling. You might empathize with a friend who had a terrible grade on a test, or with a family who needs some help getting enough food for a holiday meal.

Example sentence: The storm damage to the home caused an outpouring of support from their neighbors, who empathized with the now-struggling family.

**Endearing**—When people are endearing, they create warm feelings toward themselves. A person may have an endearing smile that makes you like them and feel kindly toward them.

Example sentence: When I joined my new school, I was seated next to a small girl with pigtails. She had the most endearing personality and we were soon great friends.

**Endeavor**—To endeavor is to try something. It can also be used as a noun, meaning "a try."

Example sentence: Once the rain stops, we will endeavor to get the garden planted.

**Endow**—To endow is to give. Quite often, this term is used to describe massive donations given to charities upon the death of a wealthy person. It can also talk about rights given to people just because of their birth or citizenship.

Example sentence: (From the Declaration of Independence) "We hold these truths to be self-evident, that all men are created equal, that they are endowed by their creator with certain unalienable rights, that among these are life, liberty, and the pursuit of happiness."

**Enhance**—To enhance something is to make it better or clearer. An umbrella enhances your experience of walking in the rain. Prescription glasses enhance your eyesight.

Example sentence: The coach added a few trick plays to the book in order to enhance our chances of success.

**Enterprise**—When you set out to do something, the process of doing it is an enterprise. This word often refers to big or difficult tasks. Think about the starship *Enterprise* from Star Trek—it has a very difficult mission: "To explore strange new worlds. To seek out new life and new civilizations. To boldly go where no man has gone before."

Example sentence: The process of building and moving to a whole new school in just a year was quite a difficult enterprise; however, the school board was committed to it as it was seen as the best option for the students' education.

**Entice**—To entice someone is to convince them to do something through the promise of reward (as opposed to coerce, which is through promise of harm). A cat can be enticed to come out from under the bed with a treat.

Example sentence: When the workers dragged their feet getting a project done, the manager enticed them to finish by promising an extra vacation day to whomever completed their portion first.

**Entrenched**—To be entrenched means to be dug in, to refuse to move, especially when it comes to thoughts and ideas. Think about how armies use trenches. They dig trenches, and then they can't easily move from the trenches without risking harm. The word entrenched comes from that idea.

Example sentence: Some people believe that debates are essentially useless since both parties often begin the debate already so entrenched in their ideas that they won't even listen to the other debater.

**Ephemeral**—Something ephemeral is very short-lived. It is fleeting and quickly gone.

Example sentence: The rainbow—one of the most beautiful natural phenomena—is quite ephemeral and generally disappears within just a few short minutes.

**Evince**—Evince is generally a verb meaning to show one's feelings.

Example sentence: The actions of the government as it tries and fails to help time and again evince anger and frustration.

**Expenditure**—An expenditure is a spending of money or other resources.

Example sentence: Buying all new china was an extravagant expenditure, but the noble felt it was necessary since he would be entertaining a duchess.

**Explanatory**—When something is explanatory, it explains something.

Example sentence: Quite often, students skip over explanatory examples and jump straight to the work; this is generally a mistake.

**Extensive**—When something is extensive, it is widespread or far-reaching. You might also say it is thorough.

Example sentence: Due to extensive cheating, the teacher shredded the tests and instead made each student meet with her for an oral examination of their knowledge.

**Feature**—A feature is a part of an item that is designed for a specific use. One feature of my car, for example, is a stereo system.

Example sentence: I was excited to check out all of the new features on my phone upgrade.

**Feeble**—To be feeble is to be weak.

Example sentence: The feeble elderly couple often needed their neighbors' help with the landscaping.

**Fetter**—To fetter is to hold someone or something back from what they want to do or accomplish.

Example sentence: While I love my parents, living under their rules often leaves me feeling fettered.

**Finite**—Finite is the opposite of infinite. When something is finite, it has a definitive beginning and ending.

Example sentence: The fact that the movie was finite saddened me—I wished it could go on and on forever.

**Fiscal**—When people describe things as fiscal (like the fiscal year), they are talking about money and the economy.

Example sentence: Because of excessive spending, the business was experiencing fiscal difficulties that threatened to bankrupt it.

**Florid**—Generally describing a person's face, this adjective means red or flushed.

Example sentence: Having run the 5K in brutal heat, the athlete rested with his florid face cradled in his hands.

**Former**—Former refers to the one before or in the past. The former president used to be the president, for example. If I give you two options and you choose the former, then you have chosen the first one that was given.

Example sentence: I was shocked when the former mayor of my town was revealed to be in the middle of a scandal, which plunged the town into a fiscal crisis.

**Forum**—A forum is a location or a meeting where people can talk about their thoughts, ideas, and opinions.

Example sentence: The teacher rearranged the desks into a circle to facilitate discussion and turn the classroom into a forum on governmental improvements.

**Frantic**—Frantic could also be expressed as desperate. When you are frantic about something, there is urgency to do all you can as you try to solve the problem.

Example sentence: The dog wandered off during the picnic, triggering a frantic search by all the family members.

**Frequent**—Frequent simply means often. When something happens frequently, it happens all the time.

Example sentence: His frequent tardiness led to a Saturday detention.

**Fundamental**—Fundamentals are basics. The fundamentals of reading would be learning the alphabet and phonics. The fundamentals of baseball are throwing, catching, and hitting.

Example sentence: After many in the class failed the math test because they weren't allowed to use calculators, the teacher made them return to fundamentals and practice adding, subtracting, multiplying, and dividing by hand.

**Germinate**—To germinate something is to take something with potential and make it start to grow. Quite often this term is used with seeds.

Example sentence: Part of the preschool's mission statement is "to germinate active and curious minds."

**Glom**—To glom is to attach to something (often in a blob-like manner).

Example sentence: Even despite continual cleaning, the boat was still covered in barnacles, which had glommed on to the hull.

**Glut**—A glut is a ridiculous abundance of something. It's having so much of something you don't even know what to do with it.

Example sentence: When the flood waters receded, there was a glut of carp left behind, flopping on the streets. The townspeople ate like kings that night and celebrated the day every year after with a Carp Festival.

**Grievance**—A grievance is a complaint. Think of it as something you would grieve over—something that makes you sad.

Example sentence: After the salesperson was seen taking a picture of my credit card, I felt it necessary to lodge a grievance against him as he was probably planning on stealing my identity.

**Haggle**—Haggling is the process two people go through as they exchange offers back and forth while trying to make a deal.

Example sentence: One reason I like garage sales so much is the opportunity to haggle with the seller and try to secure a better deal.

**Ignominious**—Something that is ignominious is undignified—it will likely cause the person experiencing it to feel shame or embarrassment.

Example sentence: My brother pulled the chair out from under me, causing me to sprawl on the ground in a very ignominious position.

**Illegible**—When something is illegible, it is unable to be read or understood.

Example sentence: With the prevalence of typing these days, many people have illegible handwriting due to lack of practice.

**Immured**—When someone is immured, they are held against their will in some way, often enclosed.

Example sentence: The young man felt trapped in the relationship, immured by his desire not to hurt her feelings.

**Impel**—To impel is to push or force someone to do something in some way.

Example sentence: Impelled by the fear of loneliness, many people resort to blind dates to try to find a companion.

**Inapplicable**—When something doesn't apply in a given situation, it is inapplicable. For example, you may have the quadratic equation memorized, which is great; however, that equation is inapplicable to many non-quadratic math problems.

Example sentence: While she had many skills, most of them were inapplicable to the current crisis; she would have to call for help.

**Incomprehensible**—Something that is incomprehensible is unable to be comprehended or understood.

Example sentence: The student's illegible handwriting and incomprehensible train of thought resulted in a very low grade on the essay.

**Incontestable**—Incontestable means unable to be contested. In other words, you can't dispute it or go against it.

Example sentence: The results of the election were incontestable; the candidate won by a landslide.

**Incorporate**—To incorporate is to fully include something. For example, you might incorporate an explanation of climate change into a paper on Antarctica.

Example sentence: The leader was harshly criticized when the press found out that he had failed to incorporate any women into the task force on family and children's rights.

**Incredulous**—When you're incredulous of something, you don't really believe it, or you have doubts about it.

Example sentence: The child looked at her friend incredulously when she tried to convince her that the monster was, in fact, not real.

**Indifference**—Indifference is that feeling of not feeling strongly about something one way or the other. You might feel indifference toward which teacher you get, or what you have for lunch, or any number of things.

Example sentence: Indifference is a dangerous emotion as it can lead to people drifting through life and never taking any risks or making any big decisions.

**Indistinguishable**—When two things are indistinguishable, they can't be told apart from one another: There are no distinguishing features.

Example sentence: Even though their mother could tell them apart, to everyone else the twins were indistinguishable.

**Ineffective**—When something is ineffective, it doesn't work. It doesn't have the effect it should.

Example sentence: Flushing ice cubes down the toilet is an ineffective strategy that kids try to ensure a snow day the next morning.

**Inefficacious**—This is pretty much the same as the previous word. Inefficacious just means not having the desired effect.

Example sentence: Studying can be inefficacious if you don't make sure to get rid of all distractions before beginning.

**Inexorable**—Inexorable is kind of like inevitable. It can't be avoided or stopped—it will occur no matter what.

Example sentence: The clock had been ticking constantly for the entire winter, counting out the inexorable passage of time.

**Ingenious**—For some reason, ingenious and genius mean the same thing.

Example sentence: The pirate queen was known for her ingenious plots to capture other ships.

**Innumerable**—When something is innumerable, it is unable to be counted. You'll notice *num* hidden away—this is also the root of the word number.

Example sentence: The grains of sand on the beach are truly innumerable.

**Institution**—An institution is an organization that has been created to fulfill a purpose (generally for the greater good). For example, governments, churches, and schools can all be examples of institutions. Generally, institutions are thought of as permanent or nearly impossible to get rid of.

Example sentence: Between churches, schools, and my mom's job as our small-town mayor, I often feel like I grew up in institutions.

**Insurrection**—An insurrection is a revolt or an uprising.

Example sentence: Though Catherine the Great is revered by Russians, the peasant insurrection during her time as ruler put a damper on her legacy.

**Integrate**—To integrate two or more things is to mix them together.

Example sentence: I don't remember the exact date, but at some point in seventh grade, the girls' lunch tables and the boys' lunch tables started to integrate and nothing was ever the same again.

**Intend**—Intend has to do with intentions. It's what you mean to do, not what you actually do. Every new year, many people intend to form new habits; what actually happens is a different story.

Example sentence: In the evenings, I always intend to get up early the next morning to increase my productivity. This rarely actually happens.

125

**Intermittent**—Intermittent just means off and on at a set interval.

Example sentence: The stoplight let cars proceed intermittently.

**Intuitive**—When something is intuitive, it is easy to use and figure out without directions. You can go based on your gut feeling and probably get it right.

Example sentence: While some people struggle to memorize math facts, other people find numbers to be intuitive and breeze through their classes.

**Inherent**—When something is inherent, it wasn't learned or created; it is naturally occurring. For example, some animals have an inherent fear of predators. You may have an inherent love of the color green or hatred of the smell of tomatoes.

Example sentence: As hard as they tried, my neighbors could not train their dog out of his inherent desire to dig holes.

**Insolent**—You might well get in trouble for acting insolent at school. Such behavior shows a general bad attitude, lack of respect, and overall grumpiness.

Example sentence: "Wouldn't you like to know," came the insolent reply from the teen when her father asked her why she had returned so late the night before.

**Intolerable**—When something is intolerable, you simply can't put up with (or tolerate) it.

Example sentence: "Your behavior is intolerable," her father responded before he grounded her.

**Invasive**—Think of the word invade. When something is invasive, it invades something or goes somewhere it isn't wanted.

Example sentence: Family get-togethers are always difficult since my great aunt likes to gossip; she goes around asking everyone highly invasive questions.

**Inversion**—To invert something is to turn it upside down. An inversion is the noun form of that word and means the act of turning upside down.

Example sentence: The scariest roller coaster in the park had the fastest speeds, the highest hills, and the most inversions.

**Irk**—When something irks you, it annoys you, but not in a major way. Someone leaving a dirty dish out, taking the middle piece of cake, not using their turn signal in traffic, or failing to do what they promised may irk you.

Example sentence: I was very irked when the teacher changed the assignment. While there was still plenty of time before the due date, I had already begun the research and had to change course due to the adjustments.

**Labyrinth**—Quite simply, a labyrinth is a maze.

Example sentence: Moving from a small family firm to a giant corporation was a big change, and I often found myself lost in the labyrinth of cubicles.

**Laden**—To be laden is to be weighed down with something physically. A shopping cart might be laden with groceries, for instance.

Example sentence: The mailman dreaded the holiday season when his bag became quite cumbersome to carry, laden as it was with packages full of presents.

**Latter**—Latter is the opposite of former. Former is the first thing mentioned, latter is the second or last.

Example sentence: I was given the option of either getting out of bed for school or getting grounded, and I foolishly choose the latter, which left me trapped at home over homecoming weekend.

**Liaison**—This is often used to mean a close connection or relationship. It can also mean a person who facilitates understanding between parties.

Example sentence: In the office, it was often my job to be a liaison between various parties.

**Magnitude**—The magnitude of something is how big it is.

Example sentence: My coworker seemed to have her head buried in the sand and didn't realize the magnitude of losing our biggest client.

**Malice**—Malice (*mal* at the beginning of the word means bad) is generally used to describe the feeling of one person wishing to do something harmful to another person.

Example sentence: It was a long-standing rivalry, and the malice off the field lead to overly aggressive behavior on the field, which resulted in the game being ended at halftime.

**Malign**—To malign someone is to say terrible things about them.

Example sentence: After he got a bad grade, he proceeded to malign the teacher to anyone who would listen.

**Manifest**—This can mean a variety of things. As a noun, it is a complete list. As a verb, it means to make appear or to make clear. As an adjective, it means obvious or clear.

Example sentence: The passenger manifest manifested to the detective the fact that the sought-after party was not on board the ship.

**Manipulate**—To manipulate something or someone is to change them to your liking. You might manipulate your parent's opinion on where to eat by casually mentioning pizza several times during the day. You might also manipulate clay into the shape of a vase.

Example sentence: While many people believe that data don't lie, in reality, data can be heavily manipulated to show just about whatever results are desired.

**Mantra**—A mantra is something that people repeat over and over to themselves in the hopes that it becomes true or as a means toward achieving a goal.

Example sentence: In the early days of January, people who appear to be just going about life are silently repeating their mantras in the hopes of fulfilling their New Years' resolutions.

**Marginalize**—This word refers to the action of making something less, often when it shouldn't be. A person's feelings may be marginalized or brushed away as not important.

Example sentence: The young girl always felt marginalized when her successful older siblings were around.

**Meander**—To meander is to wander in a non-straight line and with little or no haste or purpose.

Example sentence: If I get bored this afternoon, I may meander over to the park to see if anything is going on.

**Mechanization**—Mechanization is when something that used to be done by hand is now done by a machine.

Example sentence: Mechanization has caused great concern in the auto industry lately as workers have been laid off and their jobs replaced by robots.

**Meddle**—To meddle is to tamper with something, often human situations or emotions.

Example sentence: When my two best friends broke up, I tried to help them fix their relationship, but I only ended up making it worse. As my mom often says, "Meddling does no one any good."

**Metastasize**—When something metastasizes, it is spreading.

Example sentence: Luckily, the disease had been found before it metastasized, and so it appeared as if recovery were very likely.

**Mire**—To mire is to stick something down. When someone or something is mired, it can't be freed, but is stuck in a sticky situation either figuratively or literally.

Example sentence: I always cry during my favorite childhood book when the horse becomes mired in a bog and must be abandoned so that the quest can be completed.

**Monotony**—Monotony is the same thing over and over again.

Example sentence: As the semester progressed, I felt trapped in a scholastic monotony with nothing ever changing, each day exactly the same as the last.

150

**Motivation**—Motivation is what drives you. It's the feeling inside that makes you start that project, run that extra mile, or take the extra shift.

Example sentence: Since motivation was low, the teacher promised extra credit to the first student who turned in an "A"-worthy project.

**Mundane**—Something that is mundane is boring and normal. It's a regular everyday occurrence.

Example sentence: Until the fire alarms went off, it had just been a mundane Monday morning.

**Mutable**—Think about the math term permutation. A permutation has to do with all the different ways a set of numbers can be changed and rearranged into different orders. That root word *mut* generally has to do with change. Mutable describes something that is easy to or likely to change. Other words you might know with this root include mutate and commute.

Example sentence: The speaker was worried he would be unable to change the audience's minds, but it turned out they were much more mutable than he had anticipated.

**Mystify**—To mystify just means to confuse. Think about the word mystery with the same root. A mystery is confusing—mystifying someone confuses them.

Example sentence: The scientists were mystified at first as to the meaning of the data that they had collected.

**Net**—In describing pay, net pay is what is left after all taxes and fees are removed. In scientific terms, it could be what is left after all other considerations are removed. For example, when you weigh something and you remove the weight of the container, you are left with the net weight of what is in the container.

Example sentence: The charity race raised a net total of $3,500 after the administrative expenses and permit fees were paid out.

**Notation**—You know the word note; what you probably didn't realize is that it's a shortened version of notation. It's something you write to help you remember something or to convey information to another person.

Example sentence: By the time I bought the textbook, it had already had several other owners and the margins were filled with notations—some helpful, others decidedly not.

**Nuance**—A nuance is a subtle difference in the meaning or expression of something.

Example sentence: While the applicants responded to the question in a similar way, the nuances in their reactions helped the manager make a decision as to who would be a better fit for the job.

**Null**—Null means nothing; it's just another way of saying zero.

Example sentence: When the parties pass away, the contract becomes null and void.

**Obliterate**—To obliterate something is to completely and utterly destroy it beyond recognition.

Example sentence: The meteor obliterated the forest into which it crashed, scattering debris all over the countryside.

**Obstinate**—Obstinate is just the same as stubborn. It means refusing to give up even when wrong or faced with insurmountable forces against you.

Example sentence: Despite pleading, cajoling, and coercing, the young child obstinately refused to get in the bathtub.

**Oscillate**—To oscillate is to move back and forth in a predictable pattern at a set speed. The pendulum in a grandfather clock is a classic example of oscillation.

Example sentence: The oscillation of the carnival ride made me sick to my stomach.

**Onerous**—When something is onerous it is difficult to do, usually taking a lot of unpleasant work to complete.

Example sentence: As a veterinarian, I often have the onerous task of discussing expensive bills with clients.

**Panacea**—A panacea is a fix-all solution.

Example sentence: While most people view love as a panacea, I know from experience that it can't solve all problems.

**Parasitic**—Something that is parasitic attaches to something else and feeds off of it without giving anything back. This might be used to describe an actual parasite (like a tapeworm) or a person like the friend who always borrows money, but never returns it.

Example sentence: When one person would get wise to her parasitic ways, she would merely find someone else to leach the homework off of for the next few weeks.

**Parity**—Parity is equalness or being equal. It is the opposite of disparity, which is inequality.

Example sentence: Despite the parent's best efforts at parity, one of the children always felt that they had received less attention.

**Paradox**—A paradox is something that contradicts itself or sets up an impossible train of thought that never ends but always circles back on itself.

Example sentence: One of the most well-known paradoxes is the statement, "This statement is false."

**Partake**—To partake is the same as to participate. It is often used with food (to partake in a meal is to eat it) but can also be used with any given activity.

Example sentence: Even though I always insist I'm not hungry, my grandmother won't let me leave her home without partaking in at least one meal or snack with her and my grandfather.

**Paternal**—To be paternal is to act in a fatherly way. Paternal can also be used to describe things relating to fathers.

Example sentence: Even though I barely knew him, the old man acted in quite a paternal way to me and insisted on seeing me home safely when I became lost.

**Permeate**—To permeate is to soak through something, invading and saturating every part of it and leaving nothing untouched. Water permeates things in a flood, and smells permeate rooms and homes.

Example sentence: The smell of burned food permeated the kitchen as the family rushed to save their dinner.

**Permutation**—Remember the word mutable from above? Permutation has that same *mut* syllable indicating it's about change. Permutation has to do with all the different ways a set of items can be arranged in different orders. In how many ways can the order be changed?

Example sentence: In math class, the teacher explained permutations to us by making ten students line up in as many different ways as possible; the possibilities seemed endless.

**Perpetual**—Something that is perpetual is never-ending.

Example sentence: Life in the Arctic Circle is very difficult in the winter when whole communities are plunged into perpetual darkness for months on end.

**Perspective**—Your perspective is how you see things both literally (different seats in a theater have different perspectives of the stage) and figuratively (you and your parent may have different perspectives on your staying up until 3 A.M.).

Example sentence: Since he was the only young person in the office, he was often called into meetings to give a different perspective on various issues.

**Perturb**—To perturb is to disturb, but in an emotional way. A scary book or a strange person may perturb.

Example sentence: The teacher was quite perturbed by the actions of the small child, which were very out of character for a four-year-old.

**Pervading**—Pervading or pervade are often used as synonyms for permeate. Something (especially a smell) can be pervading when it permeates an area where it is not welcome.

Example sentence: The pervading smell was quite offensive to the students, who quickly jumped to open the windows.

**Phenomena**—Phenomena is the plural of the word phenomenon. A phenomenon is something that is known to exist or occur, the cause of which is often not clear. Planes going down in the Bermuda triangle is a well-known phenomenon.

Example sentence: A great crowd gathered to watch the strange phenomenon.

175

**Pittance**—A pittance is a pitiably small amount: not really enough to do anything with.

Example sentence: With her children and husband all gone, the widow somehow managed to live off the pittance given to her by neighborhood charities.

**Plasticity**—The plasticity of something is its ability to change and be molded.

Example sentence: The best time to learn a foreign language is when you're young; that's when you still have the most brain plasticity.

**Plenipotentiary**—A plenipotentiary is a person who has been given the authority to act on behalf of their country in foreign countries. Diplomats often act in this role, though true plenipotentiary power is rare.

Example sentence: During negotiations with France, Benjamin Franklin acted as a plenipotentiary for the United States.

**Posterity**—Posterity is the future of humankind: all of the people who will come in the future.

Example sentence: The collection of American historical artifacts at the museum is being carefully preserved for posterity.

**Postulate**—To postulate is to guess or to present an idea that is not proven. A TV personality may postulate that a certain person will be elected.

Example sentence: "Maybe there is a traffic jam," she postulated as she waited for her date who was very late.

**Potent**—Potent means very strong. Not physically, but of a high concentration. A smell or taste, for example, may be very potent.

Example sentence: As the potent fumes wafted through the laboratory, the alarms sounded to warn all the scientists to evacuate quickly.

**Prattle**—To prattle is to talk on and on while saying little of value.

Example sentence: Faced with an abundance of awkward silences, the young lady prattled endlessly to avoid the quiet.

**Predecessor**—The predecessor to something or someone is what came before. This word is often used to describe a person who held an office or job prior to the current office or job holder.

Example sentence: "My predecessor may have allowed talking in class, but I do not," the new teacher informed her students.

**Preposterous**—Something that is preposterous is so ridiculous as to be laughable.

Example sentence: The elderly man laughed and said "don't be preposterous," when his grandson suggested that he try the mechanical bull at the fair.

**Primitive**—Something that is primitive is very basic and not technologically advanced. For example, some might see flag signaling as a primitive form of long-distance communication.

Example sentence: Primitive computers took up whole buildings and had less computing power than the average flip phone does today.

**Pristine**—Something that is pristine is untouched and perfect. It is completely unmarred in any way.

Example sentence: One of my favorite sights is a field of pristine snow, untrampled by any animals or humans.

**Proliferate**—To proliferate is to grow, spread, and reproduce, often at a high rate of speed. Rumors tend to proliferate within schools, as do germs.

Example sentence: The weeds proliferated throughout the summer, and he quickly realized that having a pristine garden was impossible.

**Promulgate**—To promulgate an idea is to spread it around. There are a lot of programs, for example, that promulgate anti-bullying messages to students.

Example sentence: The man was asked to leave the gathering when he was heard to be promulgating his latest get-rich-quick scheme.

**Province**—A province is a geographical area under a government. Many countries have a province system instead of having states.

Example sentence: As a Canadian, I often simply respond with my province when Americans ask what state I'm from.

**Proxy**—A proxy is a substitute. A person standing in for another person can generally be called a proxy. In some situations, formal events like voting, getting married, and signing contracts can be done by proxy.

Example sentence: Since the CEO was incredibly busy that day, he had his assistant attend the board meeting to vote as his proxy.

**Psychological**—Things that are psychological have to do with the inner workings of our minds, which affect our feelings, emotions, and actions.

Example sentence: The doctor, having run out of tests to perform, came to the conclusion that the symptoms must have psychological causes.

**Quarrel**—To quarrel is to argue with someone. A quarrel is an argument.

Example sentence: The young nanny was constantly begging the children not to quarrel.

**Rapacious**—Someone who is rapacious is unable to be satisfied. They are very greedy and always looking to gain more of what they want.

Example sentence: The rapacious vultures searched for food all over the meadow.

**Receptive**—A person who is receptive is open to receiving things, quite often ideas.

Example sentence: While the student was nervous about asking to take the test again, the teacher was quite receptive to the idea.

**Redress**—Don't get tricked into thinking this word means to get dressed again. Instead, it means to fix or make a situation right where someone has been wronged.

Example sentence: The man who had been wrongfully imprisoned sought redress for his grievances.

**Reluctant**—To be reluctant is to act on the feeling of not wanting to do something. If you end up doing the thing, you do it in a manner that shows that you don't want to be doing it.

Example sentence: The teacher was reluctant to give up his Saturday to grade papers, but the students had already waited a week, so he sat down with his red pen and got started.

**Remonstrate**—To remonstrate is to object to something strongly or to speak out against something strongly.

Example sentence: The principal remonstrated the student's misbehavior.

**Repression**—Repression is the act of holding something down or back, especially ideas and movements.

Example sentence: The governmental repression of revolutionary societies became stronger each week.

**Reverence**—Reverence means showing great respect or a deep appreciation for something.

Example sentence: When entering the throne room, it is always necessary to show reverence for the king by bowing before him and kissing his ring.

**Rhetoric**—Rhetoric is the way in which people speak and argue to convey their points. Different people may have different styles of rhetoric: They may ask questions, they may use persuasive language, they may yell, they may trick. All of those are types of rhetoric.

Example sentence: The country quickly got tired of the candidates' loud rhetorical blustering.

200

**Sanction**—Sanction is a very interesting word as it has seemingly opposite meanings. Make sure you pay very close attention to the context. Sometimes sanction refers to officially approving or allowing something to happen. The school might sanction a dance, meaning it's officially approved by the administration. However, sanctions can also be negative—a penalty for something done that is bad. Usually the context of negative sanctions is legal; when the word is used in this manner, it often refers to one country placing sanctions on another country for things like human rights violations.

Example sentence: "Just know that I do not sanction this event," said the major when the town council voted to have the festival against her wishes.

**Scuttling**—Scuttling is a very specific type of movement. It's moving very quickly with tiny (often not smooth) steps. Think about how crabs may run along a beach—they're almost always scuttling.

Example sentence: The pickpocket checked over his shoulder one more time before scuttling down an alley with his ill-gotten gains.

**Scenario**—A scenario is the setup for a work of fiction, a book, movie, or play. It can also be any imagined situation that people put themselves in, such as discussing what could happen in the future or things that should have happened in the past.

Example sentence: My English teacher proposed an interesting scenario—what books would you take with you if you were stuck on a deserted island?

**Seamless**—Think of a shirt without seams—it's completely smooth and has no breaks in the fabric. When something is seamless, it is very smooth. This word is often used as a synonym for flawless.

Example sentence: The director was thrilled when the whole production came together seamlessly.

**Sentiment**—A sentiment is how you feel or what you say about something that has occurred.

Example sentence: While he expressed nice sentiments about being sorry, she couldn't bring herself to forgive his mistakes.

**Sentinel**—A sentinel is a soldier whose job it is to keep watch over something.

Example sentence: The sentinel rushed to the general with news of invaders.

**Sequence**—A sequence is the order that things are in or the order that they should be in.

Example sentence: The librarian got very upset when she found out that her assistant was shelving books in the wrong sequence.

**Shingled**—Something described as shingled would have the same layered look as the shingles on a roof.

Example sentence: As odd as it looked, shingled hair was quite popular in the early 2000s.

**Skeptic**—A skeptic is someone who is skeptical, or doubtful, of something.

Example sentence: Jack continued to power forward with his extravagant plans, despite the loud voices of his skeptics.

**Sluggish**—When described as sluggish, things are slow or moving like a slug.

Example sentence: I'm incredibly sluggish if I don't have any coffee in the morning.

**Squalid**—When described as squalid, things are run down, dirty, and often infested with vermin. This is often the result of war or poverty.

Example sentence: Despite her best efforts at fixing and cleaning, the apartment remained at best squalid and at worst unlivable.

**Squelch**—Squelch is an onomatopoeia; the word means the sound it makes. Squelch is the sound that might be made if you tried to pull your foot out of thick mud or if you stepped on a slug.

Example sentence: With soaking wet socks and shoes, every step squelched.

**Stagnate**—To stagnate is to stop moving forward. This is generally not physical movement.

Example sentence: The project had stagnated, which caused great concern with the management team.

**Stewardship**—A steward is someone who takes care of something. Stewardship, then, is the noun form of the act of taking care of something.

Example sentence: As the result of careful stewardship, the manor survived the 50 years of being boarded up with only a bit of dust to tell of the long emptiness.

**Stupefied**—To be stupefied is to be made temporarily stupid. This generally happens if something really sudden or unexpected occurs.

Example sentence: After witnessing the last-minute heartbreaking loss, many fans left the stadium with stupefied looks on their faces.

**Subjugate**—To subjugate a person or group of people is to put them under your total control. This is especially applicable in war-time situations when entire populations are conquered and subjugated.

Example sentence: The hero rode gallantly into town, determined to free the subjugated people.

**Subordinate**—Someone who is subordinate is lower in status, usually in a workplace. A worker is subordinate to the boss.

Example sentence: The hallmark of a good manager is when they treat their subordinates with care, kindness, and fairness.

**Subsequent**—Something that is subsequent comes after something else. For example, my birthday is subsequent to that of my older sibling.

Example sentence: After getting a D on the midterm, he resolved to study harder for any subsequent tests.

**Substantial**—When something is substantial, it is not insignificant, but almost the opposite. It is of an important size or amount.

Example sentence: The restaurant lost a substantial amount of money when it changed management.

**Sufficient**—When something is described as sufficient, it means that it is enough.

Example sentence: While I was doubtful that we'd have enough food to feed everyone, it ended up being a sufficient amount.

**Supplemental**—Something that is supplemental adds something unnecessary, but helpful, to something else. There may be supplemental information at the end of a chapter. A family may pay for a vacation with supplemental income from a part-time job.

Example sentence: The supplemental assistance from neighbors helped the family through tough times.

**Sustenance**—Sustenance is what sustains a person. Generally, this is used as a fancy word for food.

Example sentence: After having been shipwrecked for months, the sailors craved sustenance other than dried fish and leaves.

**Swayed**—To sway is to move slightly back and forth. However, this term can be used figuratively as well as literally. In an argument, you may have swayed your opponent. They didn't actually move back and forth, but maybe their opinions moved slightly.

Example sentence: As the boat swayed, I felt my stomach turn.

**Symmetric**—Something that is symmetric is the same on both sides. For example, if a person has a symmetrical face, then the left and right sides of their face would be identical.

Example sentence: By very definition, all circles must be symmetric in all directions.

**Synthetic**—Something that is synthetic is made artificially, not naturally.

Example sentence: Clothing made from synthetic material may last longer, but it also tends to breathe less, causing sweat, smells, and acne.

**Sullen**—To be sullen is to be grumpy and unenthusiastic. It is a type of bad mood wherein you do things only under protest. You might think of it as being related to sulking.

Example sentence: The sullen young man was often reprimanded by his mother for his bad attitude.

**Tactile**—Something that is tactile has to do with the sense of touch. A tactile sensation, for example, is a sensation of being touched in some way.

Example sentence: When I was young, I had a tactile disorder whereby the feeling of grass and other things against my skin caused me great distress.

**Tangible**—Something that is tangible can be seen and touched (as compared to the opposite intangible).

Example sentence: The tangible benefit of saving for retirement is obviously the money; the intangible benefit is peace of mind.

**Tedious**—Something that is tedious is repetitive and boring. It takes a long time and doesn't engage the mind.

Example sentence: The tedious task of hand stitching clothing is thankfully no longer necessary due to the advent of the sewing machine.

**Tout**—To tout is to aggressively try to sell something, to sing its praises to get someone to buy it.

Example sentence: I left quickly when I discovered the so-called party was just an excuse for the hostess to tout her overpriced essential oils.

**Transaction**—When something is a transaction, it has something to do with the purchase or exchange of goods or services.

Example sentence: The person she thought was her friend was really just interested in a transactional relationship.

**Transit**—To transit is to move from one place to another. As a noun, transit can also refer to a network of public busses, trains, and streetcars.

Example sentence: Since her car had broken down, she found it necessary to take public transit to work for a few weeks.

**Traipsing**—When one is traipsing, they are coming and going or moving in a carefree manner.

Example sentence: He finally had to put a stop to the children traipsing in and out of the house with their shoes covered in mud.

**Tributary**—A tributary is a stream or river upstream that feeds into a bigger river.

Example sentence: The Ohio River, while large, is just a tributary of the mighty Mississippi River.

**Ubiquitous**—When something is ubiquitous, it is found everywhere. It is common.

Example sentence: The flags were ubiquitous in the highly patriotic town.

**Unassuming**—When something or someone is unassuming, they are unthreatening and down to earth.

Example sentence: Everyone liked the high school principal. His unassuming nature made him easy to work with.

**Unrequited**—When feelings are unrequited, they are not returned in kind. This word is often used to describe one-sided love.

Example sentence: Driven mad by unrequited love, the story's heroine wandered the moors for the rest of her life and haunted her beloved after her death.

**Unseemly**—Something that is unseemly might otherwise be described as inappropriate for the situation.

Example sentence: While appropriate for milking cows, overalls are an unseemly choice for a fine French restaurant.

**Unstinting**—Something that is unstinting is given without pause or second thought.

Example sentence: My favorite teacher gave me unstinting support in my quest for academic excellence.

**Unveil**—To unveil is to reveal. Think of a bride walking down the aisle wearing her veil and then removing her veil to reveal her face to the groom.

Example sentence: The excitement was noticeable as the crowd waited for the mayor to unveil the new city monument.

**Usurp**—To usurp is to overthrow. This word is often used to discuss overthrowing governments and other authorities.

Example sentence: It is the duty of several agencies to find and arrest anyone who intends to usurp the government.

**Validate**—To validate something is to say that it is valid, true, or accurate. Quite often, businesses will validate parking. That is, they'll stamp the parking ticket to indicate that the person who parked had a true reason to be there.

Example sentence: Though the woman claimed that she owned the house, her words needed to be validated by calling the local public records office.

**Vantage**—Vantage is a spot with a good view to see what needs to be seen.

Example sentence: From their vantage point on the second story, they could see the whole parade while staying nice and warm.

**Verifiable**—Something that is verifiable is able to be verified, or proven correct. Facts are generally verifiable while opinions are not.

Example sentence: His alibi was not verifiable and so he was left on the list of suspects.

**Vernacular**—The vernacular is the common or slang terms that people in a given community use.

Example sentence: While parents might think it's rude or confusing, most students have vernacular terms that they and their friends use frequently.

**Versatile**—Something that is versatile can be used in many different ways.

Example sentence: Anytime you go camping you should take a good length of cording. It's a versatile tool that can help in many dangerous situations.

**Vestigial**—Something that is vestigial is a small left-behind part of something much bigger.

Example sentence: The one standing hut was the vestigial remains of a once-mighty empire.

**Virtuous**—Something that is virtuous has virtue, or a high sense of morality.

Example sentence: The virtuous young people refused to take part in the cheating ring that was quickly growing at their school.

**Wayside**—The wayside is exactly what it sounds like, the side of the road. This term is also often used in a figurative sense.

Example sentence: It is often a sad fact of life that when someone begins dating, their friends are pushed to the wayside.

**Yearning**—Yearning is to want something with all your heart. To crave it at the expense of all else.

Example sentence: Although the young man liked his hometown, he felt a sense of yearning for international travel.

250

# PART 4
# Writing

# Writing for the Digital SAT

## Introduction and Strategies

### What Is Tested on the SAT Writing?

When you write in academic settings and in your future career, you will need to use correct grammar, proper wording, logical organization, and persuasive evidence. The SAT Writing tests your skill in determining which choices lead to the highest quality essays. In addition to your knowledge of specific grammar rules, a broad understanding of written English will ensure you do your very best on this section. When in doubt about your approach to the SAT Writing, keep in mind that if you are using the same skills that would be effective in editing a paper, you are likely doing things the right way.

### How Is the SAT Writing Structured?

- Part of the Reading and Writing Section (two modules of 27 questions each, 32 minutes each)
- The first Reading and Writing module will be of standard difficulty, and the second module will be more or less difficult depending on your performance on the first module.
- Approximately 25 of the 54 total Reading and Writing questions are Writing ones.
- Out of these 25 questions, about 14 relate to Standard English Conventions and about 11 relate to the Expression of Ideas.
- The writing questions come after the reading questions in a module.

### SAT Writing Dos and Don'ts

**Do use the full amount of time available.** As you probably know from having to edit papers for school, good editing takes time. Take approximately 70 seconds to complete each of the Writing questions. Some of the writing questions may take less time than some of the reading questions, so allocate any extra time from writing questions to the earlier reading questions. When you evaluate more complicated Writing questions, you can make notes on the provided scrap paper so that you fully understand what the question is asking.

**Don't rush and make careless errors.** Students are usually aware when they have difficulty with a Math or Reading question. With SAT Writing questions, it is easy to *think* you are doing great but to actually make a careless mistake. If you are still finishing the Reading and Writing section with quite a bit of time left, you may want to slow down to be sure you are getting all of the needed information and you fully understand the question that is being asked. This is a better use of time than having a few minutes at the end of the section to just sit there.

### Example

The Roseto Effect is a concept that has expanded scientists' understanding of the effect of mental health on physical health. It has been found that there are some areas in which certain conditions, such as heart disease, are much less common. Scientists believe this may be due to the feeling of connectedness in the community contributing to greater mental health and thus positively ________ physical health.

Which choice completes the text so that it conforms to the conventions of Standard English?

(A) influenced
(B) influencing
(C) has influence
(D) had influenced

If you rush through a question like this, you will most likely make a careless mistake. The final sentence of the text says that the feeling of connectedness in the community "contributing" to greater mental health. In order to maintain a parallel structure with the "ing" ending, the only acceptable option would be (B). "Contributing" and "influencing" will maintain parallelism. Choices (A), (C), and (D) all change the verb structure such that a parallel style is not maintained. If you rush through a question like this, you might think you are in good shape, when in fact you missed a detail essential to correctly answering the question.

**Do look at enough context.** In general, be sure to read the entirety of the given text. If you have any doubt about whether you have sufficient context to make a decision, reread the context of the text just to be sure.

**Don't only consider part of a sentence.** It is easy to jump to an answer based on just a small part of a sentence. Keep an open mind as you read the entirety of a sentence. If you have difficulty with jumping to answers too quickly, try covering up the answer choices until you have carefully considered the relevant context.

### Example

Marquis went to his ________ house—he was eager to visit with both his mother and father.

Which choice completes the text so that it conforms to the conventions of Standard English?

(A) parent's
(B) parents
(C) parenting
(D) parents'

Unless you consider the information later in the sentence, you will have insufficient context to determine the correct option. The second part of the sentence states that Marquis was going to meet with "both his mother and father." This clarifies that he was meeting with both parents, and it is reasonable to infer that his mother and father shared the house. So, since there are two parents, show possession by putting an apostrophe *after* the *s* as found in choice **(D)**. Choice (A) would work if you had a singular parent. Choice (B) would work if you were using *parents* as a noun instead of using the word to show possession. And choice (C) would suggest that Marquis is going to some house where he does his own parenting, which is inconsistent with the later part of the sentence.

**Do mouth out the text as you read it.** One of the best strategies for editing a paper is to read it out loud in your head—that way, you will pick up on all sorts of errors that you would miss if you only quickly scanned your paper. Many of the correct answers on the SAT Writing can be found based on how things sound. In particular, punctuation, proper verb use, and parallel structure all lend themselves well to analysis through hearing. When taking the SAT, your job is not to go in front of a class and precisely explain the grammatical justification for an answer. Instead, you simply need to arrive at the correct answer by any means necessary, including trusting your hearing.

**Don't overly rely on intuition—know the rules.** While hearing the passage can be extremely helpful, use this approach to *supplement* rather than *replace* careful analysis based on grammar knowledge. Many potential grammar issues—like advanced punctuation concepts and subject-verb agreement—won't be clear unless you understand the underlying grammar concepts. Fortunately, this book comprehensively reviews the grammar you need to know.

### Example

Teacher letters of recommendation are a key component of a college __________ is important for students to develop good relationships with their educators.

Which choice completes the text so that it conforms to the conventions of Standard English?

(A) application; accordingly, it
(B) application, accordingly, it
(C) application; accordingly it
(D) application accordingly, it

Mouthing this out can help you determine where natural pauses are needed. First, a pause is needed between the two independent clauses (complete sentences)—after "application" and before "accordingly." Second, a pause is needed after "accordingly," since it is an introductory word before the second independent clause. This intuitive knowledge will only get you so far. It is important to know that a comma cannot join two independent clauses together unless it has a conjunction like *for, and,* or *but* along with it. Also, conjunctive adverbs like "accordingly" must have a semicolon precede them when they are used to join two independent clauses. So, the correct answer is choice **(A)** since it has a semicolon to separate the two independent clauses and a comma to separate the introductory word "accordingly" from the following independent clause. Intuition and grammar knowledge together make for an unstoppable combination on the SAT Writing questions.

**Do use the choices to help clarify your thinking.** The choices can help you see where a question is headed—look at what is different among the choices to determine what concept is being evaluated. If the choices use different verbs, watch out for subject-verb agreement. If the choices use different punctuation, watch for independent and dependent clauses. And if the choices have different lengths, watch for wordiness. Also, if two or more choices mean essentially the same thing, that is a clue that it will not be those options. For example, since both a semicolon and a period can be used to separate two independent clauses, if you see two options that only differ in that one uses a period and one uses a semicolon, it is likely *neither* of the options.

**Don't jump to a choice too quickly.** Keep an open mind as you review the choices. Be sure you have considered what the question is asking, what the surrounding context says, and what the subtle differences among the choices entail. Do not treat the SAT Writing questions like ones found on a recall test you may find in school, in which you can quickly remember the answer from class. Instead, take your time.

### Example

I stayed up late last night studying for my test. __________ I am rather tired this morning. I am afraid my test results will not reflect my true knowledge of the material.

Which choice completes the text with the most logical transition?

(A) However,
(B) In contrast,
(C) Additionally,
(D) Consequently,

The primary way you should attack this problem is to consider the logical relationship between what comes before the transitional word and what comes after it. The sentence before says that the narrator stayed up late studying for a test, and the part after says that the narrator is now rather tired. A transition that expresses a cause-and-effect relationship would be best, since it is because the narrator stayed up late that now the narrator is tired. "Consequently" in choice **(D)** signifies a cause-and-effect relationship, and it is correct. In addition to attacking the problem this way, you can look at the choices to see what clues are evident. First, all the words are transitional, making it clear that you will need to look at what comes before and after the underlined word to determine the correct answer. Second, you can look for similarities among the answers. "However" and "in contrast" are synonymous, both meaning that what comes before and what comes after are opposites. Since these two options are synonymous, you are able to eliminate them both. While this strategy is likely applicable on just a handful of problems, it can be a powerful tool if you are trying to break the tie between a couple of options.

**Do consider widely agreed upon grammar rules. There will be one definite answer.** The makers of the SAT ensure that when they ask a question, it has been thoroughly evaluated so that it clearly has a single answer. The SAT Writing questions will ask you about core grammatical concepts where there is widespread agreement, like subject-verb agreement, proper verb tense, and correct use of punctuation. It is especially important for students who are strong in math to keep this in mind, since they are used to the definitive answers found in math and sometimes feel that grammar rules are a matter of opinion. Keep in mind that while there are many ways that an essay can be crafted, out of the four options given for each SAT Writing question, there will be *one and only one correct answer*.

**<u>Don't</u> worry about stylistic preferences and pet peeves.** Here are some examples of pet peeves that some people have, which are not considered widely agreed upon grammar rules:

- Using the Oxford comma—a comma before the *and* in a list of three or more items
- Never starting a sentence with *because*
- Never using the more informal second person, *you*, and always using the more formal third person, *he, she, they*, in papers

The SAT will not test you on concepts like this because not everyone agrees on them. So, you should give the SAT Writing the benefit of the doubt—instead of overthinking a question because you think it is testing some random rule, know that there is indeed one correct answer and look at enough context until you clearly see what that correct answer is.

### Example

When preparing a college application essay, be sure to tell ______ authentic story. If you have overcome significant challenges in your life or have had interesting experiences, the application essay is a great place to showcase your story.

Which choice completes the text so that it conforms to the conventions of Standard English?

(A) one's
(B) her
(C) their
(D) your

Students are often told to avoid using the second person, "you," in their writing and instead use the third person, "he, she, or they." While this is a preference that many educators and writers may have, avoiding the second person is not technically a grammar rule. In this text, we cannot tell from the first sentence what word would be appropriate. It is only after examining the second sentence and seeing that the writer uses "you" and "your" that we realize that in order to be consistent with the wording, choice (D) is correct. This is the only option that uses "you" just like the second sentence does. By realizing that there is one definite answer and that the SAT will not test you on pet peeves, you will be able to keep an open mind as you evaluate the choices.

## How Can I Improve My Overall Grammar Knowledge?

- **Read widely.** Reading will, of course, help you improve your reading comprehension. However, it will also greatly help you with grammar. By reading high-quality books and articles, you will develop an intuitive sense of what language sounds proper and what arguments are logically organized. This is especially important when building a sense of what word choices are most appropriate. If you rely too much on a thesaurus when coming up with synonyms, you may have difficulty identifying the word that is best to use in a given context.
- **Write as much as you can.** The more you write, the better you will be at determining what arguments flow well and what organization of your essays is most appropriate. You will have a better sense of how to avoid repetition, maintain parallel structure, and maintain subject-verb agreement. When you have had to be on the lookout for good writing strategies in your own writing, you will be much more in tune with looking for good strategies in the writing of other material.

- **Take rigorous courses that encourage you to write and read high-quality material as much as possible.** While it is tempting to take easier courses where it will not be difficult to earn an (A), this will ultimately be a disservice to you when it comes to SAT Writing questions. Take courses like AP English Language and Composition, AP English Literature and Composition, and any of the other AP humanities courses. All of these courses will require you to read challenging, high-quality material and to write organized essays. The stronger your reading and writing skills, the better you will do on the SAT Writing.
- **Practice writing in your daily life.** Do not limit your writing to the classroom. Look for opportunities to write recreationally. Instead of texting, try sending an email with full paragraphs. Instead of only video chatting with a distant friend or relative, try writing a letter. Instead of just scanning online articles, give your opinions in the online comments. If you are more ambitious, try entering writing contests, writing a blog of your own, or sending well-crafted correspondence to public officials with your opinions on important issues. Rather than waiting to the last minute to write your college application essays, begin working on them in your junior year so that you can both write the best possible essays and improve your writing and editing skills.
- **Practice editing.** Use a cloud-based word processing program so that you can easily have your papers edited—encourage your friends to do the same. If you and your friends practice editing one another's papers, not only will your papers be far better, but you will also sharpen the skills needed for success on the SAT Writing.

## How Can I Use This Book to Prepare for the SAT Writing?

Practice with the specific types of questions that are most challenging for you:

- **Subject-Verb Agreement** (pages 223–228)
- **Number and Tense Agreement** (pages 229–231)
- **Punctuation** (pages 232–250)
- **Sentence Structure and Organization** (pages 251–259)
- **Transitions** (pages 260–270)
- **Rhetorical Synthesis** (pages 271–278)

Practice with the **Additional Practice Exercises**, starting on page 278, reviewing the types of material you will encounter on the actual test.

Practice with **Advanced Practice**, starting on page 284, that present the most challenging types of Writing questions you could encounter on the SAT.

Practice with the **full-length Reading and Writing tests**, carefully watching your time management.

Good luck!

# Grammar Review

## Subject-Verb Agreement

The SAT Writing tests your skill in determining whether nouns, pronouns, and verbs agree numerically. A singular subject should be paired with a singular verb, and a plural subject should be paired with a plural verb.

### Example 1

Incorrect: My friend's brand new car need to be washed.

Correct: My friend's brand new car **needs** to be washed.

Explanation: The subject is what is doing the action. In this case, the car is the thing that has to be washed. Since the subject "car" is singular, it requires a singular verb, "needs."

### Example 2

Incorrect: The pack of wolves are howling.

Correct: The pack of wolves **is** howling.

Explanation: The subject is the singular word "pack," not "wolves." Even though there are multiple wolves within a pack, the subject is still just the singular "pack." "Pack" is an example of a *collective noun*—the word refers to the singular group instead of the plural members of the group. Some other examples of collective nouns include *group, flock, class, herd, company*, and *collection*. Watch out for prepositions—words like "to," "of," "from," and "in"—that typically come before a description of the subject. In this example, "of" comes before "wolves," with "of wolves" describing the subject "pack." If a word or phrase starts with a preposition, that will likely not be the subject.

### Example 3

Incorrect: The smoke detector has dead batteries, which is why they are beeping.

Correct: The smoke detector has dead batteries, which is why **it is** beeping.

Explanation: The earlier nouns in the sentence are "detector" and "batteries." Which of these could most logically be described as "beeping?" It would have to be a detector—batteries don't beep. So, both the pronoun and the verb must change to be the singular "it is" instead of the plural "they are."

### Example 4

Incorrect: When Darnell and Liam go to the game, he always insists on paying for the tickets.

Correct: When Darnell and Liam go to the game, **Darnell** always insists on paying for the tickets.

Explanation: If a pronoun is vague, it must be clarified. In this case, the "he" could have referred to either Darnell or Liam. By revising it to have the person's actual name, the sentence becomes clear. Sometimes students worry about replacing a pronoun, thinking that they cannot be certain as to its substitute. Do not worry about that—if a pronoun needs to be replaced because it is vague, consider the potential replacements to be true.

### Example 5

Incorrect: Everybody in the school are excited for the assembly.

Correct: Everybody in the school **is** excited for the assembly.

Explanation: "Everybody" is singular, even though it refers to several people. Other singular pronouns include *everyone, anybody, no one, someone, another, either, neither*, and *each*. If you are unsure if a pronoun is singular or plural, simply take the pronoun and place it next to the verb to see if it makes sense. For example, you would say "anybody is here" instead of "anybody are here."

**Singular and Plural Agreement Practice**—select the correct choice given the context.

1. The food for both of my dogs (A) is *or* (B) are expensive.
2. My friend Andrew forgot (A) its *or* (B) his lunch money.
3. (A) These *or* (B) This books are really interesting.
4. All the cars, including mine, (A) is *or* (B) are legally parked on the street and will not be towed.
5. The flock of geese (A) are *or* (B) is migrating south for the winter.
6. My English teacher and my math teacher always (A) give *or* (B) gives detailed instructions in class.
7. The lamp, which has three light bulbs, (A) is *or* (B) are in need of some maintenance.
8. I discovered in my studies that while I enjoyed painting and sculpture, (A) it was *or* (B) they were music I found most appealing.
9. The sights and sounds of the World's Fair (A) were *or* (B) was truly memorable.
10. A dog that can still walk on all fours (A) are *or* (B) is considered mobile.
11. When starting the car, be sure that (A) the emergency brake *or* (B) it is deactivated.
12. (A) Those *or* (B) This plants really have to be watered.
13. The captain of the team (A) has led *or* (B) have led her team to victory.
14. When one is speaking to one's friends online, one should be certain that the chat is from one's friends (A) themselves *or* (B) oneself and not from a bot.
15. The car and truck were in a close race, with (A) the one *or* (B) the truck currently in the lead.
16. Anyone who loves the great outdoors (A) is *or* (B) are excited for good weather.
17. Neither terrible snow nor awful rain (A) keeps *or* (B) keep the mail from being delivered.
18. Halley's Comet, one of the solar system's short period comets, (A) is *or* (B) are projected to pass by Earth in the year 2061.
19. Since (A) it *or* (B) they will not be available on the trail, bring food and water with you for the backpacking journey.
20. Zaha Hadid, an architect known for her parametric designs (i.e., ones that embrace adaptive shapes and forms), (A) are *or* (B) is a native of Iraq.

### Answers

1. The food for both of my dogs (A) is expensive. "Food" is the subject and is singular.

2. My friend Andrew forgot (B) his lunch money. "Andrew" is a singular person, so "his" would be appropriate.

3. (A) These books are really interesting. "Books" is a plural word and "these" is used in reference to plural nouns.

4. All the cars, including mine, (B) are legally parked on the street and will not be towed. In this case, "all" is referring to the entire set of cars and is plural.

5. The flock of geese (B) is migrating south for the winter. "Flock" is a collective noun and is singular.

6. My English teacher and my math teacher always (A) give detailed instructions in class. There is a compound subject with both the English teacher and the math teacher, so the plural verb "give" is needed.

7. The lamp, which has three light bulbs, (A) is in need of some maintenance. The subject is "lamp," not "light bulbs," and "lamp" is a singular word that needs the singular verb "is."

8. I discovered in my studies that while I enjoyed painting and sculpture, (A) it was music I found most appealing. The singular subject "music" comes later in the sentence, but it is in fact the thing that the narrator finds most appealing.

9. The sights and sounds of the World's Fair (A) were truly memorable. There is a compound subject—sights and sounds—that requires a plural verb, "were."

10. A dog that can still walk on all fours (B) is considered mobile. The subject is the singular "dog," not the plural "fours." Thus, the singular verb "is" would be correct.

11. When starting the car, be sure that (A) the emergency brake is deactivated. In this case, there is a vague pronoun, so clarifying it by saying "the emergency brake" would be appropriate.

12. (A) Those plants really have to be watered. The word "plants" is plural, so the word "those" would be correct.

13. The captain of the team (A) has led her team to victory. The subject is "captain," which is singular. A singular verb "has" is needed.

14. When one is speaking to one's friends online, one should be certain that the chat is from one's friends (A) themselves and not from a bot. The word "themselves" refers to the word "friends," which is plural.

15. The car and truck were in a close race, with (B) the truck currently in the lead. The pronoun would be vague in this case, so clarify with "the truck."

16. Anyone who loves the great outdoors (A) is excited for good weather. The word "anyone" is considered to be singular, so the singular "is" would match.

17. Neither terrible snow nor awful rain (A) keeps the mail from being delivered. "Neither" and "nor" refer to objects one at a time instead of collectively, and require a singular verb; "keeps" is singular and would work.

18. Halley's Comet, one of the solar system's short period comets, (A) is projected to pass by Earth in the year 2061. The verb must agree with the singular "comet," not the plural "comets," since it is the "comet" that will be coming by Earth in the future.

19. Since (B) they will not be available on the trail, bring food and water with you for the backpacking journey. The plural word "they" refers to the plural "food and water" that should go on the trail with a hiker.

20. Zaha Hadid, an architect known for her parametric designs (i.e., ones that embrace adaptive shapes and forms), (B) is a native of Iraq. Go back to the beginning of the sentence to see that the subject is the singular person Zaha Hadid, and not the other possible nouns like "designs," "shapes," or "forms."

## Verb Agreement

The SAT Writing will test your skill in verb usage. You will often be asked to determine whether a verb is used in the correct tense. Be aware of the basics of verb conjugation, as outlined in this table (you may have learned quite a bit of verb conjugation in a world language course).

| Present | Past | Future |
|---|---|---|
| She is<br>They are<br>I am | She was<br>They were<br>I was | She will<br>They will<br>I will |
| **Present Perfect** | **Past Perfect** | **Future Perfect** |
| She has been<br>They have been<br>I have been | She had been<br>They had been<br>I had been | She will have been<br>They will have been<br>I will have been |

### Example 1

Incorrect: I went on a trip to Florida, and I have a memorable experience.

Correct: I went on a trip to Florida, and I **had** a memorable experience.

Explanation: Make sure that the verbs are used consistently in the sentence. Change "have" to "had" so that the sentence is all in the past tense.

### Example 2

Incorrect: My friend's group has been working hard on the school project, while most of the other groups are not doing so.

Correct: My friend's group has been working hard on the school project, while most of the other groups **have not been** doing so.

Explanation: The project has not yet been completed—it is an ongoing activity, so the present perfect tense is appropriate.

### Example 3

In addition to ensuring that verbs are in the correct tense, the SAT Writing will ask questions to check for both tense *and* number agreement.

Incorrect: When Eli lived across from two excellent parks, he have ample opportunities for outdoor recreation.

Correct: When Eli lived across from two excellent parks, he **had** ample opportunities for outdoor recreation.

Explanation: In the first version, "have" is incorrect with subject-verb agreement and tense. In the corrected version, "had" uses the correct past tense and is numerically consistent with the subject "Eli."

**Verb Agreement Practice**—select the correct choice given the context.

1. Yesterday, I (A) ate *or* (B) eat lunch at home.
2. Whenever I walk past that store, I always (A) felt *or* (B) feel like making a purchase.
3. My two aunts have always (A) taken *or* (B) took the bus to work.
4. The large boulder fell into the river and (A) diverted *or* (B) divert the water out of its typical path.
5. You should leave a nice review for a travel guide who (A) do *or* (B) does a good job.
6. Before watching the sequel, I (A) watching *or* (B) watched the prequel.
7. They have been swimming since early this morning and (A) is *or* (B) are continuing to do so now.
8. If you have the instructions, assembly of the new bicycle (A) were *or* (B) is easy.
9. It would (A) have *or* (B) had been an easy test if I had studied some more.
10. My neighbor will not (A) entertained *or* (B) entertain any new offers to purchase his old car.
11. When she flew to visit her relatives overseas, she (A) took *or* (B) takes only two flights.
12. The Renaissance artist (A) draws *or* (B) drew pencil sketches before he turned his ideas into paintings.
13. I will read my textbook this evening after I (A) had completed *or* (B) complete my other homework.
14. An infant may have trouble falling asleep, while teenagers rarely (A) has *or* (B) have any difficulty doing so.
15. The guard dog barked at a predator that (A) approached *or* (B) will approach the herd of sheep.
16. My father is unsure of what dish to (A) brought *or* (B) bring to the potluck dinner.
17. The flock of birds (A) have *or* (B) has taken off from the steep cliff to find food.
18. Emma did a great job on her last assignment, and I am confident she (A) will do *or* (B) had done well on the one due next week.
19. Jesse Owens, winner of four Olympic gold medals, (A) was *or* (B) were born in Oakville, Alabama.
20. What colleges have you (A) chose *or* (B) chosen for your in-person visits?

## ✓ Answers

1. Yesterday, I (A) ate lunch at home.
   "Ate" is in the past tense, which makes sense given that the sentence begins with "yesterday," putting the event in the past.

2. Whenever I walk past that store, I always (B) feel like making a purchase.
   "Feel" is in the present tense, consistent with the earlier present tense verb "walk."

3. My two aunts have always (A) taken the bus to work.
   "Have taken" is the correct conjugation, while "have took" would not work; "took" by itself is fine to express the past tense, but not in conjunction with "have."

4. The large boulder fell into the river and (A) diverted the water out of its typical path.
   The earlier verb "fell" is in the past tense, so use "diverted" to be consistent throughout the sentence.

5. You should leave a nice review for a travel guide who (B) does a good job.
   The noun "guide" is singular and therefore requires a singular verb, "does."

6. Before watching the sequel, I (B) watched the prequel.
   Using "watched" is logical given that this is a past series of events; also, using "watching" would prevent this from being a complete sentence.
7. They have been swimming since early this morning and (B) are continuing to do so now.
   "Are" is consistent with the earlier subject "they."
8. If you have the instructions, assembly of the new bicycle (B) is easy.
   "Is" will keep the sentence in the present tense, and it will be consistent with the singular subject "assembly."
9. It would (A) have been an easy test if I had studied some more.
   Use "have" in conjunction with "would have." It can be fine to say "if it had," but do not use the word "would" along with "had."
10. My neighbor will not (B) entertain any new offers to purchase his old car.
    "Will not entertain" is the proper conjugation to express that this will take place in the future; "entertained" is fine as a past tense option, but not along with "will not."
11. When she flew to visit her relatives overseas, she (A) took only two flights.
    "Took" is consistent with the earlier past tense verb "flew."
12. The Renaissance artist (B) drew pencil sketches before he turned his ideas into paintings.
    Look later in the sentence to see that it is in the past tense given the verb "turned"; therefore, use the past tense "drew" for consistency.
13. I will read my textbook this evening after I (B) complete my other homework.
    Since the textbook reading is happening in the future after the completion of the homework, it is appropriate to use the present tense for "complete."
14. An infant may have trouble falling asleep, while teenagers rarely (B) have any difficulty doing so.
    "Have" will be consistent with the plural subject "teenagers."
15. The guard dog barked at a predator that (A) approached the herd of sheep.
    "Approached" is consistent with the past tense verb "barked" earlier in the sentence.
16. My father is unsure of what dish to (B) bring to the potluck dinner.
    "To bring" is the correct infinitive form of the verb, not "to brought."
17. The flock of birds (B) has taken off from the steep cliff to find food.
    The subject is the singular noun "flock," so "has" would be consistent with it.
18. Emma did a great job on her last assignment, and I am confident she (A) will do well on the one due next week.
    Based on context clues, the correct verb will be "will do" since the next assignment is one that has not yet been evaluated.
19. Jesse Owens, winner of four Olympic gold medals, (A) was born in Oakville, Alabama.
    The subject is the singular person "Jesse Owens," not the plural "medals"; therefore, use the singular verb "was."
20. What colleges have you (B) chosen for your in-person visits?
    "Have chosen" is the correct conjugation of the verb, not "have chose."

## Number and Tense Agreement Practice Questions

1. Anyone who assembles comic book collections probably _______ superheroes. After all, Batman, Superman, Wonder Woman, and Spiderman are some of the most popular characters found in these books.

   Which choice completes the text so that it conforms to the conventions of Standard English?

   (A) enjoy
   (B) enjoying
   (C) enjoys
   (D) to enjoy

2. The two hockey teams were evenly matched—throughout the game, the team that was ahead changed many times. After a hard-fought contest, the _________________. Ultimately their goalie's defensive prowess proved pivotal.

   Which choice completes the text so that it conforms to the conventions of Standard English?

   (A) blue team won the game.
   (B) game was won by the blue team.
   (C) winning by the blue team was completed.
   (D) blue team winning of the game was done.

3. A variety of diplomats gathered at the conference to discuss the new treaty. Out of the officials present, the Secretary General of the United Nations _____ the most well-respected.

   Which choice completes the text so that it conforms to the conventions of Standard English?

   (A) will
   (B) were
   (C) are
   (D) was

4. Three years ago, she went on vacation and _______ her relatives. Now she is going to do a similar trip with her family but plans to go to a different destination.

   Which choice completes the text so that it conforms to the conventions of Standard English?

   (A) will visit
   (B) visited
   (C) visiting
   (D) visit

5. The three friends were excited to meet up for a stroll in the new city park. Jennifer and Debby couldn't wait to see _____ new dog.

   Which choice completes the text so that it conforms to the conventions of Standard English?

   (A) her
   (B) their
   (C) Pam's
   (D) whose

6. Now that we have started the new employee training, I must make my expectations about tardiness very clear. I require that everyone ____ punctual. If you cannot show up on time for the job, you might as well not show up at all.

   Which choice completes the text so that it conforms to the conventions of Standard English?

   (A) is
   (B) be
   (C) are
   (D) was

7. When you are looking for a new job, there are a few things to keep in mind. You should work on your networking skills, _______ resume, and your references.

   Which choice completes the text so that it conforms to the conventions of Standard English?

   (A) your
   (B) one's
   (C) you're
   (D) its

8. My friend and I went on a hike around the lake. We saw fish, plants, and plenty of birds. In fact, there was a flock of geese that ____ at least 30 birds.

   Which choice completes the text so that it conforms to the conventions of Standard English?

   (A) has
   (B) have
   (C) had
   (D) having

9. Make sure you are ready the day before the SAT with everything that you will need. Because _______ not provided at the testing center, a bottle of water and a snack are two things you should take with you.

   Which choice completes the text so that it conforms to the conventions of Standard English?

   (A) they are
   (B) it is
   (C) you are
   (D) we are

10. We look out the window of our apartment and can see many things happening. There are people walking on the sidewalk and kids playing on the playground. Also, ____________________

    Which choice completes the text so that it conforms to the conventions of Standard English?

    (A) the cars driving down the freeway.
    (B) the cars are driving down the freeway.
    (C) the cars are drive down the freeway.
    (D) the cars down the freeway driving.

## Answer Explanations

1. **(C)** The subject is "anyone," which is singular—it refers to each person one at a time. "Enjoys" is the only verb that would work to provide a complete sentence that aligns with a singular subject.

2. **(A)** This option puts the words in the most logical order, making it clear that the blue team won the game. Choices (B) and (C) use the passive voice with "by." Choice (D) has a convoluted word order.

3. **(D)** This verb aligns with the singular person of the "Secretary General," so the singular verb "was" works. Also, it is in the past tense, consistent with the earlier past tense verb "gathered." The other options are either in the incorrect tense, like "will," or plural, like "were" and "are."

4. **(B)** The verb "went" earlier in the sentence is in the past tense, and "visited" is the only option that is also in the past tense.

5. **(C)** Pronouns are perfectly fine to use so long as what they represent is clear. In this sentence, it is unclear who possesses the dog unless the owner is specifically named as in choice (C). The other options would leave the ownership unclear.

6. **(B)** Since this is a demand, the verb "be" is appropriate. The other options would not be typically used in a command.

7. **(A)** This is the only option that maintains parallelism with the other parts of the list—they all begin with "your."

8. **(C)** "Had" is consistent with the past tense verb "was" earlier in the sentence. The other options are not in the past tense.

9. **(A)** To see what pronoun is needed, look at what comes later in the sentence. A watch and a snack are the things that are not provided, so in reference to these two things, "they" is the only possibility.

10. **(B)** This option puts the words in a logical sequence and provides a complete sentence by saying "cars are driving." Choices (A) and (D) result in a sentence fragment. Choice (C) should use "driven" instead of "drive" in conjunction with "are."

## Punctuation

### Commas

When it comes to comma questions on the SAT, it is important to know both *when* to use a comma and *when NOT* to use a comma. You may be able to intuitively tell when to use a comma by mouthing out the sentence in your head and "hearing" where a small breath or pause would be. However, it is helpful to know specific rules about when and when not to use commas so that you can do your best.

**Do use a comma to separate an introductory phrase (dependent clause) from a complete sentence (independent clause).**

Correct: Whenever my brother sleeps, he snores loudly.

Correct: If you are happy with your grade, put the paper on your refrigerator.

Explanation: In both of these examples, there is an introductory phrase followed by a complete sentence. A comma is great for separating dependent clauses (incomplete thoughts that cannot stand on their own) from complete sentences (a complete idea with both a subject and a verb).

**Don't use a comma by itself to join two complete sentences (independent clauses).**

Incorrect: Jean went for a walk around town, she saw many different neighborhoods.

Correct: Jean went for a walk around town, **and** she saw many different neighborhoods.

Incorrect: My friend loves to paint, he makes large messes when doing so.

Correct: My friend loves to paint, **but** he makes large messes when doing so.

Explanation: A comma by itself cannot separate one complete sentence from another—this error is called a *comma splice*. If you had a word like *and, but,* or *yet* along with the comma, that would be fine. Also, a semicolon, period, and sometimes a dash or colon can work to separate complete sentences.

**Do use a comma before and after a parenthetical phrase (i.e., words that are added to a sentence without changing the original sentence's grammar or meaning).**

Correct: The first person to walk on the moon, Neil Armstrong, is a native of the state of Ohio.

Correct: Jigsaw puzzles, unlike crossword puzzles, involve visual pattern recognition.

Correct: A box of my favorite cereal, which I purchased on sale, is what my family will have for breakfast this week.

Explanation: The phrases "Neil Armstrong," "unlike crossword puzzles," and "which I purchased on sale" could be removed from the original sentences and the sentences would remain complete with their original meanings. Note that parenthetical phrases will often start with *which*. (If *which* is used without a parenthetical phrase, like "the building in which I will take the SAT," no comma before *which* is needed).

**Don't use a comma to separate the subject from the verb in a sentence.**

Incorrect: My best friend, is moving out of town.

Correct: My best friend is moving out of town.

Incorrect: Football players and basketball players, both use locker rooms to get ready.

Correct: Football players and basketball players both use locker rooms to get ready.

Incorrect: The book, that I have almost finished is very suspenseful.

Correct: The book that I have almost finished is very suspenseful.

Explanation: These sentences would work if the commas were removed. Just because a sentence has a long subject does not mean that it requires a comma. Note that phrases that do not require a comma will often start with *that*. *That* indicates that a phrase is restrictive, or essential, to the sentence's meaning.

**Do use a comma to separate words within a list.**

Correct: I will pick up apples, bananas, and oranges at the fruit stand.

**Don't use a comma right *before* a list begins.**

Incorrect: At the fruit stand, I will pick up, oranges, apples, and bananas.

Correct: At the fruit stand, I will pick up oranges, apples, and bananas.

Explanation: There is no need for a comma after "pick up" in the second sentence. Just use commas to separate the items within the list.

**Note:** The SAT uses the Oxford comma with lists: the comma before the *and* that comes before the final item. However, since the Oxford comma is more of a stylistic choice than a grammar rule, they most likely will not test you on this concept.

**Do use a comma along with coordinating conjunctions to connect two complete sentences. Coordinating conjunctions provide a strong connection between sentences. *Remember coordinating conjunctions with the acronym FANBOYS (For, And, Nor, But, Or, Yet, So).***

Correct: My sister was hungry, so she grabbed a snack from the kitchen.

Correct: I studied quite a bit for the test, but I did not perform as well as I would have liked.

**Don't just use a comma to connect two complete sentences joined by a conjunctive adverb (e.g., however, indeed, nevertheless, moreover, namely, meanwhile, subsequently, thus, furthermore). Conjunctive adverbs provide a weaker connection between sentences. Instead, use a semicolon with a comma.**

Incorrect: He was delighted to be promoted, however, he was not happy with the new work schedule.

Correct: He was delighted to be promoted; however, he was not happy with the new work schedule.

Incorrect: The tour started at the museum, subsequently, it went to the park.

Correct: The tour started at the museum; subsequently, it went to the park.

**Note:** It is fine to use conjunctive adverbs with just commas so long as they are not used to connect two complete sentences:

Correct: My friend wanted me to come to his house. Instead, I decided to stay home.

Correct: Most birds can fly. The penguin, however, cannot.

Explanation: While a comma by itself is not enough to join two complete sentences, a comma along with one of the FANBOYS words *will* be enough. Be sure that the word joining the two complete sentences is one of these FANBOYS words—if it is one of the conjunctive adverbs, use a semicolon before the conjunctive adverb and a comma after the conjunctive adverb to make the connection.

**Do** **use commas to separate adjectives if the order of the adjectives *does not* matter.**

Correct: The fluffy, friendly puppy likes to wag its tail.

Correct: The friendly, fluffy puppy likes to wag its tail.

Explanation: It does not change the meaning of the sentence whether "fluffy" or "friendly" comes first.

**Don't** **use commas to separate adjectives if the order of the adjectives *does* matter.**

Incorrect: The first, female governor won a large majority of the vote.

Incorrect: The female, first governor won a large majority of the vote.

Correct: The first female governor won a large majority of the vote.

Explanation: The order of the adjectives "first" and "female" does matter—"first" must come before "female" in order for the sentence to be logical. In this situation, do not use commas to separate the adjectives.

**Comma Practice**—select the better sentence out of the two options.

1. (A) Once upon a time, the kingdom was under attack.
   (B) Once upon a time the kingdom was under attack.
2. (A) My Advanced Placement World History class, is very interesting.
   (B) My Advanced Placement World History class is very interesting.
3. (A) I needed a quiet place to read, so I went to the library.
   (B) I needed a quiet place to read so I went to the library.
4. (A) The pedestal onto, which you place the trophies should be sturdy.
   (B) The pedestal onto which you place the trophies should be sturdy.
5. (A) If you are going to do well on your test, be sure to get a good night's sleep.
   (B) If you are going to do well on your test be sure to get a good night's sleep.
6. (A) One example of a large animal, is the blue whale.
   (B) One example of a large animal is the blue whale.
7. (A) The first person to walk across Antarctica without any assistance Colin O'Brady took 54 days to do so.
   (B) The first person to walk across Antarctica without any assistance, Colin O'Brady, took 54 days to do so.
8. (A) Essential ingredients for the cake are flour, sugar, and eggs.
   (B) Essential ingredients for the cake are flour sugar and eggs.
9. (A) The results of the study, indicate that the medicine is highly effective.
   (B) The results of the study indicate that the medicine is highly effective.
10. (A) The saw is extremely precise, cutting each edge flawlessly.
    (B) The saw is extremely precise cutting each edge flawlessly.
11. (A) Broccoli, though not my friend's favorite, is something I love to eat whenever I can.
    (B) Broccoli though not my friend's favorite is something I love to eat whenever I can.

**12.** (A) The chair that is by the window is extremely comfortable.
(B) The chair, that is by the window, is extremely comfortable.

**13.** (A) Each morning, I like to take a shower, eat breakfast, and gather my things for school.
(B) Each morning, I like to take a shower eat breakfast, and gather my things for school.

**14.** (A) Inflation is largely attributable to the ever-increasing prices of different goods and services.
(B) Inflation is largely attributable, to the ever-increasing prices of different goods and services.

**15.** (A) The ping-pong table in the middle of the gymnasium, is where I spend my time after eating lunch.
(B) The ping-pong table in the middle of the gymnasium is where I spend my time after eating lunch.

**16.** (A) Our house, which we moved into last year, is still in good condition.
(B) Our house which we moved into last year is still in good condition.

**17.** (A) The job of a lifeguard, is to vigilantly keep watch over the beach.
(B) The job of a lifeguard is to vigilantly keep watch over the beach.

**18.** (A) You did an excellent job on your group project; moreover, you aced your final exam.
(B) You did an excellent job on your group project, moreover, you aced your final exam.

**19.** (A) My newest neighbor Jian, loves to play basketball in his driveway.
(B) My newest neighbor, Jian, loves to play basketball in his driveway.

**20.** (A) If you are passionate about your profession, work will not feel like "work."
(B) If you are passionate about your profession work will not feel like "work."

**21.** (A) The new volleyball coach, was excited for the team's first game.
(B) The new volleyball coach was excited for the team's first game.

**22.** (A) Cold-brewed coffee, though not my personal favorite, has become increasingly popular.
(B) Cold-brewed coffee, though not my personal favorite has become increasingly popular.

**23.** (A) The traffic, that clogged up the highway for eight straight miles, was quite a nuisance.
(B) The traffic that clogged up the highway for eight straight miles was quite a nuisance.

**24.** (A) My videoconferencing software which I just updated helped me to meet with faraway relatives.
(B) My videoconferencing software, which I just updated, helped me to meet with faraway relatives.

**25.** (A) Several thousand years ago, people, along with many animals, traversed an ice bridge from Eurasia to the Americas.
(B) Several thousand years ago people, along with many animals traversed an ice bridge from Eurasia to the Americas.

## ✓ Answers

1. **(A)** Once upon a time, the kingdom was under attack.
Place a comma after the introductory phrase.
2. **(B)** My Advanced Placement World History class is very interesting.
Don't separate the subject from the verb with a comma.
3. **(A)** I needed a quiet place to read, so I went to the library.
"So" is one of the FANBOYS words, and can therefore be used to join two sentences along with a comma.
4. **(B)** The pedestal onto which you place the trophies should be sturdy.
This is an example of using "which" when it does not precede a parenthetical phrase—thus, no comma is needed.
5. **(A)** If you are going to do well on your test, be sure to get a good night's sleep.
Use a comma to separate the introductory phrase from the complete sentence that follows.
6. **(B)** One example of a large animal is the blue whale.
There is no need to separate the subject and the verb.
7. **(B)** The first person to walk across Antarctica without any assistance, Colin O'Brady, took 54 days to do so.
Surround the name with commas since the sentence will maintain its meaning and grammar without it.
8. **(A)** Essential ingredients for the cake are flour, sugar, and eggs.
Use commas to separate the items in the list.
9. **(B)** The results of the study indicate that the medicine is highly effective.
There is no need to separate the subject and the verb with a comma.
10. **(A)** The saw is extremely precise, cutting each edge flawlessly.
Use a comma to separate the complete sentence from the dependent clause that follows.
11. **(A)** Broccoli, though not my friend's favorite, is something I love to eat whenever I can.
Surround the parenthetical phrase with commas.
12. **(A)** The chair that is by the window is extremely comfortable.
The is no need for commas when using "that" to describe something essential to the subject.
13. **(A)** Each morning, I like to take a shower, eat breakfast, and gather my things for school.
Use commas to separate the items in the list.
14. **(A)** Inflation is largely attributable to the ever-increasing prices of different goods and services.
Do not use a comma to break up the phrase "attributable to."
15. **(B)** The ping-pong table in the middle of the gymnasium is where I spend my time after eating lunch.
Even though there is a long subject in the sentence, do not use a comma to separate the subject from the verb.
16. **(A)** Our house, which we moved into last year, is still in good condition.
Use commas around the parenthetical phrase that begins with "which."

17. **(B)** The job of a lifeguard is to vigilantly keep watch over the beach.
    Do not separate the subject from the verb.
18. **(A)** You did an excellent job on your group project; moreover, you aced your final exam.
    Use a semicolon, not a comma, to separate two sentences joined by a conjunctive adverb.
19. **(B)** My newest neighbor, Jian, loves to play basketball in his driveway.
    "Jian" is the same person as "my newest neighbor," so his name can be set off with commas.
20. **(A)** If you are passionate about your profession, work will not feel like "work."
    Use commas to separate the introductory phrase from the complete sentence that follows.
21. **(B)** The new volleyball coach was excited for the team's first game.
    Do not separate the subject from the verb.
22. **(A)** Cold-brewed coffee, though not my personal favorite, has become increasingly popular.
    Surround the parenthetical phrase with commas.
23. **(B)** The traffic that clogged up the highway for eight straight miles was quite a nuisance.
    No commas are needed to surround an essential phrase starting with "that."
24. **(B)** My videoconferencing software, which I just updated, helped me to meet with faraway relatives.
    Surround the parenthetical, nonessential phrase that begins with "which" with commas.
25. **(A)** Several thousand years ago, people, along with many animals, traversed an ice bridge from Eurasia to the Americas.
    Use a comma after "people" to separate the introductory phrase, and also use commas around the parenthetical phrase "along with many animals."

### Semicolons

**Use a semicolon (;) to separate two complete, related sentences from one another.** While a period could be substituted for a semicolon in most cases, using the semicolon allows for more stylistic variety in one's writing.

Correct: I am excited to go to the concert; I will show up early to be first in line.

Incorrect: While I am excited to go to the concert; there is no way I want to show up early to wait.

Correct: While I am excited to go to the concert, there is no way I want to show up early to wait.

Explanation: If there are complete sentences on either side of the semicolon, it is appropriate to use one. If there is a sentence fragment on either side of the semicolon, change the sentence structure (perhaps by substituting a comma for the semicolon) to make it work.

**Use a semicolon to separate items in a list when each item has internal punctuation, like a comma, within it.**

Correct: When I tour colleges, I am looking forward to checking out Boston, Massachusetts; Ithaca, New York; and Providence, Rhode Island.

Incorrect: When I tour colleges, I am looking forward to checking out Boston, Massachusetts, Ithaca, New York, and Providence, Rhode Island.

Explanation: The semicolons create a clear distinction between each place that is denoted as a city and state. Without the semicolons to separate these items, it would seem like the cities and states were different things.

**Semicolon Practice**—select the better sentence out of the two options.

1. (A) This is the best book I have ever read, I simply cannot put it down.
   (B) This is the best book I have ever read; I simply cannot put it down.
2. (A) A positive attitude can help you overcome adversity, no matter the circumstances.
   (B) A positive attitude can help you overcome adversity; no matter the circumstances.
3. (A) It was supposed to be a cloudy day, however, the weather forecast was fortunately incorrect.
   (B) It was supposed to be a cloudy day; however, the weather forecast was fortunately incorrect.
4. (A) The most critical people on the movie set are John, the director; Susan, the producer; and Harris, the lead actor.
   (B) The most critical people on the movie set are John, the director, Susan, the producer, and Harris, the lead actor.
5. (A) If the grass is dry, water the lawn.
   (B) If the grass is dry; water the lawn.

### ✓ Answers

1. **(B)** This is the best book I have ever read; I simply cannot put it down.
   Use a semicolon to separate the two complete sentences.
2. **(A)** A positive attitude can help you overcome adversity, no matter the circumstances.
   "No matter the circumstances" is not a complete sentence, so separate it from the complete sentence that comes before it with a comma.
3. **(B)** It was supposed to be a cloudy day; however, the weather forecast was fortunately incorrect.
   Recall that with conjunctive adverbs (like "however") that join two complete sentences, use a semicolon followed by a comma.
4. **(A)** The most critical people on the movie set are John, the director; Susan, the producer; and Harris, the lead actor.
   Use semicolons to separate the items in the list that have internal punctuation.
5. **(A)** If the grass is dry, water the lawn.
   A comma will work to separate the introductory phrase from the complete sentence.

## Colons

**Use a colon (:) if it comes after a complete sentence and introduces a clarification or a list.** If an idea is not fully expressed, the colon can set off the information that will complete the thought.

Correct: After many years of hard work, I have achieved my lifelong dream: hiking up a tall mountain.

Correct: French mirepoix uses these ingredients: carrots, onions, and celery.

**Colon Practice**—select the better sentence out of the two options.

1. (A) My houseplant requires the following to thrive sunlight, fertilizer, and water.
   (B) My houseplant requires the following to thrive: sunlight, fertilizer, and water.
2. (A) The office workers finally agreed on the setting for the thermostat: 72 degrees.
   (B) The office workers finally: agreed on the setting for the thermostat 72 degrees.

3. (A) You should take: your suitcase, backpack, and wallet with you on the trip.
   (B) You should take your suitcase, backpack, and wallet with you on the trip.
4. (A) We were delighted to see two of our favorite animals at the zoo: elephants and tigers.
   (B) We were delighted to see two of our favorite animals at the zoo elephants and tigers.
5. (A) No matter how you choose to season your food, salt and pepper are recommended items to have on a dinner table.
   (B) No matter how you choose to season your food: salt and pepper are recommended items to have on a dinner table.

### ✓ Answers

1. **(B)** My houseplant requires the following to thrive: sunlight, fertilizer, and water.
   The colon comes before the list of items the plant requires to thrive.
2. **(A)** The office workers finally agreed on the setting for the thermostat: 72 degrees.
   This is the correct placement for the colon since it comes after a complete sentence and before a clarification.
3. **(B)** You should take your suitcase, backpack, and wallet with you on the trip.
   Not every list will require a colon to come before it. In this case, a colon would cause a very abrupt pause.
4. **(A)** We were delighted to see two of our favorite animals at the zoo: elephants and tigers.
   The colon comes before the clarification of which animals were at the zoo.
5. **(A)** No matter how you choose to season your food, salt and pepper are recommended items to have on a dinner table.
   Since "No matter how you choose to season your food" is not a complete sentence, having a colon after it would not work. Use a comma instead.

### Dashes

**Use a dash (—) to indicate a change of thought or change of voice in a sentence.**

Correct: I would not go down that alley—it looks very spooky.

Correct: Wait—I am not ready to go.

**Use dashes to surround a parenthetical phrase.** Start and finish the parenthetical phrase using the same punctuation, like commas, dashes, or parentheses.

Correct: Las Vegas—a major tourist town—is surprisingly surrounded by desert.

Incorrect: Las Vegas—a major tourist town, is surprisingly surrounded by desert.

**Note:** With the above examples, other forms of punctuation could have been used instead of the dash. You have a great deal of flexibility in your punctuation choices in more complex sentences. *However, do not worry about whether the SAT will have two correct options.* If a colon could be used for a dash and vice versa, only one of these options will be presented.

**Dash Practice**—select the better sentence out of the two options.

1. (A) My favorite food—pizza—is easily found at many restaurants.
   (B) My favorite food, pizza—is easily found at many restaurants.

2. (A) The backpacking journey looks quite challenging—be prepared.
(B) The backpacking journey looks quite challenging be prepared.

3. (A) My science teacher—a former government researcher—is excellent at helping us see the applications of what we learn.
(B) My science teacher—a former government researcher is excellent at helping us see the applications of what we learn.

4. (A) Based on the latest data, the geologists could only come to one conclusion—a volcanic eruption was imminent.
(B) Based on the latest data, the geologists could only come to one conclusion a volcanic eruption was imminent.

5. (A) My friends Sharon and Maria are coming over to my house this evening.
(B) My friends Sharon—and Maria—are coming over to my house this evening.

### ✓ Answers

1. **(A)** My favorite food—pizza—is easily found at many restaurants.
Be consistent in using the same type of punctuation on either side of parenthetical phrases.

2. **(A)** The backpacking journey looks quite challenging—be prepared.
Have a dash toward the end of the sentence to indicate the change of thought.

3. **(A)** My science teacher—a former government researcher—is excellent at helping us see the applications of what we learn.
Surround the clarification about the science teacher's background with dashes.

4. **(A)** Based on the latest data, the geologists could only come to one conclusion—a volcanic eruption was imminent.
Have a dash before the clarification of what the conclusion was.

5. **(A)** My friends Sharon and Maria are coming over to my house this evening.
There is no need for dashes in this situation because there is no parenthetical phrase. Instead, "Maria" is part of the subject.

## Apostrophes

### Common Situations

**Use an apostrophe (') *before* an *s* to show singular possession.**

- One pet's dish
- A person's house
- Caitlin's shoes
- My car's steering wheel

**Use an apostrophe *after* an *s* to show plural possession.**

- Three pets' fence
- Seven cars' parking lot spaces
- Our books' shelf
- Three families' neighborhood

**Note:** It does not matter how many things are possessed/owned; it matters *how many owners* there are.

**Less Common Situations**

**Use an apostrophe *before* an *s* to show possession if the word is already plural.**

- The women's organization
- The children's playground

**Use just one apostrophe if both of the nouns in a compound subject *jointly* own something.**

- Pam and Andy's family (they share a family)
- The cat and dog's toys (they share the toys)

**Use apostrophes after each of the nouns in a sequence if each noun *individually* possesses an item.**

- Aliyah's and Olivia's report cards were each excellent. (Aliyah and Olivia have their own report cards.)
- My sister's and my brother's rooms are both messy. (The sister and brother individually have messy rooms.)

**TIP**

**Another way to keep these rules straight is to realize that if you remove the apostrophe and what comes after it, you will get the original non-possessive word.**

**Note:** Do not worry about apostrophe placement exceptions for names ending in s. The SAT will stick to widely agreed upon apostrophe rules.

For example:

| Possessive Form | What to Remove | Original Word |
|---|---|---|
| Dog's | 's | Dog |
| Friends' | ' | Friends |
| Men's | 's | Men |

## Apostrophes and Pronouns

**Do use an apostrophe on pronoun contractions—ones that have a pronoun and verb together.**

- It's a beautiful day outside. (same as "it is")
- They're coming over this evening. (same as "they are")
- You're doing well with your homework. (same as "you are")

**Don't use an apostrophe with pronouns that show possession.**

- The bicycle needs its tires inflated. (The tires belong to the bicycle.)
- Their clothes are now clean. (The clothes belong to the implicit people.)
- You should mind your manners at dinner. (The manners belong to you.)

**Apostrophe Practice**—select the better sentence out of the two options.

1. (A) One persons' trash is another person's treasure.
   (B) One person's trash is another person's treasure.
2. (A) The teachers' are meeting to share their best lesson ideas.
   (B) The teachers are meeting to share their best lesson ideas.
3. (A) The natural history museum's planetarium is extremely impressive.
   (B) The natural history museums planetarium is extremely impressive.
4. (A) Whenever my relatives come over, we need to order extra food.
   (B) Whenever my relatives' come over, we need to order extra food.
5. (A) Humpback whales love to swim in the open ocean.
   (B) Humpback whales' love to swim in the open ocean.

6. (A) The Broadway show's sets are difficult to move.
(B) The Broadway show's set's are difficult to move.

7. (A) When the new coach helped the men's soccer team, he made significant adjustments to the lineup.
(B) When the new coach helped the mens' soccer team, he made significant adjustments to the lineup.

8. (A) As you read the joint paper by the scientists, note how Watson's and Crick's results match their hypothesis.
(B) As you read the joint paper by the scientists, note how Watson and Crick's results match their hypothesis.

9. (A) His backpack needs it's straps repaired.
(B) His backpack needs its straps repaired.

10. (A) The three farmers' fields encompassed over 500 acres.
(B) The three farmers fields encompassed over 500 acres.

## ✓ Answers

1. **(B)** One person's trash is another person's treasure.
Since it is just one person who possesses the trash, have the apostrophe before the *s*.

2. **(B)** The teachers are meeting to share their best lesson ideas.
No apostrophe is needed since the teachers are not showing possession.

3. **(A)** The natural history museum's planetarium is extremely impressive.
The planetarium belongs to the singular museum.

4. **(A)** Whenever my relatives come over, we need to order extra food.
The relatives are doing the action of coming over, not possessing anything, so no apostrophe is needed.

5. **(A)** Humpback whales love to swim in the open ocean.
The whales are acting as a subject, not possessing anything, so no apostrophe is required.

6. **(A)** The Broadway show's sets are difficult to move.
The sets belong to the show; the sets do not possess anything.

7. **(A)** When the new coach helped the men's soccer team, he made significant adjustments to the lineup.
Since "men" is already plural, put the apostrophe before the *s*.

8. **(B)** As you read the joint paper by the scientists, note how Watson and Crick's results match their hypothesis.
Since Watson and Crick collectively own the results, just put an apostrophe before the *s* in the final name.

9. **(B)** His backpack needs its straps repaired.
Show possession with the pronoun "it" by *not* using the apostrophe.

10. **(A)** The three farmers' fields encompassed over 500 acres.
Three farmers collectively own the fields, so show possession by putting an apostrophe after the *s*.

## Parentheses

**Parentheses ( ) do not affect the grammar and meaning of the surrounding sentence.**

| Without Parentheses | With Parentheses |
|---|---|
| Once I finish the test, I will read my book for fun. | Once I finish the test (it should take about 30 minutes), I will read my book for fun. |
| Your next-door neighbor is really nice. | Your next-door neighbor (the one with the unusual mailbox) is really nice. |
| My teacher gave everyone the opportunity to earn extra credit after the difficult test. | My teacher gave everyone the opportunity to earn extra credit after the difficult test (only a handful of students took advantage of it). |

In all the above examples, the parentheses do not affect the usage of the commas and periods that surround them.

**Parentheses Practice**—select the better sentence out of the two options.

1. (A) The large dog eats quite a bit of food each day (mainly food from a bag).
   (B) The large dog eats quite a bit of food each day (mainly food from a bag.)
2. (A) When you eat breakfast (considered the most important meal of the day,) you have energy for several hours.
   (B) When you eat breakfast (considered the most important meal of the day), you have energy for several hours.
3. (A) Cricket (once an Olympic game,) is one of my favorite sports.
   (B) Cricket (once an Olympic game) is one of my favorite sports.

### ✓ Answers

1. **(A)** The large dog eats quite a bit of food each day (mainly food from a bag).
   Put the period outside of the parentheses since the parentheses will not affect the surrounding punctuation.
2. **(B)** When you eat breakfast (considered the most important meal of the day), you have energy for several hours.
   Have the comma outside of the parentheses.
3. **(B)** Cricket (once an Olympic game) is one of my favorite sports.
   There is no need for a comma within the parentheses since the parentheses already provide a needed pause.

## Question Marks

**<u>Do</u> use a question mark (?) at the end of a sentence that directly asks a question.**

- Why did you bring that toy to school with you?
- What is he planning on doing in the future?
- "Who is knocking at the door?" my father asked.

**Don't use a question mark if the sentence *indirectly* asks a question.**

- I would like to find out who my teacher will be.
- He is excited to find out what happens next in the play.
- The article addresses the central question of whether nature or nurture ultimately has a greater impact.

**Question Mark Practice**—select the better sentence out of the two options.

1. (A) If you want to do well in class, be sure to ask your teacher questions?
   (B) If you want to do well in class, be sure to ask your teacher questions.
2. (A) Where is the nearest subway station.
   (B) Where is the nearest subway station?
3. (A) While many students are quiet in class, I prefer to ask my teacher what I need to know.
   (B) While many students are quiet in class, I prefer to ask my teacher what I need to know?

### ✓ Answers

1. **(B)** If you want to do well in class, be sure to ask your teacher questions.
   This is an indirect question, so no question mark is needed.
2. **(B)** Where is the nearest subway station?
   This is a direct question, so use a question mark.
3. **(A)** While many students are quiet in class, I prefer to ask my teacher what I need to know.
   This is an indirect question, so no question mark is needed.

## Punctuation Practice Questions

### Exercise 1

1. I recently moved to a new building, and I am not so sure about some of the people who live there. ____________ quite a bit of noise when he walks around.

   Which choice completes the text so that it conforms to the conventions of Standard English?

   (A) The man who lives in the apartment above me makes
   (B) The man, who lives in the apartment above me makes
   (C) The man, who lives in the apartment above me, makes
   (D) The man who lives in the apartment, above me makes

2. I spoke to my teacher, and she gave me some good advice. "To do well on the SAT, be sure to work on improving several key ____________ reasoning, and essay editing."

   Which choice completes the text so that it conforms to the conventions of Standard English?

   (A) skills, reading comprehension, quantitative
   (B) skills: reading comprehension quantitative
   (C) skills—reading comprehension, quantitative
   (D) skills; reading comprehension, quantitative

3. The weather is lovely—there is a gentle breeze, mild temperature, and no precipitation. _____ a great afternoon to read a book for pleasure.

   Which choice completes the text so that it conforms to the conventions of Standard English?

   (A) Its
   (B) It's
   (C) Its'
   (D) It

4. The area of the park for adults had a botanical garden, a koi pond, and several artistic rock formations. The _______ playground, on the other hand, had some enormous slides and swings.

   Which choice completes the text so that it conforms to the conventions of Standard English?

   (A) children's
   (B) childrens'
   (C) childrens
   (D) childs'

5. My history teacher brings history to ___________ activities, guest speakers, and discussions about controversial topics. It is truly exciting to be a part of her class.

   Which choice completes the text so that it conforms to the conventions of Standard English?

   (A) life with stimulating,
   (B) life with: stimulating
   (C) life with; stimulating
   (D) life with stimulating

6. I came to an important realization as I worried about saving enough money for the future. Some of the best things in __________________________ completely free.

   Which choice completes the text so that it conforms to the conventions of Standard English?

   (A) life, sunshine, fresh air, and starlit nights are
   (B) life—sunshine, fresh air, and starlit nights—are
   (C) life (sunshine, fresh air, and starlit nights—are
   (D) life—sunshine, fresh air, and starlit nights, are

7. When you go shopping, please buy sugar, flour, and butter at the grocery; antacids, bandages, and a thermometer at the __________ screwdriver, and some sandpaper from the hardware store. Please come back with whatever change remains.

   Which choice completes the text so that it conforms to the conventions of Standard English?

   (A) pharmacy, and a hammer, a
   (B) pharmacy: and a hammer a
   (C) pharmacy, and a hammer a
   (D) pharmacy; and a hammer, a

8. As the human resources officer was immersed in making changes to the employee ________ neglected to enforce the policies already on the books. Ultimately, he was not very effective in his job.

   Which choice completes the text so that it conforms to the conventions of Standard English?

   (A) manual, he
   (B) manual he
   (C) manual. He
   (D) manual; he

9. While surfing the Internet, John found that ______________ been found in a nearby city. He was overjoyed to know that his companion of many years was safe and sound.

   Which choice completes the text so that it conforms to the conventions of Standard English?

   (A) Sprinkles his missing pet cat, had
   (B) Sprinkles, his missing pet cat, had
   (C) Sprinkles, his missing pet cat had
   (D) Sprinkles his missing pet cat had

10. Mitchell wrote an excellent ________ had it published in a journal. His family members were thrilled that the talents he had worked so long to fine-tune were at last being recognized by the public.

    Which choice completes the text so that it conforms to the conventions of Standard English?

    (A) poem; he
    (B) poem, he
    (C) poem he
    (D) poem, he,

## Answer Explanations

1. **(A)** It is not just any man but specifically the man who lives in the apartment above the narrator who makes noise. Since this description is essential to identifying the subject of the second sentence, there is no need for any commas to break this up.
2. **(C)** The dash provides a heavy pause before the list of the skills, each of which is separated by a comma. Choice (A) does not have a strong enough punctuation, like a colon or dash, before the list. Choice (B) does not have a comma separating the first and second items in the list. Choice (D) incorrectly uses a semicolon because what follows the semicolon is not a complete sentence.
3. **(B)** "It's" the contraction for "it is," making it the correct choice. "Its" shows possession, "its'" is always incorrect, and "it" does not have the needed verb.
4. **(A)** With a word like "children" that is already plural, you can show possession by adding an apostrophe and an "s." Choices (B) and (C) would not correctly demonstrate possession, and (D) uses the incorrect plural version of "child."

5. **(D)** The other options provide unnecessary breaks, while choice (D) allows the phrase to properly flow.

6. **(B)** When setting aside a parenthetical phrase, it is necessary to use the same punctuation to start and finish the parenthetical phrase. Choices (C) and (D) mix and match the beginning and ending punctuation, and choice (A) does not have punctuation after the end of the parenthetical phrase. Only choice (B) begins and ends the parenthetical phrase with consistent punctuation.

7. **(D)** This option correctly uses a semicolon to separate the three sets of listed items, each of which has commas within the list. The semicolon is used in this way to help avoid confusion about the separation of listed items, which would result if commas were used in this situation.

8. **(A)** This option correctly separates the dependent introductory clause from the independent clause with a comma. Choice (B) has no separation. Choices (C) and (D) would have to have a complete sentence before the punctuation to be correct.

9. **(B)** This option puts the clarification of the identity of "Sprinkles" off to the side by surrounding it with commas. The other options do not separate this phrase from the rest of the sentence.

10. **(A)** The semicolon separates the two independent clauses from one another. A comma is insufficient when used without a conjunction to separate two independent clauses.

### Exercise 2

1. The interconnectedness between mental and physical health has been consistently shown in a variety of fields in research. ________ causes relatively minor physical ailments like headaches, digestive issues, and muscle tension.

   Which choice completes the text so that it conforms to the conventions of Standard English?

   (A) In the short term mental stress, typically
   (B) In the short term, mental stress typically
   (C) In the short term; mental stress typically
   (D) In the short term, mental stress, typically

2. The most remarkable fact in connection with the season was the earlier ________ greatly delayed arrival. This was probably due almost entirely to the unusual weather conditions that seemed to prevail throughout the South during March and early April, affecting the migration of these birds.

   Which choice completes the text so that it conforms to the conventions of Standard English?

   (A) migrant's,
   (B) migrant's,
   (C) migrant
   (D) migrants'

3. A parasitic relationship is between two _________ of the organisms benefits while the other is harmed. Parasitic relationships are often associated with internal parasites like worms or some species of mites, but parasitic relationships are not limited to organisms residing within a host.

   Which choice completes the text so that it conforms to the conventions of Standard English?

   (A) organisms, one
   (B) organisms—one
   (C) organisms, while one
   (D) organisms. If one

4. With health care professionals more needed than ever, hospitals and universities are working to attract students to their health care programs. Students often head into either a nursing or premed track without ___________ there are many more jobs in healing beyond (or better yet, between) those two positions.

   Which choice completes the text so that it conforms to the conventions of Standard English?

   (A) realizing however that
   (B) realizing however, that
   (C) realizing, however, that
   (D) realizing; however that

5. Whether they like it or dislike it, most Americans are familiar with the concept of a ___________ in to save a large company that is floundering. The government does this primarily to try to save the economy from potentially crushing bankruptcies of giant corporations that employ thousands of people.

   Which choice completes the text so that it conforms to the conventions of Standard English?

   (A) government bailout: the government swoops
   (B) government bailout, the government swoops
   (C) government; bailout the government swoops
   (D) government bailout the government—swoops

6. Good health care practitioners should be able to find work in nearly any corner of the United ____________ pay in less desirable regions like rural areas and other underserved communities.

   Which choice completes the text so that it conforms to the conventions of Standard English?

   (A) States, moreover, they can earn higher
   (B) States: moreover they can earn higher
   (C) States, moreover they can earn higher
   (D) States; moreover, they can earn higher

7. The amount of time spent in making observations during the past ______ Observations were typically made independently by each of the writers and on lands differing somewhat in general character.

   Which choice completes the text so that it conforms to the conventions of Standard English?

   (A) season, is significant.
   (B) season is significant.
   (C) season is, significant.
   (D) season—is significant.

8. The migration of birds at Raleigh, N.C., during the spring of 1915 was so unusual that it is believed that a short ______ be of interest to the readers of *Bird-Lore*.

   Which choice completes the text so that it conforms to the conventions of Standard English?

   (A) account, together with a list of the records, will
   (B) account, together with a list of the records will
   (C) account—together with a list of the records, will
   (D) account together with a list of the records; will

9. Upon hatching, a baby European cuckoo's first instinct is to empty the nest. ______ back is perfectly shaped to scoop up other eggs and eject them from the nest.

   Which choice completes the text so that it conforms to the conventions of Standard English?

   (A) Its'
   (B) Its
   (C) It's
   (D) It is

10. Like the mental benefits, and thus physical benefits, that have been found from living in close-knit ______ are many activities that are known to promote physical health due to their impact on mental health.

    Which choice completes the text so that it conforms to the conventions of Standard English?

    (A) communities, there
    (B) communities there
    (C) communities; there
    (D) communities: there

## Answer Explanations

1. **(B)** This option correctly places a comma after the introductory phrase, separating the dependent clause from the independent clause that follows. Choice (A) would interrupt the independent clause, separating its subject, "mental stress," from the remainder of the sentence. Choice (C) incorrectly uses a semicolon after a dependent clause—a semicolon must have an independent clause on either side of it. Choice (D) has too many commas.

2. **(D)** Based on the context in the second sentence, there are multiple birds that are migrating. So, show possession of the "arrival" by putting the apostrophe after "migrants." It is not choice (A) or (B) since there are multiple migrants, and it is not choice (C) because this does not show possession.

3. **(B)** Use a dash before the clarification of the relationship between the two organisms since it provides a heavy pause. Choice (A) is a comma splice. Choice (C) incorrectly uses "while" to show a contrast. Choice (D) would result in a sentence fragment for the second part.

4. **(C)** The transitional word "however" should be surrounded with commas since the sentence would still be logical if this word were removed. Choices (A) and (B) do not have enough commas, and choice (D) incorrectly uses a semicolon since there is not a complete sentence after the semicolon. Moreover, there is no comma after "however" in choice (D).

5. **(A)** The colon is appropriate in this case because there is a complete sentence before it and a clarification after it. Choice (B) would result in a comma splice. Choice (C) would not have a complete and logical sentence after the semicolon, and choice (D) has a pause at an awkward spot.

6. **(D)** When joining two sentences with a conjunctive adverb like "moreover," you need a semicolon before the adverb and a comma after. Choice (D) is the only option that joins these sentences in this way.

7. **(B)** Do not separate the subject "the amount of time spent in making observations during the past season" from the verb "is." All the other options give an unnecessary pause.

8. **(A)** Surround the parenthetical phrase, "together with a list of the records," with commas. Choice (B) only begins the parenthetical phrase with a comma, but does not have one at the end. Choice (C) is inconsistent in how it starts and finishes the parenthetical punctuation. And choice (D) incorrectly uses a semicolon when no complete sentence follows it.

9. **(B)** "Its" is the correct form of the possessive for the bird's back. Choice (A) would never be correct, and choices (C) and (D) would signify "it is" instead of the possessive.

10. **(A)** A comma will correctly separate the long dependent clause from the independent clause that follows. Choice (B) provides no pause, and choices (C) and (D) would need a complete sentence preceding their punctuation.

## Sentence Structure and Organization

### Parallelism

Even though the meaning of a sentence may be clear, unless it is written in a way that has stylistic consistency, it will not flow how it should. Have stylistic consistency by looking out for *parallel structure*.

### › Example 1

Incorrect: Two of my hobbies are riding bicycles and to watch movies.

Correct: Two of my hobbies are riding bicycles and **watching** movies.

Explanation: Maintain the same way of describing the hobbies so that the sentence has a parallel structure.

### › Example 2

Incorrect: Covered in mud, leaves, and in grass, he really needed a shower.

Correct: Covered in mud, leaves, and grass, he really needed a shower.

Explanation: If all the items in the list started with "in," then it would be fine to maintain that phrasing. Since the "in" that goes with "mud" also goes with "leaves," it can also apply to "grass" so there is no need to have "in" again.

**Parallelism Practice**—select the better sentence out of the two options.

1. (A) Choose a teacher to write your letter of recommendation who knows you well, likes the work you have done, and has the time to do a good job.
   (B) Choose a teacher to write your letter of recommendation who knows you well, likes the work you have done, and time to do a good job.
2. (A) To win or losing is not really important—just enjoy the game.
   (B) Winning or losing is not really important—just enjoy the game.
3. (A) Neither the children nor the adults were ready to leave the amusement park.
   (B) Neither the children or those who were adults were ready to leave the amusement park.
4. (A) To get the most out of class, listen carefully, write detailed notes, and ask pointed questions.
   (B) To get the most out of class, listen carefully, write detailed notes, and asking pointed questions.
5. (A) Dressed in tuxedos, ballgowns, and additionally in jewels, the celebrities were ready for the awards banquet.
   (B) Dressed in tuxedos, ballgowns, and jewels, the celebrities were ready for the awards banquet.
6. (A) Having a diversified portfolio, including investments in domestic growth stocks and international items, is a sound financial strategy.
   (B) Having a diversified portfolio, including investments in domestic growth stocks and international value stocks, is a sound financial strategy.

**7.** (A) Ben, a country music lover, and Kim, an appreciator of the musical genre of classical, surprisingly found a radio station they both liked.
(B) Ben, a country music lover, and Kim, a classical music lover, surprisingly found a radio station they both liked.

**8.** (A) Be sure to pack these items for the bus trip: delicious snacks, entertaining movies, and good books.
(B) Be sure to pack these items for the bus trip: delicious snacks, movies that you find entertaining, and good books.

**9.** (A) To clean his apartment, Henry vacuumed the floor and dusting the shelves.
(B) To clean his apartment, Henry vacuumed the floor and dusted the shelves.

**10.** (A) My brother, a football fan, and my sister, a baseball fan, both enjoy watching sports in autumn.
(B) My brother, a football fan, and my sister, who is a baseball fan, both enjoy watching sports in autumn.

## ✓ Answers

1. **(A)** Choose a teacher to write your letter of recommendation who knows you well, likes the work you have done, and has the time to do a good job.
Use "has the" with the final item in the list since all the listed items begin with a verb.
2. **(B)** Winning or losing is not really important—just enjoy the game.
"Winning" and "losing" use the same phrasing.
3. **(A)** Neither the children nor the adults were ready to leave the amusement park.
"Neither" and "nor" go together, while "either" and "or" go together.
4. **(A)** To get the most out of class, listen carefully, write detailed notes, and ask pointed questions.
"Asking" is not parallel with the other verbs.
5. **(B)** Dressed in tuxedos, ballgowns, and jewels, the celebrities were ready for the awards banquet.
Using "additionally in" interrupts the parallel structure.
6. **(B)** Having a diversified portfolio, including investments in domestic growth stocks and international value stocks, is a sound financial strategy.
"International items" does not match the previous example of "domestic growth stocks."
7. **(B)** Ben, a country music lover, and Kim, a classical music lover, surprisingly found a radio station they both liked.
Simply using "lover" is sufficient and maintains the parallel structure.
8. **(A)** Be sure to pack these items for the bus trip: delicious snacks, entertaining movies, and good books.
Maintain the parallel listing structure of *adjective-noun* by saying "entertaining movies."

9. **(B)** To clean his apartment, Henry vacuumed the floor and dusted the shelves.
"Vacuumed" and "dusted" maintain a parallel style.

10. **(A)** My brother, a football fan, and my sister, a baseball fan, both enjoy watching sports in autumn.
Since the first parenthetical in the list does not have "who is," maintain that style for the next parenthetical.

### Modifier Placement

Make sure sentences follow a logical order, with descriptions and subjects in a clear sequence. Be certain that the *literal* meaning matches up with the *intended* meaning.

#### Example 1

Incorrect: After completing the long hike, a three-hour nap did Xavier take.

Correct: After completing the long hike, Xavier took a three-hour nap.

Explanation: The first sentence does not name the subject until the very end, making it difficult to follow. The second sentence makes it clear that Xavier took the hike.

#### Example 2

Incorrect: Once we left the stadium, traffic was directed.

Correct: Once we left the stadium, the police directed the traffic.

Explanation: The first sentence is vague as to who or what directed the traffic. The second sentence makes it clear that the police did so.

#### Example 3

Incorrect: Your book will not become damaged, covered with a brown paper book cover.

Correct: Your book, covered with a brown paper book cover, will not become damaged.

Explanation: The description of the book—that it is covered with a brown paper book cover—should come after the book, as the second sentence does.

**Modifier Placement Practice**—select the better sentence out of the two options.

1. (A) I helped when dinner was over to clear the table.
(B) When dinner was over, I helped to clear the table.

2. (A) The deer encountered a bear eating grass in the meadow.
(B) While eating grass in the meadow, the deer encountered a bear.

3. (A) My friend Jordan, an art aficionado, loves to go to the latest museum openings.
(B) My friend Jordan loves to go to the latest museum openings, an art aficionado.

4. (A) Widely embraced as an ethical practice, recycling is required in many municipalities.
(B) Recycling is required in many municipalities, widely embraced as an ethical practice.

5. (A) The 1960s (a decade of much social upheaval) made my relatives the people they are today.
(B) The 1960s made my relatives the people (a decade of much social upheaval) they are today.

6. (A) My classmate is very generous when I forget my own, always shares his extra pencils and erasers with me.
(B) My classmate is very generous, since he always shares his extra pencils and erasers with me when I forget my own.

7. (A) Despite my reservations about going on the trip, I ended up having a wonderful time.
(B) I ended, despite my reservations about going on the trip, up having a wonderful time.

8. (A) Astrophysicists, a mysterious force in the universe, are excited to discover the true identity of dark energy.
(B) Astrophysicists are excited to discover the true identity of dark energy, a mysterious force in the universe.

9. (A) The diameter of a circle goes through the center of the circle, which is twice the circle's radius.
(B) The diameter of a circle, which is twice the circle's radius, goes through the center of the circle.

10. (A) Even though they were delicious, the habanero peppers were so spicy they hurt my eyes.
(B) The habanero peppers were so spicy they hurt my eyes, even though they were delicious.

## ✓ Answers

1. **(B)** When dinner was over, I helped to clear the table.
This makes it clear that the narrator helped with clearing the table *after* dinner was over.

2. **(B)** While eating grass in the meadow, the deer encountered a bear.
This makes it clear that it is the deer that is eating grass, not the bear.

3. **(A)** My friend Jordan, an art aficionado, loves to go to the latest museum openings.
Jordan, not the museum openings, is the art aficionado (someone who appreciates art).

4. **(A)** Widely embraced as an ethical practice, recycling is required in many municipalities.
The ethical practice is recycling, not municipalities.

5. **(A)** The 1960s (a decade of much social upheaval) made my relatives the people they are today.
The 1960s, not the people, were the decade of much social upheaval.

6. **(B)** My classmate is very generous, since he always shares his extra pencils and erasers with me when I forget my own.
This sentence makes sense, putting the reason the classmate is generous immediately after stating that he is generous, and making the subject "he" clear in the later part of the sentence.

7. **(A)** Despite my reservations about going on the trip, I ended up having a wonderful time.
The other option breaks up the phrase "I ended up," making the sentence confusing.

8. **(B)** Astrophysicists are excited to discover the true identity of dark energy, a mysterious force in the universe.
Dark energy, not astrophysicists, can logically be described as a mysterious force in the universe.

9. **(B)** The diameter of a circle, which is twice the circle's radius, goes through the center of the circle.
   This makes it clear that the diameter is twice the circle's radius, not that the circle is twice its own radius.

10. **(A)** Even though they were delicious, the habanero peppers were so spicy they hurt my eyes.
    The habanero peppers were delicious, not the narrator's eyes.

### Logical Comparisons

When making comparisons, be sure that the things being compared match one another in their type and number. As with other sentence structure and organization ideas, be sure that the *intended* meaning corresponds to the *literal* meaning.

#### Example 1

Incorrect: The salaries at the first business are comparable to the other business.

Correct: The salaries at the first business are comparable to **<u>those of</u>** the other business.

Explanation: The salaries, not the businesses, are what are being compared. Putting "those of" in the second part of the sentence makes this clear.

#### Example 2

Incorrect: Pollen affects me the same way that ragweed.

Correct: Pollen affects me the same way that ragweed **<u>does</u>**.

Explanation: The ways that pollen and ragweed affect the narrator are what are being compared. Without putting "does" at the end, the sentence would compare "pollen affects" to the noun "ragweed."

**Logical Comparisons Practice**—select the better sentence out of the two options.

1. (A) The downtown park in my city is better than any park.
   (B) The downtown park in my city is better than any other park.

2. (A) Your assignment is better than him.
   (B) Your assignment is better than his.

3. (A) The principal at my middle school was tougher than the one at my elementary school.
   (B) The principal at my middle school was tougher than my elementary school.

4. (A) I hope that my job application is better than the other applicants.
   (B) I hope that my job application is better than the other applicants'.

5. (A) Nurse practitioners provide many of the same treatments that doctors.
   (B) Nurse practitioners provide many of the same treatments that doctors provide.

6. (A) I was disappointed to learn that students who did less work in the class earned better grades than students who put in more effort.
   (B) I was disappointed to learn that students who did less work in the class earned better grades than students of effort.

**7.** (A) Relative to the collection of my local town's art museum, that of the Louvre is far more impressive.
(B) Relative to the collection of my local town's art museum, the Louvre is far more impressive.

**8.** (A) Algebra is better understood as a study of mathematical principles than simply studying letters.
(B) Algebra is better understood as a study of mathematical principles than simply a study of letters.

**9.** (A) A general is typically more experienced than a lieutenant.
(B) A general is typically more experienced than a lieutenant does.

**10.** (A) I find walking far easier than running.
(B) I find walking far easier than the times in which I run.

## ✓ Answers

1. **(B)** The downtown park in my city is better than any other park.
Without the "other," the sentence would be comparing the downtown park to itself.

2. **(B)** Your assignment is better than his.
Compare the assignment to another assignment, not to a person.

3. **(A)** The principal at my middle school was tougher than the one at my elementary school.
Compare the principal to another principal, not to a school.

4. **(B)** I hope that my job application is better than the other applicants'.
Using the apostrophe at the end of "applicants" makes the word a substitute for the "applications of other applicants," giving us a logical comparison.

5. **(B)** Nurse practitioners provide many of the same treatments that doctors provide.
Compare the providing of the nurse practitioners to the providing of the doctors, not the doctors themselves.

6. **(A)** I was disappointed to learn that students who did less work in the class earned better grades than students who put in more effort.
Keep the phrasing of "who did less work" consistent by using the verb "put in."

7. **(A)** Relative to the collection of my local town's art museum, that of the Louvre is far more impressive.
"That of" provides a stand-in for the collection of the Louvre, so that you are comparing a collection of one museum to the collection of the other.

8. **(B)** Algebra is better understood as a study of mathematical principles than simply a study of letters.
"A study of" is consistent with the earlier phrasing, not "studying."

9. **(A)** A general is typically more experienced than a lieutenant.
The general is described with the adjective "experienced," and there is no need to use a verb like "does."

10. **(A)** I find walking far easier than running.
This comparison concisely maintains the style, ending in "ing." The other option is overly wordy and confusing.

## Sentence Structure and Organization Practice Questions

1. Michael Jordan, winner of six World Championships, is ___________. It is incredible that Jordan accumulated so many titles despite taking a hiatus from basketball for several years to pursue his interest in baseball.

   Which choice completes the text so that it conforms to the conventions of Standard English?

   (A) as a basketball player who is incredible that is universally regarded.
   (B) regarded as a basketball player universally and incredibly.
   (C) universally regarded as an incredible basketball player.
   (D) as is universally regarded a basketball player with incredible qualities.

2. The playoff match was not even close—the Tigers walloped the Lions by 20 points. Undoubtedly, the coach of the Tigers is better than ___________

   Which choice completes the text so that it conforms to the conventions of Standard English?

   (A) the Lions.
   (B) the coach of the Lions.
   (C) theirs.
   (D) the other team.

3. The restaurant was very serene, with only a handful of diners present. ___________________ He took advantage of the quiet to think about his plans for the future.

   Which choice completes the text so that it conforms to the conventions of Standard English?

   (A) My friend, chewing quietly, pensively enjoyed his dinner.
   (B) My friend pensively enjoyed his dinner chewing quietly.
   (C) My friend enjoyed his chewing quietly dinner pensively.
   (D) Chewing quietly, his dinner my friend pensively enjoyed.

4. In the adventure movie, they ran through the forest, fought fierce predators, and _______ the evil villains. I rated the film five stars for excitement but only three stars for the dialogue.

   Which choice completes the text so that it conforms to the conventions of Standard English?

   (A) stop
   (B) stopping
   (C) will stop
   (D) stopped

5. In the gym, on the field, _________ Hannah acted like a true champion. Her diligence and strength served as an excellent example for both her classmates and teammates.

   Which choice completes the text so that it conforms to the conventions of Standard English?

   (A) and the classroom,
   (B) and in the classroom,
   (C) and classroom,
   (D) and classroom as well,

6. The forecasts throughout the week predicted, high winds, heavy precipitation, and freezing temperatures. However, the weather ended up being fine; it ________ hailed. We were immensely relieved.

   Which choice completes the text so that it conforms to the conventions of Standard English?

   (A) either snowed nor
   (B) either snowed and
   (C) neither snowed and
   (D) neither snowed nor

7. Out of everyone in my city, I am _______ at solving crossword puzzles. My friend, on the other hand, is widely recognized as the best chess player in town.

   Which choice completes the text so that it conforms to the conventions of Standard English?

   (A) good
   (B) better
   (C) the best
   (D) the goodest

8. Upon receiving the notice of losing his job, ________ He took all of his belongings with him in a small box so that the next employee could use his cubicle.

   Which choice completes the text so that it conforms to the conventions of Standard English?

   (A) his desk was cleared out by him.
   (B) he cleared out his desk.
   (C) the desk cleared.
   (D) the desk was cleared.

9. The brand-new ________ Give the affordable price, I decided to buy the extended warranty and an advanced headset.

   Which choice completes the text so that it conforms to the conventions of Standard English?

   (A) phone, which cost only $30, was covered under the cell phone plan I found online.
   (B) phone was covered under the cell phone plan I found online, which cost only $30.
   (C) phone that cost only $30 was under the cell phone plan covered, that is, the one I found online.
   (D) phone which cost only $30 was online under the cell phone I found covered.

10. I find that driving the sports car is both exhilarating ________ My friends enjoy going for rides with me, especially when I retract the roof and turn the car into a convertible.

    Which choice completes the text so that it conforms to the conventions of Standard English?

    (A) and relaxed.
    (B) and relaxing.
    (C) or relaxing.
    (D) or relaxed.

## Answer Explanations

1. **(C)** This option puts the words in the most logical sequence. The other options put the words in sequences that are not very clear.

2. **(B)** By replacing the underlined portion with "the coach of the Lions," the sentence will now make a logical comparison of a coach to a coach. The other options compare the coach to illogical entities.

3. **(A)** Choice (A) is the only option that correctly has "chewing quietly" next to what it should modify—"My friend." The other options put this phrase in an awkward spot.

4. **(D)** "Stopped" is the only option that maintains the parallel structure by having a past tense verb. It is consistent with the other verbs "ran" and "fought." The other choices do not maintain parallelism.

5. **(B)** The other phrases in this sentence start with a preposition like "in" or "on." Choice (B) is the only option that begins in that similar fashion.

6. **(D)** Based on the preceding sentence and the transition "however," this sentence needs to say that no bad weather happened. "Neither . . . nor" is the appropriate way to express this idea. With "either" and "neither," use "or" not "and."

7. **(C)** Since there are surely three or more people in the city, the superlative "best" is the correct word to express this comparison. "Good" is typically used to describe a single object, "better" is used for comparing two objects, and "goodest" is not a word.

8. **(B)** This option puts the sentence in an active voice and has the words in a logical order. Choices (A) and (D) invert the word order and choice (C) would not make sense since the desk is not doing the clearing.

9. **(A)** The phrase "which cost only $30" is nonessential to the sentence and can be surrounded with commas. Moreover, the phrase needs to modify "phone" since that is the item that has the cost of $30. Choice (A) is the only option that does both tasks.

10. **(B)** This maintains parallelism with "exhilarating" by having the same ending of "ing." Also, with the word "both," you need to use "and" instead of "or."

## Transitions

The SAT tests your proficiency with transitional words—words like "but," "also," and "because" that connect phrases and sentences together. An understanding of transitional words will ensure that your writing is well-organized. Here is a list of some of the most common transitional words you will encounter on the SAT:

| General Meaning | Transitional Words |
|---|---|
| Additional Information | Also, and, besides, further, furthermore, in addition, what's more |
| Cause and Effect | As a result, because, consequently, therefore, thus, to that end |
| Clarification | At any rate, in other words, in fact |
| Comparison | Likewise, similarly, by the same token |
| Contrast | After all, alternately, although, but, by contrast, even though, however, instead, meanwhile, nevertheless, nonetheless, on the other hand, rather, still, whereas |
| Give an Example | For example, for instance |
| Obviously | Of course |
| Time Sequence | Eventually, finally, in the first place, next, ultimately |
| Typically | Traditionally |

### Example 1

Incorrect: The kitchen had virtually no food in it. Also, we managed to make dinner.

Correct: The kitchen had virtually no food in it. **Still**, we managed to make dinner.

Explanation: Even though the kitchen did not have much food, the group was still able to make dinner. Thus, a contrast is needed between the two sentences—"Still" works well. When working through transition questions, be certain to consider the surrounding context so you can determine the best logical relationship.

In the above example, you needed to look at the sentence before and after the transitional word. In some sentences, the transition is based just on what comes after the transitional word, like "Although I was excited to watch the movie, I had difficulty finding time to do so." Err on the side of considering a bit too much context just to be sure you fully understand what logical relationship is needed.

### Example 2

When school begins in the fall, seniors often ask their past teachers to write letters of recommendation on their behalf. The best teachers are typically inundated with requests, and usually have to limit the number of letters they can write. ________ it is a good idea to ask teachers in the spring or summer for letters of recommendation so that the teachers have adequate time to do them.

Which choice completes the text with the most logical transition?

(A) Also,
(B) For instance,
(C) Therefore,
(D) Furthermore,

Explanation: The correct answer to this question is **(C)**, "Therefore." This is the only option that provides a cause-and-effect relationship between the first two sentences and the final sentence of the paragraph. A cause-and-effect relationship is necessary here since it is because good teachers are flooded with letter of recommendation requests that it is sensible to ask teachers earlier to write letters on your behalf.

**Transitions Practice**—select the better sentence(s) out of the two options.

1. (A) Even though I had plenty of sleep, I still felt tired.
   (B) Consequently I had plenty of sleep, I still felt tired.
2. (A) A part-time job during high school is a great way to make extra money. Furthermore, it can help you develop skills that will serve you well in college and in your career.
   (B) A part-time job during high school is a great way to make extra money. In contrast, it can help you develop skills that will serve you well in college and in your career.
3. (A) When making bread, first preheat the oven. Therefore, put the well-kneaded dough into the oven to bake.
   (B) When making bread, first preheat the oven. Next, put the well-kneaded dough into the oven to bake.
4. (A) The yard was completely covered with weeds. Nevertheless, the gardener happily tackled the weeding and turned the yard into a beautiful site.
   (B) The yard was completely covered with weeds. Also, the gardener happily tackled the weeding and turned the yard into a beautiful site.
5. (A) Majoring in two different areas may allow for a natural synergy between subjects. For instance, a business major with an engineering major could help you learn both how to make a product and how to market it.
   (B) Majoring in two different areas may allow for a natural synergy between subjects. Whereas a business major with an engineering major could help you learn both how to make a product and how to market it.
6. (A) He did not have a good reason to run for office, and, by the same token, he did not have a reason to avoid running.
   (B) He did not have a good reason to run for office, and, in the first place, he did not have a reason to avoid running.
7. (A) A perfect score would, of course, be preferable; thus, a 99 out of 100 is truly excellent.
   (B) A perfect score would, of course, be preferable; however, a 99 out of 100 is truly excellent.
8. (A) We did not do very well in the game; consequently, our coach made us run extra laps.
   (B) We did not do very well in the game; and our coach made us run extra laps.
9. (A) The roller coaster had an awesome first hill, and what's more, it had three incredible loops.
   (B) The roller coaster had an awesome first hill and despite this, it had three incredible loops.
10. (A) The wildlife sanctuary had elephants and rhinos. In contrast, it had zebra, giraffes, and water buffalo.
    (B) The wildlife sanctuary had elephants and rhinos. Further, it had zebra, giraffes, and water buffalo.

**11.** (A) His anger at his neighbor was understandable. Therefore, it was no justification for vandalism of his neighbor's house.
(B) His anger at his neighbor was understandable. However, it was no justification for vandalism of his neighbor's house.

**12.** (A) The world-renowned orchestra conductor is nonetheless an excellent violinist.
(B) The world-renowned orchestra conductor is likewise an excellent violinist.

**13.** (A) I did not eat breakfast. As a result, I was really hungry for lunch.
(B) I did not eat breakfast. Moreover, I was really hungry for lunch.

**14.** (A) Thanksgiving is, in other words, a day on which people eat quite a bit of food.
(B) Thanksgiving is traditionally a day on which people eat quite a bit of food.

**15.** (A) Her parents did not think she wanted to join the club. In fact, she was the first one to sign up for the club at the school fair.
(B) Her parents did not think she wanted to join the club. Typically, she was the first one to sign up for the club at the school fair.

**16.** (A) Best friends are forever; despite this, you will stay connected to your best friend over many decades and great distances.
(B) Best friends are forever; in other words, you will stay connected to your best friend over many decades and great distances.

**17.** (A) At first, the athlete resisted the advice of his coach. Ultimately, he took the coach's advice and improved immensely.
(B) Initially, the athlete resisted the advice of his coach. At first, he took the coach's advice and improved immensely.

**18.** (A) I am excited for the first day of school. On the other hand, I am worried about a pop quiz over the summer reading.
(B) I am excited for the first day of school. Consequently, I am worried about a pop quiz over the summer reading.

**19.** (A) We climbed up the mountain and still reached the summit.
(B) We climbed up the mountain and eventually reached the summit.

**20.** (A) The doctor said you should eat more fruits and vegetables. Therefore, you should come to the farmer's market to buy some healthy produce.
(B) The doctor said you should eat more fruits and vegetables. Whereas you should come to the farmer's market to buy some healthy produce.

## ✓ Answers

1. **(A)** Even though I had plenty of sleep, I still felt tired.
"Even though" shows contrast between having plenty of sleep and still feeling tired.

2. **(A)** A part-time job during high school is a great way to make extra money. Furthermore, it can help you develop skills that will serve you well in college and in your career.
"Furthermore" makes sense since the idea of skill development would be an additional benefit of having a part-time job.

3. **(B)** When making bread, first preheat the oven. Next, put the well-kneaded dough into the oven to bake.
"Next" demonstrates the sequence of events that one would find in a recipe.

4. **(A)** The yard was completely covered with weeds. Nevertheless, the gardener happily tackled the weeding and turned the yard into a beautiful site.
"Nevertheless" shows a contrast between the fact that the yard was covered with weeds and the fact that the gardener could still make the yard into something beautiful.

5. **(A)** Majoring in two different areas may allow for a natural synergy between subjects. For instance, a business major with an engineering major could help you learn both how to make a product and how to market it.
"For instance" is a logical way to join the two sentences, since the second sentence provides an example of how a double major could make sense.

6. **(A)** He did not have a good reason to run for office, and, by the same token, he did not have a reason to avoid running.
"By the same token" means that the man both had a good reason to run for office *and* had a reason not to run.

7. **(B)** A perfect score would, of course, be preferable; however, a 99 out of 100 is truly excellent.
"However" shows a contrast between the acknowledgement that a perfect score would be better, but that a 99 is still outstanding.

8. **(A)** We did not do very well in the game; consequently, our coach made us run extra laps.
"Consequently" states the cause-and-effect relationship between not doing well in the game and the coach's decision to make the players run laps.

9. **(A)** The roller coaster had an awesome first hill, and what's more, it had three incredible loops.
"What's more" shows that in addition to the awesome first hill, the roller coast had three incredible loops.

10. **(B)** The wildlife sanctuary had elephants and rhinos. Further, it had zebra, giraffes, and water buffalo.
"Further" shows that along with the elephants and rhinos, the sanctuary also had other animals.

11. **(B)** His anger at his neighbor was understandable. However, it was no justification for vandalism of his neighbor's house.
"However" shows that while the man was understandably angry at his neighbor, he had no good reason to vandalize his neighbor's home.

12. **(B)** The world-renowned orchestra conductor is likewise an excellent violinist.
"Likewise" shows that the conductor is both excellent with the orchestra and with the piano.

13. **(A)** I did not eat breakfast. As a result, I was really hungry for lunch.
"As a result" shows a direct cause-and-effect relationship between not eating breakfast and being hungry for lunch.

14. **(B)** Thanksgiving is traditionally a day on which people eat quite a bit of food.
"In other words" does not make sense since the sentence is not rephrasing anything; "traditionally" works because the sentence says what typically happens on this holiday.

15. **(A)** Her parents did not think she wanted to join the club. In fact, she was the first one to sign up for the club at the school fair. "In fact" clarifies that despite what her parents thought, the daughter was actually interested in joining the club.

16. **(B)** Best friends are forever; in other words, you will stay connected to your best friend over many decades and great distances.
The part of the sentence after the semicolon clarifies what is meant by the statement that "best friends are forever," so "in other words" is logical.

17. **(A)** At first, the athlete resisted the advice of his coach. Ultimately, he took the coach's advice and improved immensely.
This sentence puts the sequence of events in a logical order, with the athlete initially resisting the coach's advice and eventually following it.

18. **(A)** I am excited for the first day of school. On the other hand, I am worried about a pop quiz over the summer reading.
"On the other hand" suggests a contrast between the excitement of the student and the worry over a quiz.

19. **(B)** We climbed up the mountain and eventually reached the summit.
This option shows a logical sequence of events with "eventually" used to mark the final part of the journey.

20. **(A)** The doctor said you should eat more fruits and vegetables. Therefore, you should come to the farmer's market to buy some healthy produce.
"Therefore" shows a cause-and-effect relationship between the doctor's recommendation about how to eat and the action necessary to acquire the recommended foods.

## Transitions Practice Questions

### Exercise 1

1. The two friends saw eye to eye on virtually everything, from food to fashion, and from literature to music. When one found something to be funny, the other was ________ amused.

   Which choice completes the text with the most logical transition?

   (A) likewise
   (B) specifically
   (C) finally
   (D) meanwhile

2. Electing Maria to be class president was a foregone conclusion. She was popular with virtually every group in school. ________ her speech made a clear and convincing case for her candidacy.

   Which choice completes the text with the most logical transition?

   (A) Notwithstanding,
   (B) Immediately,
   (C) Although,
   (D) Moreover,

3. The court proceedings were about to begin without the sole eyewitness to the crime present. The judge _______ summoned the eyewitness to appear at the next court hearing to help get to the bottom of the matter.

   Which choice completes the text with the most logical transition?

   (A) in contrast
   (B) still
   (C) accordingly
   (D) despite this

4. The play will be delayed for several minutes so that the ushers can guide the latecomers to their seats. ________ spectators can spend some time checking out the program and enjoying their concessions.

   Which choice completes the text with the most logical transition?

   (A) Centrally,
   (B) In the meantime,
   (C) To summarize,
   (D) Furthermore,

5. The meal looked and smelled a bit strange; _______, it tasted delicious. It is often helpful to be open to new experiences, not being afraid to take that first bite.

   Which choice completes the text with the most logical transition?

   (A) therefore
   (B) nevertheless
   (C) for this reason
   (D) to that end

6. When you want to chop vegetables, begin by grabbing the ingredients you will need. ______, get the cutting board and knife. Finally, begin chopping the vegetables into the shapes and sizes you need for the dish.

   Which choice completes the text with the most logical transition?

   (A) First
   (B) At last
   (C) In short
   (D) Second

7. As a father, I try to give my children the best advice I can. ________, I am no expert in psychology. However, I genuinely believe that I have my children's best interests at heart and want to help however possible.

   Which choice completes the text with the most logical transition?

   (A) Granted
   (B) Similarly
   (C) Beyond
   (D) Foundationally

8. The squirrel grabbed a large walnut and took it up a tree for storage. Only a few minutes ______ the squirrel returned to grab yet another walnut. With dedication like this, the squirrel should be in excellent shape for a long winter.

   Which choice completes the text with the most logical transition?

   (A) afterward
   (B) beyond
   (C) nevertheless
   (D) therefore

9. The baker wanted to make something that would be acceptable for diners with a gluten intolerance. ________ in mind, he found some gluten-free flour and made a wonderful dessert.

   Which choice completes the text with the most logical transition?

   (A) Unfortunate
   (B) In fact of purpose
   (C) Truly
   (D) With this object

10. When you write your term paper, be sure to give plenty of examples ________ your primary argument. The grader will carefully examine how strong the support is for your thesis.

    Which choice completes the text with the most logical transition?

    (A) with contend
    (B) of claiming
    (C) on advance
    (D) to illustrate

## Answer Explanations

1. **(A)** The two friends are similar in all their beliefs, so the transition "likewise" expresses this similarity.
2. **(D)** Maria is popular with everyone and in addition her speech was very convincing. The most appropriate transition is "moreover" since it means "also." The other options do not convey this relationship.
3. **(C)** "Accordingly" shows a cause-and-effect relationship, which makes sense given that the sole witness was absent and the judge wanted the witness to appear. The other options do not show a cause-and-effect relationship.
4. **(B)** "In the meantime" means that someone can do something else while another thing is happening. The spectators can do other things as they wait for the delayed play to begin, making "in the meantime" an appropriate transition. The other options do not convey this idea.
5. **(B)** "Nevertheless" shows a contrast, unlike the other options. A contrast is appropriate in this context since although the meal seems strange, it ended up tasting quite good.

6. **(D)** The text is outlining the steps that you should take when chopping vegetables. The second step out of the three steps is to get the cutting board and knife, making choice (D) the only logical option.
7. **(A)** "Granted" is synonymous with "it is true that . . ." In this context, the narrator Is stating that while he tries to give the children the best possible advice, he may fall short in the quality of the advice since he is not an expert in psychology. The other options do not acknowledge the truth of the situation.
8. **(A)** The squirrel returned "afterward" to get another walnut after initially grabbing and storing one. The other options would not convey the timeline of events.
9. **(D)** "With this object" means "with a goal." In this context, the baker wants to make something for diners who cannot eat gluten; given this goal, he finds flour that allows him to make something they can enjoy. The other options do not express the appropriate connection.
10. **(D)** The grader is looking for support for the thesis, so it is important "to illustrate" your argument. The other options are grammatically incorrect.

## Exercise 2

1. The parasitic European cuckoo decreases the mother bird's output and, in some cases, kills all offspring, ________ decreasing the host bird's fitness. On top of reproductive output, the mother bird must put in additional work to feed the equivalent of a nest full of babies that is just one large baby.

   Which choice completes the text with the most logical transition?

   (A) however
   (B) but
   (C) therefore
   (D) previously

2. "Ladies and gentlemen of the class of '97, wear sunscreen. If I could only offer you one tip for the future, that would be it." ______ begins a well-known commencement speech; the speaker goes on to explain why his advice about careers and life goals may or may not be helpful to the students, but the advice to wear sunscreen will always be applicable.

   Which choice completes the text with the most logical transition?

   (A) Whereas
   (B) Additionally
   (C) Thus
   (D) Also

3. In 1907 when a financial crisis (one of the foreshocks of the panic that would lead to the Great Depression) took place, Morgan took charge. Banks were on the brink of falling apart. People were going to lose their savings; the situation was dire and the government at the time did not have the power to intervene in a meaningful way. ______ Morgan did.

   Which choice completes the text with the most logical transition?

   (A) So,
   (B) Additionally,
   (C) Formerly,
   (D) Moreover,

4. The Roseto Effect was first studied in Roseto, Pennsylvania, where there lived a tight-knit community whose diets contained significant levels of fatty acids. ________ members of the town eating high levels of fats, drinking alcohol, and commonly smoking tobacco, the town's residents had significantly lower rates of cardiovascular diseases than those in surrounding areas.

   Which choice completes the text with the most logical transition?

   (A) Despite
   (B) Because of the
   (C) Given the
   (D) Whenever

5. While the concept of a government bailout is fairly new, the idea of external powers stepping in to try to boost the economy is not. Prior to the era of governmental intervention, ________ it was big business who worked to protect the economy and with it, their profits.

   Which choice completes the text with the most logical transition?

   (A) consequently,
   (B) also,
   (C) due to this,
   (D) however,

6. Easily one of the most distinctive painters associated with the surrealist movement of the early 20th century, Frida Kahlo ________ insisted adamantly throughout her career that she was by no means a surrealist herself.

   Which choice completes the text with the most logical transition?

   (A) consequently
   (B) moreover
   (C) accordingly
   (D) nonetheless

7. A good broad range sunscreen can, when used properly, prevent sunburn for hours. __________ if a product has a sun protection factor (SPF) of 30, that means that skin can be exposed for 30 times longer without burning than if no protection was used.

   Which choice completes the text with the most logical transition?

   (A) Despite this,
   (B) For example,
   (C) In contrast,
   (D) Also,

8. Despite its sinister and somewhat draconian reputation, electroconvulsive therapy (ECT) is making a rather surprising return in the treatment of chronic clinical depression. Like many of its pharmaceutical counterparts, the exact physiological mechanism responsible for ECT's alleviation of the symptoms of depression remains elusive, ______ its results are inarguably remarkable.

   Which choice completes the text with the most logical transition?

   (A) and
   (B) since
   (C) with
   (D) but

9. Sunlight is different from the light that a person experiences from a fire or a light bulb. Sunlight is mostly UV light, which has a much shorter wavelength than the light we turn on when we use the bathroom in the middle of the night. __________ if the earth's protective ozone layer didn't filter out much of the UV light, humans would risk their health just by going about their everyday lives during daylight hours.

   Which choice completes the text with the most logical transition?

   (A) Meanwhile,
   (B) Nonetheless,
   (C) Indeed,
   (D) As a result,

10. If school were operated on a year-round basis, student retention of material would be strengthened since it is much easier to forget material over a three-month break than over a two-week one. Material retention is especially vital for subjects like math and foreign language in which more advanced units will not make sense without a sound basis in the earlier material. __________ if students have more frequent breaks from the rigors of school, they are less likely to burn out.

    Which choice completes the text with the most logical transition?

    (A) However,
    (B) Consequently,
    (C) Additionally,
    (D) On the other hand,

## Answer Explanations

1. **(C)** This option is the only choice that shows a cause-and-effect relationship between the European cuckoo acting parasitically toward other birds and the resulting decrease in the host bird's overall fitness. Choices (A) and (B) show a contrast, and choice (D) unnecessarily inserts a time sequence indication.

2. **(C)** "Thus" is used to make the idiomatic phrase "Thus begins"; this phrase provides a logical transition between the quotation that started the speech and the clarification of the significance of the speech. It is not choice (A) because there is no contrast, and it is not choices (B) or (D) because this is not an additional piece of information, but a clarification.

3. **(A)** "So" correctly expresses a cause-and-effect relationship between the earlier sentence, which says that there was a dire situation with no government help, and the current sentence expresses that Morgan did intervene. The other options do not express a cause-and-effect relationship.

4. **(A)** "Despite" signifies an oppositional relationship between the first part of the sentence, which states that the diets of the town's residents are not particularly healthy, and the unexpected lack of cardiovascular disease among the residents. The other options do not convey a contrasting relationship.

5. **(D)** "However" is the appropriate transition in this context, since the sentence points out the contrast between the current era of governmental intervention and an era in the past when privately based bailouts were more commonplace. Choices (A) and (C) would show cause and effect, and choice (B) would be used to list an additional item or idea.

6. **(D)** "Nonetheless" is used to show a contrast between the fact that Frida Kahlo is considered a surrealist by society, yet she did not consider herself a surrealist. Choice (A), "consequently," and choice (C), "accordingly," show cause and effect. Choice (B), "moreover," is synonymous with "also." This is a good example where you can use the similarities among choices (A) and (C) to eliminate them.

7. **(B)** "For example" is appropriate since the current sentence provides an example of what makes a high-quality sunscreen. It is not choices (A) or (C) because there is not a contrast, and it is not choice (D) because the current sentence provides an example, not simply an extra point.

8. **(D)** The word "but" is the appropriate transition. The sentence contains a contrast—scientists do not know exactly how ECT works, but they do know that the results are remarkable. The transitions in choices (A), (B), and (C) do not indicate a contrast.

9. **(C)** "Indeed" is used to introduce a further point that elaborates on the previous point made; in this case, "indeed" connects the previous sentence that states that sunlight is mostly UV light and the current sentence that underscores the potential danger from UV light to humans. It is not choices (A) or (B) because there is not a contrast, and it is not choice (D) because there is not a cause-and-effect relationship.

10. **(C)** The word "Additionally" correctly indicates that this sentence builds upon the argument in the previous sentences. Choice (B), "Consequently," indicates a cause-and-effect relationship. Choice (A), "However," and choice (D), "On the other hand," both indicate a contrast.

## Rhetorical Synthesis Questions

A new type of question on the Digital SAT is the rhetorical synthesis, or "rhetorical analysis," question. You will be asked to consider the notes that a student has taken on a topic and determine the best way to use the information in the notes to present or emphasize a particular idea. On questions like these, be sure to really focus on what the question asks so that you can zero in on the most relevant evidence.

### Example

While researching a topic, a student has taken the following notes:

- The classical Humanist ideal of human individualism can be represented by Leonardo da Vinci's "Vitruvian Man."
- The Vitruvian Man was an emblem of Humanism and the source for the civilization model that assumes Europe is not just a location, but a universal standard of humankind.
- Posthumanism tends to turn away from the nature and culture binary and questions the distinctions between what is considered human and nonhuman.
- Posthumanism rejects individualism by discouraging human-centered, or self-centered, thought, and instead urges interconnection between self, others, and nonhuman others.

The student wants to emphasize what makes Humanism different from Posthumanism. Which choice most effectively uses relevant information from the notes to accomplish this goal?

(A) Humanism focuses on a concern for others, while Posthumanism embraces self-centeredness.
(B) Humanism argues for individualism, while Posthumanism rejects it.
(C) Humanism focuses on geography, while Posthumanism is concerned with politics.
(D) Humanism advocates compassion for all living things, while Posthumanism focuses on the needs of humans alone.

### Answers

The correct answer is choice (B). Focus on the specific question: "The student wants to emphasize what makes Humanism different from Posthumanism." Look at the bullets to determine what makes the two ideas different. The first bullet shows that individualism is associated with classical Humanism. The final bullet shows that Posthumanism rejects individualism. So, choice (B) is correct in articulating the differences between these two ideas. It is not choice (A) because this gets the two ideas backwards. It is not choice (C) because Humanism is not concerned with geography whatsoever, and Posthumanism is only loosely related to politics. It is not choice (D) because Humanism focuses on individualism rather than extensive compassion, and Posthumanism is in fact open to the consideration of the needs of nonhumans.

## Rhetorical Synthesis Practice Questions

### Exercise 1

Select the best choice out of the four options.

1. While researching a topic, a student has taken the following notes:

   - Personal trainers are fitness experts who help clients implement their health and exercise goals.
   - Trainers often personally guide their clients with customized workouts.
   - They can help clients with their greatest areas of need, like endurance, strength, or flexibility.
   - Trainers ensure that clients train safely, helping them maintain the proper exercise form.
   - Some trainers choose to pursue a four-year degree in exercise science or a related field, while others complete a one-year certificate program.
   - In addition to a formal education, trainers are almost always expected to have CPR training.

   The student wants to present a how personal trainers can prevent clients from becoming injured. Which choice most effectively uses relevant information from the notes to accomplish this goal?

   (A) Personal trainers often pursue educational credentials, like an exercise science degree, that gives their clients confidence in their skills.
   (B) For clients who need help with building their strength and endurance, a personal trainer is an excellent option.
   (C) Personal trainers can customize workouts for clients, improving their chances of achieving their fitness goals.
   (D) Through monitoring the proper exercise form of their clients, personal trainers help clients train safely.

2. While researching a topic, a student has taken the following notes:

   - More than 70 percent of the Earth's surface is covered with water.
   - Water makes up most of the human body.
   - Water is a rather simple compound: 2 hydrogen atoms covalently bonded to 1 oxygen atom.
   - Water has several unique chemical properties that make it rather suitable for life.
   - Water is considered a universal solvent, enabling cells to use nutrients and oxygen.

   The student wants to emphasize the widespread prevalence of water. Which choice most effectively uses relevant information from the notes to accomplish this goal?

   (A) Covering over 70 percent of the Earth's surface, water is widely found on our planet.
   (B) Since it is a universal solvent, water is quite useful in biological processes.
   (C) The simplicity of the composition of water belies the complexity of the organisms in which it is found.
   (D) Many chemical compounds, including water, make up the human body.

3. While researching a topic, a student has taken the following notes:

   - During the late 1800s, the private boxes at the Academy of Music Opera House were reserved for the most elite families in New York City.
   - After being excluded from the Academy of Music private boxes, some newly wealthy families met to create a new opera house.
   - The new opera house would be more extravagant than the Academy of Music one, giving the families an opportunity to display their great wealth.
   - The newly formed opera house was called the Metropolitan Opera house, known today as the "Met."
   - Just three years after the formation of the Met, the Academy of Music shut down as people flocked to the new performing center.
   - Today, the Met continues to perform at Lincoln Center in New York City

   The student wants to present a likely emotional cause for the formation of the Met. Which choice most effectively uses relevant information from the notes to accomplish this goal?

   (A) Feelings of exclusion from the elite society of the Academy of Music likely motivated wealthy families to create an alternative organization.
   (B) A pure love of musical artistry by wealthy families most likely propelled them to initially create the Academy of Music.
   (C) It is remarkable that the Met has endured over the span of three different centuries.
   (D) After the closure of the Academy of Music, wealthy families who earnestly missed operatic performances created the Met.

4. While researching a topic, a student has taken the following notes:

   - *Claire of the Sea Light* is a novel by Edwidge Danticat.
   - In the work, the woes of Haiti are addressed directly and indirectly.
   - The narrative threads through the lives of a town where everybody knows everybody and no one tragedy can exist on its own.
   - The novel emphasizes several themes:
     - displacement and exile
     - disrupted familial relationships,
     - the inheritance of trauma and loss
     - the fluidity of personal identity and belonging
   - The novel's attention to current sociopolitical issues offers a more multifaceted and activist-oriented personal account than some of Danticat's other novels.

   The student wants to summarize how Danticat treats the concept of personal identity in *Claire of the Sea Light*. Which choice most effectively uses relevant information from the notes to accomplish this goal?

   (A) Danticat articulates how family is at the core of what gives people their authentic identity.
   (B) Danticat shows that tragedy can affect not just one person but everyone in a town.
   (C) Danticat observes how activists tend to experience a reduction in social exile.
   (D) Danticat emphasizes how personal identity can be ever-changing instead of constant.

5. While researching a topic, a student has taken the following notes:

   - An adjuvant is a substance that enhances the body's immune response to an antigen.
   - Adjuvants are used in the field of medicine.
   - They are used as a possible solution to antibiotic resistant bacteria in patients.
   - Gaston Ramon, a French veterinarian, discovered adjuvants while observing and treating diseases in horses.
   - Adjuvants are coupled with antibiotics to re-sensitize bacteria to antibiotics, making the antibiotics effective again.
   - *E. coli* without the transcription factor, EF-P, are more sensitive to antibiotics than *E. coli* with it.

   The student wants to emphasize how modern doctors might use adjuvants to improve patient outcomes. Which choice most effectively uses relevant information from the notes to accomplish this goal?

   (A) Doctors might use adjuvants to help patients who are infected with antibiotic-resistant bacteria.
   (B) Adjuvants can be especially useful in helping those in emergency room settings.
   (C) An adjuvant is the most helpful treatment for patients with an *E. coli* infection.
   (D) Veterinarians discovered the extremely useful technology of adjuvants; now the technology is used on human patients.

## Answer Explanations

1. **(D)** The question asks us to present how personal trainers can prevent client injury. Choice (D) accomplishes this task by stating that through making sure clients use the proper exercise form, the clients will avoid injury. Choice (A) focuses on education instead of injury prevention. Choice (B) focuses on strength and endurance, which is not nearly as directly related to safe training as choice (D). Choice (C) vaguely mentions client workout customization.

2. **(A)** "Prevalence" means commonality—choice (A) shows just how widespread and common water is on our planet. It is not choice (B) because this is much more indirect in suggesting the prevalence of water. It is not choice (C) because this focuses on complexity instead of commonality. It is not choice (D) because this limits the discussion to the human body instead of discussing how widespread water is.

3. **(A)** The notes state that "after being excluded from the Academy of Music private boxes, some newly wealthy families met to create a new opera house." Based on this, the likely emotional cause for the formation of the Met was a feeling of exclusion, as noted in choice (A). It is not choice (B) because there is no evidence that a pure love of music was the primary motivation. It is not choice (C) because this has nothing to do with an emotional cause. It is not choice (C) because the Met was created before the end of the Academy of Music, helping to bring about its demise.

4. **(D)** The question asks us to summarize how Danticat treats the concept of personal identity in the novel. Choice (D) effectively accomplishes this task by paraphrasing the note that a theme of the novel is "the fluidity of personal identity and belonging." Choice (A) is incorrect because Danticat highlights "disrupted familial relationships," not how family is the key to personal identity. Choices (B) and (C) do not relate to personal identity.

5. **(A)** The notes state that adjuvants are used "as a possible solution to antibiotic resistant bacteria in patients." Therefore, if a student wants to show how the adjuvants can be used to improve patient outcomes, emphasizing how they reduce infection in antibiotic resistant bacteria makes sense. Choice (B) is not supported by the notes. While *E. coli* are mentioned in the final bullet, the point is not on whether adjuvants are particularly helpful but on the type of *E. coli* that is more sensitive to antibiotics—this makes choice (C) incorrect. Choice (D) does not elaborate on the relative effectiveness of adjuvants.

## Exercise 2

Select the best choice out of the four options.

1. While researching a topic, a student has taken the following notes:

   - In single-celled organisms, mitosis is used for reproduction.
   - Mitosis also occurs in more complex organisms for tissue growth and replacement of cells.
   - In mitosis, the nucleus splits to form two sets of identical chromosomes resulting in two daughter cells with the same genetic material.
   - Meiosis is cell division particular to organisms that use sexual reproduction.
   - Meiosis splits the number of chromosomes in parent cells in half so that they can combine in offspring.
   - Meiosis is essential for genetic diversity.

   The student wants to emphasize a significant similarity between mitosis and meiosis. Which choice most effectively uses relevant information from the notes to accomplish this goal?

   (A) Mitosis and meiosis are both used by living things for reproduction.
   (B) Mitosis maintains the same genetic material, while meiosis leads to greater diversity.
   (C) Mitosis and meiosis are used equally by organisms throughout the Earth.
   (D) Mitosis and mitosis both allow for exact copies of an organism to be replicated generation after generation.

2. In preparing for a physics experiment on simple harmonic motion (SHM), a student has taken the following notes:

   - SHM is periodic motion where the restoring force is proportional to the displacement of the object in motion.
   - Examples of SHM are the simple pendulum and an object on a spring.
   - Periodic motion involves the oscillation of an object about an equilibrium or lowest potential energy position.
   - Formulas for SHM assume relatively small oscillations.
   - The experiment will evaluate the impact of changing the mass of the attached object and the length of the string on the length of the oscillations

   The student wants to emphasize the type of intervals at which an object in simple harmonic motion will most likely oscillate. Which choice most effectively uses relevant information from the notes to accomplish this goal?

   (A) When moving in a simple harmonic, an object will likely have oscillations at irregular intervals.
   (B) Objects in simple harmonic motion often utilize an object on a spring.
   (C) Experiments are needed to determine more about the mass of attached objects in a simple harmonic motion.
   (D) Objects in simple harmonic motion most likely move in a regular pattern.

3. While researching a topic, a student has taken the following notes:

   - The bullroarer is an instrument made of a wooden slat typically measuring between 6 and 24 inches long, affixed at one end to a length of twisted cord.
   - The bullroarer is widespread among ancient cultures, and is also known as a "tundun," or "whizzing-stick."
   - The oldest known bullroarers were discovered in the Ukraine, and are estimated to date from the Paleolithic era, approximately 17,000 B.C.E.
   - The sound of the bullroarer is rather unique and has been likened both to an animal's roar and the approach of a distant thunderstorm.
   - Pitch modulation can be achieved by altering the speed of rotation, or the length of the cord.

   The student wants to emphasize the long duration of the bullroarer in human history. Which choice most effectively uses relevant information from the notes to accomplish this goal?

   (A) With a sound like a thunderstorm or animal roar, it is no wonder that the bullroarer has been popular for quite a while.
   (B) While Ukraine is the location of a bullroarer discovery, other locations around the world can make a similar claim to fame.
   (C) Having been by humans since at least the Paleolithic era, the bullroarer has been a part of human music for at least 17 millennia.
   (D) More ancient than any other instrument in human history, the bullroarer is a foundational component of many civilizations.

4. While researching a topic, a student has taken the following notes:

   - Feminism endeavors to create equality and empowerment for all persons.
   - Feminist theory is therefore used to analyze the reasons behind social inequality.
   - Beth Richie is an African American feminist and professor.
   - Her book *Arrested Justice: Black Women, Violence, and America's Prison Nation* is an important work in the field of feminist theory.
   - Richie's goal is to expose the ways black women have been left in particularly vulnerable and dangerous positions.
   - Richie's research concludes that Black feminist theory provides an effective and forceful counter-narrative that can help dismantle the inequality of incarceration.

   The student wants to emphasize the connections between Richie's goal and the general idea of feminist theory. Which choice most effectively uses relevant information from the notes to accomplish this goal?

   (A) *Arrested Justice: Black Women, Violence, and America's Prison Nation* is a work by the noted feminist Beth Richie.
   (B) Richie epitomizes the feminist quest to understand social inequality by endeavoring to understand why black women have been left in vulnerable positions.
   (C) Feminism examines why social inequality exists so that there can be a more equitable society.
   (D) The inequality of incarceration is something that many contemporary authors have examined.

5. While researching a topic, a student has taken the following notes:

   - A spectrometer is an instrument that spreads a wave of electromagnetic radiation into its component frequencies.
   - If you look at a simple beam of white light through a spectrometer, you will see a continuous band of colors shifting like a rainbow from red to violet.
   - When a material is heated, you can look at the flames given off through a spectrometer to determine what chemicals make up the material.
   - This is possible because the band of light is broken into a series of lines that represent specific frequencies of electromagnetic radiation that are emitted from the compound.
   - Astronomers can attach a spectrometer to a telescope to determine the chemical composition of stars.

   A student wants to present what makes the spectrometer useful to astronomical research. Which choice most effectively uses relevant information from the notes to accomplish this goal?

   (A) While a spectrometer can spread a wave of electromagnetic radiation into the frequencies that compose it, astronomers are more likely to find its capacity to create a beam of white light more useful.
   (B) Since a spectrometer can use light from a heated object to determine the object's chemical composition, astronomers can use it to determine the chemical makeup of stars.
   (C) Astronomers can use a spectrometer to determine the distance that certain astronomical bodies, like stars, are from Earth.
   (D) When astronauts take a spectrometer with them into space, they can put chemicals from meteorites into the spectrometer to determine the meteorites' chemical composition.

## Answer Explanations

1. **(A)** The student wants to emphasize a major similarity between mitosis and meiosis. According to the notes, mitosis is used by single-celled organisms for reproduction, and meiosis is used by organisms that use sexual reproduction. Therefore, both processes are used by living things for reproduction. It is not choice (B) because this shows a difference between the two. It is not choice (C) because there is no evidence presented in the notes that both processes are used equally throughout the Earth. It is not choice (D) because meiosis does not create exact copies of organisms, but instead blends parts of their genetic compositions in creating offspring.

2. **(D)** The student wants to emphasize the type of intervals at which the SHC motion will likely oscillate. Choice (D) is the only option that uses the notes to describe the intervals of oscillation—they are regular since the notes describe the motion is "periodic." It is not choice A because the oscillations will be regular, not irregular. It is not choice (B) or (C) because these do not describe the oscillation intervals.

3. **(C)** Choice (C) emphasizes the long duration of the bullroarer in human history by showing that the bullroarer has been around for millennia, since the Paleolithic era. It is not choice (A) because this focuses on the sound of the instrument instead of its duration. It is not choice (B) because this does not discuss time. It is not choice (D) because it is too vague—we have no clear sense from this just how ancient the bullroarer is.

4. **(B)** According to the notes, "Richie's goal is to expose the ways black women have been left in particularly vulnerable and dangerous positions." Moreover, according to the notes, feminist theory is generally "used to analyze the reasons behind social inequality." Choice (B) connects these two ideas. choice (A) just states a fact about Richie's authorship. Choices (C) and (D) do not directly connect to Richie.

5. **(B)** The spectrometer is useful to astronomers because it can attach it to a telescope to determine the chemical composition of stars—choice (B) makes this capacity clear. Choice (A) is not supported by the notes since the spectrometer is used to analyze beams of light, not create them. It is not choice (C) because the spectrometer is not used to determine distance. It is not choice (D) because chemicals are not inserted into the spectrometer; instead, the light emitted from the objects is analyzed.

## Additional Practice Exercises

The problems in these exercises represent the variety of SAT Writing questions you could encounter. Take about ten minutes for each exercise.

### Exercise 1

1. The European cuckoo mother bird does not randomly deposit her egg; she chooses the nests of specific species with eggs that resemble _______ the European cuckoo. She deposits her egg and leaves it with the other bird's eggs, and that is the extent of her parenting.

   Which choice completes the text so that it conforms to the conventions of Standard English?

   (A) those of
   (B) these of
   (C) this from
   (D) this of

2. On certain occasions, he is brutally ashamed of his _____________ overcompensates for his treachery by defending his father at all costs.

   Which choice completes the text so that it conforms to the conventions of Standard English?

   (A) father's deceit, on others he
   (B) fathers deceit: on others he
   (C) father's deceit; on others, he
   (D) fathers' deceit—on others, he

3. With music that is highly repetitive, Glass has been referred to as a minimalist and aligned with the work of other composers like La Monte Young, Terry Riley, and Steve Reich. ________________ marked by a nonnarrative and nonrepresentational conception of a work in progress, and represents a new approach to the activity of listening to music by focusing on the internal processes of the music.

   Which choice completes the text so that it conforms to the conventions of Standard English?

   (A) Minimalism a term that Glass has taken strides to distance himself from, is
   (B) Minimalism: a term that Glass has taken strides to distance himself from is
   (C) Minimalism—a term from which Glass has taken strides to distance himself—is
   (D) Minimalism, a term from which Glass has taken strides to distance himself—is

4. When searching for jobs, your online profile should be very thorough. Make sure to post a ________ allows the employer to see that you are a real person with real skills and makes you more likely to be interviewed.

   Which choice completes the text so that it conforms to the conventions of Standard English?

   (A) professional picture, this
   (B) professional picture: this
   (C) professional; picture this
   (D) professional picture this

5. Do ever you remember hearing in school that the sun—by far the largest body in our solar system—is composed almost entirely of the two smallest elements, ________________

   Which choice completes the text so that it conforms to the conventions of Standard English?

   (A) hydrogen, and helium.
   (B) hydrogen and helium.
   (C) hydrogen, and helium?
   (D) hydrogen and helium?

6. If you choose to teach at the secondary level, it is best to be ready to answer questions about college, career planning, and young adult issues. One thing is ________ a good teacher is there because they want to be.

   Which choice completes the text so that it conforms to the conventions of Standard English?

   (A) for sure,
   (B) for sure: a good
   (C) for sure a good
   (D) for a

7. Detractors argue that the lack of scientific oversight during underwater construction is bound to result in failure. ________ many anticipate the wealth of knowledge and new discoveries that will certainly follow underwater monitoring.

   Which choice completes the text with the most logical transition?

   (A) And,
   (B) Consequently,
   (C) Still,
   (D) Therefore,

8. While researching a topic, a student has taken the following notes:

   - Pierre-Auguste Renoir was a lead painter in the impressionist movement.
   - He was born in Limoges, Haute-Vienne, France in 1841.
   - The artists Camille Pissarro and Edouard Manet inspired his style and painting techniques.
   - His most popular paintings consist of: *Dance at Le Moulin de la Galette, Luncheon of the Boating Party*, and *The Swing*.
   - Renoir's paintings are known for their vibrant light and saturated color.

   The student wants to emphasize what makes Renoir's paintings distinctive. Which choice most effectively uses relevant information from the notes to accomplish this goal?

   (A) Renoir was uniquely influenced by the impressionist artists Pissarro and Manet.
   (B) *Dance at Le Moulin de la Galette* is one of Renoir's most famous works.
   (C) The famous impressionist artist Pierre-Auguste Renoir was born in France in 1841.
   (D) Renoir's impressionist paintings are known for having saturated color and vibrant light.

## Answer Explanations

1. **(A)** "Those of" correctly represents a logical comparison between the nests of the cuckoo and the plural nests of other birds. Choices (C) and (D) are both singular, and choice (B) incorrectly uses "these," which is improper wording in a comparative situation.

2. **(C)** The semicolon in this choice separates the two independent clauses. The apostrophe before the "s" after "father" indicates singular ownership. The comma after "others" gives a necessary break after the introductory phrase. Choice (A) creates a run-on. Choice (B) does not show possession. Choice (D) shows possession of plural fathers.

3. **(C)** The dashes set aside the parenthetical phrase, and the word choice in choice (C) is logical. Choices (A) and (B) do not set aside the parenthetical phrase. Choice (D) uses inconsistent punctuation to set aside the phrase.

4. **(B)** The colon serves to give a needed pause between the independent clause before the colon and the clarifying independent clause after the colon. Choices (A) and (D) each produce a run-on sentence. Choice (C) interrupts "professional picture."

5. **(D)** The sentence asks a question, so a question mark is needed, making choices (A) and (B) incorrect. Since just two items are listed, there is no need for a comma to separate them, making choice (C) incorrect and (D) correct.

6. **(B)** The colon is appropriate because it indicates a clarification to follow. Choice (A) results in a comma splice, while choices (C) and (D) result in run-on sentences.

7. **(C)** This is the only option that provides a needed contrast between the argument in the first sentence that the process will result in failure and the current sentence in which there is the potential for a wealth of knowledge and discoveries. The other options do not convey a contrast.

8. **(D)** The notes state that "Renoir's paintings are known for their vibrant light and saturated color." This shows what makes his paintings unique or distinctive. It is not choice (A) or (C) because these do not focus on Renoir's paintings. It is not choice (B) because this does not analyze why this painting is famous.

### Exercise 2

1. There are more ways than ever to market yourself and your skills, and to network with other professionals in your field. You will want to make sure you are competing in the online job hunt. Career websites like LinkedIn and Monster make it simple to get started. Within your online profiles, it is critical that you _______ information about your educational background, previous work experience, internships, research positions, and volunteer efforts. Now is not the time to be modest.

   Which choice completes the text so that it conforms to the conventions of Standard English?

   (A) included
   (B) include
   (C) including
   (D) to include

2. Newton's equation explained why that apple fell onto his head, _______________ and how Earth orbits the sun. It also allowed NASA scientists to send a man to the moon many years later.

   Which choice completes the text so that it conforms to the conventions of Standard English?

   (A) why on the ground one firmly stays,
   (B) on the ground one firmly stays,
   (C) why one stays firmly on the ground,
   (D) one stays firmly on the ground,

3. In his book *The Secret Life*, Dali inquires as to why in a restaurant when he requested a grilled lobster, he was never _______ a boiled telephone.

   Which choice completes the text so that it conforms to the conventions of Standard English?

   (A) brung
   (B) brought
   (C) bring
   (D) brang

4. A spectrometer is an instrument that spreads a wave of electromagnetic radiation into its component frequencies. When you look through a spectrometer at a beam of white light, ____________ a continuous band of colors shifting like a rainbow from red to violet.

   Which choice completes the text so that it conforms to the conventions of Standard English?

   (A) and you see
   (B) and one can see
   (C) and he or she can find
   (D) you see

5. By creating a metric theory of gravitation, Einstein showed that phenomena in classical mechanics correspond to inertial motion within a curved geometry of space-time. This scientific discovery laid the groundwork in both astrophysics and cosmology for years to come. Not only did the theory help to explain an irregularity in Mercury's orbit, but ________ and set the theoretical foundations for black holes.

   Which choice completes the text so that it conforms to the conventions of Standard English?

   (A) the bending of starlight was also demonstrated by it
   (B) starlight used it to bend the demonstration
   (C) it also demonstrated how starlight bends
   (D) demonstrating the starlight

6. A popular theory posits that Neanderthals met their extinction through absorption. That is—supposing Neanderthals were not a distinct species, _______ rather a subspecies of Homo sapiens—some researchers believe that they disappeared after interbreeding with humans when they arrived in Eurasia roughly 80,000 years ago.

   Which choice completes the text with the most logical transition?

   (A) but
   (B) and
   (C) or
   (D) to

7. For those interested in pursuing a career as an environmental engineer, a bachelor's degree is a must. _______ a degree in environmental engineering is necessary, related fields such as general or civil engineering can be acceptable as well.

   Which choice completes the text with the most logical transition?

   (A) If
   (B) When
   (C) While
   (D) So

8. While researching a topic, a student has taken the following notes:

    - Biltmore Estate sits on 8,000 acres of land in Asheville, North Carolina.
    - It took around six years to complete, starting in 1889 and opening for his family on Christmas Eve in 1895.
    - The mansion has an indoor swimming pool, bowling alley, conservatory, and library.
    - George Washington Vanderbilt II built the estate after falling in love with the scenery and climate of the area.
    - The Biltmore Estate is the largest privately owned house in the United States.

    The student wants to summarize some of the unique architectural features of Biltmore. Which choice most effectively uses relevant information from the notes to accomplish this goal?

    (A) The land on which Biltmore sits is approximately 8,000 acres.
    (B) Builders took approximately six years to complete Biltmore.
    (C) Biltmore boasts both a conservatory and a bowling alley.
    (D) The climate and scenery of the Asheville area made for a uniquely beautiful setting for a large home.

## Answer Explanations

1. **(B)** The text is in the present tense, and "include" is the only option that maintains this consistent tense. Moreover, "you include" demonstrates the proper conjugation of the verb.

2. **(C)** This is the only choice that is parallel to the other items listed in this sentence. Not only are the other options not parallel, they also have confused word orders.

3. **(B)** "Brought" is the correctly used tense of "to bring" in this context.

4. **(D)** "Specific" in this case means "unique," stating that the chemical signature given off by each element is unique to it. Choice (A) is too wordy. Choice (B) is incorrect because "partial to" means "to prefer" something. Choice (C) uses an adverb instead of an adjective.

5. **(C)** This choice is correct because the construction of the second part of the sentence is parallel to the first part of the sentence; additionally, it puts the words in a logical order. Choice (A) uses passive voice. Choice (B) confuses the intended meaning. Choice (D) is not parallel.

6. **(A)** "But" will logically complete the phrase "not" this, "but rather" that. The other options would not complete this phrase appropriately.

7. **(C)** The sentence conveys a contrast between what is necessary and what is acceptable. "While" is the only option that provides a contrast.

8. **(C)** The notes state that "the mansion has an indoor swimming pool, bowling alley, conservatory, and library." Since these features are architectural, citing some of them makes sense if the student wants to summarize some of the unique architectural features found at Biltmore. The other options focus on nonarchitectural features, like the land area of the property, how long it took to build, and the setting of the home.

## Advanced Practice

The following questions are designed to represent the most challenging sorts of questions you could encounter on the SAT Writing. Take about ten minutes for each exercise.

### Exercise 1

1. It wasn't until 1915 that Albert Einstein expanded on Newton's work to impart his theory of general relativity, which states that the gravity of any mass curves the space and time around it. Einstein's theory of relativity is superior to __________ because it considers special relativity and can be used when great precision is necessary.

   Which choice completes the text so that it conforms to the conventions of Standard English?

   (A) Newton
   (B) it
   (C) these
   (D) Newton's law of universal gravitation

2. While using Bernice and Marjorie to model both eras, Fitzgerald finds flaws in __________ the new approach is only relaxed on the surface.

   Which choice completes the text so that it conforms to the conventions of Standard English?

   (A) both: the old manner is a lifeless forgery, while
   (B) both, the old manner is a lifeless forgery while
   (C) both—the old manner is a lifeless, forgery, while
   (D) both; the old manner, is a lifeless forgery while

3. In these settings, occupational therapists work with clients to help them better participate _______ the areas of occupation.

   Which choice completes the text so that it conforms to the conventions of Standard English?

   (A) in all the any of
   (B) in any all of
   (C) in any or all of
   (D) in all of and any of

4. One possible justification for involving humans in the actual exploration is that __________ increase interest in funding space exploration projects.

   Which choice completes the text so that it conforms to the conventions of Standard English?

   (A) they do
   (B) it does
   (C) one do
   (D) OMIT the underlined portion

5. It can be described as one of the greatest mysteries of modern physics. In a universe that ____________ neutrality, the apparently asymmetrical distribution of the baryon charge is a singular and tantalizing puzzle.

Which choice completes the text so that it conforms to the conventions of Standard English?

(A) tends universally, as it were toward net
(B) tends—universally, as it were toward net
(C) tends—universally as it were, toward net
(D) tends—universally, as it were—toward net

6. Panes created using the glass spinning technique are usually identifiable for their bulbous centers and wavy surface ____________ the edges joining with the window frame are typically narrower than the pane's body.

Which choice completes the text so that it conforms to the conventions of Standard English?

(A) texture, additionally they are often very fragile, as
(B) texture; additionally, they are often very fragile, as
(C) texture. Additionally they are often very fragile as
(D) texture additionally, they are often very fragile, as

7. Recent studies of Neanderthal anatomy and artifacts suggest that they were remarkably well-equipped to deal with the fiercely cold and barren conditions, ____________ even thrived within them for nearly 200,000 years.

Which choice completes the text with the most logical transition?

(A) and
(B) but
(C) for it was the case that they
(D) OMIT the underlined portion.

8. While researching a topic, a student has taken the following notes:

   - In *The Republic*, Plato attempts to create a blueprint for a just city-state in which its constituents prescribe to reason and live in communal harmony.
   - In his construction of an ideal city-state, Plato reevaluates the kinship (family) relations that comprise society.
   - Plato sought to replace the kinship system with a new model in which people who aren't blood relatives still interact in ways now reserved for familial relations.
   - Plato argued that the city-state forms a communal family: "every time he meets any of them, he will assume he is meeting his brother, or sister, or mother, or son, or daughter—or the child or parent of one of these."
   - Plato claims that his new model would eliminate the familial loyalty that supersedes state loyalty.

   The student wants to present a generalization about how Plato thought about the family and the state. Which choice most effectively uses relevant information from the notes to accomplish this goal?

   (A) Those who have blood relationships to one another should be excluded from being in the same governmental state.
   (B) Loyalty to the members of one's family should rightly take precedence over loyalty to one's government.
   (C) Plato argued that the connections between members of a state should outweigh the connections from familial relations.
   (D) Kinship is at the core of what will create a monarchical system, with the monarchy passed from one generation to the next.

## Answer Explanations

1. **(D)** This is the only option that gives a logical comparison between the theory of Einstein and the theory of Newton. Be sure to compare the same sorts of objects to one another.

2. **(A)** In choice (A), the colon comes after a complete sentence right before the flaws are clarified and the comma comes before the transitional "while." Choice (B) results in a run-on sentence. Choice (C) has an unnecessary comma after "lifeless." Choice (D) has an unnecessary comma after "manner."

3. **(C)** This works because the occupational therapist could potentially help with "any" of the areas or "all" of the areas. Choices (A) and (B) do not use prepositions correctly, and choice (D) uses "and," which would not make sense because both "all of" and "any of."

4. **(B)** The "it" refers to the act of involving humans in exploration, which would be singular. "Does" is the correct form of the verb "to do" when coupled with a singular subject. Choice (D) could potentially work if instead of "that" it said "the" immediately before the underlined phrase, and if instead of "increase" it said "increased" immediately following the underlined phrase.

5. **(D)** This is the only option that sets off the parenthetical phrase with the same sort of punctuation on either side, i.e., a dash. Commas can also set up parenthetical phrases, but there must be a comma before and after the phrase.

6. **(B)** The semicolon provides a needed break between the two independent clauses, and the comma after "additionally" gives an appropriate pause separating the transition from the complete sentence that follows. Choice (A) is a run-on sentence, choice (C) lacks a needed comma after the introductory word "Additionally," and choice (D) is also a run-on.

7. **(A)** The last part of this sentence gives more support to the claim in the first part of the sentence, making "and" appropriate. Choice (B) shows contrast, choice (C) is too wordy, and choice (D) removes a needed transition.

8. **(C)** The notes state that "Plato sought to replace the kinship system with a new model in which people who aren't blood relatives still interact in ways now reserved for familial relations." In other words, Plato believed that the connections between citizens of a country should be more important than the connections between family members—this aligns with choice (C). It is not choice (A) because there is no evidence to suggest that Plato believed that people of the same family could not be in the same country. It is not choice (B) because this gets Plato's argument backwards. It is not choice (D) because the notes do not focus on the possibility of a monarchy.

## Exercise 2

1. Piketty's data on the wealthy elite makes it somewhat pioneering despite its foundations in age-old economics. ____________________ redistribution through a progressive global tax on wealth.

   Which choice completes the text so that it conforms to the conventions of Standard English?

   (A) Piketty even offers a solution; economic
   (B) Piketty, even offers a solution, economic
   (C) Piketty even offers a solution: economic
   (D) Piketty even offers, a solution economic

2. As glass enters the bath, its specific gravity and immiscibility with tin ____________ a continuous ribbon with perfectly smooth surfaces on both sides and an even width throughout.

   Which choice completes the text so that it conforms to the conventions of Standard English?

   (A) causes it to form
   (B) causes them to form
   (C) cause them to form
   (D) cause it to form

3. While Pluto is in orbit around the sun and has become nearly round, it isn't big ________________. In other words, Pluto is not gravitationally dominant in its area and shares its space with astronomical bodies of a relatively large size.

   Which choice completes the text so that it conforms to the conventions of Standard English?

   (A) enough, and therefore doesn't have enough gravity, to clear its orbit.
   (B) enough and therefore, doesn't have enough gravity, to clear its orbit.
   (C) enough and therefore doesn't have enough gravity to clear, its orbit.
   (D) enough, and, therefore, doesn't have enough gravity, to clear its orbit.

4. The Parthenon Temple itself was completed in 438 B.C., although decorative sculpting and engraving within the structure went on for several more years. Since then, the structure has served as ____________________.

   Which choice completes the text so that it conforms to the conventions of Standard English?

   (A) temple, treasury, church, and most recently, tourist attraction.
   (B) temple, treasury church, and most recently, tourist attraction.
   (C) temple treasury, church and most recently tourist attraction.
   (D) temple treasury church, and most recently tourist attraction.

5. Strindberg and Ibsen—writing in the same genre at the same point in history and emerging from both the same level of society and corner of the world—____________ developed remarkably antithetical worldviews, each powerful enough not only to weather the criticism of the opposition but to develop and grow despite it.

   Which choice completes the text with the most logical transition?

   (A) nonetheless
   (B) consequently
   (C) also
   (D) divergently

6. The exchange is notable in that it is the first time Griselda directly asserts her desires to Walter, and although she desists as soon as he raises an objection, she allows herself, finally, at ____________ she feels to be right and honorable.

   Which choice completes the text so that it conforms to the conventions of Standard English?

   (A) what she believes, to be the end of their marriage, to communicate to him what
   (B) what she believes to be the end of their marriage to communicate to him what
   (C) what she believes—to be the end of their marriage, to communicate to him what
   (D) what she believes to be the end of their marriage, to communicate to him what

7. Rognlie argues that, according to the law of diminishing returns, the rate of return will eventually _________ on to say that Piketty has an inflated idea of current return and doesn't consider depreciation.

   Which choice completes the text so that it conforms to the conventions of Standard English?

   (A) decrease; goes
   (B) decrease, goes
   (C) decrease; he goes
   (D) decrease, he goes

8. While researching a topic, a student has taken the following notes:

    - Cosmic expansion is the idea that an expanding universe could be traced back to a single point.
    - The scientist Georges Lemaître hypothesized the idea of cosmic expansion in 1927.
    - In 1929, scientist Edwin Hubble confirmed Lemaître's work when he discovered that galaxies were drifting apart.
    - For many scientists, Hubble's observations gave convincing evidence of the big bang theory.
    - The big bang theory states that after cosmic expansion, the universe cooled to form subatomic particles.
    - The theory also states that these subatomic particles that created atoms and the elements.
    - These elements went on to form stars and galaxies.

    The student wants to highlight the connection between the work of Lemaître and Hubble. Which choice most effectively uses relevant information from the notes to accomplish this goal?

    (A) Hubble provided experimental observations to support Lemaître's hypothesis.
    (B) Lemaître used the observations that Hubble made about the big bang to formulate a comprehensive scientific theory.
    (C) Modern scientists greatly appreciate the detailed observations that both Lemaître and Hubble made in the 1920s.
    (D) Lemaître's theory about subatomic particles was confirmed by Hubble's theory about the big bang.

## Answer Explanations

1. **(C)** This option correctly uses a colon to set off a clarification. Choice (B) uses a comma, which does not provide a sufficiently significant pause. Choice (D) has a pause in an awkward spot. Choice (A) needs a complete sentence after the semicolon.

2. **(D)** The compound subject of "specific gravity and immiscibility with tin" demands a plural verb; hence, "cause" works. Also, "it" is correct since the pronoun refers to the singular "glass."

3. **(A)** The parenthetical element here was tricky to diagnose. Nonetheless, "and therefore doesn't have enough gravity" was the parenthetical element; remove it from the sentence and the clause still functions perfectly well. As a rule, a parenthetical element can be surrounded by two dashes or two commas to separate it from the rest of the sentence. Choice (B) uses the two commas but splits the parenthetical element into pieces. Choice (C) omits the first comma. Choice (D) has entirely too many commas within the parenthetical element, preventing continuity. Choice (A) is the best option.

4. **(A)** This choice gives necessary breaks between all the listed items and has a break after the clarifying phrase "most recently." Choices (B), (C), and (D) all change the original meaning because of their comma placements or lack thereof.

5. **(A)** "Nonetheless" means "in spite of," which makes sense given the fact that these writers had similar backgrounds yet ended up having very different worldviews. "Consequently" in choice (B) indicates cause and effect. "Also" in choice (C) indicates the continuation of thought. "Divergently" in choice (D) could apply toward the differences in their views but does not work as a transition to show a logical contrast.

6. **(D)** The entire phrase "at what she believes to be the end of their marriage" is parenthetical. Choice (D) is the only option that both leaves this phrase intact and places a comma at the end of it so that it is set aside from the rest of the sentence.

7. **(C)** This option both clarifies the subject and uses a semicolon to give a clear break between the independent clauses. Choice (A) does not have the necessary independent clause after the semicolon. Choice (B) does not give a parallel construction. Choice (D) creates a comma splice.

8. **(A)** The notes state that Lemaître hypothesized the idea of cosmic expansion, while Hubble made observations that confirmed this theory. It is not choice (A) because Lemaître preceded Hubble. It is not choice (C) because this does not explain how Lemaître and Hubble are connected. It is not choice (D) because there is no evidence that Lemaître had a theory about subatomic particles.

# PART 5
# Math

# Math for the Digital SAT

## Introduction and Strategies

### What Is Tested on the SAT Math? What Math Classes Should I Have Taken?

The SAT Math focuses on the core math skills that you will need to be successful in a variety of college majors and future careers. No matter if you are an engineer, a nurse, a teacher, a graphic designer, or a business manager, it will be important to know how to work with numbers and interpret data. Here is a big picture summary of what is tested:

| SAT Math Question Type | Definition | Math Class(es) That Covers It |
|---|---|---|
| **Algebra** | Interpretation of linear equations and solving systems of equations | Mostly covered in Pre-Algebra and Algebra 1 |
| **Problem Solving and Data Analysis** | Demonstration of literacy with data and graphs with real-world applications | Covered throughout your Pre-Algebra, Algebra 1, and Algebra 2 coursework<br>Science classes can also provide helpful data interpretation skills. |
| **Advanced Math** | Working with more complicated equations | Mostly covered in Algebra 2 |
| **Geometry and Trigonometry** | Working with lines, angles, triangles, circles, and other geometric figures | Mainly in Geometry and Pre-Calculus |

### How Is the SAT Math Section Structured?

- Two modules, 22 questions each, 35 minutes each
- First module is of a standard difficulty, second module of an adaptive difficulty (will be easier or more difficult depending on student performance on the first module)
- Four of the questions (two per module) are experimental and will not count towards the score.
- Algebra will be about 35% of the questions; Advanced Math will be about 35% of the questions; Problem Solving and Data Analysis will be about 15% of the questions; and Geometry and Trigonometry will be about 15% of the questions.
- The questions generally become more difficult as you proceed through a given module.

## What Is *Not* Tested on the SAT Math? What Do I *Not* Need to Worry About?

If you have taken the ACT, you may recall how that test has quite a few more advanced math concepts. Some of the concepts you will NOT need to know for the SAT that are tested on the ACT include:

- Matrices
- Logarithms
- Hyperbolas
- Ellipses
- Cosecant, Secant, Cotangent
- Permutations and Combinations

## How Does the SAT Math Differ from Typical Math Tests I Have Taken in School?

Often, students have difficulty with the SAT Math because they approach it the same way as they would typical school math tests and quizzes. This is especially true for high-achieving students who consistently earn A's in their math classes—after all, if their approach works well on one math test, why wouldn't it work well on another math test like the SAT? By realizing that the SAT Math is quite a bit different from typical school math tests, students are empowered to have a different mindset to help them be successful.

| | Typical School Math Tests/ Quizzes | SAT Math |
|---|---|---|
| **Time Management** | ▪ Typically, you don't have to worry much about time management.<br>▪ Tests often do not take the entire class period, or you may be allowed to stay after class to finish up. | ▪ You will likely need the full amount of time to finish.<br>▪ Move through the test carefully and efficiently to complete every question. |
| **Scoring Curve** | ▪ If you miss a couple of questions, your grade may drop quite a bit.<br>▪ To get an A, you may need to aim for perfection. | ▪ Since the test is heavily curved, do not worry about missing a couple questions.<br>▪ To get a good score, you do not need to aim for perfection. |
| **Concepts Tested** | ▪ Usually highly focused on a particular set of concepts you have recently studied<br>▪ For example, a test on your factoring unit will focus just on factoring. You have a good sense of what each question will likely be about. | ▪ Tests on a variety of concepts from multiple years of coursework<br>▪ Cannot go on "autopilot" and just start solving the problem—have to figure out what the question is about |

(*Continued*)

| | Typical School Math Tests/ Quizzes | SAT Math |
|---|---|---|
| **Problem Solving Process** | ▪ Often, if you do not "know" the formula or problem-solving process from class, you will have trouble coming up with the answer. | ▪ While there is a good bit you need to know, the emphasis on SAT Math problems is to "figure them out" by any means necessary.<br>▪ Unconventional methods like using estimation, intuition, and plugging in answers are much more applicable. |
| **Possible Test Errors** | ▪ If there is an error on your test or quiz, just let your teacher know and it can easily be fixed. | ▪ SAT Math problems go through multiple rounds of review before they are put on an actual test.<br>▪ Rather than trying to find the flaw in the question, give the question the benefit of the doubt. |
| **Need to Explain Answer** | ▪ Your teacher may expect you to solve the problem in the way you were taught, clearly writing out every step so you can earn full credit. | ▪ You are evaluated simply on whether you answered the question correctly.<br>▪ Use whatever problem-solving method works best for you. |

## Can I Use a Calculator?

Yes—The SAT is fairly generous in terms of permitted calculators. Most scientific and graphing calculators are permitted—for a complete, updated list of approved calculators, check here: *https://collegereadiness.collegeboard.org/sat/taking-the-test/calculator-policy*. Also, there is a calculator embedded within the testing program. You can click to use it whenever you need to do so. The calculator is modeled on the popular Desmos calculator program. On the older paper-based SAT, there was a no-calculator section; on the Digital SAT, you can use a calculator on all the questions in the math modules.

## How Do the Fill-in Questions Work?

Approximately 25% of the math questions are fill-ins. Unlike the paper-based SAT in which the fill-in questions were at the end of the section, on the Digital SAT the fill-in questions come at periodic times throughout the test. Here are some important things to know about these problems.

- **It is sometimes possible to have more than one correct answer**—if you fill in any of the correct answers, you will be fine. For example, if the correct answer could be any number between 4 and 6, if you entered 5.5 you would be correct.
- Decimals that continue past the spots allowed for gridding **can be rounded or shortened**, as long as you use all of the spaces on the grid. You can also express the decimal as a fraction. For example, you can write $\frac{7}{9}$ as 7/9, .7777, or .7778 (Note that 0.8, 0.77, or, 0.78 would be considered incorrect.).
- **You don't need to reduce fractions.** For example, since $\frac{2}{3}$, $\frac{4}{6}$, and $\frac{6}{9}$ are equivalent, any of them would work as an answer.

- **Use the Answer Preview tool.** When you enter your answer, use the Answer Preview tool to check that what you intend for your answer is what you actually have down.

The bottom line on fill-ins: The SAT will not *trick* you into missing the problem. If you have a reasonable answer and enter it, you will be in good shape.

## Do They Provide Any Formulas?

The SAT will provide some of the most important geometry and trigonometry formulas. However, since most of the test covers algebra, you will need to commit algebraic formulas to memory. Here are the formulas you will be given in the testing program as a popup you can open or close as needed.

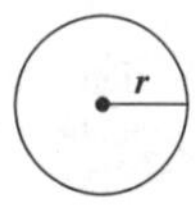


**Radius of a circle = $r$**
**Area of a circle = $\pi r^2$**
**Circumference of a circle = $2\pi r$**

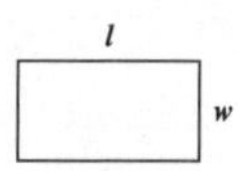


**Area of a rectangle = length × width = $lw$**

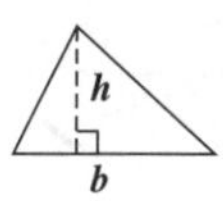


**Area of a triangle = $\frac{1}{2}$ × base × height = $\frac{1}{2}bh$**

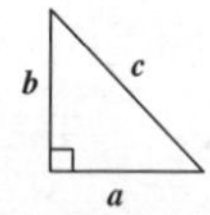


**Pythagorean theorem: $a^2 + b^2 = c^2$**

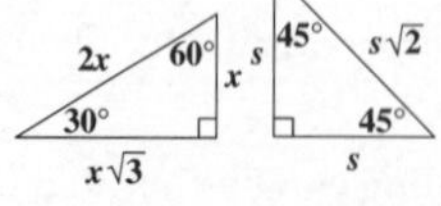


**Special right triangles: 30-60-90 and 45-45-90**

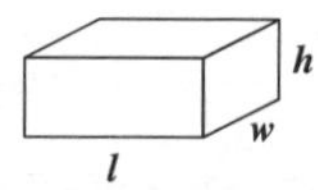


**Volume of a box =**
**length × width × height = $lwh$**

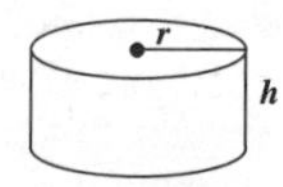


**Volume of a cylinder = $\pi r^2 h$**

**Volume of a sphere = $\frac{4}{3}\pi r^3$**

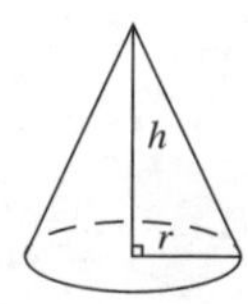


**Volume of a cone = $\frac{1}{3}\pi r^2 h$**

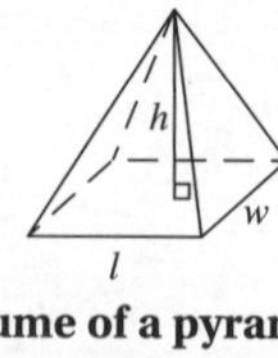


**Volume of a pyramid =**
**$\frac{1}{3}$ × length × width × height = $\frac{1}{3}lwh$**

**KEY FACTS:**

- **A circle has 360 degrees.**
- **There are $2\pi$ radians in a circle.**
- **There are 180 degrees in a triangle.**

## How Should I Pace Myself on the SAT Math?

The questions generally increase in difficulty as you progress through them. So, instead of trying to set a stopwatch for each individual question, use these general guidelines:

- **Take between 70–100 seconds per question. If it is an easier/earlier question, go closer to 60–70 seconds; if it is a harder/later question, go closer to 90–100 seconds.** Since the earlier questions are easier, you can spend about 5-6 minutes on the first five questions; since the later questions are more difficult, you can spend about 8-9 minutes on the last five questions.
- **Check your pace at reasonable intervals—every five to six questions is generally a good time to see if you are on pace.** If you check your pace with each problem, you waste time looking at the timer. On the other hand, if you do not check your pace at all, you may be surprised when the timer appears with five minutes remaining. Click on the timer whenever you need to see how much time remains. So long as the timer is not distracting, you could leave it visible throughout the section.
- **Try to do the problems <u>once</u> and <u>well</u> instead of rushing to the end.** With so many word problems on the SAT Math, it is very easy to make a careless mistake by misreading the problem the first time through. Instead of rushing to the end, focus on doing the problems carefully the first time to maximize your score.

If you cannot finish the test in a reasonable amount of time, **guess on the most difficult questions**. These questions will typically come towards the end of the math module.

If you find an earlier question to be overly difficult, go ahead and guess on it—you do not want to spend two to three minutes on a problem and not get anywhere. You can flag the question and come back to it if you have time. Try to be decisive when guessing on a problem; if there are certain problem types that you know are more difficult for you, like long word problems or particular math concepts, guess on those without investing lots of time.

## How Can I Use This Book to Prepare for the SAT Math?

- Read the strategies that follow in this section to help you with your test-taking mindset.
- Target your review by studying the math content areas where you have struggled.
- Practice your time management with the SAT problem drills throughout the chapter.
- Take full-length SAT Math tests and review your answers afterwards. Brush up on weak areas through content review.
- Challenge yourself with the advanced math drills at the end of the chapter to simulate the toughest questions you could encounter.

## SAT Math Dos and Don'ts

**<u>Do</u> fully understand the question, actively checking understanding as you go.** Read slowly and carefully, doing the problem one time well.

**<u>Don't</u> go on to the next sentence unless you fully understand the previous one.** Don't let a desire to finish quickly ultimately make you go more slowly and less accurately.

### Example

Four roommates are splitting the rent equally on an apartment. Currently, each roommate's share is \$500 a month. If they were to add one more roommate with whom they would equally split the monthly rent, by how much would the monthly rent for each of the original four roommates decrease?

(A) \$80
(B) \$100
(C) \$120
(D) \$400

### Solution

Fully understand each sentence of the question.

1. The total rent for an apartment is divided into four equal shares.
2. Each share is currently \$500. This means that the total amount of rent for the apartment is $4 \times 500 = 2{,}000$.
3. If one more roommate is added, the total rent must now be divided by 5 instead of 4. So, the new rent per person is $\frac{2{,}000}{5} = 400$.

Now does this mean the correct answer is choice (D)? No—the question asks us how much each person's monthly rent would *decrease*. So, subtract the new share from the original share to find the per-person decrease: $500 - 400 = 100$. Therefore, the correct answer is **(B)**.

**Do pay attention to the precise question that is asked.** Read the entire question, but pay especially close attention to what comes at the end of the text—that is most likely where the question wlil be found.

**Don't get bogged down in clarifying information.** Some of the information in a question may be given so there is no room for misinterpretation—do not dwell on clarifying information like this.

### Example

The formula for compound interest is $A = P\left(1 + \frac{r}{n}\right)^{nt}$ where $A$ is the amount accumulated, $P$ is the principal, $r$ is the interest rate, $n$ is the number of times interest is applied in a compounding period, and $t$ is the number of compounding periods. What is the principal in terms of the other variables?

(A) $P = \frac{1}{A\left(1 + \frac{r}{n}\right)^{nt}}$

(B) $P = \frac{1}{A\left(1 + \frac{r}{n}\right)^{-nt}}$

(C) $P = A\left(1 + \frac{r}{n}\right)^{-(nt)}$

(D) $P = A\left(1 + \frac{r}{n}\right)^{nt}$

## ✓ Solution

So that there is no room for misinterpretation (e.g., thinking that the constants could represent variables), the SAT clarifies what each constant represents in this question. You can ignore information like this and instead focus on what the questions asks you to do. The most important parts of the question are underlined below:

The formula for compound interest is $A = P\left(1+\frac{r}{n}\right)^{nt}$ where $A$ is the amount accumulated, $P$ is the principal, $r$ is the interest rate, $n$ is the number of times interest is applied in a compounding period, and $t$ is the number of compounding periods. What is the principal in terms of the other variables?

So, the problem is much easier to solve than it appears at first glance. All we must do is divide both sides by $\left(1+\frac{r}{n}\right)^{nt}$ so that the $P$ is by itself, then simplify the expression:

$$A = P\left(1+\frac{r}{n}\right)^{nt} \rightarrow$$

$$\frac{A}{\left(1+\frac{r}{n}\right)^{nt}} = \frac{P\left(1+\frac{r}{n}\right)^{nt}}{\left(1+\frac{r}{n}\right)^{nt}} \rightarrow$$

Cancel out the like terms to simplify →

$$\frac{A}{\left(1+\frac{r}{n}\right)^{nt}} = \frac{P\cancel{\left(1+\frac{r}{n}\right)^{nt}}}{\cancel{\left(1+\frac{r}{n}\right)^{nt}}} \rightarrow$$

$$\frac{A}{\left(1+\frac{r}{n}\right)^{nt}} = P \rightarrow$$

Use a negative exponent to show the part that was in the denominator:

$$A\left(1+\frac{r}{n}\right)^{-(nt)} = P$$

**Do watch out for key words that will change what you are asked to do.** In longer word problems and in questions where terms are easily confused, be especially careful.

**Don't just assume that because your calculated answer is an option, you must be correct.** The SAT will have answer choices based on common misreadings of the questions, so do not jump to conclusions.

**Exercise**—Spot the difference between the two very similarly worded questions.

**1A.** A drink stand charges \$2 for a glass of iced tea and \$1.50 for a glass of lemonade. If during an hour of operation, the stand sold a combined total of 14 glasses of tea and lemonade for a total revenue of \$25, how many glasses of lemonade were sold?

**1B.** A drink stand charges \$2 for a glass of iced tea and \$1.50 for a glass of lemonade. If during an hour of operation, the stand sold a combined total of 14 glasses of tea and lemonade for a total revenue of \$25, how many glasses of iced tea were sold?

**2A.** If the diameter of a circle is 10 units, what is the numerical difference between the area and circumference of the circle (ignore squared units)?

**2B.** If the radius of a circle is 10 units, what is the numerical difference between the area and circumference of the circle (ignore squared units)?

**3A.** Given that $a = 3$ and $b = 4$, what is the product of $a$ and $b$?

**3B.** Given that $a = 3$ and $b = 4$, what is the sum of $a$ and $b$?

## Solutions

1. Glasses of lemonade vs. glasses of iced tea
2. Diameter vs. radius
3. Product vs. sum

**Do write out your work.** Writing out your work on the scrap paper will help you avoid careless errors and recognize patterns that you might otherwise miss.

**Don't do everything in your head.** You will ultimately save time and be more accurate if you write out your work. Common incorrect answers are based on common miscalculations.

## Example

Which of the following expressions is equivalent to the polynomial below?

$$(x^2 - 3x) + (2x - 3x^2)$$

(A) $-2x^2 - x$
(B) $3x^2 - 2x$
(C) $-3x^4 + 11x^3 - 6x^2$
(D) $3x^4 - 11x^3 + 6x^2$

## Solution

This problem is not that difficult, yet it is easy to miss if you make an error with negative signs or combining exponents. If you do make a common error, it is highly likely that one of the answer choices will have your incorrect solution. Students who are good at math yet impatient to finish the test are susceptible to this sort of error. So, write out your work step-by-step to get it right:

$$(x^2 - 3x) + (2x - 3x^2) \rightarrow$$

Remove the parentheses since you are not multiplying:

$$x^2 - 3x + 2x - 3x^2 \rightarrow$$

Group like terms together and simplify:

$$x^2 - 3x^2 - 3x + 2x \rightarrow$$
$$-2x^2 - x$$

**Do use whatever is given in the problem, like scaled drawings and formulas.** All the drawings on the SAT are to scale and problems sometimes have formulas given within them, so take advantage of what you have in front of you.

**Don't let yourself be intimidated by longer, more challenging questions.** Use whatever knowledge and skills you have to attack the problem.

## Example

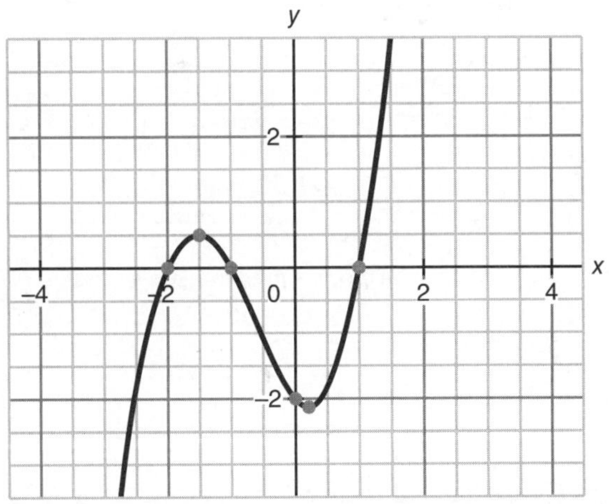


Consider the function $f(x)$ as portrayed in the $xy$-coordinate plane in the above graph. For how many values does $f(x)$ equal zero?

(A) 0
(B) 1
(C) 2
(D) 3

## Solution

Suppose that you do not remember how to work with complex functions and find zeros. You can still solve this problem without that specific knowledge. The question asks to find how many times the $f(x)$ equals zero—remember that $f(x)$ is the same as the $y$-coordinate. Examine the points on the graph where the $y$ value is equal to zero:

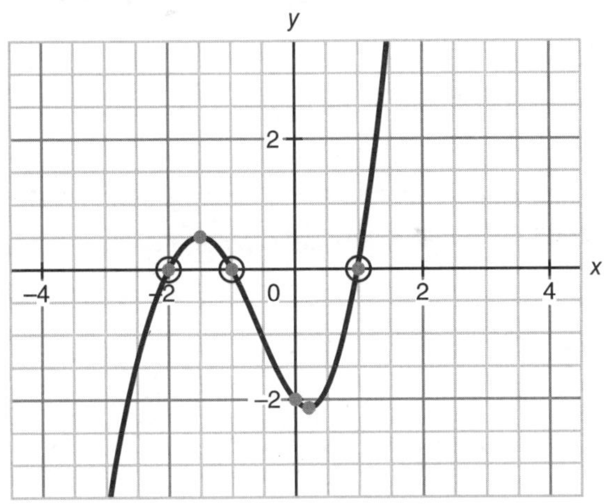


There are a total of three points where the function is equal to zero because it intersects the $x$-axis. Therefore, the correct answer is **(D)**. While this problem could also have been solved by creating an equation that had the zeros in it, make things easier for yourself and do not be intimidated.

**Do approach the problems like a puzzle that you *figure out.*** You may need to write out some work before you see the ultimate steps to solving the problem.

**Don't just give up and say you *don't know.*** The SAT Math emphasizes the core concepts from early high school math—in all likelihood, you have the background knowledge necessary to solve the problem.

## Example

$$(3x - 5)(3x + 5) + 25 = ax^2$$

In the equation above, what is the value of the constant $a$?

Fill-in: ______________

## Solution

This is not likely a problem you have typically worked with in your math classes. However, you can solve it by using concepts you probably already know—in this case, FOILing and simplifying. You do not need to know any advanced concepts about constants or equation equivalence.

$$(3x - 5)(3x + 5) + 25 = ax^2$$

FOIL the part in parentheses:

$$9x^2 + 15x - 15x - 25 + 25 = ax^2 \rightarrow$$

Add the $x$ terms and the numbers to simplify:

$$9x^2 + \cancel{15x - 15x - 25 + 25} = ax^2 \rightarrow$$

$$9x^2 = ax^2$$

Divide both sides to eliminate the $x^2 \rightarrow$

$$\frac{9x^2}{x^2} = \frac{ax^2}{x^2} \rightarrow \frac{9\cancel{x^2}}{\cancel{x^2}} = \frac{a\cancel{x^2}}{\cancel{x^2}} \rightarrow 9 = a$$

The correct answer is therefore **9**.

**Do use the choices to help see what a solution may look like.** Recognize that the answers typically go from least to greatest, so if you need to work your way backwards from the choices, start with answer (B) or (C) and then work your way up or down. Also, use the choices to recognize helpful clues as to your problem-solving process.

**Don't jump into the choices too quickly.** While plugging in the options does work sometimes, it won't be as frequent as you might like. You will be best served by carefully reading and setting up the problem step-by-step.

### Example

For what values of $x$ does $|x - 3| = 5$?

(A) 8 and 2
(B) 8 and −2
(C) −8 and 2
(D) −8 and −2

### Solution

While you could set up two absolute value equations to solve, a glance at the answer choices tells you that plugging in the possible answers will probably save you time. Because each of the numbers 8, −8, 2, and −2 is in each answer twice, you can eliminate choices more rapidly. First, let's try −8:

$$|x - 3| = 5 \rightarrow |-8 - 3| = 11 \neq 5$$

Since −8 does NOT work, we can eliminate choices (C) and (D).

Now, try −2 since it is in choice (B) and not in choice (A):

$$|x - 3| = 5 \rightarrow |-2 - 3| = 5$$

This does work, so the correct answer is choice **(B)**. There is no need to also try 8 since both choices (A) and (B) have 8 as a possibility, so trying it out would give us no new information.

**Do review and practice in a targeted way.** Focus on the problem types and math concepts that are most challenging for you.

**Don't practice by simply taking test after test, repeating the same mistakes.** Remember that practice doesn't make perfect; "perfect practice" makes perfect. Use this book to focus on areas of weakness so you may turn them into areas of strength.

*Here are the major concepts and formulas you will need to know, along with where they are covered in the book:*

**Algebra—Fundamentals**



**Algebra—Solving Equations**

**Problem Solving and Data Analysis—Unit Conversion**



**Problem Solving and Data Analysis—Percentages**



**Problem Solving and Data Analysis—Surveys**



**Problem Solving and Data Analysis—Graphs and Data Interpretation**



**Geometry—Area, Perimeter, and Volume**



**Geometry and Trigonometry—Lines, Angles, and Triangles**



**Trigonometry—Right Triangles and Trigonometry**

**Geometry—Circles**

# Algebra

This section contains comprehensive review and strategies for all of the concepts below:

**Algebra—Fundamentals**

- Order of Operations
- FOIL
- Least Common Multiple and Greatest Common Factor
- Fractions

**Algebra—Solving Equations**

- Substitution
- Elimination
- Pattern Recognition
- Plugging in Choices
- Inequalities
- Absolute Value
- Function Notation

**Algebra—Word Problems and Function Interpretation**

- Setting Up Word Problems
- Distance, Rate, and Time
- Interpreting Variables and Constants
- Functions in Table Form

**Algebra—Lines and Slope**

- Slope Formula
- Slope-Intercept Form of a Line
- Overlapping and Intersecting Lines
- Parallel and Perpendicular Lines

## Algebra—Fundamentals

### Order of Operations

To remember the correct order of operations, use the popular acronym **PEMDAS**: *Please Excuse My Dear Aunt Sally.*

| Please Excuse | My Dear | Aunt Sally |
|---|---|---|
| Parentheses ( ) and other grouping symbols, like $\sqrt{\ }$ or { }<br>Exponents<br>$x^y$ | Multiplication $x \times y$<br>Division $x \div y$ | Addition $x + y$<br>Subtraction $x - y$ |

### Example 1

$$3(2+5)^2 - 4 = ?$$

### Solution

To simplify the above expression, calculate what is within the parentheses first and square it. Then multiply that number by 3. Finally, subtract 4 to get your answer.

$$3(2+5)^2 - 4 \rightarrow 3(7)^2 - 4 \rightarrow$$
$$3 \times 49 - 4 \rightarrow 147 - 4 = 143$$

### Example 2

$$-\sqrt{\frac{64}{9}} = ?$$

### Solution

Calculate the square root of the numerator and denominator, and multiply the total by $-1$.

$$-\sqrt{\frac{64}{9}} \rightarrow -\frac{\sqrt{64}}{\sqrt{9}} \rightarrow -\frac{8}{3}$$

### Practice

Simplify the following expressions.

1. $2x + 3x = ?$
2. $5(2 - 4x) = ?$
3. $5(x^2) + 2(x - 3) = ?$
4. $\frac{3+7}{2} - \frac{4}{2} = ?$
5. $(4+2)^2 - \frac{12}{2} = ?$

### Solutions

1. $2x + 3x = 5x$
2. $5(2 - 4x) = 5 \times 2 - 5 \times 4x = 10 - 20x$
3. $5(x^2) + 2(x - 3) = 5x^2 + 2x - 6$
4. $\frac{3+7}{2} - \frac{4}{2} = \frac{10}{2} - 2 = 5 - 2 = 3$
5. $(4+2)^2 - \frac{12}{2} = (6)^2 - 6 = 36 - 6 = 30$

### FOIL

Simplify polynomials by "**FOIL**ing" the parts of an expression like $(a + b)(c + d)$ in this order: **First, Outer, Inner, Last.**

$$(a+b)(c+d) = ?$$

First $= ac$ Outer $= ad$ Inner $= bc$ Last $= bd$

Combine them: $ac + ad + bc + bd$

### Example

$$(2 + x)(3 - y) = ?$$

### Solution

$$(2 + x)(3 - y) \rightarrow$$
$$\text{First} = 2 \times 3 \;\; \text{Outer} = 2 \times (-y)$$
$$\text{Inner} = x \times 3 \;\; \text{Last} = x \times (-y)$$
$$\text{So, it equals } 6 - 2y + 3x - xy$$

### Practice

1. $(x + 1)(x + 2) = ?$
2. $(-3 + x)(-4 + x) = ?$
3. $(2 - y)(3 + y) = ?$
4. $(2x + 1)(2x - 1) = ?$
5. $(2x - 5)(3 + 4x) = ?$

### Solutions

1. $(x + 1)(x + 2) =$
   $x^2 + 2x + 1x + 2 =$
   $x^2 + 3x + 2$

2. $(-3 + x)(-4 + x) =$
   $(-3)(-4) + (-3)x + (-4)x + x^2 =$
   $12 - 7x + x^2$

3. $(2 - y)(3 + y) =$
   $2 \times 3 + 2 \times y + (-y) \times 3 + (-y) \times y =$
   $6 + 2y - 3y - y^2 =$
   $6 - y - y^2$

4. $(2x + 1)(2x - 1) =$
   $(2x)(2x) - 1(2x) + 1(2x) - 1^2 =$
   $4x^2 - 2x + 2x - 1 =$
   $4x^2 - 1$

5. $(2x - 5)(3 + 4x) =$
   $3(2x) + (2x)(4x) + (-5)(3) + (-5)(4x) =$
   $6x + 8x^2 - 15 - 20x =$
   $8x^2 - 14x - 15$

## Least Common Multiple and Greatest Common Factor

A multiple of a number is the result when the number is multiplied by a whole number, i.e., an integer. For example, multiples of 3 include 3, 6, 9, and 12.

The least common multiple (LCM) of two numbers is the *least* value that some numbers share as a *common multiple.*

### Example

What is the least common multiple of 6 and 8?

### Solution

Multiples of 6 include 6, 12, 18, and 24.

Multiples of 8 include 8, 16, and 24.

So, the least number that 6 and 8 have in common as a multiple is 24.

Factors of a number are numbers that can be multiplied together to give that number. For example, factors of 10 include 1, 2, 5, and 10 since $1 \times 10 = 10$ and $2 \times 5 = 10$.

The greatest common factor (GCF) of two numbers is the *greatest factor* that the numbers have in *common.*

### Example

What is the greatest common factor of 8 and 12?

### Solution

Factors of 8 are 1, 2, 4, and 8. Factors of 12 are 1, 2, 3, 4, 6, and 12.

So the greatest common factor between the two is 4 since it is the greatest factor that 8 and 12 share.

### Practice

1. What are five multiples of the number 4?
2. What are the factors of the number 15?
3. How many factors does 7 have?
4. What is the least common multiple of 4 and 5?
5. What is the greatest common factor of 6 and 9?

### Solutions

1. Multiples of 4 could include 4, 8, 12, 16, 20, 24, 28, and so on.
2. 1, 3, 5, and 15
3. 7 is a prime number, which has just *two* factors—1 and itself (7).
4. Multiples of 4: 4, 8, 12, 16, 20, etc. Multiples of 5: 5, 10, 15, 20, etc. So, the least common multiple between them is 20.
5. Factors of 6 are 1, 2, 3, and 6. Factors of 9 are 1, 3, and 9. So the greatest common factor between them is 3.

## Solving Fractions

Examples of fractions include numbers like $\frac{1}{3}$, $\frac{5}{7}$, and $\frac{6}{11}$. The *numerator* is on *top* of a fraction, and the *denominator* is on the *bottom*:

$$\frac{\text{Numerator}}{\text{Denominator}}$$

For example, in the fraction $\frac{2}{3}$, 2 is the numerator and 3 is the denominator.

Fractions equal one another as long as the ratio of the numerator to the denominator is equivalent. For example, $\frac{3}{4}$, $\frac{6}{8}$, and $\frac{9}{12}$ are all equivalent since they are all equal to 0.75. Putting a fraction in its "lowest term" simplifies the fraction so that the numerator and denominator only have 1 as a common factor. For the group of $\frac{3}{4}$, $\frac{6}{8}$, and $\frac{9}{12}$, $\frac{3}{4}$ is the lowest term since 3 and 4 only share 1 as a common factor.

If fractions have the same denominator, the fractions can be added or subtracted by adding or subtracting the numerators.

### Example 1

$$\frac{5}{13}+\frac{3}{13}=?$$

### Solution

$$\frac{5}{13}+\frac{3}{13}=\frac{5+3}{13}=\frac{8}{13}$$

To add and subtract fractions that do not have the same denominator, change the fractions so they have a *common denominator*.

### Example 2

$$\frac{2}{3}+\frac{1}{4}=?$$

### Solution

To provide a common denominator, 3 and 4 can be multiplied together. So that the fractions retain their values, multiply both the numerator and denominator of each fraction by a ratio equivalent to 1 (i.e., $\frac{4}{4}$ or $\frac{3}{3}$).

$$\frac{2}{3}+\frac{1}{4}=\frac{2}{3}\times\frac{4}{4}+\frac{1}{4}\times\frac{3}{3}=$$

$$\frac{2\times 4}{3\times 4}+\frac{1\times 3}{4\times 3}=\frac{8}{12}+\frac{3}{12}=\frac{11}{12}$$

## Example 3

The time it takes Henry to mop a certain floor is 10 minutes, and the time it takes Tanner to mop the same floor is 8 minutes. What is the time it takes to mop the floor if both of them work together the full amount of time to do so (use the combined work formula below to solve)?

Combined Work Formula:

$$\frac{1}{t_c}=\frac{1}{t_a}+\frac{1}{t_b}$$

$t_a$ = Time for $a$ to complete the work
$t_b$ = Time for $b$ to complete the work
$t_c$ = Time for both $a$ and $b$ to complete the work

## Solution

Using the combined worked formula above, we can calculate the time it will take both Henry and Tanner to complete the mopping. We can use 10 minutes as time $a$ and 8 minutes as time $b$.

$$\frac{1}{t_c}=\frac{1}{t_a}+\frac{1}{t_b}\rightarrow$$

$$\frac{1}{t_c}=\frac{1}{8}+\frac{1}{10}\rightarrow \text{Use 40 as the least common denominator}\rightarrow$$

$$\frac{1}{t_c}=\frac{5}{5}\times\frac{1}{8}+\frac{4}{4}\times\frac{1}{10}$$

$$\frac{1}{t_c}=\frac{5}{40}+\frac{4}{40}\rightarrow$$

$$\frac{1}{t_c}=\frac{9}{40}\rightarrow \text{Flip the fractions to solve}\rightarrow$$

$$t_c=\frac{40}{9}$$

So, it will take $\frac{40}{9}$ minutes, or about 4.44 minutes, for both of them working together to mop the floor.

Use this rule to *multiply* fractions:

$$\frac{a}{b}\times\frac{c}{d}=\frac{ac}{bd} \quad \text{(Neither } b \text{ nor } d \text{ can equal zero, or it will be undefined.)}$$

## Example 4

$$\frac{4}{7}\times\frac{2}{5}=?$$

## Solution

$$\frac{4}{7}\times\frac{2}{5}=\frac{4\times 2}{7\times 5}=\frac{8}{35}$$

Use this rule to *divide* fractions—flip the second fraction and multiply the first one by it: $\frac{a}{b}\div\frac{c}{d}=\frac{a}{b}\times\frac{d}{c}$ ($b$, $c$, and $d$ cannot equal zero, or it will be undefined.)

### Example 5

$$\frac{4}{5} \div \frac{1}{2} = ?$$

### Solution

$$\frac{4}{5} \div \frac{1}{2} = \frac{4}{5} \times \frac{2}{1} = \frac{4 \times 2}{5 \times 1} = \frac{8}{5}$$

### Practice

1. $\frac{1}{2} + \frac{1}{2} = ?$
2. $\frac{3}{4} - \frac{1}{4} = ?$
3. $\frac{2}{5} \times \frac{3}{5} = ?$
4. $\frac{3}{7} \div \frac{2}{5} = ?$
5. $\frac{3}{5} + \frac{1}{10} = ?$
6. $\frac{2}{3} - \frac{1}{6} = ?$

### Solutions

1. $\frac{1}{2} + \frac{1}{2} = \frac{1+1}{2} = \frac{2}{2} = 1$
2. $\frac{3}{4} - \frac{1}{4} = \frac{3-1}{4} = \frac{2}{4} = \frac{1}{2}$
3. $\frac{2}{5} \times \frac{3}{5} = \frac{2 \times 3}{5 \times 5} = \frac{6}{25}$
4. $\frac{3}{7} \div \frac{2}{5} = \frac{3}{7} \times \frac{5}{2} = \frac{15}{14}$
5. $\frac{3}{5} + \frac{1}{10} = \frac{3}{5} \times \frac{2}{2} + \frac{1}{10} = \frac{6}{10} + \frac{1}{10} = \frac{7}{10}$
6. $\frac{2}{3} - \frac{1}{6} = \frac{2}{3} \times \frac{2}{2} - \frac{1}{6} = \frac{4}{6} - \frac{1}{6} = \frac{3}{6} = \frac{1}{2}$

## Algebra—Solving Equations

### Substitution

When there is a system of two equations and two variables, it is often easiest to substitute an expression in terms of the other variable for one of the variables. That way, there is just one variable to work with.

### Example

What is the value of $x$ in the set of equations below?

$$y = x + 1$$
$$x + y = 3$$

### ✓ Solution

To solve for $x$, use substitution of $y$ in terms of $x$. Use the first equation, $y = x + 1$, to put everything in terms of $x$ in the second equation:

$$x + y = 3 \rightarrow$$
$$x + (x + 1) = 3 \rightarrow$$
$$2x + 1 = 3 \rightarrow 2x = 2 \rightarrow x = 1$$

## Elimination

If two equations have similar formats, eliminating variables can be the easiest approach to solving the system of equations. Use multiplication to reformat one of the equations so that it can be easily added or subtracted from the other equation, eliminating one of the variables.

### › Example 1

$$2x + y = 7$$
$$3x - y = 3$$

What is the value of $x$ in the above system of equations?

### ✓ Solution

Recognize that if you add the two equations together, the $y$ values will cancel, leaving you only with $x$.

$$2x + y = 7$$
$$+\underline{(3x - y = 3)}$$
$$5x + 0 = 10 \rightarrow 5x = 10 \rightarrow x = 2$$

### › Example 2

What are the values of $x$ and $y$ in the system of equations below?

$$3x + 4y = 1$$
$$2x - 2y = 10$$

### ✓ Solution

Use elimination to solve this. If you multiply the second equation by 2, you will be able to eliminate the $y$ variables and can then solve for $x$.

$$3x + 4y = 1$$
$$+\underline{2 \times (2x - 2y = 10)} \rightarrow$$

$$3x + 4y = 1$$
$$+\underline{4x - 4y = 20}$$
$$7x + 0 = 21 \rightarrow$$

$$7x = 21 \rightarrow x = 3$$

Then, plug 3 in for $x$ into one of the equations to solve for $y$:

$$3x + 4y = 1 \rightarrow$$
$$3(3) + 4y = 1 \rightarrow$$
$$9 + 4y = 1 \rightarrow 4y = -8 \rightarrow y = -2$$

So, the solution set is $x = 3$ and $y = -2$.

### Pattern Recognition

An excellent shortcut you can use to solve equations is to see if there is a pattern that will allow you to easily rearrange the equations without having to use substitution or elimination. If the SAT asks you to solve a problem in terms of an *expression* rather than just a *variable*, odds are that you can use pattern recognition to figure it out.

#### › Example

Given that $3(x + 4) = 2(x + 4) + 5$, what is the value of $x + 4$?

#### ✓ Solution

While you could distribute the 3 and the 2 through the values in the parentheses and solving for $x$ by itself, make things easier by just solving for $x + 4$ as a whole.

$$3(x + 4) = 2(x + 4) + 5 \rightarrow$$

Subtract $2(x + 4)$ from both sides $\rightarrow$

$$3(x + 4) - 2(x + 4) = 2(x + 4) - 2(x + 4) + 5 \rightarrow$$
$$x + 4 = 5$$

You will find far more pattern recognition types of problems on the SAT Math than you are accustomed to finding in your typical math class questions. Be on look out for them to save you time.

**Pattern Recognition: Infinite Solutions**

Building off the material in the Algebra Fundamentals, be able to recognize when there are infinite solutions to a system of equations.

If two equations with two variables can be simplified to be the same equation, there will be infinite solutions. Another way to think about it—if the lines have the same slopes and the same $y$-intercepts, they will overlap and there will be infinitely many solutions.

#### › Example

How many solutions does the following system of equations have?

$$x - 2y = 4$$
$$2x - 4y = 8$$

### ✓ Solution

Divide the second equation by 2 and you will see that it is identical to the first equation:

$$2x - 4y = 8 \rightarrow \frac{2x - 4y}{2} = \frac{8}{2} \rightarrow$$

$$x - 2y = 4$$

Since the two equations can be written the same way, there will be infinitely many sets of points that can be plugged in for $x$ and $y$ to be solutions for the set of equations.

**Pattern Recognition: Zero Solutions**

If two equations written in linear form have identical slopes and different $y$-intercepts, they will be parallel to each other and never intersect. Therefore, there will be zero solutions between them.

### › Example

How many solutions does the following system of equations have?

$$y = 3x - 4$$
$$y = 3x + 12$$

### ✓ Solution

Recall the slope-intercept form of a line: $y = mx + b$. If the lines have the same slope and different $y$-intercepts, they will run parallel to each other.

$$y = mx + b$$
$$y = 3x - 4$$
$$y = 3x + 12$$

These two lines have the same slope of 3, and different $y$-intercepts of $-4$ and 12. So, they will run parallel to each other, resulting in no solutions to the system of equations.

## Plugging in Choices

Sometimes it can save you time to simply plug in the answer choices to see what the answer would be. Do this when it looks like plugging in the choices will ultimately take you less time than solving the problem using algebra.

### › Example

$|3x + 1| = 7$

What value of $x$ is a positive number that would be a solution to the above equation?

(A) 1
(B) 2
(C) 3
(D) 4

## ✓ Solution

While it would be possible to solve this using algebra, you will likely save time by working backwards from the choices. Since the choices on the SAT Math are consistently in order from least to greatest, start with one of the middle choices like (B) or (C). That way, if your answer is too big you can try the smaller answers, and if it is too small you can try the larger answers.

Plug in choice (C) first:

$$|3x + 1| = 7 \rightarrow$$
$$|3(3) + 1| = 10$$

So, 3 is too large of an answer. Let us now try the next smallest answer, choice (B):

$$|3x + 1| = 7 \rightarrow$$
$$|3(2) + 1| = 7$$

**SAT Math Strategy**

Save time by recognizing when substitution, elimination, pattern recognition, or plugging in choices will be the most efficient way to solve a system of equations.

This works, so the correct answer is choice **(B)**.

This table breaks down how to recognize which strategy will likely be most efficient.

| | When to Use | Example | Solution |
|---|---|---|---|
| **Substitution** | If one variable can easily be expressed as the other variable, use substitution. | What is $x$ in the system of equations below?<br>$y = 7x - 4$<br>$3x + 2y = 5$ | *Plug $y = 7x + 4$ in for $y$ in the second equation to solve.*<br>$3x + 2(7x - 4) = 5 \rightarrow$<br>$3x + 14x - 8 = 5 \rightarrow$<br>$17x = 12 \rightarrow x = \frac{12}{17}$ |
| **Elimination** | If one equation can be easily modified so that one variable will cancel when the equations are combined, use elimination. | What is $x$ in the system of equations below?<br>$6x - 3y = 7$<br>$4x + 3y = 5$ | *Add the two equations together to eliminate the $y$ components.*<br>$6x - 3y = 7$<br>$+4x + 3y = 5$<br>$10x + 0 = 12 \rightarrow$<br>$x = \frac{12}{10} = \frac{6}{5}$ |
| **Pattern Recognition** | If the question asks for the value of an expression instead of a variable, watch out for pattern recognition. | What is the value of $5x - 1$ in the equation below?<br>$\frac{5x-1}{3} = 4$ | *Simplify the equation to look like by $5x - 1$ multiplying both sides by 3.*<br>$\frac{5x-1}{3} = 4 \rightarrow$<br>$5x - 1 = 4 \times 3 = 12$ |
| **Plugging in Choices** | When you can more easily plug in the answers than solve the problem with algebra, plug in the choices starting with the middle values. | What is a possible value for $x$ in this inequality?<br>$5x > -2x - 4$<br>(A) 0<br>(B) −1<br>(C) −2<br>(D) −3 | Since the algebra could be a little tricky, you could work backwards from the choices and find that choice (A), 0, is the only option that will make this true. |

## Practice

1. What is the value of $x$ in this series of equations?

$$y = x - 3$$
$$y + 2x = 9$$

2. What is the value of $y$ in this series of equations?

$$3x - 2y = 6$$
$$-6x + 5y = 4$$

3. What is the value of $3x^2$ in the equation $6x^2 - 4 = 8$?

4. What is the value of $x$ in this series of equations?

$$3x = 6y + 9$$
$$x + 2y = 7$$

5. What is the solution set for $(x, y)$ in this series of equations?

$$4x - 3y = 5$$
$$8x = 6y + 10$$

6. What is the value of $y$ in this series of equations?

$$\frac{1}{2}x + 2y = -1$$
$$2x - 3y = 7$$

7. How many solutions are there in this series of equations?

$$y = 5x + \frac{1}{2}$$
$$2y + 8 = 10x$$

8. If $|x - 4| \leq 2$, what is a possible value of $x$?

## Solutions

1. Substitute $x - 3$ in for $y$ in the second equation to solve:

$$(x - 3) + 2x = 9 \rightarrow$$
$$3x - 3 = 9 \rightarrow 3x = 12 \rightarrow x = 4$$

2. Double the first equation and then add it to the second to eliminate the $x$ components:

$$2(3x - 2y = 6)$$
$$-6x + 5y = 4 \rightarrow$$

$$6x - 4y = 12$$
$$+(\underline{-6x + 5y = 4)}$$
$$0 + y = 16 \rightarrow y = 16$$

3. Recognize that you can manipulate the equation fairly easily to isolate $3x^2$:

$$6x^2 - 4 = 8 \rightarrow$$
$$6x^2 = 12 \rightarrow$$

Divide both sides by 2 $\rightarrow$

$$3x^2 = 6$$

4. Simplify the first equation by dividing it by 3, then substitute it in to the second equation:

$$3x = 6y + 9 \rightarrow \text{Divide by } 3 \rightarrow$$
$$x = 2y + 3$$

Substitute this in the second equation $\rightarrow$

$$(2y + 3) + 2y = 7 \rightarrow$$
$$4y + 3 = 7 \rightarrow 4y = 4 \rightarrow y = 1$$

Plug 1 in for $y$ to solve for $x$:

$$x = 2y + 3 \rightarrow$$
$$x = 2(1) + 3 = 5$$

5. With a little bit of manipulation, you can see the pattern, which makes this easier to solve:

$$4x - 3y = 5$$
$$8x = 6y + 10$$

Manipulate the second equation to make it look like the first one:

$$8x = 6y + 10 \rightarrow 8x - 6y = 10 \rightarrow$$

Divide both sides by 2 →

$$4x - 3y = 5$$

So, since the second equation is equivalent to the first equation, there are infinitely many solutions.

6. Use elimination to solve—multiply the first equation by $-4$ to make it possible to add and eliminate the $x$ components:

$$-4\left(\frac{1}{2}x + 2y = -1\right) = -2x - 8y = 4 \rightarrow$$
$$-2x - 8y = 4$$
$$\underline{+2x - 3y = 7}$$
$$0 - 11y = 11 \rightarrow y = -1$$

7. Recognize the pattern here by simplifying the second equation to get it in slope-intercept form:

$$2y + 8 = 10x \rightarrow 2y = 10x - 8 \rightarrow y = 5x - 4$$

Once this equation is in slope-intercept form, you can see that it has the same slope as the first equation, 5, and a different $y$-intercept. Therefore, the lines created by these two equations will never overlap or intersect, resulting in no solutions.

8. Although this is a fill-in question, you could still try plugging in potential answers to find one that would make this statement true. Since we know that $|x - 4| \leq 2$, we could pick a value that is less than 2 and plug that in: $|x - 4| = 1$. Based on this, 5 would be a possible value for $x$.

Alternatively, you could do this algebraically as follows:

$$|x - 4| \leq 2 \rightarrow$$

Break up the absolute value like this:

$$-2 \leq x - 4 \leq 2 \rightarrow$$

Add 4 to all parts of the expression:

$$-2 + 4 \leq x - 4 + 4 \leq 2 + 4 \rightarrow$$
$$2 \leq x \leq 6$$

So, any number greater than or equal to 2 and less than or equal to 6 would work. As you can see, plugging in potential solutions would likely save you time.

## Inequalities

An inequality indicates which value is greater than or less than another value. The open end of the $>$ goes toward the larger number. For example:

$$-3 < 0 \text{ and } 10 > 4$$

A line underneath a greater/less than sign indicates that the terms on either side can possibly equal one another. For example:

$8 \geq n$ means that $n$ is less than or equal to 8, or alternatively, that 8 is greater than or equal to $n$.

Inequalities can be solved like typical equations, with an important exception:

*If multiplying or dividing a side of the inequality by a negative number, change the direction of the inequality sign.*

### Example

Simplify the expression $-4x > 3$.

### Solution

$$-4x > 3$$

Divide both sides by $-4$ and turn the $>$ around to $<$.

$$\frac{-4x}{-4} < \frac{3}{-4}$$

$$\frac{\cancel{-4}x}{\cancel{-4}} < \frac{3}{-4}$$

$$x < -\frac{3}{4}$$

### Practice

1. How would one express that $x$ represents all the numbers greater than or equal to 14?
2. If $x > 4$ and $x < 9$, what is a possible value for $x$?
3. Simplify $-2x + 4 > 6$.

### Solutions

1. $x \geq 14$
2. The values of $x$ must be greater than 4 and less than 9, so any number between 4 and 9 would work. (Note—it would not include 4 or 9 themselves since the expressions do not indicate equality.)
3. $-2x + 4 > 6 \rightarrow$
   $-2x > 2 \rightarrow$
   Divide both sides by $-2$ and flip the sign:

$$x < \frac{2}{-2} \rightarrow x < -1$$

## Absolute Value

When you take the absolute value of a number, it represents how far that number is from zero. If you took the absolute value of $-6$ or 6, both would be 6 since they are both 6 units away from zero.

Absolute value is written by putting two lines around the number—for example, the absolute value of 4 would be written as $|4|$. Calculate the absolute value of an expression by making the expression positive, no matter if the expression is originally positive or negative. Here are some absolute value expressions:

$$|8| = 8$$
$$|-5| = 5$$
$$\left|-\frac{1}{2}\right| = \frac{1}{2}$$

To solve a typical absolute value equation, set it up as two equations—one with a positive and one with a negative value. (If the absolute value expression equals zero, there will be just one solution; if the absolute value expression equals a negative number, there will be zero solutions.)

### Example

What are the possible values for $x$ in the equation $|x + 1| = 5$?

### Solution

$|x + 1| = 5$ can be set up as two different equations:

$$x + 1 = 5$$
$$x + 1 = -5$$

Solve each equation for $x$ to find the solutions:

$$x + 1 = 5 \rightarrow x = 4$$
$$x + 1 = -5 \rightarrow x = -6$$

So $x$ could be either 4 or $-6$.

### Practice

1. What is the value of $|4 - 7|$?
2. What are the possible values of $x$ in the equation $|x - 1| = 5$?
3. Given that $x$ is a real number, what is the least possible value for $|x|$?

### Solutions

1. $|4 - 7| \rightarrow |-3| \rightarrow 3$
2. Set it up as two separate equations:

$$x - 1 = 5$$
$$x - 1 = -5$$

   Then solve each equation for $x$:

$$x - 1 = 5 \rightarrow x = 6$$
$$x - 1 = -5 \rightarrow x = -4$$

   So, $x$ could be either 6 or $-4$.

3. If you take the absolute value of any real number, it will be the positive value of that number. So, the least possible value for $x$ is found when you take the absolute value of zero: $|0| = 0$. Therefore, zero is the least possible value for $|x|$.

## Function Notation

Many of the expressions you encounter on the SAT Math will be equations with $x$ and $y$ values. However, be sure you understand function notation:

$f(x) = 2x + 1$ is the same as $y = 2x + 1$; $f(x)$ corresponds to the $y$ value.

If you were told that $f(x) = 3x - 5$ and asked to find the value of $f(4)$, simply plug 4 in for $x$ into the function:

$$f(x) = 3x - 5$$

$$f(4) = 3(4) - 5 = 12 - 5 = 7$$

Finally, you may be asked to combine functions together. Be sure you work from the "inside out" to solve these.

### Example

If $f(x) = 4x - 3$ and $g(x) = 2x + 1$, what is $g(f(2))$?

### Solution

Start by calculating the value of $f(2)$:

$$f(x) = 4x - 3$$

$$f(2) = 4(2) - 3 = 8 - 3 = 5$$

Then, take 5 and plug it into $g(x)$:

$$g(x) = 2x + 1$$

$$g(5) = 2(5) + 1 = 11$$

### Practice

1. If $x$ is 4, what is $f(x)$ if $f(x) = 2x - 5$?
2. If $x$ is 8 and $f(x) = x - 4$, what is the value of $3f(x)$?
3. If $f(x) = x^2$ and $g(x) = \frac{x}{2}$, what is $f(g(4))$?

### Solutions

1. Plug 4 in for $x$ to the function:

$$f(x) = 2x - 5$$

$$f(4) = 2(4) - 5 = 8 - 5 = 3$$

2. First, determine the value of $f(x)$ by plugging in 8 for $x$:

$$f(x) = x - 4$$

$$f(8) = 8 - 4 = 4$$

Then, multiply 4 by 3 to see what $3f(x)$ would be:

$$4 \times 3 = 12$$

3. Work inside out to solve. First, determine $g(4)$:

$$g(x) = \frac{x}{2}$$
$$g(4) = \frac{4}{2} = 2$$

Then, plug 2 into $f(x)$:

$$f(x) = x^2$$
$$f(x) = 2^2 = 4$$

## Practice Drill #1—Solving Equations

*(If timing, take about 12 minutes to complete.)*

1. $6 = 5x + 1$

   What is the solution for $x$ in the equation above?

   (A) 0
   (B) 1
   (C) 2
   (D) 3

2. What value of $x$ satisfies the equation $13x + 3 = 42$?

   (A) 3
   (B) 5
   (C) 7
   (D) 10

3. $1.2x - 2.4 = 3.6$

   What value of $x$ is a solution to the above equation?

   (A) 4
   (B) 5
   (C) 6
   (D) 7

4. $-|y + 5| = -4$

   What are the solutions to the equation above?

   (A) 1 or $-3$
   (B) 1 or $-9$
   (C) $-1$ or 9
   (D) $-1$ or $-9$

5. What is the solution set for $x$ and $y$ at which these two lines would intersect?

$$3x - y = 2$$
$$-4x + 2y = 2$$

(A) (3, 7)
(B) (1, 6)
(C) (−4, 5)
(D) (2, −1)

$5(a-1) - 2(a+2) = \frac{3}{4}a$

6. What is the value of $a$ in the above equation?

(A) 2
(B) 3
(C) 4
(D) 5

$3x - 2y = 7$
$-6y + 4x = 12$

7. Consider the system of equations above. What is the value of $7x - 8y$?

(A) 7
(B) 8
(C) 14
(D) 19

8. $3x - 2 \leq 2x + 3$

What is the greatest possible number that would work for $x$ in the above inequality?

(A) 3
(B) 5
(C) 8
(D) 9

9. $2y = -6x + 14$
$\frac{2}{3}y = -2x + 1$

How many solutions are there to the above system of equations?

(A) Zero
(B) One
(C) Two
(D) Infinite

10. $\frac{1}{2}x - \frac{2}{3}y = 18$

$\frac{3}{4}x + 2y = 36$

Based on the system of equations above, what is the product of $x$ and $y$?

(A) 30
(B) 80
(C) 120
(D) 180

## Solutions

1. **(B)** $6 = 5x + 1 \rightarrow$
$5 = 5x \rightarrow$
$1 = x$

2. **(A)** $13x + 3 = 42 \rightarrow$
$13x = 39 \rightarrow$
$x = 3$

3. **(B)** $1.2x - 2.4 = 3.6 \rightarrow$
$1.2x = 6.0 \rightarrow$
$x = \frac{6.0}{1.2} = 5$

4. **(D)** $-|y + 5| = -4 \rightarrow$
$|y + 5| = 4 \rightarrow$

Make two separate equations and solve:

$$y + 5 = 4 \rightarrow y = -1$$

*or*

$$y + 5 = -4 \rightarrow y = -9$$

5. **(A)** Use elimination to solve this series of equations, since the *y*'s can be easily cancelled if you multiply the first equation by 2:

$$2(3x - y) = 2 \times 2 \rightarrow$$
$$6x - 2y = 4$$

Then, add this to the second equation to eliminate:

$$\begin{array}{r} 6x - 2y = 4 \\ \underline{-4x + 2y = 2} \\ 2x + 0 = 6 \rightarrow 2x = 6 \rightarrow x = 3 \end{array}$$

Fortunately, the only answer that has a 3 for the $x$ value is choice **(A)**, so you do not need to bother solving for $y$.

6. **(C)** $5(a-1)-2(a+2)=\frac{3}{4}a \rightarrow$

$$5a-5-2a-4=\frac{3}{4}a \rightarrow$$

$$3a-9=\frac{3}{4}a \rightarrow$$

$$-9=\frac{3}{4}a-3a \rightarrow$$

$$-9=\frac{3}{4}a-\frac{12}{4}a \rightarrow$$

$$-9=-\frac{9}{4}a \rightarrow$$

$$-9\times-\frac{4}{9}=4=a$$

7. **(D)** Although the equations present the $x$ and $y$ values in different orders, do your best to recognize that if you add these two equations together you will have the expression $7x-8y$:

$$3x-2y=7$$

$$-6y+4x=12$$

Change the order of the second equation, and add it to the first one:

$$3x-2y=7$$

$$+\underline{4x-6y=12}$$

$$7x-8y=19$$

8. **(B)** Simplify the inequality in order to see what the largest potential value for $x$ could be:

$$3x-2\leq 2x+3 \rightarrow$$

$$3x\leq 2x+5 \rightarrow$$

$$x\leq 5$$

Since $x$ can be any value less than or equal to 5, the largest possible value it could be is 5.

9. **(A)** The two equations can be simplified to be in slope-intercept form:

$$2y=-6x+14$$

$$y=-3x+7$$

And:

$$\frac{2}{3}y=-2x+1 \rightarrow$$

$$y=\frac{3}{2}(-2x+1) \rightarrow$$

$$y=-3x+1.5$$

So, the lines have the same slope, which makes them parallel. They also have different $y$-intercepts, which means they do not intersect or overlap. Therefore, there are no points of intersection for the two lines and zero solutions.

10. **(C)** Multiply the first equation by 3 so that you can add the equations together and eliminate $y$.

$$\frac{1}{2}x-\frac{2}{3}y=18 \rightarrow$$

$$\frac{3}{2}x-2y=54$$

Now, add this equation to the second equation to eliminate the *y*'s:

$$\begin{array}{r} \frac{3}{2}x - 2y = 54 \\ +\frac{3}{4}x + 2y = 36 \\ \hline \frac{9}{4}x + 0 = 90 \rightarrow \frac{9}{4}x = 90 \rightarrow \frac{4}{9} \times 90 = 40 = x \end{array}$$

Now, plug 40 back in for *x* to one of the equations to solve for *y*:

$$\frac{1}{2}x - \frac{2}{3}y = 18 \rightarrow$$

$$\frac{1}{2}(40) - \frac{2}{3}y = 18 \rightarrow$$

$$20 - \frac{2}{3}y = 18 \rightarrow -\frac{2}{3}y = 18 - 20 \rightarrow$$

$$-\frac{2}{3}y = -2 \rightarrow \left(-\frac{3}{2}\right) \times -2 = 3 = y$$

Now, multiply 3 and 40 together to give you 120.

## Practice Drill #2—Solving Equations

*(If timing, take about 12 minutes to complete.)*

1. $5x + 4 = -6$

   In the equation above, what is the value of *x*?

   (A) −2
   (B) −1
   (C) 0
   (D) 1

2. If $-5(x - 3) + 2(x + 6) = 12$, what is the value of *x*?

   (A) 3
   (B) 5
   (C) 8
   (D) 9

3. If $\frac{5a}{2} = \frac{3}{7}$, what is the value of *a*?

   (A) $\frac{6}{35}$
   (B) $\frac{10}{21}$
   (C) $\frac{14}{15}$
   (D) $\frac{7}{6}$

4. $y > 7$ and $y - 4 < 3x$

   Based on the system of inequalities above, what are the possible values for $x$?

   (A) $x < 0$
   (B) $x > 3$
   (C) $x < -11$
   (D) $x > 1$

5. If $y + 1 > 2x$ and $y > 3x + 2$, which ordered pair would satisfy the system of inequalities?

   (A) $(-3, 5)$
   (B) $(2, -4)$
   (C) $(1, 2)$
   (D) $(4, 0)$

**Fill-In Practice:** Write your answer in the underlined blank under each question.

6. $11x + 3y = 7$
   $6x + 8y = 5$

   If $(x, y)$ is a solution to the above system of equations, what is the value of $5x - 5y$?

   Answer: ________

7. Consider this series of equations:

   $x + 2y = 5$
   $y - x = -2$

   What is the value of $y$?

   Answer: ________

8. $2x - y = -1$
   $2x + y = 7$

   If $(x, y)$ is a solution to the above series of equations, what is the value of $x$?

   Answer: ________

9. For the function g, if $g(5x - 1) = x + 4$, what is the value of $g(4)$?

   Answer: ________

10. $3x - 2y = 7$
    $x + y = 9$

    In the system of equations above what is the value of $x$?

    Answer: ________

## Solutions

1. **(A)** $5x + 4 = -6 \rightarrow$

$$5x = -10 \rightarrow$$

$$x = -\frac{10}{5} = -2$$

2. **(B)** $-5(x - 3) + 2(x + 6) = 12 \rightarrow$

$$-5x + 15 + 2x + 12 = 12 \rightarrow$$

$$-3x + 27 = 12 \rightarrow$$

$$-3x = -15 \rightarrow x = 5$$

3. **(A)** $\frac{5a}{2} = \frac{3}{7} \rightarrow$ Cross Multiply the 2 $\rightarrow$

$$5a = \frac{6}{7} \rightarrow \text{Divide Both Sides by } 5 \rightarrow$$

$$a = \frac{6}{7 \times 5} = \frac{6}{35}$$

4. **(D)** Simplify $y - 4 < 3x$ to put it in terms of $y$:

$$y - 4 < 3x \rightarrow y = 3x + 4$$

Then combine the two inequalities, $y > 7$ and $y < 3x + 4$, and simplify:

$$7 < y < 3x + 4 \rightarrow$$

$$7 < 3x + 4 \rightarrow$$

$$3 < 3x \rightarrow 1 < x \rightarrow x > 1$$

5. **(A)** This is a good example of plugging in the choices to solve. Choice (A) is the only option that will be true for both the $x$ and $y$ values in the pair:

$$y + 1 > 2x \rightarrow$$

$$(5) + 1 > 2(-3) \rightarrow$$

$$6 > -6$$

And:

$$y > 3x + 2 \rightarrow$$

$$(5) > 3(-3) + 2 \rightarrow$$

$$5 > -9 + 2 \rightarrow$$

$$5 > -7$$

6. **(2)** This is a great example of a pattern recognition problem. If you subtract the second equation from the first one, you will get it to look like $5x - 5y$:

$$\begin{array}{r} 11x + 3y = 7 \\ -(6x + 8y = 5) \\ \hline 5x - 5y = 2 \end{array}$$

7. **(1)** If you add the two equations together, the $x$'s will cancel, leaving you with only the $y$ term to analyze. Rearrange the second equation, $y - x = -2$, so that the $x$ term comes first and it can be more easily added to the first equation:

$$\begin{array}{r} x + 2y = 5 \\ +\underline{(-x + y = -2)} \\ 0 + 3y = 3 \rightarrow 3y = 3 \rightarrow y = 1 \end{array}$$

8. **(1.5 or $\frac{3}{2}$)** This is a great example of an elimination question. Add the two equations together to eliminate the $y$:

$$\begin{array}{r} 2x - y = -1 \\ +\underline{2x + y = 7} \\ 4x + 0 = 6 \rightarrow 4x = 6 \rightarrow x = 1.5 \end{array}$$

9. **(5)** Since $g(4) = g(5x - 1)$, find out what the value of $x$ is by solving the equation $4 = 5x - 1$:

$$4 = 5x - 1 \rightarrow 5 = 5x \rightarrow x = 1$$

Then, plug 1 in for $x$ in the right-hand side of the function:

$$x + 4 \rightarrow 1 + 4 \rightarrow 5$$

So, the value of $g(4)$ is 5.

10. **(5)** If you double the second equation, $x + y = 9$, you can eliminate the $y$ terms and solve for $x$:

$$\begin{array}{r} 3x - 2y = 7 \\ +\underline{2x + 2y = 18} \\ 5x + 0 = 25 \rightarrow 5x = 25 \rightarrow x = 5 \end{array}$$

## Practice Drill #3—Solving Equations

*(If timing, take about 12 minutes to complete.)*

1. If $x - 3 = 0.5x$, what is the value of $x$?

(A) 2
(B) 4
(C) 6
(D) 8

2. If $5(x + 4) - 3(x + 4) = 3x - 2$, what is the value of $x$?

(A) 3
(B) 4
(C) 7
(D) 10

3. If $3x$ is 5 less than 20, what is $x + 4$?

(A) 4
(B) 6
(C) 8
(D) 9

4. $y + 5n = 3$

In the equation above, if $y = 2$, what is the value of $n$?

(A) $\frac{1}{5}$
(B) 2
(C) $\frac{7}{2}$
(D) 6

5. If $\frac{4}{3y} = \frac{2}{3}$, what is the value of $y$?

(A) 1
(B) 2
(C) 6
(D) 12

6. $y = 3x - 5$
$y = 3x + k$

Consider the system of equations above. What must the value of the constant $k$ be so that the system of equations has infinitely many solutions?

(A) $-15$
(B) $-8$
(C) $-5$
(D) 0

7. $4x + y = 3$
$-3x - 2y = 4$

In the above system of equations, what is the point in the $xy$-coordinate plane at which the lines formed by the equations would intersect?

(A) $(2, -5)$
(B) $(6, -3)$
(C) $(9, 0)$
(D) $(12, 6)$

8. $y = x + 5$
$2x + y = 11$

In the system of equations above, what is the value of $x$?

(A) 0
(B) 2
(C) 4
(D) 6

9. If $|x + 2| > 0$, which of the following statements <u>must</u> be true?

   (A) $x = -6$
   (B) $x = 5$
   (C) $x \neq -2$
   (D) $x \neq 0$

10. If $f(x) = 2x - 1$, and $g(x) = 3f(x)$, what is the slope and $y$-intercept of the line formed by $g(x)$?

    (A) Slope = 3, $y$-intercept = $-1$
    (B) Slope = 4, $y$-intercept = $-2$
    (C) Slope = 6, $y$-intercept = 3
    (D) Slope = 6, $y$-intercept = $-3$

## Solutions

1. **(C)** $x - 3 = 0.5x \rightarrow$

   $-3 = 0.5x - x \rightarrow$

   $-3 = -0.5x \rightarrow x = 6$

2. **(D)** $5(x + 4) - 3(x + 4) = 3x - 2 \rightarrow$

   $5x + 20 - 3x - 12 = 3x - 2 \rightarrow$

   $2x + 8 = 3x - 2 \rightarrow$

   $8 = x - 2 \rightarrow x = 10$

3. **(D)** Turn the words into an algebraic expression. "If $3x$ is 5 less than 20" is equivalent to:

   $$3x = 20 - 5 \rightarrow$$
   $$3x = 15$$

   Since $3x = 15 \rightarrow x = 5$

   Therefore, $x + 4 = 5 + 4 = 9$

4. **(A)** Plug 2 in for $y$ and then solve for $n$:

   $$y + 5n = 3 \rightarrow$$
   $$2 + 5n = 3 \rightarrow$$
   $$5n = 1 \rightarrow n = \frac{1}{5}$$

   In the equation above, if $y = -2$, what is the value of $n$?

5. **(B)** $\frac{4}{3y} = \frac{2}{3} \rightarrow$ Cross Multiply $\rightarrow$

   $4 = \frac{2}{3} \times 3y \rightarrow$ Cancel the 3s $\rightarrow$

   $4 = 2y \rightarrow 2 = y$

6. **(C)** Two equations will have infinitely many solutions if they overlap one another. Equations that have the same slope and $y$-intercept will overlap. Therefore, since the equations are already in slope-intercept form, make the constant $k$ identical to the $y$-intercept in the first equation:

$$y = 3x - 5$$

So, the $y$-intercept is $-5$ and $k$ should be $-5$.

7. **(A)** Use elimination to find the point of intersection. Double the first equation and add it to the second equation to eliminate the $y$ values:

$$2(4x + y) = 2(3) \rightarrow 8x + 2y = 6$$

Now add this to the second equation:

$$\begin{aligned} 8x + 2y &= 6 \\ +\underline{(-3x - 2y} &\underline{= 4)} \\ 5x + 0 = 10 \rightarrow 5x &= 10 \rightarrow x = 2 \end{aligned}$$

Fortunately, the only option that has 2 as the $x$ value is choice **(A)**, so you do not have to continue to solve for $y$.

8. **(B)** Use substitution to solve this series of equations.

$$\begin{aligned} y &= x + 5 \\ 2x + y &= 11 \end{aligned}$$

Plug the first equation into the second one, then solve for $x$:

$$\begin{aligned} 2x + (x + 5) &= 11 \rightarrow \\ 2x + x + 5 &= 11 \rightarrow \\ 3x + 5 &= 11 \rightarrow \\ 3x &= 6 \rightarrow x = 2 \end{aligned}$$

9. **(C)** Given that $|x + 2| > 0$, choices (A), (B), and (D) all *could* be true. However, the only choice that *must* be true is choice **(C)**. If $x$ were equal to $-2$, then the inequality would say that $0 > 0$, which cannot be the case.

10. **(D)** Plug $f(x) = 2x - 1$ into $g(x)$:

$$g(x) = 3(2x - 1) \rightarrow 6x - 3$$

Now, it is in slope-intercept form, and we can see that the slope is 6 and the $y$-intercept is $-3$.

## Algebra—Word Problems and Function Interpretation

### Setting Up Word Problems

So far in this section, you have worked with how to execute algebraic operations. However, many SAT Math problems have you set up the algebra by asking detailed word problems. Here are some of the most common word problem phrases along with their corresponding mathematical operations.

**SAT Math Strategy**

Know which wording corresponds to which mathematical operations to help you solve word problems.

| Wording Examples for Common Mathematical Operations | Operation |
|---|---|
| is, are, was, were, will be, equals, gives, yields, results in, costs, sells for | $=$ |
| sum, plus, increased by, more than, together, combined, total(s), added to, greater than, older than, farther than | $+$ |
| difference, decreased by, less than, fewer than, minus, after, left over, younger than, shorter than, smaller than | $-$ |
| multiplied by, times, of, product of, twice, triple, quadruple | $\times$ |
| Divided by, per, out of, split, average, ratio of, half of, one third of | $\div$ or $\frac{x}{y}$ |

### Example 1

Translate this sentence into an algebraic expression:

There are a total of 40 pets at a store, with $x$ dogs and $y$ cats.

### Solution

$$40 = x + y$$

### Example 2

Translate these sentences into algebraic expressions:

Caitlin is 6 years older than Allison, and the sum of Allison's age and Caitlin's age is 60 years.

### ✓ Solution

Let's use $C$ for Caitlin's age and $A$ for Allison's age. Be careful to not to make the equation go in the order of the words if the algebra does not correspond. For the first half of the sentence, "Caitlin is 6 years older than Allison," the equation would be:

$$C = A + 6$$

The second half of the sentence, "the sum of Allison's age and Caitlin's age is 60 years," would look like this algebraically:

$$A + C = 60$$

### › Example 3

A stoplight is always green, yellow, or red. It is green $\frac{3}{5}$ of the time and yellow $\frac{1}{4}$ of the remaining time. What fraction of the entire time is the light red?

Fill in: ________

### ✓ Solution

Read the question one step at time, writing out the relevant information. Since the stoplight is always green, yellow, or red, we can determine the fraction of time it *is not* red by subtracting the green, yellow, and red fractions from 1; the remaining fraction will indicate the fraction of the time it *is* red.

The light is green $\frac{3}{5}$ of the time. The time that it is remaining would be $1 - \frac{3}{5} = \frac{5}{5} - \frac{3}{5} = \frac{2}{5}$ of the time. Out of the $\frac{2}{5}$ of time remaining, it is yellow $\frac{1}{4}$ of time time. So, calculate the fraction of time it is yellow by multiplying $\frac{2}{5}$ and $\frac{1}{4}$:

$$\frac{2}{5} \times \frac{1}{4} = \frac{2}{20} = \frac{1}{10}$$

Then calculate the time it is red by subtracting $\frac{3}{5}$, the fraction of time it is green, and $\frac{1}{10}$, the fraction of time it is yellow, from 1:

$$1 - \frac{3}{5} - \frac{1}{10} \rightarrow$$

Use 10 as the least common denominator:

$$\frac{10}{10} - \frac{6}{10} - \frac{1}{10} = \frac{3}{10}$$

So, the light is red $\frac{3}{10}$ of the entire time.

### Practice

Turn these sentences into algebraic expressions.

1. Pam read 40 pages of her book on Monday, 30 pages of her book on Tuesday, and $x$ pages of her book on Wednesday for a total of 120 pages.
2. If Yusuf did 1 hour of homework on Sunday and twice as much homework on Monday, how many hours did he do on both of those days?
3. Dog $x$ is 5 years older than dog $y$.
4. Sofia spends two-thirds out of the 24 hours in a day awake. How would you calculate the number of hours, $h$, she is asleep in a day?
5. The average weight of person A, B, and C is 150 pounds.

### Solutions

1. $40 + 30 + x = 120$
2. $1 + 2(1) = 3$ total hours of homework
3. Be sure you don't just read this left to right. It should be set up as the following:

$$x = y + 5$$

From this expression, you can see that $x$ is 5 greater than $y$.

4. $$24 - \frac{2}{3} \times 24 = h \rightarrow$$
$$24 - 16 = h \rightarrow$$
$$8 = h$$
5. $$\frac{A + B + C}{3} = 150$$

**NOTE**

**Averages will be covered in-depth in the Problem Solving and Data Analysis section.**

### Distance, Rate, and Time

The relationship among distance, rate (speed), and time is given by the following formula:

$$DISTANCE = RATE \times TIME, \text{ or } D = RT$$

For example, if you were driving at 60 miles per hour for two hours, you would travel a total of 120 miles:

$$D = RT$$
$$120 \text{ Miles} = 60 \text{ MPH} \times 2 \text{ Hours}$$

### › Example

Julia's family took a road trip in which they drove 8 hours a day and averaged a driving speed of 50 miles per hour. If they spent a total of 6 days on the trip, how far in total did they drive?

### ✓ Solution

Start by figuring out how far they drove on a given day:

$$D = RT \rightarrow$$
$$D = 50 \times 8 \rightarrow$$
$$\text{Distance} = 400 \text{ Miles}$$

Then, multiply the daily number of miles by 6 days to find the total number of miles travelled:

$$400 \times 6 = 2{,}400$$

So, they drove a total of 2,400 miles on the trip.

## Interpreting Variables and Constants

**SAT Math Strategy**

Create your own idea of the meaning of a constant or variable before jumping into the options.

Sometimes, SAT word problems will not simply ask for you to solve for the value of a variable, but to interpret the significance of a constant or a variable.

### › Example 1

A teacher is counting up his classroom supplies for inventory at the end of the year. $T$ is equal to the number of textbooks in his classroom at the end of the year, and $L$ is the equal to the number of laptop computers in his classroom at the end of the year. In the equation

$T + L = 60$, what does the number 60 represent?

(A) The product of the number of the laptops and the number of the textbooks at the end of the year in the teacher's classroom
(B) The combined total number of laptops and textbooks at the end of the year in the teacher's classroom
(C) The difference between the number of laptops and number of textbooks in the teacher's classroom at the end of the year
(D) The predicted value of the number of laptops and textbooks a year from now

### ✓ Solution

Following our strategy for problems like these, do not jump into the choices before we have considered the meaning independently. $T$ represents the number of textbooks at the end of the year, and $L$ represents the number of laptops at the end of the year. If we add these together, we would get the sum of the textbooks and laptops the teacher has at the end of the year.

$$T + L = \text{Total number of textbooks and laptops}$$

This total is 60 in the problem. So, we can check out the choices and see that choice **(B)**, "The combined total number of laptops and textbooks at the end of the year in the teacher's classroom," corresponds to this idea.

### Example 2

The height of water in inches, $h$, in a classroom's fish tank after $w$ weeks is given by the function below.

$$h(w) = -\frac{1}{2}w + 25$$

Over a three-week period, by how much does the height of water in the tank change?

(A) Increases by .5 inches
(B) Increases by 25 inches
(C) Decreases by 1.5 inches
(D) Decreases by 2.5 inches

### Solution

To answer this, we must first understand the meaning of the numbers in the function before diving into the choices. The function is written in slope-intercept form. The $y$-intercept is 25, indicating the initial height of water in the tank before any weeks have gone by. The slope is $-\frac{1}{2}$, indicating that each week that goes by, the height of the water in the tank will decrease by $\frac{1}{2}$ an inch.

So, over a three-week period, we can see by how much the height in the tank has changed by taking $-\frac{1}{2}$ and multiplying it by 3:

$$-\frac{1}{2} \times 3 = -\frac{3}{2} = -1.5$$

Therefore, the height in the tank after three weeks have passed will decrease by 1.5 inches, corresponding to choice **(C)**.

### Functions in Table Form

Most functions you will encounter will be in the form of an equation. Sometimes, however, the SAT will provide the values of the function in a table. Here is how you attack a problem formatted in this way:

### Example

The linear function $f$ is defined by $f(x) = ax + b$, where $a$ and $b$ are constants. The values in the table below represent ordered pairs for the function:

| $x$ | $f(x)$ |
|---|---|
| 10 | 700 |
| 20 | 1200 |

What is the value of the constant $b$?

Fill In _______

**✓ Solution**

The way to read the table is to understand that each row represents an ordered pair: (10, 700) and (20, 1,200). You can solve for the constant $b$ by first calculating the value of the constant $a$, which corresponds to the slope of the line:

$$\frac{\text{Change in } y}{\text{Change in } x} = \frac{1{,}200 - 700}{20 - 10} = \frac{500}{10} = 50$$

Now we know that the function can be written as $f(x) = 50x + b$. Next, solve for $b$ by plugging in an ordered pair—let's use (10, 700) since it is smaller.

$$f(x) = 50x + b \rightarrow$$
$$700 = 50 \times 10 + b \rightarrow$$
$$700 = 500 + b \rightarrow b = 200$$

So, the value of the constant $b$ is 200.

## Practice Drill #1—Word Problems and Function Interpretation

*(If timing, take about 12 minutes to complete.)*

1. The total number of pages in a book is $T$. Eloise will read $P$ pages each day for exactly $D$ days until she completes the book at the end of the final day. Which of the following expresses the relationship between these values?

   (A) $T = PD$
   (B) $T = \frac{P}{D}$
   (C) $T = P + D$
   (D) $T = P - D$

2. Mary rented a boat that cost a \$100 flat fee plus \$3 for each gallon of gasoline used. If Mary paid a total of \$130 to rent the boat, how many gallons of gasoline did she use?

   (A) 10
   (B) 15
   (C) 30
   (D) 45

3. An average pace for a backpacker on a certain trail is to hike 10 miles per day. If Joseph is taking a weeklong backpacking trip in which he wants his average pace over the entire week to exceed this average pace each day, which inequality represents the number of miles, $m$, he will travel on his trip?

   (A) $m > 10$
   (B) $m < 10$
   (C) $m < 70$
   (D) $m > 70$

4. A bread recipe calls for 6 eggs for every 10 cups of flour. If Martin wants to use a total of 15 eggs, how many cups of flour will he need to make this larger amount of bread using this recipe?

(A) 15
(B) 16
(C) 25
(D) 60

5. The number of windmills at a windfarm starts at 200, with 6 new windmills added each year and 2 mills removed each year due to wear and tear. What function represents the number of windmills, $w$, on the windfarm $t$ years after the windfarm opens?

(A) $w(t) = 200 + 6t$
(B) $w(t) = 200 + 4t$
(C) $w(t) = 6 + 200t$
(D) $w(t) = 200 - 4t$

6. A catalog weighs enough that it requires 4 stamps for the post office to mail it. If a business is sending 500 catalogs, and each book of stamps has 20 stamps in it, how many books of stamps would the business need to purchase to mail all the catalogs?

(A) 24
(B) 80
(C) 100
(D) 2,000

7. Each student on a school trip packs 2 suitcases, 1 backpack, and 1 personal object. If there are 65 students on the trip, how many total items would the students pack?

(A) 69
(B) 130
(C) 196
(D) 260

8. The cost in dollars, $C$, of installing a sewer pipe that is $L$ feet long is modeled by the function below:

$$C(L) = 300 + 20L$$

Given that function, what is the most logical interpretation of the following equation?

$$C(20) = 700$$

(A) The cost to install a 700-foot sewer pipe is 20 dollars.
(B) 20 times the cost of a typical pipe is equivalent to 700 dollars.
(C) The cost to install a 20-foot-long sewer pipe is 700 dollars.
(D) 20 typical sewer pipes have a total installation cost of 700 dollars.

9. A plumber's compensation is \$50 per hour plus a \$5,000 profit-share at the end of the year. Which inequality represents the number of hours, $n$, she will need to work in order to make at least \$50,000 total compensation for the year?

(A) $50{,}000 \leq 50n + 5{,}000$
(B) $50{,}000 \geq 50n + 5{,}000$
(C) $\frac{n}{50} \geq 5{,}000$
(D) $\frac{n}{50} \leq 5{,}000$

10. The height in feet of an airplane, $A$, and a balloon, $B$, are modeled by these two equations, in which $t$ is the number of minutes after 12:00 P.M.

$$A = 10{,}000 - 180t$$
$$B = 20t$$

At what time that same day would the airplane and the balloon be at the same height?

(A) 12:30 P.M.
(B) 12:50 P.M.
(C) 1:00 P.M.
(D) 1:45 P.M.

## Solutions

1. **(A)** Since she will read $P$ pages each day for $D$ days, multiply $P$ and $D$ together to get the total number of pages read:

$$T = PD$$

2. **(A)** Using $x$ as the number of gallons of gasoline used, set up an equation modeling the situation like this:

$$130 = 100 + 3x$$

This means that the \$100 flat fee plus \$3 times each gallon of gas used will equal a total amount of \$130. Then, solve for $x$:

$$130 = 100 + 3x \rightarrow$$
$$30 = 3x \rightarrow$$
$$x = 10$$

So, 10 gallons of gas were used.

3. **(D)** If Joseph exceeds the average pace of 10 miles per day over the 7-day period, he will travel in excess of $10 \times 7 = 70$ miles all together. Express this as an inequality by making the number of miles, $m$, be greater than 70: $m > 70$.

4. **(C)** Set up a proportion to solve this. There are 6 eggs for every 10 cups of flour, and this ratio needs to equal the ratio when there are 15 eggs (put the flour in the numerator since you are solving for flour, making you have to use fewer steps):

$$\frac{\text{Flour}}{\text{Eggs}} = \frac{10}{6} = \frac{x}{15} \rightarrow \text{Cross multiply to solve for } x \rightarrow$$
$$\frac{10}{6} \times 15 = x \rightarrow x = 25$$

5. **(B)** Since the number of windmills begins at 200, this number can be a constant. Each year, a net of 4 windmills are added to the windfarm, since 6 are added and 2 taken away. Therefore, the function that portrays the situation is:

$$w(t) = 200 + 4t$$

6. **(C)** The business will need to purchase a total of 4 stamps for each of 500 catalogs, so to get the total number of stamps needed, multiply 4 and 500 together:

$$4 \times 500 = 2{,}000$$

Then, calculate the number of stamp books needed by taking the total of 2,000 stamps and dividing it by the number of stamps in each stamp book, 20:

$$\frac{2{,}000}{20} = 100$$

So, 100 books of stamps would be needed.

7. **(D)** Each student packs a total of $2 + 1 + 1 = 4$ personal items. Therefore, simply multiply 4 by 65 to find the total items the students would pack:

$$65 \times 4 = 260$$

8. **(C)** Consider the original equation:

$$C(L) = 300 + 20L$$

Now, take a look at the other equation:

$$C(20) = 700$$

The 20 goes in the place of the variable $L$, which represents the length of the pipe. Therefore, the length of the pipe in consideration is 20 feet. $C(L)$ represents the cost to install a pipe of length $L$, so 700 is the cost of installation for a pipe of 20 feet.

9. **(A)** The plumber's compensation is the sum of \$5,000 plus \$50 per each of $n$ hours worked. This total compensation needs to be at least \$50,000, meaning the sum of the hourly wages and the profit sharing needs to be greater than or equal to 50,000. Multiply 50 by $n$ to get the total from the hourly wages, and then add it to the \$5,000.

$50,000 \leq 50n + 5,000$ represents this situation.

10. **(B)** Set the two heights equal to each other to solve for the number of minutes after 12:00 P.M., $t$, at which they meet in the air:

$$A = 10{,}000 - 180t$$
$$B = 20t$$

Set them equal to each other and solve for $t$:

$$10{,}000 - 180t = 20t \rightarrow$$
$$10{,}000 = 200t \rightarrow$$
$$\frac{10{,}000}{200} = t \rightarrow$$
$$50 = t$$

So, take 50 minutes past 12:00 to get 12:50 P.M.

## Practice Drill #2—Word Problems and Function Interpretation

*(If timing, take about 12 minutes to complete.)*

1. If a cat eats $x$ cups of food per day, how many cups of food will the cat eat in $y$ days?

   (A) $x - y$
   (B) $x + y$
   (C) $xy$
   (D) $\frac{x}{y}$

2. The relationship between distance, $D$, rate, $R$, and time, $T$, is modeled by the equation $D = RT$. If the rate increases but the distance remains the same, what must happen to the time?

   (A) It decreases.
   (B) It increases.
   (C) It remains constant.
   (D) It cannot be determined.

3. The average price of a gallon of milk is modeled by the function $C$, in which $y$ is the number of years after the year 2000.

   $$C(y) = 2.00 + 0.08y$$

   What does the number 0.08 in the function represent?

   (A) The number of gallons of milk sold
   (B) The average yearly increase in price per gallon of milk
   (C) The unit price for each gallon of milk
   (D) The total number of gallons of milk sold in a given year

4. Out of the 50 states in the United States, all but 1, Nebraska, have bicameral legislatures—i.e., there are two legislative chambers. Nebraska has a unicameral legislature—i.e., there is just one legislative chamber. What fraction of the states in the United States are bicameral?

   (A) $\frac{1}{50}$
   (B) $\frac{1}{25}$
   (C) $\frac{24}{25}$
   (D) $\frac{49}{50}$

5. Tabitha works as a cell phone salesperson. Her pay is \$10 per hour plus \$20 commission for each new cell phone she sells. If $H$ represents the number of hours she works in a given week and $C$ represents the number of cell phones she sells that week, which equation represents her total salary (expressed in dollars before any deductions for taxes, etc.) for the week?

   (A) $Salary = 20H + 10C$
   (B) $Salary = 10H + 20C$
   (C) $Salary = 10H - 20C$
   (D) $Salary = 20H - 10C$

6. A movie theater concession counter sells a large popcorn for \$5 and a small popcorn for \$3. If the total number of both types of popcorn sold in a given day is 150, and the total revenue from the popcorn sales is \$570, how many small popcorns were sold? (Ignore sales tax in your calculations.)

   (A) 15
   (B) 30
   (C) 45
   (D) 90

7. The cost in dollars to operate a lemonade stand, $C$, is given by the function $c(x) = .25x + 20$, in which $x$ represents the number of cups of lemonade sold. What does the number 20 represent in this situation?

   (A) The fixed cost to set up the lemonade stand
   (B) The cost per each cup of lemonade sold
   (C) The total number of cups of lemonade sold
   (D) The revenue from setting up the lemonade stand

8. The linear function $f(x) = kx + b$ has constants $k$ and $b$. What is the $y$-intercept of the function based on the values of $x$ and $f(x)$ in the table below?

| $x$ | $f(x)$ |
|---|---|
| 16 | −28 |
| 21 | −38 |

   (A) 2
   (B) 4
   (C) 6
   (D) 10

9. John has \$20 to spend on his school lunch each week. A meal costs \$3 and a milk costs \$0.50. If he purchases one meal each day on Monday through Friday, what is the greatest number of milks he could purchase that week given his budget (note that sales tax is not applied to his purchases)?

   (A) 3
   (B) 7
   (C) 10
   (D) 20

10. In store A, 3 out of every 4 items are sold at a discount. In store B, 1 out of every 3 items is sold at a discount. If each store has 240 total items it is selling (both full price and at a discount), how many more discounted items will there be in store A than in store B?

   (A) 80
   (B) 100
   (C) 120
   (D) 480

## Solutions

1. **(C)** Take the $x$ cups of food and multiply it by the $y$ days the cat eats it:

$$x \times y = xy$$

2. **(A)** Take the original expression and isolate the time variable, $T$, to better understand what would happen:

$$D = RT \rightarrow \frac{D}{R} = T$$

So, if the rate increases while the distance remains the same, the fraction will decrease because the denominator will increase. Therefore, the time will decrease.

3. **(B)** In the function $C(y) = 2.00 + 0.08y$, $C$ represents the price of the gallon of milk, and $y$ is the number of years after 2000. So, 2.00 would be the price of the milk in the year 2000, and each year after 2000, the price of a gallon of milk would increase by 8 cents. Thus, the number 0.08 represents the average yearly increase in the price per gallon of milk.

4. **(D)** Since there is just 1 state, Nebraska, that does *not* have a bicameral legislature, there are 49 states that *do* have a bicameral legislature. To find the fraction, divide the number of states with a bicameral legislature, 49, by the total of 50 states:

$$\frac{49}{50}$$

5. **(B)** Tabitha makes \$10 for each of the $H$ hours a week she works and \$20 for each of the $C$ cell phones she sells in a week. Put this together to find her total salary for the week:

$$Salary = 10H + 20C$$

6. **(D)** Set up a series of equations to solve for the number of small popcorns sold. First, the sum of the large popcorns, which we can label $L$, and the small popcorns, which we can label $S$, is 150. In equation form, it is:

$$L + S = 150$$

The total revenue from the popcorn sales, \$570, is equivalent to what we get when multiplying 5 by the number of large popcorns and 3 by the number of small popcorns:

$$5L + 3S = 570$$

Now, use substitution to solve for the number of small popcorns:

$$L + S = 150 \rightarrow L = 150 - S$$

Plug this in to the second equation:

$$\begin{aligned} 5L + 3S &= 570 \rightarrow \\ 5(150 - S) + 3S &= 570 \rightarrow \\ 750 - 5S + 3S &= 570 \rightarrow \\ -2S &= -180 \rightarrow \\ S &= 90 \end{aligned}$$

So, 90 small popcorns were sold.

This problem can also be solved using elimination. Take the two equations $L + S = 150$ and $5L + 3S = 570$. Since we are solving for $S$, eliminate the $L$ by multiplying $L + S = 150$ by $-5$ and adding this to the other equation:

$$\begin{aligned} -5L - 5S &= -750 \\ +5L + 3S &= 570 \\ \hline 0 - 2S &= -180 \rightarrow S = 90 \end{aligned}$$

7. **(A)** In the function $C(x) = .25x + 20$, if zero cups of lemonade were sold, there would still be a cost of \$20 to operate the stand. Since this cost is fixed, no matter how many cups of lemonade are sold, the \$20 would be the cost to set up the lemonade stand.

8. **(B)** Since the function is a line, you can start by solving for the slope of the line using the ordered pairs presented in the table: $(16, -28)$ and $(21, -38)$.

$$\frac{\text{Change in } y}{\text{Change in } x} = \frac{-38 - (-28)}{21 - 16} = \frac{-10}{5} = -2$$

Since the function, $f(x) = kx + b$, is already in slope-intercept form, we now know that $-2$ is the slope and can be plugged in for the constant $k$:

$$f(x) = kx + b \rightarrow$$
$$f(x) = -2x + b$$

Now, we can solve for the constant $b$, which corresponds to the $y$-intercept of the function. Do so by plugging in an ordered pair for $x$ and $f(x)$. Let us use $(16, -28)$ since it is smaller:

$$\begin{aligned} f(x) &= -2x + b \rightarrow \\ -28 &= -2(16) + b \rightarrow \\ -28 &= -32 + b \rightarrow \\ 4 &= b \end{aligned}$$

Therefore, the $y$-intercept of the function is 4.

9. **(C)** If John purchases 1 meal each day on Monday through Friday, he will purchase a total of 5 meals. The cost for 5 meals is:

$$5 \times 3 = 15$$

He then has $20 - 15 = 5$ dollars remaining to purchase milks. Take the \$5 and divide it by \$0.50 to see the maximum number of milks he could purchase:

$$\frac{5}{0.50} = 10$$

Thus, John can purchase a maximum of 10 milks that week given his budget.

10. **(B)** Since there are 240 items in store A, find out how many items are being sold at a discount by multiplying $\frac{3}{4}$ by the total number of items:

$$\frac{3}{4} \times 240 = 180$$

For the discounted items in store B, do a similar calculation:

$$\frac{1}{3} \times 240 = 80$$

Then, find the difference in the number of discounted items for each store by subtracting:

$$180 - 80 = 100$$

## Practice Drill #3—Word Problems and Function Interpretation

*(If timing, take about 12 minutes to complete.)*

1. If $2x + k = 2(x + 3)$, what is the value of the constant $k$?

   (A) 2
   (B) 3
   (C) 5
   (D) 6

2. The price of a painting, $p$, is modeled by the equation $p = 800 + 20y$, in which $y$ is the number of years after the painting was created. What is the most logical interpretation of the number 20 in the equation?

   (A) The price of the painting in $y$ years
   (B) The initial price of the painting
   (C) The yearly increase in the painting's price
   (D) The change in the painting's price over a 20-year period

3. Rental of a video game costs a flat fee of $20 plus $3 for each hour the video game is used. Which equation provides the total cost, $C$, of using the game for $H$ hours?

   (A) $C(H) = 3H - 20$
   (B) $C(H) = H + 60$
   (C) $C(H) = 3H + 20$
   (D) $C(H) = 20H + 3$

| $x$ | $y$ |
|---|---|
| 6 | 0 |
| 4 | $-\frac{2}{3}$ |
| 2 | $-\frac{4}{3}$ |
| 0 | $-2$ |
| $-2$ | $-\frac{8}{3}$ |

4. The table above provides pairs of values for $x$ and $y$. Which equation below correctly shows the linear relationship between these values?

   (A) $y = \frac{1}{3}x - 2$
   (B) $y = \frac{2}{3}x - 1$
   (C) $y = \frac{1}{2}x - 5$
   (D) $y = \frac{1}{4}x$

5. A baker sells cupcakes for \$3 each and cookies for \$2 each. If he sells a total of 200 cookies and cupcakes and the total amount of revenue from selling the cookies and cupcakes is \$460, which set of equations could be used to solve for $x$ cupcakes sold and $y$ cupcakes sold?

   (A) $x + y = 460$ and $2x + 3y = 200$
   (B) $x + y = 200$ and $3x + 2y = 460$
   (C) $3x + 2y = 200$ and $x + y = 460$
   (D) $x \times y = 200$ and $(3x) \times (2y) = 460$

6. A discount bookstore sells books for \$6 each and magazines for \$3 each. In a given week, the store sells a combined total of 750 books/magazines and makes a total of \$3,600 from the book and magazine sales. In that week, how many magazines were sold?

   (A) 300
   (B) 450
   (C) 900
   (D) 10,800

7. A house is initially purchased for \$150,000 and increases in value by \$3,500 each year. Which of these expressions gives the price, $P$, of the house $t$ years after purchase?

   (A) $P = 3,500 + 150,000t$
   (B) $P = 3,500t - 150,000$
   (C) $P = 150,000 + 3,500t$
   (D) $P = 150,000 - 3,500t$

8. In the following equation, $3x + 5 = 3x + k$, what must be true about the constant $k$ equal in order for there to be no real solutions for $x$?

   (A) $k = 3$
   (B) $k = 5$
   (C) $k \neq 3$
   (D) $k \neq 5$

9. In an art class, a bin contains $C$ crayons and $M$ markers. If there are twice as many markers as crayons, and the total number of markers and crayons in the bin is 90, which of these sets of equations could be used to solve for $C$ and $M$?

   (A) $C + M = 90$
   $M = 2C$

   (B) $C \times M = 90$
   $M = \frac{C}{2}$

   (C) $\frac{C}{M} = 90$
   $2M = C$

   (D) $C \times M = 2C$
   $M - 2C = 90$

10. Chris took a bike ride through the hills near his home. On his ride, he either went uphill or downhill. His total ride was 30 miles and took 1.6 hours. If half of the distance of his journey was uphill and the other half of the distance was downhill, and his downhill speed was an average of 25 mph, what was his average uphill speed?

(A) 10 mph
(B) 12 mph
(C) 15 mph
(D) 18 mph

## Solutions

1. **(D)** Simplify the expression so that the $k$ is isolated to see its value:

$$2x + k = 2(x + 3) \rightarrow$$
$$2x + k = 2x + 6 \rightarrow$$

Subtract the $2x$ from both sides $\rightarrow$

$$k = 6$$

2. **(C)** The price of the painting is found with the equation $p = 800 + 20y$. At the year of the painting's creation, $y$ equals zero and $p$ will be 800. After one year, the price of the painting will increase by 20. So, the 20 represents the yearly increase in the painting's price.

3. **(C)** There is a flat fee of \$20, so no matter how many hours the video game is rented, there will be a constant \$20 fee. Then, for each hour the game is rented, there is a charge of \$3. The total cost is found by adding the flat fee of \$20 to the cost of \$3 for each hour it is rented:

$$C(H) = 3H + 20$$

4. **(A)** Save yourself time on this question by recognizing that all the answer choices are written in slope-intercept form, and have different $y$-intercepts. Fortunately, we can determine the $y$-intercept of the function by looking at the table: when the $x$ value is 0, the $y$ value is $-2$. Therefore, the only plausible option is choice (A): $y = \frac{1}{3}x - 2$.

5. **(B)** The total number of cupcakes sold is 200, so this equation fits the problem:

$$x + y = 200$$

The total revenue is \$460, and each of the $x$ cupcakes sells for \$3 each, and each of the $y$ cupcakes sells for \$2 each. Therefore, this equation fits the situation:

$$3x + 2y = 460$$

6. **(A)** Let's use the variable $B$ for books and $M$ for magazines and create equations to model what is described. First, there are a total of 750 books and magazines sold:

$$B + M = 750$$

Next, the total revenue from selling books at \$6 each and magazines at \$3 each is \$3,600:

$$6B + 3M = 3,600$$

Now, we can use elimination to solve for the magazines sold. Take the first equation and multiply it by $-6$ so that the $B$ term can be eliminated, then add it to the second equation:

$$\begin{aligned} -6B - 6M &= -4{,}500 \\ +\underline{6B + 3M} &\underline{= 3{,}600} \\ 0 - 3M &= -900 \end{aligned}$$

Then, solve for the number of magazines:

$$\begin{aligned} -3M &= -900 \rightarrow \\ M &= 300 \end{aligned}$$

This can also be solved using substitution. Take the two equations $B + M = 750$ and $6B + 3M = 3,600$. Since we want $M$, substitute for $B$ so everything is in terms of $M$:

$$\begin{aligned} B + M &= 750 \rightarrow \\ B &= 750 - M \end{aligned}$$

Plug this in for $B$ into the other equation:

$$\begin{aligned} 6B + 3M &= 3{,}600 \rightarrow \\ 6(750 - M) + 3M &= 3{,}600 \rightarrow \\ 4,500 - 6M + 3M &= 3{,}600 \rightarrow \\ -3M &= -900 \rightarrow \\ M &= 300 \end{aligned}$$

7. **(C)** The price starts at 150,000 (i.e., when the years are zero), and each year it goes up by \$3,500. So, the $y$-intercept of the function is 150,000, and the slope (yearly change) of the function is 3,500. Putting this in slope-intercept form, $P = 150,000 + 3,500t$ is correct even though the $y$-intercept comes first in the expression.

8. **(D)** In order for there to be no solutions, the equation must result in something that is not true for any value of $x$. If we simplify the equation, we can see that if $k$ is 5, there will be infinitely many solutions:

$$3x + 5 = 3x + k \rightarrow$$

Subtract $3x$ from both sides $\rightarrow$

$$5 = k$$

So, if $k \neq 5$, there would not be any solutions.

9. **(A)** The total number of markers and crayons in the class is 90, which can be represented by this equation:

$$C + M = 90$$

For the next equation, be careful to not just read it left to right. The correct representation of the phrase "there are twice as many markers as crayons" is:

$$M = 2C$$

Plug in a sample for $M$ and a sample for $C$ to see that this makes sense. If $M$ is 40 and $C$ is 20 then $M = 2C$. These two equations together correspond to choice **(A)**.

10. **(C)** Since half of the distance of the journey is uphill and the other downhill, 15 miles would be uphill, and 15 downhill. Let us first find how long it took to make the downhill journey—this portion would be at 25 mph. Plug it into the equation $D = RT$ and solve for time.

$$D = RT \rightarrow$$
$$15 = 25 \times T \rightarrow$$
$$\frac{15}{25} = .6 = T$$

Now that we know that .6 of an hour was spent going downhill, we know that $1.6 - .6 = 1$ hour was spent going uphill. Since this part of the journey is 15 miles, the average uphill speed will simply be 15 miles per hour.

## Algebra—Lines and Slope

### Slope Formula

The slope of a line represents its vertical increase, *rise*, divided by the horizontal increase, *run*. Calculate the slope between two points, $(x_1, y_1)$ and $(x_2, y_2)$, by plugging the coordinates of the points into this formula:

$$\text{Slope} = \frac{\text{Change in } y}{\text{Change in } x} = \frac{(y_2 - y_1)}{(x_2 - x_1)}$$

**Example**

What is the slope of a line that has the points (8, 3) and (5, 1)?

**Solution**

Be consistent in which point is point 2 and which point is point 1. In this case, let's use (8, 3) as point 2 and (5, 1) as point 1—doing so will make for an easier calculation that does not involve negative values. So, $y_2 = 3$, $y_1 = 1$, $x_2 = 8$, and $x_1 = 5$.

$$\frac{(y_2 - y_1)}{(x_2 - x_1)} = \frac{(3 - 1)}{(8 - 5)} = \frac{2}{3}$$

Thus, the slope of this line would be $\frac{2}{3}$.

### Practice

1. What is the slope of a line with the points (4, 3) and (6, 1)?
2. What is the slope of a line with the points (2.5, 7) and (−4, −8)?
3. Consider a line in the *xy*-coordinate plane in which to get from point *A* to point *B*, one must go up +5 units vertically and go over +3 units horizontally. What is the slope of this line?

### Solutions

1. $\frac{(y_2 - y_1)}{(x_2 - x_1)} = \frac{(3 - 1)}{(4 - 6)} = \frac{2}{-2} = -1$

2. $\frac{(y_2 - y_1)}{(x_2 - x_1)} = \frac{(7 - (-8))}{(2.5 - (-4))} = \frac{7 + 8}{2.5 + 4} = \frac{15}{6.5} \approx 2.31$

3. The "rise" of the line is +5 units and the "run" of the line is +3 units. So, the slope is the rise divided by the run:

$$\frac{\text{Rise}}{\text{Run}} = \frac{\text{Change in } y}{\text{Change in } x} = \frac{5}{3}$$

### Slope-Intercept Form of a Line

In order to graph a line, put its equation in **slope-intercept** form:

$y = mx + b$

$m =$ slope of the line, the "rise" over the "run"

$b = y$-intercept of the line, i.e., where the line intersects the $y$-axis

**Example 1**

What is the slope and $y$-intercept of a line with the equation $y = 5x - 7$?

**Solution**

The equation is already in slope-intercept form, so just match up the numbers in the equation to their corresponding values.

$$y = mx + b$$
$$y = 5x - 7$$
$$m = 5$$
$$b = -7$$

So, the slope of this line is 5, and the $y$-intercept of the line is $-7$.

**Example 2**

What is the equation of the line with the graph below?

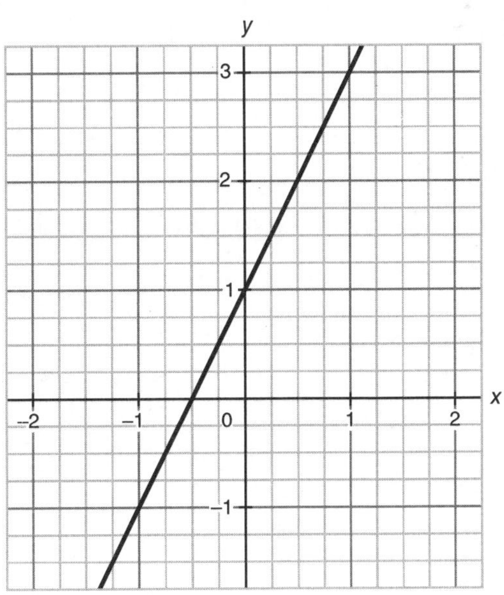

✓ **Solution**

The line intersects the $y$-axis at (0, 1), making this point the $y$-intercept. The line "rises" 2 units for every 1 unit it "runs," giving a slope of 2. So, the equation for the line is:

$$y = 2x + 1$$

### Overlapping and Intersecting Lines

Lines that have *equivalent* equations, although in different forms, will *overlap* one another. For example, $y = 3x + 4$ and $2y = 6x + 8$ overlap since the second equation is simply two times the first equation.

Lines that *meet at a single point intersect* one another. For example, $y = 2x + 3$ and $y = -2x + 1$ will intersect in the $xy$-coordinate plane when graphed:

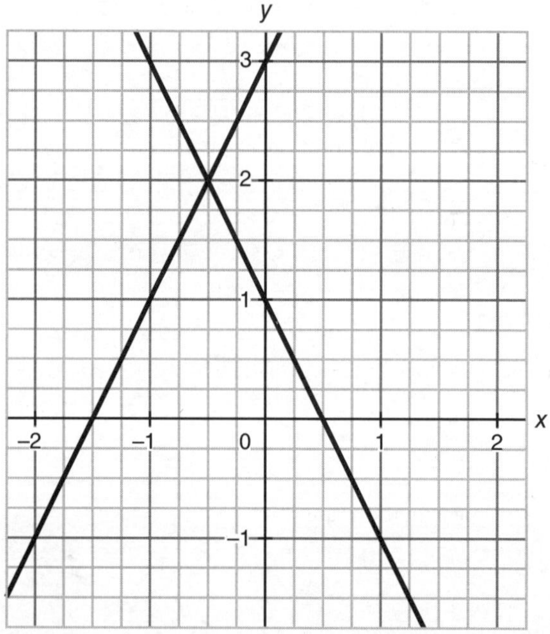

### Parallel and Perpendicular Lines

Lines that are *parallel* to one another will have the *same slope*, but different $y$-intercepts—they will never intersect or overlap one another. For example, the lines with the equations $y = \frac{1}{2}x + 1$ and $y = \frac{1}{2}x + 3$ are parallel to one another:

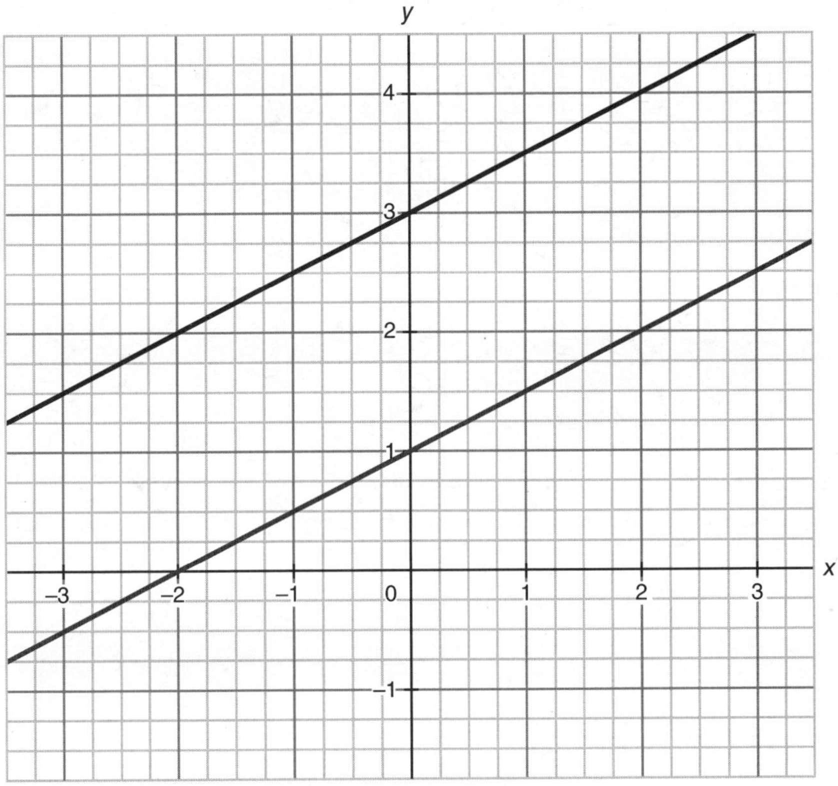


*Perpendicular* lines intersect at a right angle (90 degrees) and have slopes that are *negative reciprocals* of one another (i.e., you filp the fraction and change the sign.) For example, if one line has a slope of 3, the line perpendicular to it will have a slope of $-\frac{1}{3}$. Consider two perpendicular lines: $y = -\frac{1}{2}x + 1$ and $y = 2x + 2$.

Their graph in the *xy*-coordinate plane would be as follows:

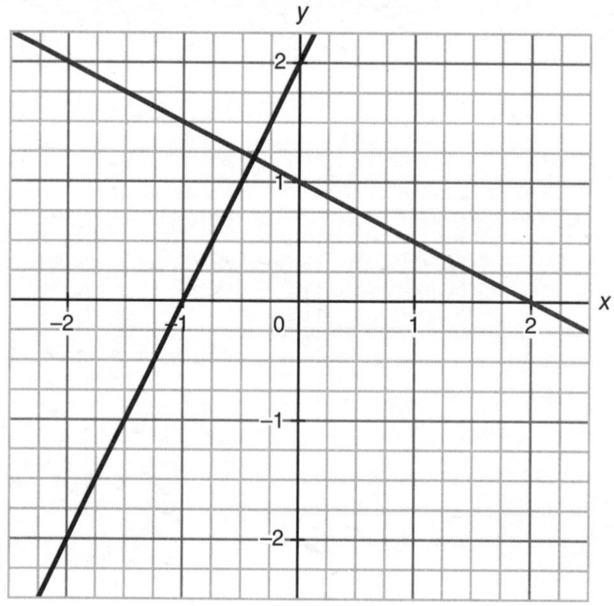


### Practice

1. What is the slope of a line with the equation $y = -3x + 8$?
2. What is the *y*-intercept of a line with the equation $y = 2x + 5$?
3. What is the slope of a line with the equation $2y = 3x + 4$?
4. What is the *y*-intercept of a line with the equation $y - 3 = 2x + 1$?
5. If the slope of a line is 4, what is the slope of a line parallel to it?
6. If a line has the equation $y = 5x - 4$, what is the slope of a line perpendicular to it?
7. Would the following sets of lines *overlap*, *intersect*, be *parallel*, or be *perpendicular* to each other?
   (A) $y = 2x + 9$ and $y = 2x - 4$
   (B) $\frac{1}{3}y = \frac{1}{3}x - 1$ and $y = x - 3$
   (C) $y = 2x$ and $y = -\frac{1}{2}x - 2$
   (D) $y = 4x - 1$ and $y = 3x + 2$

### Solutions

1. $-3$.
2. 5.
3. Divide both sides of the equation by 2 to put it in slope-intercept form.

$$2y = 3x + 4 \rightarrow \frac{2y}{2} = \frac{3x + 4}{2} \rightarrow y = \frac{3}{2}x + 2$$

   Now that it is in slope-intercept form, find the slope: $\frac{3}{2}$.

4. Put the equation in slope-intercept form to determine the *y*-intercept.

$$y - 3 = 2x + 1 \rightarrow y = 2x + 1 + 3 = y = 2x + 4$$

   Now that it is in slope-intercept form, you can see that the *y*-intercept is 4.

5. Parallel lines have the same slopes as one another, so it would just be 4.
6. The current line has a slope of 5, so take the negative reciprocal of 5:

$$5 \rightarrow -\frac{1}{5}$$

Keep in mind that the negative reciprocals have a product of $-1$.

7A. These lines have the same slope and different $y$-intercepts, so they are *parallel.*
7B. The first equation can be simplified to look like the second equation:

$$\frac{1}{3}y = \frac{1}{3}x - 1 \rightarrow 3\left(\frac{1}{3}y\right) = 3\left(\frac{1}{3}x - 1\right) \rightarrow y = x - 3$$

Since the lines have equivalent equations, they *overlap.*

7C. The product of the slopes of the two lines is $-1$.

$$2 \times \left(-\frac{1}{2}\right) = -1$$

Therefore, they are *perpendicular* to each other.

7D. The two lines have different slopes and different $y$-intercepts. They will *intersect* each other in the $xy$-coordinate plane.

### SAT Math Strategy

Memorize the key slope and line formulas so you can avoid being intimidated.

SAT Math questions using the above concepts will often integrate multiple ideas about slope and lines. If you know the formulas well, you can write out what you need to think through the problem.

## Example 1

If $ax + by = 5$ is a line in the $xy$-coordinate plane in which $a$ and $b$ are constants, which of the following expresses the slope of the line?

(A) $a$
(B) $-\frac{a}{b}$
(C) $-\frac{b}{a}$
(D) 5

## Solution

Do not let yourself be intimidated by the unusual formatting presented in the problem.

Remember the fundamental concept:

- Slope-intercept form is $y = mx + b$.

So, take the equation and put it in slope-intercept form to find the slope of the line:

$$ax + by = 5 \rightarrow by = -ax + 5 \rightarrow \frac{by}{b} = \frac{-ax + 5}{b} \rightarrow y = -\frac{a}{b}x + \frac{5}{b}$$

So, the correct answer is **(B)**, $-\frac{a}{b}$.

### Example 2

| *a* | 4 | *x* | 10 | 13 |
|---|---|---|---|---|
| *b* | 1 | 2 | 3 | 4 |

Given that the relationship between $a$ and $b$ is linear, what is the value of $x$ in the table above?

Fill in: ________

### Solution

The information is presented in a table instead of the usual $(x, y)$ style. Since the problem states that the relationship between $a$ and $b$ is linear, the *slope* of the line will be constant. We can treat $a$ as we would normally treat $x$ and treat $b$ as we would normally treat $y$. If we find the slope of the line between two points, it will be the same as it would be for two different points on the line. Let's take the point (13, 4) and (10, 3) to see what the slope of the line would be:

$$\frac{(y_2 - y_1)}{(x_2 - x_1)} = \frac{(4 - 3)}{(13 - 10)} = \frac{1}{3}$$

We can then set up an equation to solve for the unknown value of $x$. The slope of $\frac{1}{3}$ will be the same if we pick a different set of points. So, let's pick (4, 1) and $(x, 2)$ and set it equal to $\frac{1}{3}$ so that we can solve for $x$:

$$\frac{2-1}{x-4} = \frac{1}{3} \rightarrow \frac{1}{x-4} = \frac{1}{3} \rightarrow \text{Cross Multiply} \rightarrow$$

$$3 = x - 4 \rightarrow x = 7$$

Keep in mind that in a line, the $y$-value changes by the same amount with each unit increase in $x$; so the the problem can be answered by inspection (just follow the pattern and add 3 to 4).

## Practice Drill—Lines and Slope

*(If timing, take about 12 minutes to complete.)*

1. Which of the following equations represents a line in the $xy$-coordinate plane with a $y$-intercept of 6 and a slope of $-3$?

   (A) $y = 3x + 6$
   (B) $y = 6x - 3$
   (C) $y = 6x + 3$
   (D) $y = -3x + 6$

2. In the $xy$-plane, which of these linear equations has a $y$-intercept of 12?

   (A) $y = 4x + 12$
   (B) $12y = 4x - 1$
   (C) $y = 4x - 12$
   (D) $12 + y = 4x$

3. A linear equation in the $xy$-plane intercepts the $y$-axis at $-3$. For every 2 units the $y$-coordinate of the line increases, the $x$-coordinate decreases by 7 units. Which of the following is the correct equation for this line?

(A) $y = \frac{7}{2}x + 3$

(B) $y = \frac{2}{7}x - 3$

(C) $y = -\frac{2}{7}x - 3$

(D) $y = \frac{3}{2}x - 7$

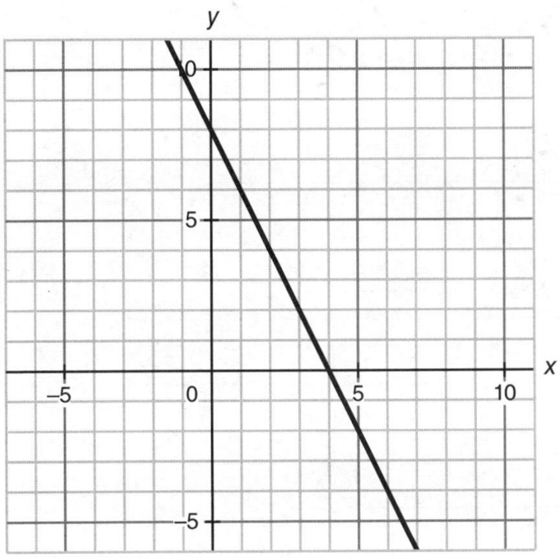


4. Consider the graph of the line above as graphed in the $xy$-coordinate plane. What is the value of $b$ if the line is presented in the equation $y = mx + b$, in which both $m$ and $b$ are constants?

(A) 4
(B) 8
(C) $-2$
(D) $-\frac{1}{2}$

5. What is the slope of a line with the equation $5x + 4y = 2$?

(A) $-\frac{1}{2}$

(B) $\frac{4}{5}$

(C) $-\frac{5}{4}$

(D) 2

6. For the equation $\frac{1}{2}y = \frac{2}{3}x - 4$, what is the $x$-intercept?

(A) $-8$
(B) $-\frac{4}{3}$
(C) 3
(D) 6

7. Two lines are graphed in the $xy$-plane. The lines have the same slope and different $y$-intercepts. How many solution(s) would the equations represented by this pair of lines have?

(A) None
(B) One
(C) Two
(D) Infinite

8. Which of these represents a linear equation in the $xy$-plane that has the points (5, 17) and (2, 5)?

(A) $y = -4x - 3$
(B) $y = -3x + 4$
(C) $y = 4x - 3$
(D) $y = 3x + 4$

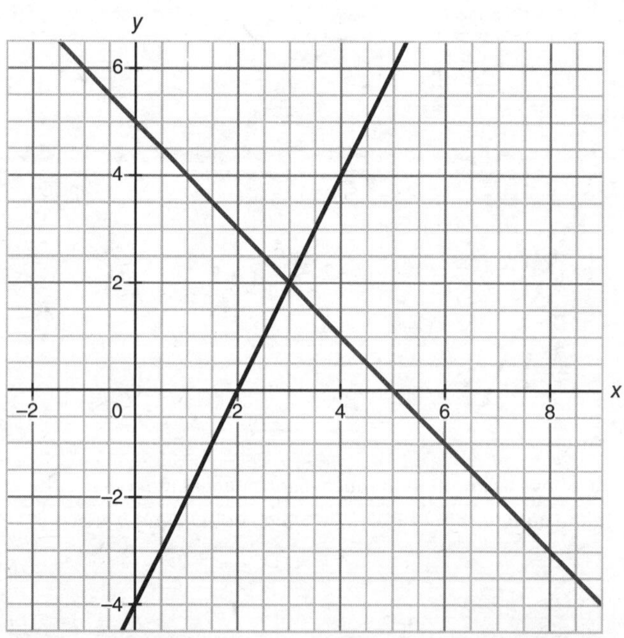


9. The above graph is represented by which of these sets of equations?

(A) $y = -4x + 2$
$y = 5x + 1$
(B) $y = 2x - 4$
$y = -x + 5$
(C) $y = \frac{1}{2}x - 4$
$y = -5x + 1$
(D) $y = \frac{1}{4}x - 1$
$y = -2x + 5$

10. Which of the following equations has a slope perpendicular to the slope of a line with the equation $y = ax + b$, given that $a$ and $b$ are constants?

(A) $y = -\frac{1}{a}x + 2b$
(B) $y = -ax + 2b$
(C) $y = -\frac{1}{b}x + 2a$
(D) $y = -bx - 2a$

## Solutions

1. **(D)** Use the slope-intercept form of a line, and plug in the value for the slope, $m$, and the $y$-intercept, $b$.

$$y = mx + b \rightarrow y = -3x + 6$$

2. **(A)** When a line is written in slope-intercept form, the $y$-intercept corresponds to the constant $b$. The only option that has positive 12 for $b$ is choice **(A)**.

$$y = mx + b \rightarrow y = 4x + 12$$

3. **(C)** From the description of the line in the problem, we can determine the line's slope. The line decreases horizontally 7 units for every 2 units it increases vertically. Therefore, the slope of the line will be $\frac{2}{(-7)} = -\frac{2}{7}$. The only option that has $-\frac{2}{7}$ for its slope is choice **(C)**.

4. **(B)** The line intersects the $y$-axis at the point (0, 8). Therefore, the $y$-intercept of the line is 8.

5. **(C)** Put the line in slope-intercept form in order to determine the slope of the line:

$$5x + 4y = 2 \rightarrow$$
$$4y = -5x + 2 \rightarrow$$
$$y = -\frac{5}{4}x + \frac{2}{4} \rightarrow y = -\frac{5}{4}x + \frac{1}{2}$$

So, the slope of the line is $-\frac{5}{4}$.

6. **(D)** This is an easy question to misread—you are asked to find the $x$-intercept, not the $y$-intercept. The $x$-intercept is the point at which the line intersects the $x$-axis; for this to happen, the $y$ value at the point must be zero. So, plug zero in for $y$ and see what the value of $x$ is:

$$\frac{1}{2}y = \frac{2}{3}x - 4 \rightarrow$$
$$\frac{1}{2}(0) = \frac{2}{3}x - 4 \rightarrow$$
$$0 = \frac{2}{3}x - 4 \rightarrow 4 = \frac{2}{3}x \rightarrow$$
$$x = 4 \times \left(\frac{3}{2}\right) \rightarrow x = \frac{12}{2} = 6$$

7. **(A)** Lines that have the same slope and different $y$-intercepts run parallel to one another. At no point will they intersect, so the answer is "none."

8. **(C)** Looking ahead to the answers, all of the choices have different values for the line's slope. So, calculate the slope of the line with the given information and see which of the options matches:

$$\text{Slope} = \frac{y_2 - y_1}{x_2 - x_1} = \frac{17 - 5}{5 - 2} = \frac{12}{3} = 4$$

The only one of the lines that has 4 as its slope is choice **(C)**, $y = 4x - 3$.

9. **(B)** Fortunately, the different options given have different $y$-intercepts. So you can save time in solving this by identifying the $y$-intercepts of the two lines and then matching them with a choice. The two $y$-intercepts are 5 and $-4$, and the only option that has both of those values as $y$-intercepts is choice **(B)**:

$$y = 2x - 4$$
$$y = -x + 5$$

10. **(A)** Since the equation of the line is already in slope-intercept form, we can see that its slope is $a$. We then can take the negative reciprocal of $a$ to get the slope of a line perpendicular to it:

$$a \rightarrow -\frac{1}{a}$$

The only option that has $-\frac{1}{a}$ as its slope is choice **(A)**.

# Advanced Math

This section contains comprehensive review and strategies for all of the concepts below:

**Polynomials and Factoring**

- Polynomial Manipulation
- Common Factoring Patterns

**Exponents and Roots**

- Exponent Rules
- Problems with Exponents and Roots

**Solving Quadratic Equations**

- Factoring Quadratic Equations
- Square Root Method
- Quadratic Formula
- Completing the Square
- Plugging in the Answers
- Undefined Functions
- Extraneous Solutions
- Synthetic Division

**Zeros, Parabolas, and Polynomial Graphing**

- Zeros of a Function
- Parabola Graphing
- Function Transformations
- Visualizing Polynomial Graphs

**Function Interpretation and Manipulation**

- Putting Variables in Terms of Other Variables
- Identifying Constants
- Interpreting Functions

## Polynomials and Factoring

### Polynomial Manipulation

The SAT Math section will have you simplify polynomial expressions using addition, subtraction, multiplication, and division. How should you approach these types of problems?

Students typically miss polynomial simplification problems not because of their mathematical difficulty, but because of careless mistakes, like with manipulating negative signs.

> **SAT Math Strategy**
>
> When simplifying polynomials, write out all your steps to avoid making careless errors.

### Example

$(-2x^2 + 3x + 1) - (x^2 + x + 2)$ is equivalent to which of these expressions?

(A) $x^2 + 3x - 1$
(B) $-x^2 + 3x + 1$
(C) $-3x^2 + 2x - 1$
(D) $-3x^2 - 2x - 1$

### Solution

Combine the $x^2$ components, the $x$ components, and the numerical components in order to simplify. Write out all your steps to avoid careless errors.

$$(-2x^2 + 3x + 1) - (x^2 + x + 2)$$

Remove the parentheses, and distribute the $-1$ throughout the second half of the expression:

$$-2x^2 + 3x + 1 - x^2 - x - 2$$

Now, group like terms together to simplify:

$$(-2x^2 - x^2) + (3x - x) + (1 - 2) \rightarrow$$
$$-3x^2 + 2x - 1$$

This corresponds to answer choice (C).

### Practice

Simplify the following expressions.

1. $2x + 6x - 9x$
2. $3x^2 - 4x^2$
3. $2x^2 - x + x^2$
4. $3x^3 - 2x + x^3 + 4x$
5. $8x^4 + 2(x^2 - 3x^4)$
6. $3(4x^2 - 2x) - 2(3x^2 + 5)$
7. $x(-x + 4) - 2x(x + 3)$

### Solutions

1. $2x + 6x - 9x \rightarrow 8x - 9x \rightarrow -x$
2. $3x^2 - 4x^2 \rightarrow -x^2$
3. $2x^2 - x + x^2 \rightarrow (2x^2 + x^2) - x \rightarrow 3x^2 - x$
4. $3x^3 - 2x + x^3 + 4x \rightarrow$
   $(3x^3 + x^3) + (-2x + 4x) \rightarrow$
   $4x^3 + 2x$
5. $8x^4 + 2(x^2 - 3x^4) \rightarrow$
   $8x^4 + 2x^2 - 6x^4 \rightarrow$
   $(8x^4 - 6x^4) + 2x^2 \rightarrow$
   $2x^4 + 2x^2$

6. $3(4x^2 - 2x) - 2(3x^2 + 5) \rightarrow$
   $12x^2 - 6x - 6x^2 - 10 \rightarrow$
   $(12x^2 - 6x^2) - 6x - 10 \rightarrow$
   $6x^2 - 6x - 10$
7. $x(-x + 4) - 2x(x + 3) \rightarrow$
   $-x^2 + 4x - 2x^2 - 6x \rightarrow$
   $(-x^2 - 2x^2) + (4x - 6x) \rightarrow$
   $-3x^2 - 2x$

### Common Factoring Patterns

Since the SAT primarily evaluates your skill in problem solving and pattern recognition, as opposed to evaluating your skill in doing tedious calculations, memorize these common factoring patterns so that you can solve the problems most efficiently.

> **SAT Math Strategy**
>
> The SAT math consistently has problems in form that can be easily factored. Be on the lookout for common factoring patterns.

#### Square of Binomial (with Plus Sign)

$$(a + b)(a + b) = a^2 + 2ab + b^2$$

**Example**

$$(x + 5)(x + 5) = x^2 + 10x + 25$$

#### Difference of Squares

$$(a + b)(a - b) = a^2 - b^2$$

**Example**

$$(x + 5)(x - 5) = x^2 - 25$$

#### Square of Binomial (with Negative Sign)

$$(a - b)(a - b) = a^2 - 2ab + b^2$$

**Example**

$$(x - 5)(x - 5) = x^2 - 10x + 25$$

#### Sum of Cubes

$$(a + b)(a^2 - ab + b^2) = a^3 + b^3$$

**Example**

$$(x + 5)(x^2 - 5x + 25) = x^3 + 5^3 = x^3 + 125$$

#### Difference of Cubes

$$(a - b)(a^2 + ab + b^2) = a^3 - b^3$$

### Example

$$(x - 5)(x^2 + 5x + 25) = x^3 - 5^3 = x^3 - 125$$

### Practice

Write the following expressions in factored form.

1. $n^2 + 2n + 1 = ?$
2. $a^2 - 14a + 49 = ?$
3. $y^2 - 16 = ?$
4. $4x^2 - 9y^2 = ?$
5. $27 - n^3 = ?$
6. $9x^2 - 25y^2 = ?$
7. $\frac{1}{4}x^2 - \frac{1}{9}y^2 = ?$
8. $125a^3 + 64b^3 = ?$

### Solutions

1. $n^2 + 2n + 1 = (n + 1)(n + 1)$
2. $a^2 - 14a + 49 = (a - 7)(a - 7)$
3. $y^2 - 16 = (y + 4)(y - 4)$
4. $4x^2 - 9y^2 = (2x)^2 - (3y)^2 = (2x + 3y)(2x - 3y)$
5. $27 - n^3 = \rightarrow$

   $a^3 - b^3 = (a - b)(a^2 + ab + b^2) \rightarrow$

   $3^3 - n^3 = (3 - n)(9 + 3n + n^2)$
6. $9x^2 - 25y^2 = (3x)^2 - (5y)^2 = (3x + 5y)(3x - 5y)$
7. $\frac{1}{4}x^2 - \frac{1}{9}y^2 = ?$

   $\left(\frac{1}{2}x + \frac{1}{3}y\right)\left(\frac{1}{2}x - \frac{1}{3}y\right)$
8. $(a + b)(a^2 - ab + b^2) = a^3 + b^3$

   $125a^3 + 64b^3 = (5a)^3 + (4b)^3 \rightarrow$

   $a^3 + b^3 = (a + b)(a^2 - ab + b^2) \rightarrow$

   $(5a + 4b)(25a^2 - 20ab + 16b^2)$

## Practice Drill—Polynomials and Factoring

*(If timing, take about 12 minutes to complete.)*

1. Which of the following is equivalent to $3n(n^2 + 2n - 1)$?

   (A) $3n^3 + 6n^2 - 3n$
   (B) $3n^2 + 6n - 3$
   (C) $3n^3 + 6n^2 + 3n$
   (D) $3n^6 + 6n^4 - 3n^2$

2. $x^3 + 6x^2 + 9x$

Which of the following is equivalent to the above expression?

(A) $x(x + 3)(x - 3)$
(B) $(x + 3)^3$
(C) $x(x + 3)^2$
(D) $(x + 3)(x + 3)$

3. $x^2 + 12x = -36$ is equivalent to which of the following?

(A) $(x + 6) = (x - 6)$
(B) $x(x + 12 + 36) = 0$
(C) $(x + 6)^2 = 0$
(D) $(x - 6)^2 = 4$

4. Which of the following expresses the result when $x^3 + x$ is subtracted from $3x^3 + 2x^2$?

(A) $2x^3 + 2x^2 - x$
(B) $4x^3 + 2x^2 + x$
(C) $-2x^3 - 2x^2 + x$
(D) $4x^3 + 2x^2 - x$

5. The expression $-(x^2 + 2)(-x - 1)$ is equivalent to which of the following?

(A) $x^3 - x^2 + 2x - 2$
(B) $x^3 + 2x^2 - x - 2$
(C) $x^3 + x^2 + 2x + 2$
(D) $-x^3 - x^2 + 2x + 1$

6. $(x + y^2)(-x - y^2)$

Which of the following options is an equivalent form of the expression above?

(A) $x^2 - 2xy^2 + y^4$
(B) $-x^2 - 2xy^2 - y^4$
(C) $2x^2 - xy^2 - 4y^4$
(D) $-x^2 - y^4$

7. $\frac{5}{3} + \frac{2}{x - 3}$ is equivalent to which of the following, given that $x \neq 3$?

(A) $\frac{7}{3x}$

(B) $\frac{7}{3x - 9}$

(C) $\frac{10}{3(x - 3)}$

(D) $\frac{5x - 9}{3x - 9}$

**Fill-In Practice:** Write your answer in the underlined blank under each question.

8. For the function $f(x) = (2x - 10)^2$, what is the value of $f(13)$?

   Answer: ________

9. If $\frac{2x}{5} - \frac{3y}{10} = 0$, what is the value of $\frac{x}{y}$?

   Answer: ________

10. If $\frac{3}{9 + 6x + x^2} = \frac{3}{4}$, what is the value of $(x + 3)$ if $(x + 3) > 0$?

    Answer: ________

## Solutions

1. **(A)**

   $3n(n^2 + 2n - 1) \rightarrow$

   Distribute the $3n \rightarrow$

   $3n^3 + 6n^2 - 3n$

2. **(C)**

   $x^3 + 6x^2 + 9x \rightarrow$

   Factor out an $x \rightarrow$

   $x(x^2 + 6x + 9) \rightarrow$

   Factor the part in parentheses $\rightarrow$

   $x(x + 3)(x + 3) \rightarrow x(x + 3)^2$

3. **(C)**

   $x^2 + 12x = -36 \rightarrow$

   $x^2 + 12x + 36 = 0 \rightarrow$

   $(x + 6)(x + 6) = 0 \rightarrow (x + 6)^2 = 0$

4. **(A)** Be careful to put this in the correct order. It should look like this:

   $(3x^3 + 2x^2) - (x^3 + x) \rightarrow$

   $3x^3 + 2x^2 - x^3 - x \rightarrow$

   $2x^3 + 2x^2 - x$

5. **(C)**

   $-(x^2 + 2)(-x - 1) \rightarrow$

   FOIL the parts within the parentheses $\rightarrow$

   $-(-x^3 - x^2 - 2x - 2) \rightarrow$

   Distribute the $-1 \rightarrow$

   $x^3 + x^2 + 2x + 2$

6. **(B)**
$(x + y^2)(-x - y^2) \rightarrow$
FOIL the expression $\rightarrow$
$-x^2 - xy^2 - xy^2 + y^4 \rightarrow$
$-x^2 - 2xy^2 - y^4$

7. **(D)** Make each fraction have a common denominator and then add them together.
$\frac{5}{3} + \frac{2}{x-3} \rightarrow$
$\frac{5(x-3)}{3(x-3)} + \frac{2(3)}{3(x-3)} \rightarrow$
$\frac{5(x-3)+6}{3(x-3)} \rightarrow$
$\frac{5x-15+6}{3(x-3)} \rightarrow$
$\frac{5x-9}{3(x-3)} \rightarrow$
$\frac{5x-9}{3x-9}$

8. **(256)**
$f(x) = (2x - 10)^2 \rightarrow$
$f(13) = (2(13) - 10)^2 \rightarrow$
$f(13) = (26 - 10)^2 \rightarrow$
$f(13) = 16^2 = 256$

9. **($\frac{3}{4}$ or 0.75)**
$\frac{2x}{5} - \frac{3y}{10} = 0 \rightarrow$
$\frac{2x}{5} = \frac{3y}{10} \rightarrow$
Divide both sides by $y \rightarrow$
$\frac{2x}{5y} = \frac{3}{10} \rightarrow$
Multiply both sides by $\frac{5}{2} \rightarrow$
$\frac{x}{y} = \frac{3}{10} \times \frac{5}{2} = \frac{15}{20} = \frac{3}{4}$

10. **(2)** Recognize that the denominator is the square of $(x + 3)$, and this will be much easier to solve:
$\frac{3}{9+6x+x^2} = \frac{3}{4} \rightarrow$
$\frac{3}{(x+3)(x+3)} = \frac{3}{4} \rightarrow$
$\frac{3}{(x+3)^2} = \frac{3}{4} \rightarrow$
Divide both sides by 3 $\rightarrow$
$\frac{1}{(x+3)^2} = \frac{1}{4} \rightarrow$

Cross multiply to bring the values to the numerator →

$4 = (x + 3)^2 \rightarrow$

Take the square root of both sides →

$2 = x + 3$

Fortunately, we don't need to worry about imaginary solutions since the value of $(x + 3)$ is greater than zero.

If you do not see the pattern, you can also solve this by finding the value of $x$:

$\frac{3}{9 + 6x + x^2} = \frac{3}{4} \rightarrow$

$\frac{1}{9 + 6x + x^2} = \frac{1}{4} \rightarrow$

$9 + 6x + x^2 = 4 \rightarrow$

$x^2 + 6x + 5 = 0 \rightarrow$

$(x + 5)(x + 1) = 0$

$x = -5$ or $x = -1$

Since $(x + 3)$ must be greater than zero, the only possible solution for $x$ is $-1$. Plugging this in to the expression gives us the same answer of 2:

$(x + 3) \rightarrow -1 + 3 = 2$

## Advanced Math—Exponents and Roots

### Exponent Rules

Memorize these exponent rules that are frequently tested on the SAT Math:

| Exponent Rule | Example | How to Remember |
|---|---|---|
| $x^a x^b = x^{(a+b)}$ | $x^2 x^3 = x^{(2+3)} = x^5$ | *Use the acronym* ***MADSPM*** Multiply exponents, Add them Divide exponents, Subtract them Parentheses with exponents, Multiply them |
| $\frac{x^a}{x^b} = x^{a-b}$ | $\frac{x^5}{x^2} = x^{5-2} = x^3$ | |
| $(x^a)^b = x^{(ab)}$ | $(x^2)^3 = x^{(2 \times 3)} = x^6$ | |
| $x^{-a} = \frac{1}{x^a}$ | $x^{-3} = \frac{1}{x^3}$ | "Negative" things go to the bottom. |
| $x^{\frac{a}{b}} = \sqrt[b]{x^a}$ | $x^{\frac{2}{3}} = \sqrt[3]{x^2}$ | The root of a tree is on the bottom. The bottom part of the fraction is identical to the root. |

### Practice

Write these expressions in simplified, alternative forms.

1. $a^2 a^6 = ?$
2. $\frac{x^7}{x^4} = ?$
3. $y^{\left(\frac{3}{4}\right)} = ?$
4. $b^{-4} = ?$
5. $(n^3)^4 = ?$
6. $(x^2 x^3)^2 = ?$
7. $\frac{1}{a^{-3}} = ?$
8. $\sqrt[3]{216x^{12}} = ?$

### Solutions

1. $a^2 a^6 = a^{(2+6)} = a^8$
2. $\frac{x^7}{x^4} = x^{(7-4)} = x^3$
3. $y^{\left(\frac{3}{4}\right)} =$ the fourth root of $y^3 = \sqrt[4]{y^3}$
4. $b^{-4} = \frac{1}{b^4}$
5. $(n^3)^4 = n^{(3\times4)} = n^{12}$
6. $(x^2 x^3)^2 = \left(x^{(2+3)}\right)^2 = (x^5)^2 = x^{(5\times2)} = x^{10}$
7. $\frac{1}{a^{-3}} \rightarrow$

   Bring the denominator up to the top since it has a negative exponent $\rightarrow$

   $\rightarrow a^3$
8. $\sqrt[3]{216x^{12}} \rightarrow$

   $\sqrt[3]{(6\times6\times6)\times(x^4)(x^4)(x^4)} \rightarrow$

   $6x^4$

### Problems with Exponents and Roots

SAT Math problems that involve exponents and roots will often ask you to integrate multiple concepts to arrive at a solution.

#### Example

If $x^{\left(-\frac{1}{3}\right)} = y$ and $x$ is positive, what is $x$ in terms of $y$?

(A) $y = x^3$

(B) $y = \sqrt[3]{x}$

(C) $x = \frac{1}{y^3}$

(D) $x = y^3$

#### Solution

When a problem asks you to put $x$ in terms of $y$, it means that you should have $x$ by itself and an expression in terms of $y$ on the other side. So, we should isolate the $x$ variable to arrive at a solution:

$$x^{\left(-\frac{1}{3}\right)} = y \rightarrow$$

Take each side to the $-3$ power to get a simple $x \rightarrow$

$$\left(x^{\left(-\frac{1}{3}\right)}\right)^{(-3)} = y^{-3} \rightarrow$$

$$x^{\left(-\frac{1}{3} \times -3\right)} = y^{-3} \rightarrow$$

$$x^1 = y^{-3} \rightarrow$$

$$x = \frac{1}{y^3}$$

**SAT Math Strategy**

Memorize the values of simple numbers to different powers to more easily recognize patterns.

The SAT Math heavily emphasizes pattern recognition and does *not* emphasize tedious calculations. As a result, you will frequently find that problems involving exponents and roots will involve simple numbers and their exponential values and roots. Memorizing these equivalences will save you time.

$x^0 = 1$ Anything to the zero power is simply one. $1^0 = 1$ $2^0 = 1$ $10^0 = 1$

$2^1 = 2$ Anything to the 1st power is simply itself. $3^1 = 3$ $20^1 = 20$ $(-5)^1 = -5$

$2^2 = 4$ $2^3 = 8$ $2^4 = 16$ $2^5 = 32$ $2^6 = 64$

$\sqrt{4} = 2$ $\sqrt[3]{8} = 2$ $\sqrt[4]{16} = 2$ $\sqrt[5]{32} = 2$ $\sqrt[6]{64} = 2$

$3^2 = 9$ $3^3 = 27$ $3^4 = 81$

$\sqrt{9} = 3$ $\sqrt[3]{27} = 3$ $\sqrt[4]{81} = 3$

$4^2 = 16 \quad 4^3 = 64 \quad 4^4 = 256$

$\sqrt{16} = 4 \quad \sqrt[3]{64} = 4 \quad \sqrt[4]{256} = 4$

---

$5^2 = 25 \quad 5^3 = 125$

$\sqrt{25} = 5 \quad \sqrt[3]{125} = 5$

---

$6^2 = 36 \quad 6^3 = 216$

$\sqrt{36} = 6 \quad \sqrt[3]{216} = 6$

---

$7^2 = 49 \quad 8^2 = 64 \quad 9^2 = 81$

$\sqrt{49} = 7 \quad \sqrt{64} = 8 \quad \sqrt{81} = 9$

---

$10^2 = 100 \quad 10^3 = 1{,}000 \quad 10^4 = 10{,}000$

$\sqrt{100} = 10 \quad \sqrt[3]{1{,}000} = 10 \quad \sqrt[4]{10{,}000} = 10$

---

### Example 1

If $2^{(x-5)} = 8$, what is the value of $x$?

(A) 4
(B) 5
(C) 7
(D) 8

### ✓ Solution

Use your knowledge of the exponential values of 2 to see a shortcut. Since $2^3 = 8$, simply set the exponent of 2 equal to 3 to solve for $x$:

$$x - 5 = 3 \rightarrow x = 8$$

So, choice **(D)** is correct. Alternatively, you could work your way backwards from the answer choices. When you plug in choice (D), you will also arrive at the correct answer:

$$2^{(x-5)} = 8 \rightarrow \text{Plug in 8 for } x \rightarrow$$
$$2^{(8-5)} = 8 \rightarrow 2^3 = 8$$

Your knowledge of the exponential values of 2 will also help you quickly see the correct answer when you solve by plugging in the answer choices.

### Example 2

| x | f(x) |
|---|---|
| 1 | 1 |
| 2 | 4 |
| 3 | 9 |
| 4 | 16 |

In the table above, which of the following defines the function $f(x)$?

(A) $f(x) = x + 3$
(B) $f(x) = x^2$
(C) $f(x) = -x^2$
(D) $f(x) = x^3$

### Solution

Use your knowledge of the exponential values of simple numbers to recognize the pattern.

$$1^2 = 1$$
$$2^2 = 2$$
$$3^2 = 9$$
$$4^2 = 16$$

Choice **(B)**, $f(x) = x^2$, therefore correctly models this relationship.

## Practice Drill—Exponents and Roots

*(If timing, take about 12 minutes to complete.)*

1. Which of these expressions is equivalent to $\sqrt[4]{x^3}$?

(A) $x^{\left(\frac{4}{3}\right)}$
(B) $\frac{x^3}{x^4}$
(C) $\frac{x^4}{x^3}$
(D) $x^{\left(\frac{3}{4}\right)}$

2. If $3x^2 - 27 = 0$, and $x > 0$, what is the value of $x$?

(A) 1
(B) 2
(C) 3
(D) 4

3. $f(x) = \frac{5^x}{2^x}$

What is the value of $f(2)$ in the function above?

(A) $\frac{25}{4}$
(B) $\frac{5}{2}$
(C) $\frac{10}{4}$
(D) 8

4. If $f(x) = \frac{\sqrt{x}}{x}$, what is $f(9)$?

(A) $\frac{1}{9}$
(B) $\frac{1}{3}$
(C) 1
(D) 3

5. If $x$ is positive, which expression is equivalent to $\sqrt[3]{27x^6}$?

(A) $3x$
(B) $3x^2$
(C) $6x^2$
(D) $9x^3$

| x | f(x) |
|---|---|
| 1 | 2 |
| 2 | 5 |
| 3 | 10 |
| 4 | 17 |
| 5 | 26 |

6. Based on the values in the table above, which of the following correctly expresses the value of $f(x)$?

(A) $f(x) = x + 1$
(B) $f(x) = x^2$
(C) $f(x) = x^3$
(D) $f(x) = x^2 + 1$

7. $\dfrac{x^a y^{-b}}{x^{-a} y^b}$

Consider the expression above, in which $x$ and $y$ are both positive, and $a$ and $b$ are positive constants. Which of the following would be an equivalent form of the expression?

(A) $\dfrac{x^a}{y^b}$

(B) $\dfrac{x^{(a^2)}}{y^{(b^2)}}$

(C) $\dfrac{x^{2a}}{y^{2b}}$

(D) $\dfrac{y}{x}$

**Fill-In Practice:** Write your answer in the underlined blank under each question.

8. $\sqrt[3]{125} + \sqrt[3]{64} = x^2$

Given that $x > 0$, what is the value of $x$ in the above equation?

Answer: ________

9. If $x^{-2}y^{-1} = \frac{1}{5}$, what is the value of $x^4y^2$?

Answer: ________

10. If $\sqrt{\frac{x}{2}} = 4$, what is $\sqrt[5]{x}$?

Answer: ________

## Solutions

1. **(D)**

$\sqrt[4]{x^3} \rightarrow$ The root, 4, is on the outside $\rightarrow$
$= x^{\left(\frac{3}{4}\right)}$

2. **(C)**

$3x^2 - 27 = 0 \rightarrow$
$3x^2 = 27 \rightarrow$
$x^2 = 9 \rightarrow$
$x = 3$

Alternatively, you could have tried plugging in the answer choices to the original equation.

3. **(A)**

$f(x) = \dfrac{5^x}{2^x} \rightarrow$

$f(2) = \dfrac{5^2}{2^2} \rightarrow$

$f(2) = \dfrac{25}{4}$

4. **(B)**

$f(x) = \frac{\sqrt{x}}{x} \rightarrow$

$f(9) = \frac{\sqrt{9}}{9} \rightarrow$

$f(9) = \frac{3}{9} = \frac{1}{3}$

5. **(B)**

$\sqrt[3]{27x^6} \rightarrow$

Take the cube root of both 27 and $x^6 \rightarrow$

$= 3x^2$

6. **(D)** Try plugging some sample values into the answer choices to determine the answer. When you try the first ordered pair, (1, 2), choices (B) and (C) can be eliminated. When you try the next ordered pair, (2, 5), choice (A) can be eliminated. Only choice **(D)**, $f(x) = x^2 + 1$, correctly models the function.

7. **(C)** On a problem like this, it can be helpful to look ahead to the answers to have a sense of what the answer might look like. It appears we want a solution that has only the $x$ values on either the numerator or denominator and only the $y$ values on the opposite side. With that in mind, simplify the expression:

$\frac{x^a y^{-b}}{x^{-a} y^b} \rightarrow$

$\frac{x^a x^a}{y^b y^b} \rightarrow$

$\frac{x^{2a}}{y^{2b}}$

8. **(3)**

$\sqrt[3]{125} + \sqrt[3]{64} = x^2 \rightarrow$

$5 + 4 = 9 = x^2 \rightarrow 3 = x$

9. **(25)**

$x^{-2}y^{-1} = \frac{1}{5} \rightarrow$

Flip both sides $\rightarrow$

$x^2y = 5 \rightarrow$

Square both sides to make it the desired expression $\rightarrow$

$x^4y^2 = 25$

10. **(2)**

$\sqrt{\frac{x}{2}} = 4 \rightarrow$

Square both sides $\rightarrow$

$\frac{x}{2} = 16 \rightarrow$

$x = 32$

Take the fifth root of 32 $\rightarrow$

$\sqrt[5]{32} = 2$

## Advanced Math—Solving Quadratic Functions

### Factoring Quadratic Equations

*If a quadratic function can be easily factored to identify the solutions, use factoring to solve.*

**Example 1**

$$x^2 - 9x + 20 = 0$$

What are the solutions for $x$ in the equation above?

**Solution**

Factor the expression to solve for the solutions.

$$x^2 - 9x + 20 = 0 \rightarrow$$
$$(x - 4)(x - 5) = 0$$

With the equation in this form, you can identify which values of $x$ will make the expression zero:

$$x - 4 = 0 \rightarrow x = 4$$
or
$$x - 5 = 0 \rightarrow x = 5$$

So, $x$ could equal 4 or 5.

**Example 2**

$$3x^2 - 3x = 6$$

What are the solutions for $x$ in the equation above?

### ✓ Solution

Even though this equation is not as obviously factorable as the previous example, with a little bit of manipulation you can get it in a factorable form:

$$3x^2 - 3x = 6 \rightarrow$$

Divide both sides by 3 →

$$x^2 - x = 2 \rightarrow$$

$$x^2 - x - 2 = 0$$

Factor the expression →

$$(x - 2)(x + 1) = 0$$

Based on this, the two values that would be solutions are 2 and $-1$, since either value if plugged in for $x$ would make the entire expression equal to zero.

### Practice

Use factoring to find the solutions to the equations.

1. $x^2 - 6x + 8 = 0$
2. $x^2 - 10x + 21 = 0$
3. $x^2 - 6x - 16 = 0$
4. $x^3 - 4x = 0$
5. $x^3 + 5x^2 + 6x = 0$

### Solutions

1. $x^2 - 6x + 8 = 0 \rightarrow$
   $(x - 4)(x - 2) = 0 \rightarrow$
   $x = 4$ or $x = 2$

2. $x^2 - 10x + 21 = 0 \rightarrow$
   $(x - 7)(x - 3) = 0 \rightarrow$
   $x = 7$ or $x = 3$

3. $x^2 - 6x - 16 = 0 \rightarrow$
   $(x - 8)(x + 2) = 0 \rightarrow$
   Solutions: 8, $-2$

4. $x^3 - 4x = 0 \rightarrow$
   $x(x^2 - 4) = 0 \rightarrow$
   $x(x + 2)(x - 2) = 0$
   Solutions are 0, $-2$, or 2

5. $x^3 + 5x^2 + 6x = 0 \rightarrow$
   $x(x^2 + 5x + 6) = 0 \rightarrow$
   $x(x + 3)(x + 2) = 0$
   Solutions are 0, $-3$, or $-2$

### Square Root Method

If a quadratic equation does *not* have an x term, you may want to use the square root method—take the square root of both sides of the equation to arrive at the solution(s). The positive and negative cases will be solutions.

#### Example

$$x^2 - 16 = 0$$

What are the solutions for $x$ in the equation above?

#### Solution

This equation lacks an $x$ term, so we can use the square root method to solve:

$$x^2 - 16 = 0 \rightarrow$$
$$x^2 = 16 \rightarrow$$
$$x = \pm 4$$

### Practice

Use the square root method to solve these equations.

1. $x^2 = 81$
2. $y^2 - 64 = 0$
3. $(x - 3)^2 = 25$

### Solutions

1. $x^2 = 81 \rightarrow$
   $\sqrt{x^2} = \sqrt{81} \rightarrow$
   $x = \pm 9$

2. $y^2 - 64 = 0 \rightarrow$
   $\sqrt{y^2} = 64 \rightarrow$
   $y = \pm 8$

3. $(x - 3)^2 = 25 \rightarrow$
   $\sqrt{(x - 3)^2} = \sqrt{25} \rightarrow$
   $x - 3 = \pm 5$

   Then, set up two equations to solve for the potential values of $x$:

   $$x - 3 = 5 \rightarrow x = 8$$

   or

   $$x - 3 = -5 \rightarrow x = -2$$

   So, the solutions are 8 and $-2$.

### Quadratic Formula

An equation with constants *a*, *b*, and *c* and a variable *x* that is written in the form $ax^2 + bx + c = 0$ may be solved using the *quadratic formula*:

$$x = \frac{-b \pm \sqrt{b^2 - 4ac}}{2a}$$

Use the quadratic formula when factoring the equation looks challenging, often when the $x^2$ term has a constant other than 1 in front of it (examples: $6x^2$ or $\frac{1}{3}x^2$).

**Example**

$$3x^2 + 5x - 2 = 0$$

What are the solutions for *x* in the equation above?

**Solution**

The values of the constants are $a = 3$, $b = 5$, and $c = -2$. Plug these values into the quadratic formula to solve for *x*.

$$x = \frac{-b \pm \sqrt{b^2 - 4ac}}{2a} \rightarrow$$

$$x = \frac{-5 \pm \sqrt{5^2 - 4(3)(-2)}}{2(3)} \rightarrow$$

$$x = \frac{-5 \pm \sqrt{25 + 24}}{6} \rightarrow$$

$$x = \frac{-5 \pm \sqrt{49}}{6} \rightarrow$$

$$x = -\frac{5}{6} \pm \frac{\sqrt{49}}{6} \rightarrow -\frac{5}{6} \pm \frac{7}{6}$$

So, the solutions are:

$$-\frac{5}{6} + \frac{7}{6} = \frac{2}{6} = \frac{1}{3}$$

or

$$-\frac{5}{6} - \frac{7}{6} = -\frac{12}{6} = -2$$

### Practice

1. $3x^2 + 5x + 2 = 0$
2. $2x^2 - 5x - 7 = 0$
3. $5x^2 + 3x = 2$
4. $3x^2 + 4x - 5 = 0$
5. How many real solutions does the equation $5x^2 - 3x + 2 = 0$ have?

## Solutions

1. $x = \dfrac{-b \pm \sqrt{b^2 - 4ac}}{2a}$

   $3x^2 + 5x + 2 = 0 \rightarrow$

   $x = \dfrac{-5 \pm \sqrt{5^2 - 4(3)(2)}}{2(3)} \rightarrow$

   $x = \dfrac{-5 \pm \sqrt{25 - 24}}{6} \rightarrow$

   $x = \dfrac{-5 \pm 1}{6} \rightarrow x = -1 \text{ or } -\dfrac{2}{3}$

2. $2x^2 - 5x - 7 = 0 \rightarrow$

   $x = \dfrac{-b \pm \sqrt{b^2 - 4ac}}{2a} \rightarrow$

   $x = \dfrac{-(-5) \pm \sqrt{(-5)^2 - 4(2)(-7)}}{2(2)} \rightarrow$

   $x = \dfrac{5 \pm \sqrt{25 + 56}}{4} \rightarrow$

   $x = \dfrac{5 \pm \sqrt{81}}{4} \rightarrow$

   $x = \dfrac{5 \pm 9}{4} \rightarrow$

   $x = \dfrac{5 + 9}{4} = 3.5 \text{ or } x = \dfrac{5 - 9}{4} = -1$

3. $5x^2 + 3x = 2 \rightarrow$

   $5x^2 + 3x - 2 = 0 \rightarrow$

   $x = \dfrac{-b \pm \sqrt{b^2 - 4ac}}{2a} \rightarrow$

   $x = \dfrac{-3 \pm \sqrt{3^2 - 4(5)(-2)}}{2(5)} \rightarrow$

   $x = \dfrac{-3 \pm \sqrt{9 + 40}}{10} \rightarrow$

   $x = \dfrac{-3 \pm \sqrt{49}}{10} \rightarrow$

   $x = \dfrac{-3 \pm 7}{10} \rightarrow$

   $x = \dfrac{-3 + 7}{10} = \dfrac{4}{10} = 0.4$

   or

   $x = \dfrac{-3 - 7}{10} = \dfrac{-10}{10} = -1$

4. $3x^2 + 4x - 5 = 0 \rightarrow$

$$x = \frac{-b \pm \sqrt{b^2 - 4ac}}{2a} \rightarrow$$

$$x = \frac{-4 \pm \sqrt{4^2 - 4(3)(-5)}}{2(3)} \rightarrow$$

$$x = \frac{-4 \pm \sqrt{16 + 60}}{6} \rightarrow$$

$$x = \frac{-4 \pm \sqrt{76}}{6} \rightarrow$$

Simplify the $\sqrt{76}$ by factoring out the square root of 4 $\rightarrow$

$$x = \frac{-4 \pm \sqrt{4(19)}}{6} \rightarrow \frac{-4 \pm 2\sqrt{19}}{6} \rightarrow \frac{-2 \pm \sqrt{19}}{3}$$

So, $x$ can be:

$$-\frac{2}{3} + \frac{\sqrt{19}}{3} \text{ or } -\frac{2}{3} - \frac{\sqrt{19}}{3}$$

5. To see how many real solutions there are, find the value of the *discriminant*, i.e., the component of the quadratic formula underneath the square root sign: $b^2 - 4ac$. If it is positive, there are two real solutions. If it is zero, there is just one real solution. And if it is negative, there are no real solutions since you would have to take the square root of a negative number.

In the equation $5x^2 - 3x + 2 = 0$, $b^2 - 4ac = (-3)^2 - 4(5)(2) = 9 - 40 = -31$.

So, there are *zero* real solutions to the equation.

### Completing the Square

Use completing the square particularly to work with problems involving parabolas. Completing the square will enable you to more easily identify key information about the parabola. (Note—parabolas will be covered later in the chapter.)

**Example**

$$x^2 + 8x = 20$$

What are the values for $x$ in the above equation?

**Solution**

Here is how you can use *completing the square* to solve this equation.

First, take half of 8 (which is 4), square it, and add it to both sides of the equation.

$$x^2 + 8x = 20 \rightarrow$$
$$x^2 + 8x + 16 = 20 + 16 \rightarrow$$
$$x^2 + 8x + 16 = 36$$

Now, you can factor the left-hand side in a squared form:

$$(x + 4)^2 = 36$$

Then, take the square root of both sides:

$$\sqrt{(x+4)^2} = \sqrt{36} \rightarrow$$
$$x + 4 = \pm 6$$

Finally, solve for $x$:

$$x + 4 = 6 \rightarrow x = 6 - 4 = 2$$

or

$$x + 4 = -6 \rightarrow x = -6 - 4 = -10$$

So, $x$ could be either 2 or $-10$.

### Practice

Solve each of these using completing the square.

1. $x^2 + 6x = -8$
2. $x^2 + 8x = 9$
3. $4x^2 + 3x = 1$

### Solutions

1. $x^2 + 6x = -8 \rightarrow$
   $x^2 + 6x + 9 = -8 + 9 \rightarrow$
   $(x+3)^2 = 1 \rightarrow$
   $x + 3 = \pm 1$
   So, $x$ could equal $-4$ or $-2$.

2. $x^2 + 8x = 9 \rightarrow$
   $x^2 + 8x + 16 = 9 + 16 \rightarrow$
   $(x+4)^2 = 25 \rightarrow$
   $x + 4 = \pm 5$
   So, $x$ could equal 1 or $-9$.

3. $4x^2 + 3x = 1 \rightarrow$
   $x^2 + \frac{3}{4}x = \frac{1}{4} \rightarrow$
   Take half of $\frac{3}{4}$, $\frac{3}{8}$, square it, and add to both sides:
   $x^2 + \frac{3}{4}x + \left(\frac{3}{8}\right)^2 = \frac{1}{4} + \left(\frac{3}{8}\right)^2 \rightarrow$
   $x^2 + \frac{3}{4}x + \frac{9}{64} = \frac{1}{4} + \frac{9}{64} \rightarrow \frac{16}{64} + \frac{9}{64} = \frac{25}{64} \rightarrow$
   $\left(x + \frac{3}{8}\right)^2 = \frac{25}{64} \rightarrow \sqrt{\frac{25}{64}} = +/-\frac{5}{8}$
   So, $x$ could equal:
   $x + \frac{3}{8} = \frac{5}{8} \rightarrow x = \frac{2}{8} = \frac{1}{4}$
   or
   $x + \frac{3}{8} = -\frac{5}{8} \rightarrow x = -\frac{8}{8} = -1$

### Plugging in the Answers

*Try plugging in the answer choices in a quadratic equation if solving the problem algebraically will take longer than working backwards from the four options.*

#### Example

$$\frac{1}{x+2}+\frac{3}{2x+4}=\frac{1}{2}$$

What is the value of $x$ in the equation above?

(A) 1
(B) 2
(C) 3
(D) 4

#### Solution

While this problem could be solved algebraically, it will likely save you time to work backwards from the answer options. Since the answers are in order from least to greatest, start with one of the middle options to minimize the potential trial and error.

Start with 2:

$$\frac{1}{x+2}+\frac{3}{2x+4}=\frac{1}{2}\rightarrow$$

$$\frac{1}{2+2}+\frac{3}{2(2)+4}=\frac{1}{2}\rightarrow$$

$$\frac{1}{4}+\frac{3}{8}=\frac{5}{8}\neq\frac{1}{2}$$

This option did not work. Since the sum was larger than $\frac{1}{2}$, we should try another answer choice that will make the expression have a smaller fraction—this comes from having a larger denominator. So, we will next try choice (C), 3:

$$\frac{1}{x+2}+\frac{3}{2x+4}=\frac{1}{2}\rightarrow$$

$$\frac{1}{3+2}+\frac{3}{2(3)+4}=\frac{1}{2}\rightarrow$$

$$\frac{1}{5}+\frac{3}{10}=\frac{2}{10}+\frac{3}{10}=\frac{5}{10}=\frac{1}{2}$$

This checks out, so choice **(C)**, 3, is correct.

## Practice

Use plugging in the answers to solve.

1. $4(x-2)^2+2=2x$

   Which of the following is a value of $x$?

   (A) 1
   (B) 2
   (C) 3
   (D) 4

2. $\frac{1}{x+2}+\frac{1}{x+3}=\frac{3}{2}$

   Which of the following is a value of $x$?

   (A) $-2$
   (B) $-1$
   (C) 0
   (D) 1

3. Which of the following is/are solutions for $x$ in the following equation?

   $8x^2-7x=x^3$

   I. Zero
   II. One
   III. Two

   (A) I only
   (B) II only
   (C) I and II only
   (D) All of the above

## Solutions

1. $4(x-2)^2+2=2x \rightarrow$
   $4(3-2)^2+2=2(3) \rightarrow$
   $4(1)^2+2=6 \rightarrow$
   $6=6$

   So, choice **(C)**, 3, works.

2. $\frac{1}{x+2}+\frac{1}{x+3}=\frac{3}{2} \rightarrow$

   $\frac{1}{-1+2}+\frac{1}{-1+3}=\frac{3}{2} \rightarrow$

   $\frac{1}{1}+\frac{1}{2}=\frac{3}{2}$

   So, choice **(B)**, $-1$, works.

3. First, let's try zero:

   $8x^2 - 7x = x^3 \rightarrow$

   $8(0)^2 - 7(0) = 0^3 \rightarrow$

   $0 = 0$

   So, option I, zero, does work.

   Next, let's try 1:

   $8x^2 - 7x = x^3 \rightarrow$

   $8(1)^2 - 7(1) = 1^3 \rightarrow$

   $8 - 7 = 1 \rightarrow$

   $1 = 1$

   So option II, 1, does work.

   Finally, let's try 2:

   $8x^2 - 7x = x^3 \rightarrow$

   $8(2)^2 - 7(2) = 2^3 \rightarrow$

   $32 - 14 = 8 \rightarrow$

   $18 \neq 8$

   So option III, 2, does NOT work. Therefore, the correct answer is choice **(C)**. You could also approach this in an efficient way by realizing that if option III DOES work, choice (D) will have to be the answer since it is the only option with option III. Further, if you are evaluating quadratics on the calculator section, you may want to graph the function to more quickly identify its roots.

### Undefined Functions

When a function is divided by zero, it may be undefined—that is, it will have no solutions. If you were to divide a number like 3 by 0, it would be undefined since it is impossible to divide 3 into zero parts.

#### › Example

When is this function undefined?

$$f(x) = \frac{x^3 - x^2 + 2}{x - 4}$$

#### ✓ Solution

Determine the value of $x$ that would cause the function to have zero in the denominator. Set the denominator equal to zero and solve for $x$:

$$x - 4 = 0 \rightarrow x = 4$$

Therefore, the function is undefined when $x$ is equal to 4.

### Practice

Find the values of $x$ that will make the expression undefined.

1. $\frac{5}{x}$
2. $\frac{12x+1}{x+4}$
3. $\frac{7}{x^2-9}$

### Solutions

1. $\frac{5}{x} \rightarrow \frac{5}{0}$

   So, the function is undefined when $x$ is 0.

2. $\frac{12x+1}{x+4} \rightarrow \frac{12x+1}{0} \rightarrow$

   $x+4=0 \rightarrow x=-4$

   So, the function is undefined when $x$ is $-4$.

3. $\frac{7}{x^2-9} \rightarrow \frac{7}{0} \rightarrow$

   $x^2-9=0 \rightarrow$

   $x^2=9 \rightarrow x=\pm 3$

   So, the function is undefined when $x$ is 3 or $-3$.

### Extraneous Solutions

When dealing with equations involving roots, it is a good idea to test the solutions to see if they are *extraneous*—meaning, they do not work in the original equation. The reason they typically do not work is that they would require taking the square root of a negative number, which would result in an imaginary solution.

**Example**

$$\sqrt{x-1}=x-7$$

What are the solutions for $x$ in the equation above?

**Solution**

Start by squaring both sides to get rid of the radical sign:

$$\sqrt{x-1}=x-7 \rightarrow$$
$$x-1=x^2-14x+49$$

Then, simplify the equation and factor to find the potential solutions:

$$x-1=x^2-14x+49 \rightarrow$$
$$x^2-15x+50=0 \rightarrow$$
$$(x-10)(x-5)=0$$

So, the potential solutions are 10 and 5. Now, to be sure we don't have any extraneous solutions, plug 10 and 5 back in to the original equation to see if they work:

$$\sqrt{x-1} = x - 7 \rightarrow$$
$$\sqrt{10-1} = 10 - 7 \rightarrow$$
$$\sqrt{9} = 3$$

So, 10 works in the original equation. Now let's try 5.

$$\sqrt{5-1} = 5 - 7 \rightarrow$$
$$\sqrt{5-1} = 5 - 7 \rightarrow$$
$$\sqrt{4} \neq -2$$

The square root of 4 cannot be equal to $-2$ in this case, since we would need an imaginary number to make it work. Therefore, 5 is an extraneous solution and the only solution is 10.

### Practice

Solve each of these equations for $x$, watching out for extraneous solutions.

1. $x = \sqrt{12 - x}$
2. $\sqrt{x+1} + 5 = x$
3. $\sqrt{x-6} = x - 8$

### Solutions

1. $x = \sqrt{12 - x} \rightarrow$

   $x^2 = 12 - x \rightarrow$

   $x^2 + x - 12 = 0 \rightarrow$

   $(x + 4)(x - 3)$

   So, $-4$ and 3 are potential solutions. Check to see if either is extraneous.

   $-4 = \sqrt{12 - (-4)} \rightarrow$

   $-4 \neq 4$

   So, $-4$ does NOT work.

   $3 = \sqrt{12 - 3} \rightarrow$

   $3 = 3$

   So, 3 does work.

2. $\sqrt{x+1} + 5 = x \rightarrow$

   $\sqrt{x+1} = x - 5 \rightarrow$

   $x + 1 = x^2 - 10x + 25 \rightarrow$

   $0 = x^2 - 11x + 24 \rightarrow$

   $0 = (x - 8)(x - 3)$

   8 and 3 are potential solutions. Check to see if either is extraneous.

   $\sqrt{8+1} + 5 = 8 \rightarrow$

   $3 + 5 = 8 \rightarrow$

   $8 = 8$

8 does work.

$\sqrt{3+1}+5=3 \rightarrow$
$\sqrt{4}+5=3 \rightarrow$
$2+5 \neq 3$

3 does NOT work.

3. $\sqrt{x-6}=x-8 \rightarrow$
$x-6=(x-8)^2 \rightarrow$
$x-6=x^2-16x+64 \rightarrow$
$0=x^2-17x+70 \rightarrow$
$0=(x-10)(x-7)$

10 and 7 are potential solutions. Check to see if either is extraneous.

$\sqrt{x-6}=x-8 \rightarrow$
$\sqrt{10-6}=10-8 \rightarrow$
$\sqrt{4}=2$

So, 10 does work.

$\sqrt{x-6}=x-8 \rightarrow$
$\sqrt{7-6}=7-8 \rightarrow$
$\sqrt{1}=1 \neq -1$

So, 7 does NOT work.

## Synthetic Division

On occasion, the SAT will ask you to divide a polynomial. The easiest way to do this is using synthetic division.

### Example 1

What is the result when $2x^2+5x-3$ is divided by $x-4$?

### Solution

Set up the problem by taking the coefficients of the terms of the polynomial and placing the numerical term of the divisor to the left of them like this:

$$\begin{array}{r|rrr} 4 & 2 & 5 & -3 \\ \hline \end{array}$$

Next, bring down each of the coefficients, multiplying the columns one-by-one by the divisor 4, and create sums to see what the divided polynomial and remainder would be:

$$\begin{array}{r|rrr} 4 & 2 & 5 & -3 \\ & & 8 & 52 \\ \hline & 2 & 13 & 49 \end{array}$$

The answer would be $2x+13$ with a remainder of $\frac{49}{x-4}$.

### Example 2

Based on the previous problem, is $x - 4$ a factor of $2x^2 + 5x - 3$?

### Solution

For an expression to be a factor of the polynomial, you must be able to divide the polynomial by that expression and NOT have a remainder, i.e., the remainder must be zero. Since there is a remainder of $\frac{49}{x-4}$ when the expression is divided, $x - 4$ is NOT a factor of $2x^2 + 5x - 3$.

## Practice

1A. What is the result when $x^2 + 2x - 15$ is divided by $x + 5$?
1B. Is $x + 5$ a factor of $x^2 + 2x - 15$?
2A. What is the result when $4x^2 - 3x - 5$ is divided by $x - 3$?
2B. Is $x - 3$ a factor of $4x^2 - 3x - 5$?

## Solutions

1A.

| $-5$ | 1 | 2 | $-15$ |
|---|---|---|---|
| | | $-5$ | 15 |
| | 1 | $-3$ | 0 |

Therefore, the answer is $x - 3$.

1B. Since there was no remainder when it was divided, this is a factor of the expression.

2A.

| 3 | 4 | $-3$ | $-5$ |
|---|---|---|---|
| | | 12 | 27 |
| | 4 | 9 | 22 |

So, the result is $4x + 9$ with a remainder of $\frac{22}{x-3}$.

2B. Since there was a remainder when it was divided, this is NOT a factor of the expression.

> **SAT Math Strategy**
>
> Many SAT quadratic function problems can be solved in different ways. Use whatever approach is easiest for you.

### Example

If $2x^2 - 6x = 20$, what are the solutions for $x$?

(A) $-2$ or $-5$
(B) $-2$ or $5$
(C) $2$ or $-5$
(D) $2$ or $5$

### ✓ Solution

**Method 1: Factoring.** If you notice that all the numbers in the problem have 2 as a factor, you can take a 2 out of everything to simplify. Then factoring will probably appear to be the easiest method.

$$2x^2 - 6x = 20 \rightarrow$$
$$2x^2 - 6x - 20 = 0 \rightarrow$$
$$x^2 - 3x - 10 = 0 \rightarrow$$
$$(x + 2)(x - 5) = 0$$

The correct answer is therefore **(B)**, $-2$ or 5.

**Method 2: Quadratic Formula.** If you do not see an easy way to factor the equation, you can put the equation in standard form and use the quadratic formula to solve. This can be a good approach if you are quick and careful with your calculations.

$$2x^2 - 6x = 20 \rightarrow$$
$$2x^2 - 6x - 20 = 0 \rightarrow$$
$$x = \frac{-b \pm \sqrt{b^2 - 4ac}}{2a} \rightarrow$$
$$x = \frac{-(-6) \pm \sqrt{(-6)^2 - 4(2)(-20)}}{2(2)} \rightarrow$$
$$x = \frac{6 \pm \sqrt{36 + 160}}{4} \rightarrow$$
$$x = \frac{6 \pm \sqrt{196}}{4} \rightarrow$$
$$x = \frac{6 \pm 14}{4}$$

So, $x$ could be either $\frac{6 + 14}{4} = \frac{20}{4} = 5$ or $\frac{6 - 14}{4} = \frac{-8}{2} = -2$

**Method 3: Plug in the Answers.** Look ahead to the answer choices to notice that all of them are variations of $\pm 2$ and $\pm 5$. So, you essentially just have four numbers to plug in to the original equation.

$2(-2)^2 - 6(-2) = 20 \rightarrow$
$8 + 12 = 20$
$-2$ works.

$2(2)^2 - 6(2) = 20 \rightarrow$
$8 - 12 \neq 20$
2 does NOT work.

$2(-5)^2 - 6(-5) = 20 \rightarrow$
$2(25) + 30 = 20 \rightarrow$
$50 + 30 \neq 20$
$-5$ does NOT work.

$2(5)^2 - 6(5) = 20 \rightarrow$
$2(25) - 30 = 20 \rightarrow$
$50 - 30 = 20$
5 does work.

If there were more numbers to plug in, this approach would have been more difficult.

On school tests, you can often get in a rhythm with the questions you are solving. Each question on a test or quiz may be a variation of "solve for *x*." On the SAT Math, be careful on quadratic function questions to first understand what the question is asking, then start working on the solution.

**SAT Math Strategy**

Do not go on autopilot with the questions—carefully consider what you are asked to do.

### Example

Variables $x$ and $y$ are related to each other in a quadratic function of the form $y = kx^2$, in which $k$ is a constant. If $y$ is 12 when $x$ is 2, and $y$ is 48 when $x$ is 4, what is the value of $y$ when $x$ is 5?

(A) 30
(B) 45
(C) 60
(D) 75

### Solution

This is not a problem that can be solved in a typical fashion, like using the quadratic formula or factoring. We must fully understand what the question tells us.

- The variables are related to each other in an equation like $y = kx^2$.
- $x$ and $y$ are variables while $k$ is a constant.
- We have ordered pairs of values—(2, 12) and (4, 48)—that we can plug in to see what the constant $k$ would be.

Given that information, let's plug in the ordered pair (2, 12) into the equation, since it is smaller and easier to work with than (4, 48):

$$y = kx^2 \rightarrow$$
$$12 = k(2)^2 \rightarrow$$
$$12 = 4k \rightarrow$$
$$k = 3$$

So, the function in the question is $y = 3x^2$. We now can see what the value of $y$ is when $x$ is 5:

$$y = 3x^2 \rightarrow$$
$$y = 3(5)^2 \rightarrow$$
$$y = 3(25) = 75$$

The answer is therefore **(D)**, 75.

## Practice Drill #1—Solving Advanced Equations

*(If timing, take about 12 minutes to complete.)*

1. For what positive value of $x$ is this function undefined?

$$f(x) = \frac{1}{x^2 - 1}$$

(A) 1
(B) 2
(C) 3
(D) 4

2. If $x^2 - 3x - 10 = 0$, for what value of $x$ is this equation true given that $x > 0$?

(A) 3
(B) 4
(C) 5
(D) 6

3. Which of the following would be a solution to this equation?

$$21 - \sqrt{x} = 10$$

(A) 11
(B) 18
(C) 55
(D) 121

4. Which of the following provides the two solutions to this equation?

$$3x^2 + 5x + 2 = 0$$

(A) $-\frac{2}{3}$ or $-1$
(B) $\frac{1}{6}$ or $\frac{2}{5}$
(C) $-\frac{3}{4}$ or 7
(D) $\frac{6}{11}$ or $-8$

5. $x^2 - 15 = x + 5$

What is the product of the solutions to the above equation?

(A) −35
(B) −20
(C) 1
(D) 9

6. $\dfrac{x^2 - y^2}{3} = 0$

What value of $y$ would always make the above equation true?

(A) $x$
(B) $x^2$
(C) $4x$
(D) $8x$

**Fill-In Practice:** Write your answer in the underlined blank under each question.

7. If $\dfrac{(x+2)}{(x-3)} - 2 = \dfrac{7}{(x-3)}$, what is the solution for $x$?

Answer: ________

8. If $2\sqrt{x} + 1 = 10 - \sqrt{x}$, what is the solution for $x$?

Answer: ________

9. $(x+b)(x+b) = x^2 + 4x + 4$

If the above equation has infinitely many solutions, what is the value of the constant $b$?

Answer: ________

10. If $\dfrac{6x^2 - 5x + 8}{2} = x^2 - 3$, how many real solutions are there for $x$?

Answer: ________

## Solutions

1. **(A)** For the function $f(x) = \dfrac{1}{x^2 - 1}$ to be undefined, we need a value of $x$ that will make the denominator equal to zero. So, set up an equation to solve for the positive value of $x$ needed:

$$x^2 - 1 = 0 \rightarrow$$
$$(x+1)(x-1) = 0$$

So, $x$ could equal 1 or $-1$. Since we need a positive value of $x$, the correct answer is 1.

2. **(C)** Solve this by factoring:

$$x^2 - 3x - 10 = 0 \rightarrow$$
$$(x-5)(x+2) = 0$$

So, $x$ could be either 5 or $-2$. Since the answer must be positive, the correct answer is 5.

3. **(D)** Use the square root method to solve:

$$21 - \sqrt{x} = 10 \rightarrow$$
$$11 - \sqrt{x} = 0 \rightarrow$$
$$11 = \sqrt{x} \rightarrow$$
$$121 = x$$

4. **(A)** Given that there is a 3 in front of the $x^2$ term, the quadratic formula will be the best way to solve this:

$$3x^2 + 5x + 2 = 0 \rightarrow$$

$$x = \frac{-b \pm \sqrt{b^2 - 4ac}}{2a} \rightarrow$$

$$x = \frac{-5 \pm \sqrt{5^2 - 4(3)(2)}}{2(3)} \rightarrow$$

$$x = \frac{-5 \pm \sqrt{25 - 24}}{6} \rightarrow$$

$$x = \frac{-5 \pm 1}{6} \rightarrow$$

$$x = -\frac{5}{6} + \frac{1}{6} = -\frac{4}{6} = -\frac{2}{3}$$

and

$$x = -\frac{5}{6} - \frac{1}{6} = -\frac{6}{6} = -1$$

5. **(B)** Simplify and factor the equation to determine the two solutions, then multiply them together to find their product:

$$x^2 - 15 = x + 5 \rightarrow$$

$$x^2 - x - 20 = 0 \rightarrow$$

$$(x - 5)(x + 4) = 0$$

The solutions are therefore 5 or $-4$. The product of them is $5 \times (-4) = -20$.

6. **(A)** Solve for $y$ by simplifying the equation, then using the square root method:

$$\frac{x^2 - y^2}{3} = 0 \rightarrow$$

$$x^2 - y^2 = 0 \rightarrow$$

$$x^2 = y^2 \rightarrow$$

$$\sqrt{x^2} = \sqrt{y^2} \rightarrow$$

$$x = y$$

7. **(1)** Multiply the equation by $(x - 3)$ to remove the $(x - 3)$ from the denominator:

$$(x - 3) \times \left(\frac{(x + 2)}{(x - 3)} - 2\right) = (x - 3) \times \left(\frac{7}{(x - 3)}\right) \rightarrow$$

$$(x + 2) - 2(x - 3) = 7 \rightarrow$$

$$x + 2 - 2x + 6 = 7 \rightarrow$$

$$-x + 8 = 7 \rightarrow$$

$$-x = -1 \rightarrow x = 1$$

8. **(9)** Simplify and use the square root method:

$$2\sqrt{x} + 1 = 10 - \sqrt{x} \rightarrow$$
$$3\sqrt{x} = 9 \rightarrow$$
$$\sqrt{x} = 3 \rightarrow$$
$$(\sqrt{x})^2 = 3^2 \rightarrow$$
$$x = 9$$

9. **(2)** For there to be infinitely many solutions, the equation must be equivalent on both sides. FOIL the left-hand side to see what the value of $b$ must be for this to be true.

$$(x + b)(x + b) = x^2 + 4x + 4 \rightarrow$$
$$x^2 + 2bx + b^2 = x^2 + 4x + 4$$

If $b$ is equal to 2, both sides are equivalent, giving us infinitely many solutions.

10. **(0)** Simplify this equation to get it in standard form.

$$\frac{6x^2 - 5x + 8}{2} = x^2 - 3 \rightarrow$$
$$6x^2 - 5x + 8 = 2x^2 - 6 \rightarrow$$
$$4x^2 - 5x + 14 = 0$$

Now, use the quadratic formula to solve:

$$x = \frac{-b \pm \sqrt{b^2 - 4ac}}{2a} \rightarrow$$
$$x = \frac{-(-5) \pm \sqrt{(-5)^2 - 4(4)(14)}}{2(4)} \rightarrow$$
$$x = \frac{5 \pm \sqrt{25 - 224}}{8}$$

Since the discriminant (the $\sqrt{25 - 224}$ term) is negative, there will be 0 real solutions.

## Practice Drill #2—Solving Advanced Equations

*(If timing, take about 12 minutes to complete.)*

1. If $x^2 - 14x + 49 = 0$, what is the value of $x$?

(A) 3
(B) 5
(C) 7
(D) 9

2. If $n^2 - 6n + 9 = 25$, which of the following is a possible value of $n - 3$?

(A) 4
(B) 5
(C) 6
(D) 9

3. If $\frac{3x}{6-x} = x$, what are the value(s) of $x$ that would satisfy the equation?

(A) 1 and −6
(B) 2 and −3
(C) 3 and 0
(D) 6 and 4

4. What is the largest value of $n$ that satisfies the following equation?

$$\frac{(n+4)(n-6)}{2} = 0$$

(A) −4
(B) −6
(C) 4
(D) 6

5. $f(x) = \frac{2x-13}{2x^2-16x+32}$

For what value of $x$ is the above function $f(x)$ undefined?

(A) −8
(B) −4
(C) 2
(D) 4

6. What are the solutions to the equation $5x^2 - 7x + 1 = 0$?

(A) $\frac{5 \pm \sqrt{23}}{14}$
(B) $\frac{7 \pm \sqrt{29}}{10}$
(C) $\frac{3 \pm \sqrt{37}}{11}$
(D) $\frac{12 \pm \sqrt{43}}{7}$

7. $\sqrt{x+4} = -4$

What is the set of real solutions for the above equation?

(A) 2 only
(B) 2 and −4
(C) 4 and −2
(D) There are no real solutions.

8. What is the remainder when $2x^2 + 3x - 1$ is divided by $x - 4$?

(A) $\frac{43}{x-4}$
(B) $\frac{22}{x-4}$
(C) $\frac{16}{x-1}$
(D) 0

9. If $\sqrt{x+5}=4$, what is the value of $x$?

(A) −9
(B) −5
(C) 2
(D) 11

10. $\frac{3x^2-27}{3x-9}=5$

What value of $x$ is a solution to the equation above?

(A) 2
(B) 5
(C) 6
(D) 18

## Solutions

1. **(C)** Solve by factoring:

$$x^2-14x+49=0\rightarrow$$
$$(x-7)(x-7)=0$$

So, 7 is the only solution.

2. **(B)** Factor the expression, then use the square root method:

$$n^2-6n+9=25\rightarrow$$
$$(n-3)(n-3)=25\rightarrow$$
$$\sqrt{(n-3)^2}=\sqrt{25}\rightarrow$$
$$n-3=5$$

3. **(C)** Plugging and chugging would be a viable approach on this problem, but you can also solve it fairly easily by cross multiplying and then solving for $x$.

$$\frac{3x}{6-x}=x\rightarrow$$
$$3x=x(6-x)\rightarrow$$
$$3x=6x-x^2\rightarrow$$
$$x^2-3x=0\rightarrow$$
$$x^2=3x\rightarrow$$

So zero is a solution.
Also, 3 is a solution because

$$x^2=3x\rightarrow x=3.$$

4. **(D)** This is easiest to solve by plugging in the answers. Start with the largest choice and work your way smaller if needed:

$$\frac{(n+4)(n-6)}{2} = 0 \rightarrow$$

$$\frac{(6+4)(6-6)}{2} = 0 \rightarrow$$

$$\frac{10 \times 0}{2} = 0$$

So, 6 works. Alternatively, keep in mind that a polynomial written in factored form automatically shows what the zeroes are.

5. **(D)** For the function $f(x) = \dfrac{2x - 13}{2x^2 - 16x + 32}$ to be undefined, the denominator must be zero. So, set up an equation in which just the denominator is equal to zero.

$$2x^2 - 16x + 32 = 0 \rightarrow$$

$$x^2 - 8x + 16 = 0 \rightarrow$$

$$(x-4)(x-4) = 0$$

So, if $x$ equals 4, the denominator will equal zero and the function will be undefined.

6. **(B)** Use the quadratic formula to solve this equation.

$$5x^2 - 7x + 1 = 0 \rightarrow$$

$$x = \frac{-b \pm \sqrt{b^2 - 4ac}}{2a} \rightarrow$$

$$x = \frac{-(-7) \pm \sqrt{(-7)^2 - 4(5)(1)}}{2(5)} \rightarrow$$

$$x = \frac{7 \pm \sqrt{49 - 20}}{10} \rightarrow$$

$$x = \frac{7 \pm \sqrt{29}}{10}$$

7. **(D)** Plugging in the potential answers of 2, 4, −2, and −4 is an excellent way to solve the problem. You can also solve it algebraically:

$$\sqrt{x+4} = -4 \rightarrow$$

$$(\sqrt{x+4})^2 = (-4)^2 \rightarrow$$

$$x + 4 = 16 \rightarrow$$

$$x = 12$$

Now, when you plug 12 back in to the original equation, you can see that it does not work:

$$\sqrt{x+4} = -4 \rightarrow$$

$$\sqrt{12+4} = -4 \rightarrow$$

$$4 \neq -4$$

In fact, if you notice that in the original equation it states that the square root of $x + 4$ must equal a negative number, you can stop right there since the least that the square root of the number could be would be zero. We would need imaginary numbers to arrive at a negative solution.

8. **(A)** Use synthetic division to solve:

$$\begin{array}{r|rrr} 4 & 2 & 3 & -1 \\ & & 8 & 44 \\ \hline & 2 & 11 & 43 \end{array}$$

Take the 43 and divide it by $x - 4$ to get the remainder of $\frac{43}{x-4}$.

9. **(D)** Plugging in the answers will work well on this problem. Also, you can solve it algebraically:

$$\sqrt{x+5} = 4 \rightarrow$$
$$(\sqrt{x+5})^2 = 4^2 \rightarrow$$
$$x + 5 = 16 \rightarrow$$
$$x = 11$$

10. **(A)** You could use plugging in the answers to solve this, but you could also do it algebraically.

$$\frac{3x^2 - 27}{3x - 9} = 5 \rightarrow$$

Divide the numerator and the denominator of the left side by 3 $\rightarrow$

$$\frac{x^2 - 9}{x - 3} = 5 \rightarrow$$
$$\frac{(x+3)(x-3)}{(x-3)} = 5 \rightarrow$$
$$\frac{(x+3)\cancel{(x-3)}}{\cancel{(x-3)}} = 5 \rightarrow$$

$x + 3 = 5 \rightarrow x = 2$ (Note that 3 is an extraneous solution if you plug it back into the original equation.)

## Advanced Math—Zeros, Parabolas, and Polynomial Graphing

### Zeros of a Function

The *root* or *zero* of a function is the value of $x$ for which a function like $f(x)$ has a value of zero. When an equation of the function is provided, you can identify the zeros by solving for when $f(x)$ is 0 (i.e., finding the $x$-intercepts or solutions). When a graph of the function is provided, you can identify the zeros by looking at the values of $x$ for which the $f(x)$values have coordinates at 0.

### Example

What are the zeros of the parabola of the equation $f(x) = x^2 - 6x + 5$ and with the graph below?

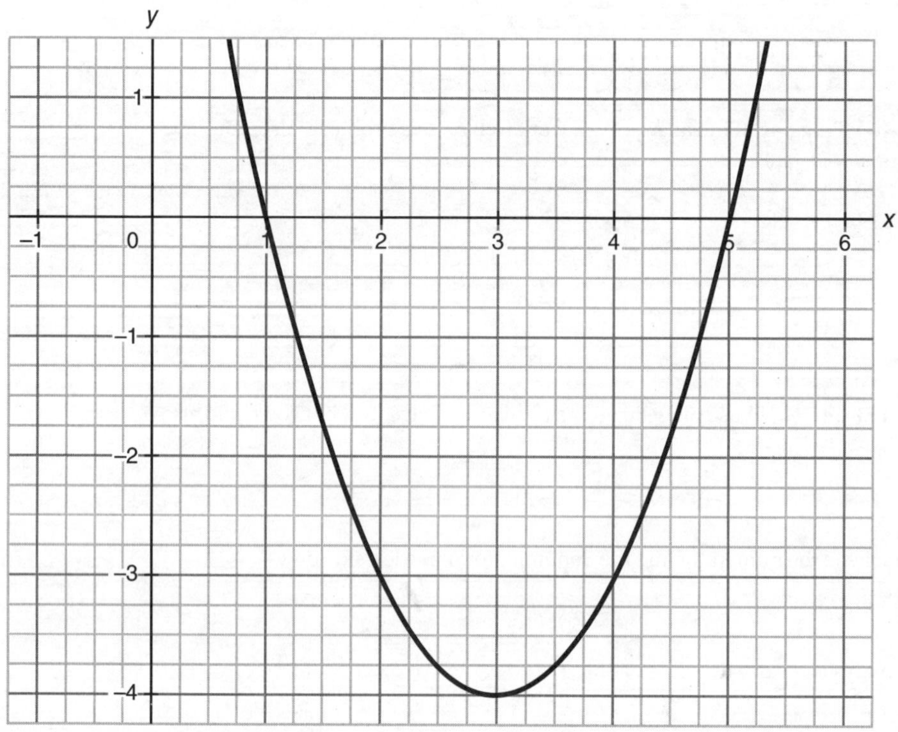


### Solution

The first way you can find the zeros is by factoring the equation:

$$f(x) = x^2 - 6x + 5 \rightarrow$$

$$f(x) = (x - 5)(x - 1)$$

So, there are zeros at $x$ values of 5 and 1 since plugging those two values in to the function will cause the value of $f(x)$ to be 0.

The second way you can find the zeros is by examining the graph above. Look at the points where the function intersects the $x$-axis, since the value of $f(x)$, or $y$, will be zero there. At points (1, 0) and (5, 0), the function intersects the $x$-axis, so 5 and 1 are zeros of the function.

### Practice

1. What are the zeros of the function $y = (x + 3)(x - 5)$?
2. What are the zeros of the function $f(x) = x^2 + 4x - 12$?

3. What are the zeros of the function graphed below?

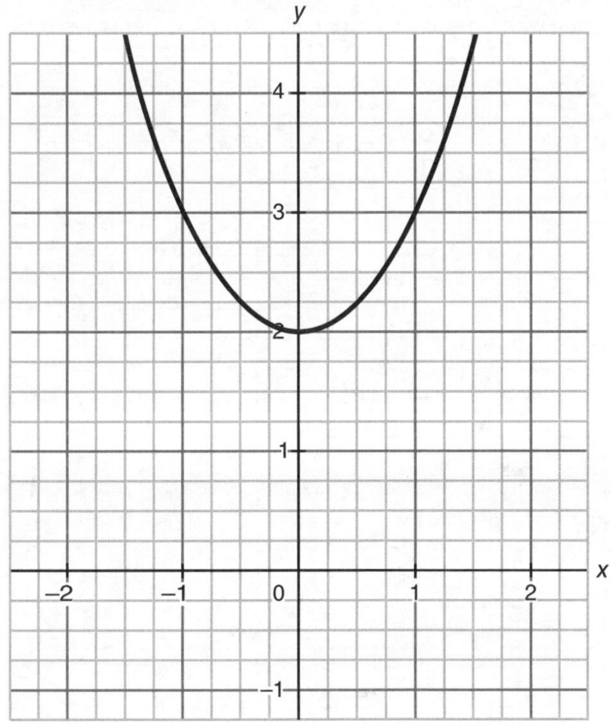


4. What are the zeros of $f(x) = x(x - 1)(x + 2)(x - 9)$?

## Solutions

1. Since the function is already in factored form, it is easy to identify which values of $x$ would make $y$ have a value of zero. If $x$ is either $-3$ or 5, $y$ will be zero. Therefore, the zeros are $-3$ and 5.

2. Factor the equation to identify the zeros:

$$f(x) = x^2 + 4x - 12 \rightarrow$$
$$f(x) = (x + 6)(x - 2)$$

   So, the zeros are at $-6$ and 2.

3. Since the function does not intersect the $x$-axis, there are no points at which $y$ will be zero. Therefore, there are NO real zeros in the function.

4. Examine the equation to determine the values of $x$ that will make $f(x) = 0$. Fortunately, the equation is already factored, $f(x) = x(x - 1)(x + 2)(x - 9)$, making it easier to identify the zeros. 0, 1, $-2$, and 9 if plugged in for $x$ would all make the function equal to 0, so these numbers are all zeros of the function.

### Parabola Graphing

A parabola is a function with a u-shaped curve that has certain properties. Here is an example of a parabola with the equation $y = 2(x - 3)^2 + 1$:

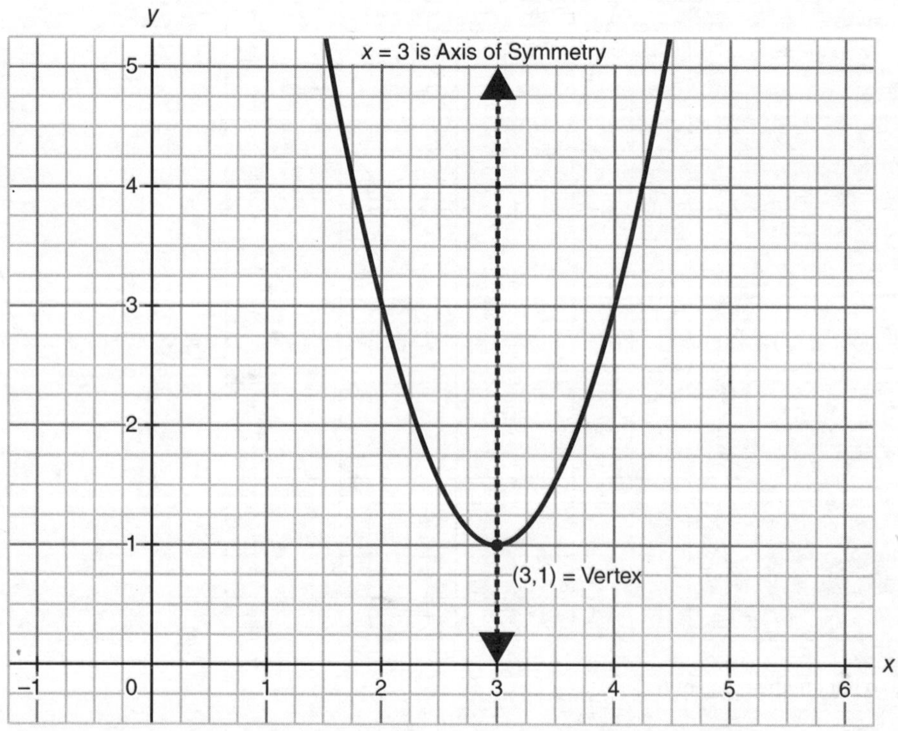


- The vertex form of a parabola is $y = a(x - h)^2 + k$. In the above example, $y = 2(x - 3)^2 + 1$ is written in vertex form, with $a = 2$, $h = 3$, and $k = 1$.
- The value of the constant $a$ determines the direction of the parabola—if it is positive, it opens upward, and if it is negative, it opens downward. In the example, $a$ is $+2$, so the parabola opens upward.
- The vertex (the bottom point of the u-shape) has the coordinates $(h, k)$. The vertex of the parabola in the example is $(3, 1)$.
- The $x$-coordinate of the vertex gives the *axis of symmetry* for the parabola. The axis of symmetry in the example is $x = 3$.

The SAT Math questions involving parabolas focus heavily on identify the vertex of a parabola. There are four major approaches to doing this.

**Method 1: Identify points $h$ and $k$ when the parabola is in vertex form.**

### Example

What is the vertex of the parabola with the equation $y = 3(x - 4)^2 - 7$?

### Solution

Notice that the equation is already in vertex form, making it easy to identify the vertex:

$$y = a(x - h)^2 + k \rightarrow$$

$$y = 3(x - 4)^2 - 7$$

Since 4 corresponds to the $h$ and $-7$ corresponds to the $k$, the vertex will be $(4, -7)$.

**Method 2: Use the formula $x = -\frac{b}{2a}$.**

When a parabola is written in the form $y = ax^2 + bx + c$, you can determine the $x$-coordinate of the parabola's vertex by using this formula:

$$x = -\frac{b}{2a}$$

Then, you can plug the $x$ value back in to the original equation to solve for the $y$ value of the vertex.

### Example

What is the vertex of the parabola with the equation $y = 4x^2 - 2x - 3$?

### Solution

Find the $a$ and $b$ values in the equation and then plug them into the formula. Constant $a$ is 4 and constant $b$ is $-2$. Now, plug them in:

$$x = -\frac{b}{2a} \rightarrow$$

$$x = -\frac{(-2)}{2(4)} = \frac{2}{8} = \frac{1}{4}$$

Now that we know the $x$-coordinate of the vertex, we can plug this value back into the original equation to solve for the $y$-coordinate of the vertex:

$$y = 4x^2 - 2x - 3 \rightarrow$$

$$y = 4\left(\frac{1}{4}\right)^2 - 2\left(\frac{1}{4}\right) - 3 \rightarrow$$

$$y = 4\left(\frac{1}{16}\right) - \frac{1}{2} - 3 \rightarrow$$

$$y = \frac{1}{4} - \frac{1}{2} - 3 = -3\frac{1}{4}$$

So, the vertex of the parabola is $\left(\frac{1}{4}, -3\frac{1}{4}\right)$.

**Method 3: Identify the $x$ value halfway between the zeros.**

**Example**

What is the $x$-coordinate of the vertex of the parabola with the equation $y = (x - 6)(x - 2)$?

**Solution**

The zeros of the parabola are at $x$-coordinates of 6 and 2. The $x$-coordinate of the vertex comes halfway between these two zeros. So the $x$-coordinate of the vertex will be at 4 since it is halfway between 6 and 2. Here is a graph of the parabola to more easily visualize this:

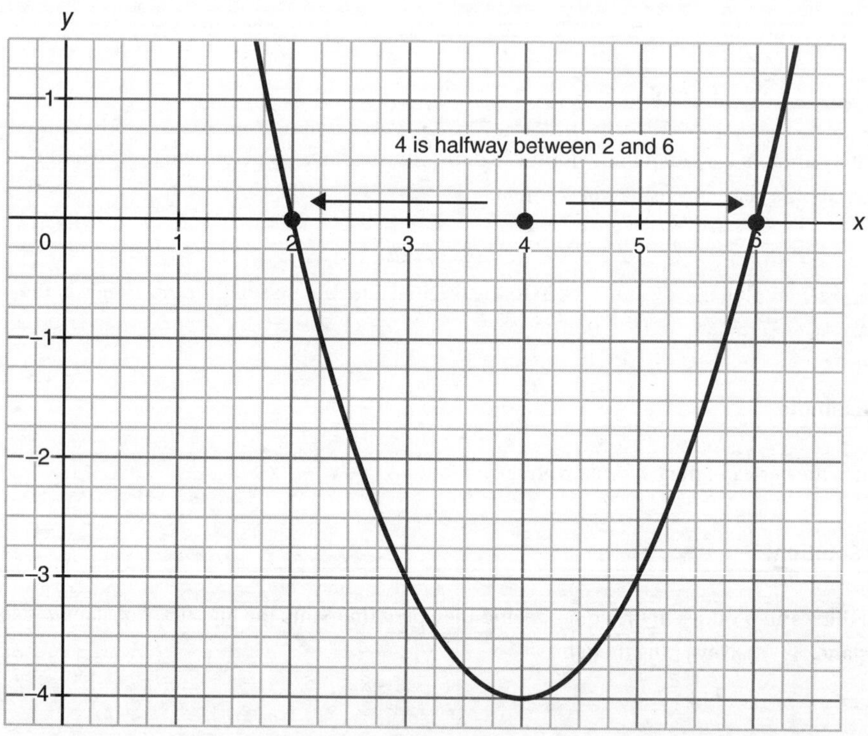

**Method 4: Identify the vertex from the graph.**

## Example

What is the vertex of the parabola with the graph below?

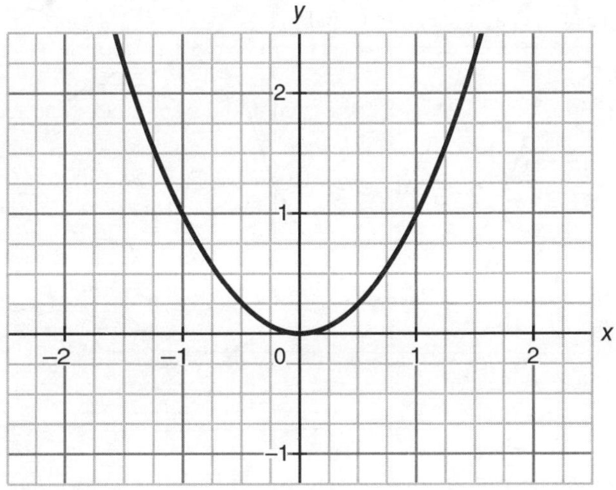


## Solution

Look for the very bottom point of the parabola to identify the vertex. The parabola has a bottom at (0, 0), so the vertex of the parabola is at (0, 0):

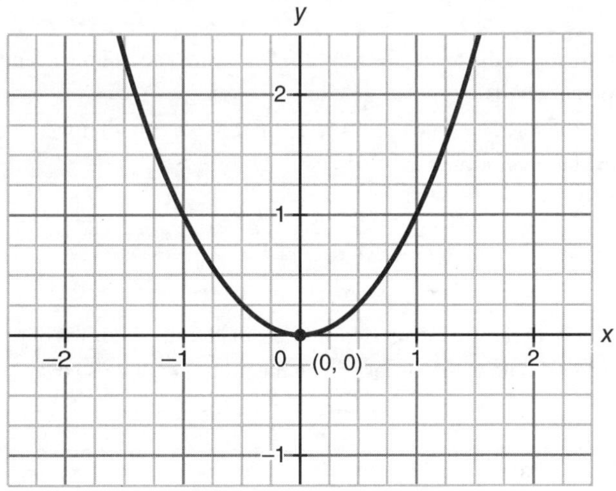

## Practice

1. Does the parabola $y = 3(x - 2)^2 + 9$ open upwards or downwards?
2. What is the vertex of the parabola with the equation $y = 4(x - 1)^2 + 6$?
3. What is the $x$-coordinate of the vertex of a parabola with the equation $y = (x + 4)(x - 8)$?
4. What is the $x$-coordinate of the vertex of a parabola with the equation $y = 3x^2 - 8x + 4$?
5. What is the vertex of the parabola graphed below?

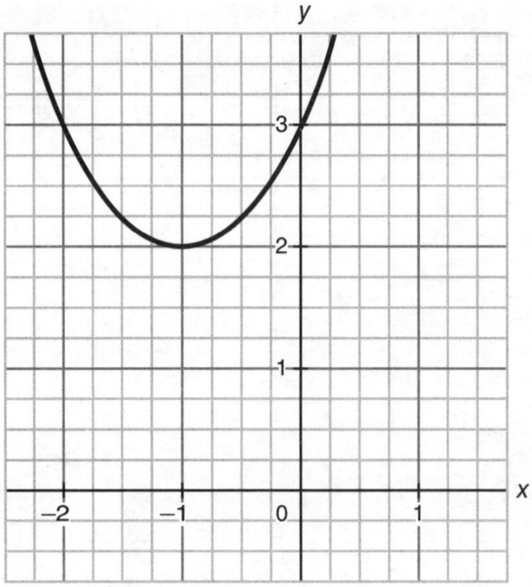


## Solutions

1. The parabola is already in the form $y = a(x - h)^2 + k$, with 3 equalling $a$. Since $a$ is positive, the parabola will open upwards.
2. The parabola is in the form $y = a(x - h)^2 + k$. From this, we can identify the values of the constants $h$ and $k$ to identify the vertex.

$$y = a(x - h)^2 + k \rightarrow$$
$$y = 4(x - 1)^2 + 6 \rightarrow ?$$
$$(h, k) = (1, 6)$$

3. Since the equation is already in factored form, we can identify the zeros of $y = (x + 4)(x - 8)$ as $-4$ and 8. The $x$-coordinate of the vertex will be the midpoint of these two values:

$$\frac{-4 + 8}{2} = \frac{4}{2} = 2$$

4. Use the formula $x = -\frac{b}{2a}$ to solve:

$$y = ax^2 + bx + c \rightarrow$$
$$y = 3x^2 - 8x + 4 \rightarrow$$
$$x = -\frac{b}{2a} \rightarrow \frac{-8}{2(3)} = \frac{8}{6} = \frac{4}{3}$$

5. From the graph, we can identify that the vertex of the parabola is at its lowest point, $(-1, 2)$.

### Function Transformations

It is useful on some SAT Math problems to know how changes to a function's equation can impact its graph. Here are some key relationships to know.

Suppose we have the function $y = x^2$ with the graph below:

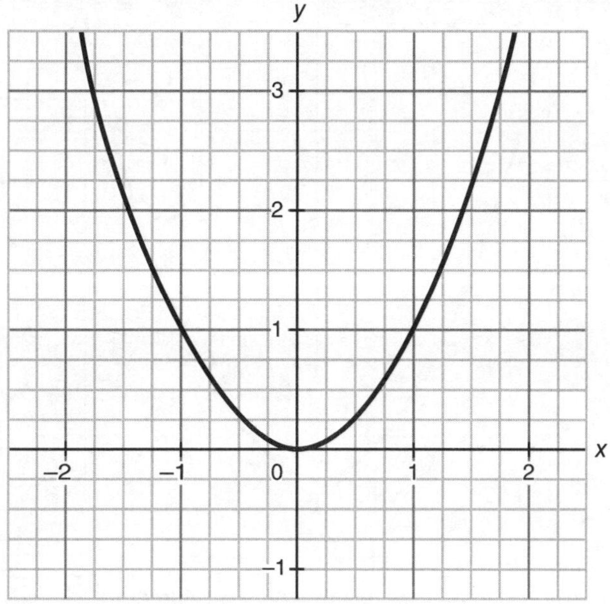


**Treat *h* and *k* as constants for these rules.**

**Rule 1: If you transform $f(x)$ to $f(x) + k$, the function will shift UP *k* units.**

The graph of $y = x^2 + 2$ is this:

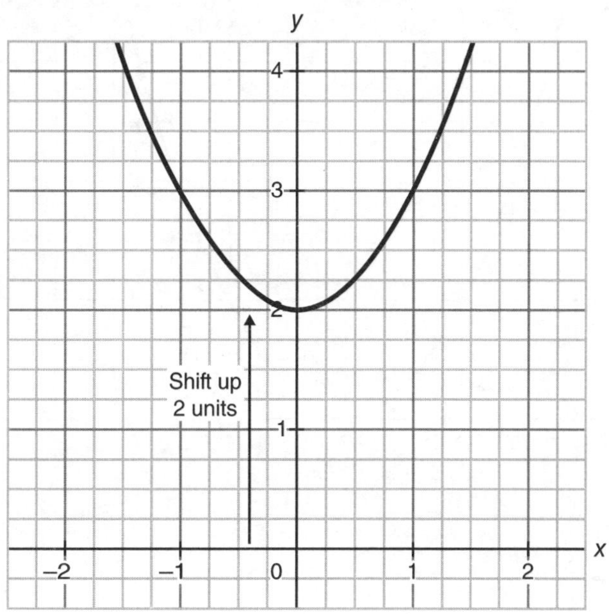

**Rule 2: If you transform $f(x)$ to $f(x) - k$, the function will shift DOWN $k$ units.**

The graph of $y = x^2 - 2$ is this:

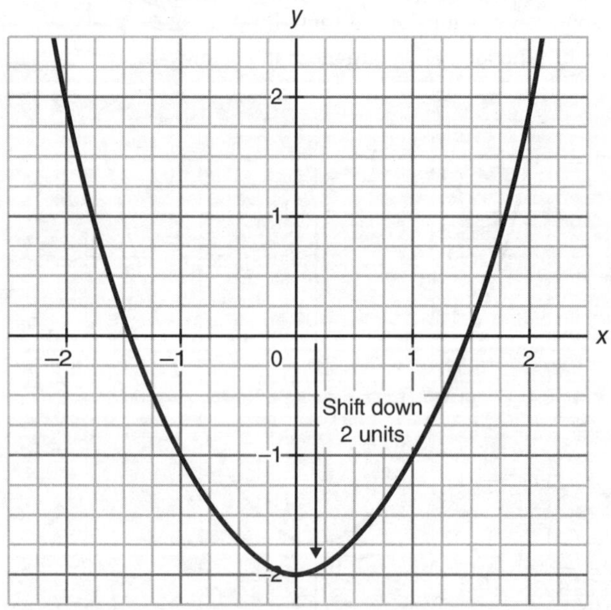


**Rule 3: If you transform $f(x)$ to $f(x + h)$, the function will shift LEFT $h$ units.**

The graph of $y = (x + 2)^2$ is this:

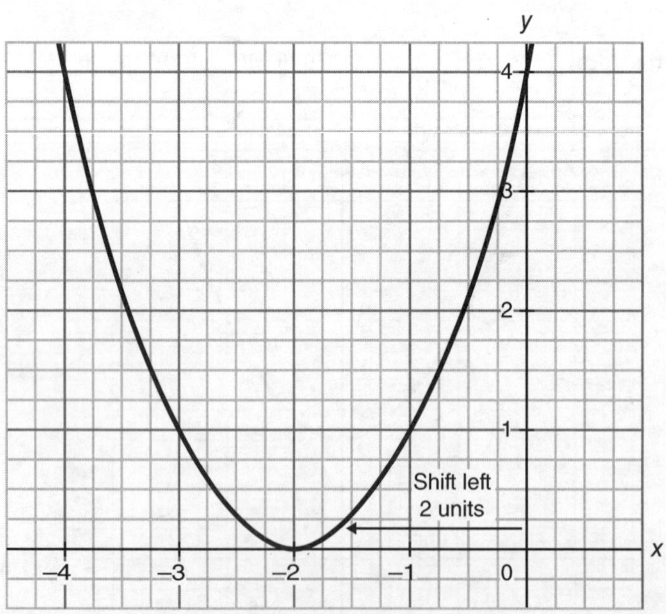

**Rule 4: If you transform $f(x)$ to $f(x - h)$, the function will shift RIGHT $h$ units.**

The graph of $y = (x - 2)^2$ is this:

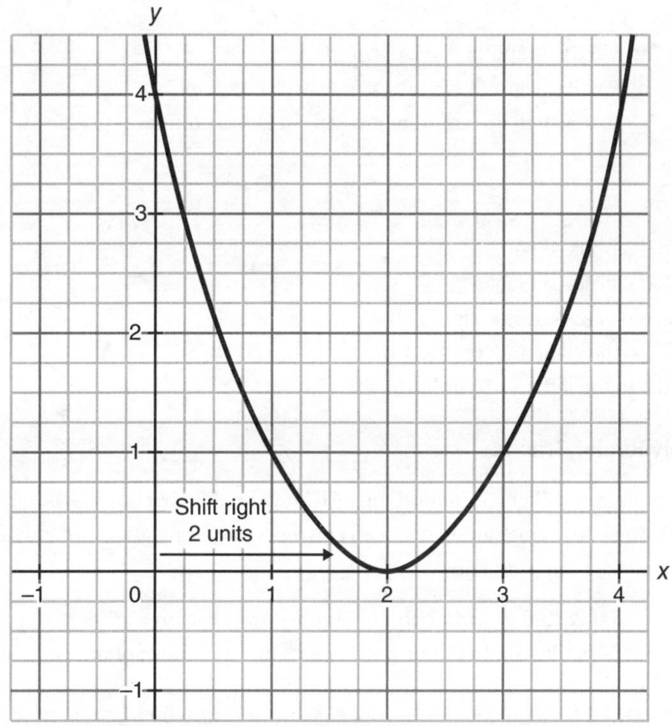


**Rule 5: If you transform $f(x)$ to $-f(x)$, the function will be REFLECTED across the $x$-axis.**

The graph of $y = -x^2$ is this:

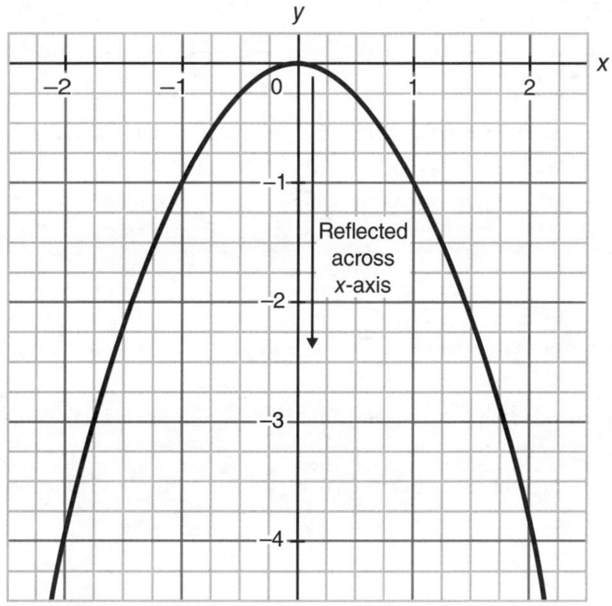

### Practice

1. If $y = 3x^3$, how will the graph of $y = 3x^3 - 5$ compare?
2. If $y = 4x^2$, how will the graph of $y = 4(x + 2)^2$ compare?
3. If $y = -2x^3$, how will the graph of $y = 2x^3$ compare?
4. If $y = 6x^2 - 5$, how will the graph of $y = 6(x - 1)^2 - 8$ compare?
5. If $y = 2(x - 4)^5 + 5$, how will the graph of $y = 2(x + 1)^5 - 5$ compare?

### Solutions

1. It will be shifted 5 units down.
2. It will be shifted 2 units to the left.
3. It will be reflected across the $x$-axis.
4. It will be 1 unit to the right and 3 units down.
5. It will be 5 units to the left and 10 units down.

### Visualizing Polynomial Graphs

Most of the functions you will encounter on the SAT Math are lines or parabolas. Occasionally, there will be questions involving more advanced concepts about the graphs of polynomial functions. Here are some key things to know.

**Consider a polynomial with the term with the highest power term $ax^n$.**

- The greatest possible number of turns (changes in $y$ direction) of this function will be at most $n - 1$.
- If the constant $a$ is positive, the function will ultimately point upwards as the $x$ values increase; if the constant $a$ is negative, the function will ultimately point downwards as the $x$ values increase.
- If the exponent $n$ is even, the ends of the function go the same direction; if the exponent $n$ is odd, the ends of the function go in different directions.

#### Example 1

Consider the polynomial $y = x^3 - 7x^2 + 7x + 15$.

- How many times will the polynomial turn with respect to its $y$ values?
- Will the function ultimately point upwards or downwards?
- Will the ends of the function go in the same or different directions?

#### ✓ Solutions

The greatest number exponential value in the polynomial is $x^3$; so the greatest possible number of turns it can have will be $3 - 1 = 2$.

Since the coefficient of $x^3$ is positive 1, the function will ultimately increase as the $x$ values increase.

Since the greatest exponent in the function, 3, is odd, the ends of the function go in different directions.

All of this is easiest to see in the graph below:

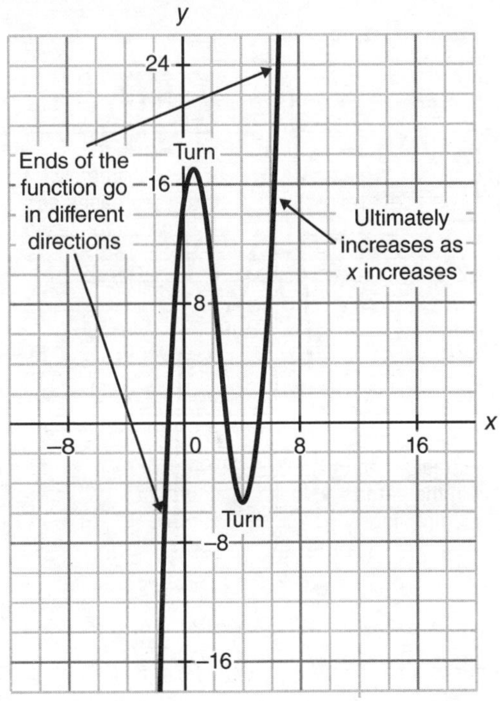


## Example 2

Consider the polynomial $y = -x^4 + 5x^3 - 5x^2 - 5x + 6$.

- How many times will the polynomial turn with respect to its $y$ values?
- Will the function ultimately point upwards or downwards?
- Will the ends of the function go in the same or different directions?

## ✓ Solution

The greatest number exponential value in the polynomial is $x^4$, so the greatest number of turns it can have will be $4 - 1 = 3$.

Since the coefficient of $x^4$ is negative 1, the function will ultimately decrease as the $x$ values increase.

Since the greatest exponent in the function, 4, is even, the ends of the function go in the same direction.

All of this is easiest to see in the graph below:

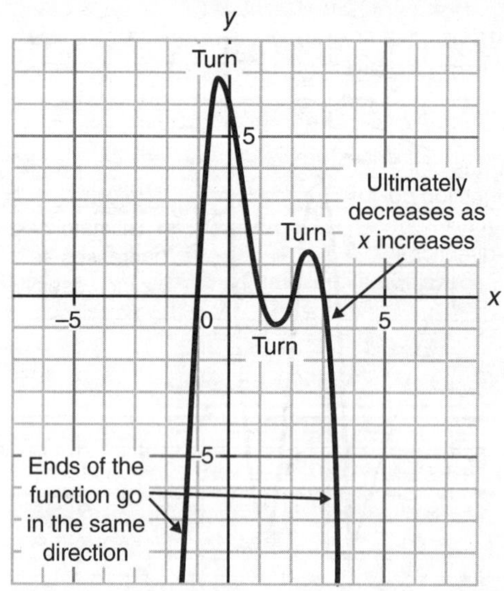


## Practice

1. What is the most number of turns a function of the form $f(x) = ax^2$ can have?
2. Will the end values of the function $f(x) = x^3$ go in the same or different directions?
3. Will the $y$ values in $y = 4x^5$ ultimately point upwards or downwards as $x$ increases?
4. Will the end values of the function $f(x) = x^6 + 3x^5 - 2x$ go in the same or different directions?
5. Will the $y$ values in $y = -6x^5 + 3x^4 + 7x^2 - 9$ ultimately point upwards or downwards as $x$ increases?

## Solutions

1. The greatest number exponential value in the polynomial is $x^2$; so the greatest number of turns it can have will be $2 - 1 = 1$.
2. Since the greatest exponent in the function, 3, is odd, the ends of the function go in different directions.
3. Since the coefficient of $x^5$ is positive 4, the function will ultimately increase as the $x$ values increase.
4. Since the greatest exponent in the function, 6, is even, the ends of the function go in the same direction.
5. Since the coefficient of $x^5$ is negative 6, the function will ultimately decrease as the $x$ values increase.

Many SAT Math problems involving zeros and parabolas will require you to use different concepts in unique ways. Write out what is given and what concepts you know to see how to put it all together.

**SAT Math Strategy**

Integrate your knowledge about zeros, parabolas, and polynomial graphing to solve problems.

### Example 1

$$x^2 + nx + 25 = 0$$

In the quadratic equation above, $n$ is a constant. For what value of $n$ will the function intersect the $x$-axis only once?

(A) $-13$
(B) $-12$
(C) $-11$
(D) $-10$

### Solution

This question does not ask us to do something straightforward like identifying the zeros or the vertex. We need to find out what value of the constant $n$ will make the function have only one point of intersection with the $x$-axis.

To have only one point of intersection with the $x$-axis, the function should have *only one zero*. So, if we could factor the equation and it would have only one zero in factored form, that would tell us what the constant would need to be. Notice that 25 is a perfect square—the square root of it is 5. So, if we were to write the equation in factored form, it would look like this:

$$(x - 5)(x - 5) = 0$$

When the equation is in this form, it has only ONE zero—the number 5. Next, to identify the constant $n$, we can FOIL the equation to see what it looks like in the form described by the problem.

$$(x - 5)(x - 5) = 0$$

$$x^2 - 10x + 25 = 0$$

Based on this, $n$ is $-10$, choice **(D)**. So, we were able to integrate some of the different concepts we know about zeros to solve this problem.

## Example 2

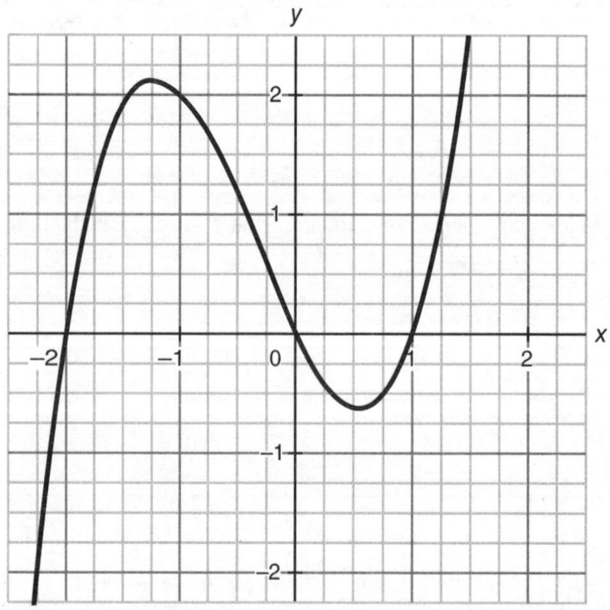


The graph above is represented by which of the following equations?

(A) $y = x(x + 2)(x - 1)$
(B) $y = x^2(x + 1)(x - 2)$
(C) $y = x(x - 2)(x + 1)$
(D) $y = x^2(x + 2)(x - 1)$

## Solution

We can integrate our knowledge about zeros and polynomial graphing to solve this problem. First, the ends of the function go in *different* directions, so the largest exponential value in the function must be *odd*. Based on this, we can eliminate choices (B) and (D) since when they are written in expanded form, the largest exponential value would be $x^4$. Choices (A) and (C) could potentially work since when they are written in expanded form, the largest exponential value would be $x^3$.

Now that we know it must be either choice (A) or (C), we can identify the zeros of the function from the graph: they are −2, 0, and 1. This makes choice **(A)** correct with respect to zeros of the function, since the outside term $x$ would work with 0, the term $(x + 2)$ would work with −2, and the term $(x - 1)$ would work with 1. Therefore, the correct answer is **(A)**.

## Practice Drill—Zeros, Parabolas, and Polynomial Graphing

*(If timing, take about 12 minutes to complete.)*

1. How many zeros does the function $y = x^3 + 2$, portrayed in the graph below, have?

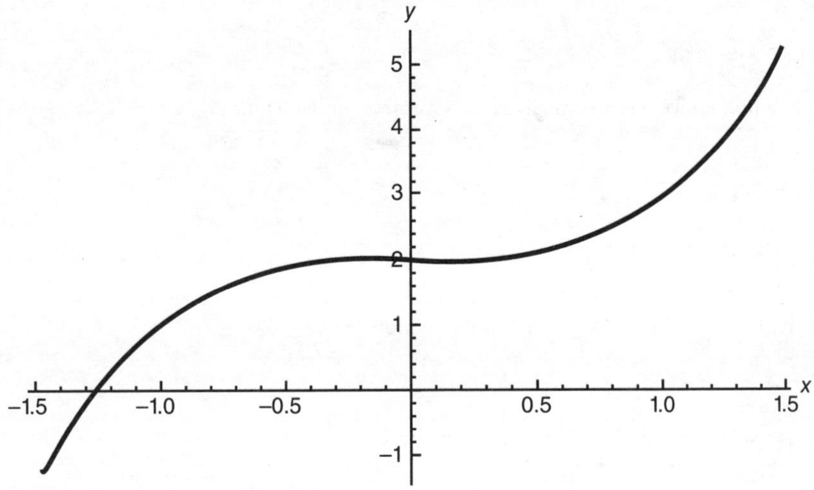


(A) 0
(B) 1
(C) 2
(D) 3

2. $f(x) = (x + 4)(x - 6)$

In the function above, what is the straight-line distance in units in the *xy*-coordinate plane between the function's zeros?

(A) 4
(B) 6
(C) 10
(D) 24

3. What is the *y*-intercept of the function $y = x^2 - 4$?

(A) −4
(B) −2
(C) 1
(D) 4

4. What is the vertex in the parabola with the equation $\frac{y+4}{2} = (x-5)^2$?

(A) (5, 4)
(B) (−5, −4)
(C) (−5, 4)
(D) (5, −4)

5. What are the $x$-intercepts of the function $f(x) = x^2 - 3x - 10$?

(A) $-2$ and 5
(B) $-2$ and $-5$
(C) 2 and 5
(D) 10 and 2

6. $y = (x - 3)(x + 5)$

The function above has a vertical axis of symmetry on which line?

(A) $x = -5$
(B) $x = -3$
(C) $x = -1$
(D) $x = 15$

7. Which of the following is a graph of the equation $y = x^2 - 3$?

(A)

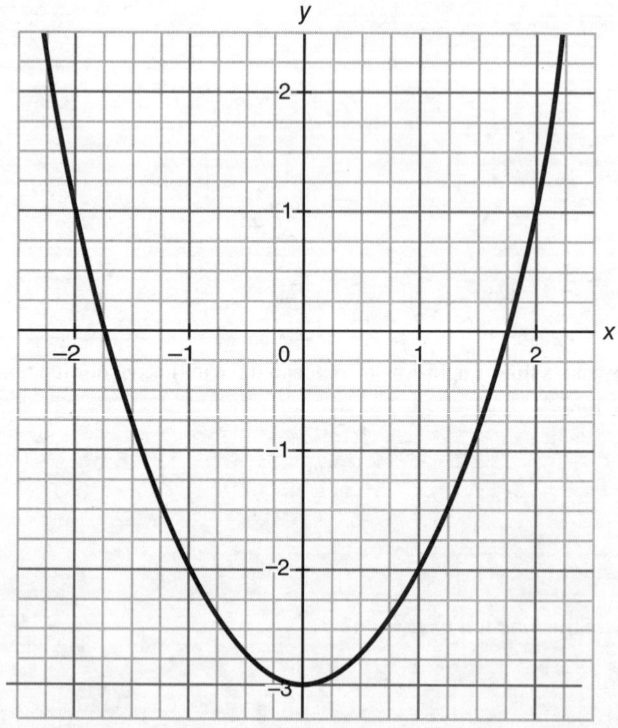

(B)

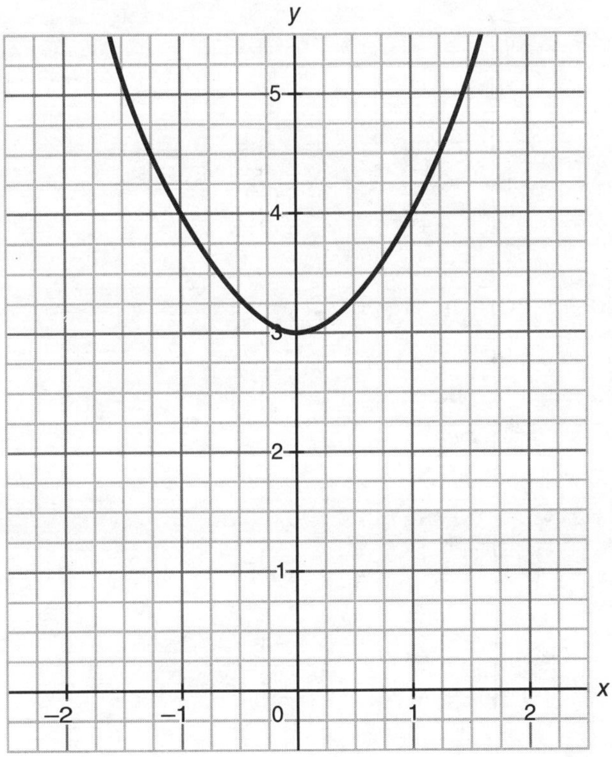


(C)

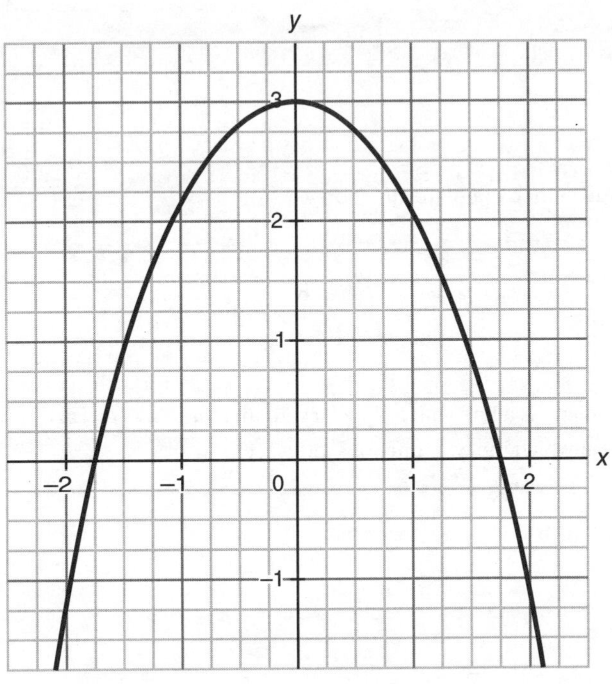

(D)

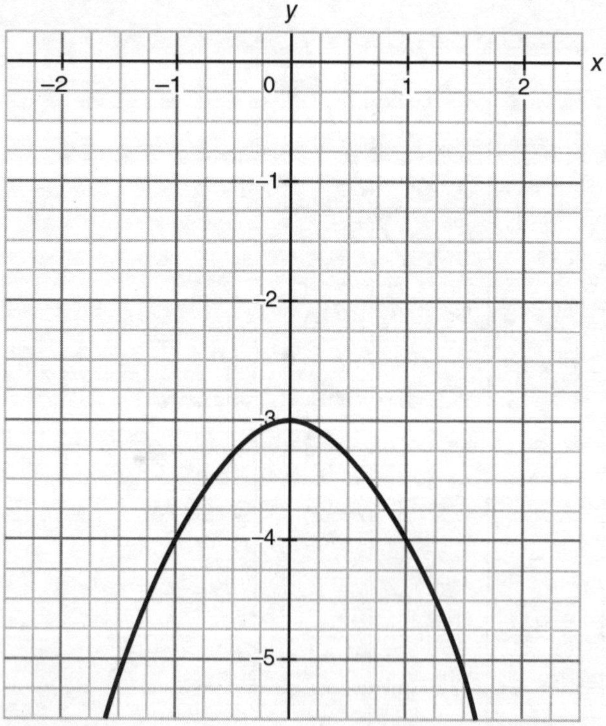


8. Which of the following functions intersects the $x$-axis at exactly 3 points?

(A) $y = x^2 - 3$
(B) $y = x(x - 2)(x + 3)$
(C) $y = (x + 4)^3$
(D) $y = 5(x - 2)(x - 2)$

9. What is the $y$ value of the $y$-intercept of the function $y = (5)^x$?

(A) 0
(B) 1
(C) 2
(D) 3

10. If $f(x) = (x - 5)^2 + 4$ and $g(x)$ is a line with a slope of zero that intersects $f(x)$ at only one point, what is the point at which the two functions intersect?

(A) (−3, −4)
(B) (−2, 5)
(C) (0, 8)
(D) (5, 4)

## Solutions

1. **(B)** From the graph, you can see that the function only intersects the $x$-axis at one point. Therefore, there is just one zero of the function.

2. **(C)** The function is already in factored form, so we can see that the zeros are at $-4$ and 6. So, to find the distance between the two zeros, just measure the difference between $-4$ and 6 on the $x$-axis. This will be:

$$6-(-4) = 10$$

3. **(A)** To find the $y$-intercept, we must find the $y$ value when $x$ is equal to zero. So, plug zero in for $x$ to solve:

$$y = x^2 - 4 \rightarrow$$
$$y = 0^2 - 4 \rightarrow$$
$$y = -4$$

4. **(D)** Manipulate the equation to get it in the form $y = a(x - h)^2 + k$ so the vertex can be easily identified:

$$\frac{y+4}{2} = (x-5)^2 \rightarrow$$
$$y + 4 = 2(x-5)^2 \rightarrow$$
$$y = 2(x-5)^2 - 4$$

Since the vertex corresponds to $(h, k)$, the vertex will be $(5, -4)$.

5. **(A)** Factor the function to identify the zeros—these are the same as the $x$-intercepts of the function since they are the points at which the $y$ value is zero.

$$f(x) = x^2 - 3x - 10 \rightarrow$$
$$f(x) = (x-5)(x+2)$$

Therefore, the $x$-intercepts are $-2$ and 5.

6. **(C)** The vertical axis of symmetry will be the line that bisects the parabola through the vertex. Find the $x$-coordinate of the vertex and make an equation in which every $x$ value is equal to that point. The zeros of $y = (x - 3)(x + 5)$ are 3 and $-5$, so the $x$-coordinate of the vertex will be halfway between them at $-1$. So, the vertical axis of symmetry will be $x = -1$.

7. **(A)** The equation is already in the form $y = a(x - h)^2 + k$, which makes it easy to identify the vertex and the direction of the parabola. The vertex is $(0, -3)$ and $a$ is $+1$, so the parabola will open upward. The parabola graphed in choice **(A)** has this vertex and direction.

8. **(B)** Determine which of the four functions has three zeros:

   $y = x^2 - 3$ has 2 zeros at $\sqrt{3}$ and $-\sqrt{3}$.

   $y = x(x-2)(x+3)$ has 3 zeros at 0, 2, and $-3$.

   $y = (x+4)^3$ has 1 zero at $-4$.

   $y = 5(x-2)(x-2)$ has 1 zero at $+2$.

   So, choice **(B)** is correct.

9. **(B)** The $y$-intercept for this function is the point at which the $x$ value is 0. So, plug 0 in for $x$ to see the corresponding $y$ value.

$$y = (5)^x \rightarrow$$

$$y = 5^0 = 1$$

10. **(D)** The two functions will intersect at the vertex of the parabola—if the flat, horizontal line intersected above the vertex, it would intersect at two points. Since the function is already in the form $y = a(x - h)^2 + k$, the vertex of $f(x) = (x - 5)^2 + 4$ can be identified as (5, 4). This is the point at which the functions will intersect.

## Advanced Math—Function Interpretation and Manipulation

### Putting Variables in Terms of Other Variables

**SAT Math Strategy**

When asked for the value of a variable or an expression, manipulate the equation to isolate that variable or expression.

#### Example 1

The energy, $E$, of a planet in an elliptical orbit around the sun is given by the equation

$$E = -\frac{GmM}{2a}$$

in which $G$ is the gravitational constant, $M$ is the mass of the sun, $m$ is the mass of an orbiting planet, and $a$ is the length of the semimajor axis of the ellipse made by the planetary orbit. What is the value of a planet's mass in terms of the other values?

#### Solution

Typically, when you solve an equation, you find the numerical value of $x$ or some other variable. In a question like this, you should isolate the variable for mass, $m$, to see what $m$ is "in terms of" the other variables.

$$E = -\frac{GmM}{2a} \rightarrow$$

Multiply both sides by $2a \rightarrow$

$$2aE = -GmM \rightarrow$$

Divide both sides by $-GM \rightarrow$

$$m = -\frac{2aE}{GM}$$

### Example 2

What is the value of $2n - 1$ in the equation below?

$$\frac{2n-1}{3} + 11 = 8n - 4$$

### Solution

As a general rule, *when the SAT asks you to find the value of an expression, there will be a straightforward way to find it by treating the expression as a whole unit.* This problem is no exception. We do not need to solve for $n$ individually—instead, we can manipulate the equation to isolate the expression $2n - 1$:

$$\frac{2n-1}{3} + 11 = 8n - 4 \rightarrow$$

Factor the right side $\rightarrow$

$$\frac{(2n-1)}{3} + 11 = 4(2n - 1) \rightarrow$$

Multiply both sides by 3 $\rightarrow$

$$(2n - 1) + 33 = 12(2n - 1) \rightarrow$$

Subtract $(2n - 1)$ from both sides $\rightarrow$

$$33 = 11(2n - 1) \rightarrow$$
$$3 = (2n - 1)$$

So, the value of $2n - 1$ is 3.

## Identifying Constants

**SAT Math Strategy**

Recognize that the SAT will make it easy to identify constant terms.

### Example 1

If $(x + 4)^2 + 5 = ax^2 + bx + c$, what is the sum of the constants $a$, $b$, and $c$?

### Solution

You do not need to use any special formulas to solve this. Just expand the left side of the expression and simplify so you can identify the constants $a$, $b$, and $c$:

$$(x + 4)^2 + 5 \rightarrow$$
$$(x + 4)(x + 4) + 5 \rightarrow$$
$$x^2 + 4x + 4x + 16 + 5 \rightarrow$$
$$x^2 + 8x + 16 + 5 \rightarrow$$
$$x^2 + 8x + 21$$

So,

$$a = 1,\ b = 8, \text{ and } c = 21$$

$$1 + 8 + 21 = 30$$

### Example 2

$$f(x) = (x - 4)(x + 11)$$

In the equation above, which of these values is displayed as a constant or constants?

(A) $y$-intercepts
(B) $x$-intercepts
(C) $x$-coordinate of the vertex
(D) $y$-coordinate of the vertex

### Solution

In the function, we see the numbers 4 and 11 displayed as constants. What do we know about this function based on what we have previously covered? The *zeros* of the function are going to be 4 and $-11$. Since a zero is where the function intersects the $x$-axis, we can say that the $x$-intercepts are displayed as constants in the function.

## Interpreting Functions

**SAT Math Strategy**

Apply what you have already learned about algebra and graphs to interpret functions—you will only be tested on what is reasonable to know.

### Example 1

A company's profit, $P$, for selling $n$ products is modeled by the following function:

$$P = -10n^2 + 300n - 1{,}000$$

How many products should the company sell to achieve its maximum profit?

(A) 10
(B) 12
(C) 15
(D) 18

### Solution

While it would be possible to work your way backwards from the solutions, that could be time-consuming in this case. Instead, use your knowledge of quadratic functions to solve. The maximum of a parabola that is facing downwards can be found at the vertex of the parabola. The $n^2$ term is the largest power term, and it has $-10$ as its coefficient, meaning the parabola will face downwards. So, if we can find the vertex of the parabola, we can find the $x$-coordinate at which the parabola is at its maximum.

Use the formula $x = -\frac{b}{2a}$ to find the vertex since the equation is in standard form. The constant $a$ will be $-10$, and the constant $b$ will be 300, and we can substitute $n$ for $x$.

$$x = -\frac{b}{2a} \rightarrow$$

$$n = -\frac{b}{2a} \rightarrow$$

$$n = -\frac{300}{2(-10)} = \frac{300}{20} = 15$$

Thus, the number of products that should be sold to maximize the profit is 15, choice **(C)**.

### Example 2

In the equation $nx^2 + m = 5x^2 + 4$, there are infinitely many solutions for $x$. What is the product of the constants $m$ and $n$?

(A) 10
(B) 14
(C) 18
(D) 20

### Solution

Think through what you know about equations. For there to be infinitely many solutions, the equation can be formatted so that what is on the left side and the right side are identical. For example, $x + 5 = x + 5$ would have infinitely many solutions since any number can be plugged in for $x$ to make this equation true.

So, let's apply the same idea to this problem. For this equation to have infinitely many solutions, the two sides should be equal:

$$nx^2 + m = 5x^2 + 4 \rightarrow$$

$$5x^2 + 4 = 5x^2 + 4$$

Therefore, $n$ equals 5 and $m$ equals 4. The product comes from multiplying the two numbers together. Thus, the product of 5 and 4 is $5 \times 4 = 20$, choice **(D)**.

## Practice Drill #1—Function Interpretation and Manipulation

*(If timing, take about 12 minutes to complete.)*

1. In the equation $E = mc^2$, what is the value of $c$ in terms of the other values?

(A) $Em$
(B) $\frac{m}{E}$
(C) $\sqrt{\frac{E}{m}}$
(D) $\sqrt{\frac{m}{E^2}}$

2. The formula to model the height, $h$, in meters of an object $t$ seconds after being dropped is $h(t) = -4.9t^2 + h_0$ in which $h_0$ is the height from which the object is dropped. If the height of an object 3 seconds after being dropped is 0, what is the initial height of the object?

(A) 9.8 meters
(B) 17.2 meters
(C) 24.4 meters
(D) 44.1 meters

3. Body mass index is calculated by taking the mass of a person in pounds and the height of a person in inches and plugging these values into this formula:

$$BMI = \frac{mass}{height^2} \times 703$$

What is the mass of a person in terms of the other values?

(A) $mass = \frac{BMI \times height^2}{703}$

(B) $mass = \frac{BMI \times height}{703}$

(C) $mass = \frac{703}{BMI \times height^2}$

(D) $mass = \frac{703}{BMI \times height}$

4. The height of a rock thrown off a ledge relative to the ground beneath the ledge is graphed below.

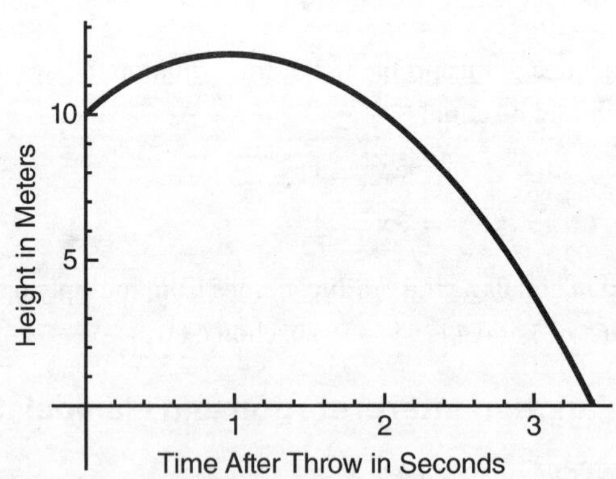


At what time did the rock reach its maximum height?

(A) At the time of the throw
(B) 1 second after the throw
(C) 2 seconds after the throw
(D) 3.5 seconds after the throw

5. If $x - 5 = \frac{2x^2 + ax - 20}{2x + 4}$, what is the value of the constant $a$?

   (A) $-6$
   (B) $-3$
   (C) $\frac{1}{2}$
   (D) 8

6. The moon orbits Earth once approximately every 27 days. Titan, a moon of the planet Saturn, orbits Saturn once approximately every 16 days. For every full planetary orbit the moon of Earth makes, $M$, how many orbits of Saturn (or fractions thereof) will Titan make of Saturn, $T$?

   (A) $T = \frac{16}{27}M$
   (B) $T = \frac{4}{9}M$
   (C) $T = \frac{27}{16}M$
   (D) $T = \frac{9}{4}M$

**Fill-In Practice:** Write your answer in the underlined blank under each question.

7. The number of geese at a lake tripled each year, when compared to the number of geese on January 1 of each year between January 1, 2017, and January 1, 2020. If there were 810 geese on January 1, 2020, how many geese would there have been on January 1, 2017?

   Answer: ________

8. What is the $y$-intercept of the graph of the following equation?

$$y = \frac{2x^2 - 18}{x - 3}$$

   Answer: ________

9. If $2(3x^2 - 4x + 2) = ax^2 + bx + c$, what is the value of $c$?

   Answer: ________

10. $y = \frac{4x^2 - 36}{2x + 6}$

    What is the slope of the line formed by the equation above?

    Answer: ________

## Solutions

1. **(C)** Isolate the $c$ to arrive at your solution:

$$E = mc^2 \rightarrow$$

$$\frac{E}{m} = c^2 \rightarrow$$

$$\sqrt{\frac{E}{m}} = \sqrt{c^2} \rightarrow$$

$$c = \sqrt{\frac{E}{m}}$$

2. **(D)** The value of $h_0$ is the initial height of the object. So, plug in 3 for $t$ and 0 for the final height, $h(t)$:

$$h(t) = -4.9t^2 + h_0 \rightarrow$$
$$0 = -4.9(3)^2 + h_0 \rightarrow$$
$$0 = -44.1 + h_0 \rightarrow$$
$$h_0 = 44.1$$

3. **(A)** Manipulate the equation until mass is isolated.

$$BMI = \frac{mass}{height^2} \times 703 \rightarrow$$
$$\frac{BMI}{703} = \frac{mass}{height^2} \rightarrow$$
$$mass = \frac{BMI \times height^2}{703}$$

4. **(B)** Find the point on the graph where the height is at its maximum:

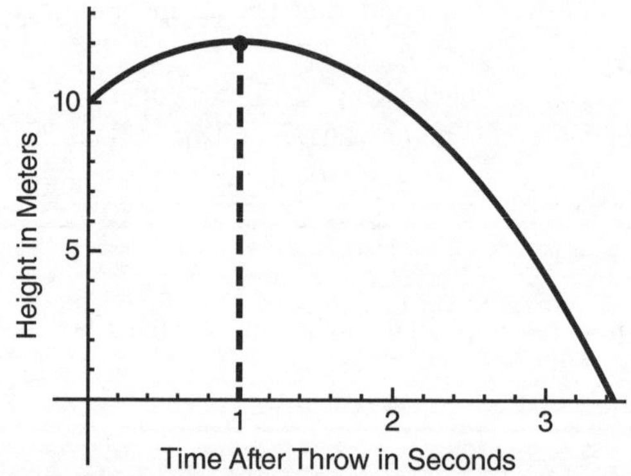


So, the rock reached its maximum height at 1 second after the throw.

5. **(A)**

$$x - 5 = \frac{2x^2 + ax - 20}{2x + 4} \rightarrow$$
$$(x - 5)(2x + 4) = 2x^2 + ax - 20 \rightarrow$$
$$2x^2 - 10x + 4x - 20 = 2x^2 + ax - 20 \rightarrow$$
$$2x^2 - 6x - 20 = 2x^2 + ax - 20$$

The constant $a$ corresponds to $-6$.

6. **(C)** It takes the moon 27 days to make a complete orbit of Earth, and it takes Titan 16 days to make a complete orbit of Saturn. So, if the moon has made one full orbit, 27 days have gone by—in that time, Titan would have made nearly two orbits since it orbits more quickly. To be precise, it would make $\frac{27}{16}$ orbits. Therefore, the answer is choice **(C)**, $T = \frac{27}{16}M$.

Another way to think about this: Titan makes $\frac{1}{16}$ of an orbit in one day. Since it takes the moon 27 days to make a complete orbit, Titan would make $\frac{1}{16} \times 27 = \frac{27}{16}$ of an orbit in the time it takes the moon to make a single orbit.

7. **(30)** Since the number of geese triples each year, work your way backwards to the number of geese in 2017 by taking $\frac{1}{3}$ of each previous year's total.

   In 2020, there were 810 geese.

   In 2019, there would be $\frac{1}{3}$ of 810, which is 270.

   In 2018, there would be $\frac{1}{3}$ of 270, which is 90.

   And in 2017, there would be $\frac{1}{3}$ of 90, which is 30.

8. **(6)**

$$y = \frac{2x^2 - 18}{x - 3} \rightarrow$$

$$y = \frac{2(x+3)(x-3)}{x-3} \rightarrow$$

   Cancel the $x - 3 \rightarrow$

$$y = 2(x+3) \rightarrow$$

$$y = 2x + 6$$

   Since the equation is now in slope-intercept form, we can see that the $y$-intercept is 6. Alternatively, just plug in 0 for $x$ and evaluate the $y$ value.

9. **(4)** Distribute the 2 to put the left-hand side of the equation in a similar form to the right-hand side:

$$2(3x^2 - 4x + 2) = ax^2 + bx + c \rightarrow$$

$$6x^2 - 8x + 4 = ax^2 + bx + c$$

   So, the constant $c$ is equal to the constant 4.

10. **(2)** Manipulate this equation to get it in slope-intercept form:

$$y = \frac{4x^2 - 36}{2x + 6} \rightarrow$$

$$y = \frac{4(x^2 - 9)}{2(x+3)} \rightarrow$$

$$y = 2\frac{(x+3)(x-3)}{(x+3)} \rightarrow$$

$$y = 2\frac{\cancel{(x+3)}(x-3)}{\cancel{(x+3)}} \rightarrow$$

$$y = 2x - 6$$

   So, the slope, $m$, of the line is 2 since the equation is in the form $y = mx + b$.

## Practice Drill #2—Function Interpretation and Manipulation

*(If timing, take about 12 minutes to complete.)*

1. In physics, force, $F$, is equal to the mass, $m$, multiplied by acceleration, $a$:

$$F = ma$$

What is acceleration in terms of force and mass?

(A) $a = F + m$

(B) $a = \frac{m}{F}$

(C) $a = \frac{1}{Fm}$

(D) $a = \frac{F}{m}$

2. In a sphere, the surface area, $S$, is calculated using the formula $S = 4\pi r^2$, where $r$ is the radius of the sphere. What is the value of the radius in terms of the surface area?

(A) $r = \frac{S}{4\pi}$

(B) $r = 16\pi S^2$

(C) $r = \sqrt{\frac{S}{4\pi}}$

(D) $r = \sqrt{\frac{4\pi}{S}}$

3. If $a$ is a positive constant, what is the value of $a$ in the equation below?

$$(2x + a)(3x + a) = 6x^2 + 5ax + 16$$

(A) 4
(B) 5
(C) 6
(D) 30

4. The solute potential of a solution $\Psi_S$ is calculated as follows:

$$\Psi_S = -iCRT$$

In this equation, $i$ is the ionization constant, $C$ is the molar concentration, $R$ is the pressure constant, and $T$ is the temperature in degrees Kelvin. What is the molar concentration in terms of the other values?

(A) $C = -\frac{R\Psi_S}{iT}$

(B) $C = -\frac{TR}{i\Psi_S}$

(C) $C = -\frac{iRT}{\Psi_S}$

(D) $C = -\frac{\Psi_S}{iRT}$

5. The height, $h$, of a ball thrown from the top of a ladder that is 10 feet above the ground, and $t$ seconds after being thrown, is calculated using this function:

$$h(t) = -16t^2 + 20t + 10$$

After how many seconds would the ball reach its maximum height?

(A) 0.25 seconds
(B) 0.48 seconds
(C) 0.625 seconds
(D) 0.895 seconds

6. $(2x - 3y)(4x + y) = 8x^2 + axy + bxy - 3y^2$

In the equation with variables $x$ and $y$ above, what is the sum of the constants $a$ and $b$?

(A) $-10$
(B) $-6$
(C) 4
(D) 12

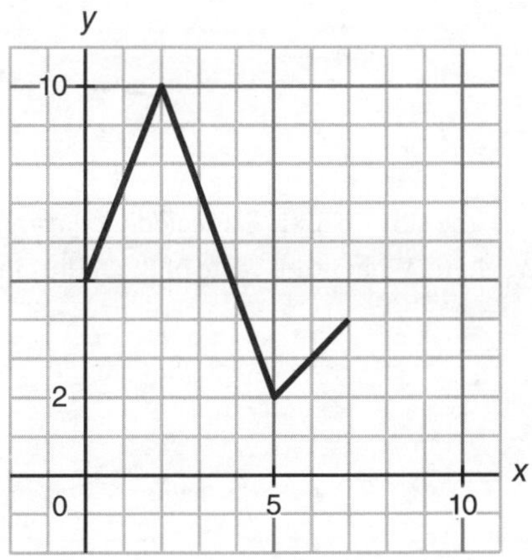


7. The graph above represents all the values for the function $g(x)$ as graphed in the $xy$-coordinate plane. What is the difference between the minimum and the maximum value of the function?

(A) 5
(B) 7
(C) 8
(D) 10

8. $k(ax^2 + bx + 5) = 6x^2 - 21x + 15$

In the expression above, in which $k$, $a$, and $b$ are constants, what is the value of $k$?

(A) 3
(B) 7
(C) 21
(D) 75

9. If $f(x) = x^2 - 4$ and $f(x + n) = x^2 + 6x + 5$, what is the value of the constant $n$?

(A) 1
(B) 2
(C) 3
(D) 4

10. If $2y = 3x - 4$ and $y + 1 = z - 5$, what is $x$ in terms of $z$?

(A) $x = \frac{2}{3}z - \frac{8}{3}$
(B) $x = \frac{4}{5}z + 2$
(C) $x = -\frac{3}{5}z - \frac{4}{9}$
(D) $x = -3z + \frac{1}{4}$

## Solutions

1. **(D)** Manipulate the equation so that $a$ is isolated:

$$F = ma \rightarrow$$

Divide both sides by $m \rightarrow$

$$a = \frac{F}{m}$$

2. **(C)** Solve the equation for the radius, $r$: In a sphere, the surface area, $S$, is calculated using the formula $S = 4\pi r^2$, where $r$ is the radius of the sphere. What is the value of the radius in terms of the surface area?

$$S = 4\pi r^2 \rightarrow$$
$$r^2 = \frac{S}{4\pi} \rightarrow$$
$$\sqrt{r^2} = \sqrt{\frac{S}{4\pi}} \rightarrow$$
$$r = \sqrt{\frac{S}{4\pi}}$$

3. **(A)** FOIL the left-hand side of the equation so you can identify what values are equivalent:

$$(2x + a)(3x + a) = 6x^2 + 5ax + 16 \rightarrow$$
$$6x^2 + 2ax + 3ax + a^2 = 6x^2 + 5ax + 16 \rightarrow$$
$$6x^2 + 5ax + a^2 = 6x^2 + 5ax + 16 \rightarrow$$
$$a^2 = 16$$

So, $a$ could equal 4. Plugging this back in, you can see that having 4 for $a$ makes the equation work:

$$(2x + a)(3x + a) = 6x^2 + 5ax + 16 \rightarrow$$
$$(2x + 4)(3x + 4) = 6x^2 + 5(4)x + 16 \rightarrow$$
$$6x^2 + 8x + 12x + 16 = 6x^2 + 20x + 16 \rightarrow$$
$$6x^2 + 20x + 16 = 6x^2 + 20x + 16$$

4. **(D)** Manipulate the equation to isolate for $C$, the molar concentration.

$$\Psi_S = -iCRT \rightarrow$$

Divide both sides by $-iRT \rightarrow$

$$C = -\frac{\Psi_S}{iRT}$$

5. **(C)** The function is a parabola that is facing downwards, given the $-16$ in front of the largest power term, $t^2$. The maximum value for the height will therefore be at the parabola's vertex. To find the value of $t$ at the vertex, the easiest way to proceed is to use the formula $x = -\frac{b}{2a}$. The constant $a$ is $-16$, and the constant $b$ is 20. Instead of $x$, we can use the variable $t$:

$$x = -\frac{b}{2a} \rightarrow$$

$$t = -\frac{b}{2a} \rightarrow$$

$$t = -\frac{20}{2(-16)} \rightarrow$$

$$t = \frac{20}{32} = 0.625$$

6. **(A)** FOIL the left-hand side of the equation so you can identify the components that correspond to the values on the right side:

$$(2x - 3y)(4x + y) = 8x^2 + axy + bxy - 3y^2 \rightarrow$$

$$8x^2 + 2xy - 12xy - 3y^2 = 8x^2 + axy + bxy - 3y^2 \rightarrow$$

Subtract the $8x^2$ and $-3y^2$ from both sides $\rightarrow$

$$2xy - 12xy = axy + bxy \rightarrow$$

Divide both sides by $xy \rightarrow$

$$2 - 12 = a + b \rightarrow$$

$$-10 = a + b$$

So, $-10$ equals the sum of $a$ and $b$.

7. **(C)** The $y$ value of the highest point on the function is 10, and the $y$ value of the lowest point on the function is 2. So, the difference between the maximum and the minimum of the function will be $10 - 2 = 8$.

8. **(A)** Distribute the $k$ to see potential equivalences:

$$k(ax^2 + bx + 5) = 6x^2 - 21x + 15 \rightarrow$$

$$kax^2 + kbx + 5k = 6x^2 - 21x + 15$$

Based on this, we have three different equivalences:

$$ka = 6,\ kb = -21, \text{ and } 5k = 15$$

Since we do not know the values of $a$ and $b$, the easiest way to solve this is to solve $5k = 15$:

$$5k = 15 \rightarrow$$
$$\frac{5k}{5} = \frac{15}{5} \rightarrow$$
$$k = 3$$

9. **(C)** Plug $x + n$ into $f(x) = x^2 - 4$, then make this expression equivalent to $x^2 + 6x + 5$ to solve for $n$:

$$(x + n)^2 - 4 \rightarrow$$
$$(x + n)(x + n) - 4 \rightarrow$$
$$x^2 + 2xn + n^2 - 4 = x^2 + 6x + 5$$

Given this equation, the easiest way to proceed is probably to set $2xn$ equal to $6x$ and solve for $n$:

$$2xn = 6x \rightarrow$$
$$2n = 6 \rightarrow$$
$$n = 3$$

10. **(A)** Solve this by making an equation that has only $x$ and $z$ in it, eliminating the $y$.

$$2y = 3x - 4 \rightarrow$$
$$y = \frac{3}{2}x - 2 \rightarrow$$

Substitute this for $y$ in the other equation:

$$\left(\frac{3}{2}x - 2\right) + 1 = z - 5 \rightarrow$$
$$\frac{3}{2}x - 1 = z - 5 \rightarrow$$
$$\frac{3}{2}x = z - 4 \rightarrow$$
$$x = \frac{2}{3}z - \frac{8}{3}$$

## Problem Solving and Data Analysis

This section contains comprehensive review and strategies for all of the concepts below:

**Problem Solving and Data Analysis—Measures of Center**

- Mean
- Median
- Mode
- Outliers
- Range and Standard Deviation

**Problem Solving and Data Analysis—Unit Conversion**

**Problem Solving and Data Analysis—Surveys**

- Sampling Methods
- Drawing Conclusions

**Problem Solving and Data Analysis—Percentages**

- Percentage Essentials
- Percent Increase and Decrease
- Simple Interest
- Compound Interest

**Problem Solving and Data Analysis—Graphs and Data Interpretation**

- Probability
- Graph Interpretation
- Scatterplots
- Histograms
- Tables
- Box Plots
- Linear and Exponential Growth
- Interpreting Constants and Functions

## Problem Solving and Data Analysis—Measures of Center

The SAT Math will assess your understanding of different ways of calculating averages. Mean, median, and mode are the three major concepts to know.

### Mean

$$\frac{\text{Sum of Items}}{\text{Number of Items}} = \text{Mean}$$

This is what you typically would do if asked to find the average of a set of terms.

**Example 1**

What is the mean of the numbers 2, 4, 7, 12, 14, and 18?

**Solution**

$$\frac{\text{Sum of Items}}{\text{Number of Items}} = \frac{2+4+7+12+14+18}{6} = \frac{57}{6} = 9.5$$

**Example 2**

There are four numbers in a set: 4, 10, 12, and $x$. If the mean of the four terms is 10, what is the value of $x$?

**Solution**

Set up an equation for the mean of the set, keeping $x$ as an unknown value:

$$\frac{\text{Sum of Items}}{\text{Number of Items}} = \text{Mean} \rightarrow$$

$$\frac{4 + 10 + 12 + x}{4} = 10 \rightarrow$$

$$\frac{26 + x}{4} = 10 \rightarrow$$

$$26 + x = 40 \rightarrow$$

$$x = 14$$

So, the value of $x$ is 14.

### Median

The *middle term* of a set of numbers when arranged from *least to greatest.* (If there is an even number of terms and the two middle terms are different, take the mean of the two middle terms to find the median of the set of numbers.)

**Example 1**

What is the median of this set of numbers? {1, 3, 6, 9, 12, 17, 22}

**Solution**

The numbers are already arranged from least to greatest, so find the middle term. In this case, since there are seven terms, the fourth term will be the middle term. The answer is therefore 9.

**Example 2**

What is the median of this set of numbers? {6, 4, 3, 10, 13, 14}

**Solution**

First, arrange the numbers from least to greatest.

{3, 4, 6, 10, 13, 14}

Notice that there are six numbers, and the two middle numbers are different. So, to find the median of this set, we must take the mean of 6 and 10:

$$\frac{6 + 10}{2} = \frac{16}{2} = 8$$

### Mode

This is the *most frequent* number in a set. (Note that if a set of numbers has each number appear just once, there will be zero modes. If a set of numbers has two or more numbers tied for appearing the most times, it will have multiple modes.)

**Example**

What is the mode of this set of numbers? {1, 5, 3, 9, 2, 4, 8, 9}

**Solution**

Every number in the set appears just once, except for 9, which appears twice. Therefore, 9 is the mode of the set.

## Outliers

A number in a set that is quite different from the other values in the set.

**Example**

Which value in this set would be considered an outlier? {2, 3, 5, 6, 8, 240}

**Solution**

While the first five numbers in the set are rather small, 240 is far larger than the others and would be considered an outlier.

### Practice

1. What is the mean of this set of numbers? {1, 4, 9, 10}
2. What is the median of this set of numbers? {2, 4, 8, 9, 12}
3. What is the mode of this set of numbers? {4, 5, 7, 8, 4, 2, 9}
4. There are a total of four numbers in a set. The sum of the three smallest terms is 80. If the average of the set of four numbers is 30, what is the value of the largest number in the set?
5. What is the median of 4, 3, 8, 10, 20, and 12?
6. In this set of numbers, {1, 2, 4, 5, 5, 20, 56), is the mean, median, or mode the largest?
7. If an outlier is added to a set of numbers, would it most likely affect the mode, median, or mean of the set?

### Solutions

1. $\frac{\text{Sum of Items}}{\text{Number of Items}} = Mean \rightarrow$

   $\frac{1+4+9+10}{4} = \frac{24}{6} = 6$

2. There are five terms in the set, with 8 being the middle term since they are already in order from least to greatest. Therefore, 8 is the median.

3. All the numbers appear just once, except for 4, which appears twice. Thus, 4 is the mode of the set.
4. Calculate the value of the missing term, which we can call $x$, using the mean formula. Since the smallest three terms add up to 80, we can add 80 and $x$ to get the sum of the items.

$$\frac{\text{Sum of Items}}{\text{Number of Items}} = \text{Mean} \rightarrow$$

$$\frac{80 + x}{4} = 30 \rightarrow$$

$$80 + x = 120 \rightarrow$$

$$x = 40$$

5. Put the numbers in order from least to greatest:

3, 4, 8, 10, 12, 20

There are six terms and the third and fourth terms are different. So, to calculate the median of the set, we must take the mean of 8 and 10:

$$\frac{8 + 10}{2} = \frac{18}{2} = 9$$

6. Rather than calculating the individual values of the median, mean, and mode for the set—{1, 2, 4, 5, 5, 20, 56)—you can take a shortcut. Since the set has two numbers, 20 and 56, that are far greater than the others, they will cause the mean to be greater than the mode and median.

Alternatively, you can calculate the individual values of the mean, median, and mode:

The mean is $\frac{1 + 2 + 4 + 5 + 5 + 20 + 56}{7} \approx 13.3$

The median is 5 since the fourth number out of the set of seven numbers is 5.

The mode is 5 since it appears most frequently.

So, however you find it, the mean will be the greatest.

7. An outlier would most likely affect the *mean* of a set of numbers, since it would be included in the mathematical calculation of the average. It is possible that an outlier would not change the median, so long as the middle value remained the same. It is also possible that an outlier would not change the mode, so long as the outlier was not repeated.

## Range and Standard Deviation

To analyze properties of data sets, understand the concepts of range and standard deviation. *Range* is the difference between the smallest and largest values in a set of data.

### Example

What is the range of this set of numbers? {1, 3, 7, 9, 15}

### ✓ Solution

Take the difference between the largest and smallest values in the set to find the range:

$$15 - 1 = 14$$

Therefore, the range is 14.

*Standard deviation* indicates how significant the *spread* of the data in a set is.

Mathematically, it is calculated as:

$$\sqrt{\text{Average of the squared distances of the data points from their mean}}$$

Fortunately, instead of having you calculate the precise value of the standard deviation, the SAT tests your understanding of the *concept* of standard deviation.

If the standard deviation in a set of numbers is *small*, there is little variation in the data.

If the standard deviation in a set of numbers is *large*, there will be greater variation in the data.

### › Example

Which of the following sets will have a greater standard deviation?

Set X: {5, 6, 7, 8, 9}
Set Y: {1, 20, 40, 80, 95}

### ✓ Solution

Set Y will have a greater standard deviation because the numbers deviate more greatly from its mean. The values in Set X are much more closely clustered around one another.

### Practice

1. What is the range of this set of numbers? {−5, 3, 8, 20, 28}
2. Which of the following numbers, if added to the set {2, 5, 8, 11, 15} would most likely *decrease* its standard deviation?

   (A) 2
   (B) 5
   (C) 8
   (D) 15

3. What positive number could be added to the set {2, 4, 8, 9, 18} to double its range?
4. Would a sample of ages among students in an elementary school or a sample of ages among residents of a city more likely have a greater standard deviation?

## Solutions

1. Find the difference between the least and greatest values in the set to calculate the range:

$$28 - (-5) = 28 + 5 = 33$$

2. Since the standard deviation is calculated by the

$$\sqrt{\text{Average of the squared distances of the data points from their mean}}$$

if you add a data point that *is equal* to the mean, that would certainly reduce the standard deviation of the set. Since the number 8 is equal to the mean, adding it would ensure that the average of the squared distances of the data points from their mean would decrease. So, the answer is **(C)**, 8.

3. First, let's calculate the original range of the set by subtracting the least value from the greatest value:

$$18 - 2 = 16$$

Now, let's double this range:

$$16 \times 2 = 32$$

Since the question asks us to find a *positive* number that could be added to the set that would cause it to have this doubled range of 32, we can add the least value to this range to find the needed value to be added:

$$2 + 32 = 34$$

So, if 34 were added to the set, the range of the set would double.

4. Standard deviation provides a measure of the *spread* of data points—the greater the spread, the greater the standard deviation. In an elementary school, the ages of students would most likely be clustered around lower ages, like 5–12. In a town, the residents would range in age from very young to very old. So, it is more likely that the standard deviation of ages in the town would be greater.

## Practice Drill—Measures of Center

*(If timing, take about 12 minutes to complete.)*

1. $\{2, 7, 9, x, 12, 15\}$

Consider the data set above. What must the value of $x$ be so that the median of the data set is 10?

(A) 9
(B) 10
(C) 11
(D) 12

2. What is the mean of the fractions $\frac{1}{3}$, $\frac{1}{4}$, and $\frac{1}{6}$?

(A) $\frac{1}{5}$

(B) $\frac{3}{13}$

(C) $\frac{1}{4}$

(D) $\frac{1}{3}$

3. For a fundraiser, 8 students sold fewer than 5 coupon books. Ten students sold at least 5 and no more than 10 coupon books. Fifteen students sold 11 or more coupon books. Assuming that the previously mentioned students represent the entire set of students, which of the following could have been the median number of coupon books for this group based on this information?

(A) 4
(B) 8
(C) 10.5
(D) 12

| Number of Apps on a Phone (Range of Values) | How Many Students with Number of Apps in Range |
|---|---|
| 0–5 | 2 |
| 6–10 | 5 |
| 11–15 | 7 |
| 16–20 | 4 |
| More than 20 | 2 |

4. Twenty students were asked how many apps they had on their phones. The results are provided in the table above. If two students are added to this set, one of whom has just 3 apps and the other of whom has 26 apps, how would the median number of apps per student be affected?

(A) Increases
(B) Decreases
(C) Remains the same
(D) Cannot determine from the given information

5. Five students purchased a computer that costs \$1,000. The students split the cost equally among themselves. In order for the share per person to decrease by \$75, how many additional students would they need to share in the purchase, given that they would all share the cost equally?

(A) 3
(B) 4
(C) 6
(D) 8

6. $\{1, 4, 5, 5.5, 6, 6.5, 9.5\}$

   In the above set of numbers, the two values that are the greatest outliers from the others are removed. Once these two values are removed, what is the range of the remaining values?

   (A) 2.5
   (B) 3
   (C) 7
   (D) 8.5

7. The maximum weight a certain elevator can hold is 3,000 pounds. For a group of 15 people to go on the elevator, what is the maximum the mean of their weights could be?

   (A) 170 pounds
   (B) 190 pounds
   (C) 200 pounds
   (D) 240 pounds

8. A student had scores of 80, 90, 85, 100, 75, and 85 on his tests in a history class. If the teacher threw out his worst test grade, which of these values describing the set of his scores would change?

   (A) Mean
   (B) Median
   (C) Mode
   (D) None of the above

9. Jake has a smartwatch that helps him keep track of the number of steps he takes each day. On Monday, he walked 8,000 steps; Tuesday, 13,000; Wednesday, 7,000; and Thursday, 8,500. Which inequality expresses the number of steps, $n$, that Jake could walk on Friday so that the average for the 5 days is at least 10,000 steps per day?

   (A) $\frac{8,000 + 13,000 + 7,000 + 8,500 + n}{5} \leq 10,000$

   (B) $\frac{8,000 + 13,000 + 7,000 + 8,500 + n}{5} \geq 10,000$

   (C) $\frac{8,000 + 13,000 + 7,000 + 8,500}{n} \geq 10,000$

   (D) $\frac{8,000 + 13,000 + 7,000 + 8,500 + n}{4} \leq 10,000$

10. The heights in inches of 10 people in a room is given below:

    $\{60, 49, 72, 75, 54, 58, 76, 44, 51, 53, 62\}$

    If someone new comes in to the room and has a height of 74 inches, which of these is an accurate statement about the range and standard deviation of the set?

    (A) Only the standard deviation would change.
    (B) Only the range would change.
    (C) Both the standard deviation and range would change.
    (D) Neither the standard deviation nor range would change.

## Solutions

1. **(C)** There are 6 numbers in this set, so the median will be the average of the two middle terms. If the two middle terms were 7 and 9, the median would be 8; if the two middle terms were 9 and 12, the median would be 10.5. So, $x$ must be between 9 and 12 and must average out to 10. You can therefore solve for $x$ by solving the following equation:

$$\frac{x+9}{2} = 10 \rightarrow$$
$$x + 9 = 20 \rightarrow$$
$$x = 11$$

Thus, 11 would be the value of $x$ that would cause the set of numbers to have a median of 10.

2. **(C)** First, modify all the fractions so they have the same denominator, 12:

$$\frac{1}{3} = \frac{4}{12}, \frac{1}{4} = \frac{3}{12}, \text{ and } \frac{1}{6} = \frac{2}{12}$$

Then, add the fractions together and divide by 3 to solve for the mean.

$$\frac{\left(\frac{4}{12} + \frac{3}{12} + \frac{2}{12}\right)}{3} = \frac{\left(\frac{9}{12}\right)}{3} = \frac{3}{12} = \frac{1}{4}$$

3. **(B)** Let us find the total number of students in the set: $8 + 10 + 15 = 33$. The middle value will be the 17th value, since there would be 16 values less than it and 16 values greater than it.

Since there are 8 who sold fewer than 5, and 10 students who sold between 5–10 books, the 17th term if the terms were placed in order from least to greatest would be within the range of 5–10 books. The answer is therefore 8 because it is the only number within this range.

4. **(C)** Because there are 20 students, the initial median will be the average of the 10th and 11th terms. The 10th and 11th terms will both fall between the range of 11–15 apps based on the table. If a student with 3 apps and a student with 26 apps were added to this set, they would balance each other out and there would be no impact on the median of the set. Therefore, the median of the set would remain the same.

5. **(A)** First, let's find the original cost per student by calculating the mean when there are 5 students and a total price of $1,000:

$$\frac{1,000}{5} = 200$$

So, the initial share per student is $200. If the amount of the share per student is to decrease by $75, the new share per student would be $200 - 75 = 125$ dollars. Set up a new calculation of the mean to solve for the number of students, $x$, who would need to be added to the initial 5 students to get a new average of $125:

$$\frac{1,000}{5+x} = 125 \rightarrow$$
$$1,000 = 125(5 + x) \rightarrow$$
$$1,000 = 625 + 125x \rightarrow$$
$$375 = 125x \rightarrow$$
$$x = 3$$

Therefore, if 3 students were added to the total, there would be a total of 8 students who could share the cost at an equal amount of $125 a person.

6. **(A)** The two greatest outliers in the set are the values that are farthest from the mean: 1 and 9.5. If we remove these values, the new set is {4, 5, 5.5, 6, 6.5}. To calculate the range of this new set, subtract the smallest value from the largest value:

$$6.5 - 4 = 2.5$$

7. **(C)** Since the maximum weight is 3,000 pounds, divide 3,000 by 15 to find the mean under these conditions:

$$\frac{3,000}{15} = 200$$

8. **(A)** Let's see how the mean, median, and mode will be affected by this change of removing the score of 75, the worst test grade, from the set. The original set, when the numbers are put in order from least to greatest, is {75, 80, 85, 85, 90, 100}. The new set would be {80, 85, 85, 90, 100}.

| Original Set: {75, 80, 85, 85, 90, 100} | New Set: {80, 85, 85, 90, 100} |
|---|---|
| Original Mean: $\frac{75+80+85+85+90+100}{6} = \frac{515}{6} \approx 85.83$ | New Mean: $\frac{80+85+85+90+100}{5} = \frac{440}{5} = 88$ |
| Original Median: {75, 80, 85, 85, 90, 100}: The third and fourth terms are both 85, so the median is 85. | New Median: {80, 85, 85, 90, 100}: The third term is 85, so the median is still 85. |
| Original Mode: 85 is the most frequent term. | New Mode: 85 is still the most frequent term. |

Therefore, only the mean of the set will change. If you notice that the mode and median will not be affected, you can see that just the mean will be affected since removing one value that is less than the original mean will inevitably change the mean of the set.

9. **(B)** This is a question where looking ahead to the answers can help, since the answers show that you just need to set up the calculation, rather than doing it all the way to completion. Be careful to avoid careless mistakes, especially with the direction of the inequality sign. Jake wants to average *at least* 10,000 steps per day, so the average number of steps must be *greater than or equal to* 10,000: *average* ≥ 10,000. The average is calculated by adding the known values together and treating $n$ as the one day that is not known. There are 5 total days including $n$. Therefore, the calculation will be:

$$\frac{8,000 + 13,000 + 7,000 + 8,500 + n}{5} \geq 10,000$$

10. **(A)** The range of the set is the difference between the least and greatest terms in the set: $76 - 44 = 32$. The range will not change if 74 were added to the set, since the values of the least and greatest numbers in the set would remain at 44 and 76.

The standard deviation of the set *would* change since the variation of the numbers from the mean will be different with the relatively large value of 74 added to the group. Therefore, the answer is **(A)**.

## Problem Solving and Data Analysis—Unit Conversion

**SAT Math Strategy**

Use proportions to solve simple unit conversions, and use unit cancellation to solve more complex unit conversions.

If an SAT Math problem involves a straightforward calculation between just two units, you can probably solve it using a proportion.

### Example 1

There are 5,280 feet in 1 mile. If Susan runs 3.5 miles, how many feet did she run?

### Solution

Set up a proportion to solve for the $x$ number of feet that Susan ran in the race. It is easier if you place the variable for which you are solving *in the numerator* so the algebra is less complex.

$$\frac{5,280 \text{ feet}}{1 \text{ mile}} = \frac{x \text{ feet}}{3.5 \text{ miles}} \rightarrow$$

Multiply both sides by 3.5 miles to solve for $x \rightarrow$

$$\frac{5,280 \text{ feet}}{1 \text{ mile}} \times 3.5 \text{ miles} = \frac{x \text{ feet}}{3.5 \text{ miles}} \times 3.5 \text{ miles} \rightarrow$$

Cancel out the miles units and the 3.5 on the right side $\rightarrow$

$$\frac{5,280 \text{ feet}}{1 \cancel{\text{mile}}} \times 3.5 \cancel{\text{miles}} = \frac{x \text{ feet}}{\cancel{3.5 \text{ miles}}} \times \cancel{3.5 \text{ miles}} \rightarrow$$

$$5,280 \text{ feet} \times 3.5 = x$$

$$18{,}480 \text{ feet} = x$$

### Example 2

Ahmad has 300 U.S. dollars that he wants to convert to euros. His bank offers an exchange rate of 0.83 euros for 1 U.S. dollar. Assuming there are no fees or taxes, if Ahmad converts all 300 of his dollars to euros, how many euros will he have?

### Solution

Set up a proportion to solve for euros:

$$\frac{0.83 \text{ Euros}}{1 \text{ Dollar}} = \frac{x \text{ Euros}}{300 \text{ Dollars}} \rightarrow$$

Multiply both sides by 300 dollars to solve for $x \rightarrow$

$$\frac{0.83 \text{ Euros}}{1 \text{ Dollar}} \times 300 \text{ Dollars} = \frac{x \text{ Euros}}{300 \text{ Dollars}} \times 300 \text{ Dollars} \rightarrow$$

Cancel out the dollars units and the 300 on the right side →

$$\frac{0.83 \text{ Euros}}{1 \cancel{\text{Dollar}}} \times 300 \cancel{\text{Dollars}} = \frac{x \text{ Euros}}{\cancel{300 \text{ Dollars}}} \times \cancel{300 \text{ Dollars}} \rightarrow$$

$$0.83 \text{ Euros} \times 300 = x$$

$$249 \text{ Euros} = x$$

So, Ahmad would have 249 euros after the currency conversion.

### Example 3

Emily took a bike ride that was 8 kilometers long. Given that there are approximately 0.6214 miles in a kilometer and 5,280 feet in a mile, approximately how many *feet* was Emily's bike ride?

### Solution

Ultimately, your unit conversion will end with feet. Use *dimensional analysis* or the *unit-factor method* (different ways of labelling the same idea) to cancel out units and end with the desired unit. The ride is 8 kilometers, and there are 0.6214 miles in a kilometer and 5,280 feet in a mile. So, set up the unit conversion like this:

$$8 \text{ kilometers} \times \frac{0.6214 \text{ miles}}{1 \text{ kilometer}} \times \frac{5,280 \text{ feet}}{1 \text{ mile}} \rightarrow$$

Cancel out units that are in both the numerator and denominator:

$$8 \cancel{\text{kilometers}} \times \frac{0.6214 \cancel{\text{miles}}}{1 \cancel{\text{kilometer}}} \times \frac{5,280 \text{ feet}}{1 \cancel{\text{mile}}} \rightarrow$$

$$8 \times 0.6214 \times 5,280 \approx 26,248 \text{ feet}$$

### Example 4

Timothy has 1 gallon of milk. There are approximately 3.785 liters in 1 gallon. How many milliliters of milk does Timothy have?

### Solution

While the SAT will give you many conversion ratios, there are some that it will be helpful to memorize:

- 12 inches in 1 foot
- 60 seconds in 1 minute
- 60 minutes in 1 hour
- 100 centimeters in 1 meter (Prefix *centi* means "one-hundredth.")
- 1,000 millimeters in 1 meter (Prefix *milli* means "one-thousandth.")
- 1,000 milliliters in 1 liter (Prefix *milli* means "one-thousandth.")
- 1,000 meters in 1 kilometer (Prefix *kilo* means "thousand.")

In this problem, we will ultimately end up with milliliters. Use *dimensional analysis* or the *unit-factor method* to cancel out units and end with the desired unit of milliliters:

$$1 \text{ gallon} \times \frac{3.785 \text{ liters}}{1 \text{ gallon}} \times \frac{1,000 \text{ milliliters}}{1 \text{ liter}} \rightarrow$$

$$1 \cancel{\text{gallon}} \times \frac{3.785 \cancel{\text{liters}}}{1 \cancel{\text{gallon}}} \times \frac{1,000 \text{ milliliters}}{1 \cancel{\text{liter}}} \rightarrow$$

$$1 \times 3.785 \times 1,000 = 3,785 \text{ milliliters}$$

## Practice Drill—Problem Solving and Data Analysis: Unit Conversion

*(If timing, take about 12 minutes to complete.)*

1. Approximately how many kilometers are in a marathon, given that a marathon is 26.22 miles and that there are 1.609 kilometers in a mile?

   (A) 16.3 km
   (B) 27.8 km
   (C) 42.2 km
   (D) 74.5 km

2. The Empire State Building in New York City has a height of 1,250 feet, while if its pinnacle is included, it has a height of 1,454 feet. What is the height of just the pinnacle to the nearest whole meter given that there are 3.28 feet in 1 meter?

   (A) 62 meters
   (B) 85 meters
   (C) 204 meters
   (D) 669 meters

3. If 1 ounce of platinum sells for $700 and 1 ounce of gold sells for $1,700, how much more expensive would a pound of gold be than a pound of platinum, given that there are 16 ounces in a pound?

   (A) $7,000
   (B) $16,000
   (C) $27,200
   (D) $38,400

4. A barrel has a volume of 42 gallons. If you have 105 gallons of a liquid, what would be the equivalent number of barrels of the liquid?

   (A) 0.4 barrels
   (B) 1.5 barrels
   (C) 2.5 barrels
   (D) 6.8 barrels

5. The depth in *feet* of water, $D$, in a lake $x$ days after it was dammed is given by this equation:

$$D = 0.5x + 30$$

Based on this equation, how many *inches* does the depth of the water in the lake increase each day?

(A) 0.5
(B) 3.5
(C) 6
(D) 30

6. In 1875, Matthew Webb was the first person to successfully swim across the English Channel. He took about 22 hours to make the roughly 22-mile swim. Given that there are about 1.61 kilometers in a mile, what was his approximate average swimming speed for this trip in kilometers per hour?

(A) 0.62 km/hour
(B) 1.61 km/hour
(C) 35 km/hour
(D) 44 km/hour

7. The speed of sound as it travels through rubber is approximately 60 meters per second. How fast does sound travel through rubber in kilometers per hour?

(A) Approximately 216 km/hour
(B) Approximately 642 km/hour
(C) Approximately 36,000 km/hour
(D) Approximately 216,000 km/hour

**Fill-In Practice:** Write your answer in the underlined blank under each question.

8. Mark rides his bicycle 30 feet in 2 seconds. At that rate, how many feet would he travel in 1 minute on his bicycle?

Answer: ________

9. The key on a map indicates that 1 inch on the map corresponds to ½ of a mile in actual distance. If the distance on the map between two points is 6 inches, how many miles apart would they be in real life?

Answer: ________

10. The number of cloves in a head of garlic is between 10 and 12. If a recipe called for 3.5 heads of garlic, what would a possible value for the number of cloves that would meet this requirement?

Answer: ________

## Solutions

1. **(C)** Use a proportion to solve for the number of kilometers in a marathon:

$$\frac{1.609 \text{ kilometers}}{1 \text{ mile}} = \frac{x \text{ kilometers}}{26.22 \text{ miles}} \rightarrow$$

Cross Multiply:

$$\frac{1.609 \text{ kilometers}}{1 \text{ mile}} \times 26.22 \text{ miles} = x$$

Cancel out the miles:

$$\frac{1.609 \text{ kilometers}}{1 \cancel{\text{mile}}} \times 26.22 \cancel{\text{miles}} = x \rightarrow$$

$$1.609 \text{ kilometers} \times 26.22 \approx 42.2 \text{ kilometers}$$

2. **(A)** First, determine the height of the pinnacle by itself by subtracting the height of just the building from the height of the building and pinnacle combined:

$$1,454 - 1,250 = 204$$

Then, set up a proportion to solve for the height of the pinnacle in meters:

$$\frac{1 \text{ meter}}{3.28 \text{ feet}} = \frac{x \text{ meters}}{204 \text{ feet}} \rightarrow$$

$$\frac{1 \text{ meter}}{3.28 \text{ feet}} \times 204 \text{ feet} = x \rightarrow$$

$$\frac{1 \text{ meter}}{3.28 \cancel{\text{feet}}} \times 204 \cancel{\text{feet}} = x \rightarrow$$

$$\frac{204}{3.28} \approx 62 \text{ meters}$$

3. **(B)** First, recognize that we need to convert the difference between the price of gold and platinum:

$$1,700 - 700 = 1,000$$

Then, multiply $1,000 by 16 ounces to find the total difference in price per pound:

$$1,000 \times 16 = 16,000$$

4. **(C)** Use a proportion to solve this problem:

$$\frac{1 \text{ barrel}}{42 \text{ gallons}} = \frac{x \text{ barrels}}{105 \text{ gallons}} \rightarrow$$

$$\frac{1 \text{ barrel}}{42 \text{ gallons}} \times 105 \text{ gallons} = x \rightarrow$$

$$\frac{1 \text{ barrel}}{42 \cancel{\text{gallons}}} \times 105 \cancel{\text{gallons}} = x \rightarrow$$

$$\frac{105}{42} = 2.5 \text{ barrels} = x$$

5. **(C)** The equation is written in slope-intercept form, so to see how much the depth is increasing in feet each day, look at the slope—0.5. Then, convert .5 feet to inches. Since there are 12 inches in a foot, multiply 0.5 feet by 12 inches to get the converted number of inches:

$$0.5 \times 12 = 6$$

So, each day the depth of water increases by 6 inches.

6. **(B)** We want to have the units result in kilometers per hour, so use unit cancellation to determine this speed:

$$\frac{22 \text{ miles}}{22 \text{ hours}} \times \frac{1.61 \text{ kilometers}}{1 \text{ mile}} \rightarrow$$

$$\frac{22 \cancel{\text{miles}}}{22 \text{ hours}} \times \frac{1.61 \text{ kilometers}}{1 \cancel{\text{mile}}} \rightarrow$$

$$\frac{22}{22} \times 1.61 = 1.61 \frac{\text{km}}{\text{hr}}$$

Alternatively, you could have noticed that the speed is 1 mile per hour, so just multiply 1 mile per hour by 1.61.

7. **(A)** Use unit-cancellation to solve for the speed in kilometers per hour:

$$\frac{60 \text{ meters}}{1 \text{ second}} \times \frac{1 \text{ kilometer}}{1{,}000 \text{ meters}} \times \frac{3{,}600 \text{ seconds}}{1 \text{ hour}} =$$

$$\frac{60 \cancel{\text{meters}}}{1 \cancel{\text{second}}} \times \frac{1 \text{ kilometer}}{1{,}000 \cancel{\text{meters}}} \times \frac{3{,}600 \cancel{\text{seconds}}}{1 \text{ hour}} \approx 216 \frac{\text{km}}{\text{hr}}$$

8. **(900)** Use unit-cancellation to solve for the distance he will travel in 1 minute:

$$\frac{30 \text{ feet}}{2 \text{ seconds}} \times \frac{60 \text{ seconds}}{1 \text{ minute}} \rightarrow$$

$$\frac{30 \text{ feet}}{2 \cancel{\text{seconds}}} \times \frac{60 \cancel{\text{seconds}}}{1 \text{ minute}} \rightarrow$$

$$\frac{30 \times 60}{2} = 900 \frac{\text{feet}}{\text{minute}}$$

9. **(3)** Use a proportion to solve for the miles:

$$\frac{0.5 \text{ mile}}{1 \text{ inch}} = \frac{x \text{ miles}}{6 \text{ inches}} \rightarrow$$

$$\frac{0.5 \text{ mile}}{1 \text{ inch}} \times 6 \text{ inches} = x \rightarrow$$

$$\frac{0.5 \text{ mile}}{1 \cancel{\text{inch}}} \times 6 \cancel{\text{inches}} = x \rightarrow$$

$$0.5 \times 6 = 3 \text{ miles} = x$$

10. **(Any number greater than or equal to 35 and less than or equal to 42.)** Find the lower number by multiplying 10 by 3.5, and the greater number by multiplying 12 by 3.5:

$$10 \times 3.5 = 35$$

$$12 \times 3.5 = 42$$

So, the range of garlic cloves would be between 35 and 42, inclusive (meaning including 35 and 42 also).

## Problem Solving and Data Analysis—Percentages

### Percentage Essentials

Percent calculations are heavily emphasized on the SAT Math. To be successful on percent problems, there are several key formulas it is helpful to memorize.

$$\frac{\text{Part}}{\text{Whole}} \times 100 = \text{Percent}$$

In most situations you will come across, the "part" will be the smaller number and the "whole" will be the larger number.

#### Example 1

If there are 200 students in a graduating class, and 40 of them graduated with honors, what percent of students in the class graduated with honors?

#### ✓ Solution

The "part" is 40, and the "whole" is 200. Plug these values into the above formula to calculate the percent:

$$\frac{\text{Part}}{\text{Whole}} \times 100 = \text{Percent} \rightarrow$$

$$\frac{40}{200} \times 100 = 0.2 \times 100 = 20\%$$

#### Example 2

If 60% is considered a passing grade on a particular test, and the test has 30 questions, how many questions would a test taker have to answer correctly to pass the test?

#### ✓ Solution

Use 60% as the "percent," and use 30 as the "whole," since 30 represents the total number of questions. Then, use the percent formula to solve for the "part"—the number of questions that must be answered correctly to pass:

$$\frac{\text{Part}}{\text{Whole}} \times 100 = \text{Percent} \rightarrow$$

$$\frac{\text{Part}}{30} \times 100 = 60 \rightarrow$$

$$\text{Part} = \frac{60 \times 30}{100} = \frac{1,800}{100} = 18$$

So, one would need to answer at least 18 questions correctly to pass the test.

#### Example 3

If 30% of the cars in a parking lot have bumper stickers, what fraction of the cars in the parking lot would have bumper stickers?

### ✓ Solution

Manipulate the percent formula so we can convert this situation to a fraction:

$$\frac{\text{Part}}{\text{Whole}} \times 100 = \text{Percent} \rightarrow$$

$$\frac{\text{Part}}{\text{Whole}} = \frac{\text{Percent}}{100}$$

Use 30 as the percent, then reduce the fraction:

$$\frac{30}{100} = \frac{3}{10}$$

So, $\frac{3}{10}$ of the cars in the parking lot have bumper stickers.

### › Example 4

Michal took a test that had 20 points, and she earned 2 points of extra credit in addition to a perfect score on the test. What was her percentage score?

### ✓ Solution

In this situation, the "part" will be 22 to include the perfect score and the extra credit. The "whole" will be 20, given that total number of points on the test. So, calculate her percentage scores as follows:

$$\frac{\text{Part}}{\text{Whole}} \times 100 = \text{Percent} \rightarrow$$

$$\frac{22}{20} \times 100 = 110\%$$

For problems like these, it can be helpful to know the conversions of fractions to percentages off the top of your head:

$$10\% = \frac{1}{10}$$

$$25\% = \frac{1}{4}$$

$$50\% = \frac{1}{2}$$

$$75\% = \frac{3}{4}$$

The part/whole formula will always work, so you can stick to that approach if you are more comfortable. There are, however, a number of ways to work with percentages more efficiently depending on the type of problem.

> When asked to find the percent of a number, take the percent and move the decimal point *to the left two spots and then multiply.*

### Example 1

What is 75% of 500?

### Solution

Rather than using the previous percent formula to solve, start by taking the 75% and moving the decimal point to the left by two spots:

$$75.0 \rightarrow 0.75$$

Now multiply by 500:

$$500 \times 0.75 = 375$$

So, 375 represents 75% of 500.

### Example 2

What is 4% of 20?

### Solution

Move the decimal point of 4% to the left by two spots:

$$4.0 \rightarrow 0.04$$

Now multiply by 20:

$$0.04 \times 20 = 0.8$$

So, 0.8 is 4% of 20.

### Example 3

What is 150% of 70?

### Solution

Move the decimal point of 150 to the left by two spots:

$$150.0 \rightarrow 1.5$$

Then, multiply by 70:

$$70 \times 1.5 = 105$$

### Practice

1. What is 40% of 240?
2. Two out of every five students at a school pack their lunches each day. What percent of students at the school pack their lunches each day?

3. What is 5% of 125?
4. With extra credit, Chris had a 105% as his grade for the semester in a class. If he scored 100% on every assignment throughout the semester, and there were a total of 400 points from all the regular assignments (not including extra credit), how many points in extra credit did he get that semester?
5. If 60 employees in a business work part-time, and these employees represent 30% of all the employees at the business, how many total employees does the business have?

### Solutions

1. $0.4 \times 240 = 96$
2. $\frac{2}{5} \times 100 = 40\%$
3. $0.05 \times 125 = 6.25$
4. Just take 5% of the total points from the regular assignments to find the points in extra credit he earned:

$$0.05 \times 400 = 20$$

5. Plug in values to the general percentage formula to solve for the total number of employees:

$$\frac{\text{Part}}{\text{Whole}} \times 100 = \text{Percent} \rightarrow$$

$$\frac{60}{\text{Whole}} \times 100 = 30 \rightarrow$$

Cross multiply →

$$\frac{60}{30} \times 100 = \text{Whole} \rightarrow$$

$$200 = \text{Whole}$$

So, the business has a total of 200 employees.

### Percent Increase and Decrease

To find the percent by which something has increased or decreased, use this formula, being careful on what you plug in for the "original" and "new" values:

$$\frac{\text{New} - \text{Original}}{\text{Original}} \times 100 = \text{Percent Change}$$

If the value of the percent change is positive, the change is increasing. If the value is negative, the change is decreasing.

### Example 1

Melanie's height is 40 inches. A year later, her height is 44 inches. By what percent did her height increase?

### ✓ Solution

The original value is 40, and the new value is 44, so the calculation is

$$\frac{\text{New} - \text{Original}}{\text{Original}} \times 100 = \text{Percent Change}$$

$$\frac{44 - 40}{40} \times 100 = \frac{4}{40} \times 100 = 10\%$$

So, Melanie's height has increased by 10%.

### › Example 2

William has \$800 in his checking account. If he spends \$200 out of his checking account, by what percent did his checking account decrease?

### ✓ Solution

The new value is \$600 (\$800 − \$200), and the original value is \$800, so the calculation is

$$\frac{\text{New} - \text{Original}}{\text{Original}} \times 100 = \text{Percent Change} \rightarrow$$

$$\frac{600 - 800}{2} \times 100 = \text{Percent Change} \rightarrow$$

$$\frac{-200}{800} \times 100 = -25\%$$

Since this value is *negative*, there has been a 25% *decrease* in his checking account.

What are easy ways to calculate the new amount if we know the percent by which something has increased or decreased?

> When the percentage is expressed as a decimal, $r$:
> Increased Total = (Original Amount) × $(1 + r)$
> Decreased Total = (Original Amount) × $(1 - r)$

### › Example 1

If the cost of a gallon of milk, originally at \$2 a gallon, increased by 20%, what would be the new cost of a gallon of milk?

### ✓ Solution

Use the increased total formula, plugging in 2 for the original amount, and using 0.20 as the $r$ since we must express 20% as a decimal:

$$\text{Increased Total} = (\text{Original Amount}) \times (1 + r) \rightarrow$$
$$\text{New Price} = (2) \times (1 + 0.2) = 2 \times 1.2 = 2.40$$

So, the new price of a gallon of milk would be \$2.40.

### Example 2

If a toy is originally \$30 and is on sale for 40% off, what would its new price be?

### Solution

Use the decreased total formula, plugging in 30 for the original amount and 0.40 for $r$ since 40% must be expressed as a decimal:

$$\text{Decreased Total} = (\text{Original Amount}) \times (1 - r) \rightarrow$$
$$\text{Decreased Total} = (30) \times (1 - 0.40) = 30 \times 0.6 = 18$$

Therefore, the discounted price of the toy is \$18.

## Practice

1. What number is 60% more than 40?
2. The amount of monthly rainfall in a town in January was 10 inches, and in February it was 7 inches. By what percent did the monthly rainfall decrease?
3. A car originally sells for \$20,000, but is on sale for 10% off. How much money would a buyer save by purchasing the car on sale? (Do not include sales tax in your calculations.)
4. During the school year, Ashra would read 3 hours a week for fun. Over the summer, she would read 9 hours a week for fun. By what percent did her weekly leisure reading in the summer increase compared to what she did during the school year?
5. A book typically sells for \$30, but there is a 20% discount. After including a 7% sales tax, what is the sale price of the book?

## Solutions

1. Use this formula, Increased Total = (Original Amount) × (1 + $r$), plugging in 40 as the original amount and 0.4 as $r$, since the percent must be expressed as a decimal:

$$\text{Increased Total} = (\text{Original Amount}) \times (1 + r) \rightarrow$$
$$\text{Increased Total} = (40) \times (1 + 0.6) = 40 \times 1.6 = 64$$

2. Use this formula, $\frac{\text{New} - \text{Original}}{\text{Original}} \times 100 = \text{Percent Change}$, plugging in 10 as the original amount and 7 as the new amount to solve for the percent it has changed:

$$\frac{\text{New} - \text{Original}}{\text{Original}} \times 100 = \text{Percent Change} \rightarrow$$
$$\frac{7 - 10}{10} \times 100 = \frac{-3}{10} \times 100 = -30\%$$

Since this is negative, the monthly rainfall has decreased by 30%.

3. Rather than using the percent change formula, recognize that you simply need to calculate 10% of \$20,000 to find the amount saved:

$$20{,}000 \times 0.10 = 2{,}000$$

So, the amount of money saved is \$2,000.

4. Calculate the percent increase using this formula, $\frac{\text{New} - \text{Original}}{\text{Original}} \times 100 = \text{Percent Change}$, plugging in 3 for the original amount and 9 for the new amount:

$$\frac{\text{New} - \text{Original}}{\text{Original}} \times 100 = \text{Percent Change} \rightarrow$$

$$\frac{9-3}{3} \times 100 = \frac{6}{3} \times 100 = 200\%$$

Since this is positive, there is a 200% increase in her weekly leisurely reading.

5. First, use this formula to find the discounted price:

$$\text{Decreased Total} = (\text{Original Amount}) \times (1 - r)$$

Use 30 as the original amount and $r$ as 0.2 to represent the 20% discount:

$$\text{Decreased Total} = (30) \times (1 - 0.2) \rightarrow$$

$$\text{Decreased Total} = 30 \times 0.8 = 24$$

Now, use Increased Total $=$ (Original Amount) $\times (1 + r)$ to find the price after adding the 7% sales tax, using 24 as the original amount and 0.07 as the $r$ (since 7% would be expressed as a decimal):

$$\text{Increased Total} = (\text{Original Amount}) \times (1 + r) \rightarrow$$

$$\text{Increased Total} = (24) \times (1 + 0.07) = 24 \times 1.07 = 25.68$$

So, the sale price after tax is added is \$25.68.

### Simple Interest

The SAT will frequently test your skill in calculating how interest applied over time will affect the amount. First, *simple interest* enables you to calculate the interest over a set period of time.

#### Simple Interest

$$I = P \times r \times t$$

$I$ = Amount of Interest
$P$ = Principal (Original Amount)
$r$ = Interest rate expressed as a decimal
$t$ = Time period the interest is applied (usually years)

#### Example 1

Andrew has \$500 in his savings account, and it receives 1% interest over a year. How much interest would he have accumulated after the end of the year?

#### Solution

Use the formula $I = P \times r \times t$ to solve for the amount of interest. The principal is \$500, the interest rate expressed as a decimal is 0.01, and the time period is one year.

$$I = P \times r \times t \rightarrow$$
$$I = 500 \times 0.01 \times 1 = 5$$

So, Andrew would earn \$5 in interest in one year.

**Example 2**

Bridget's home price increases by 4% in simple interest (not compounded) over a three-year period. If her home at the beginning of the three-year period costs $100,000, what is the price at the end of the period?

**Solution**

Use $I = P \times r \times t$ to find the amount of interest over the three-year period. The principal is $100,000, the rate is 0.04, and the time period is 3:

$$I = P \times r \times t \rightarrow$$
$$I = 100{,}00 \times 0.04 \times 3 = 12{,}000$$

Then, add 12,000 to the original price to find out the price of the house at the end of the period:

$$100{,}000 + 12{,}000 = 112{,}000$$

So, the price of her house after three years would be $112,000.

### Compound Interest

More frequently, the SAT Math will ask about *compound interest*:

**Compound Interest**

$$A = P\left(1 + \frac{r}{n}\right)^{nt}$$

$A$ = Future Value
$P$ = Initial Value (Principal)
$r$ = Interest Rate Expressed as a Decimal ($r$ is positive if increasing, negative if decreasing)
$t$ = Time
$n$ = Number of Times Interest is Compounded over Time Period $t$

**Example 1**

A savings bond has an initial value of $500. The interest on the bond is 4%, compounded annually. What is the value of the savings bond after 2 years?

**Solution**

Use the compound interest formula to solve. The initial value is $500, the interest rate expressed as a decimal is 0.04, the time is 2 years, and the number of times it is compounded each year is 1.

$$A = P\left(1 + \frac{r}{n}\right)^{nt} \rightarrow$$
$$A = 500\left(1 + \frac{.04}{1}\right)^{(1 \times 2)} \rightarrow$$
$$A = 500(1.04)^2 = 540.80$$

So, the savings bond would have a value of $540.80 after a 2-year time period.

### Example 2

The depth in a lake is 40 meters, and is decreasing by 1.2% each month, compounded. After 1 year, what will the depth of the lake be to the nearest hundredth of a meter?

### Solution

Use the compound interest formula, with 40 as $P$, $-0.012$ as $r$ (since the depth is decreasing), $n$ as 12 (since there are 12 months in a year), and $t$ as 1 since there is 1 year.

$$A = P\left(1 + \frac{r}{n}\right)^{nt} \rightarrow$$

$$A = 40\left(1 + \frac{-0.012}{12}\right)^{12(1)} \rightarrow$$

$$A = 40(0.999)^{12} \approx 39.52$$

So, the depth of the lake after 1 year to the nearest hundredth of a meter is 39.52 meters.

**SAT Math Strategy**

In order to visualize percentage changes with variables, use 100 as an initial value.

### Example

The price, $P$, after $n$ years for a television that initially costs $x$ dollars is given in the function below.

$$P = xk^n$$

If the price of a television decreases by 10% each year, what is the value of the constant $k$?

(A) 0.1
(B) 0.9
(C) 10
(D) 90

### Solution

Most of the SAT Math problems you encounter will have concrete numbers in them. On the occasion that you have one with pure variables, it can often be difficult to visualize the potential changes. To make things easier, use 100 as an initial value—that way you can efficiently calculate the percent change from the initial value.

With this problem, let's then use 100 as the initial value for $x$. If the initial value decreases by 10%, it would be 90 the following year. So, we can plug in 90 for $P$, 100 for $x$, and 1 for $n$, then solve for $k$:

$$P = xk^n \rightarrow$$

$$90 = 100k^1 \rightarrow$$

$$90 = 100k \rightarrow$$

$$\frac{90}{100} = k \rightarrow$$

$$k = 0.9$$

So, the answer is **(B)**, 0.9 as the $k$ value.

## Practice Drill #1—Problem Solving and Data Analysis: Percentages

*(If timing, take about 12 minutes to complete.)*

1. What is 150% of 3,000?

   (A) 1,500
   (B) 2,000
   (C) 4,500
   (D) 5,500

2. At a certain university, 25% of graduating seniors earned an honors diploma. What is the number of students graduating with an honors diploma if there were a total of 480 graduating seniors at the university?

   (A) 100
   (B) 120
   (C) 200
   (D) 600

3. If a computer that regularly costs $800 is on sale for 20% off, what would its sale price be (do not include sales tax in your calculation)?

   (A) $160
   (B) $200
   (C) $600
   (D) $640

| Average Commute Time from Home to Work | Percentage of Respondents |
|---|---|
| Less than 10 minutes | 25% |
| 10–30 minutes | 45% |
| Over 30 minutes | 30% |

4. If the number of respondents with an average commute of greater than 30 minutes is 240, how many people all together responded to this survey?

   (A) 480
   (B) 620
   (C) 800
   (D) 960

5. Sam purchases a total of 25 gift cards for his friends, with the gift cards being for retail stores or for restaurants. If he purchases 50% more retail store gift cards than restaurant gift cards, how many retail store gift cards did he purchase?

   (A) 12.5
   (B) 15
   (C) 20
   (D) 37.5

6. In a park, 15% of the parkgoers were children, 45% were male adults, and the remaining 8 were adult females. How many parkgoers were there all together?

   (A) 20
   (B) 24
   (C) 30
   (D) 36

7. Chelsea has a temperature of 98.6°F. The next day, she has a fever, with a temperature of 103.2°F. By what percentage, calculated to the nearest tenth of a percent, did her temperature increase from the first day to the second day?

   (A) 4.5%
   (B) 4.7%
   (C) 5.1%
   (D) 5.4%

8. The U.S. stock market has returned a historical average of approximately 10% per year. If this rate of return were to continue into the future, what function would model the value, $V$, of an initial investment of $V_O$ in the stock market $t$ years from now?

   (A) $V(t) = V_O(10)^t$
   (B) $V(t) = V_O(110)^t$
   (C) $V(t) = V_O(1.1)^t$
   (D) $V(t) = V_O(0.1)^t$

9. A new car is on sale for 15% off the sticker price. Maxwell is trading in his old car for a total of \$5,000—all of this counts as a credit toward the price paid for a new car purchase. Assuming there is no sales tax, if the car has a sticker price of $x$ dollars, what amount will Maxwell have to pay, $P$, for a new car, accounting for the sale discount and the trade-in credit?

   (A) $P = 0.85x - 5,000$
   (B) $P = 0.85 + 5,000$
   (C) $P = 0.15x - 5,000$
   (D) $P = 0.15x + 5,000$

10. The gravitational force, $F$, is related to the gravitational constant, $G$, mass of one object, $m_1$, and mass of another object, $m_2$, and the distance between the centers of the objects, $r$, using the following equation:

$$F = \frac{Gm_1 m_2}{r^2}$$

By what percent would the gravitational force between two objects change if the distance between them were doubled and the other quantities remained the same?

   (A) It would decrease by 50%.
   (B) It would decrease by 75%.
   (C) It would increase by 100%.
   (D) It would increase by 200%.

## Solutions

1. **(C)** Take 150 and move the decimal point over two spots to the left. Then multiply this by 3,000:

$$1.5 \times 3,000 = 4,500$$

2. **(B)** Calculate 25% of 480 by moving the decimal point two spots to the left in 25, then multiplying it by 480:

$$0.25 \times 480 = 120$$

3. **(D)** Use the formula Decreased Total = (Original Amount) × (1 − *r*), with 800 as the original amount and *r* as 0.2:

$$\text{Decreased Total} = (\text{Original Amount}) \times (1 - r) \rightarrow$$

$$\text{Decreased Total} = 800 \times (1 - 0.2) = 800 \times 0.8 = 640$$

4. **(C)** Use the formula $\frac{\text{Part}}{\text{Whole}} \times 100 = \text{Percent}$ to calculate the total number of survey participants. Let's use $x$ as the unknown number of total survey participants, 30 as the percent, and 240 as the "part":

$$\frac{\text{Part}}{\text{Whole}} \times 100 = \text{Percent} \rightarrow$$

$$\frac{240}{x} \times 100 = 30 \rightarrow$$

Cross multiply →

$$\frac{240}{30} \times 100 = x \rightarrow$$

$$8 \times 100 = x \rightarrow$$

$$800 = x$$

5. **(B)** Set up an equation modeling the situation. The total number of gift cards is 25, and he purchased 50% more retail cards than restaurant cards. Use $x$ as the number of restaurant cards and use $1.5x$ as the number of retail cards, since it is 50% more:

$$x + 1.5x = 25 \rightarrow$$

$$2.5x = 25 \rightarrow$$

$$x = 10$$

Then, using the formula Number of Retail Gift Cards = (Original Amount) × (1 + *r*), calculate the number of retail gift cards purchased; 10 will be the original amount, and *r* will be 0.5:

$$\text{Number of Retail Gift Cards} = (\text{Original Amount}) \times (1 + r) \rightarrow$$

$$\text{Number of Retail Gift Cards} = 10 \times 1.5 = 15$$

Therefore, he will purchase 15 retail store gift cards. You could also try plugging in the answers to see which would fit the criteria.

6. **(A)** The percent of female parkgoers will be what remains after subtracting the children and males:

$$100\% - 45\% - 15\% = 40\%$$

So, 40% of the parkgoers are female, and this number will be 8. Now, we can solve for the total number of parkgoers by using the equation $\frac{\text{Part}}{\text{Whole}} \times 100 = \text{Percent}$; let's use $x$ as the "whole," 40 as the "percent," and 8 as the "part."

$$\frac{\text{Part}}{\text{Whole}} \times 100 = \text{Percent} \rightarrow$$

$$\frac{8}{x} \times 100 = 40 \rightarrow$$

Cross Multiply →

$$\frac{8}{40} \times 100 = x \rightarrow$$

$$0.2 \times 100 = x \rightarrow$$

$$20 = x$$

So, the total number of parkgoers is 20.

7. **(B)** Use the formula $\frac{\text{New} - \text{Original}}{\text{Original}} \times 100 = \text{Percent Change}$ to calculate the percent change. The original value is 98.6 and the new value is 103.2:

$$\frac{\text{New} - \text{Original}}{\text{Original}} \times 100 = \text{Percent Change} \rightarrow$$

$$\frac{103.2 - 98.6}{98.6} \times 100 \rightarrow$$

$$\frac{4.6}{98.6} \times 100 \approx 4.7\%$$

8. **(C)** Use the formula $A = P\left(1 + \frac{r}{n}\right)^{nt}$ to model the future value of the investment. $V(t)$ will be $A$, $P$ will be $V_O$, $r$ will be 0.1, $n$ will be 1, and $t$ will stay as a variable.

$$A = P\left(1 + \frac{r}{n}\right)^{nt} \rightarrow$$

$$V(t) = V_O\left(1 + \frac{0.1}{1}\right)^{1(t)} \rightarrow$$

$$V(t) = V_O(1.1)^t$$

You could also solve this by looking at what makes the answer choices different and noticing that the only one that would show a 10% increase is choice **(C)**.

9. **(A)** Take a 15% discount off the price of the new car to find what he will have to pay before the trade-in value is included:

$$\text{Decreased Total} = (\text{Original Amount}) \times (1 - r) \rightarrow$$

$$\text{Discounted Price} = x \times (1 - 0.15) = 0.85x$$

Then, subtract \$5,000 from the price paid to include the trade-in value:

$$P = 0.85x - 5{,}000$$

10. **(B)** In doing the comparison, keep everything constant that remains constant, and change only what is different. The gravitational force, $F$, and the distance, $r$, are the only things that will change. Consider the original force:

$$F = \frac{Gm_1 m_2}{r^2}$$

Now, double the distance, $r$, and see how the original force would change:

$$F = \frac{Gm_1 m_2}{r^2} \rightarrow$$

$$\text{New } F = \frac{Gm_1 m_2}{(2r)^2} = \frac{Gm_1 m_2}{4r^2} = \frac{1}{4}\left(\frac{Gm_1 m_2}{r^2}\right) = \frac{1}{4}F$$

So, the new force is $\frac{1}{4}$ of the original value, which means it has decreased by $\frac{3}{4}$ its original value. Convert $\frac{3}{4}$ to a percentage by using a proportion:

$$\frac{3}{4} = \frac{x}{100} \rightarrow$$

$$0.75 = \frac{x}{100} \rightarrow$$

$$75\% = x$$

Therefore, the gravitational force between the two objects would decrease by 75% if the distance between them were doubled.

## Practice Drill #2—Problem Solving and Data Analysis: Percentages

*(If timing, take about 12 minutes to complete.)*

**Fill-In Practice:** Write your answer in the underlined blank under each question.

1. What number is 130% of 50?

   Answer: ________

2. In the United States in 2019, approximately 62% of utility electricity came from fossil fuels, 20% from nuclear, and 18% from renewable sources. What fraction of U.S. utility electricity in 2019 came from nuclear?

   Answer: ________

3. A wind turbine has a maximum electrical generating capacity of 200 kilowatts per hour, and it operates on average at 25% of this maximum capacity. If the turbine operates at its average capacity for an entire day, how many kilowatts of electricity would it produce?

   Answer: ________

| Mascot Preference | Percent of Students Who Prefer Mascot |
|---|---|
| Tiger | 10% |
| Lion | 15% |
| Bear | 30% |
| Eagle | 25% |
| Dog | 20% |

4. A college had all of its students vote on their preference for a new school mascot. If the number of students who preferred Bear exceeded the number who preferred Dog by 240 students, how many students selected Eagle?

   Answer: ________

5. A toy store sells only dolls and games; 70% of the toys it sells are dolls and 30% are games. The store sells a total of 400 toys. How many more dolls than games does the store sell?

   Answer: ________

**Multiple-Choice Practice**

6. A house was initially listed for sale at $200,000. After three months, the sellers still had not sold it and decided to drop the price by 15%. What would the new price be?

   (A) $170,000
   (B) $185,000
   (C) $215,000
   (D) $230,000

7. A school district is doing a ten-year projection of its student enrollment. If at the start of the ten years there are 2,000 students in the district, and the student enrollment increases by 5% each year, what would be the enrollment $t$ years from now?

   (A) $2,000(1.5)^t$
   (B) $2,000(1.05)^t$
   (C) $2,000(.05)^t$
   (D) $2,000(5)^t$

8. In the year 2010, New York City had a population density of 27,016 people per square mile, and San Francisco had a population density of 17,246 people per square mile. The population density in San Francisco was what percent lower than the population density in New York in 2010, calculated to the nearest tenth of a percent?

   (A) 36.2%
   (B) 41.6%
   (C) 53.4%
   (D) 63.8%

9. The elimination half-life of a medicine is the amount of time it takes for the concentration of the medicine in the body to be reduced by half. If a particular medicine starts at a dose of 100 mg that is fully absorbed in the body and has an elimination half-life of 8 hours, how much of the medicine remains in the body after 1 day?

   (A) 6.25 mg
   (B) 12.5 mg
   (C) 25 mg
   (D) 36 mg

10. One serving of a cereal is $\frac{2}{3}$ of a cup and has 20% of the daily recommended amount of only fiber, which is 6 grams. If another cereal has a serving size of 1 cup, how many grams of fiber should it have to provide 30% of the daily value of fiber?

   (A) 4 grams
   (B) 6 grams
   (C) 9 grams
   (D) 12 grams

## Solutions

1. **(65)** Move the decimal point in 130 to the left two spots, then multiply by 50:

$$1.3 \times 50 = 65$$

2. **(0.2 or $\frac{1}{5}$)** Convert the 20% from nuclear to a percentage by reducing the fraction to its simplest form:

$$\frac{20}{100} \rightarrow \frac{1}{5}$$

   This could also be expressed as a decimal, 0.2.

3. **(1,200)** Multiply the number of kilowatts per hour, 200, by 0.25 to get the 25% operational level. Then, multiply this by 24 since there are 24 hours in a day:

$$200 \times 0.25 \times 24 = 1,200$$

   So, it would produce 1,200 kilowatts of electricity in a day.

4. **(600)** The Bear students are 30% of the total, and the Dog students are 20% of the total. The difference between them is 10%, so 10% of the total is 240. Multiply 240 by 10 to get the total number of students (since 10% multiplied by 10 is 100%):

$$240 \times 10 = 2,400$$

   Then, take 25% of the total:

$$0.25 \times 2,400 = 600$$

5. **(160)** Calculate the number of dolls sold (70% of 400):

$$0.7 \times 400 = 280$$

   Then, calculate the number of games sold (30% of 400):

$$0.3 \times 400 = 120$$

Then, subtract 120 from 280 to find how many more dolls are sold than games:

$$280 - 120 = 160$$

Alternatively, if you notice the difference between them must equal 40% of the total toys sold, you could just take 40% of 400 and get the same result of 160.

6. **(A)** Calculate the discounted price by using this formula,

Decreased Total = (Original Amount) × (1 − *r*), with 200,000 as the original amount and *r* as 0.15:

$$\text{Decreased Total} = (\text{Original Amount}) \times (1 - r) \rightarrow$$

$$\text{Sale Price} = 200,000 \times (1 - 0.15) = 200,000 \times 0.85 = 170,000$$

7. **(B)** Use the formula $A = P\left(1 + \frac{r}{n}\right)^{nt}$ to determine what the enrollment would be. *A* represents the enrollment, *P* is the original number of 2,000 students, *r* is 0.05 (5% expressed as a decimal), *n* is 1 since the compounding is annual, and *t* will remain a variable:

$$A = P\left(1 + \frac{r}{n}\right)^{nt} \rightarrow$$

$$\text{Enrollment} = 2,000\left(1 + \frac{0.05}{1}\right)^{(1)t} \rightarrow$$

$$\text{Enrollment} = 2,000(1.05)^{t}$$

8. **(A)** Use the formula $\frac{\text{New} - \text{Original}}{\text{Original}} \times 100 = \text{Percent Change}$ to calculate the percent difference between the population density of New York City and San Francisco. The "original" value will be 27,016 and the "new" will be 17,246:

$$\frac{\text{New} - \text{Original}}{\text{Original}} \times 100 = \text{Percent Change} \rightarrow$$

$$\frac{17,246 - 27,016}{27,016} \times 100 \rightarrow$$

$$\frac{-9,770}{27,016} \times 100 \approx -36.2\%$$

*Since this is negative, the population density in San Francisco is about 36.2% lower than it is in New York City.*

9. **(B)** During a one-day period of 24 hours, the medicine will have gone through three half-life cycles, since each half-life cycle is 8 hours and 8 goes into 24 three times. So, to find out how much of the medicine is left after three half-life cycles, take 50% of the original amount of 100 three times:

$$100 \times 0.5 \times 0.5 \times 0.5 = 12.5$$

10. **(C)** Sort out the essential information here, as there is irrelevant information given. The serving sizes of the cereal are not important—what is important is providing the correct amount of fiber. The first cereal provides 20% of the daily value of fiber in its serving; the second cereal provides 30% of the daily value of fiber in its serving. Set up a proportion to solve for *x*, the number of grams of fiber in the second cereal:

$$\frac{30}{20} = \frac{x}{6} \rightarrow$$

$$1.5 = \frac{x}{6} \rightarrow$$

$$6 \times 1.5 = 9 = x$$

## Problem Solving and Data Analysis—Surveys

Surveys are a part of everyday life, and the SAT will assess your skill in interpreting surveys. One of the biggest things emphasized will be determining whether a sampling method is appropriate.

### Sampling Methods

**Let's first look at some ways a survey could be POORLY conducted.**

- **Sample is chosen non-randomly:**
    - Example: Researcher interviews only parents and caregivers at a playground on their thoughts about increased funding for extracurricular activities at schools to determine what all the citizens in the community think about increased extracurricular funding. *Why is this problematic?* If the researcher is interested in sampling the community as a whole, by limiting the respondents to parents and caregivers who have congregated at a playground, the researcher will oversample those who are already interested in children's activities and/or have children.
    - Example: A city worker samples city residents who have memberships to the city's community center about whether they would support a tax levy for an additional city community center. *Why is this problematic?* If the respondents are all members of the city's community center, they are using this service already. So, it is more likely they will support increased funding for a city service they enjoy. The worker should instead include respondents who are not already members of the community center.
- **Participants can volunteer:**
    - Example: A politician has a survey on her website asking whether she or her opponent won a political debate. *Why is this problematic?* Supporters are more likely to be on her website and believe their preferred candidate—i.e., the politician conducting the survey—won the debate. This will result in a sample of respondents skewed toward those who already supported the candidate.
    - Example: A theme park worker asks people who are leaving the theme park to complete a 10-minute customer survey about their experience. *Why is this problematic?* This will result in a sample skewed toward those who have the time to complete the survey and feel passionately enough about their experience (for good or for bad) to want to answer questions.
- **Sample size is too small:**
    - Example: A student, who lives in a city of 100,000 people, surveys four city residents about their favorite restaurant in the city and draws conclusions about the city's favorite restaurant. *Why is this problematic?* Four people is too small of a sample when the population of the city is 100,000.

> **SAT Math Strategy**
>
> In general, to get the best results in a survey, have the sample be as large and as random as possible. The larger and more random the survey, the less the potential bias will be in the results.

**Now, let's consider some ways a survey could be conducted WELL.**

- **Responses are randomly collected.**
    - Example: To survey a group of 1,000 people, a random number generator selects which of the 1,000 people will be respondents.
    - Example: To select 100 respondents for a political survey in a state, a researcher randomly selects phone numbers from a database of all mobile phones and landlines in the state.
- **The sample size is sufficiently large.**
    - Example: To predict the winner of an upcoming senatorial election, a random sample of 1,000 likely voters is conducted.

- **All groups in a survey are fairly represented.**
  - Example: To test the effectiveness of a medicine in the population as a whole, a university ensures that there are sufficient patients in the study from different genders, ages, and ethnicities.
  - Example: To determine the popularity of a shift in the school schedule among staff members, a school superintendent ensures that adequate representation from all types of school district workers is given—teachers, administrators, custodians, bus drivers, etc.

Use *margin of error* to quantify the quality of a survey's conclusions. Margin of error is the maximum expected difference between the actual parameter and the sample parameter. If a survey is conducted poorly, it will have a HIGH margin of error. If it is conducted well, it will have a LOW margin of error.

### Example

If a pollster conducts a poll that says 40% of the voters will vote in favor of Candidate 1, with a 3% margin of error, which of the following could be the actual value of the percent of votes cast in the election for Candidate 1?

(A) 35%
(B) 38%
(C) 44%
(D) 47%

### ✓ Solution

Since the margin of error is 3%, that means that the actual results are projected to be between $\pm 3\%$ of 40%, so between 37% and 43%. So, the correct answer is choice **(B)**, since 38% falls within this range.

### Drawing Conclusions

**SAT Math Strategy**

Limit generalizations about a survey to what is directly supported by the results.

### Example 1

A researcher asks 100 randomly selected survey participants in a city their favorite place for outdoor exercise. The survey has a low response rate, and the researcher concludes that the residents are not exercising sufficiently and that a "Get Outdoors Health Campaign" is needed to motivate city residents to exercise outdoors. Is this conclusion warranted based on the given information?

### ✓ Solution

No, it is not supported by the given information since there are many potential reasons why the response rate to the survey could be low:

- Perhaps the deadline to return the survey was too short.
- Perhaps the surveys did not reach the participants.
- Perhaps the potential respondents did not want to participate in research.

Moreover, the survey did not ask participants if they exercise outside—instead, it only asked their favorite location to do so. Given what the survey asked, a conclusion about whether or not city residents are exercising outside and need to be motivated with an advertising campaign cannot be drawn.

### › Example 2

A city worker wants to determine the percent of the city's residents that are fluent in both Spanish and English. The worker writes the survey in Spanish and mails it to 400 randomly selected addresses in the city. Thirty of the surveys are returned, and 90% of them state that their household members are fluent in both Spanish and English. Would it be correct to generalize that 90% of the town's residents are fluent in both Spanish and English?

### ✓ Solution

No, because of the survey design. If household members were not able to read Spanish, they would not be able to understand the survey and could not respond. Therefore, households in which the residents were only fluent in English would be far less likely to be included in the results. Households that were able to read Spanish would understand the instructions and would be much more likely to respond, skewing the results to show a higher proportion of bilingual households.

## Practice Drill—Problem Solving and Data Analysis: Surveys

*(If timing, take about 12 minutes to complete.)*

1. To find out which world language they wanted to study in high school, 250 junior high students were surveyed. Of the students surveyed, 75 indicated they wanted to study Chinese. Which conclusion is best supported by this data?

   (A) Approximately 30% of the junior high students surveyed were interested in studying Chinese.

   (B) Approximately 75% of the junior high students surveyed were interested in studying Chinese.

   (C) Approximately 25% of all students in the town were interested in studying Chinese.

   (D) Approximately 35% of all students in the town were interested in studying Chinese.

2. According to a recent student survey, 40% of high school seniors in the United States have taken a college credit class while in high school. If there are 3.7 million students in this year's high school graduating class in the United States, approximately how many of these graduating students likely took a college credit class while in high school?

(A) 148,000
(B) 222,000
(C) 1,480,000
(D) 2,220,000

3. For an upcoming election, a pollster estimates that 55% of voters will vote for Ballot Issue #1, given a margin of error of $\pm 3\%$. If there are 200,000 voters in the upcoming election, what would the pollster estimate to be the number, $x$, who will vote for Ballot Issue #1?

(A) $90,000 < x < 96,000$
(B) $104,000 < x < 116,000$
(C) $120,000 < x < 124,000$
(D) $224,000 < x < 248,000$

4. A newspaper surveyed 2,000 likely voters about their preference for a candidate in the upcoming election. The results are compiled in the table below:

| Candidate | Vote Total |
|---|---|
| Candidate A | 980 |
| Candidate B | 764 |
| Candidate C | 155 |
| No Preference | 101 |

Based on these results, which of the following would be a true statement?

(A) 49% of the survey respondents preferred candidate A.
(B) 98% of the survey respondents preferred candidate A.
(C) 16% of survey respondents preferred candidate C.
(D) 46% of survey respondents preferred candidate C.

5. A randomly selected survey of 2,000 dentists finds that 600 prefer Brand A dental floss. Based on this information, out of a group of 1,000 randomly selected dentists, how many will likely prefer Brand A dental floss?

(A) 200
(B) 300
(C) 800
(D) 900

6. A political scientist conducts a survey about approval for a state's governor. The results of the random sample of registered voters in the state are given in the table below:

| % Who Approve | % Who Disapprove | Margin of Error |
|---|---|---|
| 55 | 45 | 5 |

What action by the political scientist would most likely decrease the survey's margin of error?

(A) Conduct an identical survey in a different state
(B) Conduct an identical survey in a different country
(C) Decrease the survey sample size
(D) Increase the survey sample size

7. A travel agency wanted to determine which types of vacation destinations would be most popular for potential clients. They randomly sampled 100 adults within the boundaries of the travel agency's city and found that the majority of the respondents preferred a beach destination. What is the largest group for which these results of the market survey could accurately be generalized?

(A) The child residents of the travel agency's city
(B) The adult residents of the travel agency's city
(C) All residents of the travel agency's city
(D) All citizens of the travel agency's country

8. A medical researcher surveyed a random sample of nursing home residents and estimated between 46% and 54% of the residents had a family member who lived within 25 miles. What is another way she could report her estimate?

(A) 25% with an 8% margin of error
(B) 46% with an 8% margin of error
(C) 50% with a 4% margin of error
(D) 54% with a 4% margin of error

9. At an arboretum, a botanist found that out of 100 randomly selected trees from the arboretum, 30 were evergreen and 70 were deciduous. If there were a total of 1,000 trees in the arboretum, which inequality expresses how many of the remaining trees, $E$, would have to be evergreen if more than half of all the trees in the arboretum were evergreen?

(A) $E > 470$
(B) $E < 470$
(C) $E > 590$
(D) $E < 590$

10. One hundred randomly selected users of a television streaming service were surveyed as to their preferred use for the service. Of these, 35% preferred to "binge watch" one show until they had seen all the episodes for that show, and 65% preferred to skip around to watch different shows. What is the most accurate conclusion based on these results?

    (A) It is more likely that a randomly selected user of the service prefers binge watching to show skipping.
    (B) It is more likely that a randomly selected user of the service prefers show skipping to binge watching.
    (C) Exactly 65% of all users of the streaming service prefer binge watching over show skipping.
    (D) Exactly 65% of all users of the streaming service prefer show skipping over binge watching.

## Solutions

1. **(A)** We can eliminate choices (C) and (D) since the survey is limited to students at the junior high and would not be representative of all students in the town. The correct answer is choice **(A)** because 75 of the 250 junior high students said they wanted to study Chinese—this equates to 30%.

$$\frac{75}{250} \times 100 = 30\%$$

2. **(C)** Based on the survey data, 40% of high school seniors in the United States have taken a college credit class. Therefore, if we take 40% of the total number of students in the United States who are graduating from high school, we will get the approximate number of the graduating students who likely took a college credit class:

$$0.40 \times 3,700,000 = 1,480,000$$

3. **(B)** Since the margin of error is 3%, the likely number of voters will be between 52% and 58% of the 200,000 total.

$$0.52 \times 200,000 = 104,000$$
$$0.58 \times 200,000 = 116,000$$

So, the estimated number of voters who will vote for Ballot Issue #1 is $104,000 < x < 116,000$.

4. **(A)** There are 2,000 total respondents to the survey, so determine what percent of this total Candidate A would be:

$$\frac{980}{2,000} \times 100 = 49\%$$

Thus, 49% of survey respondents preferred Candidate A. The other options are based on incorrect calculations with the vote totals in the table.

5. **(B)** Set up a proportion to solve for the number of dentists out of the 1,000 randomly selected ones who will prefer Brand A:

$$\frac{600}{2,000} = \frac{x}{1,000} \rightarrow$$

Cross multiply →

$$\frac{600}{2,000} \times 1,000 = x \rightarrow$$

$$300 = x$$

6. **(D)** To decrease the margin of error, make the survey sample as large and as random as possible. Choices (A) and (B) are incorrect because conducting the same survey in a different location will not better inform us about the approval within the state; they would be conducting the studies outside the considered population. Choice **(D)** is correct because increasing the sample size will make the survey data set larger, therefore decreasing the margin of error.

7. **(B)** The travel agency did a random sample of adults within the boundaries of the travel agency's city, so the generalization will be for adult residents of that city. It will not be choice (A) since children were not surveyed. It will not be choice (C) because that would include both children and adults in the generalization. And it will not be choice (D) because we do not know the specifics of other areas in the country and how they would respond.

8. **(C)** The number 50 is halfway between 46 and 54, with 4 units separating 46 from 50 and 4 units separating 54 from 50. So, the researcher could report the estimate as 50% with a 4% margin of error since this would encompass values between 46% and 54%.

9. **(A)** One hundred trees have already been selected, so there would be $1,000 - 100 = 900$ trees remaining. Half of all the trees in the arboretum would be 500. In the survey sample, there were 30 evergreen trees. So, there must be enough evergreen trees in the remaining 900 to give a total of over 500. Solve this inequality to reach the solution:

$$E > 500 - 30 \rightarrow$$

$$E > 470$$

10. **(B)** Choices (C) and (D) assert too much precision by stating that "exactly" 65% of the users must have a particular preference. Since 65% of the survey respondents said they like to skip around to different shows, and only 35% of the respondents preferred to binge watch, it would be reasonable to conclude that a randomly selected user of the service prefers show skipping to binge watching.

## Problem Solving and Data Analysis—Graphs and Data Interpretation

### Probability

Probability is defined as "the likelihood that a given event will happen," expressed as a decimal or fraction.

- If the probability that it will rain tomorrow is 0.5, there is a 50% chance it will rain.
- If the probability that it will snow tomorrow is 0, there is a 0% chance it will snow.
- If the probability that it will be cloudy tomorrow is 1, there is a 100% chance it will be cloudy.

To calculate probability, take the number of ways an event can happen and divide it by the total number of possible outcomes:

$$\frac{\text{Number of Ways Event Can Happen}}{\text{Total Number of Possible Outcomes}} = \text{Probability of Event}$$

## Example

If I have a total of 30 books on my bookshelf and 10 of them are novels, what is the probability that a randomly selected book from my bookshelf would be a novel?

## Solution

The "number of ways an event can happen" is 10 and the "total number of possible outcomes" is 30, so divide 10 by 30 to determine the probability:

$$\frac{10}{30} = \frac{1}{3}$$

So, the probability that a randomly selected book from the bookshelf would be a novel is $\frac{1}{3}$.

### Practice

1. On a multiple-choice test, there are four choices per question: (A), (B), (C), and (D). What is the probability that on a given question a test taker who is randomly selecting his answer will select choice (B)?
2. In John's wallet, he has five one-dollar bills, two five-dollar bills, and three ten-dollar bills. If a bill is selected at random from his wallet, what is the possibility it will be a five-dollar bill?
3. An advertiser finds that for 200 randomly selected online ad placements, six users will click through to the business website. Based on this data, what is the probability that a randomly selected ad placement will result in the user clicking through to the business website?

### Solutions

1. There are a total of four possible events, and choice (B) is one of the potential outcomes. So, divide 1 by 4 to find the probability: $\frac{1}{4}$.
2. John has a total of $5 + 2 + 3 = 10$ bills in his wallet. Out of these ten bills, two are five-dollar bills. So, divide 2 by 10 to find the probability:

$$\frac{2}{10} = \frac{1}{5}$$

3. There are 6 possible events out of 200 potential outcomes, so divide 6 by 200 to determine the probability:

$$\frac{6}{200} = 0.03$$

So, the probability that a randomly selected ad placement will result in the user clicking through to the business website is 0.03.

**SAT Math Strategy**

Carefully examine the units on the axes to avoid careless errors.

### Graph Interpretation

The SAT will assess your skill in interpreting a variety of graphs—you will be asked to find maximums, minimums, overall trends, and more.

**Example**

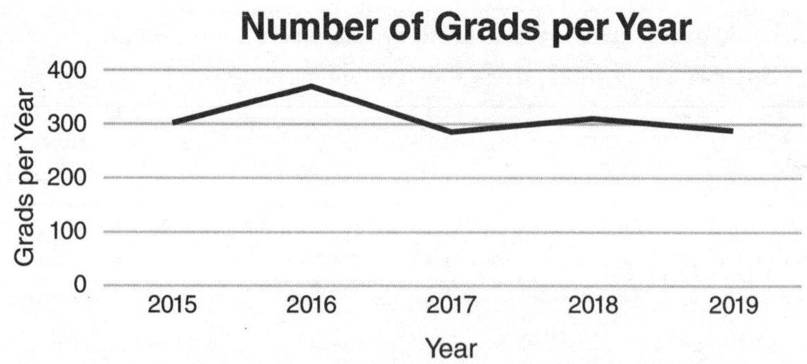


The number of graduates per year from Jackson High School are given in the line graph above. During what year of this time period was the number of graduates the greatest?

**Solution**

Examine the graph to see that the *x*-axis has the "years" and the *y*-axis has "grads per year." So, we need to find where the "grads per year" are at their highest value and the corresponding year.

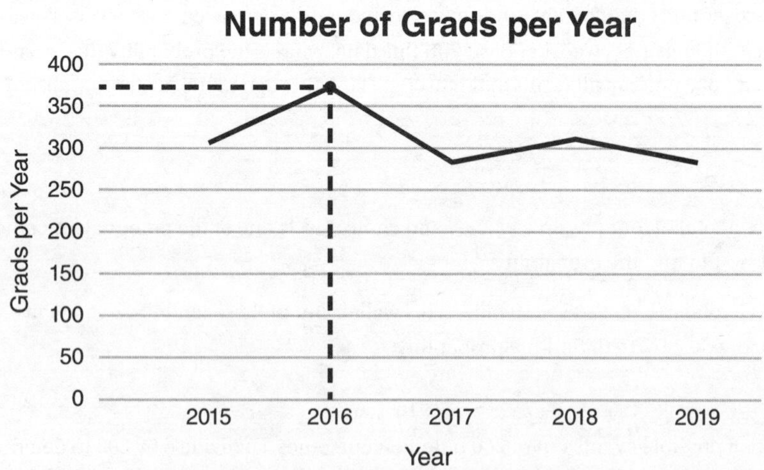


Drawing on the graph will help you visualize that the greatest number of grads per year is approximately 370, and that this occurs in year 2016. So, the answer is 2016.

## Practice

A delivery driver plots how far he is from his home throughout his workday.

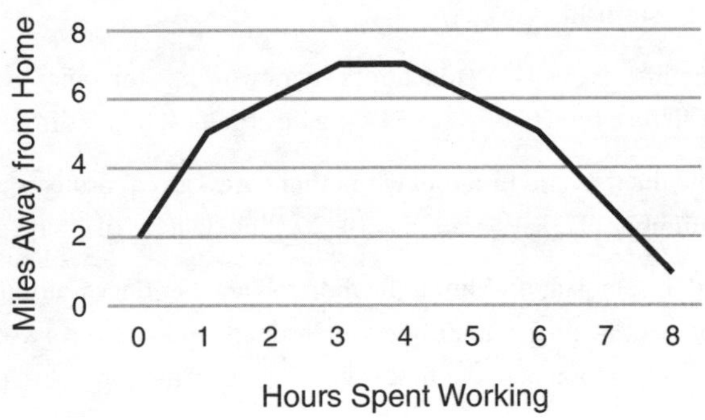


1. How far from home is the worker when he starts his workday?
2. For approximately how long is the driver at least 5 miles from home?

   A teacher has a total of 100 minutes he can spend grading essays and group projects. The various ways he could allocate his time are graphed below:

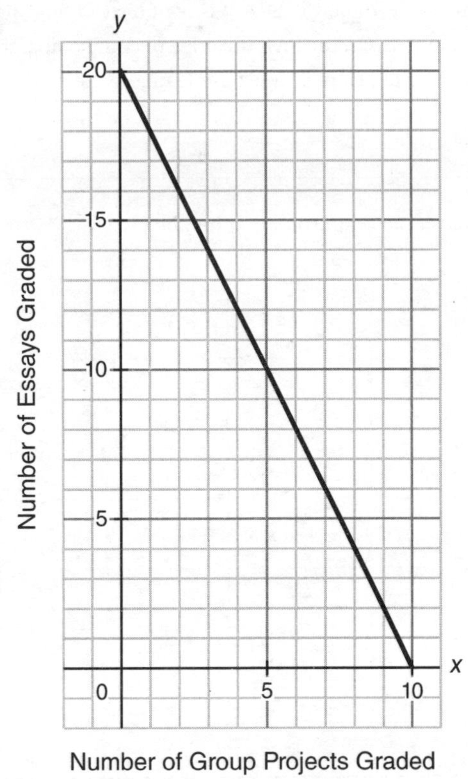


3. If the teacher spends the full 100 minutes grading projects and essays, and he grades 5 group projects, how many essays will he grade within this time?
4. How long does it take for him to grade an essay?

## Solutions

1. **2 miles.** Zero hours of working would correspond to the beginning of the driver's workday. At an $x$ value of 0, the $y$ value is 2 for the number of miles away from home. So, he will be 2 miles from home when he starts his workday.

2. **5 hours.** From 1 hour spent working to 6 hours spent working, the miles away from home is at least 5. So, there will be a total of $6 - 1 = 5$ hours he is at least 5 miles from home.

3. **10 essays.** Examine the line and find that when there are 5 group projects graded, the $y$- value representing the number of essays graded is 10. So, there will be 10 essays graded in this time.

4. **5 minutes.** To find this, look at the situation when the teacher does nothing but grade essays. This is at the point (0, 20)—no group projects are graded, and 20 essays would be graded. Since the teacher is spending a total of 100 minutes grading, find the number of minutes it takes to grade a single essay by dividing 100 minutes by 20 essays:

$$\frac{100}{20} = 5$$

## Scatterplots

Scatterplots provide a graph of different points that together will show a relationship among data. To see the relationship among the data, visualize a **line of best fit** that shows a line that would best approximate the data points. (On the SAT, the edge of your scrap paper can give you a great way to approximate a straight line.) Here is an example of a scatterplot with a line of best fit:

### Examples

Consider the line of best fit for the scatterplot graphed below.

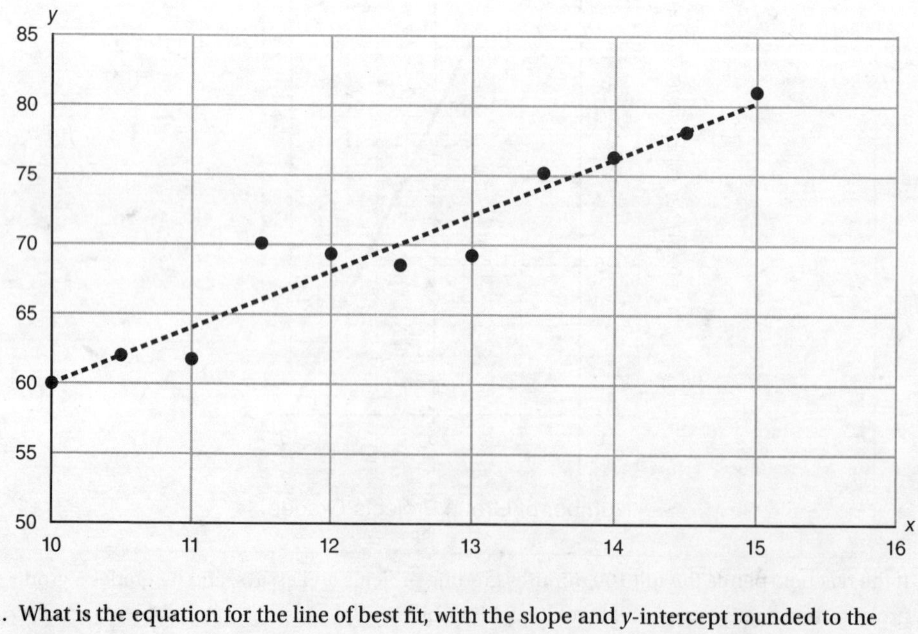


1. What is the equation for the line of best fit, with the slope and $y$-intercept rounded to the nearest whole integer values?

### ✓ Solution

Be careful to examine the $x$- and $y$-coordinates in the graph—they do not begin at (0, 0). First, pick two points for which it will be easy to find the slope: (10, 60) and (15, 80) will work.

$$\frac{\text{Change in Y}}{\text{Change in X}} = \frac{80 - 60}{15 - 10} = \frac{20}{5} = 4$$

So, the slope of the line is 4. Now, plug in a point that is in the line of best fit, such as (10, 60), to solve for the $y$-intercept:

$$y = mx + b \rightarrow$$

Plug in 4 for $m$, the slope:

$$y = 4x + b \rightarrow$$

Plug in (10, 60) as a point to solve for $b$:

$$60 = 4(10) + b \rightarrow$$
$$60 = 40 + b \rightarrow$$
$$20 = b$$

So, the equation for the line of best fit is $y = 4x + 20$ since the line has a slope of 4 and a $y$-intercept of 20.

2. Which point is an "outlier"—an observation that lies farthest from the values predicted by the line of best fit?

### ✓ Solution

Find the point that is most distant from the line of best fit:

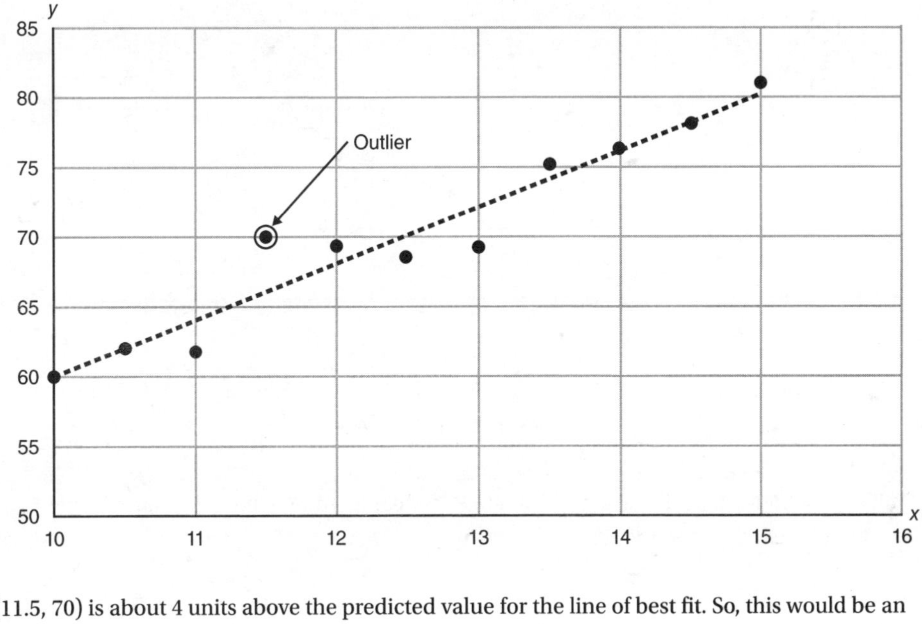


(11.5, 70) is about 4 units above the predicted value for the line of best fit. So, this would be an outlier in the graph.

### Practice

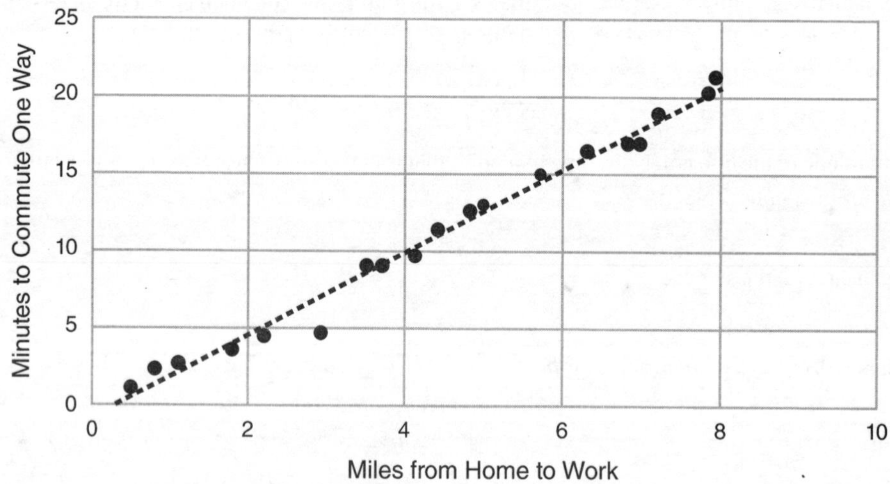


Twenty commuters recorded the distance from their homes to work and the time of their commutes on a particular day.

1. Based on the line of best fit, if someone lived 4 miles from work, how long would their commute time most likely be?
2. What value on the graph is most different from what would be predicted based on the trend?
3. For how many of the commuters was their actual commute time shorter than what would be predicted?

### Solutions

1.

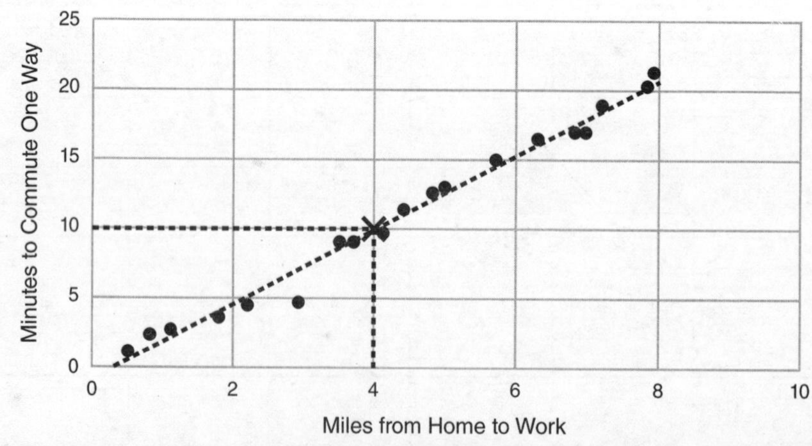


At 4 miles from home to work, the predicted number of commuting minutes is approximately 10, as you can see in the graph above.

2.

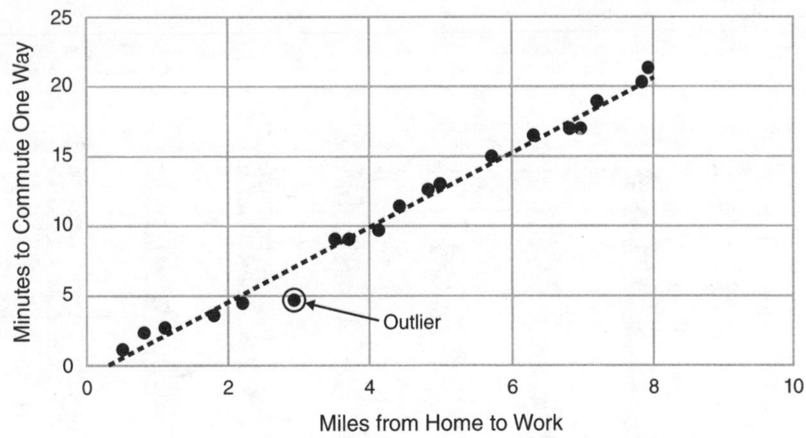


The value that is most different from what is predicted is the point (2.9, 4.6)—this point is an "outlier" since it is far away from the line of best fit.

3. Mark and count the number of points that fall *underneath* the line of best fit:

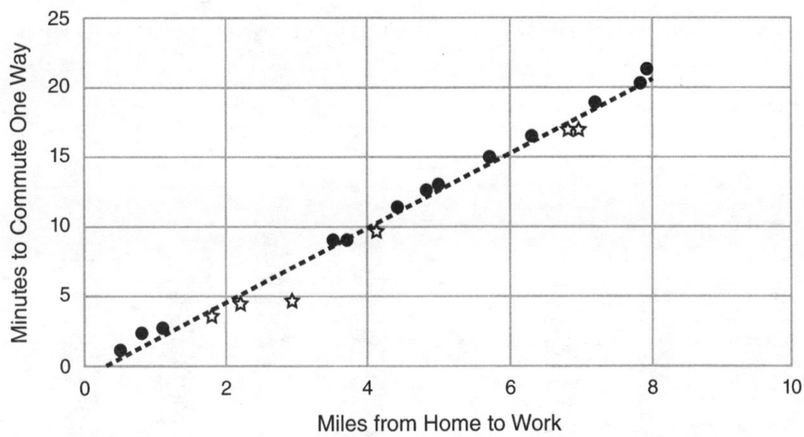


There are 6 points that fall underneath the line of best fit, so there are 6 commuters for whom the commute was shorter than predicted.

### Histograms

Histograms are also known as **bar graphs**—they show the frequency of different values in a data set.

**Example**

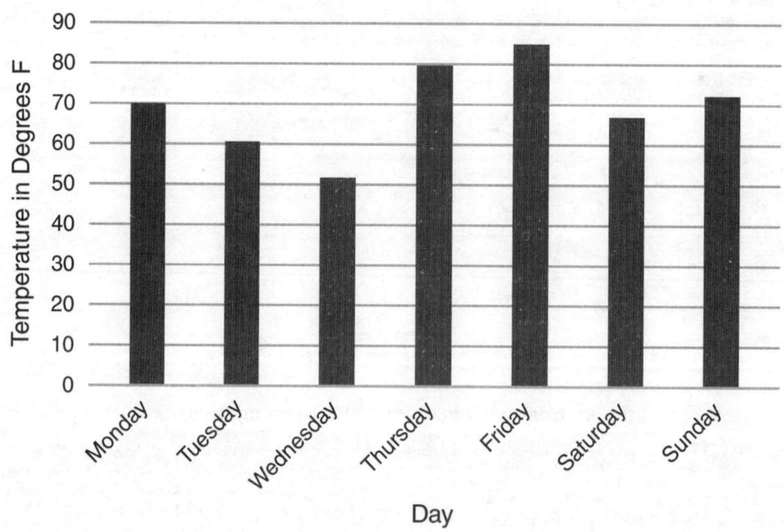


Based on the above graph, between what two days was there the largest increase in temperature?

**Solution**

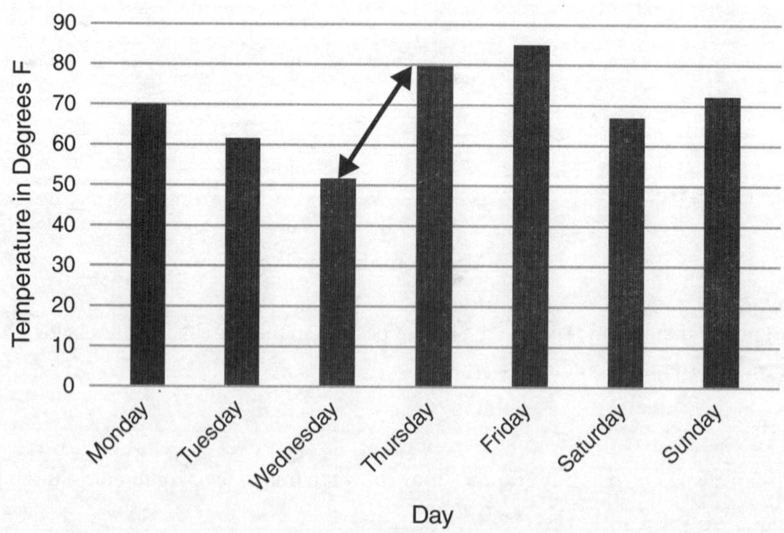


From Wednesday to Thursday, the temperature increases from approximately 52 degrees to 80 degrees. From the graph, this is clearly the largest increase from day to day.

## Practice

1.

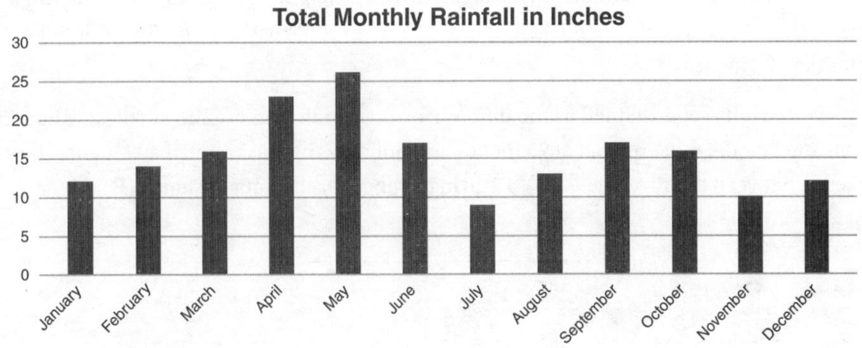


During which months was the total monthly rainfall greater than 20 inches?

2. Which of the following best approximates the range in monthly rainfall over the course of a year?

(A) 9
(B) 17
(C) 22
(D) 26

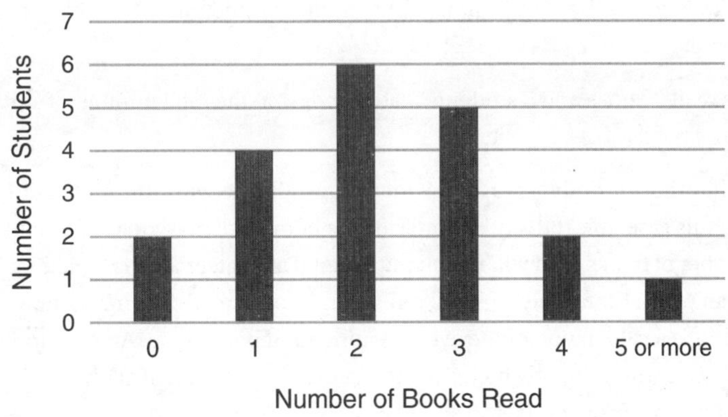


The graph above shows the distribution of the number of 20 total students who read a certain number of books over the summer. Use this graph to answer questions 3–4.

3. How many total students read just 2 or just 3 books?

4. If another student is added to the set who read 7 books over the summer, what will be the effect on the median number of books read and mean number of books read?

(A) Median decreases, while the mean remains the same.
(B) Both the median and the mean decrease.
(C) Median remains the same, and the mean increases.
(D) Both the median and the mean increase.

## Solutions

1. April has rainfall of 23 inches, and May has rainfall of 26 inches, while all the other months have less than 20 inches of rain. So, just April and May would have total monthly rainfall greater than 20 inches.

2. The range of a data set is defined as the difference between the largest and smallest values in the set. May has the most rainfall at 26 inches, and July has the least rainfall at 9 inches. So, the difference between the two is $26 - 9 = 17$ giving a range for the data of choice **(B)**, 17.

The graph above shows the distribution of the number of students who read a certain number of books over the summer.

3. Six students read 2 books and 5 students read 3 books, so the total number of students who read just 2 or 3 books is $6 + 5 = 11$.

4. Given that there are 20 students total, the median will fall between the 10th and 11th terms in the set. In this case, the 10th and 11th terms are both students who read 2 books, so the median number of books read will not change even if a greater value is added to the set since a new median with 21 total students will remain at 2 books read. The mean, however, will change since it is a calculation of the average number of books read. An additional student who read 7 books would slightly increase the mean since the sum of all the books read would be greater. Thus, the answer is **(C)**.

## Tables

The SAT will frequently present data in a table form. When analyzing tables, be sure you clearly understand what the numbers in each cell represent. Do so by carefully matching the cells up with the corresponding descriptions.

### Example

Air Quality Index, or AQI, is a measure used to determine how safe it is to be outside given the air pollution that is in an area. The index ranges between 0 and 500, and measures of 151 or above are considered unsafe for the general public. Sixty cities in a country had their average AQI for two months measured, with the results tabulated below:

| | AQI less than 151 in February | AQI greater than 151 in February | Total |
|---|---|---|---|
| **AQI less than 151 in January** | 40 | 4 | 44 |
| **AQI greater than 151 in January** | 10 | 6 | 16 |
| **Total** | 50 | 10 | 60 |

What is the probability that one of the surveyed cities would have an unsafe AQI for the general population over both months surveyed?

### Solution

Let's be clear about what the numbers in the table represent (don't worry—you don't need to be this thorough for every problem; this is so you can clearly see how these tables work):

- 40 is the number of cities that had the lower AQI in both January and February.
- 10 is the number of cities that had a greater AQI in January and a lower AQI in February.
- 4 is the number of cities that had a greater AQI in February and a lower AQI in January.
- 6 is the number of cities that had a greater AQI in both January and February.
- 44 is the total number of cities that had a lower AQI in January.
- 16 is the total number of cities that had a higher AQI in January.
- 50 is the total number of cities that had a lower AQI in February.
- 10 is the total number of cities that had a higher AQI in February.
- There are 60 cities all together that were presented.

So, to calculate the probability that one of the surveyed cities would have an *unsafe* AQI (over 151) over *both* months, first see how many cities had the greater AQI in both January and February—there were 6 such cities. Then, divide this by the total number of cities presented, 60.

$$\frac{6}{60} = 0.1$$

So the probability that one of the surveyed cities would have an unsafe AQI over both months is

$$0.1.$$

## Practice

**Type of Math Class and Type of Class Instructor at a University**

| | Graduate Student | Professor | Totals |
|---|---|---|---|
| **Lower-Level Class** | 80 | 40 | 120 |
| **Upper-Level Class** | 20 | 45 | 65 |
| **Totals** | 100 | 85 | 185 |

1. How many instructors in total taught lower-level classes?
2. How many instructors were there all together at the university?
3. What percent of all the math classes are taught by professors, calculated to the nearest whole percent?
4. If a math class is taught by a graduate student, what is the probability the class is an upper-level class?

## Solutions

1. **120.** Match up the Lower-Level Class with the Totals and see that there are 120 total instructors for lower-level classes.

2. **185.** The bottom right cell shows how many total instructors of all types and all classes were at the university—185.

3. **46%.** There are a total of 185 classes, and out of these 185 classes, 85 are taught by professors. So, calculate the percent of classes taught by professors like this:

$$\frac{85}{185} \times 100 \approx 46\%$$

4. **0.2.** There are 100 total math classes taught by graduate students, and 20 of these classes are upper level. So, to calculate the probability, divide 20 by 100:

$$\frac{20}{100} = 0.2$$

### Box Plots

On occasion, you may come across box plots (a.k.a. whisker plots) on the SAT Math, called this because the two quartiles (fourths) of the data that are in the middle make a box (the least and most quartiles make "whiskers" on either side). These plots break up the values in the data set into four quadrants so you can more easily visualize the spread of the data and the median.

**Example**

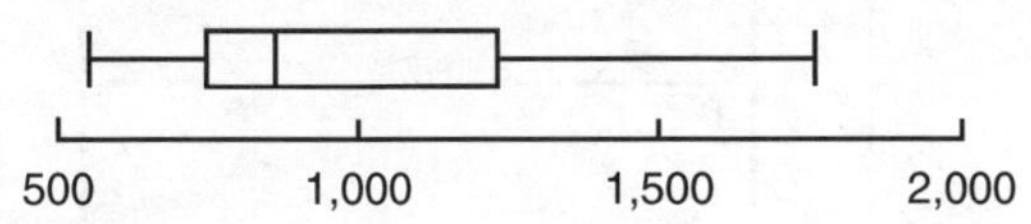


The box plot above summarizes the values for the average monthly apartment rental price in a particular neighborhood. Which of the following would be closest to the median monthly apartment rental price in this neighborhood?

(A) 500
(B) 600
(C) 800
(D) 1,200

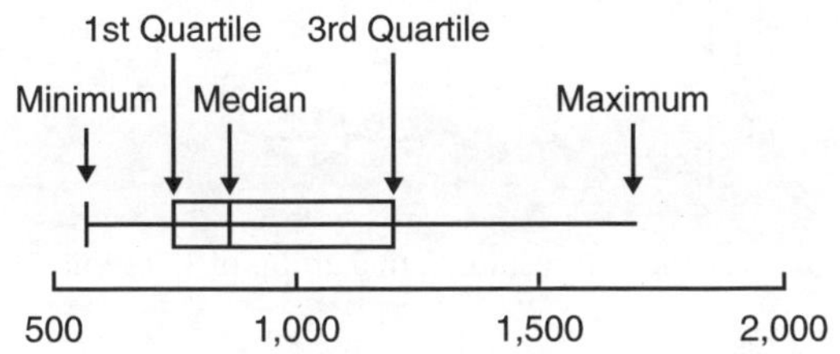


**Solution**

From this, you can see that the median value would be approximately 800, making choice **(C)** the correct answer.

## Practice

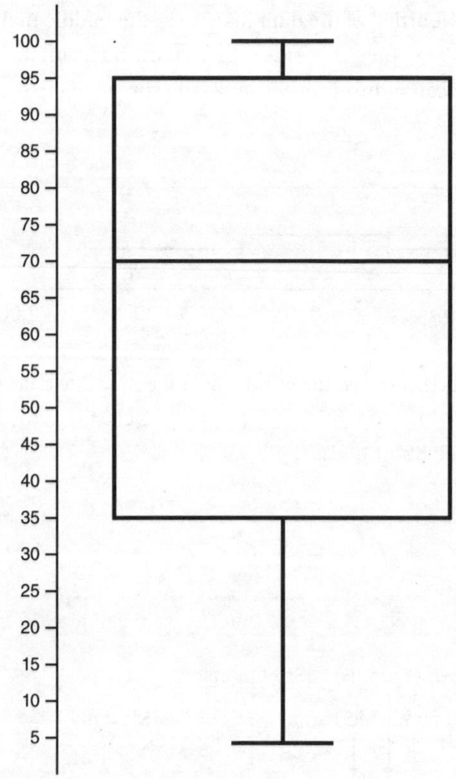


The above box plot summarizes the test results from a group of 300 seniors at a high school.

1. What is the minimum test score?
2. What is the median test score?
3. Which expression would give the test results, $x$, between the 50th and 75th percentiles?

   (A) $5 < x < 35$
   (B) $35 < x < 70$
   (C) $70 < x < 95$
   (D) $95 < x < 100$

## Solutions

1. The very least value in the plot is 5.
2. In the middle of the box is the value 70, which would represent the median.
3. The test results between the 50th and 75th percentiles would be between the 2nd and 3rd quartiles. This would be between the median, 70, and the 3rd quartile, 95. So, the correct answer is choice **(C)**.

## Linear and Exponential Growth

A constant relationship between two variables is called a *linear relationship*. Linear *growth* occurs when the equation formed by the variables has a positive slope; as the $x$ value increases, the $y$ value also increases. Linear *decay* occurs when the equation formed by the variables has a negative slope; as the $x$ value increases, the $y$ value decreases.

### Example 1

Linear growth for the equation $y = x + 1$

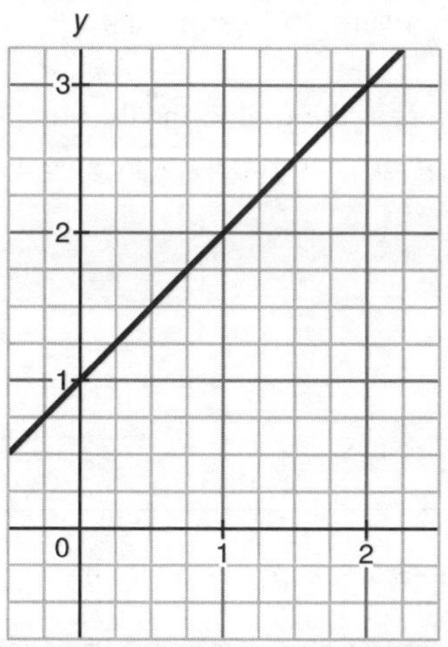


### Example 2

Linear decay for the equation $y = -x + 3$

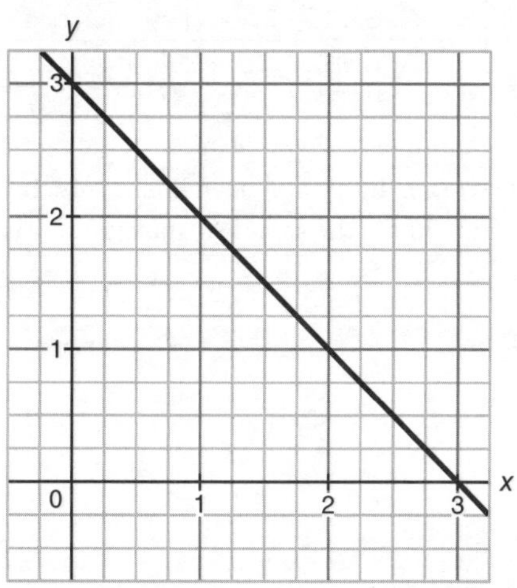


A relationship between two variables $x$ and $y$ that is expressed in the form $y = ab^x$ or $y = ab^x + c$ is *exponential*. Exponential *growth* occurs when as the $x$ value increases, the $y$ value increases exponentially. Exponential *decay* occurs when as the $x$ value increases, the $y$ value decreases exponentially.

### Example 3

Twenty sheep were introduced to an island where they had no natural predators. The population of the sheep on the island over time is given in the table below.

| Year | Number of Sheep |
|---|---|
| 1800 | 20 |
| 1810 | 28 |
| 1820 | 38 |
| 1830 | 51 |
| 1840 | 65 |

If a function were made with the year as the $x$ value and the number of sheep as $f(x)$, what would best describe the relationship between $x$ and $f(x)$ if it were graphed in the $xy$-coordinate plane?

(A) Exponential growth
(B) Exponential decay
(C) Linear growth
(D) Linear decay

### Solution

Let's examine how much the number of sheep changes from year to year:

| Year | Number of Sheep | Increase from 10 Years Prior |
|---|---|---|
| 1800 | 20 | Not applicable |
| 1810 | 28 | +8 |
| 1820 | 38 | +10 |
| 1830 | 51 | +13 |
| 1840 | 65 | +14 |

We can see that not only is the number of sheep *increasing*, the number by which it is increasing in each interval is also *increasing*. If this had been linear growth, the number by which it increases in each interval would remain the same. So, the correct answer is choice **(A)**, exponential growth.

## Practice

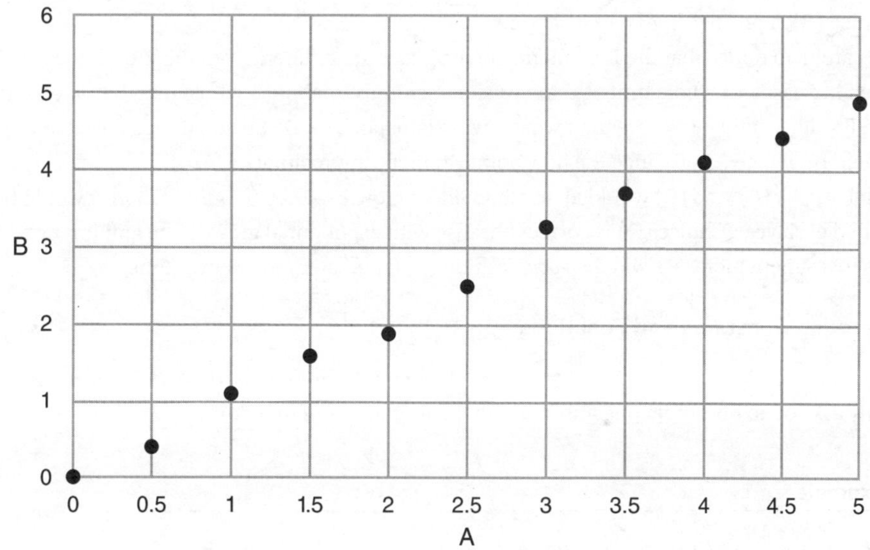


1. The line of best fit for the points given in the graph above would show what type of relationship between *A* and *B*?

   (A) Negative linear association
   (B) Positive linear association
   (C) Negative exponential association
   (D) Positive exponential association

2. If the trend given in the above graph were to continue, what would be closest to the projected value of B when A is 6?

   (A) 5
   (B) 5.5
   (C) 6
   (D) 6.5

3. John wishes to place $1,000 in an investment. Which of these circumstances would provide him with the greatest amount of money after a ten-year period?

   (A) An investment that grows linearly at 7% of the original amount each year
   (B) An investment that has exactly $60 added each year
   (C) An investment in which 2% of the original amount and $45 is added each year
   (D) An investment that grows exponentially at 6% a year, compounded annually

## Solutions

1. As the $x$ values increase, the $y$ values also increase at a steady rate. Therefore, this will be choice **(B)**, a positive linear association.
2. Be careful to notice that the increments on the $x$-axis are different from those on the $y$-axis. For each increase in 1 whole unit of $x$, the $y$ value increases by about 1 whole unit. So, when A is 6, the B value would be 1 more than what it was at the point (5, 5). So, the projected value for B would be choice **(C)**, 6, since the new point would be approximately (6, 6).
3. Choices (A), (B), and (C) would all result in linear growth—a set amount of money would be added each year. Choice **(D)** is correct because with exponential growth, the amount by which the investment increases will *increase*, resulting in far greater growth over time.

## Interpreting Constants and Functions

In order to assess your skill in understanding the meaning of functions, the SAT Math will frequently ask you to interpret constants and other components of functions.

### Example

Mary's investment in a stock portfolio, $S$, is modeled by the function

$$S(y) = 1000(1.15)^y$$

in which $y$ is the number of years Mary holds the stock. What is the best interpretation of the number 1.15 in the context of this function?

(A) When Mary holds the investment for 1.15 years, her overall investment increases by $1,000.
(B) When Mary holds the investment for 0.15 years, her overall investment decreases by $1,000.
(C) For each year that Mary owns the stock portfolio, her investment balance increases by $15.
(D) For each year that Mary owns the stock portfolio, her investment balance increases by 15% compounded annually.

### Solution

Use your knowledge of other concepts to help you interpret the meaning of constants in functions. Recall from the review of percentages that the formula for compound interest is $A = P\left(1 + \frac{r}{n}\right)^{nt}$, which has the same structure as the function $S(y) = 1000(1.15)^y$. The number 1.15 will correspond to $1 + \frac{r}{n}$. Since the intervals at which the investment value is compounded are one year, given the exponent $y$, $1 + \frac{r}{n}$ will equal $1 + \frac{0.15}{1} = 1.15$. This means that the percent increase each year is 15%. Therefore, the correct answer is choice **(D)**, since each year that she owns the portfolio, her investment balance will increase by 15%.

You could also use process of elimination to figure this out, since choices (A), (B), and (C) would all correspond to linear growth.

## Practice

A chemist measured the amount of caffeine in different volumes of coffee:

| Fluid Ounces | Milligrams of Caffeine |
|---|---|
| 2 | 25 |
| 5 | 60 |
| 8 | 95 |
| 12 | 143 |

1. Which of the following functions best approximates the relationship between fluid ounces, $F$, and milligrams of caffeine, $C$?

   (A) $C = 4F$
   (B) $C = 8F$
   (C) $C = 12F$
   (D) $C = 16F$

2. Given the relationship in the above table, which of the following would best approximate the milligrams of caffeine in 15 fluid ounces of coffee?

   (A) 150
   (B) 165
   (C) 180
   (D) 195

**Questions 3–4 refer to the following information:**

The half-life formula for a given substance is

$$N(t) = N_0\left(\frac{1}{2}\right)^{\frac{t}{h}}$$

in which $N(t)$ is how much of the original amount of a substance, $N_0$, remains after a certain amount of time $t$ elapsed, and $h$ is the half-life of the substance.

3. What would the value of $N(5)$represent?

   (A) How long it takes for half of a substance to decay
   (B) How much of the substance would remain after 5 years had elapsed
   (C) The number of years it takes for a substance to fully decay
   (D) The original mass of a substance before calculation of its half-life

4. Suppose that a particular substance has a half-life of 20 years. What fraction of the substance in the year 2000 would remain in the year 2080?

(A) $\frac{1}{16}$

(B) $\frac{1}{8}$

(C) $\frac{1}{4}$

(D) $\frac{1}{2}$

## Solutions

1. Glance ahead to the solutions to see that all of them are written in slope-intercept form. Determine which equation is correct by approximating the slope of the line. Let's use the points (2, 25) and (5, 60):

$$\frac{60-25}{5-2}=\frac{35}{3}\approx 11.67$$

This corresponds to choice **(C)**, since 12 is the closest slope value to 11.67.

2. When there is an increase of 3 fluid ounces from 5 to 8, the milligrams of caffeine increases by 35, from 60 to 95. So, when going from 12 fluid ounces to 15 fluid ounces, the milligrams of caffeine will increase by a similar amount: $143+35=178$. This is closest to choice **(C)**, 180.

Alternatively, you could have used the equation from the previous problem to solve for the number of milligrams, plugging in 15 for $F$.

3. $N(5)$ would represent the choice **(B)** since $t$ is the amount of time that would go by, and if $t$ is 5, then $N(5)$ would represent how much of the substance would remain after 5 half-lives had elapsed.

4. If the half-life is 20 years, according to the equation, half of the original amount of the substance would decay in a 20-year period. Since the time span is 80 years, going from 2000 to 2080, the original amount of the substance would be halved a total of 4 times:

$$\frac{1}{2}\times\frac{1}{2}\times\frac{1}{2}\times\frac{1}{2}=\frac{1}{16}$$

So, the correct answer is **(A)** since there would be $\frac{1}{16}$ of the original amount.

## Practice Drill #1—Problem Solving and Data Analysis Graphs and Data Interpretation

*(If timing, take about 12 minutes to complete.)*

The complete distribution of letter grades on a final exam are given in the table below:

| Letter Grade | Number of Students |
|---|---|
| A | 12 |
| B | 16 |
| C | 10 |
| D | 7 |
| F | 5 |

1. What is the total number of students who completed the exam?

(A) 40
(B) 50
(C) 60
(D) 70

2. Which set of grades represents $\frac{3}{10}$ of the total number of students?

(A) A and B
(B) A and D
(C) C and D
(D) C and F

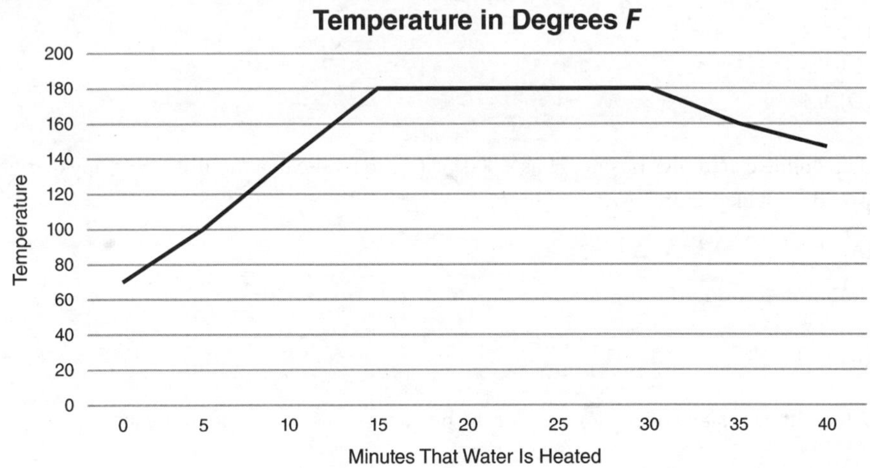


3. According to the graph above, what best approximates the initial temperature of the water?

(A) 70 degrees
(B) 90 degrees
(C) 100 degrees
(D) 120 degrees

4. Consider the graph above. A cook wanted to cook pasta during a 15-minute time period when the water temperature was steady. To accomplish this goal, between what times after starting to heat the water did the cook have the pasta in the water?

(A) 0–10 minutes
(B) 10–15 minutes
(C) 15–30 minutes
(D) 30–40 minutes

**Questions 5–7 are about the following information.**

A marketing agency surveyed clients from different online businesses to find the e-commerce conversion rate, i.e., what percentage of website visitors purchased something from the business. The results are compiled below:

| Business Type | Conversion Rate |
|---|---|
| Industrial Supplies | 4% |
| Pet Supplies | 9% |
| Booksellers | 10% |
| Electronics | 26% |
| Toys | 12% |
| Business Supplies | 21% |

5. Based on the above table, what is the probability that a visitor to an online bookstore will make a purchase?

(A) 0.1
(B) 0.2
(C) 0.3
(D) 0.4

6. If an online electronics business has 2,000 visitors to its site in a month, how many of them would most likely purchase something?

(A) 440
(B) 520
(C) 650
(D) 860

7. What is the median conversion rate for the business types presented in the table?

(A) 5%
(B) 7%
(C) 9%
(D) 11%

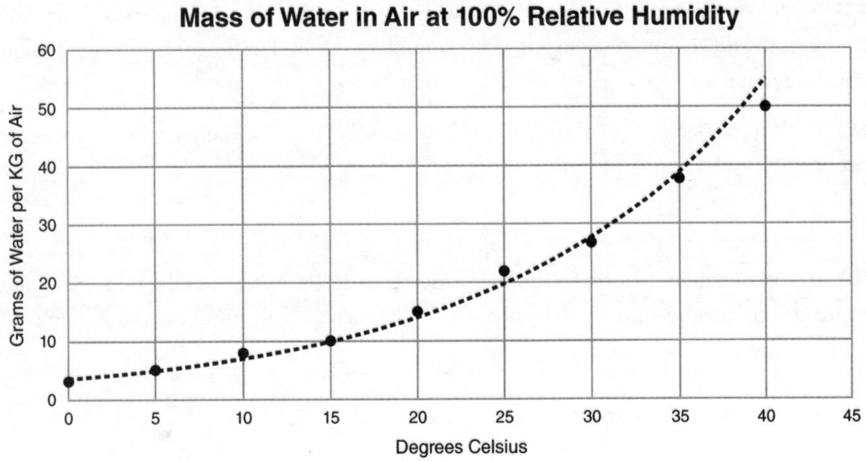


8. The relationship between temperature and grams of water per kilogram of air in the above graph is best described as which of the following?

   (A) Exponentially increasing
   (B) Exponentially decreasing
   (C) Linear increasing
   (D) Linear decreasing

9. What is the predicted value of grams of water per kilogram of air at 25 degrees C?

   (A) 16
   (B) 20
   (C) 24
   (D) 28

10. The greatest outlier presented in the above graph is found at what temperature?

   (A) 10 degrees
   (B) 20 degrees
   (C) 30 degrees
   (D) 40 degrees

## Solutions

1. **(B)** Add up the total number of students from the right column to find the total number of students who completed the exam:

$$12 + 16 + 10 + 7 + 5 = 50$$

2. **(D)** Find what $\frac{3}{10}$ of the total of 50 students would be:

$$\frac{3}{10} \times 50 = 15$$

   Then, examine which combination will add up to 15. The only one that does is choice **(D)**, *C and F*, since $10 + 5 = 15$.

3. **(A)** The initial temperature of the water is the temperature when 0 minutes have passed. At an *x* value of 0, the *y* value for temperature is closest to 70 degrees.

4. **(C)** For the temperature to be steady, the line must be horizontal, having a slope of zero. Between 15 and 30 minutes, the line is horizontal, so it is in that range that the cook should cook the pasta.

5. **(A)** Look at the percentage of conversion for booksellers—10%. Then, expresses this as a probability:

$$\frac{10}{100} = \frac{1}{10} = 0.1$$

6. **(B)** The conversion rate for electronics businesses is 26% according to the table. So, find 26% of 2,000 to predict how many of the business's visitors will likely purchases something:

$$0.26 \times 2{,}000 = 520$$

7. **(D)** Put the percentages in order from least to greatest:

$$4, 9, 10, 12, 21, 26$$

Since there are an even number of terms, and the two middle terms are different, find the median of the set by averaging 10 and 12:

$$\frac{10 + 12}{2} = 11$$

So, the median conversion rate is 11%.

8. **(A)** As the temperature increases, the grams of water per kg of air increase more and more. Had this been a constant increase, it would be linear. Since the increase accelerates, it would be an exponential increase.

9. **(B)** The predicted value and measured value differ—the measured value is indicated by the dot, while the predicted value will be on the curved, dotted line. At 25 degrees Celsius, the grams of water per kilogram of air would be 20.

10. **(D)** The greatest outlier is the value that most differs from the predicted value; in other words, it is the measured value that is farthest from the curve. At 40 degrees, the measured value of the grams is 50, while the curve would predict approximately 55. This point is farther away from the predicted values than any of the other dots presented in the graph.

## Practice Drill #2—Problem Solving and Data Analysis Graphs and Data Interpretation

*(If timing, take about 12 minutes to complete.)*

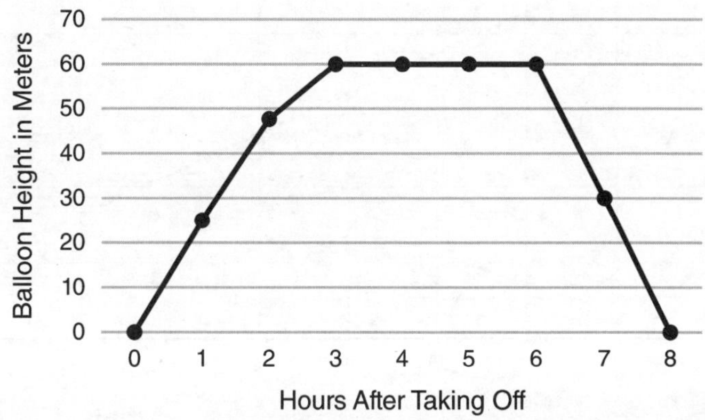


1. Sam took a balloon ride, in which he ascended to a height of 60 meters and remained there for a period of time. His height in meters above the ground as it relates to hours after taking off is graphed above.

   For how many hours in his ride did he stay at his maximum height?

   (A) 1
   (B) 2
   (C) 3
   (D) 4

2. During what interval did Sam's height make the greatest change?

   (A) Between 0–2 hours
   (B) Between 2–4 hours
   (C) Between 4–6 hours
   (D) Between 6–8 hours

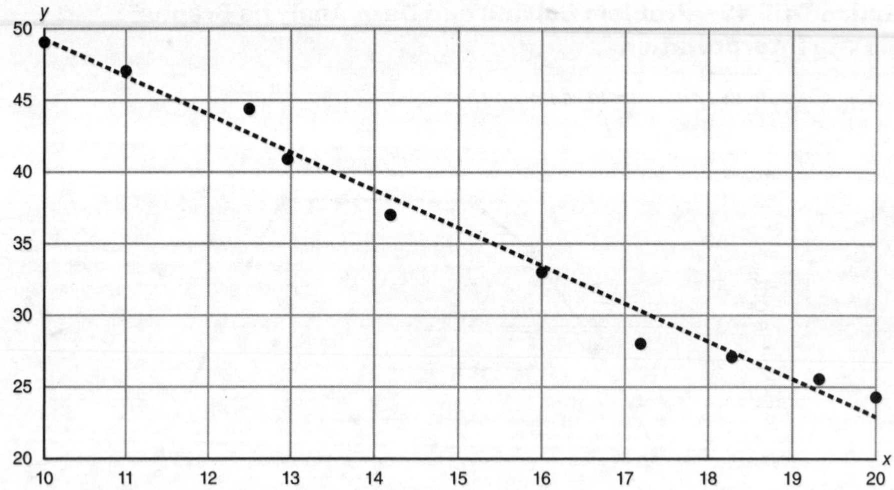


3. Consider the set of data in the scatterplot above.

   Assuming the trend in the above graph were to continue, what would most likely be the $y$ value of the predicted point with an $x$ value of 25?

   (A) 5
   (B) 10
   (C) 15
   (D) 20

4. If a linear equation were made to represent this data, which of the following would most closely estimate its $y$-intercept?

   (A) 48
   (B) 60
   (C) 75
   (D) 90

A survey of 200 online shoppers asked respondents their favorite product to purchase on the internet. Their responses are summarized in the table below.

| Item | Percent of Those Surveyed |
|---|---|
| Books/Music | 17 |
| Technology | 18 |
| Clothing | 22 |
| Online Education | 6 |
| Trips | 11 |
| Reused Goods | 19 |
| Other | 7 |

5. Based on this table, how many of the 200 respondents primarily preferred reused goods, trips, or clothing?

 (A) 104
 (B) 132
 (C) 150
 (D) 178

| Fund Name | Share Price | Expected Yearly Management Expenses per Share |
|---|---|---|
| Fund A | $140 | $1.12 |
| Fund B | $80 | $0.64 |
| Fund C | $200 | $1.60 |
| Fund D | $64 | $0.51 |
| Fund E | $50 | $0.40 |

6. The table above shows the price per share and the estimated yearly expenses for five different actively managed mutual funds (investment products that purchase stocks in many different companies).

 If Jennifer purchased 200 shares of Fund C, what would her yearly fund expenses most likely be?

 (A) $100
 (B) $190
 (C) $240
 (D) $320

7. Which function best approximates the relationship between the share price, $S$, and expenses, $E$, given that the two quantities have a linear relationship?

    (A) $(0.008)S = E$
    (B) $(0.08)S = E$
    (C) $(0.8)S = E$
    (D) $(8)S = E$

8. If William purchased 100 shares of Fund D, what inequality shows the percentage return on the investment that would allow him to make enough money to cover his expected yearly management expenses, calculated to the nearest tenth of a percent?

    (A) Percent $\leq 0.8$
    (B) Percent $\geq 0.8$
    (C) Percent $\geq 1.2$
    (D) Percent $\leq 1.2$

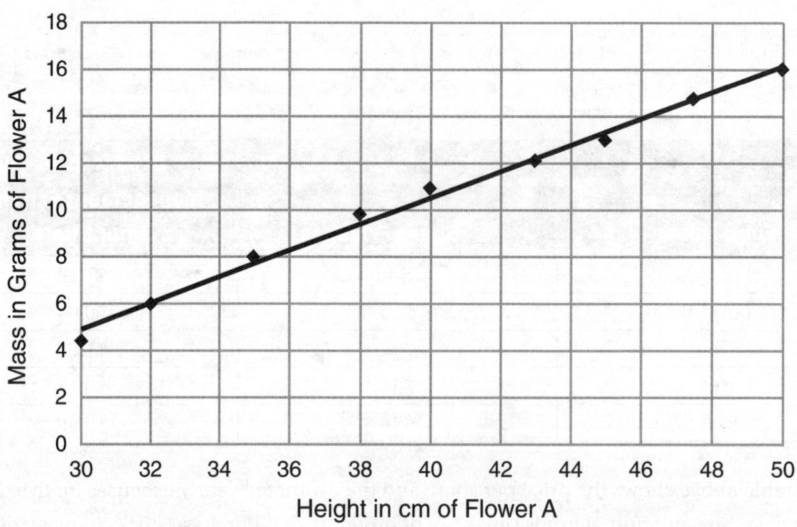


**Figure 1**

9. Assuming the trend of the best fit line in Figure 1 continues, what would be the mass of flower A if it has a height of 55 cm?

    (A) Approximately 12.5 grams
    (B) Approximately 16 grams
    (C) Approximately 19.5 grams
    (D) Approximately 24 grams

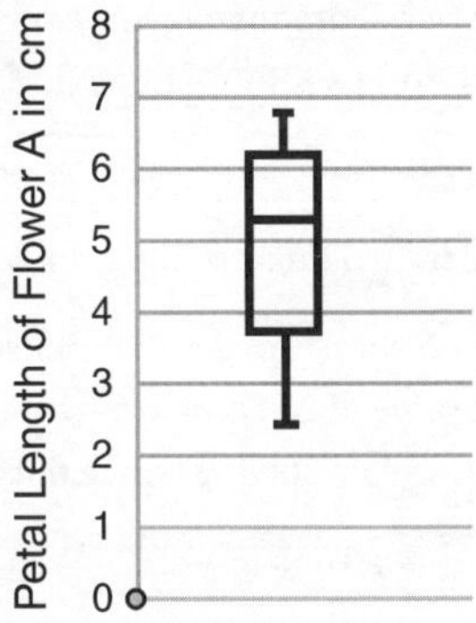


**Figure 2**

10. Based on Figure 2, in which of the following ranges would one find the median petal length of flower A?

(A) 3–4 cm
(B) 4–5 cm
(C) 5–6 cm
(D) 6–7 cm

## Solutions

1. **(C)** The maximum height of the balloon is at 60 meters, and Sam is at this height between 3 and 6 hours of flight, for a total of 3 hours.

2. **(D)** During the interval between 6 and 8 hours, Sam's height decreased by 60 meters. This is a greater change than that of any of the other intervals, including between 0–2 hours when Sam's height increased by 50 meters.

3. **(B)** Continue the same trend as illustrated in the graph. Since 25 is 5 more than 20, determine how much the *y* value decreases during a similar interval. Between *x* values of 15 and 20, the *y* value decreases from approximately 36 to 23, for a decrease of 13 units. So, to predict the *y* value when *x* is 20, subtract 13 from 23 (which is the *y* value when *x* is 20):

$$23 - 13 = 10$$

Therefore, the predicted value would be 10.

4. **(C)** Be careful to examine the units of the graph—the *x*-axis begins at 10 rather than 0. So, to find the *y*-intercept, we need to determine what that point of intersection on the *y*-axis would be if we expanded the graph by 10 lesser *x* units. This could be accomplished by plugging in sample values, finding the slope of the equation, and then solving for the *y*-intercept. Fortunately, you can save time in this problem—determine how much the *y* value increases as the *x* value decreases from 20 to 10. This number will be identical to how much the *y* value increases as the *x* value decreases from 10 to 0, enabling us to find the *y*-intercept. Between 20 and 10, the *y* value increases from 23 to 49, for a total increase of $49 - 23 = 26$. So, increase the *y* value at the *x* value of 10, namely 49, by 26 units to find the *y*-intercept: $49 + 26 = 75$.

5. **(A)** Add the percentages who preferred reused goods (19), trips (11), and clothing (22): $19\% + 11\% + 22\% = 52\%$. Then, take 52% of 200:

$$0.52 \times 200 = 104$$

6. **(D)** Each share of Fund C has a per-share management expense of \$1.60. So, multiply 1.60 by 200 to find her likely yearly fund expenses:

$$1.6 \times 200 = 320$$

Therefore, her yearly fund expenses would most likely be \$320.

7. **(A)** Find the relationship between share price and expenses by setting up an equation using sample values. Let's use a share price of 200 and a corresponding expense amount of 1.60, and call $k$ the constant for which we are solving (since the terms have a linear relationship):

$$kS = E \rightarrow$$
$$k(200) = 1.60 \rightarrow$$
$$k = \frac{1.60}{200} = 0.008$$

So, $(0.008)S = E$ would best approximate the relationship between the share price and expenses.

8. **(B)** For a single share of Fund D, the percent of fund expenses are calculated as follows:

$$\frac{0.51}{64} \times 100 \approx 0.797$$

The percent of fund expenses would remain the same no matter how many shares William had. So, to express the percentage return on his investment that he would need to have to cover his expected yearly management expenses, William would need Percent $\geq 0.8$, since 0.8 would approximate 0.797 to the nearest tenth.

9. **(C)** When the height of the flower increases from 45–50 centimeters, the mass of the flower increases by approximately 3 grams, going from 13.5 to 16.5 grams. So, increase the flower's mass when it is at 50 cm in height by a similar amount of 3 grams, since there is a steady, linear relationship between the flower's height and mass. $16.5 + 3 = 19.5$ grams, corresponding to choice **(C)**.

10. **(C)** In a box plot, the line at which the two boxes meet is the median. In this graph, this occurs at approximately 5.25 cm. Therefore, the median will be within the range of 5–6 cm.

## Geometry and Trigonometry

This section contains comprehensive review and strategies for all of the concepts below:

**Area, Perimeter, and Volume**

- Rectangle Area
- Triangle Area
- Perimeter of Polygons
- Parallelogram Area
- Trapezoid Area
- Surface Area
- Volume of a Box, Cylinder, Sphere, Cone, and Pyramid

**Lines, Angles, and Triangles**

- Supplementary Angles
- Vertical Angles
- Parallel Lines and a Transversal

**Angles, Triangles, and Quadrilaterals**

- Equilateral Triangles
- Isosceles Triangles
- Similar Triangles
- Angles in a Quadrilateral

**Right Triangles and Trigonometry**

- Pythagorean Theorem and Special Right Triangles
- Sine, Cosine, Tangent
- Area of an Equilateral Triangle
- Sine and Cosine of Complementary Angles

**Circles**

- Radius and Diameter
- Area and Circumference
- 360° in a Circle
- Inscribed Angle
- Arc Length
- Sector Area
- Circle Formula
- Radians

### Area, Perimeter, and Volume

At the beginning of each math test section, the SAT will provide you with a formula sheet that covers much of what you will need for problems related to area, perimeter, and volume.

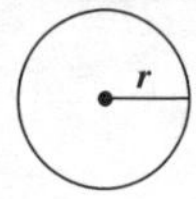


**Radius of a circle = $r$**

**Area of a circle = $\pi r^2$**

**Circumference of a circle = $2\pi r$**

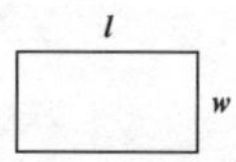


**Area of a rectangle = length × width = $lw$**

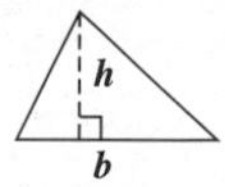


**Area of a triangle = $\frac{1}{2}$ × base × height = $\frac{1}{2}bh$**

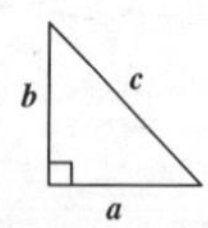


**Pythagorean theorem: $a^2 + b^2 = c^2$**

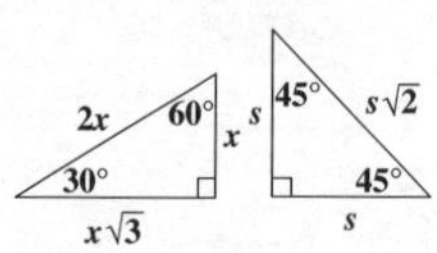


**Special right triangles: 30-60-90 and 45-45-90**

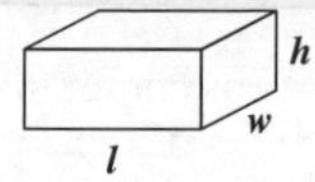


**Volume of a box = length × width × height = $lwh$**

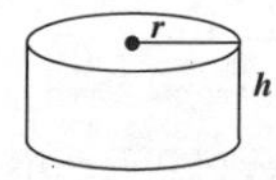


**Volume of a cylinder = $\pi r^2 h$**

**Volume of a sphere = $\frac{4}{3}\pi r^3$**

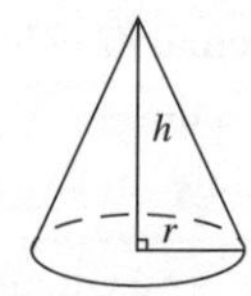


**Volume of a cone = $\frac{1}{3}\pi r^2 h$**

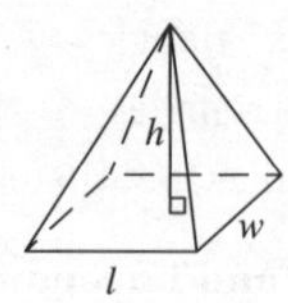


**Volume of a pyramid =**
**$\frac{1}{3}$ × length × width × height = $\frac{1}{3}lwh$**

**KEY FACTS:**

- **A circle has 360 degrees.**
- **There are $2\pi$ radians in a circle.**
- **There are 180 degrees in a triangle.**

### SAT Math Strategy

Even though many geometry formulas are provided, you should memorize these formulas so you have them at your fingertips. Memorizing the formulas will help you quickly remember what formula you will need for a given problem. Also, if you memorize the formulas, you will have a better sense of what all the variables and constants mean and how to apply them.

As you can see from above, the SAT provides you with area formulas for two important shapes: the rectangle and the triangle.

### Rectangle Area

The area of a rectangle is calculated as follows:

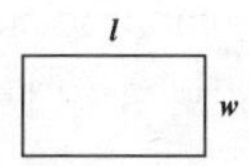


**Area of a rectangle = length × width =** $lw$

### Example

What is the area of a rectangle with a length of 6 units and a width of 4 units?

### Solution

Multiply the length by the width to find the area:

$$6 \times 4 = 24$$

So, the area of the rectangle would be 24 square units.

### Triangle Area

The SAT also provides you with the formula for the area of a triangle:

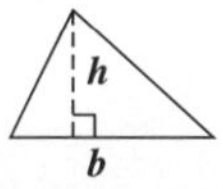


**Area of a triangle** $= \frac{1}{2} \times \text{base} \times \text{height} = \frac{1}{2}bh$

**Note:** In your math class, you may have learned this formula as $A = \frac{bh}{2}$. This formula is perfectly fine to use as well.

### Example

What is the area of the triangle drawn below?

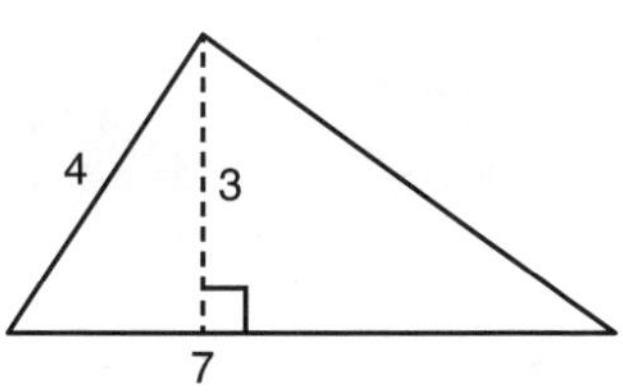

### Solution

When calculating the area of triangles, parallelograms, and trapezoids, remember that the **height is perpendicular to the base**. On this particular problem, the base is 7 and the height is 3 (not 4). To calculate the area of the triangle, use the triangle area formula:

$$\text{Area} = \frac{1}{2} \times \text{Base} \times \text{Height} \rightarrow$$
$$\text{Area} = \frac{1}{2} \times 7 \times 3 = \frac{21}{2} = 10.5$$

So, the triangle's area will be 10.5 square units.

Now, let's consider the polygon concepts the SAT expects you to know, but for which you **do not** receive formulas.

## Perimeter of Polygons

The *perimeter* of a shape is the length of its sides added together.

### Example 1

What is the perimeter of the rectangle below?

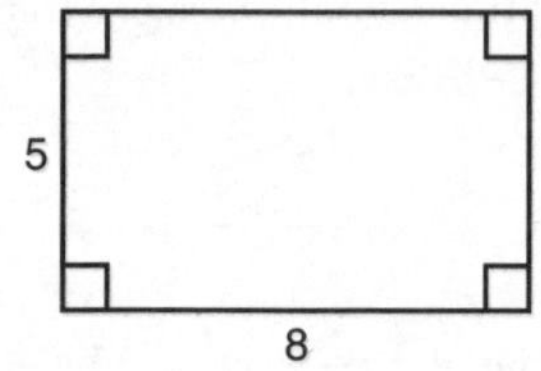


### Solution

In a rectangle, the sides opposite one another are equal. So the total length of the sides of the rectangle would be $5 + 5 + 8 + 8 = 26$ units.

### Example 2

What is the perimeter for the triangle below?

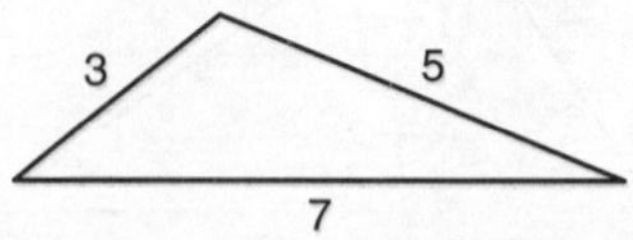


### Solution

Add the three side lengths of the triangle to find the perimeter:

$$3 + 5 + 7 = 15 \text{ units}$$

### Parallelogram Area

A parallelogram is a four-sided figure that has opposite sides that are parallel. (A rectangle is a special form of a parallelogram that has only 90° angles.) The area for a parallelogram is given below:

*Base × Height = Area*

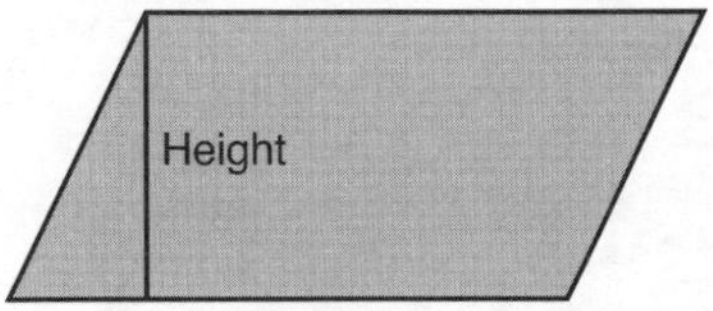


Be careful that you do not count one of the slanted edges as the height. Like with the triangle, the height will always be perpendicular to the base.

**Example**

What is the area of the parallelogram drawn below?

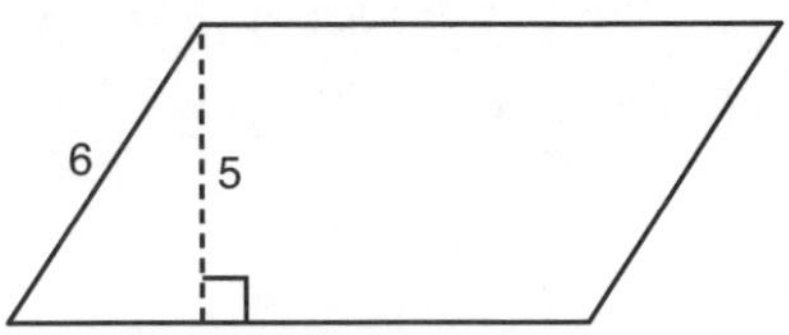


**Solution**

The base of the parallelogram is 10, and the height is 5 since it is perpendicular to the base. (The height is not 6 since this side is not perpendicular to the base.) So, the area is the base multiplied by the height:

$$\text{Base} \times \text{Height} = 10 \times 5 = 50$$

The area is therefore 50 square units.

### Trapezoid Area

A trapezoid is a four-sided figure that has a pair of opposite sides parallel to one another. The area for a trapezoid is calculated as follows:

$$\frac{(B1 + B2)}{2} height = Area$$

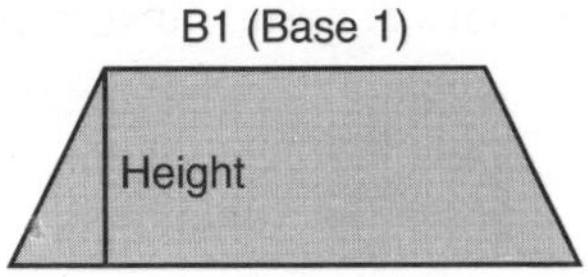

In essence, you are finding the "average" of the two bases and multiplying this average by the height of the trapezoid. As with the triangle and parallelogram, be mindful that the height must be perpendicular to the base.

**Example**

What is the area of the trapezoid drawn below?

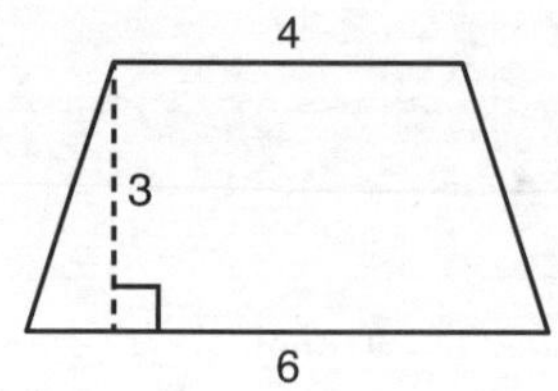


**Solution**

Use 4 as B1, 6 as B2, and 3 as the height, plugging these values into the trapezoid formula:

$$\frac{(B1 + B2)}{2} height = Area \rightarrow$$

$$\frac{(4 + 6)}{2} \times 3 = 5 \times 3 = 15$$

So, the area of the trapezoid is 15 square units.

### Surface Area

The SAT may ask you to calculate the surface area of a *right rectangular prism*—this is a fancy way of saying *box*. To calculate the surface are of a box, take the area of each face of the box and add them together using this formula:

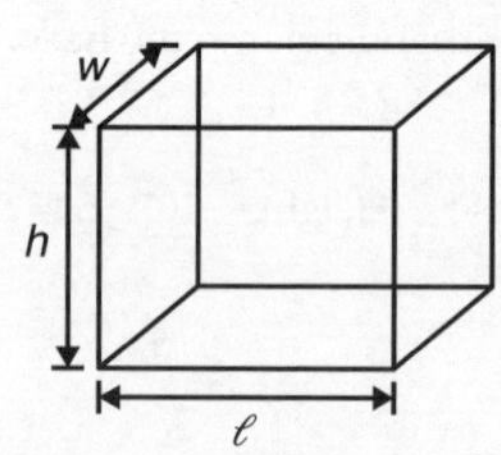


Surface Area = $2(lw) + 2(lh) + 2(wh)$

**Example**

What is the surface area of a right rectangular prism with a height of 3 units, a length of 5 units, and a width of 4 units?

## ✓ Solution

Carefully plug 3, 4, and 5 into the surface area formula to find the surface area:

$$\text{Surface Area} = 2(lw) + 2(lh) + 2(wh) \rightarrow$$
$$\text{Surface Area} = 2(5 \times 4) + 2(5 \times 3) + 2(4 \times 3) \rightarrow$$
$$2(20) + 2(15) + 2(12) =$$
$$40 + 30 + 24 = 94$$

So, the surface area is 94 square units.

### Practice

1. What is the area of a triangle with a height of 3 units and a base of 4 units?
2. What is the perimeter of a rectangle with a width of $x$ and length of $2x$?
3. What is the area of the parallelogram below?

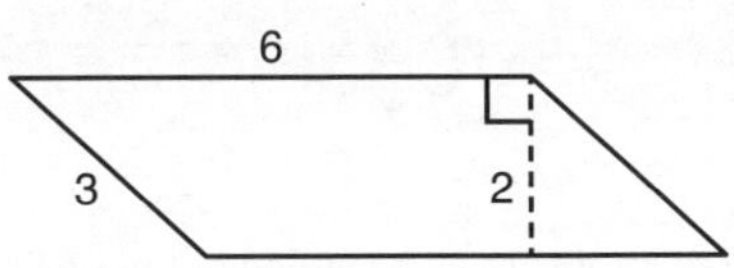


4. If a trapezoid has a height $h$ and an area of $6h$ square units, what would be the area of a trapezoid with bases of the same length but a height twice that of the original?
5. What is the surface area of a cube with an edge length of 3?
6. If the perimeter of a rectangle is 24 inches, what would be the value of the length and the width of the rectangle in order to *maximize* the rectangle's area?

### Solutions

1. $\frac{1}{2} \times \text{Base} \times \text{Height} = \frac{1}{2} \times 4 \times 3 = 6$
2. There are two sides of length $x$ and two sides of length $2x$:

$$2(x) + 2(2x) = 2x + 4x = 6x$$

3. $\text{Base} \times \text{Height} = 6 \times 2 = 12$
4. Consider the area formula for a trapezoid:

$$\frac{(B1 + B2)}{2} \textit{height} = \textit{Area}$$

   If the bases remain the same, and the height is doubled, the original area will be doubled since the only thing that changes is the height. So, the new area would be $12h$.

5. In a cube, all the edges are of the same length:

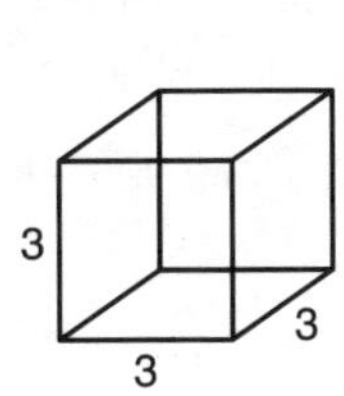

So, plug 3 in for length, width, and height in the surface area formula:

$$\text{Surface Area} = 2(lw) + 2(lh) + 2(wh) \rightarrow$$
$$\text{Surface Area} = 2(3^2) + 2(3^2) + 2(3^2) \rightarrow$$
$$\text{Surface Area} = 18 + 18 + 18 = 54$$

Alternatively, you could calculate the surface area for one of the sides, $3 \times 3 = 9$, and multiply this by 6 since there are 6 total sides: $6 \times 9 = 54$ square units.

6. To maximize the area of the rectangle while minimizing the perimeter, the rectangle should be a *square*. You can see why this would be by trying out some sample values for length and width (that would allow for a perimeter of 24):

   Length: 6 inches, width: 6 inches. Area is 36 square inches.
   Length: 7 inches, width 5 inches. Area is 35 square inches.
   Length: 8 inches, width 4 inches. Area is 32 square inches.
   Length: 9 inches, width 3 inches. Area is 27 square inches.
   So, the length and width should each be 6 inches in order to maximize the area of the rectangle.

## Volume Calculations

The volume formulas you need to know are all provided at the beginning of each math section. Here are examples showing how to apply each of these formulas.

**Volume of a Box (Right Rectangular Prism)**

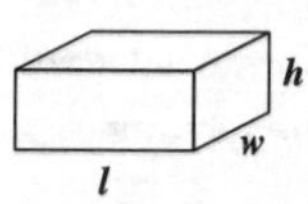


**Volume of a box = length × width × height = *lwh***

A common error students make is to confuse area and volume. Area will only be a calculation of two dimensions, like length × width. Volume will be a calculation of three dimensions, as we can see above.

### Example

What is the volume of box with a length $2x$ inches, a width of $3x$ inches, and a height of $y$ inches?

### Solution

Even though this asks you to calculate expressions with $x$ and $y$, you can still use the same formula as above and multiply the length, width, and height together.

$$lwh = (2x)(3x)(y) = 6x^2y$$

So, the volume would be $6x^2y$ cubic inches.

**Volume of a Cylinder**

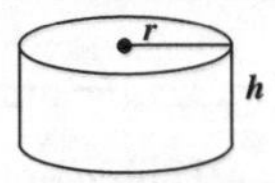


**Volume of a cylinder = $\pi r^2 h$**

Think about calculating the volume of a cylinder as taking the area of the circle on top, then multiplying it by the height all the way down.

## Example

What is the volume of a cylinder with a height of 8 inches and a diameter of 4 inches, as shown below?

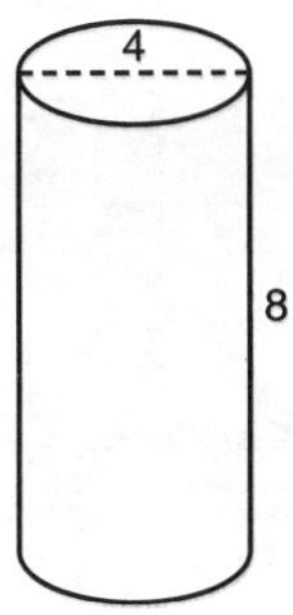


## ✓ Solution

Be careful to distinguish between the radius and the diameter. The radius is *half* the length of the diameter, so the radius for the above cylinder would be 2. Then, plug 2 in for the radius and 8 in for the height to solve for the volume:

$$\pi r^2 h = \pi(2)^2(8) = 32\pi$$

So, the volume would be $32\pi$ cubic inches.

**Volume of a Sphere**

**Volume of a sphere = $\frac{4}{3}\pi r^3$**

## Example

Consider the volume of a sphere with a radius of $x$ units. How much greater will the volume of a sphere with double the radius be?

**Solution**

The volume of the original sphere will be $\frac{4}{3}\pi x^3$ cubic units. The radius of the second sphere will be $2x$, so its volume will be $\frac{4}{3}\pi(2x)^3 = \frac{4}{3}\pi(8x^3)$ cubic units. Divide the second volume by the first to see the multiple by which it is greater than the first:

$$\frac{\frac{4}{3}\pi(8x^3)}{\frac{4}{3}\pi x^3} \rightarrow \frac{\cancel{\frac{4}{3}}\cancel{\pi}(8\cancel{x^3})}{\cancel{\frac{4}{3}}\cancel{\pi}\cancel{x^3}} = 8$$

So, the volume of the second sphere will be 8 times greater than the first. If you realize that the only thing that will change from one sphere to the next is the radius, you can simply calculate the ratio of the cubes of the radii to arrive at your solution.

**Volume of a Cone**

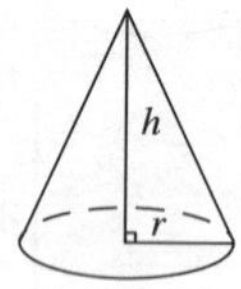


**Volume of a cone** $= \frac{1}{3}\pi r^2 h$

**Example**

How many cones of with radius 4 and height 6 will have the same total volume as a cylinder with the same radius and height?

**Solution**

The SAT will frequently test your proficiency in manipulating algebraic expressions instead of doing long calculations. This question is a great example of this. Rather than calculating the volume of each cone, look at the relationship between the two formulas:

$$\text{Cone Volume} = \frac{1}{3}\pi r^2 h$$

$$\text{Cylinder Volume} = \pi r^2 h$$

The cylinder volume is three times that of the cone volume, since everything in the two formulas is the same except for the $\frac{1}{3}$ in front of the cone volume formula. Since $\frac{1}{3}$ goes into 1 three times, three cones could fit into a cylinder with the same radius and height as the cone.

**Volume of a Pyramid**

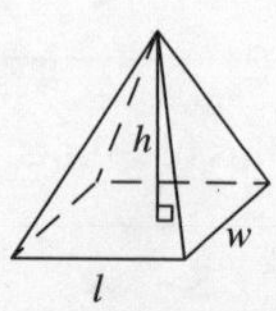


**Volume of a pyramid =**

$\frac{1}{3}$ × **length** × **width** × **height** $= \frac{1}{3}lwh$

## Example

Consider a pyramid with a volume of 20 cubic inches. If the width is cut in half and the height is doubled, what would be the volume of the resulting pyramid?

## Solution

Focus on how the changes to the width and height would affect the volume calculation. For the original pyramid, the volume calculation would be as follows:

$$20 = \frac{1}{3}lwh$$

For the second pyramid, the new width is $\frac{1}{2}w$ and the new height is $2h$. So, the volume would be:

$$\frac{1}{3}l\left(\frac{1}{2}w\right)(2h) = \frac{1}{3}l\left(\frac{\cancel{1}}{\cancel{2}}w\right)(\cancel{2}h) = \frac{1}{3}lwh$$

Therefore, the volume of the new pyramid will be identical to the volume of the first: 20 cubic inches.

### Practice

1. What is the volume of a box with dimensions 3 inches by 2 inches by 5 inches?
2. What is the volume of a cone with a radius and height both of $y$ centimeters?
3. What is the volume of a sphere with a diameter of 6 inches?
4. How many pyramids with dimensions 1 by 1 by 1 inch would fit in a box with dimensions 1 inch by 2 inches by 2 inches?
5. If the height of a cylinder were tripled and its radius halved, what would the volume of the new cylinder be as a multiple of the volume of the original?

### Solutions

1. $lwh = 3 \times 2 \times 5 = 30$ cubic inches
2. Cone Volume $= \frac{1}{3}\pi r^2 h \rightarrow \frac{1}{3}\pi y^2 y = \frac{1}{3}\pi y^3$
3. Be sure to use the radius and not the diameter—the radius for this sphere is 3 inches. Plug 3 in to the sphere volume formula:

   $$\text{Volume} = \frac{4}{3}\pi r^3 \rightarrow \frac{4}{3}\pi 3^3 = \left(\frac{4}{3}\right)(27)\pi = 36\pi \text{ cubic inches}$$

4. Divide the volume of a 1 by 2 by 2 inch pyramid by that of a 1 by 1 by 1 inch pyramid to see how many of the smaller pyramids would fit within the larger one.

   $$\frac{\left(\frac{1}{3}(1 \times 2 \times 2)\right)}{\left(\frac{1}{3}(1 \times 1 \times 1)\right)} = \frac{\frac{1}{3} \times 4}{\frac{1}{3} \times 1} = \frac{\frac{\cancel{1}}{\cancel{3}} \times 4}{\frac{\cancel{1}}{\cancel{3}} \times 1} = \frac{4}{1} = 4$$

   So, four of the smaller pyramids would fit in the larger pyramid.

5. Use the formula for Cylinder Volume $= \pi r^2 h$. For the original cylinder, let's just use $r$ as the radius and $h$ as the height, making the volume $\pi r^2 h$. For the new cylinder, the height is tripled and the radius is halved. So, use $3h$ for the height and $\frac{1}{2}r$ for the radius and calculate the new volume:

$$\pi\left(\frac{1}{2}r\right)^2(3h) = \pi\left(\frac{1}{4}r^2\right)(3h) = \frac{3}{4}\pi r^2 h$$

So, the volume of the new cylinder would be $\frac{3}{4}$ the volume of the original one.

## Practice Drill—Area, Perimeter, and Volume

*(If timing, take about 12 minutes to complete.)*

**Fill-In Practice:** Write your answer in the underlined blank under each question.

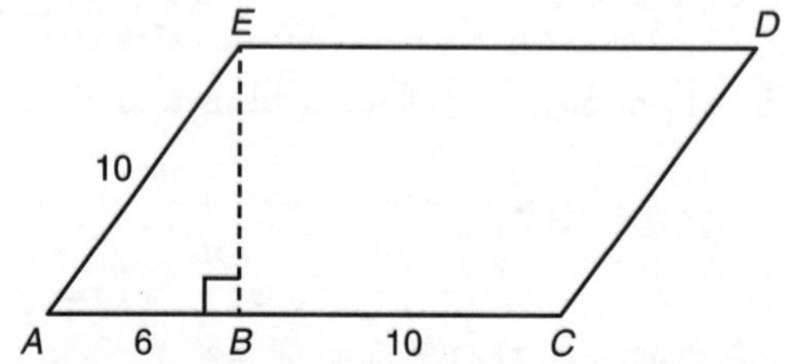


1. $AEDC$ is a parallelogram, with the length of $\overline{AB}$ 6 units, the length of $\overline{BC}$ 10 units, and the length of $\overline{AE}$ 10 units. Point B is on $\overline{AC}$ and $\overline{BE}$ is perpendicular to $\overline{AC}$. What is the area of the parallelogram in square units?

   Answer: ____________

2. A rectangular plot of land has a length twice its width. If the perimeter of the land is 90 feet, what is its area in square feet?

   Answer: ____________

3. If a cube has a volume of 125 cubic centimeters, what is the combined length of all the edges of the cube in centimeters?

   Answer: ____________

4. A cylinder has a volume of $150\pi$ square units and a height of 6 units. What is the diameter of the base of the cylinder in units?

   Answer: ____________

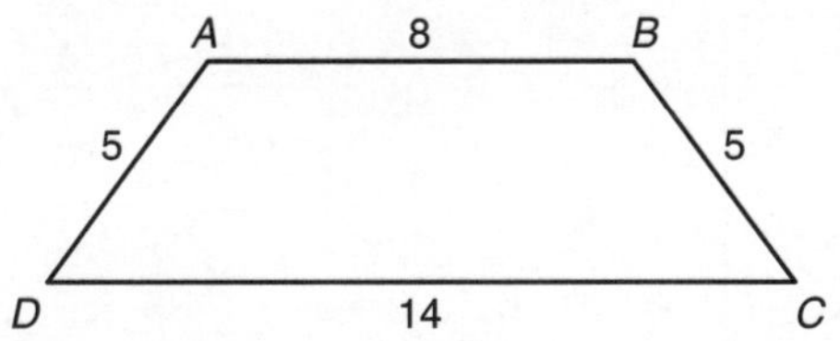


5. What is the area in square units of the trapezoid above, in which $\overline{AB}$ and $\overline{CD}$ are parallel?

Answer: ____________

**Multiple-Choice Practice**

6. Each gallon of wall paint that Julius purchases covers 400 square feet. If Julius is going to paint 3 walls, each with dimensions 40 feet by 12 feet, what is the minimum number of gallons of paint he needs to purchase, assuming he can only buy whole gallons and that there are no windows or other irregularities on the walls?

(A) 2
(B) 3
(C) 4
(D) 5

7. A basket maker designs cylindrical baskets with a radius of $x$ centimeters, for which the height of the basket is twice the radius of the basket. Which of the following would correctly express the volume, $V$, in cubic centimeters, of such baskets?

(A) $V = 2\pi x^3$
(B) $V = \pi x^2$
(C) $V = 4\pi x^2$
(D) $V = 4\pi x^3$

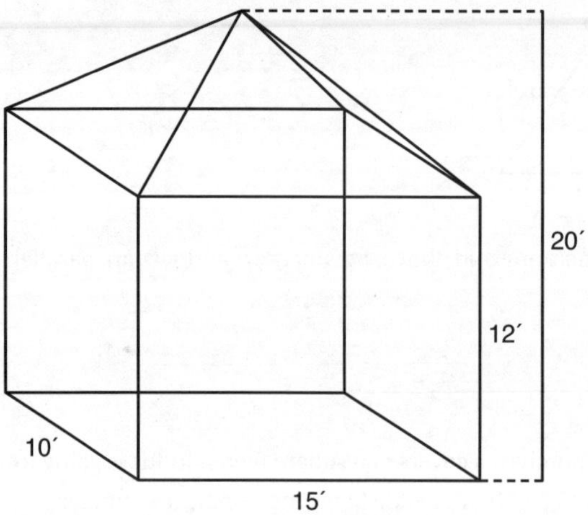


8. In the three-dimensional figure above, a rectangular prism with dimensions 12 feet by 10 feet by 15 feet has a pyramid with a base of 10 by 15 feet on top of it. The height of the rectangular prism and pyramid together is 20 feet. What is the volume of this entire figure?

(A) 900 cubic feet
(B) 1,460 cubic feet
(C) 2,200 cubic feet
(D) 3,000 cubic feet

9. A shoebox in the shape of a rectangular prism is supposed to have a volume between 432 and 504 cubic inches, inclusive. The box needs to have a length of 12 inches and a width of 6 inches. What is the range for a possible value for the height of the box?

(A) 5–6 inches inclusive
(B) 6–7 inches inclusive
(C) 7–8 inches inclusive
(D) 8–9 inches inclusive

10. A cylindrical tank is 3 meters deep and has a diameter of 10 meters. If the density of water is $997 \frac{kg}{m^3}$, how would one correctly calculate the mass in kilograms of the water in the tank if it is filled to the top with nothing but water?

(A) $\pi \times (10^2) \times 3 \times 997$
(B) $\pi \times (10^2) \times (1.5) \times 997$
(C) $\pi \times (5^2) \times (1.5) \times 997$
(D) $\pi \times (5^2) \times 3 \times 997$

## Solutions

1. **(128)** $\overline{BE}$ is the height of the parallelogram, so use the Pythagorean theorem to solve for its length:

$$a^2 + b^2 = c^2 \rightarrow$$
$$6^2 + b^2 = 10^2 \rightarrow$$
$$36 + b^2 = 100 \rightarrow$$
$$b^2 = 64 \rightarrow b = 8$$

Then, multiply the height 8 by the base of 16 (add $\overline{AB}$ and $\overline{BC}$) to find the area of the parallelogram:

$$8 \times 16 = 128$$

2. **(450)** Let's call $x$ the length of the rectangle and $y$ the width of the rectangle. Since the length is twice that of the width, we can say that $x = 2y$. The perimeter of the rectangle is $2x + 2y$, and since $x = 2y$, we can use substitution to solve for either the width or length—let's solve for the width:

$$2x + 2y = 90 \rightarrow$$
$$2(2y) + 2y = 90 \rightarrow$$
$$4y + 2y = 90 \rightarrow$$
$$6y = 90 \rightarrow$$
$$y = 15$$

So, the width of the rectangle is 15, and the length would be twice 15: 30. Then multiply 30 and 15 together to find the area of the rectangle:

$$15 \times 30 = 450$$

3. **(60)** The volume, $V$, of a cube of side length $x$ is $V = x^3$. Solve for $x$ given that the volume is 125 cubic centimeters:

$$V = x^3 \rightarrow$$
$$125 = x^3 \rightarrow$$
$$\sqrt[3]{125} = x \rightarrow$$
$$5 = x$$

There are 12 total edges in a cube, so multiply 5 by 12 to find the combined length of all the edges of the cube:

$$5 \times 12 = 60$$

4. **(10)** Plug the volume and the height into the cylinder volume formula:

$$\text{Cylinder Volume} = \pi r^2 h \rightarrow$$
$$150\pi = \pi r^2 (6) \rightarrow$$
$$150 = r^2 (6) \rightarrow$$
$$25 = r^2 \rightarrow r = 5$$

Now, double the radius to solve for the base diameter:

$$5 \times 2 = 10$$

5. **(44)** First, determine the height of the trapezoid. The trapezoid is isosceles which makes it easier to find the height using the Pythagorean theorem, since $3^2 + 4^2 = 5^2$.

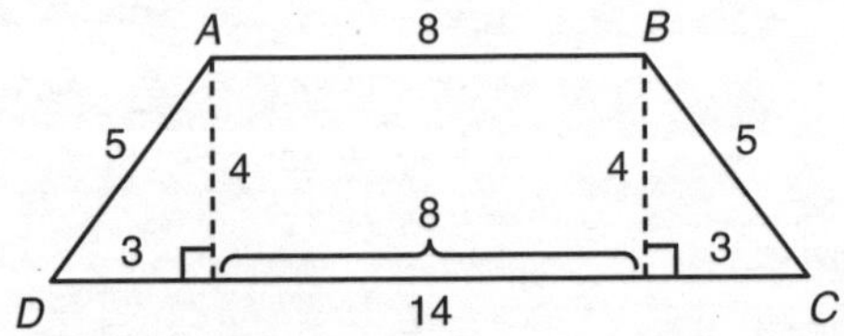


Now, use the area formula for a trapezoid to solve:

$$\frac{(B1 + B2)}{2}\textit{height} = \textit{Area} \rightarrow$$

$$\frac{(8 + 14)}{2}(4) = \frac{22}{2}(4) = 11 \times 4 = 44$$

6. **(C)** Find the surface area of each individual wall:

$$40 \times 12 = 480$$

Then multiply 480 by 3 to get the total area of the three walls:

$$480 \times 3 = 1{,}440$$

Now, divide 1,440 by 400 to see how many gallons of paint would be needed:

$$\frac{1{,}440}{400} = 3.6$$

Since Julius cannot purchase a partial gallon of paint, he must buy 4 full gallons to accomplish his task.

7. **(A)** Since the height of the basket is twice the radius of the basket, the height will be $2x$. Plug $x$ in for the radius and $2x$ in for the height to express the volume:

$$V = \pi r^2 h \rightarrow$$
$$V = \pi x^2(2x) \rightarrow$$
$$V = 2\pi x^3$$

8. **(C)** The figure is a box with dimensions 12 by 10 by 15 with a pyramid on top of it. The pyramid has a base of 10 by 15 and a height of 8, since $20 - 12 = 8$. Find the volumes of these two figures and add them together. First, the volume of the box:

$$lwh = 10 \times 15 \times 12 = 1{,}800$$

Next, the volume of the pyramid:

$$V = \frac{1}{3}lwh = \frac{1}{3} \times 10 \times 15 \times 8 = 400$$

Finally, add these separate volumes together to find the total volume:

$$1{,}800 + 400 = 2{,}200$$

9. **(B)** Pick a value that is within the range of 432 and 504 and solve for the possible height. Halfway between 432 and 504 is 468, so we can use that as a sample volume. The length and width are given, so let's plug in 468 for the volume and solve for the potential height:

$$V = lwh \rightarrow$$

$$468 = 12 \times 6 \times h \rightarrow$$

$$\frac{468}{(12 \times 6)} = 6.5 = h$$

The only option that has 6.5 as a possibility for the height is choice **(B)**.

10. **(D)** Multiply the density by the volume of the tank so we can find the mass of water in the tank—when doing this, we are left with kilograms as the resulting unit. Use 5 meters as the radius, since radius is half the diameter:

$$\pi r^2 h \times \text{Density} \rightarrow$$

$$\pi \times (5^2) \times 3 \times 997$$

## Lines, Angles, and Triangles

**SAT Math Strategy**

Unless the question states otherwise, the drawings on the SAT math will all be done to scale, so do not hesitate to estimate based on the drawings. The angle rules below are very helpful to know, but if you forget them on test day, making estimates is an excellent backup plan.

### Supplementary Angles

Supplementary angles add up to 180 degrees. The most common example of supplementary angles is when two angles are formed with a straight line across the bottom.

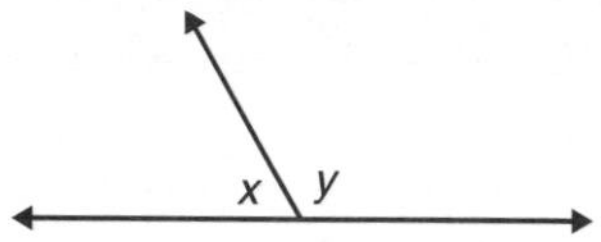


The sum of $x$ and $y$ is 180 degrees.

**Example**

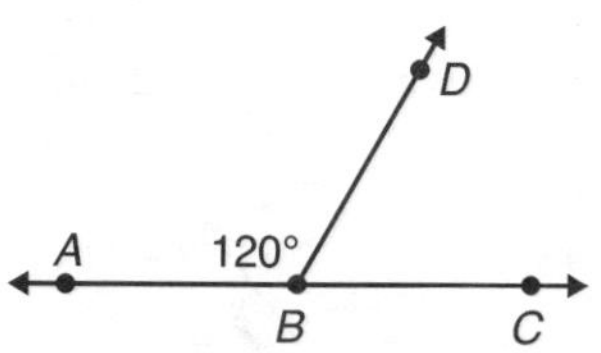


Given that $\overline{ABC}$ is a straight line that is intersected at point $B$ by $\overline{BD}$, and that $\angle ABD$ is 120°, what is the measure of $\angle DBC$?

### Solution

The two angles add up to 180°, so subtract to find the answer, using $x$ as the unknown angle measure:

$$x + 120 = 180 \rightarrow$$

$$x = 180 - 120 = 60$$

So, $\angle DBC = 60°$

### Vertical Angles

When two lines intersect, the angles that are across from one another are called *vertical angles*. Vertical angles are equal to one another.

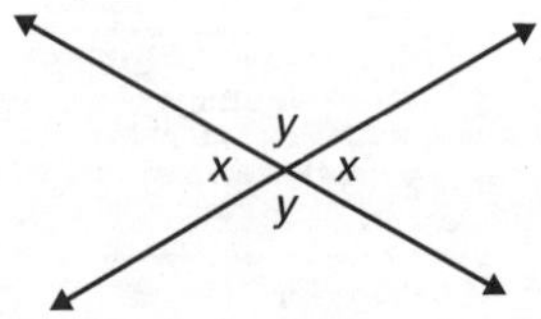


$x = x$ and $y = y$

### Example

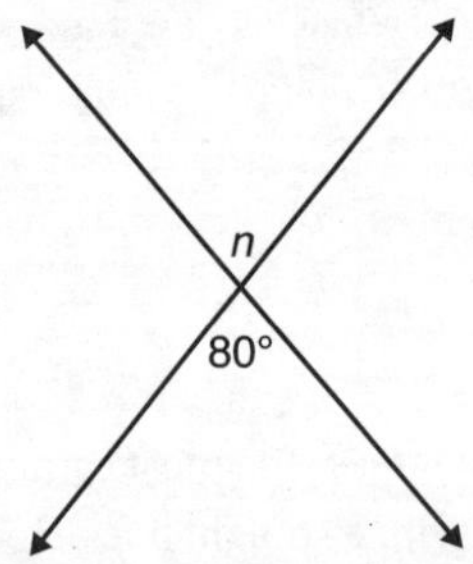


Two lines intersect one another in the figure above. What is the measure of $\angle n$?

### Solution

Since $\angle n$ is a vertical angle to the angle of 80° across from it, $\angle n$ will be equal to this angle and will therefore have a measure of 80°.

### Parallel Lines and a Transversal

When two parallel lines are cut by a *transversal*, a line that intersects both lines, there are angle equivalencies as labelled below:

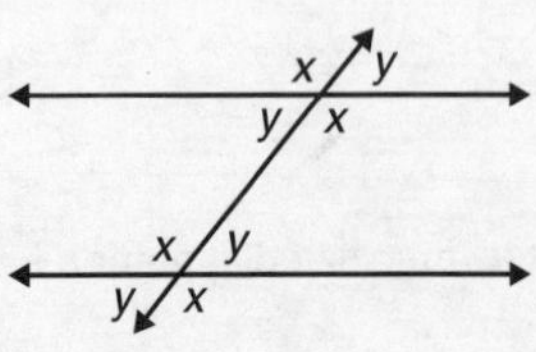


It can help to remember that the "big" angles (in this case $x$) are all equivalent and the "small" angles (in this case $y$) are all equivalent.

## Example

Two parallel lines have a transversal running through them, as indicated in the drawing below. What is the measure of $\angle a$?

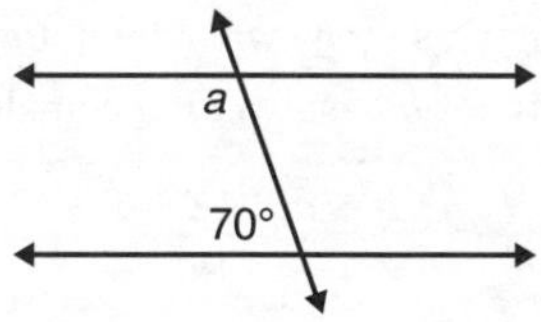


## Solution

The measures of all the angles are labelled below:

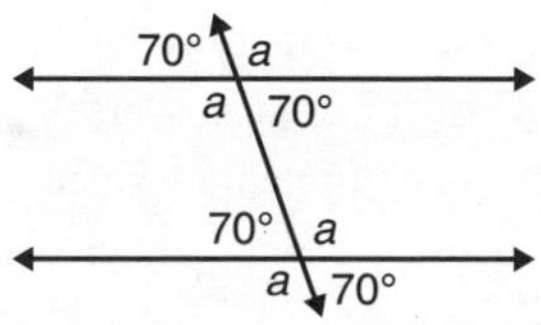


As you can see, the "big" angles are all equivalent and the "small" angles are all equivalent. To calculate the value of $a$, subtract 70° from 180° since $a$ and 70° are supplementary:

$$180 - 70 = 110$$

So, $a$ is equal to 110°.

### Practice

1. If $\angle x$ is supplementary to an angle of 40 degrees, what is the measure of $\angle x$?

2. 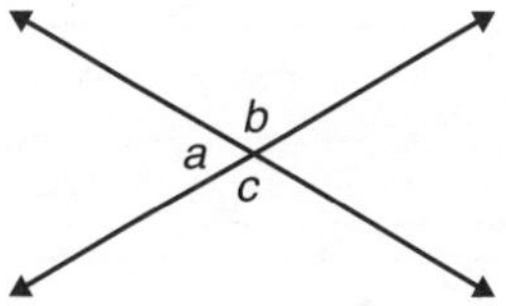


   Two lines intersect above, forming angles with measures $a$, $b$, and $c$ degrees. If $\angle b$ is twice the measure of $\angle a$, what is the measure of $\angle c$?

3. 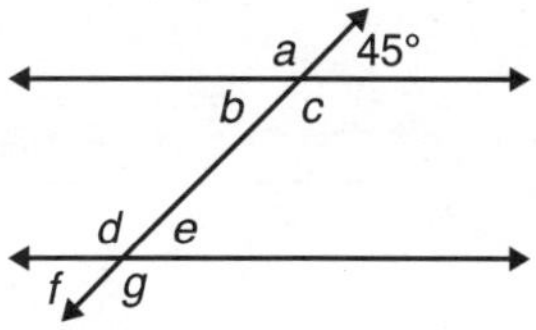


   Two parallel lines are intersected by a transversal, as given above. What are the measures of the labelled angles?

### Solutions

1. **(140)** Since $\angle x$ is supplementary to 40°, $\angle x$ is equal to 180° minus 40°.

$$180 - 40 = 140$$

2. **(120)** $\angle b$ and $\angle a$ are supplementary, so they will add up to 180°. Since $\angle b$ is twice the measure of $\angle a$, $b = 2a$. Now, plug $2a$ in for $b$ to solve for the angle measure of $a$:

$$b + a = 180 \rightarrow$$
$$(2a) + a = 180 \rightarrow$$
$$3a = 180 \rightarrow$$
$$a = 60$$

Since $\angle b$ and $\angle a$ are supplementary, find the value of $\angle b$ by subtracting 60 from 180: $180 - 60 = 120$. $\angle b$ is 120°, and since $\angle c$ and $\angle b$ are vertical angles, $\angle c$ is also equal to 120°.

3. $\angle a$ is supplementary to 45°, so it has a measure of $180 - 45 = 135$. $\angle b$, $\angle e$, and $\angle f$ are all equal to 45°, given that these are parallel lines with a transversal. $\angle a$, $\angle c$, $\angle d$, and $\angle g$ are all equal to 135°. This is an excellent example of a problem in which you can think it through using the facts that the "big" angles are equal and the "small" angles are equal.

## Angles, Triangles, and Quadrilaterals

The SAT gives you this important information on the formula sheet at the beginning:

*The sum of the measures in degrees of the angles of a triangle is 180.*

Even though this is given, it is extremely helpful to commit this fundamental concept to memory.

**Example**

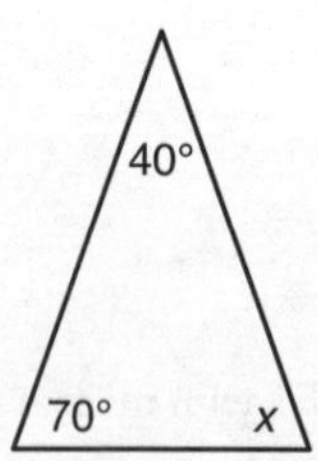


In the triangle above, what is the measure of $\angle x$?

**Solution**

Subtract 70 and 40 from 180 to find the measure of $\angle x$:

$$180 - 70 - 40 = 70$$

So, $\angle x$ is 70°.

The SAT does NOT give you reminders of these concepts—be sure you memorize them.

- **Equilateral** triangles have all three angles equal (each measuring 60 degrees) and all three sides equal.
- **Isosceles** triangles have only two angles equal and two sides equal.

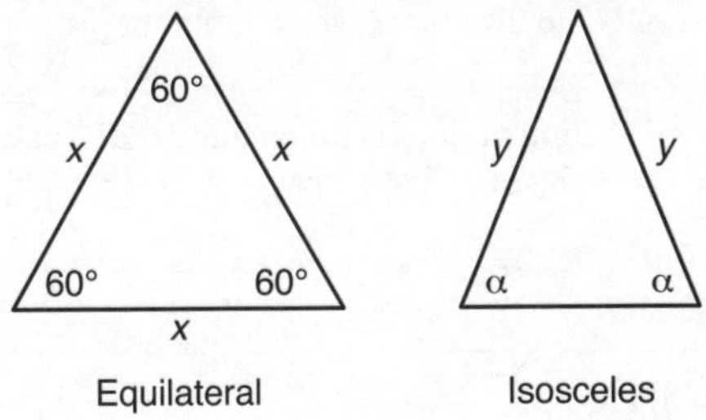


## Example

Is an equilateral triangle also isosceles?

## Solution

Yes—it is a special form of an isosceles triangle. If two of the angles and corresponding sides are equivalent, the triangle is isosceles. An equilateral triangle does have two angles and sides equivalent. This situation is similar to saying that a square is a special form of a rectangle.

**Similar triangles** are ones with the same angles, but not necessarily the same sides.

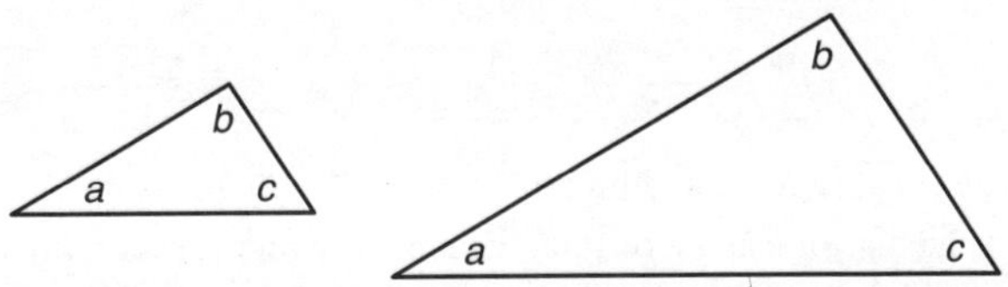


The triangle on the right is larger than the one on the left, yet they are similar—they have the same angle measures and their sides are *proportional* to each other.

## Example

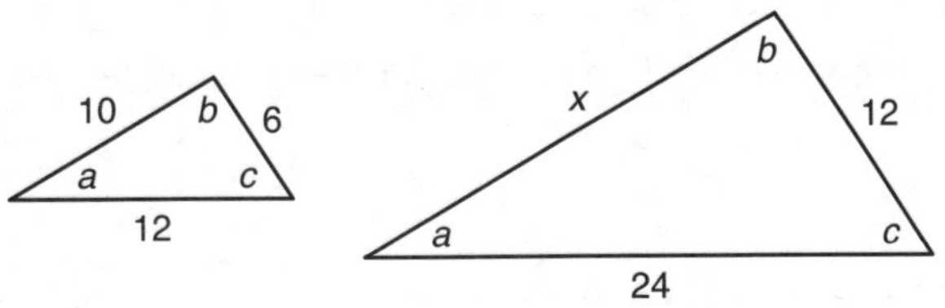


Suppose that the two triangles above are similar to one another. What is the length of side $x$?

## Solution

Since the triangles are similar, their corresponding sides are proportional:

$$10:6:12$$

$$x:12:24$$

So, set up a proportion to solve for $x$:

$$\frac{x}{12} = \frac{10}{6} \rightarrow$$

$$x = \frac{12 \times 10}{6} = 20$$

$x$ is therefore 20 units long. You could also have used a different proportion to solve this given the numbers provided.

A final important fact to know about angles is that **a quadrilateral has internal angles that add up to 360 degrees.** This is true for squares, rectangles, parallelograms, trapezoids, and so on.

### Example

In the parallelogram below, what is the measure of $\angle x$?

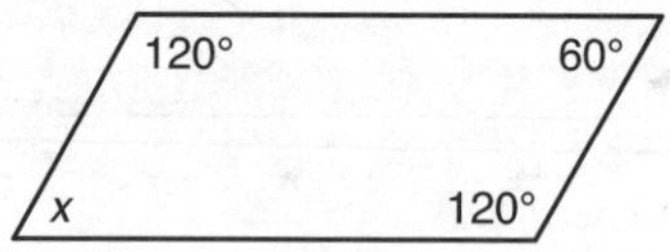


### Solution

Subtract the other angles from 360° to find the measure of $\angle x$:

$$360 - 120 - 60 - 120 = 60$$

$\angle x$ is equal to the angle opposite it, 60°.

### Practice

1. If three of the angles in a trapezoid add up to 300°, what is the measure of the fourth angle?
2. If an isosceles triangle has one angle of 100°, what are the measures of the other two angles?
3. A triangle has two sides with a length of 7 units and two angles that each measure 60°. Based on this information, what is the length of the third side of the triangle?

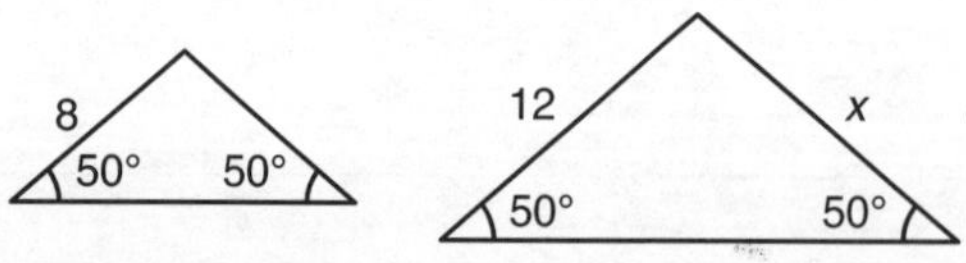


4. Based on the drawing of the two triangles above, what is the measure of side $x$?

### Solutions

1. **(60°)** Since a trapezoid is a quadrilateral, its internal angles will add up to 360°. To find the measure of the fourth angle, subtract 300 from 360:

$$360 - 300 = 60$$

So, the fourth angle has a measure of 60°.

2. **(40°)** A triangle has a total internal degree measure of 180°. Since one of the angles is 100°, it must be the case that the other two angles are equivalent and would add up to 80°. (If the 100° angle were duplicated, the total sum of the internal angles in the isosceles triangle would exceed 200°, which is not possible.) So, subtract 100 from 180 to find the sum of the other two angles:

$$180 - 100 = 80$$

Then, divide 80 by 2 to find the measure of each of the other two angles:

$$\frac{80}{2} = 40$$

So, each of the other two angles will measure 40°.

3. **(7)** Since two of the angles in the triangle are each 60°, the measure of the third angle must also be 60° so that the three angles can have a sum of 180°. Since all the angles are equivalent, the triangle must be equilateral. By definition, an equilateral triangle will have equal angles *and* equal sides. Therefore, the measure of the third side of the triangle will be equivalent to the measures of the other two sides—7 units.

4. **(12)** The two triangles are both isosceles with angle measures of 50°, 50°, and 100°. Since they are similar to one another, the side lengths will be proportional.

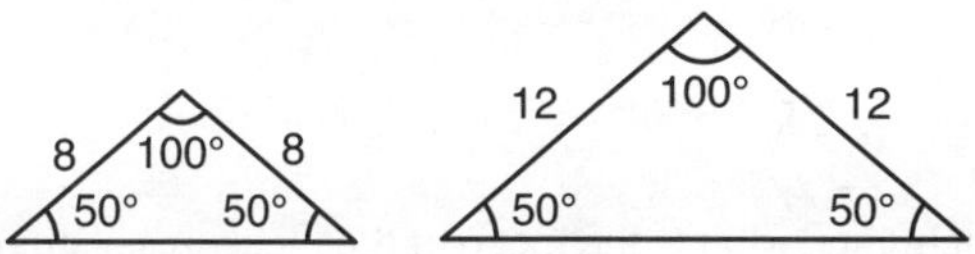


As you can see from the drawings above, the measure of side $x$ will therefore be 12.

## Practice Drill—Lines, Angles, and Triangles

*(If timing, take about 12 minutes to complete.)*

**Fill-In Practice:** Write your answer in the underlined blank under each question.

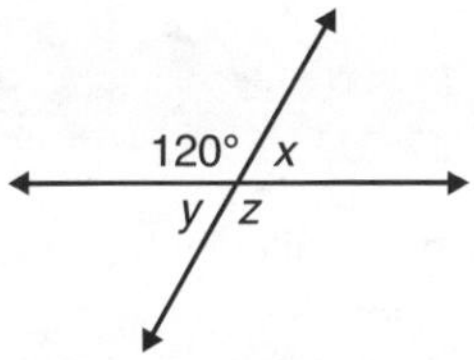


1. In the drawing above of the two intersecting lines, how many of the angles $x$, $y$, and $z$ is/are equal to 120°?

   Answer: ____________

2. An equilateral triangle has sides of the following lengths in units: 8, $x - 7$, and $-2x + 38$. What is the value in units of $x$?

   Answer: ____________

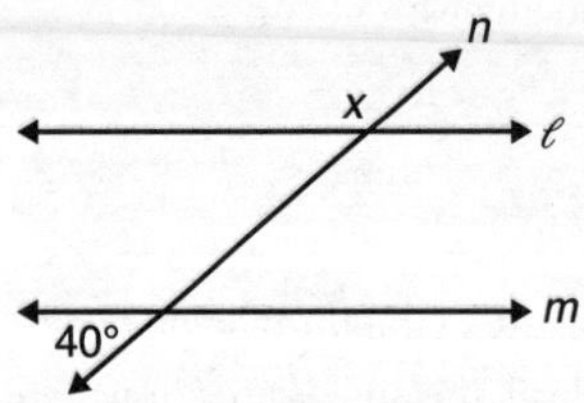


3. For parallel lines *l* and *m* with an intersecting line *n*, what is the measure of angle *x* in degrees?

Answer: ________

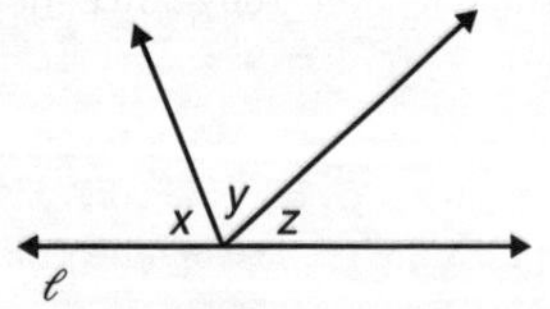


4. Given that *l* is a straight line, what is the mean of the measures of angles *x*, *y*, and *z* in degrees?

Answer: ________

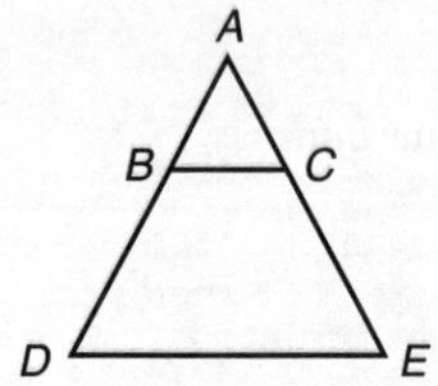


5. In $\Delta ADE$, *B* is a point on $\overline{AD}$ and *C* is a point on $\overline{AE}$, and $\overline{BC}$ and $\overline{DE}$ are parallel. If $\overline{AE}$ is 12 units, $\overline{AC}$ is 4 units, and $\overline{BC}$ is 3 units, what is the measure of $\overline{DE}$ in units?

Answer: ________

**Multiple-Choice Practice**

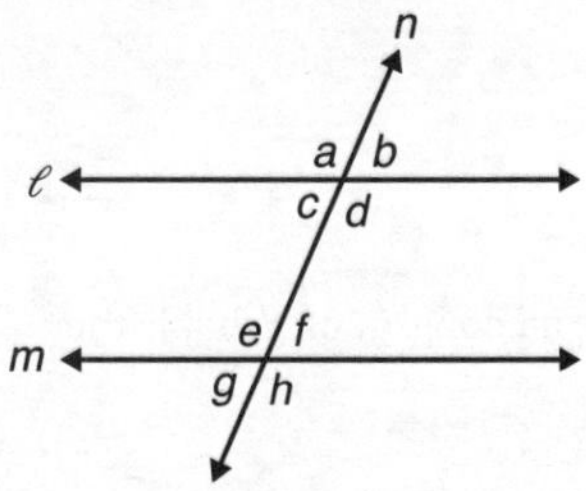


6. If lines $l$ and $m$ are parallel, and line $n$ intersects both line $l$ and line $m$, which pairs of angles must be congruent?

   I. $\angle a$ and $\angle h$

   II. $\angle c$ and $\angle f$

   III. $\angle e$ and $\angle b$

   (A) I only
   (B) III only
   (C) I and II only
   (D) All of the above

7. If triangle $ABC$ has one angle greater than 90°, what is the maximum number of sides of the triangle that can be equal in length?

   (A) 1
   (B) 2
   (C) 3
   (D) Cannot be determined with the given information

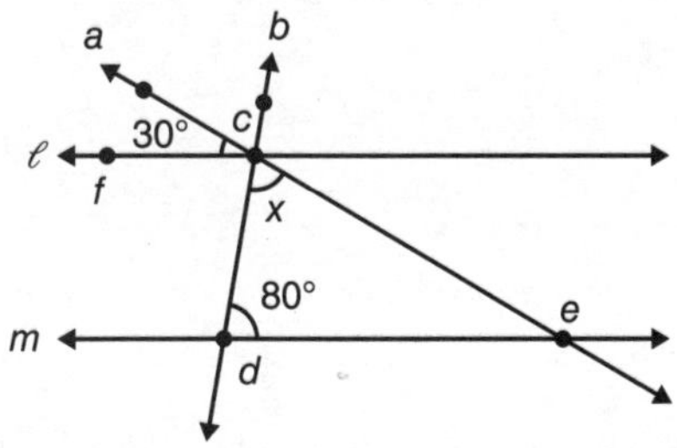


8. In the above figure, lines $l$ and $m$ are parallel, and lines $a$ and $b$ intersect at point $C$. If $\angle CDE$ is 80° and $\angle ACF$ is 30°, what is the measure of $\angle x$?

   (A) 70°
   (B) 80°
   (C) 100°
   (D) 150°

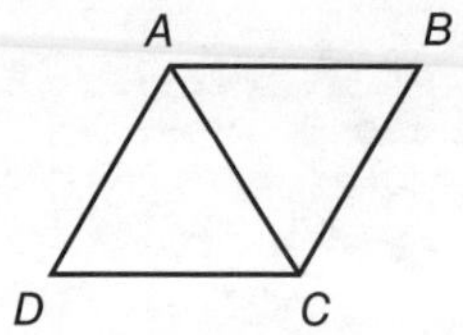


9. In parallelogram $ABCD$ above, $\overline{AB}$, $\overline{BC}$, $\overline{CD}$, $\overline{DA}$, and $\overline{AC}$ are all congruent. What is the measure of angle $\angle BAC$?

(A) 60°
(B) 80°
(C) 90°
(D) 120°

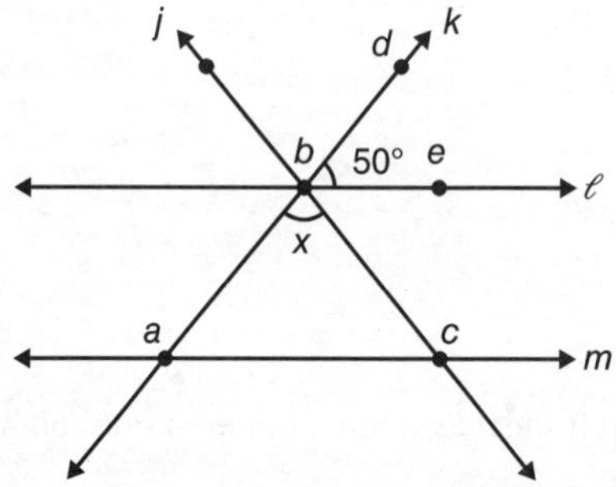


10. In the graph above, lines $l$ and $m$ are parallel, $\overline{AB}$ and $\overline{BC}$ are congruent, $\angle DBE$ is 50°, and lines $j$ and $k$ intersect at point $B$. What is the measure of angle $x$?

(A) 60°
(B) 80°
(C) 100°
(D) 120°

## Solutions

1. **(1)** Only the vertical angle that is across from the angle of 120° will also have a measure of 120°. $\angle x$ and the angle across from it each measure 60°.

2. **(15)** All of the sides in an equilateral triangle are equivalent, so set up an equation to solve for $x$:

$$8 = x - 7 \rightarrow$$
$$8 + 7 = x \rightarrow$$
$$15 = x$$

3. **(140)** $\angle x$ is identical to the angle that is supplementary to 40°. Therefore,

$$40 + x = 180 \rightarrow$$
$$x = 140$$

4. **(60)** All three of the angles add up to 180°, so calculate the mean by dividing 180 by 3:

$$\frac{180}{3} = 60$$

5. **(9)** Triangles *ABC* and *ADE* are similar to one another because their angles are congruent, so their sides are proportional. Set up a proportion to solve for $\overline{DE}$.

$$\frac{\overline{AC}}{\overline{AE}} = \frac{\overline{BC}}{\overline{DE}} \rightarrow$$

$$\frac{4}{12} = \frac{3}{x} \rightarrow$$

$$x = \frac{3 \times 12}{4} = \frac{36}{4} = 9$$

6. **(C)** With parallel lines and a transversal, match up the "large" and the "small" angles to establish equivalences. $\angle a$ and $\angle h$ are alternate exterior angles that are congruent, and $\angle c$ and $\angle f$are alternate interior angles that are congruent. $\angle e$ and $\angle b$ are not congruent, which you see from estimation in addition to knowing the general rule.

7. **(B)** It will be impossible for the triangle to have all sides equal, since an equilateral triangle has all angles equal to 60°. However, it is possible to have two of the sides equal since an isosceles triangle could be formed. For example, if the largest angle were 100° and the other two angles were both 40°, the sides opposite the 40° angles would be equivalent.

8. **(A)** Since lines *l* and *m* are parallel with a transversal, $\angle CED$ will equal 30°. $\angle x$, $\angle CED$, and $\angle CDE$ add up to 180° because they are within a triangle. Therefore, you can solve for $\angle x$ as follows:

$$x + 80 + 30 = 180 \rightarrow$$

$$x = 180 - 80 - 30 = 70$$

9. **(A)** If all the sides are equivalent, two equilateral triangles, *ABC* and *ACD*, will form. Since all the angles in an equilateral triangle are equal to 60°, $\angle BAC$ will equal 60°.

10. **(B)** Use the fact that vertical angles are equal and the angles across from equal sides in an isosceles triangle (i.e., *ABC*) are equal to establish equivalences as drawn below:

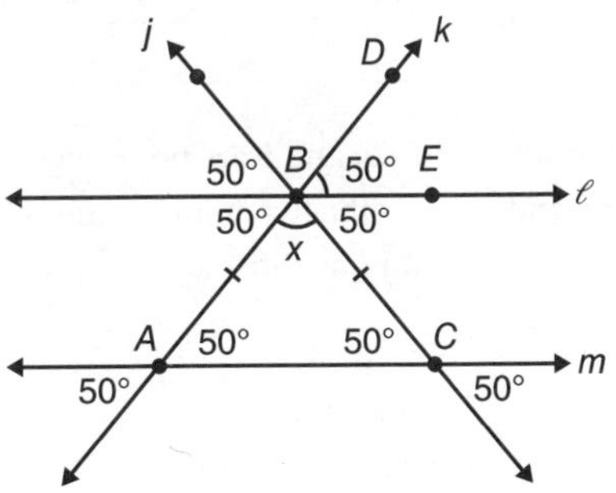


Since $\overline{AB}$ and $\overline{BC}$ are congruent, $\angle BAC = \angle BCA$ (triangle *ABC* is isosceles). Since lines *l* and *m* are parallel and $\angle KBE$ and $\angle BAC$ are corresponding angles, $\angle BAC = 50°$. Therefore, $\angle BCA = 50°$ and $\angle x = 180° - 50° - 50° = 80°$.

## Right Triangles and Trigonometry

### Pythagorean Theorem and Special Right Triangles

The SAT provides you with these two important right triangle formulas that enable you to determine the side lengths and even some angles in right triangles (triangles that have a 90° angle):

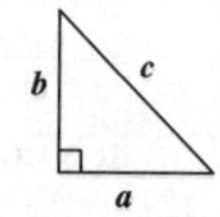


**Pythagorean theorem: $a^2 + b^2 = c^2$**

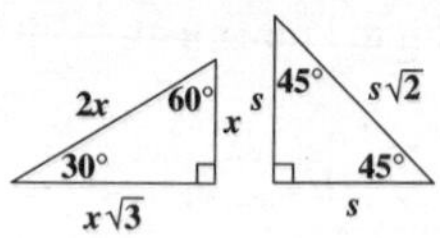


Even though they are provided, it is extremely helpful to have these formulas memorized so that you can more instantaneously and intuitively determine right angle relationships.

**Example 1**

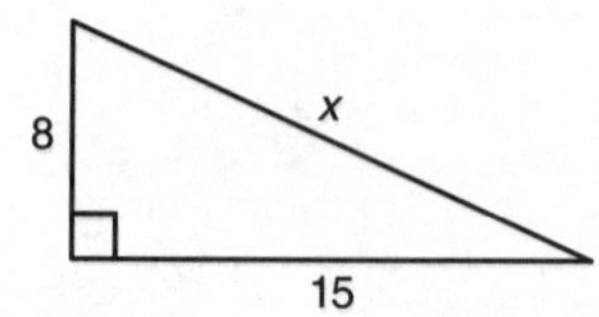


What is the length of $x$ in the right triangle above?

**Solution**

Use the Pythagorean theorem to solve. Sides $a$ and $b$ are both "legs" of the right triangle (the sides NOT across from the 90° angle), and side $c$ is the hypotenuse (the side that is across from the 90° angle). Let's use 8 as side $a$, 15 as side $b$, and $x$ as side $c$.

$$a^2 + b^2 = c^2 \rightarrow$$
$$8^2 + 15^2 = x^2 \rightarrow$$
$$64 + 225 = 289 = x^2 \rightarrow$$
$$\sqrt{289} = 17 = x$$

So, side $x$ is equal to 17 units.

**Example 2**

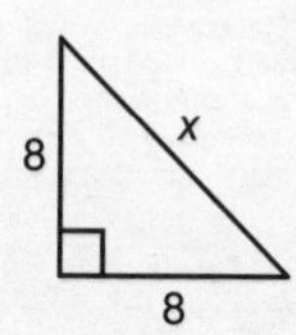


What is the length of side $x$ in the right triangle above?

## ✓ Solution

While you could use the Pythagorean theorem to solve for $x$, it will be more efficient to recognize that this is a special right triangle in which the sides have a relationship of $s$, $s$, $s\sqrt{2}$. The legs of the triangle are both 8, so you can find the hypotenuse of the triangle by multiplying 8 by $\sqrt{2}$. Therefore, the length of $x$ is $8\sqrt{2}$.

## › Example 3

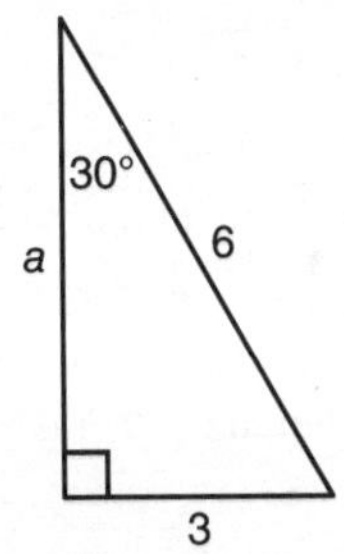


What is the length of side $a$ in the right triangle above?

## ✓ Solution

The above triangle has angles of 90°, 30°, and 60° (since $180 - 30 - 90 = 60$). So, the sides will have a relationship of $x$, $x\sqrt{3}$, and $2x$. So, instead of having to use the Pythagorean theorem to solve for $a$, realize that $a$ will simply be $\sqrt{3}$ multiplied by 3, given where the sides are in the triangle. Therefore, $a = 3\sqrt{3}$.

Another way of solving for the unknown sides of right triangles is to use **Pythagorean triples**. These are combinations of side lengths in right triangles for which each value is an integer. The most important ones to know are the following:

**3-4-5, 5-12-13, and 7-24-25**

Not only will the above combinations work as sides for right triangles, but *multiples* of them will also work. Just as 5-12-13 could be sides of a right triangle, 10-24-26 could also be sides of a right triangle, since each side is twice the value of the sides in the original triple.

## › Example

What is the measure of side $x$ in the triangle below?

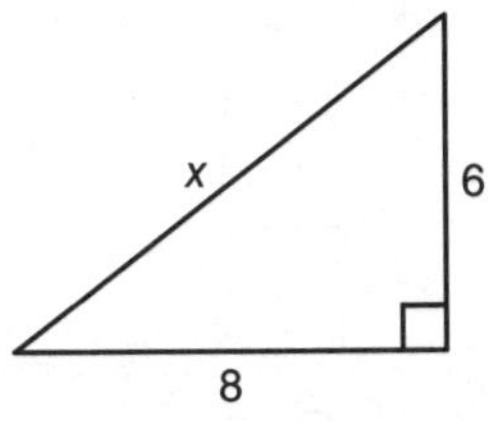

### ✓ Solution

While you could solve for $x$ by using the Pythagorean theorem, you can solve this more quickly by recognizing that the sides in this triangle are multiples of a 3-4-5 triple. The 6 is twice 3, the 8 is twice 4, so the $x$ is twice 5. So, to solve for $x$, just double 5:

$$2 \times 5 = 10$$

Side $x$ therefore has a length of 10 units.

### Practice

1. If two legs in a right triangle are 9 and 40, what is the length of the hypotenuse?
2. If the hypotenuse in a right triangle is 61 and one of the legs is 60, what is the length of the other leg?
3. Two legs in a right triangle are equal to $y$. What is the value of the hypotenuse in terms of $y$?
4. If the hypotenuse in a right triangle is equal to 50 and the smaller leg is equal to 14, what is the length of the third side?
5. If the sides in a right triangle are 4, $4\sqrt{3}$, and 8, what is the measure of the smallest angle in the triangle?

### Solutions

1. Use the Pythagorean theorem to solve:

$$a^2 + b^2 = c^2 \rightarrow$$
$$9^2 + 40^2 = c^2 \rightarrow$$
$$81 + 1{,}600 = 1{,}681 = c^2 \rightarrow$$
$$\sqrt{1{,}681} = 41 = c$$

So, the hypotenuse has a length of 41 units.

2. Use the Pythagorean theorem to solve for the unknown leg. Use 61 as the $c$ and 60 as $a$:

$$60^2 + b^2 = 61^2 \rightarrow$$
$$3{,}600 + b^2 = 3{,}721 \rightarrow$$
$$b^2 = 121 \rightarrow$$
$$b = 11$$

So, the unknown side has a length of 11 units.

3. With two of the legs equal in this triangle, we know that the relationship of the sides is $s$, $s$, $s\sqrt{2}$. Plugging in $y$ for $s$, the hypotenuse will be $y\sqrt{2}$.

4. While you could use the Pythagorean theorem to solve this, you will save time if you recognize that these values are twice what we would find in the Pythagorean triple of 7-24-25. So, double the 24 to find the third side: $24 \times 2 = 48$.

5. Since the sides have the ratios $x$, $x\sqrt{3}$, and $2x$ (with $x = 4$), the triangle will have angles of 30°, 60°, and 90°. The smallest angle will therefore have a measure of 30°.

### Sine, Cosine, Tangent

In a right triangle (a triangle with a 90° angle), the three sides are called the following:

*Hypotenuse*: This side is across from the 90° angle, and is always the longest side of the triangle.

*Opposite*: The side that is opposite, or across from, a particular angle. It could be either of the legs of the triangle depending on where the angle is.

*Adjacent*: The side that is adjacent to, or next to, a particular angle. It also could be either of the legs of the triangle depending on where the angle is and will never be the hypotenuse.

For example, in the right triangle below, the hypotenuse and the sides opposite and adjacent to angle $x$ are labelled:

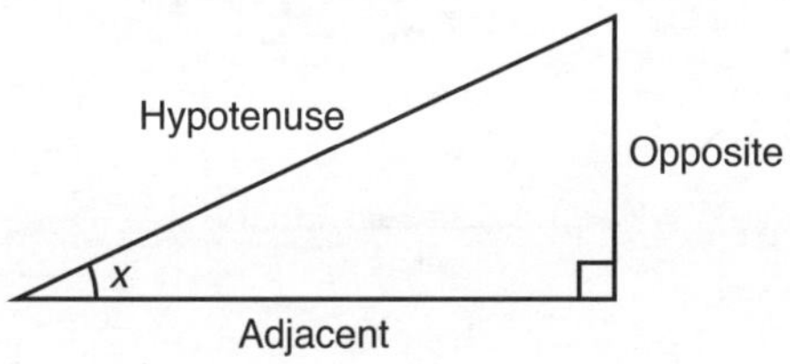


The popular acronym SOH-CAH-TOA will help you remember which sides to use when calculating *sine, cosine,* and *tangent.*

| S-O-H | C-A-H | T-O-A |
|---|---|---|
| $\sin\theta = \dfrac{\text{Opposite}}{\text{Hypotenuse}}$ | $\cos\theta = \dfrac{\text{Adjacent}}{\text{Hypotenuse}}$ | $\tan\theta = \dfrac{\text{Opposite}}{\text{Adjacent}}$ |

Let's take a look at an example to see what the different trigonometry values would be.

$$\sin\theta = \frac{a}{c}$$
$$\cos\theta = \frac{b}{c}$$
$$\tan\theta = \frac{a}{b}$$

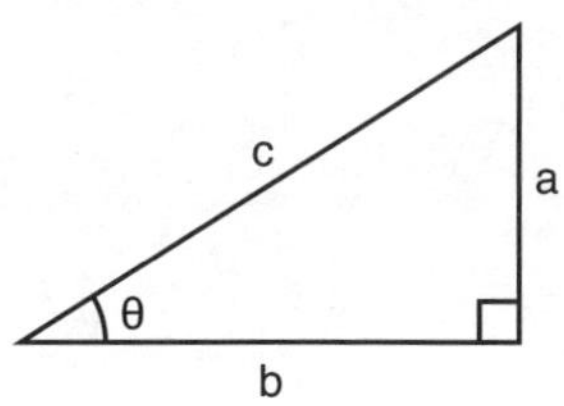


### Example

What is the tangent for angle $x$ in the right triangle below?

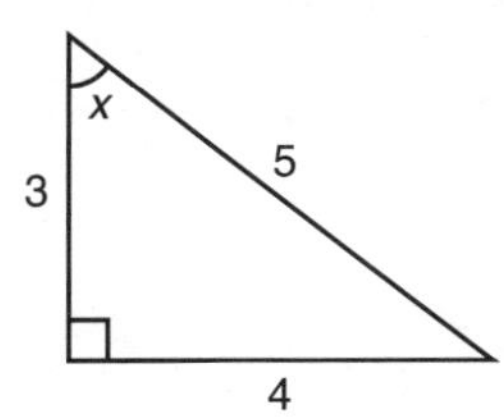

### ✓ Solution

To find the tangent, we need the opposite side and the adjacent side. The side of length 4 is opposite $\angle x$, and the side of length 3 is adjacent to $\angle x$. So, calculate the tangent of $\angle x$ as follows:

$$\tan\theta = \frac{\text{Opposite}}{\text{Adjecent}} \rightarrow$$

$$\tan x = \frac{4}{3}$$

### Practice

Consider the triangle below:

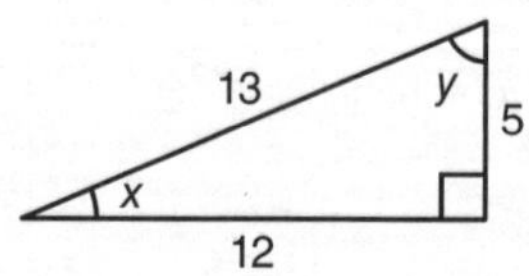


1. What is sin *x*?
2. What is cos *y*?
3. What is tan *y*?
4. In a 45-45-90 triangle, which values will be identical?

    I. $\cos 45$

    II. $\sin 45$

    III. $\tan 45$

### Solutions

1. $\sin x = \frac{\text{Opposite}}{\text{Hypotenuse}} = \frac{5}{13}$
2. $\cos y = \frac{\text{Adjacent}}{\text{Hypotenuse}} = \frac{5}{13}$
3. $\tan y = \frac{\text{Opposite}}{\text{Adjacent}} = \frac{12}{5}$
4. In a 45-45-90 triangle, the sides have a ratio of $s{:}s{:}s\sqrt{2}$. I and II are equal since $\cos(45)$ and $\sin(45)$ are both $\frac{1}{\sqrt{2}}$. III is not equal to the others since $\tan(45)$ is just 1.

### Area of an Equilateral Triangle

While it is manageable to solve for the area of an equilateral triangle without knowing this formula, memorizing it will save you time should you come across a problem that asks about it.

The area, *A*, of an equilateral triangle with sides of length *a* is:

$$A = \frac{\sqrt{3}}{4}a^2$$

### › Example

What is the area of an equilateral triangle with sides that are 4 inches long?

### ✓ Solution

Plug 4 in for $a$ into the equilateral triangle area formula:

$$A = \frac{\sqrt{3}}{4}a^2 \rightarrow$$

$$A = \frac{\sqrt{3}}{4}(4)^2 = \frac{\sqrt{3}}{4}(16) = 4\sqrt{3}$$

So, the area of the triangle would be $4\sqrt{3}$ square inches.

### Sine and Cosine of Complementary Angles

Complementary angles add up to 90°. The relationship of the sine and cosine of complementary angles is:

$$\sin(x) = \cos(90° - x)$$

### › Example

If the sine of 30° is 0.5, what is the cosine of 60°?

### ✓ Solution

While you could use a calculator for a problem like this on the calculator-permitted test section, if this were on the non-calculator test section you would have to know an alternative way to approach it. Use the relationship between the sine and cosine of complementary angles to solve. Since $30 + 60 = 90$, 30° and 60° are complementary. Because $\sin(x) = \cos(90° - x)$, $\sin(30) = \cos(60)$, and the cosine of 60° will also equal 0.5.

## Practice Drill—Right Triangles and Trigonometry

*(If timing, take about 12 minutes to complete.)*

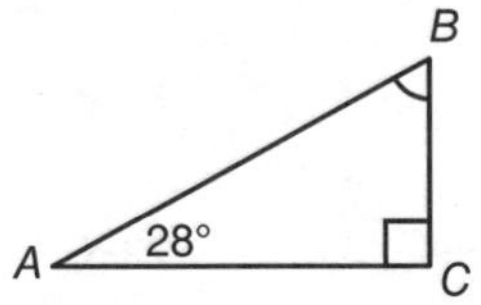


1. Triangle $ABC$ is portrayed above. If triangle $DEF$ is similar to triangle $ABC$, and angle $B$ corresponds to angle $E$, what is the measure of angle $E$?

   (A) 28°
   (B) 52°
   (C) 62°
   (D) 84°

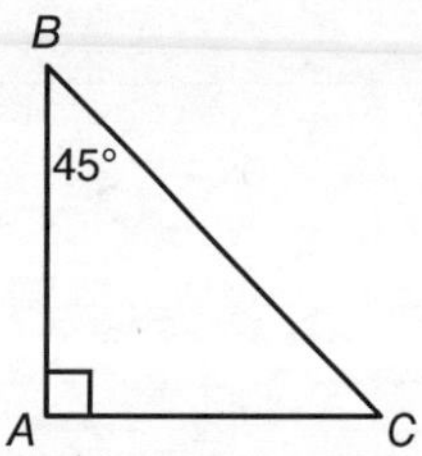


2. In $\Delta ABC$, $\angle A$ is 90° and $\angle B$ is 45°. If $\overline{BC}$ has a length of 4 units, what is the length of $\overline{AC}$?

(A) 2
(B) $2\sqrt{2}$
(C) $2\sqrt{3}$
(D) 4

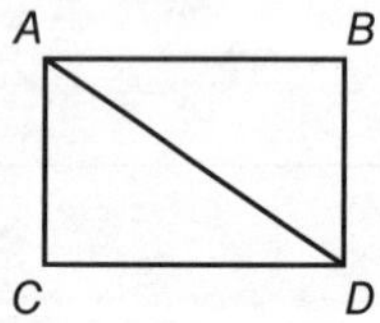


3. If rectangle *ABCD* has a side length of 7 for *AC* and a side length of 24 for *CD*, what is the length of the diagonal *AD*?

(A) 14
(B) 25
(C) 28
(D) 35

4. For an equilateral triangle with a side length of 8 units, what is the triangle's area in square units?

(A) $8\sqrt{2}$
(B) $8\sqrt{3}$
(C) $16\sqrt{2}$
(D) $16\sqrt{3}$

5. Triangle *DEF* is similar to triangle *ABC*, with vertex *D* corresponding to vertex *A*, vertex *E* corresponding to vertex *B*, and vertex *F* corresponding to vertex *C*. The measure of $\angle C$ is 90° and the measure of $\angle B$ is 30°. What is the cosine of $\angle D$?

(A) $\frac{1}{3}$
(B) $\frac{1}{2}$
(C) $\frac{2}{3}$
(D) $\frac{3}{4}$

6. What is the difference between sin($x$) and cos($90° - x$) if $x$ is an angle between 20 and 30 degrees?

(A) 0
(B) $\frac{1}{2}$
(C) $\frac{3}{5}$
(D) $\frac{3}{4}$

7. What is the sine of the smallest angle in a right triangle with sides 7, 24, and 25?

(A) $\frac{7}{25}$
(B) $\frac{7}{24}$
(C) $\frac{24}{7}$
(D) $\frac{25}{7}$

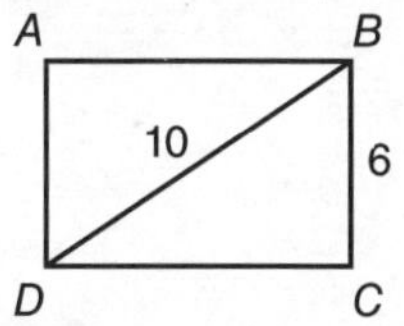


8. In rectangle $ABCD$ above, diagonal $\overline{DB}$ is 10 units long, and side $\overline{BC}$ is 6 units long. What is the area of the rectangle $ABCD$?

(A) 30 square units
(B) 36 square units
(C) 48 square units
(D) 60 square units

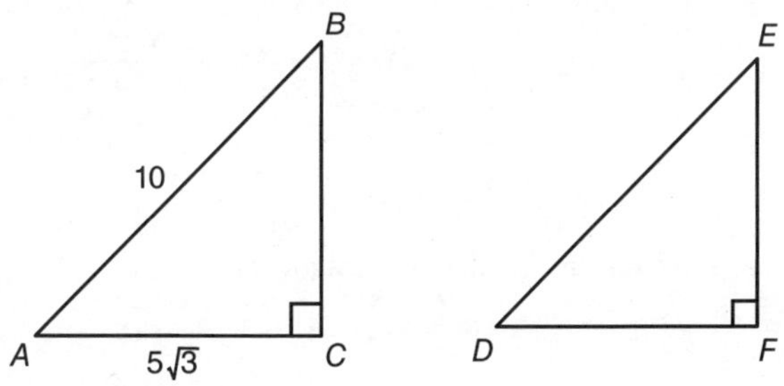


9. Right triangles $ABC$ and $DEF$ are similar to each other. What is the tangent of $\angle EDF$?

(A) $\frac{1}{\sqrt{3}}$
(B) $\frac{\sqrt{2}}{3}$
(C) $\frac{1}{2}$
(D) 2

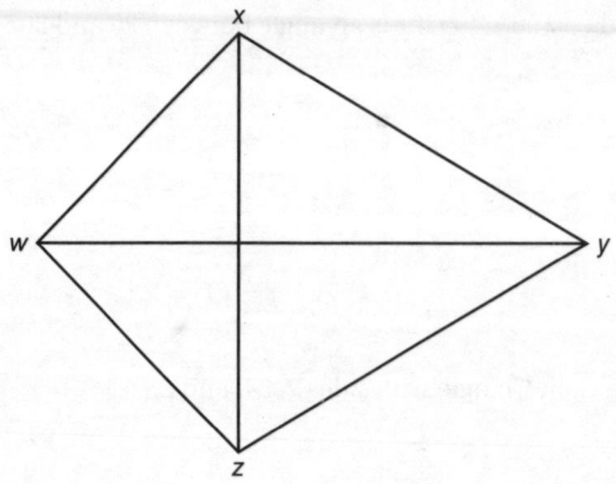


10. In the figure above, $\overline{XZ}$ and $\overline{WY}$ are perpendicular, and $\overline{WY}$ bisects $\overline{XZ}$. $\overline{XY}$ and $\overline{ZY}$ are of equal length, $\overline{WX}$ and $\overline{WZ}$ are of equal length, and $\angle XWY = 45°$. If $\overline{XY}$ is 4 and $\overline{WX}$ is $2\sqrt{2}$, what is the length of $\overline{WY}$?

    (A) $2\sqrt{2}$
    (B) $2\sqrt{3}$
    (C) 4
    (D) $2 + 2\sqrt{3}$

## Solutions

1. **(C)** Calculate $\angle B$ as follows:

$$90 - 28 = 62$$

Since $\angle B$ and $\angle E$ correspond to one another, $\angle E$ will have the same measure of 62°.

2. **(B)** In a 45-45-90 triangle, the hypotenuse is $\sqrt{2}$ multiplied by the length of one of the legs. So, in this situation, solve for the length of one of the legs by using a proportion:

$$\frac{\overline{BC}}{\overline{AC}} = \frac{\sqrt{2}}{1} \rightarrow$$

$$\frac{4}{\overline{AC}} = \frac{\sqrt{2}}{1} \rightarrow$$

$$\overline{AC} = \frac{4}{\sqrt{2}} = 2\sqrt{2}$$

3. **(B)** Use the Pythagorean theorem to solve for the length of the diagonal:

$$a^2 + b^2 = c^2 \rightarrow$$
$$7^2 + 24^2 = c^2 \rightarrow$$
$$625 = c^2 \rightarrow$$
$$\sqrt{625} = 25 = c$$

Alternatively, you could recognize that this is a Pythagorean triple of 7-24-25, thereby avoiding the need to calculate.

4. **(D)** Plug 8 in for $a$ into the area formula for an equilateral triangle:

$$A = \frac{\sqrt{3}}{4}a^2 \rightarrow$$

$$A = \frac{\sqrt{3}}{4}(8)^2 = \frac{\sqrt{3} \times 64}{4} = 16\sqrt{3}$$

5. **(B)** $\angle D$ will have a measure of 60°, since it corresponds to $\angle A$ in the other triangle. Calculate the cosine of $\angle D$ using your calculator (be sure your calculator is set to calculate in degrees, not radians), or realize that this is a 30-60-90 triangle so the side adjacent to 60° will be like 1 and the hypotenuse will be like 2. Since the cosine equals the adjacent divided by the hypotenuse, its value will be $\frac{1}{2}$.

6. **(A)** Given that $\sin(x) = \cos(90° - x)$, the two expressions will be equal to one another.

   Therefore, the value when the $\cos(90° - x)$ is subtracted from $\sin(x)$ will be zero, regardless of what particular value you would select for $x$.

7. **(A)** The smallest angle is marked below—it is the one across from the smallest side, 7.

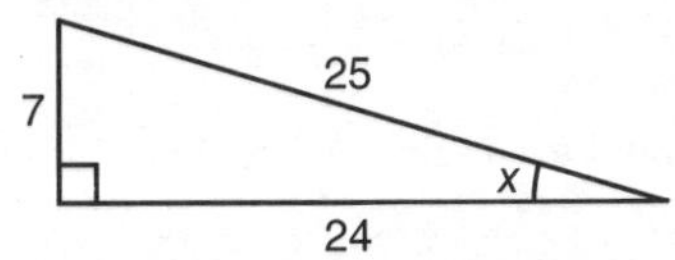


   The sine of this angle is equal to the opposite side divided by the hypotenuse: $\frac{7}{25}$.

8. **(C)** Solve for the length of the rectangle so that you can then multiply by the width of 6 to find the rectangle's area. Save time by recognizing that the numbers 10 and 6 are double the values found in the 3-4-5 Pythagorean triple. So, the length will be twice 4: 8. Then, multiply 8 by 6 to find the area of the rectangle: $8 \times 6 = 48$.

9. **(A)** Because the triangles are similar to one another, their corresponding sides will be proportional. The tangent of $\angle EDF$ will be the same as the tangent of $\angle BAC$. Recognize that triangle $ABC$ is a special right triangle: 30-60-90 with sides relating to each other as $x$, $x\sqrt{3}$, and $2x$. Therefore, the unknown side in the triangle $ABC$ will be 5. You can then calculate the tangent of $\angle BAC$ by dividing the oppposite side of 5 by the adjacent side of $5\sqrt{3}$:

$$\frac{5}{5\sqrt{3}} = \frac{1}{\sqrt{3}}$$

10. **(D)** Label the figure below to find the angle and side values based on the 30-60-90 triangles and 45-45-90 triangles within:

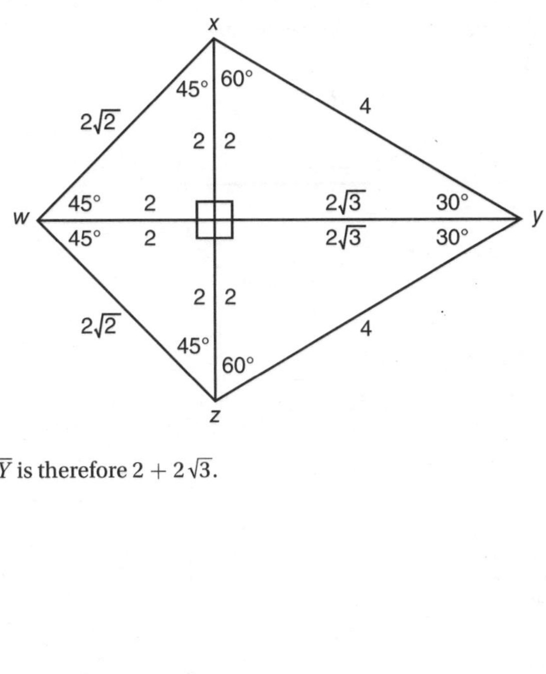


   The length of $\overline{WY}$ is therefore $2 + 2\sqrt{3}$.

## Circles

At the beginning of each math test section, you are provided with these facts and formulas about circles:

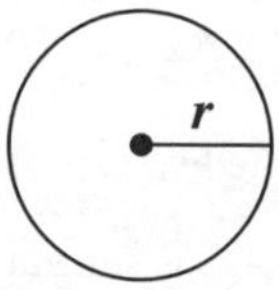


- $r$ = **Radius of the Circle**
- **Area of a Circle** $= \pi r^2$
- **Circumference of a Circle** $= 2\pi r$
- **A circle has 360 degrees.**

Memorize these facts so you do not have to flip back to the beginning of the section. Here is how to apply these essential concepts.

### Radius and Diameter

- The *radius* goes the distance from the center of the circle to the circle itself, and is half the length of the diameter.
- The *diameter* goes from one side of a circle to another side through the center, and is twice the measure of the radius.

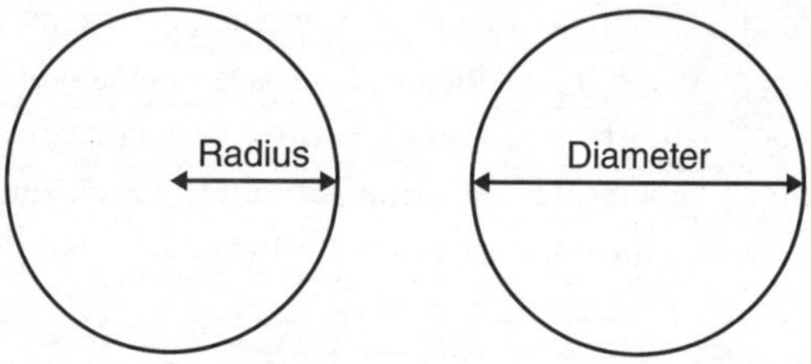


**Example**

What is the radius and the diameter in the circle drawn below?

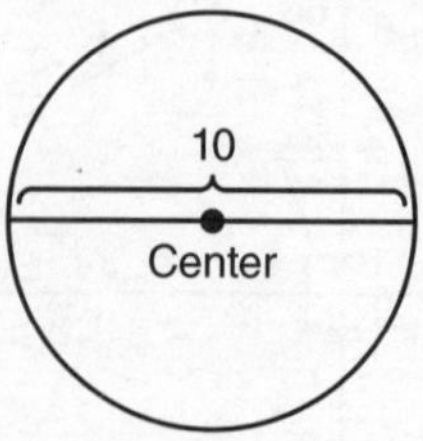


**Solution**

The diameter is 10 and the radius will be half the diameter, so the radius is 5.

### Area and Circumference

The *area* of a circle is calculated using the radius, *r*:

$$\text{Area} = \pi r^2$$

The *circumference* of a circle is calculated using the radius, *r*:

$$\text{Circumference} = 2\pi r$$

Keep these two concepts clear by remembering that the area will give you square units, while the circumference will give you units of length.

**Note:** It is fine to use the formula Circumference $= \pi \times$ Diameter if you would prefer.

**Example**

What is the area and the circumference of a circle with a radius of 5 inches?

**Solution**

Calculate each value using the above formulas, plugging 5 in for *r*.

$$\text{Area} = \pi r^2 \rightarrow \pi 5^2 = 25\pi \text{ square inches}$$

$$\text{Circumference} = 2\pi r = 2 \times \pi \times 5 = 10\pi \text{ inches}$$

### 360° in a Circle

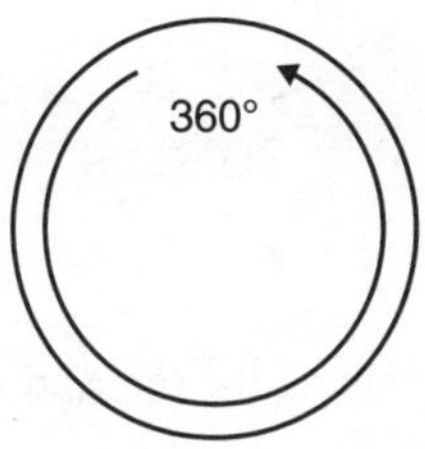


A full rotation of a circle will be 360°.

**Example**

A circle can be divided into how many right angles?

**Solution**

Since there are a total of 360° in a circle, and a right angle is 90°, a circle can be divided into $\frac{360}{90} =$ 4 right angles.

## Inscribed Angle

This is a less common concept related to degree measure that is good to understand, just in case a problem about it comes up.

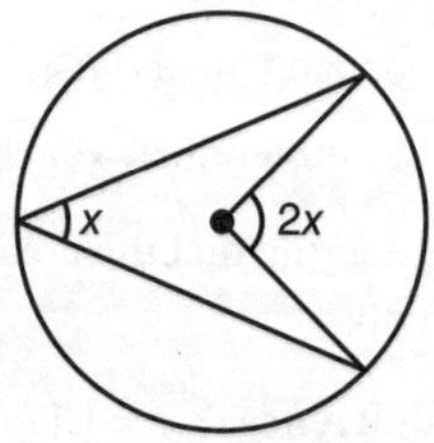


In the graph above, 2x corresponds to a central angle and $x$ corresponds to an inscribed angle. When the inscribed angle and the central angle have the same arc, the central angle is *twice* the measure of the inscribed angle.

### Example

In the circle graphed below with a central angle of 80°, what is the measure of $\angle x$?

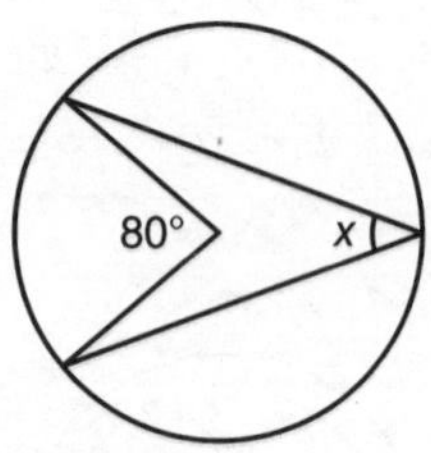


### Solution

Given that $\angle x$ is an inscribed angle that shares the same arc as the central angle of 80°, $\angle x$ will be half the measure of 80°:

$$\frac{80^\circ}{2} = 40^\circ$$

## Practice

1. If the radius of a circle is $x$ units, what will be the diameter of the circle in terms of $x$?
2. What is the area of a circle with a radius of 10 inches?
3. What is the circumference of a circle with a diameter of 4 inches?
4. If a circular pie is to be divided into 12 equal pieces, what will be the measure of the angle formed at the central tip of each piece of pie after the pieces are cut?
5. What is the measure of the central angle $a$ of the sector drawn in the figure below?

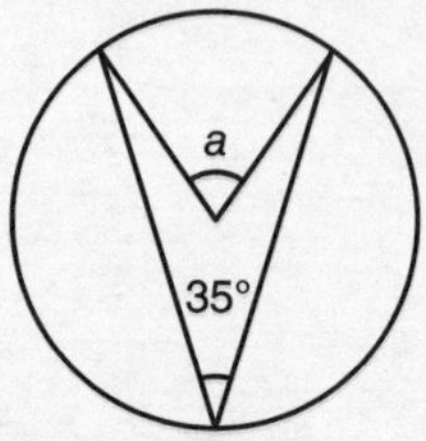

## Solutions

1. The diameter of a circle is twice that of the radius, so the diameter will be $2x$.
2. Area $= \pi r^2 \rightarrow \pi 10^2 = 100\pi$
3. Be sure you use 2 for the radius, not 4. Circumference $= 2\pi r \rightarrow 2 \times \pi \times 2 = 4\pi$
4. Take 360° and divide it by 12 to find the angle:

$$\frac{360^\circ}{12} = 30^\circ$$

5. The central angle will be twice the measure of the inscribed angle, 35°. So $35^\circ \times 2 = 70^\circ$.

The SAT will have you apply the general concepts about circle area, circumference, and degree measure to calculate the length of an arc or the area of a sector.

## Arc Length

$$\frac{\text{Part}}{\text{Whole}} = \frac{\text{Angle}}{360^\circ} = \frac{\text{Length of Arc}}{\text{Circumference}}$$

### Example

In a circle of radius 3 with an arc of 60°, what is the length of the arc?

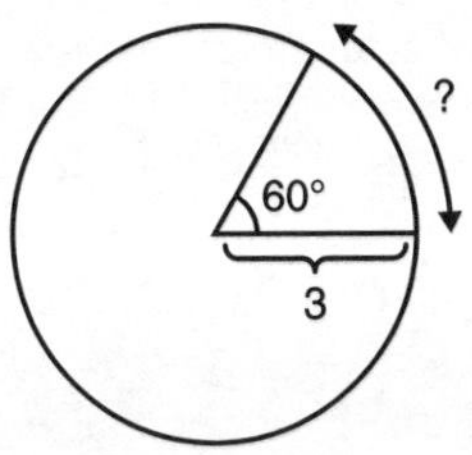


### Solution

$$\frac{\text{Part}}{\text{Whole}} = \frac{60^\circ}{360^\circ} = \frac{1}{6} = \frac{\text{Length of Arc}}{\text{Circumference}} = \frac{x}{2 \times \pi \times 3}$$

So, set up a proportion to solve for the arc length:

$$\frac{1}{6} = \frac{x}{6\pi} \rightarrow \frac{6\pi}{6} = x \rightarrow \pi = x$$

The length of the arc is therefore $\pi$ units.

### Sector Area

$$\frac{\text{Part}}{\text{Whole}} = \frac{\text{Angle}}{360°} = \frac{\text{Area of Sector}}{\text{Area of Circle}}$$

**Example**

In a circle with a radius of 3 and a sector of 60°, what is the area of the sector?

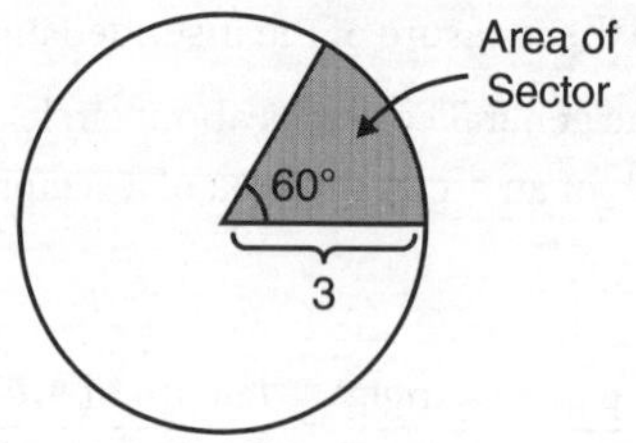


**Solution**

$$\frac{\text{Part}}{\text{Whole}} = \frac{60°}{360°} = \frac{1}{6} = \frac{\text{Area of Sector}}{\text{Area of Circle}} = \frac{x}{\pi 3^2} = \frac{x}{9\pi}$$

So, set up a proportion to solve for the sector area:

$$\frac{1}{6} = \frac{x}{9\pi} \rightarrow \frac{9\pi}{6} = x \rightarrow \frac{3}{2}\pi = x$$

The area of the sector is therefore $\frac{3}{2}\pi$ square units.

### Practice

1. What is the length of a 45° arc in a circle that has a radius of 5 inches?
2. What is the area of a 30° arc in a circle with a radius of 4 inches?
3. A circular pizza has a surface area of $64\pi$ square inches. If the pizza is divided into 8 equal pieces made by cutting along the diameter through the center point of the pizza, what is the length of the crust on the edge of each piece?

### Solutions

1.
$$\frac{\text{Part}}{\text{Whole}} = \frac{45°}{360°} = \frac{1}{8} = \frac{\text{Length of Arc}}{\text{Circumference}} = \frac{x}{2 \times \pi \times 5}$$

So, set up a proportion to solve for the arc length:

$$\frac{1}{8} = \frac{x}{10\pi} \rightarrow \frac{10\pi}{8} = x \rightarrow \frac{5}{4}\pi = x$$

2.
$$\frac{\text{Part}}{\text{Whole}} = \frac{30°}{360°} = \frac{1}{12} = \frac{\text{Area of Sector}}{\text{Area of Circle}} = \frac{x}{\pi 4^2} = \frac{x}{16\pi}$$

So, set up a proportion to solve for the sector area:

$$\frac{1}{12} = \frac{x}{16\pi} \rightarrow \frac{16\pi}{12} = x \rightarrow \frac{4}{3}\pi = x$$

3. First, solve for the radius of the pizza by using its area:

$$64\pi = \pi r^2 \rightarrow 64 = r^2 \rightarrow 8 = r$$

Next, find the angle for the sector formed by each of the 8 pieces:

$$\frac{360^\circ}{8} = 45^\circ$$

Then, calculate the length of a sector in a circle with a radius of 8 inches and a sector angle of 45°:

$$\frac{\text{Part}}{\text{Whole}} = \frac{45^\circ}{360^\circ} = \frac{1}{8} = \frac{\text{Length of Arc}}{\text{Circumference}} = \frac{x}{2 \times \pi \times 8}$$

So, set up a proportion to solve for the arc length:

$$\frac{1}{8} = \frac{x}{16\pi} \rightarrow \frac{16\pi}{8} = x \rightarrow 2\pi = x$$

So, the length of the crust on each piece would be approximately 6.3 inches.

## Circle Formula

To graph a circle in the *xy*-coordinate plane, use this formula:

$$(x - h)^2 + (y - k)^2 = r^2$$
$$(h, k) = \text{Center}$$
$$r = \text{Radius}$$

### Example

What is the graph of a circle with the equation $(x - 3)^2 + (y - 2)^2 = 16$?

### ✓ Solution

Based on the equation, the center of the circle will be (3, 2), and the radius will be the square root of 16, which is 4. Here is the graph of this circle:

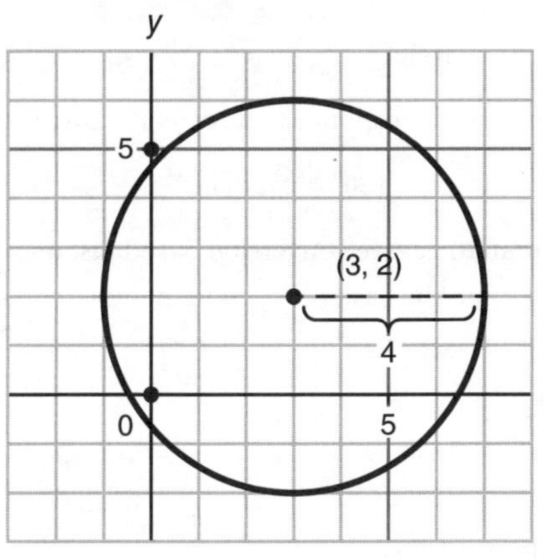

## Practice

1. What is the radius of a circle with the equation $(x - 2)^2 + (y + 5)^2 = 81$?
2. What is the center of a circle with the equation $(x + 5)^2 + (y - 6)^2 = 14$?
3. What is the equation of the circle graphed below?

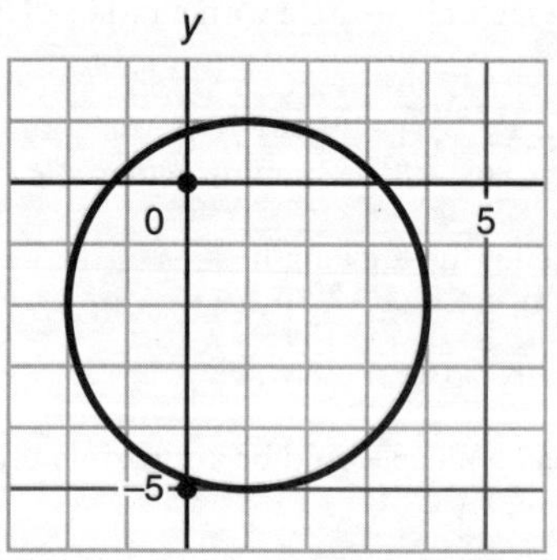


## Solutions

1. Take the square root of 81 to find the radius:

$$\sqrt{81} = 9$$

2. Be careful with the negative signs, keeping in mind that in the original circle formula, there are negative signs in front of the $h$ and $k$. So, $+5$ will give an $x$-coordinate for the center of $-5$ and $-6$ will give a $y$-coordinate for the center of $+6$. Therefore, the center point $(h, k)$ will be $(-5, 6)$.
3. The center of the circle is at $(1, -2)$ and the radius is 3 units. So, the equation for the circle will be $(x - 1)^2 + (y + 2)^2 = 9$.

## Radians

A radian is a different way of measuring angles. The SAT says the following at the beginning of the test section:

- **There are $2\pi$ radians in a circle.**

Since there are 360° in a circle, 360° corresponds to $2\pi$ radians. Divide this by 2 to find:

$$180° = \pi \text{ radians}$$

While you could figure out radian to degree conversion based just on what the SAT provides at the beginning of the section, it might be easier for you to memorize this conversion formula:

$$\frac{\text{Radians}}{\pi} = \frac{\text{Degrees}}{180}$$

### Example

How many radians are in 90 degrees?

### ✓ Solution

$$\frac{\text{Radians}}{\pi} = \frac{90}{180} \rightarrow$$

$$\frac{\text{Radians}}{\pi} = \frac{1}{2} \rightarrow$$

$$\text{Radians} = \frac{\pi}{2}$$

So, there are $\frac{\pi}{2}$ radians in 90°.

In addition to doing this conversion, you can memorize several common unit circle points and radian to degree conversions as given in the graph of the *unit circle* below.

**Common Unit Circle Points and Degree to Radian Conversions:**

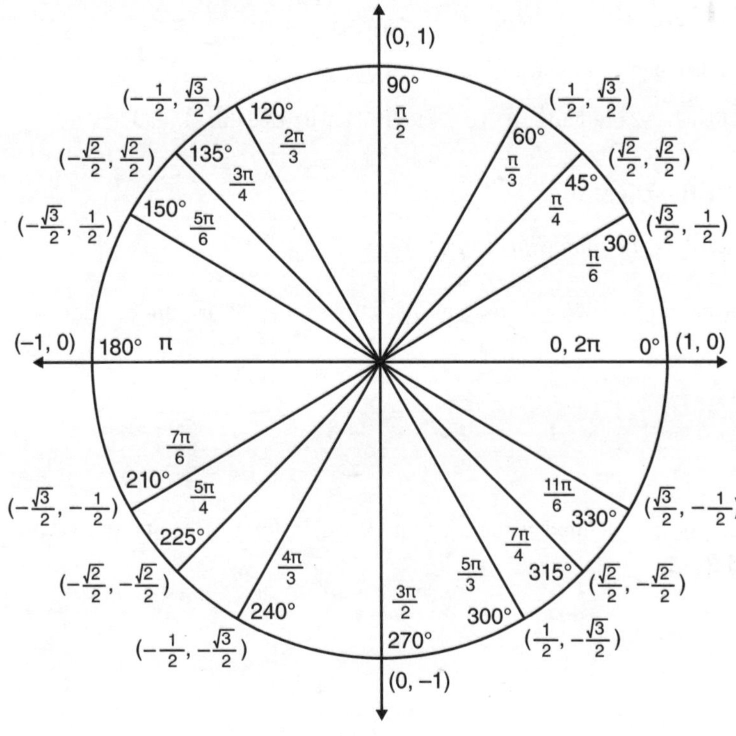


### Practice

1. How many radians are in 270°?
2. How many degrees are in $\pi$ radians?
3. How many total radians would there be in two circles?

## Solutions

1.
$$\frac{\text{Radians}}{\pi} = \frac{270}{180} \rightarrow$$
$$\frac{\text{Radians}}{\pi} = \frac{3}{2} \rightarrow$$
$$\text{Radians} = \frac{3\pi}{2}$$

You could also use the graph of the circle with the radian to degree conversions.

2.
$$\frac{\text{Radians}}{\pi} = \frac{\text{Degrees}}{180} \rightarrow$$
$$\frac{\pi}{\pi} = \frac{\text{Degrees}}{180} \rightarrow$$
$$1 = \frac{\text{Degrees}}{180} \rightarrow$$
$$180 = \text{Degrees}$$

You could also memorize that 180° are in $\pi$ radians.

3. A single circle has $2\pi$ radians, so two circles will have twice this: $4\pi$ radians.

## Practice Drill—Circles

*(If timing, take about 12 minutes to complete.)*

1. If a circle has an area of $64\pi$ units, how many units long is its circumference?

   (A) $8\pi$
   (B) $12\pi$
   (C) $16\pi$
   (D) $32\pi$

2. Consider the circle defined by the equation $(x + 4)^2 + (y - 8)^2 = 144$. What is the radius of this circle?

   (A) 4
   (B) 8
   (C) 12
   (D) 72

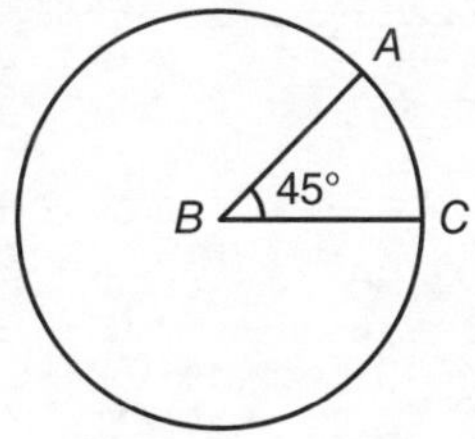


3. The above circle has points $A$ and $C$ and a center of $B$. What percentage of the circle's area is within the sector designated by the central angle $\angle ABC$?

(A) 8%
(B) 12.5%
(C) 14.5%
(D) 25%

4. A square with a perimeter of 16 inches is inscribed within a circle, all of the square's vertices intersecting the circle itself. What is the diameter of the circle?

(A) 4
(B) $4\sqrt{2}$
(C) $4\sqrt{3}$
(D) 8

5. Circle $A$ has a radius of 2 units and an area of $x$ square units. If circle $B$ has a radius twice that of circle $A$, and the area of circle $B$ is expressed in the form $nx$, in which $n$ is a constant, what is the value of $n$?

(A) 1
(B) 2
(C) 3
(D) 4

6. A circle has a diameter of 10 units. The function graphed below could represent what about the circle?

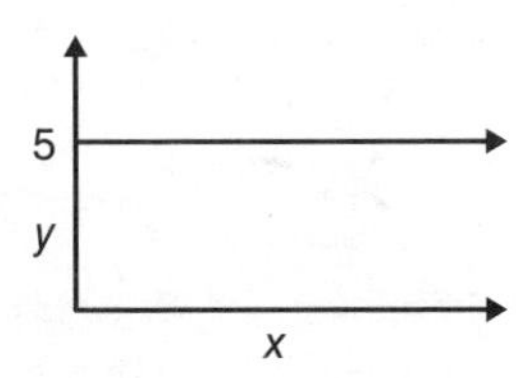


(A) The distance $y$ from a point $x$ on the circle to its center.
(B) The area of the circle, $y$, depending on its radius, $x$.
(C) The circumference of the circle, $y$, depending on its diameter, $x$.
(D) The diameter of the circle measured at different points in the coordinate plane, $(x, y)$.

7. What is the radius of the circle with the equation $x^2 - 4x + y^2 + 2y = 11$?

(A) 3
(B) 4
(C) 6
(D) 7

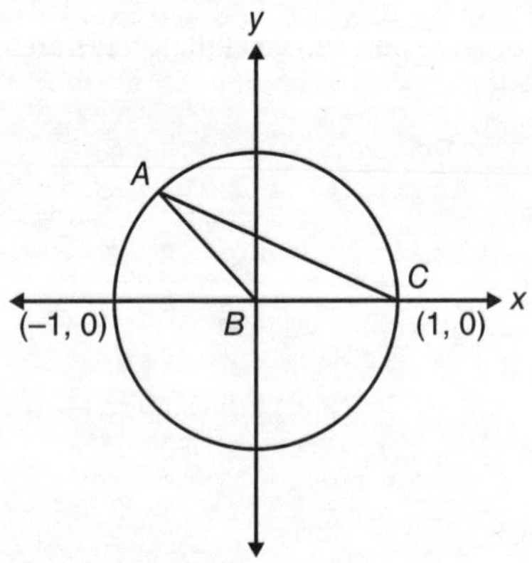


8. The circle above is centered at the origin with a radius of 1 unit; $\overline{AB}$ and $\overline{BC}$ are both radii of the circle. In triangle $ABC$ above, $\angle BAC$ is 40°. What is the measure of $\angle ACB$ in radians?

(A) $\frac{2}{9}\pi$
(B) $\frac{3}{4}\pi$
(C) $\pi$
(D) $\frac{7}{6}\pi$

9. At what point will a circle with the equation $(x - 4)^2 + (y - 5)^2 = 9$ and the line $y = -2$ intersect?

(A) $(-5, -2)$
(B) $(3, -2)$
(C) $(4, 5)$
(D) They will not intersect.

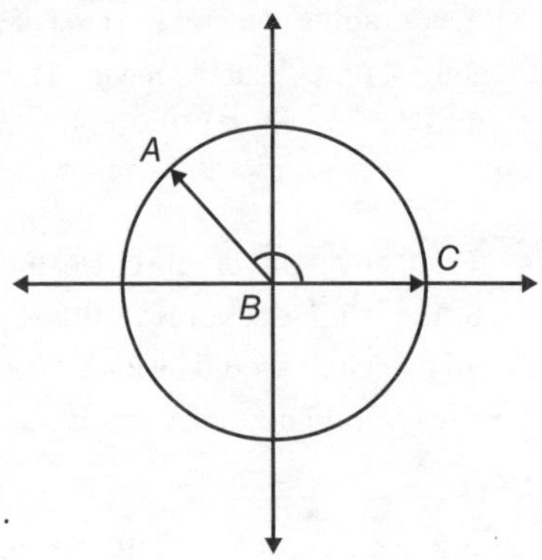


10. If the cosine of $\angle ABC$ in the unit circle above is $-\frac{1}{\sqrt{2}}$, what is the tangent of $\angle ABC$?

(A) $-1$
(B) $-0.5$
(C) 1
(D) 1.8

## Solutions

1. **(C)** Use the formula for area to find the radius of the circle:

$$\pi r^2 = 64\pi \rightarrow$$
$$r^2 = 64 \rightarrow r = 8$$

Now, use the formula for circumference, using 8 as the radius:

$$2\pi r \rightarrow 2 \times \pi \times 8 = 16\pi$$

2. **(C)** In the circle formula, the right side is the radius squared. So, find the square root of 144 to find the radius: $\sqrt{144} = 12$.

3. **(B)** There are 360° in a circle, so find the percentage that 45° is out of 360°:

$$\frac{45}{360} \times 100 = 12.5\%$$

4. **(B)** If the square has a perimeter of 16 inches, each side on the square is 4 inches. The square is inscribed within the circle, making the situation look like this:

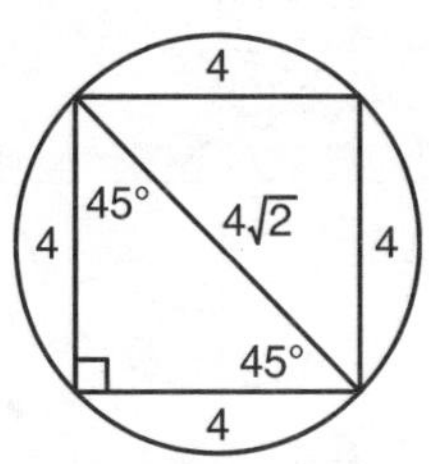


The triangle formed by two of the sides and the diameter of the circle is a 45-45-90 triangle, so the diameter will be $4\sqrt{2}$ units.

5. **(D)** Circle $A$ will have an area of $4\pi$ square units, since it has a radius of 2 and the area of a circle is $\pi r^2$. Circle $B$ has twice the radius of circle $A$, meaning 4 units, thereby having $16\pi$ square units of area. Comparing the two areas, if $x = 4\pi$, and the area of $B$ is $16\pi$, then $n$ must equal 4 since $\frac{16\pi}{4\pi} = 4$.

6. **(A)** Since the diameter of the circle is 10, the radius is 5. From any point on the circle, the distance from the point to the center of the circle will be 5. The graph does portray this relationship. It is not going to be choice (B) because the area of this circle would be $25\pi$. It is not going to be choice (C) because the circumference of the circle would be $10\pi$. And it is not going to be choice (D) because the diameter is 10, not 5.

7. **(B)** Complete the square for both the $x$ and $y$ components to get the equation into the format of the circle formula, enabling you to see the radius:

$$x^2 - 4x + y^2 + 2y = 11 \rightarrow$$
$$x^2 - 4x + 4 + y^2 + 2y + 1 = 11 + 4 + 1 \rightarrow$$
$$(x - 2)^2 + (y + 1)^2 = 16$$

The radius is the square root of 16, 4.

8. **(A)** Sides $\overline{AB}$ and $\overline{BC}$ are equivalent, since they are both radii of the circle. Therefore, triangle $ABC$ is isosceles, with $\angle BAC$ and $\angle ACB$ both 40°. So, we need to convert 40° to radians using the radian conversion formula:

$$\frac{\text{Radians}}{\pi} = \frac{\text{Degrees}}{180} \rightarrow$$
$$\frac{\text{Radians}}{\pi} = \frac{40}{180} \rightarrow$$
$$\frac{\text{Radians}}{\pi} = \frac{2}{9} \rightarrow$$
$$\text{Radians} = \frac{2}{9}\pi$$

9. **(D)** The circle has a center at (4, 5) and a radius of 3. So, it has no points that will be below the $x$-axis, and therefore will never intersect the line $y = -2$.

10. **(A)** We can label the graph as following given the information in the problem, since sides of this ratio will form a 45-45-90 triangle:

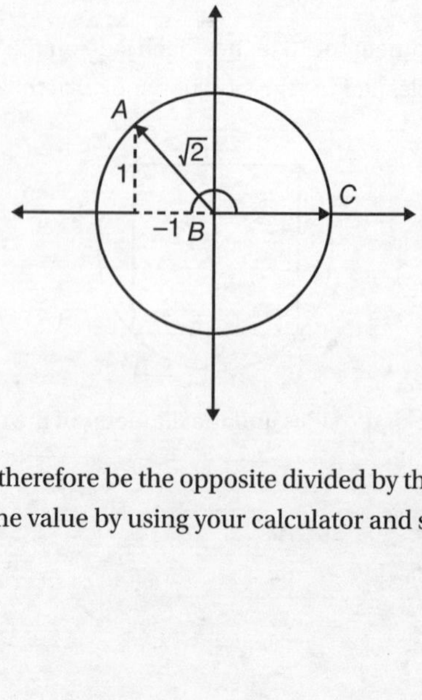


The tangent of $\angle ABC$ will therefore be the opposite divided by the adjacent, which is $\frac{-1}{1} = -1$. You could also calculate the value by using your calculator and solving $\tan(135) = -1$.

## Advanced Drills

Use these drills to push yourself with the toughest types of problems you are likely to encounter on SAT test day. Each drill has ten questions, with solutions that follow.

- Algebra Drill 1
- Algebra Drill 2
- Advanced Math Drill 1
- Advanced Math Drill 2
- Problem Solving and Data Analysis
- Geometry and Trigonometry
- Mixed Problems

If you are doing a drill under timed conditions, allow about 15 minutes to complete (longer than the chapter drills because of the increased average difficulty of the problems). Good luck!

### Algebra Drill 1

1. Solve for $x$:

$$1\frac{7}{8}x + \frac{5}{32} = 3\frac{3}{4}x - 1\frac{1}{4}$$

(A) $\frac{3}{4}$

(B) $2\frac{17}{32}$

(C) $\frac{15}{16}$

(D) $-\frac{45}{76}$

2. When 2 times a number is subtracted from 14, the result is 2 greater than the number. What is the number in question?

(A) $\frac{16}{3}$

(B) 4

(C) 12

(D) 16

3. In 2015, Andre had 210 coins in his collection. If Andre adds 5 new coins a year starting in 2015 through the end of 2022 and then adds 8 coins a year starting in 2023, how many coins will he have in his collection at the end of 2045?

(A) 224

(B) 421

(C) 429

(D) 434

4. How many pairs $(x, y)$ satisfy both $x - y > 3$ and $y - 5 > x$?

(A) 0
(B) 1
(C) 2
(D) Infinitely many

5. What is the solution $(x, y)$ to the following set of equations?

$$4x - 3y = \frac{11}{3} \text{ and } -\frac{2}{3}x + \frac{1}{4}y = -\frac{13}{18}$$

(A) $\left(\frac{4}{3}, \frac{5}{4}\right)$
(B) $\left(\frac{5}{4}, \frac{4}{9}\right)$
(C) $\left(-\frac{37}{12}, -\frac{16}{3}\right)$
(D) $\left(\frac{7}{4}, 10\right)$

6. How many ordered pairs $(x, y)$ satisfy the following system of equations?

$$(x - 2)(y + 5) = 0 \text{ and } 3x + y = 1$$

(A) 0
(B) 1
(C) 2
(D) Infinitely many

7. What are the solutions to the following series of equations?

$$\frac{3}{8}a + \frac{2}{3}b = 4.3 \text{ and } -12.9 + 1.125a = -2b$$

(A) $a = 0.8$ and $b = 6$
(B) $a = 16.8$ and $b = -3$
(C) No solutions
(D) Infinitely many solutions

8. Candidate M and Candidate N are the only candidates running for city mayor. If the total number of votes the two candidates receive is 50,000 and if Candidate M receives 3 times as many votes as Candidate N, what is the total number of votes Candidate N receives?

(A) 12,500
(B) 16,667
(C) 21,500
(D) 37,500

9. Jennifer's yearly salary, $S$, is modeled using the equation $S = 2{,}500Y + 40{,}000$, where $Y$ represents how many years she has been working at the company. What does the number 2,500 represent in this equation?

(A) The amount Jennifer's salary increases for each year she has been working
(B) Jennifer's starting salary
(C) The amount of money Jennifer has made in year $Y$
(D) The number of hours Jennifer has worked in year $Y$

10. If Avinash reads 2 fiction articles per day and 14 nonfiction articles per week, which expression models the total number of articles he would read in $w$ weeks?

(A) $2w + 14$
(B) $16w$
(C) $28w$
(D) $112w$

## Solutions

1. **(A)** To make solving this problem a bit easier, let's convert all of our mixed numbers into improper fractions:

$$\frac{15}{8}x + \frac{5}{32} = \frac{15}{4}x - \frac{5}{4}$$

We eventually want to combine our $x$ terms and combine our constant terms. So our $x$ terms need a common denominator (8), and our constant terms need a common denominator (32). Thus, let's rewrite our fractions with these common denominators. Our full equation is now:

$$\frac{15}{8}x + \frac{5}{32} = \frac{30}{8}x - \frac{40}{32}$$

To avoid dealing with negatives, let's bring the constants to the left by adding $\frac{40}{32}$ to both sides:

$$\frac{15}{8}x + \frac{45}{32} = \frac{30}{8}x$$

We then want to get all $x$ terms on the right by subtracting $\frac{15}{8}x$ from both sides:

$$\frac{45}{32} = \frac{15}{8}x$$

To solve for $x$, divide both sides by $\frac{15}{8}$ (in other words, multiply both sides by $\frac{8}{15}$):

$$\frac{45(8)}{32(15)} = x \text{ so } \frac{360}{480} = x$$

This reduces to $\frac{3}{4} = x$, which is choice **(A)**.

2. **(B)** Let $x$ be the number we are trying to find.

"2 times a number is subtracted from 14" can be written as $14 - 2x$. (We are subtracting 2 times a number, or $2x$, from the 14.)

"The result is" means an equals sign.

"2 greater than the number" can be written as $x + 2$. Thus, the whole sentence can be written as:

$$14 - 2x = x + 2$$

Add $2x$ to both sides to get all $x$ terms on the right. Then subtract 2 from both sides to get all constants on the left:

$$12 = 3x$$

Dividing by 3 tells us that $x = 4$, which is answer **(B)**.

3. **(D)** Between 2015 and 2022, Andre adds 5 coins 8 times:

2015, 2016, 2017, 2018, 2019, 2020, 2021, and 2022

Adding 5 coins 8 times means he added a total of $5(8) = 40$ coins in those years.

Between 2023 and 2045, he added 8 coins 23 times:

2023, 2024, 2025, 2026, 2027, 2028, 2029, 2030, 2031, 2032, 2033, 2034, 2035, 2036, 2037, 2038, 2039, 2040, 2041, 2042, 2043, 2044, and 2045

Thus, from 2023 to 2045, he added a total of $8(23) = 184$ coins.

Andre started with 210 coins. So the sum of the coins in his collection will be the original 210 plus the number of coins he added:

$$210 + 40 + 184 = 434$$

This is choice **(D)**.

4. **(A)** Since we have two inequalities, we can use elimination to get rid of one variable. Let's add both equations together:

$$\begin{array}{r} x - y > 3 \\ +\ \underline{y - 5 > x} \\ x - 5 > 3 + x \end{array}$$

Subtracting $x$ from both sides and adding 5 to both sides leaves you with $0 > 8$. Because we know that under no circumstances is 0 greater than 8, there are no solutions.

5. **(B)** In a system of two equations, we can either use substitution or elimination to solve.

If we multiply the second equation by 12 and add the equations together, our $y$ terms will cancel out. Start by multiplying the second equation by 12:

$$12\left(-\frac{2}{3}x + \frac{1}{4}y = -\frac{13}{18}\right) = -8x + 3y = -\frac{26}{3}$$

Now we can add this equation to the first equation:

$$\begin{array}{r} 4x - 3y = \frac{11}{3} \\ \underline{+-8x + 3y = -\frac{26}{3}} \\ -4x = -\frac{15}{3} \end{array}$$

To solve for $x$, divide by $-4$:

$$x = \frac{15}{12} = \frac{5}{4}$$

This is enough to narrow down the answer to choice (B). However, you could plug this $x$ value into one of your functions to solve for $y$ if you wanted.

Alternatively, you could have used substitution by solving for $x$ in the first equation and then plugging that equation back into the second equation.

To solve for $x$, first add $3y$ to both sides:

$$4x = 3y + \frac{11}{3}$$

Then divide both sides by 4 to isolate $x$:

$$x = \frac{3y}{4} + \frac{11}{12}$$

Now you can plug this expression into the second equation for $x$:

$$-\frac{2}{3}\left(\frac{3y}{4} + \frac{11}{12}\right) + \frac{1}{4}y = -\frac{13}{18}$$

Next, distribute the $-\frac{2}{3}$:

$$-\frac{6}{12}y - \frac{22}{36} + \frac{1}{4}y = -\frac{13}{18}$$

Some of these fractions can be reduced. For our purposes, though, it doesn't really matter. Next, we need to combine our $y$ terms, but first we need a common denominator.

Let's convert $\frac{1}{4}y$ to $\frac{3}{12}y$:

$$-\frac{6}{12}y - \frac{22}{36} + \frac{3}{12}y = -\frac{13}{18}$$

Now combine like terms:

$$-\frac{1}{4}y - \frac{22}{36} = -\frac{13}{18}$$

To add $\frac{22}{36}$ to both sides, we need to first convert $-\frac{13}{18}$ to $-\frac{26}{36}$ so that our constants have a common denominator:

$$-\frac{1}{4}y - \frac{22}{36} = -\frac{26}{36}$$
$$-\frac{1}{4}y = -\frac{1}{9}$$

To solve for $y$, divide both sides by $-\frac{1}{4}$ (multiply both sides by $-4$):

$$y = \frac{4}{9}$$

This is enough to narrow it down to choice **(B)**. However, we can solve for $x$ by plugging the $y$ value into our equation for $x$:

$$x = \frac{3}{4}y + \frac{11}{12} = \frac{3}{4}\left(\frac{4}{9}\right) + \frac{11}{12} = \frac{12}{36} + \frac{11}{12} = \frac{12}{36} + \frac{33}{36} = \frac{45}{36} = \frac{5}{4}$$

Finally, we could have solved this problem by plugging each answer choice into the two equations to see which set of points work. If using this method, be careful to check that the points satisfy BOTH equations. For instance, choice (C) works when plugged into the first equation but not the second.

6. **(B)** In the first equation, one of those factors must equal 0 for the whole equation to equal 0. Therefore, we will find the possible solutions by setting each factor equal to 0:

$$x - 2 = 0$$

Adding 2 to both sides tells us that $x = 2$ is a possible solution:

$$y + 5 = 0$$

Subtracting 5 from both sides tells us that $y = -5$ is another possible solution.

Plugging these values into the second equation will tell us the solutions to it:

$$3(2) + y = 1$$

So $6 + y = 1$.

Subtracting 6 from both sides tells us that $y = -5$, which is the original $y$ value we got from the first equation.

Let's try the $y$ value that we already determined:

$$3x + -5 = 1$$

So $3x = 6$. Dividing by 3 tells us that $x = 2$. However, this is the $x$ solution that we already tried. Therefore, there is only one solution:

$$(2, -5)$$

This is choice **(B)**.

7. **(D)** Let's use substitution. Solve for $b$ in the second equation by dividing both sides by $-2$:

$$6.45 - 0.5625a = b$$

Let's now plug the left side of this equation into the first equation for $b$:

$$\frac{3}{8}a + \frac{2}{3}(6.45 - 0.5625a) = 4.3$$

Distributing the $\frac{2}{3}$ leaves us with:

$$\frac{3}{8}a + 4.3 - 0.375a = 4.3$$

Let's get that $\frac{3}{8}a$ into decimal form so that we can easily combine our like terms:

$$0.375a + 4.3 - 0.375a = 4.3$$

Combining both $a$ terms results in:

$$4.3 = 4.3$$

We know that this is always true, meaning we have an infinite number of solutions.

Alternatively, you may have noticed that if you multiply the second equation by $-\frac{1}{3}$ and convert any fractions in the two equations into decimals, the two equations are exactly the same. Since they are the same line, there are infinitely many solutions.

8. **(A)** Let's turn what we know into equations. Let $m$ equal the number of votes that Candidate M receives and let $n$ equal the number of votes that Candidate N receives.

First, we know that the sum of the votes that the two candidates receive is 50,000. In other words:

$$m + n = 50{,}000$$

Additionally, we know that the number of votes Candidate M receives is 3 times the number of votes that Candidate N receives. This can be expressed by the equation

$$m = 3n$$

Now we can plug in $3n$ for $m$ in the first equation:

$$3n + n = 50{,}000$$

Combining like terms results in:

$$4n = 50{,}000$$

We can solve for $n$ by dividing both sides by 4:

$$n = 12{,}500$$

This is choice **(A)**.

9. **(A)** We're told that $Y$ is the number of years Jennifer has worked at the company. We can see that each time $Y$ increases by 1, her salary goes up \$2,500. For instance, when $Y = 0$, Jennifer's salary is \$40,000. When $Y = 1$, her salary is \$42,500. When $Y = 2$, her salary is \$45,000. Therefore, choice **(A)** is correct.

   Choice (B) is incorrect because it can be shown that Jennifer's starting salary (when $Y = 0$) is \$40,000.

   Choice (C) is incorrect because the amount of money made is given by the variable $S$.

   Choice (D) is incorrect because the equation tells us nothing about the number of hours Jennifer worked.

10. **(C)** We want to know how many articles Avinash reads in $w$ weeks. So we first need to figure out how many articles he reads per week. We can then multiply this number by $w$ to give the number of articles he reads in $w$ weeks.

    Avinash reads 2 fiction articles per day. Since there are 7 days in a week, he reads $2(7) = 14$ fiction articles per week. He also reads 14 nonfiction articles per week. So Avinash reads $14 + 14 = 28$ fiction and nonfiction articles per week.

    Therefore, the number of articles Avinash reads in $w$ weeks is given by the expression $28w$, which is choice **(C)**.

## Algebra Drill 2

1. If $-(2x - 4) + 3(x - 5) = -4$, what is the value of $x$?

   (A) $-3$
   (B) 5
   (C) 7
   (D) 15

2. If $g(x + 2) = 5x - 4$, what is the value of $g(7)$?

   (A) 21
   (B) 29
   (C) 31
   (D) 41

3. John is having an undetermined number of people over for dinner. He needs to have 6 serving utensils (used by everyone collectively), plus a knife, fork, and spoon for each diner. Which of the following equations correctly models the total number of utensils, $U$, John will need for $x$ number of diners, himself included?

   (A) $U = 3x$
   (B) $U = 9x$
   (C) $U = 3x + 6$
   (D) $U = 6x + 3$

4. If $f(x) = 4x + 7$ and if $g(x) = -3x + 2$, what is the value of $f(g(3))$?

(A) $-27$
(B) $-21$
(C) $-7$
(D) 19

5. Under a new state law, a massage therapist will be required to charge sales tax on her services. If the sales tax rate is 7%, by what ratio would she need to multiply the current price of her services to determine the new total amount customers will pay under the new law?

(A) $\frac{7}{100}$
(B) $\frac{7}{10}$
(C) $\frac{107}{100}$
(D) $\frac{170}{100}$

6. If $6(2a - b) = 4b$, what is the ratio of $b$ to $a$?

(A) $\frac{2}{3}$
(B) $\frac{5}{6}$
(C) $\frac{6}{5}$
(D) $\frac{12}{5}$

7. The total operational costs $C$ for a restaurant are modeled by the equation $C = 2M + 50{,}000$, where $M$ represents the number of meals served. What does the 50,000 represent in the equation?

(A) The total operational costs
(B) The fixed operational costs
(C) The cost per meal
(D) The minimum number of meals served

8. The total costs $C$ to operate a factory are represented by the function $C(n) = an + b$, where $n$ is the number of days the factory is operational. If the daily operations costs were to increase beyond the given rate and if the initial startup costs were to decrease beyond the given rate, how would this affect the constants $a$ and $b$?

(A) $a$ would increase, and $b$ would increase.
(B) $a$ would increase, and $b$ would decrease.
(C) $a$ would decrease, and $b$ would increase.
(D) $a$ and $b$ would remain the same.

9. How will the function $f(x) = 4x - 5$ be affected by the translation

$$g(x) = f(x - 1) + 2?$$

(A) It will be shifted up 2 units and 1 unit to the left.
(B) It will be shifted down 1 unit and 2 units to the left.
(C) It will be shifted up 2 units and 1 unit to the right.
(D) It will be shifted down 1 unit and 2 units to the right.

10. A company is conducting an online campaign to increase its social media followers. The number of social media followers, $N$, is estimated by the equation $N = 30W + 250$, where $W$ represents the number of weeks of the campaign (and $W > 0$). What does the number 250 represent in the equation?

    (A) The number of weeks of the campaign
    (B) The number of new social media followers each week
    (C) The number of social media followers at the start of the campaign
    (D) The number of social media followers at the end of $W$ weeks

## Solutions

1. **(C)** First, we need to distribute. Don't forget to distribute the negative sign to the$(2x - 4)$ term. Distributing gives us:

$$-2x + 4 + 3x - 15 = -4$$

   Combining like terms on the left side gives:

$$x - 11 = -4$$

   Adding 11 to both sides tells us that $x = 7$, which is choice **(C)**.

   Note that you could also plug each answer choice into the equation to see which one gives the correct equality, but doing this could be more time-consuming.

2. **(A)** First, we must determine what number we should plug in for $x$. Our original function is $g(x + 2)$, and we're looking for $g(7)$. That means that we want $x$ such that $x + 2 = 7$. Subtracting 2 from both sides gives $x = 5$. So to find $g(7)$, we simply plug in 5 for $x$ in the original function:

$$g(5 + 2) = 5(5) - 4 = 25 - 4 = 21$$

   The correct answer is choice **(A)**.

3. **(C)** John needs 6 utensils no matter how many people come, so +6 will be a constant. He also needs 3 utensils per person, which can be represented as $3x$. Thus, he needs $3x + 6$ utensils, choice **(C)**.

   Choice (A) is incorrect because although it correctly depicts the 3 utensils needed for each person, it neglects the 6 serving utensils.

   Choice (B) is incorrect because it states that each person needs 9 utensils.

   Choice (D) is incorrect because it states that there are 3 utensils needed no matter how many people come, rather than the 6 utensils actually needed.

   Alternatively, you could have imagined a scenario in which John invited 1 other person over, making a total of 2 people at dinner. They need 6 serving utensils, plus each one of them needs a knife, spoon, and fork. This makes a total of 2 knives, 2 spoons, and 2 forks, or 6 more utensils. The total number of utensils needed in this case is $6 + 6 = 12$.

   You could have then plugged in 12 for $U$, plugged in 2 for $x$, and chosen the answer choice that worked, which is choice **(C)**:

$$12 = 3(2) + 6$$

4. **(B)** First, we have to find the value of $g(3)$ by plugging in 3 wherever there's an $x$ in $g(x)$:

$$g(3) = -3(3) + 2 = -9 + 2 = -7$$

Now we have to find $f(-7)$ by plugging in $-7$ wherever there is an $x$ in $f(x)$:

$$f(-7) = 4(-7) + 7 = -28 + 7 = -21$$

The answer is choice **(B)**.

5. **(C)** Let's imagine that a massage therapist currently charges \$100 for a massage. If the tax rate is 7%, or 0.07, tax on that service will be:

$$0.07(\$100) = \$7$$

Therefore, the price of the massage including the sales tax will be:

$$\$100 + \$7 = \$107$$

The ratio of the new price to the old price is:

$$\frac{107}{100}$$

The massage therapist can find the new prices for all of her services by multiplying the old prices by this ratio.

6. **(C)** First, distribute the 6:

$$12a - 6b = 4b$$

Bring the $b$ terms to the right side by adding $6b$ to both sides:

$$12a = 10b$$

To find the ratio of $b$ to $a$, we want to solve for $\frac{b}{a}$. First, divide both sides by $a$:

$$12 = 10\frac{b}{a}$$

To isolate $\frac{b}{a}$, we need to divide both sides by 10:

$$\frac{b}{a} = \frac{12}{10} = \frac{6}{5}$$

The correct ratio is choice **(C)**.

7. **(B)** This \$50,000 is some sort of cost that stays the same whether the restaurant serves 0 meals or serves 1,000 meals. Because the \$50,000 doesn't vary with the variable meals, it's a fixed cost, which is choice **(B)**.

Choice (A) is incorrect because $C$ represents the total costs, and $C$ varies with the number of meals served.

Choice (C) is incorrect because 2 is the cost per meal, as shown by the $2M$ in the equation.

Choice (D) is incorrect because the minimum number of meals served could be any positive integer.

8. **(B)** Total cost is found by adding together the variable costs and the fixed costs. In this problem, the variable cost is $an$ since this value depends on $n$, the number of days the factory is operational. Since $an$ is a cost and since $n$ is a number of days, it follows that the daily operational cost is given by $a$. Therefore, if the daily operational cost increases, $a$ will increase.

The initial startup costs, or fixed costs, are given by variable $b$ because $b$ is a constant that isn't affected by the variable $n$. Therefore, if the startup costs decrease, $b$ will decrease.

The correct scenario is depicted in choice **(B)**.

9. **(C)** In general, if $f(x)$ is our original function and if $c$ is a constant, then:

   - $f(x-c)$ shifts $f(x)$ to the right by $c$ units.
   - $f(x+c)$ shifts $f(x)$ to the left by $c$ units.
   - $f(x)+c$ shifts $f(x)$ up by $c$ units.
   - $f(x)-c$ shifts $f(x)$ down by $c$ units.

   In this particular problem, $g(x)=f(x-1)+2$. Using the above properties, $f(x-1)$ tells us that $f(x)$ is shifted to the right by 1 unit. The $+2$ in the expression tells us that $f(x)$ is shifted up by 2 units. This corresponds to choice **(C)**.

10. **(C)** The number 250 is in the equation regardless of the value of $W$. Therefore, it makes sense that 250 would be the initial number of followers the campaign had. We can see this by plugging 0 in for $W$ in the equation. This gives us the initial number of followers before the company starts campaigning:

$$N=30(0)+250=0+250=250$$

So we can see that when $W=0$, $N=250$.

## Advanced Math Drill 1

1. An element's half-life is the amount of time that it takes for the element to decay by half. If there is $x$ amount of element Z initially, which of the following represents the amount $A$ of Z that would remain after $n$ whole half-lives of Z had passed?

   (A) $A=\frac{x}{2n}$

   (B) $A=\frac{x}{2^n}$

   (C) $A=\frac{n}{2x}$

   (D) $A=\frac{x}{2^{n-1}}$

2. $\sqrt[5]{32x^8y^{11}}$ is equivalent to which of the following?

   (A) $2xy^2\sqrt[5]{x^3y}$

   (B) $2x^5y^{10}\sqrt[5]{x^3y}$

   (C) $2x^3y^6\sqrt[5]{xy}$

   (D) $2xy^2\sqrt[5]{2x^3y^2}$

3. If $x>0$, then $\frac{1}{2x}+\frac{1}{3x}$ is equivalent to which of the following?

   (A) $\left(\frac{25}{6x^2}\right)^{\frac{1}{2}}$

   (B) $\left(\frac{4}{25x^2}\right)^{\frac{1}{2}}$

   (C) $\left(\frac{5}{6x}\right)^{2}$

   (D) $\left(\frac{25}{36x^2}\right)^{\frac{1}{2}}$

4. If $x^2 + ax = b$, where $a$ and $b$ are constants, what are the solutions for $x$?

(A) $x = -\frac{a}{2} \pm \sqrt{2b + \frac{a^2}{2}}$
(B) $x = -\frac{a}{2} \pm \sqrt{b + \frac{a^2}{4}}$
(C) $x = -\frac{b}{2} \pm \sqrt{\frac{a^2}{2} - 2b}$
(D) $x = -\frac{a}{2} \pm \sqrt{b^2 + \frac{a^2}{4}}$

5. $6x^2 + 15xy + 6y^2 = ?$

(A) $3(2x + y)^2$
(B) $(3x + y)(x + 3y)$
(C) $(3x + 3y)(2x + 2y)$
(D) $3(x + 2y)(2x + y)$

6. What are the solution(s) for $x$ in the equation below?

$$x - 6 = \sqrt{75 - 2x}$$

(A) 13
(B) 13 and −3
(C) −3 and 3
(D) No solution

7. At what points will $f(x) = 8x^2 - 22x + 15$ intersect the $x$-axis?

(A) 15
(B) $\frac{3}{2}$ and $\frac{5}{4}$
(C) $-\frac{5}{4}$ and $-\frac{3}{2}$
(D) $\frac{5}{4}$ and $\frac{15}{2}$

8. Which value of $n$ will cause the value of $f(x) = xn$ to be consistently positive and increase the most rapidly, given that $x$ is greater than 1 and that $n$ is an even integer?

(A) −2
(B) −1
(C) 1
(D) 2

9. To see if two sets of data are correlated, one can calculate the correlation coefficient between two populations, $r_{xy}$, using the formula $r_{xy} = \frac{s_{xy}}{s_x s_y}$, where $s_{xy}$ is the covariance of the population, $s_x$ is the standard deviation of population $x$, and $s_y$ is the standard deviation of population $y$. If the dispersion of population $x$ and the dispersion of population $y$ both increase while the covariance between the populations remains the same, what would happen to the correlation coefficient of the two populations?

(A) It would decrease.
(B) It would increase.
(C) It would stay the same.
(D) It cannot be determined.

10. If the function $f(x) = x^n + 3^{xm}$ has 5 zeros and if $f(x)$ is multiplied by $-1$, how many zeros will the resulting function have?

(A) $-5$
(B) 4
(C) 5
(D) 6

## Solutions

1. **(B)** The amount after one half-life is $\frac{1}{2}x$. After the second half-life, half of this new amount decays, and we're left with:

$$\frac{1}{2}\left(\frac{1}{2}x\right) = \frac{1}{4}x = \left(\frac{1}{2^2}\right)x$$

After the third half-life, half of that amount left decays. We now have left:

$$\frac{1}{2}\left(\frac{1}{4}x\right) = \frac{1}{8}x = \left(\frac{1}{2^3}\right)x$$

We can start to see a pattern: each time a half-life passes, we multiply the amount we previously had by $\frac{1}{2}$. So after $n$ half-lives, $A = \left(\frac{1}{2^n}\right)x$ remains, or $A = A = \frac{x}{2^n}$. This matches choice **(B)**.

2. **(A)** $\sqrt[5]{32} = 2$. So go ahead and bring a 2 outside of the radical before dealing with the variables:

$$\sqrt[5]{32x^8y^{11}} = 2\sqrt[5]{x^8y^{11}}$$

Let's deal with the $x$ term under the root next. Notice the following:

$$\sqrt[5]{x^8} = \sqrt[5]{x^5x^3} = \sqrt[5]{x^5}\sqrt[5]{x^3} = x\sqrt[5]{x^3}$$

Similarly, we can rewrite the $y$ term under the root as follows:

$$\sqrt[5]{y^{11}} = \sqrt[5]{y^5y^5y} = \sqrt[5]{y^5}\sqrt[5]{y^5}\sqrt[5]{y} = y \cdot y\sqrt[5]{y} = y^2\sqrt[5]{y}$$

Thus, the entire expression can be rewritten as:

$$\sqrt[5]{32x^8y^{11}} = 2\sqrt[5]{x^8y^{11}} = 2\sqrt[5]{x^8}\sqrt[5]{y^{11}} = 2xy^2\sqrt[5]{x^3y}$$

This is choice **(A)**.

3. **(D)** All of the answer choices are a single fraction. So first find a common denominator and add the two fractions. The least common denominator is $6x$. Multiply the first fraction by $\frac{3}{3}$ and the second by $\frac{2}{2}$:

$$\frac{3}{6x} + \frac{2}{6x} = \frac{5}{6x}$$

We can rule choice (C) out because it's our answer squared, so it will not equal our answer.

The rest of the answers are being raised to the $\frac{1}{2}$ power, which is equivalent to taking the square root. In order to find out what should be inside the parentheses, we must work backward by doing the opposite to our function. Because the answer choices take the square root of an expression, we must square our expression to find what should go inside the parentheses:

$$\left(\frac{5}{6x}\right)^2 = \frac{5^2}{(6x)^2} = \frac{25}{36x^2}$$

Therefore, the answer is choice **(D)**.

Alternatively, we could have taken the square root of choices (A), (B), and (D) to see which one is equivalent to $\frac{5}{6x}$:

$$\left(\frac{25}{6x^2}\right)^{\frac{1}{2}} = \frac{\sqrt{25}}{\sqrt{6x^2}} = \frac{5}{\sqrt{6}x}$$

So, choice (A) is incorrect.

$$\left(\frac{4}{25x^2}\right)^{\frac{1}{2}} = \frac{\sqrt{4}}{\sqrt{25x^2}} = \frac{2}{5x}$$

So, choice (B) is incorrect.

$$\left(\frac{25}{36x^2}\right)^{\frac{1}{2}} = \frac{\sqrt{25}}{\sqrt{36x^2}} = \frac{5}{6x}$$

This matches the expression we obtained, so choice **(D)** is correct.

4. **(B)** In their structure, the answer choices all look like the quadratic formula. So subtract $b$ from both sides:

$$x^2 + ax - b = 0$$

Now you can use the quadratic formula:

$$x = \frac{-b \pm \sqrt{b^2 - 4ac}}{2a}$$

We have to be careful, though. Our equation has $a$ and $b$ coefficients, but they don't match up exactly with the $a$ and $b$ given in the quadratic formula. In the quadratic formula, $a$ is the coefficient in front of the $x^2$ term, $b$ corresponds to the coefficient in front of the $x$ term, and $c$ represents the constant. In our case, however, the coefficient in front of the $x^2$ term is 1, the coefficient of the $x$ term is $a$, and the constant is $b$. Keep this in mind while using the quadratic formula to get:

$$x = \frac{-a \pm \sqrt{a^2 - 4(1)(-b)}}{2(1)} = \frac{-a \pm \sqrt{a^2 + 4b}}{2}$$

This doesn't match any of the answer choices, so we need to simplify further. All of the answer choices have the leading term over 2, so let's divide this into two fractions:

$$\frac{-a \pm \sqrt{a^2 + 4b}}{2} = -\frac{a}{2} \pm \frac{\sqrt{a^2 + 4b}}{2}$$

From the leading term, you can narrow it down to choices (A), (B), and (D). It looks like the answer choices have pulled the denominator of the second term into the square root. Because 2 equals $\sqrt{4}$, we can change the denominator to $\sqrt{4}$:

$$-\frac{a}{2} \pm \frac{\sqrt{a^2 + 4b}}{2} = -\frac{a}{2} \pm \frac{\sqrt{a^2 + 4b}}{\sqrt{4}} = -\frac{a}{2} \pm \sqrt{\frac{a^2 + 4b}{4}}$$

In all of the answer choices, the fraction inside the square root appears to be broken up, so do that:

$$-\frac{a}{2} \pm \sqrt{\frac{a^2 + 4b}{4}} = -\frac{a}{2} \pm \sqrt{\frac{a^2}{4} + \frac{4b}{4}} = -\frac{a}{2} \pm \sqrt{\frac{a^2}{4} + b}$$

Reordering what's inside the root gives you choice **(B)**.

5. **(D)** One easy way to solve this problem is to use FOIL on the answer choices and see which matches the original:

Choice (A):

$$3(2x + y)^2 = 3[(2x + y)(2x + y)] = 3(4x^2 + 4xy + y^2) = 12x^2 + 12xy + 3y^2$$

This does not match our expression, so we can rule out this choice.

Choice (B):

$$(3x + y)(x + 3y) = 3x^2 + 10xy + 3y^2$$

This does not match the original.

Choice (C):

$$(3x + 3y)(2x + 2y) = 6x^2 + 12xy + 6y^2$$

This does not quite match the original.

Choice (D):

$$3(x + 2y)(2x + y) = 3(2x^2 + 5xy + 2y^2) = 6x^2 + 15xy + 6y^2$$

This matches the original expression, so the answer is choice **(D)**.

Another way to solve the problem is to factor. Since each term is divisible by 3, we can factor out a 3 to get:

$$3(2x^2 + 5xy + 2y^2)$$

Next, we factor the expression inside the parenthesis as follows:

$$3(2x + y)(x + 2y)$$

This matches choice **(D)**.

6. **(A)** Look at the answer choices. There are only three possible $x$ values in the answer choices (13, 3, and −3), so it's probably easiest to just plug in these three values for $x$ in our original equation to see which ones work:

$$13 - 6 = \sqrt{75 - 2(13)}$$

$$7 = \sqrt{49}$$

The square root of 49 is 7, so 13 works.

$$-3 - 6 = \sqrt{75 - 2(-3)}$$

$$-9 = \sqrt{81}$$

Square roots always give nonnegative answers, so this one doesn't work.

$$3 - 6 = \sqrt{75 - 2(3)}$$

$$-3 = \sqrt{69}$$

Only 13 works, so the answer is choice **(A)**.

You could also solve this directly by squaring both sides of the equation:

$$(x - 6)^2 = (\sqrt{75 - 2x})^2$$

Squaring gives:

$$x^2 - 12x + 36 = 75 - 2x$$

This is a quadratic equation. So we move everything over to one side, combine like terms, and factor:

$$x^2 - 10x - 39 = 0$$

Factoring gives:

$$(x-13)(x+3)=0$$

So $x = 13$ or $x = -3$. Since we initially squared our equation, we have to check our answers since this procedure can lead to extraneous answers. Indeed, only $x = 13$ works. So 13 is the only solution to the equation.

7. **(B)** Functions intersect the $x$-axis at their zeros. Zeros can be found by setting the function equal to 0 and either factoring or using the quadratic formula to solve for possible values of $x$.

The polynomial can be factored to $(4x - 5)(2x - 3) = 0$. Set each factor equal to 0 and solve for $x$:

$$4x-5=0$$

Adding 5 to both sides and then dividing by 4 gives you $x = \frac{5}{4}$.

$$2x-3=0$$

Adding 3 to both sides then dividing by 2 gives you $x = \frac{3}{2}$.

Choice **(B)** is the answer.

Alternatively, you could have used the quadratic formula:

$$x=\frac{-b\pm\sqrt{b^2-4ac}}{2a}=\frac{22\pm\sqrt{(-22)^2-4(8)(15)}}{2(8)}=\frac{22\pm\sqrt{4}}{16}=\frac{22\pm2}{16}$$

$$x=\frac{24}{16}=\frac{3}{2}\text{ or }x=\frac{20}{16}=\frac{5}{4}$$

8. **(D)** We are told that $x$ is greater than 1, so the function will always be positive regardless of $n$. We are also told that $n$ is an even integer, so this narrows down the answer to 2 or $-2$. In order for the function to increase most rapidly, you want the exponent $n$ to be the largest even number possible, which is choice **(D)**.

9. **(A)** If the dispersion of population $x$ increases, the standard deviation of $x$ increases. If the dispersion of population $y$ increases, the standard deviation of $y$ increases. Therefore, you'd be holding the numerator constant while increasing the denominator. Therefore, the correlation coefficient would decrease, which is choice **(A)**.

10. **(C)** Multiplying a function by $-1$ will flip it about the $x$-axis. The new function will still cross the $x$-axis the same number of times at the same values of $x$ as the original function. So the zeros will not change. If $f(x)$ has 5 zeros, $-f(x)$ will also have 5 zeros.

Consider this simpler function to see how multiplying it by $-1$ would affect its graph.

The graph of $y = x^2 - 5$ is shown:

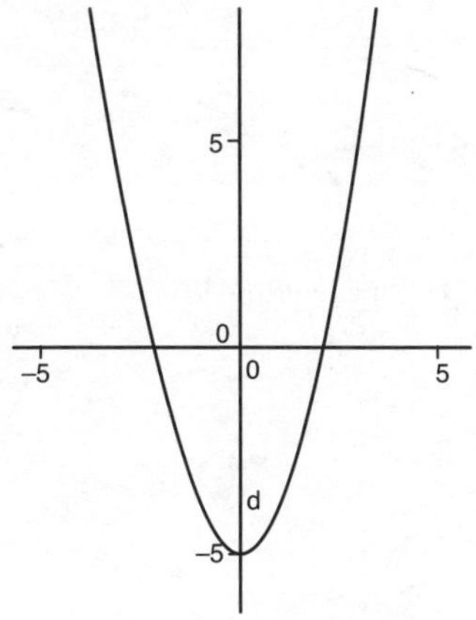


If the function is multiplied by $-1$ on the right-hand side, it will give the function $y = -x^2 + 5$, which is shown:

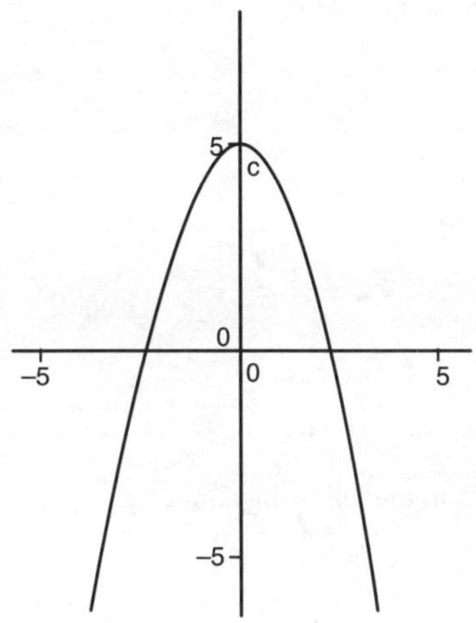


So the functions have the same zeros even though they are mirror images of one another.

## Advanced Math Drill 2

1. A particular savings account provides no interest in the first year of a deposit and 3% annual compounded interest on a deposit for each year thereafter. If $x$ dollars are deposited initially, which of the following equations expresses the total amount of money $A(n)$ in the account $n$ years later, where $n$ is an integer greater than 2?

   (A) $A(n) = x[(0.03)^n]$
   (B) $A(n) = x[(0.97)^n]$
   (C) $A(n) = x[(0.03)^{n-1}]$
   (D) $A(n) = x[(1.03)^{n-1}]$

2. What is the value of $x$ in the following equation?

$$x^2 + 9 = -6x$$

(A) $-3$
(B) 0
(C) 3
(D) No solution

3. For $y < 0$, which of the following is equivalent to $\frac{3}{x^2 y}$?

(A) $\frac{3x^{-2}}{\sqrt[4]{y^2}}$

(B) $\frac{3x^{-2}}{-\sqrt[4]{y^4}}$

(C) $\frac{3x^{\frac{1}{2}}}{\sqrt[4]{y^4}}$

(D) $\frac{3x^{-2}}{\sqrt[4]{y^4}}$

4. For positive $x$ and $y$, $x^{-\frac{3}{4}} y^{\frac{4}{3}}$ is equivalent to

(A) $-\frac{x^3 y^4}{x^4 y^3}$

(B) $\frac{\sqrt[4]{y^3}}{\sqrt[3]{x^4}}$

(C) $\frac{y\sqrt[3]{y}}{\sqrt[4]{x^3}}$

(D) $\frac{y^4 \sqrt[3]{y}}{x^3 \sqrt[4]{x}}$

5. What are the possible values of $x$ in the following equation?

$$3x^2 + 12x + 6 = 0$$

(A) $-12 \pm \sqrt{3}$
(B) $-2 \pm \sqrt{2}$
(C) $-2 \pm \sqrt{3}$
(D) $2 \pm \sqrt{2}$

6. If $x^2 + x - 12 = 0$ and if $x < 0$, what is the value of $x$?

(A) $-6$
(B) $-4$
(C) $-3$
(D) 3

7. $64x^6 - 16y^8$ is equivalent to which of the following expressions?

(A) $16(4x^3 + y^4)(x^3 - y^4)$
(B) $16(4x^3 - y^4)(x^3 - y^4)$
(C) $16(2x^3 + y^4)(2x^3 - y^4)$
(D) $16(2x^6 - y^8)(2x - y)$

8. Solve the following equation for all possible $x$ values.

   (A) 3
   (B) 3 and 8
   (C) −3 and −8
   (D) Infinitely many solutions

9. The graph of $x - 4 = y^4$ has a minimal $x$ value that compares in what way to the minimal $x$ value of the graph $x = y^4$?

   (A) It is 4 less.
   (B) It is 4 greater.
   (C) They are the same.
   (D) The answer cannot be determined.

10. Which of the following functions represents the reflection across the $x$ axis of

$$y = 3(x - 5)^2 + 4?$$

   (A) $y = -3(x + 5)^2 - 4$
   (B) $y = -3(x - 5)^2 - 4$
   (C) $y = 3(-x - 5)^2 + 4$
   (D) $y = 3(-x + 5)^2 + 4$

## Solutions

1. **(D)** If 3% is added annually after the first year is complete, after the second year, 3% will have been added. Thus, after 2 years, the total amount of money in the account can be represented as:

$$x + 0.03x$$

By combining like terms, it can also be expressed as:

$$1.03x = x(1.03)^1$$

After three years, another 3% is added to the new amount:

$$1.03x + 0.03(1.03x) = 1.03(x + 0.03x) = 1.03(1.03x) = x(1.03)^2$$

Continue in this manner. So after the fourth year, the amount of money in the account is $x(1.03)^3$.

Keeping this pattern in mind, the money in the account after $n$ years is $x(1.03)n^{-1}$, which is choice **(D)**.

Note that raising 1.03 to the $n - 1$ power means that you're multiplying $x$ by 1.03 one time less than the number of years that have passed. This is because no interest is added in the first year.

2. **(A)** Add the $6x$ to both sides so that the polynomial is equal to 0:

$$x^2 + 6x + 9 = 0$$

You can either factor this or use the quadratic formula. This is easily factorable:

$$(x + 3)(x + 3) = 0$$

You can set each factor equal to 0 to solve for the possible values of $x$. However, since they're the same factor, you need to do it only once:

$$x + 3 = 0$$

Subtracting 3 from both sides tells you that $x = -3$, which is choice **(A)**.

3. **(B)** The key here is to notice that in the problem, $y < 0$. In the original expression, $x$ is squared. So regardless of its sign, $x^2$ will be positive. Therefore, $\frac{3}{x^2 y}$ will be negative when $y$ is negative. Thus, the new expression must also be negative.

Simplify the answer choices to see which matches the original expression.

Choice (A):

Negative exponents get sent to the denominator:

$$\frac{3x^{-2}}{\sqrt[4]{y^2}} = \frac{3}{x^2 \sqrt[4]{y^2}}$$

Roots can be expressed as fractional exponents:

$$\frac{3}{x^2 \sqrt[4]{y^2}} = \frac{3}{x^2 y^{\frac{2}{4}}}$$

However, $y^{\frac{2}{4}} \neq y$. So this is different than our original expression. We can rule out choice (A).

Choice (B):

Following the same process as the previous answer choice, we can rewrite this answer as:

$$\frac{3x^{-2}}{-\sqrt[4]{y^4}} = -\frac{3}{x^2 \sqrt[4]{y^4}}$$

Now consider $\sqrt[4]{y^4}$. It is tempting to say that this just equals $y^{\frac{4}{4}} = y$, but we have to be careful not to ignore a subtle point. When we take the fourth root of something, or in general the even root of something, we necessarily get a result that is nonnegative. In particular, $\sqrt[4]{y^4}$ must be non-negative. However, $y$ is negative, so the expression can't equal $y$. The expression actually equals $-y$, which is positive since $y$ is negative.

(Convince yourself of this. For example, let $y = -2$ and consider $\sqrt[4]{y^4} = \sqrt[4]{(-2)^4}$. This expression is equal to $\sqrt[4]{16} = 2 = -(-2) = -y$ since $y = -2$.)

Thus, plugging in ı/$y$ for $\sqrt[4]{y^4}$ in our expression gives the following after canceling out the negative signs:

$$\frac{3x^{-2}}{-\sqrt[4]{y^4}} = -\frac{3}{x^2 \sqrt[4]{y^4}} = -\frac{3}{x^2(-y)} = \frac{3}{x^2 y}$$

This is our original expression, so choice **(B)** must be the correct answer.

If you wanted to explore the other answer choices, you could.

Choice (C):

By the same logic as before, this simplifies to:

$$\frac{3x^{\frac{1}{2}}}{\sqrt[4]{y^4}} = \frac{3\sqrt{x}}{-y} = -\frac{3\sqrt{x}}{y}$$

This clearly doesn't match the original expression, so it can be eliminated.

Choice (D):

Simplifying gives:

$$\frac{3x^{-2}}{\sqrt[4]{y^4}} = \frac{3}{x^2(-y)} = -\frac{3}{x^2 y}$$

This is close to our original expression but has a negative sign in front, so we can eliminate this choice.

4. **(C)** Remember that negative exponents can be made positive by moving whatever is being raised to that exponent to the denominator:

$$x^{-\frac{3}{4}} y^{\frac{4}{3}} = \frac{y^{\frac{4}{3}}}{x^{\frac{3}{4}}}$$

Fractional exponents are the same as roots:

$$\frac{y^{\frac{4}{3}}}{x^{\frac{3}{4}}} = \frac{\sqrt[3]{y^4}}{\sqrt[4]{x^3}}$$

This doesn't match any answer choices, so we need to simplify further. The $y$ is being raised to a power higher than its root, so we should be able to pull something out of the root.

Since $y$ is positive:

$$\sqrt[3]{y^4} = \sqrt[3]{y^3 y} = \sqrt[3]{y^3}\sqrt[3]{y} = y\sqrt[3]{y}$$

Therefore, our whole expression can be rewritten as:

$$\frac{y\sqrt[3]{y}}{\sqrt[4]{x^3}}$$

Choice **(C)** is the correct answer.

5. **(B)** Factor out a 3:

$$3(x^2 + 4x + 2) = 0$$

Divide both sides by 3:

$$x^2 + 4x + 2 = 0$$

This isn't easily factorable, so use the quadratic formula:

$$x = \frac{-b \pm \sqrt{b^2 - 4ac}}{2a} = \frac{-4 \pm \sqrt{4^2 - 4(1)(2)}}{2(1)} = \frac{-4 \pm \sqrt{8}}{2} = \frac{-4 \pm 2\sqrt{2}}{2} = -2 \pm \sqrt{2}$$

Choice **(B)** is the answer.

6. **(B)** We need to find all solutions less than 0. This equation is easily factorable:

$$x^2 + x - 12 = (x + 4)(x - 3) = 0$$

If $x + 4$ or $x - 3$ equaled 0, the whole expression would equal 0. Therefore, setting both factors equal to 0 will tell us the two potential values of $x$:

$$x + 4 = 0 \text{ so } x = -4$$

$$x - 3 = 0 \text{ so } x = 3$$

The question asks for only the value of $x$ that's less than 0, so the answer is $x = -4$, which is choice **(B)**.

7. **(C)** All of the answers have a 16 factored out, so do that first:

$$64x^6 - 16y^8 = 16(4x^6 - y^8)$$

When anything is in the form $(a^2 - b^2)$, it can be factored using the difference of squares formula: $(a + b)(a - b)$. The trick to this problem is figuring out what $a$ and $b$ are. Set $4x^6$ equal to $a^2$ to find $a$:

$$4x^6 = a^2$$
$$a = \sqrt{4x^6}$$

Take the square root of both 4 and the $x$ term:

$$a = 2x^{\frac{6}{2}} = 2x^3$$

Next, set $y^8$ equal to $b^2$ to solve for $b$:

$$y^8 = b^2$$
$$b = \sqrt{y^8} = y^{\frac{8}{2}} = y^4$$

Therefore, if you wanted to express $(4x^6 - y^8)$ in the form of $(a + b)(a - b)$, it would be:

$$(2x^3 + y^4)(2x^3 - y^4)$$

Putting the 16 in front gives you choice **(C)**.

8. **(B)** Get rid of the square root by squaring both sides:

$$x^2 = 11x - 24$$

To find the possible values of $x$, subtract $11x$ and add 24 to both sides, setting the left side equal to 0. Then factor or use the quadratic formula to solve:

$$x^2 - 11x + 24 = 0$$

This equation factors as:

$$(x - 3)(x - 8) = 0$$

This statement would hold true if $x - 3 = 0$ or if $x - 8 = 0$. In other words, the statement would hold true if $x = 3$ or if $x = 8$, which is choice **(B)**.

Be careful, though. When we squared both sides of the equation, we were no longer guaranteed to get the same exact solutions as our original equation. In other words, because we square both sides, it is possible that we get extraneous solutions. So we should get in the habit of checking that both of our solutions are indeed solutions. We can do this by plugging both answer choices into our original equation:

$$x = 3$$
$$\sqrt{11(3) - 24} = \sqrt{9} = 3 = x$$

This solution checks out.

$$x = 8$$
$$\sqrt{11(8) - 24} = \sqrt{64} = 8 = x$$

This solution checks out as well.

In this problem, both solutions check out. However, you should be cautious in general when squaring equations.

9. **(B)** The first function can be expressed as $y = \sqrt[4]{x-4}$. It's an even root. This means that the value within the root must be greater than or equal to 0 since we can find only the even root of a nonnegative number:

$$x - 4 \geq 0$$
$$x \geq 4$$

Therefore, the domain of the function is $[4, \infty)$.

The second function can be expressed as $y = \sqrt[4]{x}$. Again, it's an even root. So what's within the root must be greater than or equal to 0:

$$x \geq 0$$

The domain of this function then is $[0, \infty)$.

Therefore, the minimal $x$ value of the first function is 4 more than the minimal $x$ value of the second function. Choice **(B)** is the answer.

10. **(B)** To reflect something across the $x$-axis, multiply the entire equation by $-1$:

$$-y = -[3(x-5)^2 + 4] = -3(x-5)^2 - 4$$

Alternatively, notice that our original function gives the equation of a parabola; think about what this parabola looks like. Recall that the vertex form of a parabola is $y = a(x-h)^2 + k$. Our original parabola will open upward since $a = 3$ is positive. This parabola will also have a vertex at $(h, k) = (5, 4)$. If you want to reflect this across the $x$- axis, it would need to open downward and have a vertex at $(5, -4)$. Therefore, the vertex form of this new parabola would be:

$$y = -3(x-5)^2 - 4$$

The answer is choice **(B)**.

## Problem Solving and Data Analysis Drill

1. If there are 4 cars for every 5 trucks in the parking lot (with no other types of vehicles), what is the ratio of cars to the total number of vehicles in the parking lot?

(A) 1 to 5
(B) 4 to 9
(C) 5 to 9
(D) 4 to 5

2. On Monday, the highest temperature reached was 70 degrees Fahrenheit. On Tuesday, the highest temperature increased by 20%. On Wednesday, the highest temperature decreased by 25% from the previous day. What was the difference between Monday's and Wednesday's highest temperatures in degrees Fahrenheit?

(A) 5
(B) 7
(C) 14
(D) 21

3. A recipe calls for 3 cups of sugar. There are 16 tablespoons in a cup and 3 teaspoons in a tablespoon. If a cook has 1.5 cups of sugar available in the pantry, how many teaspoons of sugar must the cook obtain from other sources to follow the recipe?

(A) 72
(B) 104
(C) 144
(D) 216

| Price per Gallon of Milk | Number of Gallons Sold |
|---|---|
| $1.50 | 650 |
| $0.90 | 780 |
| $1.95 | 530 |
| $2.80 | 330 |
| $3.40 | 190 |

4. Which of these functions best models the relationship between the number of gallons of milk sold, $N(g)$, and the price per gallon of milk, $g$?

(A) $N(g) = 530 + 590(g - 1.95)^2$
(B) $N(g) = 1{,}000 - 240g$
(C) $N(g) = 1{,}000 + 240g$
(D) $N(g) = 780 - 360(g - 0.9)^2$

| | Employed | Unemployed |
|---|---|---|
| Population X | 890 | 112 |
| Population Y | 748 | 205 |

5. What is the difference between the unemployment percentage in Population Y and the unemployment percentage in Populations X and Y combined, calculated to the nearest tenth?

(A) 5.0%
(B) 5.3%
(C) 5.8%
(D) 6.2%

**Questions 6—7 use the following table.**

**Election Results**

| | Candidate A | Candidate B | Total |
|---|---|---|---|
| Columbus | 350,000 | 270,000 | 620,000 |
| Cleveland | 180,000 | 195,000 | 375,000 |
| Total | 530,000 | 465,000 | 995,000 |

6. Of all eligible voters in Columbus, 40% actually voted in the election. How many total eligible voters did Columbus have?

(A) 248,000
(B) 875,000
(C) 1,550,000
(D) 2,487,500

7. Suppose that a survey of total 200 randomly selected voters from both cities accurately predicted the results of the election. How many of the people surveyed would have been supporters of Candidate A from Columbus?

(A) 50
(B) 70
(C) 113
(D) 132

**Questions 8–9 use the following table.**

| Grade | Test 1 | Project 1 | Test 2 | Project 2 | Total |
|---|---|---|---|---|---|
| A | 5 | 8 | 9 | 7 | 29 |
| B | 7 | 6 | 5 | 10 | 28 |
| C | 6 | 7 | 4 | 5 | 22 |
| D | 4 | 1 | 3 | 2 | 10 |
| F | 1 | 1 | 3 | 0 | 5 |
| Total | 23 | 23 | 24 | 24 | 94 |

8. The median letter grade for assignments in the class is:

(A) A
(B) B
(C) C
(D) D

9. For which assignment is the standard deviation of the grade results the least?

(A) Test 1
(B) Project 1
(C) Test 2
(D) Project 2

10. An online shopping site allows customers to post 1-star, 2-star, 3-star, 4-star, and 5-star reviews for products. If an item currently has an average star rating of 2.3 based on a total of 10 reviews, what is the minimum number of reviews that could bring up the overall average rating to at least a 3.0?

(A) 2
(B) 3
(C) 4
(D) 5

## Solutions

1. **(B)** Let's imagine the simplest version of this ratio: there are only 4 cars and 5 trucks in the parking lot. So how many total vehicles are there?

   $$4 \text{ cars} + 5 \text{ trucks} = 9 \text{ vehicles}$$

   So the ratio of cars to vehicles is 4 cars to 9 vehicles, choice **(B)**.

2. **(B)** If the highest temperature on Tuesday increased 20% from the highest temperature on Monday, then the highest temperature on Tuesday was 120%, or 1.2, of Monday's temperature. Find 120% of 70 degrees:

   $$1.2(70) = 84$$

   So Tuesday's high temperature was 84 degrees Fahrenheit. Wednesday's high was 25% lower than Tuesday's temperature, so it was only 75%, or 0.75, of Tuesday's temperature. Find 75% of 84 degrees:

   $$0.75(84) = 63$$

   The highest temperature on Wednesday was 63 degrees Fahrenheit. We want to know the difference between Monday's high temperature and Wednesday's high. The difference is given by $70 - 63 = 7$, which is choice **(B)**.

3. **(A)** If a cook has 1.5 cups of sugar in the pantry but needs 3 cups, he needs $3 - 1.5 = 1.5$ more cups from other sources. We want to convert this to teaspoons:

   $$1.5 \text{ cups} \times \frac{16 \text{ tablespoons}}{\text{cup}} \times \frac{3 \text{ teaspoons}}{\text{tablespoon}} = 72 \text{ teaspoons}$$

   The answer is choice **(A)**.

4. **(B)** Test the answer choices.

   Choice (A):

   $$N(1.50) = 530 + 590(1.50 - 1.95)^2 = 649.48$$

   This is a fairly good estimate, so let's try another value:

   $$N(0.90) = 530 + 590(0.90 - 1.95)^2 = 1{,}180.48$$

   We can rule out choice (A).

   Choice (B):

   $$N(1.50) = 1{,}000 - 240(1.50) = 640$$

   This is also a fairly good estimate, so let's try the other values:

   $$N(0.90) = 1{,}000 - 240(0.90) = 784$$
   $$N(1.95) = 1{,}000 - 240(1.95) = 532$$
   $$N(2.80) = 1{,}000 - 240(2.80) = 328$$
   $$N(3.40) = 1{,}000 - 240(3.40) = 184$$

   All of these values are pretty close to the actual values, so this answer choice may be correct. However, the question asks for the best model, so we need to make sure that there are no better models.

Choice (C):

$$N(1.50) = 1{,}000 + 240(1.50) = 1{,}360$$

We can rule out choice (C).

Choice (D):

$$N(1.50) = 780 - 360(1.50 - 0.9)^2 = 650.4$$
$$N(0.90) = 780 - 360(0.90 - 0.9)^2 = 780$$
$$N(1.95) = 780 - 360(1.95 - 0.9)^2 = 383.1$$

We can rule out choice (D).

Choice **(B)** is the best model of the relationship.

5. **(B)** In Population Y, 205 of the 748 + 205 = 953 people are unemployed. Therefore, the unemployment percentage is:

$$\frac{205}{953} \times 100\% = 21.51\%$$

In both populations combined, there are a total of 112 + 205 = 317 unemployed people, and a total population of 890 + 112 + 748 + 205 = 1,955. Therefore, the unemployment rate is:

$$\frac{317}{1{,}955} \times 100\% = 16.21\%$$

The difference between the two unemployment rates is 21.51% − 16.21% = 5.3%, which is choice **(B)**.

6. **(C)** The number of people who voted in Columbus was 620,000. If this number represents only 40% of eligible voters, you can set up a proportion to solve for 100% of the number of eligible voters:

$$\frac{620{,}000}{40} = \frac{x}{100}$$

In the proportion, $x$ represents the number of eligible voters in Columbus. Cross multiply to get:

$$620{,}000(100) = 40x$$
$$62{,}000{,}000 = 40x$$

Dividing by 40 tells you that $x = 1{,}550{,}000$, which is choice **(C)**.

Another way we can solve this problem is as follows. We know that 620,000 is 40% of the eligible voters, $x$, in Columbus. In other words, $620{,}000 = 0.4x$. Dividing by 0.4 gives 1,550,000, which is choice **(C)**.

7. **(B)** Since there are 350,000 Columbus voters who support Candidate A and 995,000 voters in the two cities combined, we know that $\frac{350{,}000}{995{,}000} = 0.352$ of the voters in the table were supporters of Candidate A from Columbus. We would expect the same proportion of the 200 randomly surveyed voters to be supporters of Candidate A from Columbus. This can be found by taking 0.352(200) = 70.4. Thus, we could expect about 70 of the randomly surveyed to fall into this category. So the correct answer is choice **(B)**.

8. **(B)** There are 94 total grades. To find the median term in a series with an even number of terms, you have to take the mean of the two middle terms. To find these two middle terms, first divide the total number of terms by 2. This will tell you the number of the 1st term you'll use in your average. Then add 1 to that number to find the number of the 2nd term you'll use in your average.

If we listed all 94 grades starting with the lowest grades, the F's, and ending with the highest grades, the A's, the median terms would be the average of the $\frac{94}{2} = 47$th term and the $\frac{94}{2} + 1 = 48$th term.

F's take us through the first 5 terms.

D's take us through 10 more, to the 15th term.

C's take us through another 22, to the $15 + 22 = 37$th term.

B's take us through another 28 to the $37 + 28 = 65$th term. The 47th and 48th terms will then both be B's, so the median grade is a B, which is choice **(B)**.

9. **(D)** Standard deviation is usually lowest when range is lowest because it means that more values are centered near the mean. Because no one received an F on project 2, the range was only between an A and a D, with only two people receiving D's. Because this project has a rather small range, it will have a rather small standard deviation. In all of the other assignments, at least one student earned an A and at least one earned an F, so the ranges will be higher for all other answer choices. Thus, choice **(D)** is the best choice.

10. **(C)** An average (in other words, a mean) is given by the following expression:

$$\text{Mean} = \frac{\text{Sum}}{n}$$

In the expression, "sum" is the total of the terms you're averaging and $n$ is the number of terms you're averaging. In order to calculate the minimum number of reviews needed to raise the mean to a 3.0, we'll need to know the sum of the current ratings. Plugging the numbers into the equation gives:

$$2.3 = \frac{\text{Sum}}{10}$$

Therefore, the sum of the current ratings is $2.3(10) = 23$.

In order to raise the average with the minimum number of reviews, the reviews need to all be as high as possible, so they must all be 5-star reviews.

Let's test our answer choices. When plugging in answer choices, start with one of the middle answers since answers tend to be arranged from smallest to largest or from largest to smallest.

Choice (B):

If the product gets 3 new 5-star reviews, this will add $3(5) = 15$ to our current sum. This will also add 3 to our current $n$:

$$\text{Mean} = \frac{23 + 15}{10 + 3} = \frac{38}{13} = 2.92$$

The mean is not high enough yet, so we need more reviews.

Choice (C):

If the product gets 4 new 5-star reviews, this will add $4(5) = 20$ to our current sum and 4 to our current $n$:

$$\text{Mean} = \frac{23 + 20}{10 + 4} = \frac{43}{14} = 3.07$$

This mean is higher than our desired mean, so 4 is the minimum number of reviews needed, choice **(C)**.

Alternatively, you could have solved this algebraically. Adding $x$ more 5-star reviews will add $5x$ to the sum and $x$ to $n$, the total number of reviews. Therefore, the mean can be represented with the following equation:

$$\text{Mean} = \frac{23 + 5x}{10 + x}$$

Since we know we want the mean to be 3.0, we can set the right side of our equation equal to 3.0:

$$3.0 = \frac{23 + 5x}{10 + x}$$

Let's get rid of the denominator by multiplying both sides by $(10 + x)$:

$$30 + 3.0x = 23 + 5x$$

Combine like terms by subtracting $3.0x$ and 23 from both sides:

$$7 = 2.0x$$

Dividing both sides by 2.0 tells you that the minimum number of new reviews needed is 3.5. Recall that we want the minimum number of reviews needed to raise the average to a 3.0. Since 3 reviews would not be enough and a person can't give 0.5 of a review, we must round up to the nearest integer, 4. Therefore, to raise the average to a 3.0, you need 4 new reviews.

## Geometry and Trigonometry Drill

1. A box in the shape of a rectangular prism has dimensions 20 inches by 30 inches by 12 inches. Inside the box are four solid cubes, each with edge lengths of 4 inches. If the inside of the larger box is empty except for the solid cubes, what is the volume of empty space in the box?

   (A) 248 cubic inches
   (B) 1,800 cubic inches
   (C) 6,944 cubic inches
   (D) 7,200 cubic inches

2. A right triangle has a hypotenuse of 10 inches and legs that measure 8 inches and 6 inches. What is the area of the triangle in square inches?

   (A) 12
   (B) 18
   (C) 24
   (D) 36

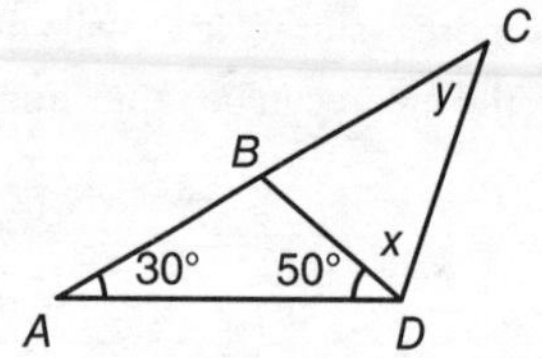


3. In triangle $ACD$ above, point $B$ is on $\overline{AC}$, and $B$ and $D$ form a line. What is the sum of $\angle x$ and $\angle y$ in degrees?

(A) 100
(B) 110
(C) 120
(D) 140

4. If a circle has the equation $(x - 4)^2 + (y - 6)^2 = 9$, what is the equation of the circle if it is reflected directly across the $x$-axis?

(A) $(x + 4)^2 + (y + 6)^2 = -9$
(B) $(x - 4)^2 - (y + 6)^2 = -9$
(C) $(x + 4)^2 - (y + 6)^2 = 9$
(D) $(x - 4)^2 + (y + 6)^2 = 9$

5. If the area of an equilateral triangle is $2\sqrt{3}$ square units, what is the perimeter of the triangle?

(A) 6
(B) $4\sqrt{3}$
(C) $6\sqrt{2}$
(D) $6\sqrt{3}$

6. Given that $\angle X$ is between 0 and 90 degrees, and that $\cos X = Y$, what is the *sine* of an angle with the measure $(90 - X)$ degrees?

(A) $90 - Y$
(B) $Y$
(C) $\frac{2}{3}$
(D) 90

7. An angle measuring $3\pi$ radians would be equivalent to how many angles with a measure of 45°?

(A) 4
(B) 8
(C) 9
(D) 12

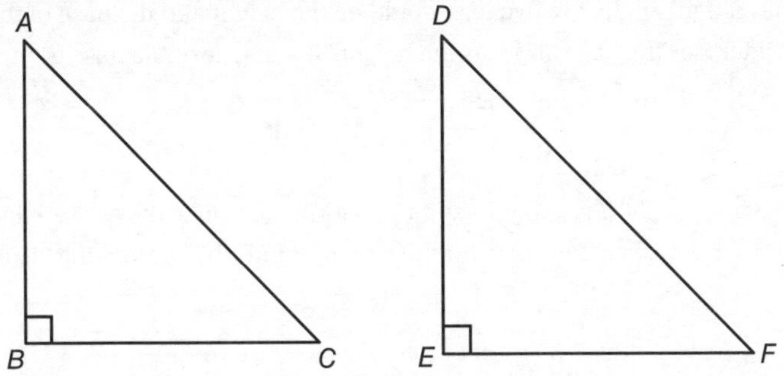


8. Triangles $ABC$ and $DEF$ are similar to one another. If the cosine of $\angle BAC$ is $\frac{12}{13}$, and the length of $\overline{DE}$ is 24 units, what is the length of $\overline{DF}$?

   (A) 14
   (B) 20
   (C) 26
   (D) 30

9. Over a 20-second time period, Jeff runs in a circle of 8 feet in radius around a pole. Assuming that Jeff starts the time period at a radius of 8 feet from the pole, the graph during this interval of his time (as the $x$-coordinates) and his distance from the pole (as the $y$-coordinates) would have a slope of what?

   (A) $-1$
   (B) 0
   (C) 1
   (D) 2

10. A rectangular dog park is $x$ feet wide and $y$ feet long. The park is to be fenced in along its sides with wooden material, except for part of one side where there will be a metal gate that is $g$ feet long. How long must the fence material be in order to meet these conditions?

   (A) $2x + 2y - g$
   (B) $2x + 2y + g$
   (C) $xy - g$
   (D) $xyg$

## Solutions

1. **(C)** Calculate the volume of the larger box, and then subtract the volume of the 4 solid cubes to find the volume of empty space. Use $V = lwh$ to calculate the volume of each rectangular prism.

$$\text{Volume of larger prism} - \text{Volume of 4 smaller cubes} \rightarrow$$
$$(20 \times 30 \times 12) - 4(4 \times 4 \times 4) =$$
$$7{,}200 - 256 = 6{,}944$$

2. **(C)** Since the triangle has a right angle, the two legs would be the height and the base of the triangle. So, we can consider 8 as the base and 6 as the height. The area formula for a triangle is $\frac{1}{2} \times B \times H$. Plug in 8 and 6 to this formula to get your answer:

$$\frac{1}{2} \times 6 \times 8 = 24$$

3. **(A)** The angles with measures 30°, 50°, *x*, and *y* all add up to form 180° since they are angles within the triangle *ACD*. Therefore, you can solve for the sum of *x* and *y* by subtracting 30 and 50 from 180:

$$180 - 30 - 50 = 100$$

4. **(D)** Based on the circle equation, in which $(x - h)^2 + (y - k)^2 = r^2$, with $(h, k)$ as the center and $r$ as the radius, the original circle will have a center at (4, 6) and radius of 3. To reflect this circle, which is entirely in the first quadrant, across the *x*-axis, just change the *y*-coordinate of its center to −6. The reflected circle will have an equation of $(x - 4)^2 + (y + 6)^2 = 9$ and the reflection is drawn below:

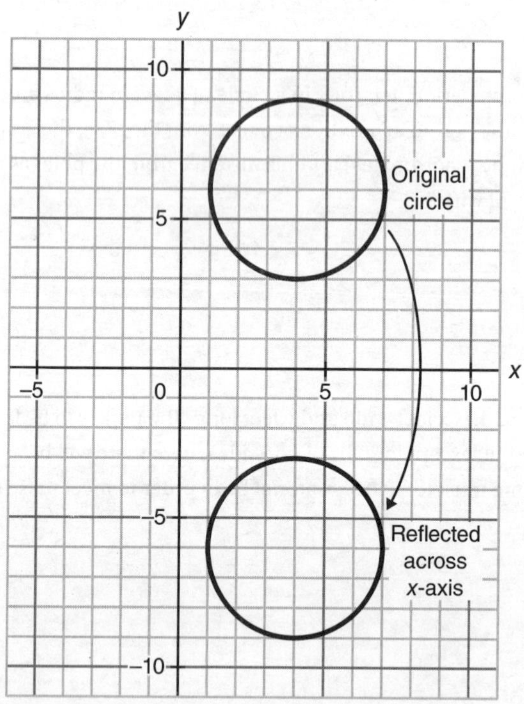


5. **(C)** To find the perimeter of the of the triangle, we must add up the three side lengths of the triangle. The formula for the area of an equilateral triangle is $A = \frac{\sqrt{3}}{4}a^2$, in which $a$ is the side length. So, solve for the side length of the triangle given that we know its area:

$$2\sqrt{3} = \frac{\sqrt{3}}{4}a^2 \rightarrow$$

$$2 = \frac{a^2}{4} \rightarrow$$

$$8 = a^2 \rightarrow$$

$$2\sqrt{2} = a$$

Now, just triple the side length to find the perimeter:

$$3 \times (2\sqrt{2}) = 6\sqrt{2}$$

6. **(B)** Since $X$ and $(90 - X)$ are complementary, the sine of one will equal the cosine of the other. Therefore, the sine of $(90 - X)$ is simply $Y$.

7. **(D)** There are $\pi$ radians in 180°, so set up a proportion to make a conversion to the total number of degrees in an angle measuring $3\pi$ radians:

$$\frac{180}{\pi} = \frac{x}{3\pi} \rightarrow$$

$$\frac{180}{\pi} \times (3\pi) = x \rightarrow$$

$$180 \times 3 = x \rightarrow$$

$$540 = x$$

Now, divide 540 by 45 to see how many angles of 45° would go into 540:

$$\frac{540}{45} = 12$$

8. **(C)** Set up a proportion to solve for the length of $\overline{DF}$. The cosine of $\angle BAC$ is the same as the cosine of $\angle EDF$ since the triangles are similar to one another. Set the cosine of $\angle BAC$ equal to the cosine of $\angle EDF$, using 24 as the "adjacent" side and the unknown $\overline{DF}$ as the hypotenuse:

$$\frac{12}{13} = \frac{24}{x} \rightarrow$$

$$x = \frac{24 \times 13}{12} = 26$$

9. **(B)** Since the distance that Jeff is from the center remains 8 over the time period, the slope of the line formed by these values would simply be zero since the line would be horizontal.

10. **(A)** Find the perimeter of the rectangular dog park by adding the width twice and the length twice:

$$2x + 2y$$

Then, subtract the length of the metal gate from this total to find the total amount of wooden material required:

$$2x + 2y - g$$

## Mixed Drill

1. Which of the following lines is perpendicular to $5y - 2.5x = -10$?

(A) $y = -2x + 8$
(B) $y = 0.5x + 2$
(C) $y = 2x - 7$
(D) $y = 0.4x + 10$

**Questions 2–3 use the following table.**

**Hours of Sleep per Night**

| | More Than 8 | 6–8 | Less Than 6 | Total |
|---|---|---|---|---|
| **Under Age 13** | 15 | 8 | 1 | 24 |
| **Ages 13–18** | 13 | 17 | 14 | 44 |
| **Ages 19–22** | 18 | 12 | 20 | 50 |
| **Total** | 46 | 37 | 35 | 118 |

2. The least possible median age of those surveyed would be which of the following?

(A) 13
(B) 15
(C) 19
(D) Cannot be determined from the given information

3. The mean number of hours of sleep of all those surveyed is

(A) 6.5
(B) 7.5
(C) 8.5
(D) Cannot be determined from the given information

4. For values of *a* not equal to zero, $\left(\frac{2}{\sqrt[3]{a}}\right)^6$ equals

(A) 2a−2
(B) 12a−2
(C) $64a\frac{1}{2}$
(D) $64a^{-2}$

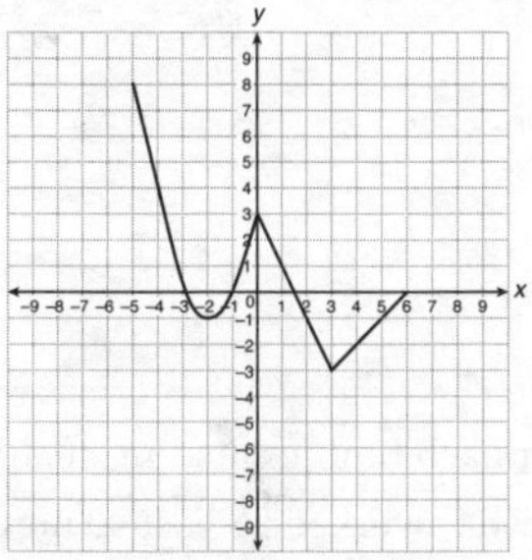

5. The graph of $y = f(x)$ is shown above. Which of the following graphs best represents the graph of $y = |f(x)|$?

(A)

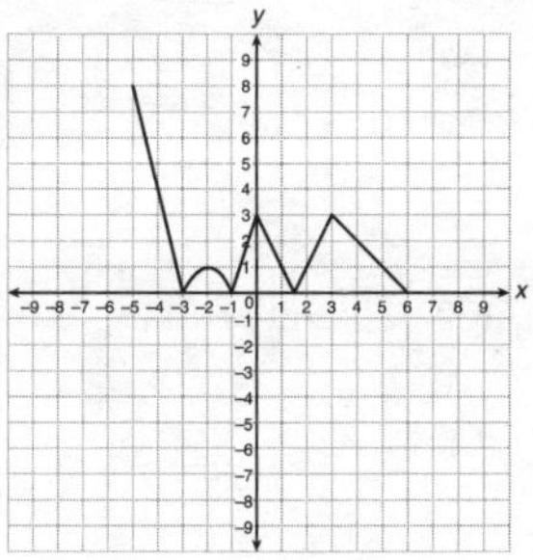

(B)

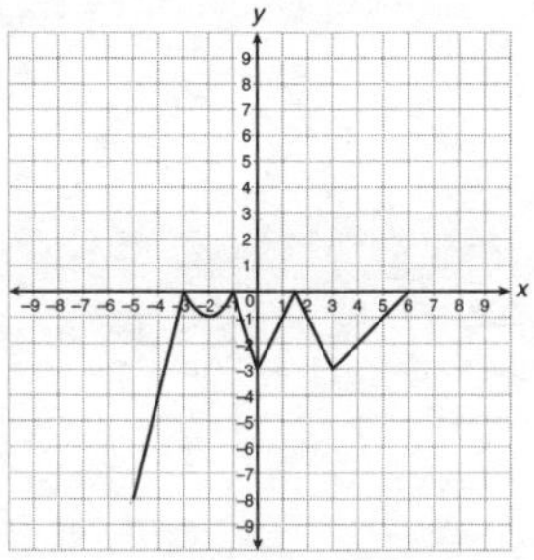

(C)

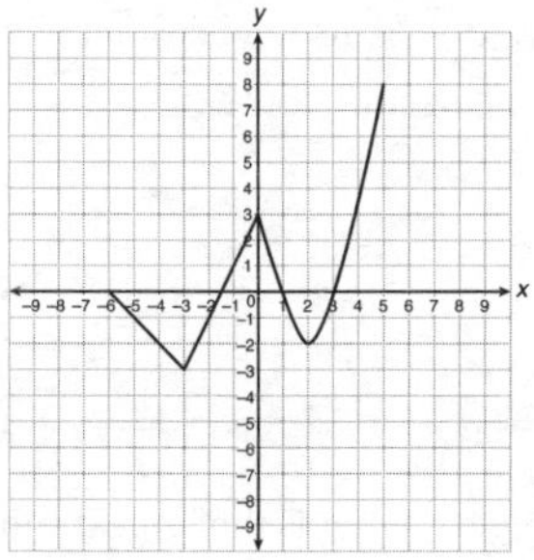

(D)

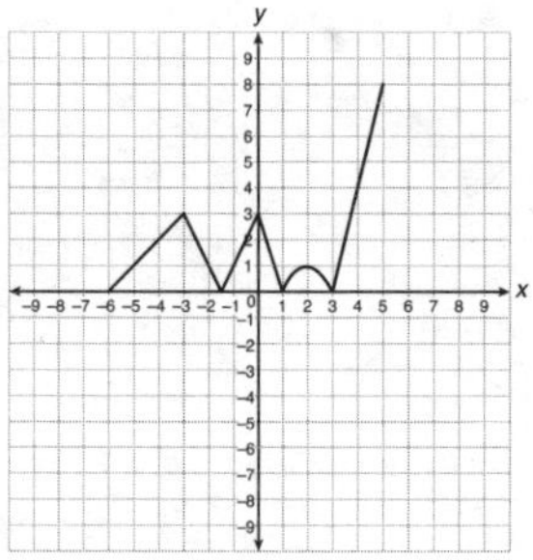

6. Which of the following is equivalent to $(6x^3 + 3x^2 - 1) + (4x^3 - 4x^2 + 2x + 3)$?

(A) $11x^6 + 2$
(B) $10x^3 - 7x^2 + 2x + 2$
(C) $10x^3 - x^2 + x + 3$
(D) $10x^3 - x^2 + 2x + 2$

7. Peter makes \$15 per hour when he works 40 hours a week. For each hour exceeding 40, he is paid 50% more than his usual hourly rate. Assuming that Peter has worked at least 40 hours in a particular week, which inequality properly expresses the range of hours, $h$, he must work to make over \$800 in that week?

(A) $800 < 600 + 22.5 \times (h - 40)$
(B) $800 < 600 + 22.5h$
(C) $800 < 600 + 7.5 \times (h - 40)$
(D) $800 < 40 + 15h$

8. In the $xy$-plane below, $ABC$ is an equilateral triangle with sides of length 2. If point $A$ has coordinates $(-2, 0)$, what are the coordinates of point $B$?

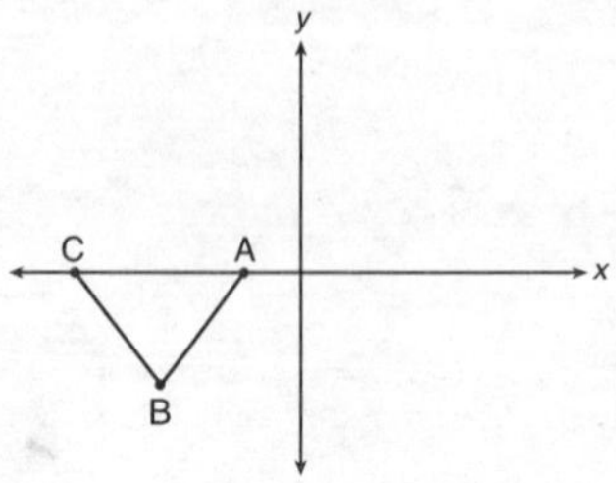


(A) $(-\sqrt{3}, -3)$
(B) $(-2, -\sqrt{3})$
(C) $(-3, \sqrt{2})$
(D) $(-3, -\sqrt{3})$

9. In a pet store with 30 customers, 60% of the customers like dogs and 11 customers like cats. What is the minimum number of customers who like both cats and dogs?

(A) 0
(B) 1
(C) 4
(D) 7

10. The function $f$ is defined below. If $f(n)$ and $n$ are both integers, what is the largest value that $n$ can be?

$$f(n) = \frac{2}{\sqrt[4]{n - 300}}$$

(A) 0
(B) 301
(C) 316
(D) 426

## Solutions

1. **(A)** We first need to get the given line into slope-intercept form, i.e., $y = mx + b$, so that we can easily see the slope. Begin by adding $2.5x$ to both sides:

$$5y = 2.5x - 10$$

Now divide by 5:

$$y = \frac{1}{2}x - 2$$

The slope of this line is $\frac{1}{2}$. The slope of a line perpendicular to this will have a slope that is the negative reciprocal of $\frac{1}{2}$. The negative reciprocal of $\frac{1}{2}$ is $-2$, and only choice (A) has a slope of $-2$.

2. **(A)** There were 118 people surveyed. If you lined up the people by age, the median age would be the average of the 59th and 60th persons. (Prove this to yourself. If you have a series of four terms, the median is between your second and third term. Divide your even number by 2 to get the first term, and add 1 to get the next.)

The first 24 people are younger than 13.

People numbered 25–68 are between ages 13 and 18. Therefore, the 59th and 60th people are both within this age category. If this whole age group were 13 (or even if all but 8 of them were), then the median age would be 13. This is the least possible age in this category, so it is the least possible median age.

3. **(D)** Without knowing everyone's exact response or the average number of hours slept per group, we can't calculate the mean. There's no way to add up the responses without knowing the responses or averages of the responses.

4. **(D)** Raising a fraction to an exponent raises both the numerator and the denominator to that exponent:

$$\left(\frac{2}{\sqrt[3]{a}}\right)^6 = \frac{2^6}{\sqrt[3]{a^6}}$$

Roots can be written as fractional exponents. So the expression can be rewritten as:

$$\frac{64}{a^{\frac{6}{3}}}$$

$a^{\frac{6}{3}}$ simplifies to $a^2$:

$$\frac{64}{a^{\frac{6}{3}}} = \frac{64}{a^2}$$

An exponent in the denominator of a fraction can be expressed as a negative exponent in the numerator:

$$\frac{64}{a^2} = 64a^{-2}$$

Choice **(D)** is the answer.

5. **(A)** If the new function is the absolute value of the old function, the graphs should be the same in all of the places where $y$ is already 0 or positive. This includes the intervals from $-5 \leq x \leq -3$ and from $-1 \leq x \leq 1.5$. The values for when the function is below the $x$-axis, $-3 < x < -1$ and $1.5 < x < 6$, will simply be their positive counterparts; they will be reflected above the $x$-axis.

   The only graph that shows this relationship is choice **(A)**.

6. **(D)** There's nothing to distribute, so you can just get rid of the parentheses and combine like terms:

$$6x^3 + 3x^2 - 1 + 4x^3 - 4x^2 + 2x + 3$$

   It's probably easiest if you start with the highest degree of $x$ and move downward:

   There's a $6x^3$ term and a $4x^3$ term. Combine these:

$$10x^3 + 3x^2 - 1 - 4x^2 + 2x + 3$$

   Next, there's $3x^2$ and $-4x^2$:

$$10x^3 - x^2 - 1 + 2x + 3$$

   There's only one term with an $x$ in it, so move on to the constant terms: $-1$ and 3:

$$10x^3 - x^2 + 2x + 2$$

   This corresponds to choice **(D)**.

7. **(A)** If Peter wants to make at least \$800, we can come up with an expression for the amount of money that he'll make working $h$ number of hours and set that expression greater than 800:

$$\text{Amount of money Peter makes weekly} > 800$$

   The problem states that he makes \$15/hour for his first 40 hours, and we assume that he's already worked 40 hours this week. Thus, Peter will make $\$15(40) = \$600$ for those 40 hours. This is a fixed constant.

   For every hour after his 40th hour, he makes 50% more than his original hourly wage, for a total of 150% of his hourly wage. Thus, every hour Peter works after his 40th hour, he makes $1.5(\$15) = \$22.50$.

   However, we can't just express this as $22.5h$, because that would imply that Peter makes \$22.50 for every single hour that he works rather than for just the hours past 40. Thus, it must be expressed as $22.5(h - 40)$.

   To see that this is true, we can plug 41 in for $h$ to see that for the 41st hour he works, Peter makes an extra:

$$22.5(41 - 40) = 22.5(1) = 22.5$$

   This is what we would expect.

   Our total expression for the amount of money Peter makes for working $h$ hours, then, is:

$$600 + 22.5(h - 40)$$

   Plug this into our original inequality to get:

$$600 + 22.5(h - 40) > 800$$

   This is the same as choice **(A)**.

8. **(D)**

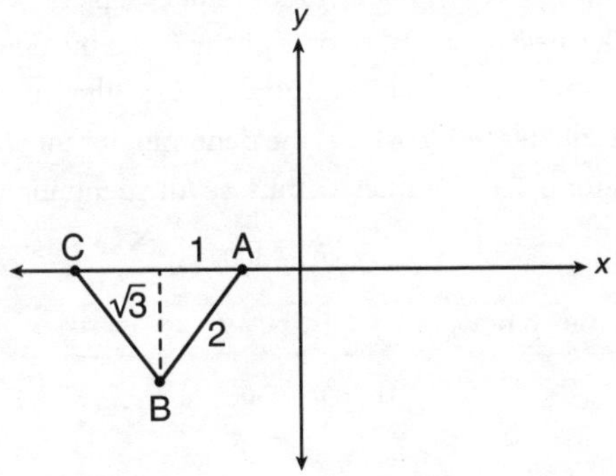


We are told that this triangle is equilateral, so each of the three angles is 60°. We are also told that point *A* has coordinates (−2, 0). Since point *C* is on the *x*-axis and is 2 units to the left of point *A*, point *C* must have coordinates (−4, 0). By drawing a line that starts halfway between points *A* and *C* and bisects the angle at point *B*, as shown in the drawing, we can split this equilateral triangle into two 30-60-90 triangles. Because the equilateral triangle has side lengths of 2 and the line splits the side along the *x*-axis in half, the new triangles have side lengths of 1 along the *x*-axis.

You can see, then, that point *B* has an *x* value 1 unit from both point *A*'s and point *C*'s *x* values. Because points *A* and *C* have *x* values of −2 and −4, respectively, point *B* will have an *x* value of −3.

You may remember that a 30-60-90 triangle is a special right triangle that has opposite side lengths of 1, $\sqrt{3}$, and 2, respectively. Since you've already found side lengths of 1 and 2, the dotted line will have a length of $\sqrt{3}$. Because it's in the negative *y* direction, it will have a *y*-coordinate of $-\sqrt{3}$. Therefore, the coordinates for point *B* are $\left(-3,\ -\sqrt{3}\right)$.

Alternatively, if you didn't remember the 30-60-90 triangle, you could have used the Pythagorean theorem with the two known side lengths to find the third length:

$$a^2 + b^2 = c^2$$
$$(1)^2 + b^2 = (2)^2$$
$$1 + b^2 = 4$$

Subtract 1 from both sides:

$$b^2 = 3$$

To find *b*, take the square root of both sides:

$$b = \sqrt{3}$$

So the third side has a length of $\sqrt{3}$.

9. **(A)** We are told that 60% of the customers like dogs. Since there are 30 customers, $0.6(30) = 18$ customers like dogs. We are also told that 11 people like cats. It is possible that 18 customers like only dogs, 11 people like only cats, and $30 - 18 - 11 = 1$ person likes neither. Thus, the minimum number of customers who necessarily like both is 0, choice **(A)**.

10. **(C)** If $f(n)$ needs to be an integer and we want a number in the denominator ($n$) to be as large as possible, that means we're looking for the smallest possible integer for $f(n)$. This integer must be positive. Because the numerator is positive and the denominator is being raised to an even root, the denominator must be positive as well. The smallest possible positive integer is 1, so set $f(n)$ equal to 1. If $f(n)$ is 1, the denominator must be 2 since $\frac{2}{2}$ is the only fraction with a numerator of 2 that equals 1. Thus, set the denominator equal to 2:

$$2 = \sqrt[4]{n - 300}$$

Raise both sides to the fourth power:

$$16 = n - 300$$

Add 300 to both sides:

$$n = 316$$

You can plug this number back in to the original expression to verify.

# PART 6
# Practice Tests 1 and 2

# SAT Test Overview

This SAT Practice Test is made up of a Reading and Writing section and a Math section. On these two non-adaptive practice tests, the second module of each section is more challenging than the first module of each section.

**Note:** In this book, there is an answer sheet you can use to write down your letter choices and math answers. Feel free to use the sheet to record your answers or simply circle and write down your answers in the test as you go.

**Section 1:** Reading and Writing (54 Questions)

There are two 27-question modules in the Reading and Writing section.

**Section 2:** Math (44 Questions)

There are two 22-question modules in the Math section. You can use a calculator throughout the math section.

## Modules

The modules in each section are timed separately. You can review your answers in each module before time expires. When the time reaches zero, you will automatically move on to the next section. You are unable to return to a completed module.

## Directions

At the beginning of each section, there are directions for answering the questions.

# ANSWER SHEET
## Practice Test 1

### Section 1, Module 1: Reading and Writing

| | | |
|---|---|---|
| 1. ____ | 10. ____ | 19. ____ |
| 2. ____ | 11. ____ | 20. ____ |
| 3. ____ | 12. ____ | 21. ____ |
| 4. ____ | 13. ____ | 22. ____ |
| 5. ____ | 14. ____ | 23. ____ |
| 6. ____ | 15. ____ | 24. ____ |
| 7. ____ | 16. ____ | 25. ____ |
| 8. ____ | 17. ____ | 26. ____ |
| 9. ____ | 18. ____ | 27. ____ |

# ANSWER SHEET
## Practice Test 1



### Section 1, Module 2: Reading and Writing

| | | |
|---|---|---|
| 1. ____ | 10. ____ | 19. ____ |
| 2. ____ | 11. ____ | 20. ____ |
| 3. ____ | 12. ____ | 21. ____ |
| 4. ____ | 13. ____ | 22. ____ |
| 5. ____ | 14. ____ | 23. ____ |
| 6. ____ | 15. ____ | 24. ____ |
| 7. ____ | 16. ____ | 25. ____ |
| 8. ____ | 17. ____ | 26. ____ |
| 9. ____ | 18. ____ | 27. ____ |

# ANSWER SHEET
## Practice Test 1

### Section 2, Module 1: Math

| | | | |
|---|---|---|---|
| 1. | _____ | 12. | _____ |
| 2. | _____ | 13. | _____ |
| 3. | _____ | 14. | _____ |
| 4. | _____ | 15. | _____ |
| 5. | _____ | 16. | _____ |
| 6. | _____ | 17. | _____ |
| 7. | _____ | 18. | _____ |
| 8. | _____ | 19. | _____ |
| 9. | _____ | 20. | _____ |
| 10. | _____ | 21. | _____ |
| 11. | _____ | 22. | _____ |

# ANSWER SHEET
## Practice Test 1

### Section 2, Module 2: Math

| | |
|---|---|
| 1. _____ | 12. _____ |
| 2. _____ | 13. _____ |
| 3. _____ | 14. _____ |
| 4. _____ | 15. _____ |
| 5. _____ | 16. _____ |
| 6. _____ | 17. _____ |
| 7. _____ | 18. _____ |
| 8. _____ | 19. _____ |
| 9. _____ | 20. _____ |
| 10. _____ | 21. _____ |
| 11. _____ | 22. _____ |

# Practice Test 1

## Section 1, Module 1: Reading and Writing

32 MINUTES, 27 QUESTIONS

**DIRECTIONS**

You will be tested on a variety of important reading and writing skills. Each question has one or more passages, possibly including a graph or table. Carefully read each passage and question and choose the best answer to the question based on the passage(s).

Every question in this section is multiple-choice with four possible answers. Each question has only one best answer.



The boss said to _______. The rain made the work impossible, and half the materials hadn't been delivered on time. He was too frustrated to think!

**1**

Which choice completes the text with the most logical and precise word or phrase?

(A) do what you can
(B) start the work
(C) appreciate the sunlight
(D) call it a day

Emily had _________ about being invited to Kayla's house. The last time they hung out it hadn't gone very well. In fact, Emily had stormed out angrily after Kayla made some rude comments.

**2**

Which choice completes the text with the most logical and precise word or phrase?

(A) detainments
(B) territories
(C) reservations
(D) anticipation

1 MODULE 1 1

The basic engineering degrees—mechanical, electrical, chemical, and civil—are consistently ranked in the top ten degrees in terms of ________ after graduation. As such, someone who wants to earn a high salary in a job after graduation may find an engineering degree to be a good fit.

**3**

Which choice completes the text with the most logical and precise word or phrase?

Ⓐ expenditure
Ⓑ compensation
Ⓒ enterprises
Ⓓ reimbursement

The issue is that car testers just don't use female dummies. A female dummy was first requested by testers in the 1980s and wasn't incorporated into tests by the National Highway Safety and Traffic Administration (NHSTA) until 2003. That female dummy is not adjusted in any way to make up for the difference in shape and composition between men and women—it is just a miniaturized model of the male dummy. In fact, it is so ________ that it only represents the smallest 5 percent of women. In addition, it is only used as a passenger in testing, never as a driver.

**4**

Which choice completes the text with the most logical and precise word or phrase?

Ⓐ augmented
Ⓑ built up
Ⓒ scaled down
Ⓓ abbreviated

Psychological researchers should be more modest about the certainty of data that involves human behavior. After all, human behavior is more difficult to ________ measure than criteria that other scientific fields assess, like temperature or velocity.

**5**

Which choice completes the text with the most logical and precise word or phrase?

Ⓐ impulsively
Ⓑ subjectively
Ⓒ irrationally
Ⓓ objectively

# 1 MODULE 1 1

Nobody wants to feel easily influenced. Yet, I beg you to hear me out: advertising is everywhere because it works. U.S. companies spend an annual $70 billion in television ads, and this is before we take a look at other mediums of advertising like radios, magazines, website cookies, and even social media "sponsored" ads.

**6**

Which choice best describes the function of the underlined sentence in the text as a whole?

Ⓐ To explain the process by which advertising is created

Ⓑ To critique corporations for misleading, unethical practices

Ⓒ To give concrete evidence to illustrate the expanse of advertising

Ⓓ To demonstrate instances when consumers feel consciously manipulated

The following text is from Walt Whitman's 1891 poem "A Promise to California." The poem was written in the aftermath of the U.S. Civil War when the country was trying to heal its emotional wounds.

A promise to California,
Also to the great Pastoral Plains, and for Oregon:
Sojourning east a while longer, soon I travel
toward you, to remain, to teach robust
American love;
For I know very well that I and robust love
belong among you, inland, and along the
Western Sea;
For These States tend inland, and toward the
Western Sea—and I will also.

**7**

Which choice best states the main purpose of the text?

Ⓐ It outlines how with the skilled narrator's leadership the United States will gain new territory.

Ⓑ It draws a comparison between how just as the United States has spread, so will the narrator's love spread.

Ⓒ It compares the geographic and economic features of several U.S. states.

Ⓓ It sketches a plan for national harmony amidst an ongoing bloody conflict.

8. The following text is adapted from F. Scott Fitzgerald's 1920 novel *This Side of Paradise*. The novel opens with the following character introduction of Fitzgerald's semi-autobiographical protagonist, Amory Blaine.

> "Amory."
>
> "Yes, Beatrice." (Such a quaint name for his mother; she encouraged it.)
>
> "Dear, don't think of getting out of bed yet. I've always suspected that early rising in early life makes one nervous. Clothilde is having your breakfast brought up."
>
> "All right."
>
> "I am feeling very old to-day, Amory," she would sigh, her face a rare cameo of pathos, her voice exquisitely modulated, her hands as facile as Bernhardt's. "My nerves are on edge—on edge. We must leave this terrifying place to-morrow and go searching for sunshine."

**8**

Amory's relationship with his mother is best described as

Ⓐ traditionally pious.
Ⓑ unusually friendly.
Ⓒ blatantly disrespectful.
Ⓓ cold and distant.



An English professor analyzes the 1917 poem titled "The River Merchant's Life: A Letter" by Li Bai, translated by Ezra Pound. The professor claims that the poem emphasizes the narrator's desire for reunification with her departed husband:

__________

**9**

Which quotation from the poem most effectively illustrates the claim?

Ⓐ "While my hair was still cut straight across my forehead / I played about the front gate, pulling flowers."
Ⓑ "Lowering my head, I looked at the wall. / Called to, a thousand times, I never looked back."
Ⓒ "You went into far Ku-to-en, by the river of swirling eddies, / And you have been gone five months."
Ⓓ "If you are coming down through the narrows of the river, / Please let me know beforehand, / And I will come out to meet you."

**Table 1**

| Crop | Yield (Unit/ Acre) | Nitrogen Removal (Pounds/Acre) |
|---|---|---|
| Barley | 40 | 30 |
| Corn | 50 | 35 |
| Soybeans | 30 | 103 |
| Wheat | 40 | 42 |
| Corn Silage | 15 | 116 |
| Grass-Legume Hay | 2 | 87 |

All data is sourced from the University of Delaware, *Nitrogen Removal by Delaware Crops.*

In general, crop rotation is fairly simple. In one year, a nitrogen-fixing plant, like a legume, will be planted. These crops deposit nitrogen into the soil. The following year a nitrogen-depleting crop should be planted and will thrive. This process can be repeated with different crops, all of which will either fix or remove nitrogen. For example, after planting a legume in a field for a growing season, a farmer would be well advised to plant ________.

**10**

Which choice most effectively uses data from the graph to complete the example?

Ⓐ barley, because it has a relatively high rate of nitrogen removal

Ⓑ corn silage, because it has a relatively high rate of nitrogen removal

Ⓒ corn, because it has a relatively low rate of nitrogen removal

Ⓓ wheat, because it has a relatively low rate of nitrogen removal

The following is an adaptation of remarks given by Don Evans (the secretary of commerce under George W. Bush) as part of a panel at an economics conference in December of 2004. Note: A tort is a type of lawsuit.

> I was in Missouri this last year, and I had a chance to really see up close and personal how [increased costs from healthcare lawsuits are] impacting the health care industry. I talked to a David Carpenter, who is the CEO of North Kansas City Hospital, and what he told me was that there had been 30 doctors that had moved from Missouri to Kansas because Kansas had, indeed, passed tort reform and had put some caps in place. So, you see it happening all across America, where doctors are moving around and trying to find a more friendly environment.

**11**

Which of the following findings, if true, would best support Evans's overall argument as presented in the text?

Ⓐ A survey of medical doctors indicated that 85% of them prefer to work close to the community of patients they treat.

Ⓑ Cities with unlimited caps on business lawsuit payouts had 15% overall greater life satisfaction among residents than cities that limited such payouts.

Ⓒ States with tort reforms in place saw 20% more businesses relocate to their territories than states without such reforms.

Ⓓ Medical practices are 30% more likely to move to states with populations in excess of 10,000,000 residents.

"An Encounter" is part of James Joyce's 1914 short story collection, *Dubliners*. A young, unnamed narrator searches for release from the constraints of daily routine. An English student claims that the narrator's willingness to follow the intellectual requirements of his school could best be described as "half-hearted: ________"

**12**

Which quotation from "An Encounter" most effectively illustrates this claim?

Ⓐ "Everyone was incredulous when it was reported that he had a vocation for the priesthood. Nevertheless it was true."

Ⓑ "This page or this page? This page? Now, Dillon, up! *'Hardly had the day'*... Go on! What day? *'Hardly had the day dawned'*... Have you studied it? What have you there in your pocket?"

Ⓒ "I'm surprised at boys like you, educated, reading such stuff. I could understand it if you were... National School boys. Now, Dillon, I advise you strongly, get at your work or..."

Ⓓ "But when the restraining influence of the school was at a distance I began to hunger again for wild sensations, for the escape which those chronicles of disorder alone seemed to offer me."

Many studies suggest that while exercising and having a healthy diet can drastically reduce the concentration of cholesterol in our blood, genes do play a crucial role in an individual's risk of cardiovascular disease. The strong role genes play in cholesterol processing is seen in bears, especially polar bears. Polar bears are among the most fat-obsessed members of the animal kingdom, yet they do not experience any cardiovascular complications. About half of a polar bear's weight is fat and its blood cholesterol levels are high enough that they would cause serious cardiovascular disease in humans; even so, ________

**13**

Which choice most logically completes the text?

Ⓐ polar bears have a varied diet despite the harsh environment in which they live.

Ⓑ heart attacks are not a concern for polar bears.

Ⓒ polar bears are equally susceptible to cardiac issues.

Ⓓ cardiovascular disease remains a leading cause of death.

# 1 MODULE 1 1

As Mendeleev assembled the periodic table, he had noticed several gaps in the pattern of properties which—cleverly—he hypothesized to be areas held by yet undiscovered elements. Apart from reserving space on the table for these elements, he went so far as to predict not only their existence, but their chemical properties as well. Several years later, the spectroscopic discovery of one of these elements—specifically gallium—and the confirmation of Mendeleev's predictions caused the popularity of his theory to skyrocket, and ________

**14**

Which choice most logically completes the text?

Ⓐ his contemporaries allowed Mendeleev a limited degree of credit for his work.

Ⓑ applications to anatomical and zoological research naturally followed.

Ⓒ Mendeleev's scientific curiosity finally found an outlet.

Ⓓ the periodic table quickly became a standard fixture in the study of chemistry.

Birdfeeders attract birds, but they also attract foragers like squirrels and chipmunks. There are several methods for keeping them away from feeders; a common one is putting the feeder on a tall pole at least five feet away from bushes and trees and adding a ________

**15**

Which choice completes the text so that it conforms to the conventions of Standard English?

Ⓐ baffle; a cone-shaped device that prevents squirrels from climbing the pole.

Ⓑ baffle: a cone-shaped device that prevents—squirrels from climbing the pole.

Ⓒ baffle (a cone-shaped device that prevents squirrels from climbing the pole).

Ⓓ baffle, a cone-shaped device, that prevents squirrels from climbing the pole.

In a situation where CPR is being administered in a public space, oftentimes no one calls medics because they assume someone else already ________

**16**

Which choice completes the text so that it conforms to the conventions of Standard English?

Ⓐ has.

Ⓑ have had.

Ⓒ have.

Ⓓ are.

Today, the concept of the high school rock band __________ yet students still have lofty dreams of making a career out of something equally improbable: social media.

**17**

Which choice completes the text so that it conforms to the conventions of Standard English?

Ⓐ is out of a bit of style,
Ⓑ is of style out a bit,
Ⓒ style is a bit out of,
Ⓓ is a bit out of style,

The possibility of becoming a physician assistant or a nurse practitioner allows students to become health care professionals who ________ people without the rigors of medical school and the associated student debt.

**18**

Which choice completes the text so that it conforms to the conventions of Standard English?

Ⓐ helps
Ⓑ helping
Ⓒ helped
Ⓓ help

Rodents only make up a portion of a ____________ Servals will also use their large ears to listen carefully for the flutter of bird wings overhead or the buzz of an insect nearby.

**19**

Which choice completes the text so that it conforms to the conventions of Standard English?

Ⓐ serval's diet.
Ⓑ servals diets.
Ⓒ servals' diet.
Ⓓ serval's diets'.

Schrödinger posited the issue of when superposition collapses into reality—when multiple occupying states simultaneously ________ one or the other.

**20**

Which choice completes the text so that it conforms to the conventions of Standard English?

Ⓐ becomes
Ⓑ become
Ⓒ have becoming
Ⓓ had becoming

# 1 MODULE 1 1

Even in his short life, Cannon managed to make an enduring difference. ______________ In his wake, Native American art was refreshed, moving away from strict rules that had governed traditional forms and into a new space where artists could be more expressive by using traditional styles and concepts while incorporating modern ideas and inspirations.

**21**

Which choice completes the text so that it conforms to the conventions of Standard English?

Ⓐ Art historians trace the resurgence and change; in Native American art to a movement that started with Cannon.

Ⓑ Art historians trace the resurgence, and change in Native American art to a movement that started with Cannon.

Ⓒ Art historians trace the resurgence and change in Native American art to a movement that started with Cannon.

Ⓓ Art historians trace the resurgence and change in Native American art—to a movement—that started with Cannon.

Melodies are so loved that people will hum them even when they are trying to concentrate on other things. Beats are so universally loved that babies will dance to them, and hard-of-hearing people will seek out their vibrations. ____________ in music. Humans, since the very beginning of our species, have used them to express joy, sadness, heartache, love, and pain.

**22**

Which choice completes the text so that it conforms to the conventions of Standard English?

Ⓐ These two things (the melodical notes and the beats), come together

Ⓑ These two things the melodical notes and the beats, come together

Ⓒ These two things—the melodical notes and the beats—come together

Ⓓ These two things—the melodical notes and the beats, come together

Technology has transformed how job seekers should present their qualifications to prospective employers. _________ the old paper resume needed to be concise and fit within the scope of one or two pages, your online career profile can be much more thorough.

**23**

Which choice completes the text with the most logical transition?

Ⓐ Whereas

Ⓑ Since

Ⓒ Because

Ⓓ Moreover

Working class families will continue to buy only in neighborhoods where they can afford homes, and where home values are unpredictable. __________ they will face further financial instability; meanwhile, the privileged few who can afford to purchase real estate in New York, Chicago, London, and so on, will see their returns peak.

**24**

Which choice completes the text with the most logical transition?

Ⓐ Unexpectedly,
Ⓑ Paradoxically,
Ⓒ In contrast,
Ⓓ Hence,

While conducting research, a student took these notes:

- Gyoja monks, also known as Marathon monks, are a Buddhist group in Japan.
- Each monk, over seven years, walks around 27,000 miles, generally at a rate of 25 miles per day for months on end.
- Toward the end of the seven years, the monks will walk up to 52 miles per day.
- The grueling physical demands of completing this task on little food or sleep often proves to be fatal—only around 50 monks have completed the task in the past 135 years.
- This challenge of prayer, meditation, and physical discipline, when completed, leads to the monk being known as a living saint.

**25**

The student wants to emphasize the physical demands of being a Gyoja monk. Which choice most effectively uses relevant information from the notes to accomplish this goal?

Ⓐ The Gyoja monks walk up to an incredible 52 miles per day on very little food and sleep.
Ⓑ Gyoja monks sometimes walk about 25 miles per day, a task that many people might find challenging.
Ⓒ Those who want to become Gyoja monks must dedicate seven straight years of their lives to this challenge.
Ⓓ While the spiritual introspection might be psychologically burdensome, the public recognition makes the work worthwhile.

# 1 MODULE 1 1

While researching a topic, a student has taken the following notes:

- The type of springs used in the seating surface of furniture impacts comfort and durability.
- Furniture constructed with eight-way hand-tied coil springs can be expected to be extremely durable and very comfortable to sit on.
- Eight-way hand-tied coil springs involve a labor-intensive fabrication process.
- Sinuous springs are more common than eight-way hand-tied coil springs.
- Sinuous springs have a wide range of costs due to flexibility in the quality of the materials used.

**26**

The student wants to make a generalization about the makeup of typical furniture. Which choice most effectively uses relevant information from the notes to accomplish this goal?

Ⓐ Since most consumers seek to maximize comfort, it is more likely that coil springs would be found in a typical piece of furniture than would sinuous springs.

Ⓑ Most pieces of furniture are made using a labor-intensive crafting process.

Ⓒ It is more likely that the springs in an everyday piece of furniture are sinuous than coil.

Ⓓ Both sinuous and coil springs are found throughout the components of typical furniture, from the backs to the seats.

While researching a topic, a student has taken the following notes:

- Offshore wind farms are an increasingly viable source of renewable energy.
- These wind farms are typically located on the surface of the ocean near coastal cities.
- The average wind speed offshore tends to be higher than on land since there are fewer geographical obstacles to wind gusts.
- Wind farms can often be placed relatively close to major coastal urban areas, thereby reducing the distance needed for electricity transmission.
- While wind farms offshore are promising, increased research should be done to minimize the maintenance costs for these facilities.

**27**

The student wants to point out a reason why an offshore wind farm would be better than a land-based wind farm. Which choice most effectively uses relevant information from the notes to accomplish this goal?

Ⓐ Since offshore wind farms provide the possibility of renewable energy, builders should utilize them instead of land-based wind farms.

Ⓑ Given the higher typical wind speeds offshore, offshore wind farms are more sensible than land-based ones.

Ⓒ The convenience of having the source of electricity closer to major urban areas makes land-based wind farms more promising than offshore ones.

Ⓓ The higher maintenance costs associated with offshore wind farms make them less viable than land-based ones.

# Section 1, Module 2, Reading and Writing

32 MINUTES, 27 QUESTIONS

**DIRECTIONS**

You will be tested on a variety of important reading and writing skills. Each question has one or more passages, possibly including a graph or table. Carefully read each passage and question and choose the best answer to the question based on the passage(s).

Every question in this section is multiple-choice, with four possible answers. Each question has only one best answer.



We rarely pause mid-recipe to consider the chemistry of cooking, but understanding the chemical reactions occurring in our food will help us to become better cooks. Isn't that <u>some food for thought?</u>

**1**

As used in the text, what does the phrase "some food for thought" most nearly mean?

Ⓐ An appetizing situation
Ⓑ A next step for researchers
Ⓒ A plan for actionable change
Ⓓ Something worth considering

Despite the wide applicability of the ABC-X model, like any other theory, it has faced critiques of its usefulness. One of the major critiques is its focus on serious stressor events and inaccessibility to smaller, everyday stressors. Another _________ is its inability to consider how multiple stressors may affect the current stressor situation.

**2**

Which choice completes the text with the most logical and precise word or phrase?

Ⓐ drawback
Ⓑ assessment
Ⓒ trauma
Ⓓ rumination

Tests should operate as an assessment of what is practiced daily inside the classroom. Classroom teachers who teach to well-written standards __________ that students are prepared for the next grade level.

**3**

Which choice completes the text with the most logical and precise word or phrase?

Ⓐ assure
Ⓑ insure
Ⓒ ensure
Ⓓ reassure

# 1 MODULE 2 1

A folklorist may enter a city or village or subculture and begin to participate in that population's day-to-day life. Possibly, they may end up studying a story, a joke, a dance, a dish, or even a child's game—an apparently trivial practice that, when looked at closely, turns out to be quite ________.

**4**

Which choice completes the text with the most logical and precise word or phrase?

Ⓐ insignificant
Ⓑ substantive
Ⓒ imbecilic
Ⓓ exuberant

In the 1990s, amidst concern for its effect on wildlife, DDT was largely banned; bedbugs slowly began their comeback. By 2010 their numbers were spiking. Because of a huge increase in personal travel since the last time the bugs were an issue, they spread faster than ever. Laundromats, hotels, and libraries became __________ for transmission. Bug eggs can get tucked into suitcases when traveling, or into books that you check out from the library. In communal living areas (like apartment buildings), they can crawl from one apartment to another as they look for human hosts on which to feed.

**5**

Which choice completes the text with the most logical and precise word or phrase?

Ⓐ agents
Ⓑ excursions
Ⓒ hygienics
Ⓓ meanderings

Studies show that younger children are much better suited to learn multiple languages at one time, with the effects reaching from elevated attentiveness to enhanced musical abilities. According to the Cornell Language Acquisition Lab, elementary language learners are 70% more likely to reach an intermediate level of communication compared to those who begin in high school. The incorporation of multiple language study at an early age creates more culturally aware students, but it results in more measurable impacts as well: students who study language before the age of 10—when brain capacity is at its highest—test better in all core subjects, including English, Reading, and Math. Greater cognitive development encourages exceptional creativity and divergent thinking.

**6**

Which choice best states the main purpose of the text?

Ⓐ To convince the reader to study a specific world language to become more culturally aware
Ⓑ To provide an evidence-based argument in favor of early learning of multiple languages
Ⓒ To suggest a curriculum for graduate-level studies in multiple language acquisition
Ⓓ To argue that the biological obstacles to learning language at an early age are difficult to overcome

**Text 1**

Film star Charlie Chaplain was much more than a mere entertainer. In his 1939 film *The Great Dictator,* Chaplin delivers an impassioned speech in which he condemns dictators, prejudice, and xenophobia. Knowing the historical context, Chaplin was clearly making a commentary on Hitler, Mussolini, and fascism. This speech is widely regarded as one of the most powerful performances in film history, which is rather ironic—Chaplin was famous as a silent film star, after all.

**Text 2**

Stephen Spielberg is a master of the close-up—nearly every Spielberg film features an extended close-up on a wide-eyed, shocked face experiencing awe or terror. Some critics find this technique manipulative, alleging that this technique suggests that the audience should likewise respond with shock or awe at the events onscreen, even if such a response has not been emotionally "earned" by the scene. But what some call a cheap trick, others call engaging cinema.

**7**

Based on the texts, what would the "critics" in Text 2 most likely say about Chaplin's impassioned speech as described in Text 1?

Ⓐ The emotional response it evokes is well earned.
Ⓑ It is overly focused on political activism.
Ⓒ Without a vocal accompaniment, a silent film cannot be poignant.
Ⓓ Attempts to prompt a visceral reaction to what is on the screen are unwarranted.

The following text is from Willa Cather's 1918 novel *My Ántonia*.

When Jim was still an obscure young lawyer, struggling to make his way in New York, his career was suddenly advanced by a brilliant marriage. Genevieve Whitney was the only daughter of a distinguished man. Her marriage with young Burden was the subject of sharp comment at the time. It was said she had been brutally jilted by her cousin, Rutland Whitney, and that she married this unknown man from the West out of bravado. She was a restless, headstrong girl, even then, who liked to astonish her friends.

**8**

Based on the text, the narrator likely believes that Jim married his wife

Ⓐ out of a love for her intellect.
Ⓑ because of professional ambition.
Ⓒ due to his sincere love for her.
Ⓓ given her sympathy for his poverty.

The following text is adapted from Octave Uzanne's 1894 work "The End of Books." In this story, a group of gentlemen gathers after dinner to discuss what they think the future holds. Eventually they come to the topic of the future of books and the following monologue is given by one of the group.

> If by books you are to be understood as referring to our innumerable collections of paper, printed, sewed, and bound in a cover announcing the title of the work, I own to you frankly that I do not believe (and the progress of electricity and modern mechanism forbids me to believe) that Gutenberg's invention can do otherwise than sooner or later fall into desuetude as a means of current interpretation of our mental products.
>
> Printing... which has changed the destiny of Europe, and which, especially during the last two centuries, has governed opinion through the book, the pamphlet, and the newspaper—printing, which since 1436 has reigned despotically over the mind of man, is, in my opinion, threatened with death by the various devices for registering sound which have lately been invented, and which little by little will go to perfection.

**9**

Based on the text, the narrator believes that the impact of printing on history up to the time period when the article was written could be described as

Ⓐ extremely significant.
Ⓑ largely irrelevant.
Ⓒ indisputably oppressive.
Ⓓ uniformly militaristic.

Author Mary Shelly composed a novel called *The Last Man* in 1826. The narrator of this story suggests that the greatest obstacle to his father's success is an inability to follow through on his commitments: ________________

**10**

Which quotation from *The Last Man* most effectively illustrates the claim?

Ⓐ "During the short years of thoughtless youth, he was adored by the high-bred triflers of the day, nor least by the youthful sovereign."

Ⓑ "The fiend of gambling, which fully possessed [my father], made his good resolutions transient, his promises vain."

Ⓒ "With the quick sensibility peculiar to his temperament, he perceived his power in the brilliant circle to be on the wane."

Ⓓ "The king married; and the haughty princess of Austria, who became, as queen of England, the head of fashion, looked with harsh eyes on his defects, and with contempt on the affection her royal husband entertained for him."

1 MODULE 2 1

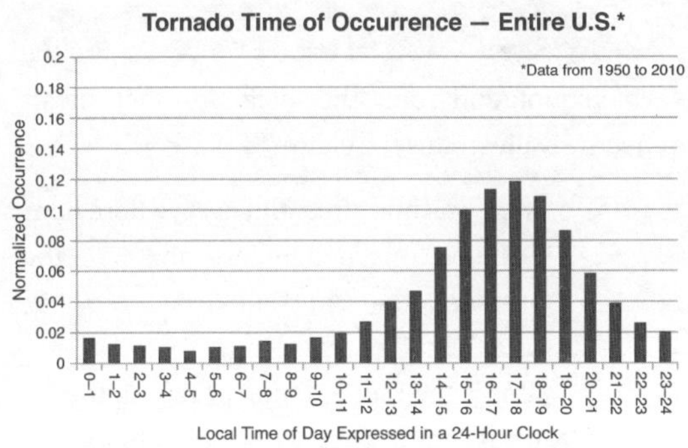


Source: *www1.ncdc.noaa.gov/pub/data/cmb/images/tornado/clim/US_nationa_timeofday.png*

**Figure 1**

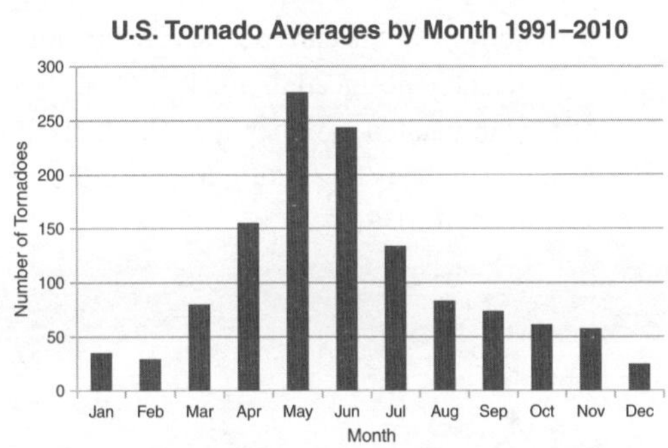


Source: *www1.ncdc.noaa.gov/pub/data/cmb/images/tornado/clim/tornadoes_bymonth.png*

**Figure 2**

Meteorologists in the Northern Hemisphere hypothesize that by observing the most common conditions in which a tornado might form, they can better predict the likelihood of tornado creation. With this knowledge in place, meteorologists can build public awareness about the increased possibility of tornadoes during certain conditions, helping citizens become more aware of potential danger. Given the meteorologists' goal, they would be well-served to inform the public that there is an increased likelihood of tornado formation at ______________

**11**

Which choice most effectively uses data from the table to complete the statement?

Ⓐ midday in the summer.
Ⓑ nighttime in the fall.
Ⓒ sunset in the springtime.
Ⓓ sunrise in the winter.

"The Social Contract" is a 1763 treatise of political philosophy by Jean-Jacques Rousseau. During the unsettled time in which the work was written, Rousseau advocated social cohesion. In fact, the central tenet of the social contract is that man must give himself entirely to the state to ensure social order: ____________

**12**

Which quotation from "The Social Contract" most effectively illustrates the claim?

Ⓐ "Man was born free, but everywhere he is in chains. This man believes that he is the master of others, and still he is more of a slave than they are."

Ⓑ "This is the fundamental problem; the social contract offers a solution to it."

Ⓒ "And so it follows that each individual immediately recovers his primitive rights and natural liberties whenever any violation of the social contract occurs and thereby loses the contractual freedom for which he renounced them."

Ⓓ "The individual member alienates himself totally to the whole community together with all his rights."

1 MODULE 2 1

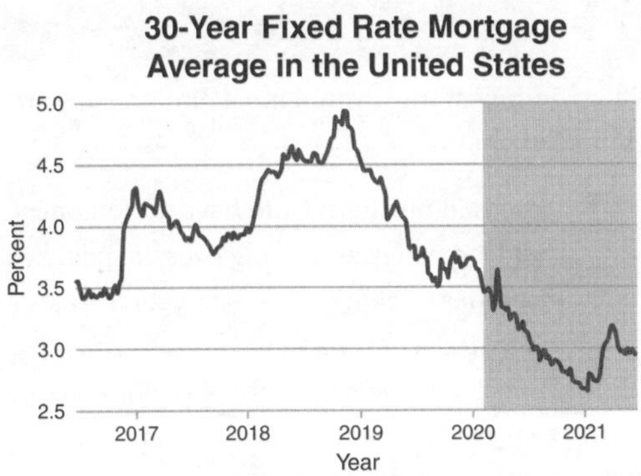


Freddie Mac, 30-Year Fixed Rate Mortgage Average in the United States [MORTGAGE30US], retrieved from FRED, Federal Reserve Bank of St. Louis; https://fred.stlouisfed.org/series/MORTGAGE30US, June 22, 2021.

Economists have observed that during times of economic recession, central banks tend to lower interest rates to help make the cost of having loans less expensive. Since interest payments comprise a major component of any loan, lowering interest rates will help consumers save money. If consumers can save money on interest, they have more money available to purchase goods and services, thereby stimulating the economy and helping the country emerge successfully from a recession. Economists hypothesize that in the relatively recent recession that started in early 2020, interest rates on a variety of loan products would decrease: ______________

**13**

Which choice most effectively uses data from the chart to support the economists' hypothesis?

Ⓐ While the U.S. mortgage rate is relatively low by historical standards, it stayed fairly constant during the duration of the recession.

Ⓑ The interest rate on U.S. 30-year fixed mortgages rose to as high as 3.7% in the aftermath of the recession.

Ⓒ U.S. 30-year fixed mortgage rates, for example, generally decreased throughout 2020 to a five year low of less than 3 percent.

Ⓓ Mortgage payments for the average American homebuyer increased in the immediate aftermath of the recent recession.

An area in southern Ohio has been undergoing construction for the past two decades. New apartment complexes are replacing the forests that used to cover that area. Surprisingly, researchers have found that a type of bird, Species X, has been growing in population over that same period. Group 1 hypothesizes that the growth is due to detrimental environmental changes in another area, causing Species X to move from their preferred area into southern Ohio. Group 2 hypothesizes that the new landscape of southern Ohio is more suitable for Species X, leading more of them to move into the new area.

**14**

Which finding, if true, would most directly support Group 2's hypothesis?

Ⓐ Areas in northern Ohio have undergone widespread tree clearing over the past two decades, making it necessary for Species X to find a new habitat.

Ⓑ Species X preferred habitat is along the edges of tree lines, so with all the fragmentation of land, there are more edges.

Ⓒ The number of natural predators of Species X in southern Ohio has increased in recent years due to reintroduction of some predators to the wild.

Ⓓ Over the past two decades, there has been an increase in river-based pollutants throughout the southern Ohio region.

The mite reproductive process causes significant distress to bee colonies since the mites themselves reproduce within a bee colony. The female mite plants herself into the brood cells of the honeycomb where the queen has laid an egg. The cell is then sealed as the egg hatches and the larva grows. During that time, the female mite lays her eggs on the larva so that when the new bee emerges from the cell to join the workforce, it already has mites and is in a weakened state. Since worker bees and beekeepers alike can't see into the capped cell, no one knows how many of the capped cells are infested, and once the cell is uncapped, several more mites can harm the colony. This reproduction method makes the mites very difficult to get rid of as, at any given time, ______________

**15**

Which choice most logically completes the text?

Ⓐ the queen bee will have the resilience to overcome any infestation that manifests.

Ⓑ the number of worker bees in a colony exceeds the number of drone bees.

Ⓒ a beekeeper can utilize thermal imagery to detect the presence of mites in the cells.

Ⓓ there are more mites breeding in capped cells that mite treatments may not reach.

Originating in13th-century Japan, haikus were originally used as openings for longer poems called renga poems. But it wasn't until Matsuo Bashō redefined haiku poetry that it __________ what it is today.

**16**

Which choice completes the text so that it conforms to the conventions of Standard English?

Ⓐ becoming
Ⓑ becomed
Ⓒ became
Ⓓ becomes

When taking out a loan, the fine print is key. It is important to understand the differences between fixed __________ throughout the term of the loan, and adjustable interest rates, which can change over time.

**17**

Which choice completes the text so that it conforms to the conventions of Standard English?

Ⓐ interest rates, that remain constant
Ⓑ interest rates, which remain constant
Ⓒ interest rates which remain constant
Ⓓ interest rates; remain constant

After the varnish is removed, repair can finally begin. New varnish can be applied and, before it dries, new paint can be mixed into the varnish on damaged areas to replace damaged paint. This method __________ for the old paint to be preserved under the varnish, but for the painting to have a "face lift" and look like new on the surface.

**18**

Which choice completes the text so that it conforms to the conventions of Standard English?

Ⓐ allowed
Ⓑ would of allowed
Ⓒ will have allowed
Ⓓ allows

For most students, social media is just a part of life. __________ inundated with pictures and videos from "influencers" who appear to live lavish lifestyles and pay for it through sponsorships and ad revenues that come from having a large social media following.

**19**

Which choice completes the text so that it conforms to the conventions of Standard English?

Ⓐ Regardless of what platform they're on; they are
Ⓑ Regardless of what platform their on they are
Ⓒ Regardless of what platform they're on, they are
Ⓓ Regardless, of what platform there on their

The layperson merely associates Newton with gravity and laws of motion, and Einstein with relativity and mass-energy equivalence, failing to understand the magnitude of __________ contribution.

**20**

Which choice completes the text so that it conforms to the conventions of Standard English?

Ⓐ either scientist's
Ⓑ either scientists'
Ⓒ each scientists
Ⓓ each scientists'

For the duration of the expedition, Commerson and Baret were aboard two different ships called the *Boudeuse* and the *Étoile*. During their trip, they went to the city of Montevideo, Uruguay; ____________________ and New Ireland, in the present-day Papua New Guinea.

**21**

Which choice completes the text so that it conforms to the conventions of Standard English?

Ⓐ the city of Rio de Janeiro, Brazil
Ⓑ the city of Rio de Janeiro: Brazil
Ⓒ the city of Rio de Janeiro, Brazil;
Ⓓ the city, of Rio de Janeiro Brazil,

Sweden's aggressive new policies during the Great Depression came with a price tag, particularly from its massive investment in public works projects. ______ creating a large federal deficit, in 1934 Sweden became the first country to fully emerge from the Depression, and foreign creditors were quickly recompensed.

**22**

Which choice completes the text with the most logical transition?

Ⓐ Despite
Ⓑ For
Ⓒ By
Ⓓ With

Humorism held medical discovery back for centuries at a time when the pure sciences were preparing for a renaissance; it established a systemic insularity in the field that cut medicine off from discoveries in biology, chemistry, and physics, and generated a remarkably long-lived illusion of comprehensiveness that categorically rejected revision and innovation. ________ humorism was a far more persistent enemy of medical science than was superstition because it wore the guise of naturalism.

**23**

Which choice completes the text with the most logical transition?

Ⓐ Somewhat
Ⓑ In contrast,
Ⓒ Further,
Ⓓ Because of this,

When people understand the idea of time and diversification, they need one final thing to help them be successful in the marketplace: a sense of calm. Panic buying and selling is never a good idea. If an account was started early and properly diversified, ______ severe market downturns should not incite panic. Instead, clear-thinking investors will see that the market will correct; rather than "selling low," investors wait for the upswing (and maybe longer) in order to see the payout on their investments.

**24**

Which choice completes the text with the most logical transition?

Ⓐ thus
Ⓑ even
Ⓒ so
Ⓓ while

While conducting research, a student took these notes:

- In addition to the well-known IQ (Intelligence Quotient), people also have varying levels of EQ (Emotional Quotient), SQ (Social Quotient), and AQ (Adversity Quotient).
- People who develop IQ but not any emotional or social skills may struggle to succeed even if they are incredibly intelligent.
- AQ is a measure of how well people bounce back from adversarial events.
- A person without a degree of AQ may quickly give up in the face of adversity and may see failures as permanent situations instead of learning opportunities.
- Parents should work to ensure that a variety of skills, not just academic prowess, are developed in early childhood.

**25**

The student wants to introduce the concept of AQ to an audience already familiar with the concept of IQ. Which choice most effectively uses relevant information from the notes to accomplish this goal?

Ⓐ In contrast to IQ, AQ examines the personal characteristic most important to personal success.
Ⓑ Unlike IQ, AQ is less focused on intelligence and more on personal grit when faced with adversity.
Ⓒ While people can succeed without AQ, it is impossible to do so without IQ.
Ⓓ Between IQ and AQ, AQ is more important to academic achievement.

While researching a topic, a student has taken the following notes:

- There are many high- and low-tech ways to implement sustainable agriculture.
- Stover mulching uses leftover plant material to regenerate the soil and reduce water run-off.
- Genome editing of plants like rice can increase the efficiency with which the plant uses nutrients in the soil.
- Silt traps prevent agricultural run-off from reaching vulnerable waterways.
- Companion planting involves planting mutually beneficial crops closely to increase their success.

**26**

The student wants to suggest a low-tech way of implementing a sustainable agricultural practice. Which choice most effectively uses relevant information from the notes to accomplish this goal?

Ⓐ Factory manufacturing of silt traps can prevent river pollution.

Ⓑ When two companion plants are grown near one another, they both benefit.

Ⓒ Scientists should utilize gene editing to decrease fertilizer waste.

Ⓓ Stover mulch can potentially be turned into renewable biofuels for transportation.

While researching a topic, a student has taken the following notes:

- There are different ethical theories about how to determine the morality of different actions.
- Utilitarianism considers if the benefits of an action outweigh its costs—if they do, then the action is considered ethical.
- Some summarize the idea behind utilitarianism as "the ends justify the means."
- Deontology is a competing ethical theory that considers actions to be ethical if they follow universal moral laws.
- Deontologists argue that people should follow ethical rules like "do not kill" or "do not steal," even if the costs to humanity outweigh the benefits; they believe following duty is more important than a cost-benefit analysis.

**27**

The student wants to give an example of an action that would be approved by a utilitarian but disapproved by a deontologist. Which choice most effectively uses relevant information from the notes to accomplish this goal?

Ⓐ A politician lies to secure higher office but implements helpful polices when elected.

Ⓑ A teacher strongly penalizes cheating, making students less likely to collaborate.

Ⓒ A mathematician makes a calculator error that results in a bridge collapsing.

Ⓓ A computer programmer creates a new programming language to enable improved virtual reality.

## Section 2, Module 1: Math

35 MINUTES, 22 QUESTIONS

**DIRECTIONS**

- All expressions and variables use real numbers.
- All figures are drawn to scale.
- Every figure lies in a plane.
- The domain of given functions is the set of all real numbers for which the corresponding value of the function is real.

For **multiple-choice questions**, solve the problem and pick the correct answer from the provided choices. Each multiple-choice question has only one correct answer.

For **student-produced response questions,** solve each problem and enter your answer following these guidelines:

- If you find **more than one correct answer,** enter just one answer.
- You can enter up to five characters for a **positive** answer and up to six characters (this includes the negative sign) for a **negative** answer.
- If your answer is a **fraction** that does not fit in the given space, enter the decimal equivalent instead.
- If your answer is a **decimal** that does not fit in the given space, enter it by stopping at or rounding up at the fourth digit.
- If your answer is a **mixed number** (like $4\frac{1}{2}$), enter it as an improper fraction (9/2) or its decimal equivalent (4.5).
- Do not enter **symbols** like a comma, dollar sign, or percent sign.

## Examples

| Answer | Acceptable Entries | Unacceptable Entries That Will Receive Zero Credit |
|---|---|---|
| 4.5 | 4.5<br>4.50<br>9/2 | $4\frac{1}{2}$<br>41/2 |
| $\frac{8}{9}$ | 8/9<br>.8888<br>.8889<br>0.888<br>0.889 | 0.88<br>.88<br>.89<br>0.89 |
| $-\frac{1}{9}$ | −1/9<br>−.1111<br>−0.111 | −.11<br>−0.11 |

**REFERENCE**

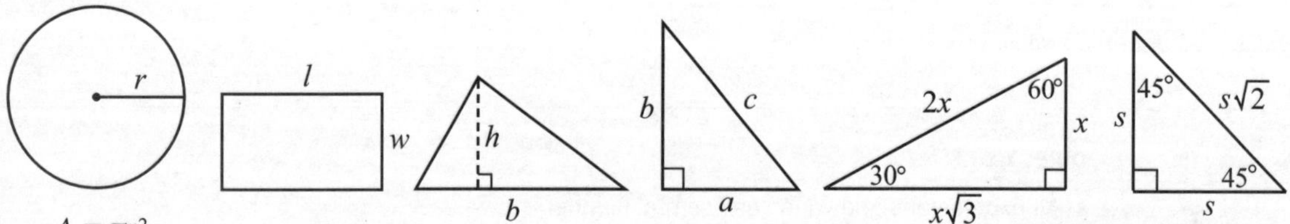


$A = \pi r^2$
$C = 2\pi r$

$A = lw$

$A = \frac{1}{2}bh$

$c^2 = a^2 + b^2$

Special Right Triangles

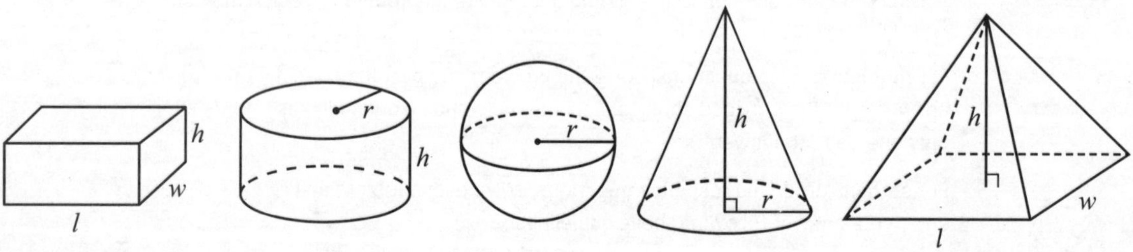


$V = lwh$

$V = \pi r^2 h$

$V = \frac{4}{3}\pi r^3$

$V = \frac{1}{3}\pi r^2 h$

$V = \frac{1}{3}lwh$

The number of degrees of arc in a circle is 360.
The number of radians of arc in a circle is $2\pi$.
The sum of the measures in degrees of the angles of a triangle is 180.

# 2 MODULE 1 2

**1**

If $x = 5$, what is $3(x + 2) - 2x$?

Ⓐ 5
Ⓑ 9
Ⓒ 11
Ⓓ 13

**2**

$-3(x^2 - 2x + 4)$ is equivalent to which of the following expressions?

Ⓐ $-3x^2 - 6x + 12$
Ⓑ $-3x^2 - 6x - 12$
Ⓒ $-3x^2 - 6x + 12$
Ⓓ $-3x^2 + 6x - 12$

**3**

| Letter Grade | Percentage of Students with That Grade |
|---|---|
| **A** (90–100%) | 26 |
| **B** (80–99%) | 33 |
| **C** (70–79%) | 21 |
| **D** (60–69%) | 13 |
| **F** (<60%) | 7 |

The table above presents the percentage of students in a class with particular letter grades. What letter grade is the median grade for the class?

Ⓐ A
Ⓑ B
Ⓒ C
Ⓓ D

**4**

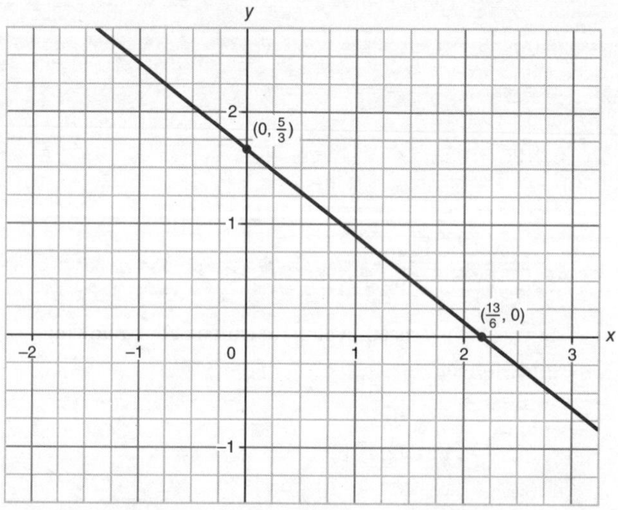


What is the slope of the line in the above graph in the *xy*-coordinate plane?

Ⓐ $-\frac{13}{4}$

Ⓑ $-\frac{10}{13}$

Ⓒ $-\frac{1}{3}$

Ⓓ $\frac{7}{4}$

**5**

What is the product of the solutions to the equation $0 = \left(x + \frac{1}{4}\right)\left(x - \frac{2}{3}\right)$ ?

Ⓐ $-\frac{1}{12}$

Ⓑ $-\frac{1}{6}$

Ⓒ $\frac{1}{4}$

Ⓓ $\frac{5}{12}$

2 MODULE 1 2

6

At a certain college, 27% of all students majored in science or mathematics. If there were a total of 4,000 students at the college, how many of the students would have a science or mathematics major?

Ⓐ 1,080
Ⓑ 2,920
Ⓒ 14,815
Ⓓ 108,000

7

Mark consistently sleeps for 8 hours per day. Which expression gives the number of hours that Mark would sleep in $W$ weeks?

Ⓐ $56 \times W$
Ⓑ $8 \times W$
Ⓒ $8 + W$
Ⓓ $56 + W$

8

If $x^3 = \frac{27}{8}$, what is the value of $x$?

Ⓐ $\frac{1}{3}$
Ⓑ $\frac{3}{4}$
Ⓒ $\frac{3}{2}$
Ⓓ $\frac{9}{4}$

9

$$B = 2P + 3E$$

A bagel store charges $2 for each plain bagel, $P$, and $3 for each everything bagel, $E$. The equation above represents the total amount, $B$, that Samantha paid for a box of bagels. If the box cost a total of $40 and Samantha purchased 4 everything bagels, how many plain bagels did she purchase?

**10**

A circle with an original area of $16\pi$ units increases in area by 56.25%. What is the radius of the new circle?

Ⓐ 5 units
Ⓑ 6 units
Ⓒ 10 units
Ⓓ 25 units



**11**

$$3x - 4y = -2$$
$$x + y = 11$$

Given that $(x, y)$ is a solution to the above system of equations, what is the value of $x$?

**12**

If the city of Detroit has a population of 4,900 persons per square mile, and there are 139 square miles of land within the city, what would most closely approximate the total population of the city?

Ⓐ 35,000
Ⓑ 47,000
Ⓒ 681,000
Ⓓ 1,240,000

**13**

If $\frac{x^2 - 4}{3} = 7$ and $x - 2 = 3$, what is the value of $x + 2$?

2 MODULE 1 2

**14**

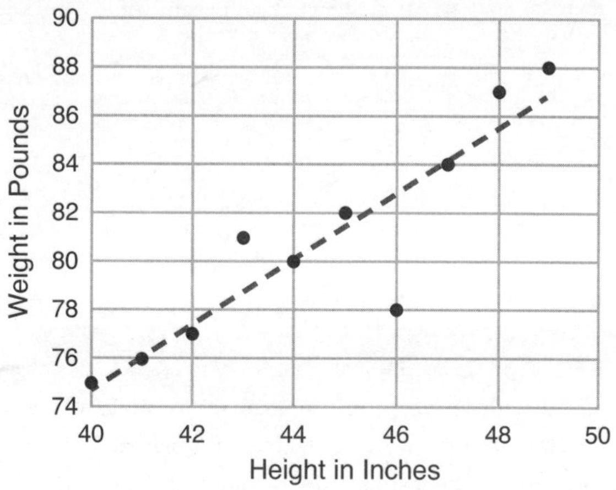


The height in inches and weight in pounds for several female orangutans is graphed in the scatterplot above. Based on the data in the graph, which of these statements best summarizes the overall trend in the data?

Ⓐ The greater the height of the orangutan, the greater the weight.
Ⓑ The lower the height of the orangutan, the greater the weight.
Ⓒ The greater the height of the orangutan, the lower the weight.
Ⓓ The height and the weight of the orangutan are equivalent throughout the set of data.

**15**

A cylindrical tank has base with a diameter of 10 feet and a volume of $300\pi$ cubic feet. What is the height of this tank in feet?

Ⓐ 8
Ⓑ 10
Ⓒ 12
Ⓓ 16

2 MODULE 1 2

16

If the function $f(x) = \frac{x^2 + 3}{2x}$ when $x \neq 0$, what is the value of $f(6)$ ?

Ⓐ $-\frac{7}{3}$

Ⓑ $\frac{2}{9}$

Ⓒ 1

Ⓓ $\frac{13}{4}$



17

After a presidential debate, viewers could go to an online poll and vote for which of the two candidates they thought won the debate. Approximately 2,500 viewers chose to fill out responses. Would the results from the online poll provide an accurate representation of opinions of all likely voters as to whom they thought won the debate?

Ⓐ Yes, because the sample of viewers was random.

Ⓑ Yes, because the number of respondents was sufficiently large.

Ⓒ No, because the respondents were self-selected instead of randomly selected.

Ⓓ No, because the number of respondents was insufficient.

18

| $x$ | $y$ |
|---|---|
| 2 | 5 |
| 6 | 15 |
| 10 | 25 |

The relationship between the values in the table above can be expressed as the function $y = kx$, in which $k$ is a constant value. What is the value of $k$?

**19**

In the *xy*-plane, which of these equations would represent the graph of $y = x^2 - 4$ shifted upward five units?

Ⓐ $y = x^2 - 5$
Ⓑ $y = x^2 - 1$
Ⓒ $y = x^2 + 1$
Ⓓ $y = 5x^2 - 4$

**20**

$$y \geq x + n$$

When the ordered pair $(2, 5)$ is a solution for $(x, y)$ in the inequality above, what is the greatest possible value for $n$?

Ⓐ 3
Ⓑ 5
Ⓒ 8
Ⓓ 12

**21**

| | Actually Has Illness | Actually Does Not Have Illness |
|---|---|---|
| **Positive Test Result** | 5 | 20 |
| **Negative Test Result** | 0 | 800 |

If a randomly selected patient who participated in the study with the results given above has a positive test result (i.e., the test indicates that someone has an illness), what is the probability that the result is a *false* positive?

Ⓐ 0.5
Ⓑ 0.8
Ⓒ 0.9
Ⓓ 1.2

22

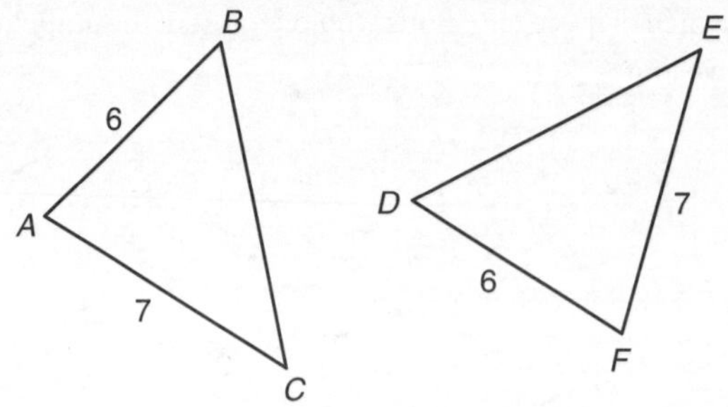


Triangles *ABC* and *DEF* both have sides of length 6 and 7 as shown above. Which of the following would, if true, be sufficient to prove that the triangles are congruent?

Ⓐ That angle *BAC* equals angle *DEF*
Ⓑ That angle *CBA* equals angle *EDF*
Ⓒ That angle *BAC* equals angle *DFE*
Ⓓ That angle *ABC* equals angle *FED*

# Section 2, Module 2: Math

35 MINUTES, 22 QUESTIONS

**DIRECTIONS**

- All expressions and variables use real numbers.
- All figures are drawn to scale.
- Every figure lies in a plane.
- The domain of given functions is the set of all real numbers for which the corresponding value of the function is real.

For **multiple-choice questions**, solve the problem and pick the correct answer from the provided choices. Each multiple-choice question has only one correct answer.

For **student-produced response questions,** solve each problem and enter your answer following these guidelines:

- If you find **more than one correct answer,** enter just one answer.
- You can enter up to five characters for a **positive** answer and up to six characters (this includes the negative sign) for a **negative** answer.
- If your answer is a **fraction** that does not fit in the given space, enter the decimal equivalent instead.
- If your answer is a **decimal** that does not fit in the given space, enter it by stopping at or rounding up at the fourth digit.
- If your answer is a **mixed number** (like $4\frac{1}{2}$), enter it as an improper fraction (9/2) or its decimal equivalent (4.5).
- Do not enter **symbols** like a comma, dollar sign, or percent sign.

## Examples

| Answer | Acceptable Entries | Unacceptable Entries That Will Receive Zero Credit |
|---|---|---|
| 4.5 | 4.5<br>4.50<br>9/2 | $4\frac{1}{2}$<br>41/2 |
| $\frac{8}{9}$ | 8/9<br>.8888<br>.8889<br>0.888<br>0.889 | 0.88<br>.88<br>.89<br>0.89 |
| $-\frac{1}{9}$ | −1/9<br>−.1111<br>−0.111 | −.11<br>−0.11 |

PRACTICE TEST 1

**REFERENCE** ∨

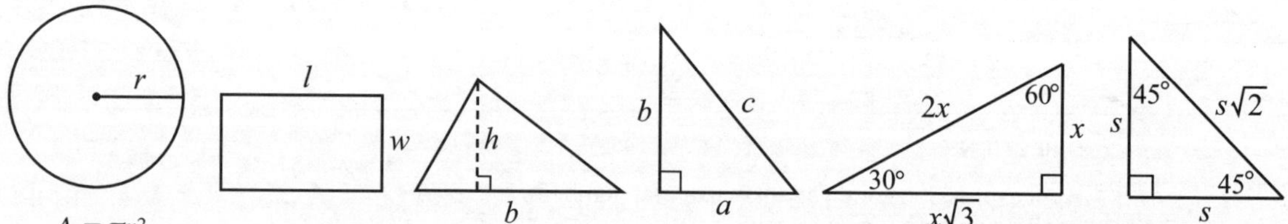


$A = \pi r^2$
$C = 2\pi r$

$A = lw$

$A = \frac{1}{2}bh$

$c^2 = a^2 + b^2$

Special Right Triangles

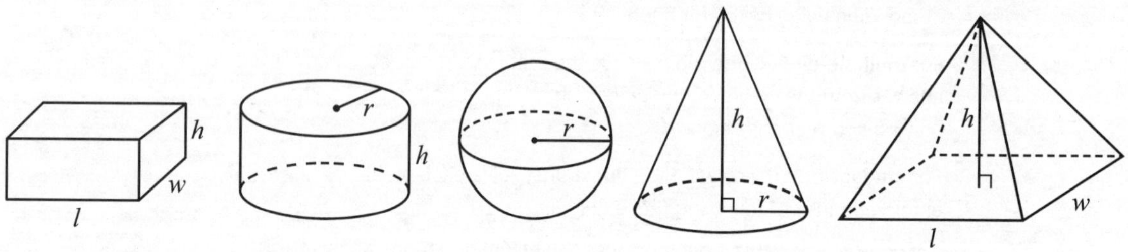


$V = lwh$

$V = \pi r^2 h$

$V = \frac{4}{3}\pi r^3$

$V = \frac{1}{3}\pi r^2 h$

$V = \frac{1}{3}lwh$

The number of degrees of arc in a circle is 360.
The number of radians of arc in a circle is $2\pi$.
The sum of the measures in degrees of the angles of a triangle is 180.

# 2 MODULE 2 2

**1**

If $5x + 2 = 4(x - 3)$, what is the value of $x$?

Ⓐ $-14$
Ⓑ $-11$
Ⓒ $-7$
Ⓓ $3$

**2**

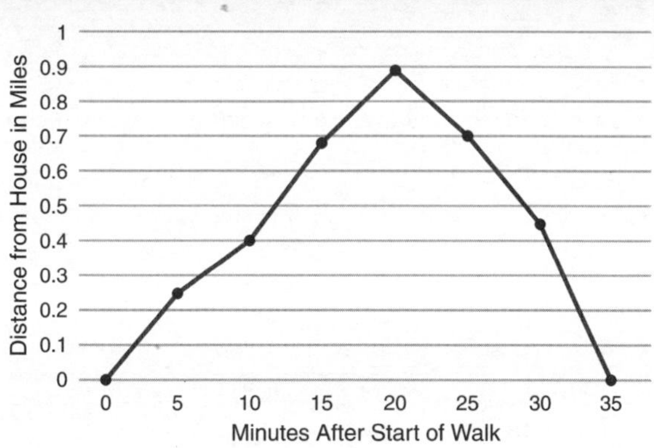


Tyrese takes a walk around his neighborhood. The distance he is in miles from his house at a particular number of minutes after beginning his walk is represented in the graph above. At what interval of time in his walk did the distance he is from his house decrease most rapidly?

Ⓐ 0–5 minutes
Ⓑ 15–20 minutes
Ⓒ 25–30 minutes
Ⓓ 30–35 minutes

**3**

If $\frac{1}{3}(x - 2) = y$ and $x = 5$, what is the value of $y$?

PRACTICE TEST 1

**4**

If a line has a slope of 5 and a $y$-intercept of $k$, what is the value of $k$ if the points $(1, 8)$ and $(3, 18)$ are in the line?

Ⓐ 3
Ⓑ 5
Ⓒ 9
Ⓓ 24

**5**

$$\frac{x^2 - 9}{x - 3}$$

Which of the following is equivalent to the above expression, in which $x \neq 3$ ?

Ⓐ $x^2 - 2$
Ⓑ $x^3 - 1$
Ⓒ $x - 9$
Ⓓ $x + 3$

**6**

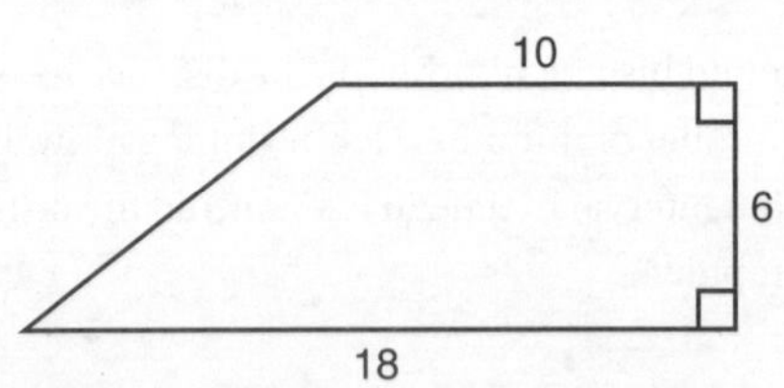


How many units is the perimeter of the above trapezoid?

# 2 MODULE 2 2

**7**

A fruit stand charges a different amount depending on the number of pieces of fruit in a box:

| Number of Pieces of Fruit in the Box | Cost of Box |
|---|---|
| 6 | $13.40 |
| 12 | $25.40 |
| 20 | $41.40 |
| 32 | $65.40 |

What function could be used to determine the total cost, $C$, of a box that has $x$ pieces of fruit?

Ⓐ $C(x) = -x + 2.40$
Ⓑ $C(x) = 2x + 1.40$
Ⓒ $C(x) = 1.4x + 3$
Ⓓ $C(x) = 2.8x + 1$

**8**

Kinetic energy, $K$, is calculated using the following formula, in which $m =$ mass, and $v =$ velocity.

$$K = \frac{1}{2}mv^2$$

What is the velocity in terms of the other variables?

Ⓐ $v = 2Km$
Ⓑ $v = \sqrt{\frac{2K}{m}}$
Ⓒ $v = \sqrt{\frac{2m}{K}}$
Ⓓ $v = 2m^2\sqrt{K}$

**9**

A data set of 15 different numbers has a median of 25 and a mean of 30. If the smallest member of the set has 5 subtracted from it and the largest member has 20 added to it, while all the other elements remain the same, which of these is a correct statement?

Ⓐ The standard deviation of the set changes more than the range of the set
Ⓑ The range of the set changes more than the standard deviation of the set.
Ⓒ The range of the set remains the same.
Ⓓ The standard deviation of the set remains the same.

**10**

Consider the sum of the expressions $-x^2 + 4x - 3$ and $5x^2 - 2x + 8$. If the sum is written in the form $gx^2 + hx + k$, where $g$, $h$, and $k$ are constants, what is the value of $k$?

Ⓐ 1
Ⓑ 3
Ⓒ 4
Ⓓ 5

**11**

In the $xy$-plane, a line passes through the points $(5, 0)$ and $(0, 3)$. Another line is perpendicular to this line. What would be this perpendicular line's slope?

**12**

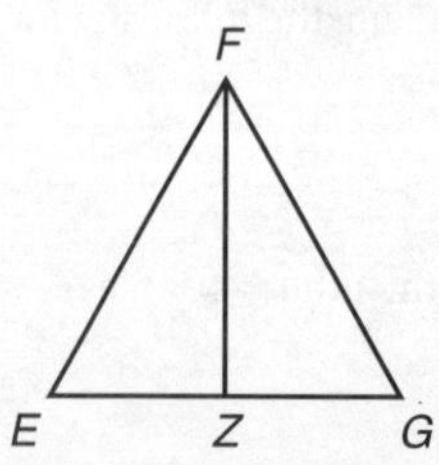


Triangle $EFG$ is equilateral. If $\overline{EF}$ is 10 units long, and $\angle EFZ$ is 30°, what is the length of $\overline{FZ}$?

Ⓐ $5\sqrt{3}$
Ⓑ $5\sqrt{2}$
Ⓒ 10
Ⓓ $10\sqrt{2}$

2 MODULE 2 2

13

A particular multivitamin provides 300 mg of calcium, giving 23% of the recommended daily value of calcium for an adult. If another multivitamin provides 210 mg of calcium, approximately what percentage of a recommended daily value of calcium for an adult would it provide, to the nearest whole percent?

Ⓐ 8%
Ⓑ 16%
Ⓒ 20%
Ⓓ 44%

14

The measure of an angle is $\frac{2}{3}\pi$ radians. How many angles of this measure would be equivalent to 360 degrees?

15

For the system of inequalities $y \leq x + 2$ and $y \leq -x + 4$, when $y$ is at its greatest possible value, what is the corresponding value of $x$?

Ⓐ $-6$
Ⓑ $-2$
Ⓒ 1
Ⓓ 4

2 MODULE 2 2



**16**

| $x$ | $y$ |
|---|---|
| 1 | 2 |
| 2 | $\frac{1}{2}$ |
| 3 | $\frac{2}{9}$ |
| 4 | $\frac{1}{8}$ |
| 5 | $\frac{2}{25}$ |

Which function expresses the relationship between $x$ and $y$?

Ⓐ $y = \frac{2}{x^2}$

Ⓑ $y = \frac{4}{x^2}$

Ⓒ $y = \frac{1}{2}x^2$

Ⓓ $y = \frac{1}{6}x^3$

**17**

What is the result when $4x^2 - 3x + 2$ is divided by $x - 3$?

Ⓐ $4x - 9$

Ⓑ $12x^2 + 9$

Ⓒ $2x - 3 + \frac{1}{(x-3)}$

Ⓓ $4x + 9 + \frac{29}{(x-3)}$

**18**

$$y = x(x - 4)^2(x + 3)^2$$

In the above equation, how many unique $x$-intercepts does the graph of the function have?

Ⓐ 0

Ⓑ 1

Ⓒ 3

Ⓓ 5

# 2 MODULE 2 2

**19**

| | Bus | Walk | Total |
|---|---|---|---|
| **Elementary** | $a$ | $b$ | $c$ |
| **Middle** | $d$ | $e$ | $f$ |
| **Total** | 80 | 70 | 150 |

Consider the information in the table above with the variables representing numerical values. There are twice as many elementary school students as there are middle school students, and 60% of elementary school students take the bus. How many middle school students walk to school?

Ⓐ 20
Ⓑ 30
Ⓒ 40
Ⓓ 60

**20**

What values of $x$ would make the product of $\frac{2}{x}$ and $\frac{3}{(x-1)}$ undefined?

Ⓐ 0 only
Ⓑ −1 only
Ⓒ 0 and 1 only
Ⓓ −1 and 0 only

**21**

For a parabola with the equation $y = 7(x-5)(x+2)$, what is the distance between the $x$ intercepts of the parabola?

**22**

If $(x+5)(x+3) = ax^2 + bx + c$, in which $a$, $b$, and $c$ are all constants, what is the value of $c$?

# ANSWER KEY
## Practice Test 1

### Section 1, Module 1: Reading and Writing

1. **D**
2. **C**
3. **B**
4. **C**
5. **D**
6. **C**
7. **B**
8. **B**
9. **D**
10. **B**
11. **C**
12. **D**
13. **B**
14. **D**
15. **C**
16. **A**
17. **D**
18. **D**
19. **A**
20. **B**
21. **C**
22. **C**
23. **A**
24. **D**
25. **A**
26. **C**
27. **B**

### Section 1, Module 2: Reading and Writing

1. **D**
2. **A**
3. **C**
4. **B**
5. **A**
6. **B**
7. **A**
8. **B**
9. **A**
10. **B**
11. **C**
12. **D**
13. **C**
14. **B**
15. **D**
16. **C**
17. **B**
18. **D**
19. **C**
20. **A**
21. **C**
22. **A**
23. **C**
24. **B**
25. **B**
26. **B**
27. **A**

# ANSWER KEY
## Practice Test 1

### Section 2, Module 1: Math

1. **C**
2. **D**
3. **B**
4. **B**
5. **B**
6. **A**
7. **A**
8. **C**
9. **14**
10. **A**
11. **6**
12. **C**
13. **7**
14. **A**
15. **C**
16. **D**
17. **C**
18. **2.5 or $\frac{5}{2}$**
19. **C**
20. **A**
21. **B**
22. **C**

### Section 2, Module 2: Math

1. **A**
2. **D**
3. **1**
4. **A**
5. **D**
6. **44**
7. **B**
8. **B**
9. **B**
10. **D**
11. **1.666, 1.667, or $\frac{5}{3}$**
12. **A**
13. **B**
14. **3**
15. **C**
16. **A**
17. **D**
18. **C**
19. **B**
20. **C**
21. **7**
22. **15**

## Digital SAT Scoring Chart

This will give you an approximation of the score you would earn on the Digital SAT.[1] Tally the number of correct answers from the Reading and Writing section (out of 54) and the Math section (out of 44). Take the total for each of these and find the corresponding section score in the tables below.

| Number of Correct Reading and Writing Questions (Out of 54) | Reading and Writing Test Score (Out of 800) |
|---|---|
| 0 | 200 |
| 1 | 210 |
| 2 | 220 |
| 3 | 230 |
| 4 | 240 |
| 5 | 250 |
| 6 | 260 |
| 7 | 270 |
| 8 | 280 |
| 9 | 290 |
| 10 | 300 |
| 11 | 310 |
| 12 | 330 |
| 13 | 340 |
| 14 | 350 |
| 15 | 360 |
| 16 | 380 |
| 17 | 390 |
| 18 | 400 |
| 19 | 410 |
| 20 | 430 |
| 21 | 440 |
| 22 | 460 |
| 23 | 470 |
| 24 | 490 |
| 25 | 500 |
| 26 | 510 |
| 27 | 520 |
| 28 | 530 |
| 29 | 540 |
| 30 | 550 |
| 31 | 560 |
| 32 | 570 |
| 33 | 580 |
| 34 | 590 |
| 35 | 600 |
| 36 | 610 |
| 37 | 620 |
| 38 | 630 |
| 39 | 640 |
| 40 | 650 |
| 41 | 660 |
| 42 | 670 |
| 43 | 680 |
| 44 | 690 |
| 45 | 700 |
| 46 | 710 |
| 47 | 720 |
| 48 | 730 |
| 49 | 740 |
| 50 | 750 |
| 51 | 760 |
| 52 | 770 |
| 53 | 790 |
| 54 | 800 |

[1] Keep in mind that some of the questions on an actual SAT test will be research questions that will not count towards your actual score. For the sake of simplicity, we are including possible research questions in your calculation.

| Number of Correct Math Questions (Out of 44) | Math Section Score (Out of 800) |
|---|---|
| 0 | 200 |
| 1 | 220 |
| 2 | 230 |
| 3 | 240 |
| 4 | 250 |
| 5 | 280 |
| 6 | 300 |
| 7 | 320 |
| 8 | 340 |
| 9 | 350 |
| 10 | 360 |
| 11 | 380 |
| 12 | 390 |
| 13 | 400 |
| 14 | 410 |
| 15 | 430 |
| 16 | 440 |
| 17 | 450 |
| 18 | 460 |
| 19 | 480 |
| 20 | 490 |
| 21 | 500 |
| 22 | 510 |

| Number of Correct Math Questions (Out of 44) | Math Section Score (Out of 800) |
|---|---|
| 23 | 520 |
| 24 | 530 |
| 25 | 540 |
| 26 | 550 |
| 27 | 560 |
| 28 | 570 |
| 29 | 580 |
| 30 | 590 |
| 31 | 600 |
| 32 | 610 |
| 33 | 620 |
| 34 | 630 |
| 35 | 650 |
| 36 | 660 |
| 37 | 680 |
| 38 | 690 |
| 39 | 700 |
| 40 | 720 |
| 41 | 750 |
| 42 | 770 |
| 43 | 790 |
| 44 | 800 |

Add the Reading and Writing section score and the Math section score to find your total SAT test score:

____________ Reading and Writing Section Score +

____________ Math Section Score =

____________ **Total SAT Test Score (between 400 and 1600)**

Approximate your testing percentiles (1st to 99th) using this chart:[2]

| Total Score | Section Score | Total Percentile | Reading and Writing Percentile | Math Percentile |
|---|---|---|---|---|
| 1600 | 800 | 99+ | 99+ | 99 |
| 1500 | 750 | 98 | 98 | 96 |
| 1400 | 700 | 94 | 94 | 91 |
| 1300 | 650 | 86 | 86 | 84 |
| 1200 | 600 | 74 | 73 | 75 |
| 1100 | 550 | 59 | 57 | 61 |
| 1000 | 500 | 41 | 40 | 42 |
| 900 | 450 | 25 | 24 | 27 |
| 800 | 400 | 11 | 11 | 15 |
| 700 | 350 | 3 | 3 | 5 |
| 600 | 300 | 1 | 1 | 1 |
| 500 | 250 | 1 | 1 | 1 |
| 400 | 200 | 1 | 1 | 1 |

[2] Scoring Data based on information at *collegeboard.org*

# Answer Explanations

## Section 1, Module 1: Reading and Writing

1. **(D)** "To call it a day" means to give up working. The boss in this text acknowledges that work is too difficult under the conditions, so it would be logical for him to suggest that everyone give up working. It is not choice (A) or (B) because continuing the work under these circumstances would not be advisable. It is not (C) because the focus is on work not pleasure.

2. **(C)** In this context, "reservations" means "doubts." This would be logical given that the two people had not gotten along very well the last time they hung out. It is not choice (A) because to detain someone is to hold them as a prisoner, which is not logical here. Choice (B) does not make sense because someone would not have land or "territories" when thinking about an invitation. It is not (D) because this is the opposite of the needed meaning.

3. **(B)** While all of the choices are in some way related to money or business, only "compensation" makes sense in terms of referring to the likely salaries that engineers could receive. "Expenditures" refers to general spending, "enterprises" refers to business activities, and "reimbursement" refers to receiving a refund for one's paid expenses.

4. **(C)** Later in the sentence with the underlined portion, the narrator states that the crash test dummy only represents the "smallest 5 percent of women," indicating that it is a smaller size. To say something is "scaled down" means that it is made to be smaller, making choice (C) the most logical option. It is not choice (A) or (B) because these would show that the model is increased in size. It is not (D) because this word means to shorten a non-physical object, like time or a word.

5. **(D)** The sentence is focused on scientific measurement, so "objectively" would be most appropriate. The other options would not be used to describe high-quality scientific measurement, but would instead apply to human emotions.

6. **(C)** This sentence provides a statistic and other context intended to show that advertising is pervasive, so choice (C) is correct. The other options don't consider the context prior to the sentence in which the author tries to persuade the reader that advertising is effective despite common opinion that one is immune to influence.

7. **(B)** The final line makes the comparison made throughout the poem most clear in that just as the United States now spans toward the Western Sea, so will the narrator's love. It is not choice (A) because the narrator does not indicate that he intends to lead the country. It is not (C) because the economic features of the states are not compared. It is not (D) because no direct allusion is made to the need for national harmony and a bloody conflict.

8. **(B)** Amory's relationship with his mother can be best seen through their dialogue. Amory's use of his mother's first name indicates that their affiliation is familiar, while her anxiety over him rising too early shows that it is a kindly relationship. So, choice (B) works best here, in which "friendly" refers to "approachable and informal." Using his mother's first name is far from traditional, as in choice (A). Since the mother finds it agreeable, there is no evidence that Amory is disrespectful as in (C). Choice (D) can be tempting because Amory not only uses Beatrice's first name in addressing her, but the narrator also tells us that Amory holds no illusions about his vain mother. However, "cold" and "distant" are too negative.

9. **(D)** This option most directly shows that the narrator wishes to reunify with her departed husband, since she states that if he is coming, he should be sure to let her know ahead of time so that she can meet him. Choice (A) focuses on the narrator's appearance and outdoor actions. Choice (B) would show that the narrator was not especially eager for a reunification. Choice (C) does not express emotion about missing the husband, but just states information about his journey.

10. **(B)** The final sentence of the text is providing an example to elaborate on the claim made in the previous sentence, which is that crops can aid the crop rotation process by either fixing or removing nitrogen. Since the text indicates that a legume is a nitrogen-fixing plant, the example would be completed by presenting a crop that would remove nitrogen from the soil—choice (B) is the best option since corn silage has the highest rate of nitrogen removal of any of the crops in the table. It is not choice (A) because barley has the lowest rate of nitrogen removal. It is not choice (C) or (D) since these incorrectly suggest that something with a low rate of nitrogen removal would be needed.

11. **(C)** The author makes an anecdotal argument in favor of lawsuit reform in this paragraph—the argument would be bolstered by using concrete statistics in support. Choice (C) would provide direct statistical support to make the case that implementing tort reform would result in businesses relocating to more tort-friendly locations. It is not choice (A) because this does not connect to tort reform. It is not choice (B) because this would undermine the author's argument, showing that having a greater possibility of lawsuit payouts would lead to greater social happiness. It is not choice (D) because this gives a reason unrelated to tort reform for business relocation.

12. **(D)** In these lines, our narrator voices his discontent with the requirements of school and his attention toward other "wild sensations," supporting the idea that his interest toward his studies is only half-hearted. Choices (A), (B), and (C) are incorrect because they do not provide evidence of the character's attitude toward following and participating in school requirements.

13. **(B)** The final sentence of the text starts by giving information that would seem to indicate that polar bears may be at risk for heart problems given their high bodily fat content and cholesterol levels. The transition "even so" shows that what follows in the sentence should contrast with what comes before. Choice (B) is the most logical option since it states that polar bears are in fact not at risk for heart attacks. Choice (A) does not provide a contrast, and choices (C) and (D) would be in agreement with the first part of the sentence instead of showing a contrast with it.

14. **(D)** Since the text states that Mendeleev's predictions cause the popularity of his theory to skyrocket, it makes sense that the periodic table would become extremely popular, making choice (D) the most logical option. It is not choice (A) because it would not make sense to state that Mendeleev received only a limited degree of credit because his theory skyrocketed in popularity. It is not choice (B) because these fields would not directly relate to chemistry. It is not choice (C) because Mendeleev had outlets in chemistry years before the periodic table became quite popular.

15. **(C)** Choice (C) properly uses parentheses to set aside the parenthetical phrase that describes what a baffle is. Choice (A) does not have an independent clause after the semicolon. Choice (B) incorrectly inserts a dash, which provides an unnecessary interruption. Choice (D) is too choppy with an unnecessary comma after "device."

16. **(A)** "Someone else" is a singular subject that agrees with the singular verb "has." All the other verbs are plural.

17. **(D)** Choice (D) puts the words in the most logical order, starting with a verb and then using the idiom "a bit out of style." The other options have illogical word order.

18. **(D)** "Help" would match both the plural subject of "professionals" and the present tense of the sentence as indicated by the verb "allow." Choice (A) is a singular verb, and (B) and (C) are not present tense plural verbs.

19. **(A)** Choice (A) uses the apostrophe to show that the singular serval possesses its diet. "Serval" must be singular since the word "a" precedes it. Choice (B) does not show possession, and (C) and (D) inappropriately use plural apostrophes on servals' and diets' respectively.

20. **(B)** The verb refers to the plural "states" and so requires a plural verb—"become." Also, the tense of the other verbs in the sentence is present, so "become" makes sense because it is also in the present tense. Choice (A) is singular, and (C) and (D) use incorrect verb tense.

21. **(C)** No punctuation is needed to break up this sentence. Choice (A) is incorrect since there is not a complete sentence after the semicolon. Choice (B) incorrectly breaks up a two-part list with a comma. Choice (D) incorrectly inserts a parenthetical phrase.

22. **(C)** Choice (C) appropriately uses dashes to set aside the parenthetical phrase that clarifies what the two things are. Choice (A) has an unnecessary comma after the parentheses—the parentheses would be sufficient by themselves to set this phrase off to the side. Choice (B) does not have a comma before the parenthetical phrase, and (D) uses inconsistent punctuation around the parenthetical phrase.

23. **(A)** "Whereas" is the only option that provides a contrast within the sentence between the ideas that a resume should be concise and that an online profile can be more thorough.

24. **(D)** "Hence" is the only option to indicate a cause-and-effect relationship between the fact that the housing market is challenging with its cost and unpredictability and the fact that as a result, many working-class families will face further financial instability.

25. **(A)** Choice (A) best emphasizes the physical demands of being a Gyoja monk since it states that they walk an incredible 52 miles a day with very little food and sleep. While choice (B) also refers to the physical demands, 25 miles a day is not as rigorous as 52 miles a day. Choices (C) and (D) do not focus on the physical demands of becoming Gyoja monks, instead focusing on the time and spiritual commitment involved.

26. **(C)** Choice (C) succeeds in making a generalization about the makeup of typical furniture since it states that the springs in the everyday furniture are more likely to be sinuous than coil, which is consistent with the notes. It is not choice (A) because this is the opposite of what the notes indicate. It is not choice (B) because the labor-intensive process only applies to coil springs as described in the notes. It is not choice (D) because the notes indicate that sinuous springs are more common, not that the springs are equally likely to be found.

27. **(B)** According to the notes, the wind speeds offshore "tend to be higher than on land," making choice (B) a logical reason why having an offshore wind farm could be better than a land-based one. It is not choice (A) because both offshore and land-based wind farms would provide renewable energy. It is not choice (C) because this is an argument in favor of land-based wind farms. It is not choice (D) because it points out a cost drawback of offshore wind farms.

## Section 1, Module 2: Reading and Writing

1. **(D)** The author uses an idiom in an ironic way, stating that despite a lack of common understanding, chemistry is extremely applicable to cooking, implying that this is something to think about. Choice (A) incorrectly understands it as stimulating one's appetite. Choices (B) and (C) inaccurately assume action rather than contemplation.

2. **(A)** "Drawback" is another way of stating that something is a shortcoming or problem. The narrator is discussing the problems with the ABC-X model, so "drawback" would make sense to introduce a sentence that describes another problem with this theory. It is not "assessment" or "rumination" as the narrator already has a negative opinion on the theory. It is not "trauma" because this is too negative.

3. **(C)** To "assure" is to remove doubt, and it is generally done to another person. I assured my father that I would be home by curfew. To "ensure" means to make sure a thing will or won't happen. I studied last night to ensure that I wouldn't fail the test. To "insure" refers to car insurance, life insurance, health insurance, etc. To "reassure" is simply to "assure" someone multiple times. In this sentence, the classrooms are ensuring that something will happen—students will be prepared for the next grade. Choice (C) is the correct answer.

4. **(B)** The narrator is drawing a contrast between something that may appear to be "trivial" while in actuality turning out to be significant—therefore, "substantive" makes the most sense because it means that whatever is being evaluated has substance. Choices (A) and (C) are overly negative, while "exuberant" does not draw a logical contrast with "trivial."

5. **(A)** The text asserts that certain things help cause the spread of bedbugs, making "agent" an appropriate word since in one of the less common definitions of "agent," it can mean something that helps bring about a specific effect. It is not "excursions" or "meanderings" since these buildings do not travel anywhere. It is not "hygienics" because the buildings are not sanitary.

6. **(B)** The text begins by stating that since young children are better suited to learning multiple languages, they can benefit from a wide range of positive effects. The text goes on to highlight some of these effects, such as increased cultural awareness and overall improvement in academic skill. Thus, choice (B) makes the most sense because the text provides evidence in favor of early learning of multiple languages. It is not choice (A) because the narrator does not argue that a specific language should be learned; rather, the narrator argues that multiple language learning in general is beneficial. It is not (C) because no specific curriculum is suggested. It is not (D) because the narrator argues that biological obstacles to early language learning are minimized if the language is learned earlier in life.

7. **(A)** The second text suggests that some emotional responses that Spielberg tries to evoke in his films may not always be "earned" because they are prompted by watching the character reactions instead of considering the content of what happened. The example in Text 1 has quite a bit of intellectual activity behind it, implying that an emotional response to this speech is based on something substantive instead of something manipulative. It is not choice (B) because the author of Text 2 does not express a concern with political activism. It is not choice (C) because the author of Text 2 clearly believes that emotion can be prompted by the expressions that actors have on the screen. It is not (D) because the author of Text 2 implies that some emotional responses can be earned.

8. **(B)** The text tells us that Jim was struggling to make it in New York. Then, he had a "brilliant marriage." The connection to "the daughter of a distinguished man" helped Jim advance in life. The implication, then, is that Jim married his wife for her connections. Additionally, the marriage between them prompted "sharp comment" at the time, suggesting that the motives for the marriage were considered suspicious. This makes choice (B) the best answer—the narrator believes Jim married his wife to advance his career. Choices (A) and (C) are incorrect as there is no evidence that Jim and his wife share any love. (D) is incorrect as we have no evidence that his wife sympathized with his poverty.

9. **(A)** In the second paragraph, the author describes the tremendous impact that printing has had on human history, saying that it "changed the destiny of Europe," and that it has "governed opinion," reigning over the mind of man. So, this influence can best be described as "extremely significant." It is not choice (B) because the influence of printing is relevant, not irrelevant. It is not (C) because the author suggests that printing has had a widespread influence, not that it has had a serious negative impact on society. It is not (D) because the impact of printing is more cultural, not militaristic.

10. **(B)** This option shows that the speaker believes that the "fiend of gambling" has made his father's "good resolutions transient, his promises vain," showing that he has an inability to follow through on his commitments. This is a great obstacle to the narrator's father since it has "fully possessed him." Choice (A) describes the father's early adulthood but does not indicate that it is a great obstacle. Choices (C) and (D) show a single obstacle his father faced (the declining favor of the king) but do not indicate that this was a large overall issue in his life.

11. **(C)** We can see in Figure 1 that the evening hours have the highest normalized occurrence rates of any time of day. We also see that in Figure 2, the Northern Hemispheric spring months of April, May, and June have the highest rate of tornado formation. Combined, this makes the evening hours in the spring the most likely time for a tornado to form. Choice (C) is the best option. The other options all have a lower likelihood of spawning a tornado.

12. **(D)** To give oneself entirely to the state means that someone would give up their personal ambitions and desires so that the society as a whole can benefit. Choice (D) most directly illustrates this since the individual would "alienate" himself to the whole community, giving up his rights. Choices (A) and (B) do not address the individual sacrifice of rights. It is not (C) because this suggests an opportunity for individuals to recover their rights should the social contract be violated.

13. **(C)** The economists hypothesize that if we look at the months after 2020, interest rates should decrease. Choice (C) correctly points out that mortgage rates generally decreased during this time period, providing an example in support of the claim. Choice (A) would not show a decrease. Choices (B) and (D) would show the opposite of what would support the hypothesis.

14. **(B)** Group 2 argues that the reason why Species X has been growing in population despite a loss of habitat is that the landscape has become more suitable for the bird. Choice (B) would directly support this idea because if there is more construction taking place, it stands to reason that there might be more fragmentation of land creating more edges along tree lines that the birds might prefer. It is not choice (A) because this does not show why south Ohio would be a good choice for the birds. It is not (B) because an increase in predators would likely kill

some of the birds, making the habitat less desirable. Also, choice (D) is incorrect because having more pollution in southern Ohio would be likely be detrimental to the birds.

15. **(D)** The text states that the bees cannot see into the capped cell, so they do not know if mites are growing inside the cells. Thus, choice (D) makes the most sense because it underscores how there are mites breeding that the treatments may not reach because they are inside the capped cells. It is not choice (A) or (C) because these options would instead show that the mites could be gotten rid of. It is not (B) because this would not be directly relevant to the claim made in the final sentence of the text.

16. **(C)** "Became" is consistent with the past tense seen in surrounding verbs, like "wasn't," "used," and "called." The other options are not in the proper conjugation for past tense.

17. **(B)** "Which" is used to set aside a nonessential description, while "that" is used at the beginning of an essential description. In this case, the clarification about the constancy of interest rates could be removed from the sentence and the sentence would still be logical. Therefore, surrounding the description of the fixed interest rates with commas make sense. It is not choice (A) because this is a nonessential description, and commas typically do not precede the word "that". It is not (C) because there is no pause before "which." It is not (D) because there is not a complete sentence after the semicolon.

18. **(D)** The surrounding sentences use verbs that are in the present tense, like "can" and "have." So, "allows" is both consistent with the present tense and the singular subject of "method." The other options are not in the present tense.

19. **(C)** This option uses the correct form of "they're," which means "they are." Also, it puts a comma after the dependent clause that introduces the sentence. Choices (B) and (D) use "their" and "there," which are incorrect in this context. Choice (A) incorrectly uses a semicolon to provide a break after a dependent clause—there needs to be an independent clause on either side of the semicolon when it is used to break up sentences.

20. **(A)** This needs a possessive to match the idea: the contribution of either scientist. As possession and an apostrophe are required, eliminate choice (C). Eliminate choices (B) and (D) for using the plural word "scientists" since the initial idea was the contribution of either scientist, not the contribution of both scientists.

21. **(C)** Choice (C) is the only option that correctly uses the comma and semicolon to indicate that this is part of a list—the items within the list have commas within them (separating each city name and country name/description), so semicolons are logically used to separate items in this list.

22. **(A)** The text begins by stating that Sweden had to spend quite a bit of money during the Great Depression, which would make it understandable if Sweden had not been able to repay its debts. The text goes on to state that Sweden quickly paid back its creditors, making a contrast to introduce the second sentence necessary. "Despite" is the only option that expresses a contrast.

23. **(C)** "Further" correctly indicates that what follows in this sentence will build upon the argument already presented. Choice (A) does not make a strong tie to the argument, (B) shows contrast, and (D) shows cause and effect.

24. **(B)** "Even" in this context is used to emphasize that severe market downturns should not incite panic. (A) causal link is already established with the "if" at the beginning of the sentence, making "thus" and "so" unnecessary. It is not "while" because there is not a contrast.

PRACTICE TEST 1

25. **(B)** If an audience is already familiar with the concept of IQ, they will know that IQ is associated with intelligence. Choice (B) builds off this understanding by drawing a contrast between AQ and IQ. It is not choice (A) because the notes indicate that AQ is an important component to success but does not indicate that it is the most important component. It is not choice (C) because the text does not suggest that IQ is totally unimportant to success. It is not (D) because the last bullet point implies that AQ is not necessarily key to academic prowess.

26. **(B)** While there are many ways that sustainable agriculture could be implemented, the student wishes to suggest a way of doing so that does not involve much technology. The last bullet point suggests that simply planting crops close to each other will increase their success, making (B) the most logical answer. The other options all involve more high-tech ways of implementing sustainable agricultural practices.

27. **(A)** According to the notes, a utilitarian looks at the outcomes of an action to determine if it is ethical, while a deontologist looks at whether the action was carried out in a rule-based way. Choice (A) is a good example of something that would be approved of by a utilitarian but not a deontologist: the politician is violating a rule against lying, but while in office the politician carries out policies that serve the greater good. It is not choice (B) because a utilitarian would not like the resulting lack of collaboration among the students. It is not choice (C) because a utilitarian would not appreciate the outcome of a collapsed bridge. It is not choice (D) because it is not clear whether any ethical rules would be violated in this action, making it uncertain as to whether a deontologist would disapprove.



## Section 2, Module 1: Math

1. **(C)** Plug 5 in for $x$ into the expression to find its value:

$$3(x+2)-2x \rightarrow$$
$$3(5+2)-2(5) \rightarrow$$
$$3(7)-10=21-10=11$$

2. **(D)**

$$-3(x^2-2x+4) \rightarrow$$
$$\text{Distribute the } -3 \rightarrow$$
$$-3x^2+6x-12$$

3. **(B)** The total number of students in the class is $26+33+21+13+7=100$. So, the median grade will be the average of the 50th and 51st term. The 50th and 51st terms, when the grades are put in order from least to greatest, are both (B). So, the median grade for the class is (B).

4. **(B)**

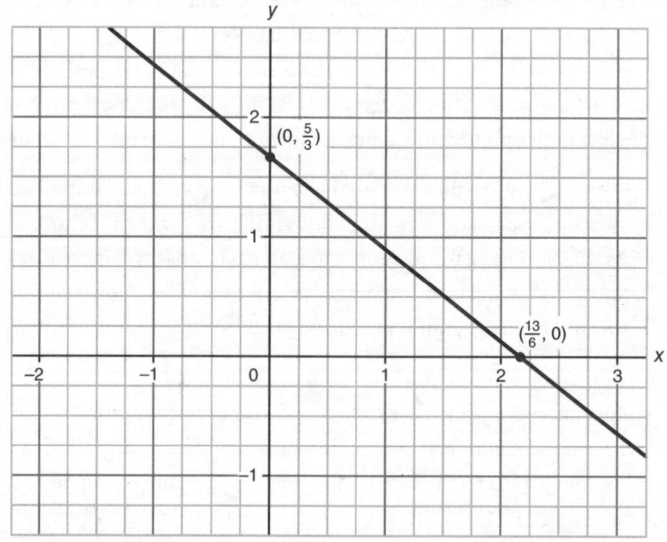


Take the change in $y$ divided by the change in $x$ to find the slope of the line. Use the points $\left(0, \frac{5}{3}\right)$ and $\left(\frac{13}{6}, 0\right)$, and the formula $slope = \frac{y_2 - y_1}{x_2 - x_1}$:

$$\frac{y_2 - y_1}{x_2 - x_1} = \frac{\frac{5}{3} - 0}{0 - \frac{13}{6}} = \frac{\frac{5}{3}}{-\frac{13}{6}} = \frac{5}{3} \times -\frac{6}{13} = -\frac{5 \times 2}{13} = -\frac{10}{13}$$

5. **(B)** The equation is already in a factored form that allows you to identify the solutions. If $x$ is $-\frac{1}{4}$ or $\frac{2}{3}$, the value of the right-hand side of the equation would be zero. Therefore, these two numbers are solutions. So, multiply them together to find the product:

$$-\frac{1}{4} \times \frac{2}{3} = -\frac{2}{12} = -\frac{1}{6}$$

6. **(A)** Find 27% of 4,000 to see how many of the students would have a science or math major. Move the decimal point of 27 to the left two spots, then multiply this by 4,000 to find the number of students:

$$0.27 \times 4{,}000 = 1{,}080$$

7. **(A)** There are 7 days in one week, so multiply the 8 hours Mark sleeps per day by 7 to find out the total number of hours he sleeps in a week: $7 \times 8 = 56$. Then, multiply 56 by the number of weeks, $W$, to find the number of hours that Mark would sleep in $W$ weeks: $56 \times W$.

8. **(C)** Take the cube root of both sides of the equation to solve for $x$:

$$x^3 = \frac{27}{8} \rightarrow$$

$$\sqrt[3]{x^3} = \sqrt[3]{\frac{27}{8}} \rightarrow$$

$$x = \frac{3}{2}$$

If $x^3 = \frac{27}{8}$, what is the value of $x$?

9. **(14)** Plug 40 in for $B$ and 4 in for $E$. Then solve for $P$:

$$B = 2P + 3E \rightarrow$$
$$40 = 2P + 3(4) \rightarrow$$
$$40 = 2P + 12 \rightarrow$$
$$40 - 12 = 2P \rightarrow$$
$$28 = 2P \rightarrow$$
$$P = 14$$

10. **(A)** Multiply $16\pi$ by 1.5625 to find what the area of a circle that is 56.25% greater in area would be. (This would represent 156.25% of the original circle—that is why we multiply by 1.5625 instead of just 0.5625.)

$$16\pi \times 1.5625 = 25\pi$$

Note that we only multplied the 16 by the 1.5625 so that we can identify the radius more easily. So, the new circle will have a radius of 5, since the area of a circle is $\pi r^2$ and the square root of 25 is 5.

11. **(6)** You can use substitution to solve for $x$. Take the second equation and find the value of $y$ in terms of $x$:

$$x + y = 11 \rightarrow$$
$$y = 11 - x$$

Then, substitute this in to the first equation to solve for $x$:

$$3x - 4y = -2 \rightarrow$$
$$3x - 4(11 - x) = -2 \rightarrow$$
$$3x - 44 + 4x = -2 \rightarrow$$
$$7x = 42 \rightarrow$$
$$x = 6$$

12. **(C)** Multiply the number of persons per square mile by the total number of square miles to find an approximation of the total population of the city:

$$4{,}900 \times 139 \approx 681{,}000$$

13. **(7)** Be sure to solve for "$x + 2$" and not just for $x$. The expression $x^2 - 4$ can be rewritten as $(x + 2)(x - 2)$, enabling you to plug in 3 for $x - 2$ and solve for $x + 2$:

$$\frac{x^2 - 4}{3} = 7 \rightarrow$$
$$\frac{(x - 2)(x + 2)}{3} = 7 \rightarrow$$
$$\frac{3(x + 2)}{3} = 7 \rightarrow$$
$$x + 2 = 7$$

14. **(A)** As the height of the orangutans increases, their weight also increases. Choice (A), "The greater the height of the orangutan, the greater the weight," correctly summarizes this trend.

15. **(C)** Use the volume formula for a cylinder, $V = \pi r^2 h$, in which $r$ is the radius and $h$ is the height. Note that this formula is provided in the formulas at the beginning of the section, so refer to it if you do not remember the formula. Since the tank has a base with a diameter of 10 feet, the radius will be 5. Plug in the volume and the radius into the formula to solve for height:

$$V = \pi r^2 h \rightarrow$$
$$300\pi = \pi(5^2)h \rightarrow$$
$$300\pi = 25\pi h \rightarrow$$
$$\frac{300\pi}{25\pi} = h \rightarrow$$
$$12 = h$$

16. **(D)** Plug 6 in for $x$ to solve for the value of $f(6)$:

$$f(x) = \frac{x^2 + 3}{2x} \rightarrow$$
$$f(6) = \frac{6^2 + 3}{2(6)} = \frac{36 + 3}{12} = \frac{39}{12} = \frac{13}{4}$$

17. **(C)** The number of respondents is sufficient to generalize on the voter preferences. However, the respondents were not randomly selected—they all chose to go to an online poll to vote for a particular candidate. People who chose to respond to the online poll are more likely enthusiastic about their political preferences; this self-selected group would therefore not accurately represent a cross-section of voters. The survey would have been more accurate if the respondents had been randomly selected instead of self-selected.

18. $\left(\mathbf{2.5 \text{ or } \frac{5}{2}}\right)$ Pick an ordered pair, (2, 5) would work, and plug it in to the equation $y = kx$ to solve for the constant $k$:

$$y = kx \rightarrow$$
$$5 = k(2) \rightarrow$$
$$k = 2.5$$

19. **(C)** Add 5 to the equation to shift the equation upwards by 5 units:

$$y = x^2 - 4 \rightarrow y = x^2 - 4 + 5 \rightarrow y = x^2 + 1$$

You can see the effect of this translation in the following graph:

PRACTICE TEST 1

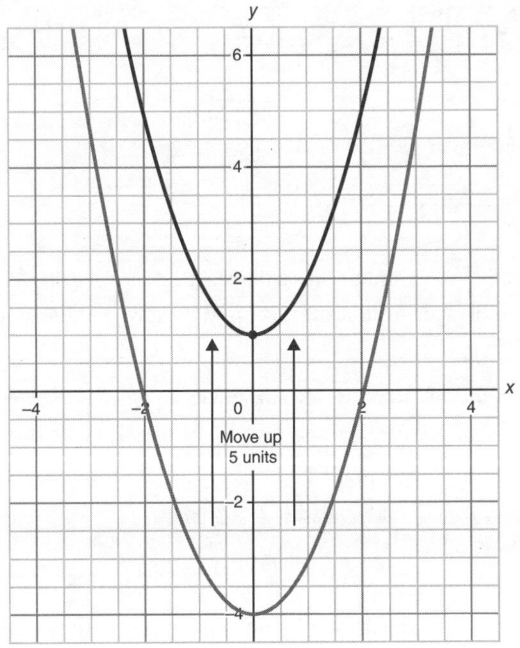


20. **(A)** Plug in 2 for $x$ and 5 for $y$, since this ordered pair represents a solution to the inequality:

$$y \geq x + n \rightarrow$$
$$5 \geq 2 + n \rightarrow$$
$$3 \geq n$$

Since $n$ must be less than or equal to 3, the greatest possible value for $n$ is 3.

21. **(B)** There are 25 patients who had a positive test result. Out of those 25 patients, 20 actually did not have the illness, meaning they had a false positive. So, divide 20 by 25 to find the probability that one of the positive test results was actually a false positive:

$$\frac{20}{25} = 0.8$$

22. **(C)**

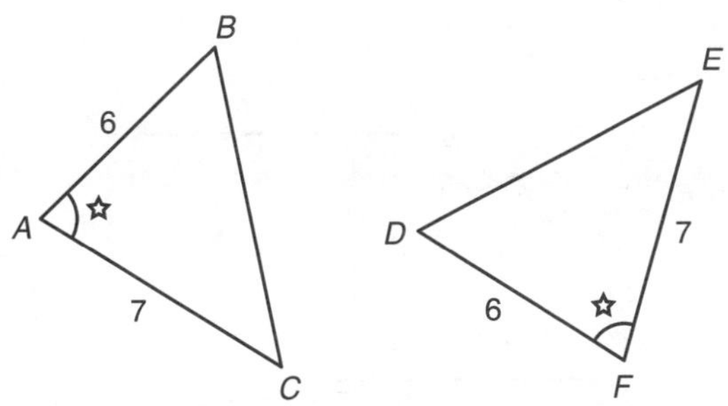


If angle *BAC* equals angle *DFE*, as labelled above, the triangles would be congruent because of the Side-Angle-Side theorem. This theorem states that if two sides and the angle formed by these two sides are equal to two sides and the included angle in another triangle, the two triangles are congruent.

## Section 2, Module 2: Math

1. **(A)**

$$5x + 2 = 4(x - 3) \rightarrow$$
$$5x + 2 = 4x - 12 \rightarrow$$
$$x + 2 = -12 \rightarrow$$
$$x = -14$$

2. **(D)** The interval from 30–35 minutes has a decrease in distance of 0.45 miles. This is the greatest decrease in distance over any time period portrayed in the graph, so choice (D) is the correct answer.

3. **(1)** Plug in 5 for $x$ to the equation to solve for the value of $y$:

$$\frac{1}{3}(x - 2) = y \rightarrow$$
$$\frac{1}{3}(5 - 2) = y \rightarrow$$
$$\frac{1}{3}(3) = 1 = y$$

4. **(A)** The equation can be written in slope-intercept form since it is a line. Use $k$ as the $y$-intercept:

$$y = mx + b$$
$$y = 5x + k$$

Now, plug in a point—we can use (1, 8)—for $x$ and $y$ to solve for $k$:

$$y = 5x + k \rightarrow$$
$$8 = 5(1) + k \rightarrow$$
$$3 = k$$

5. **(D)**

$$\frac{x^2 - 9}{x - 3} \rightarrow \frac{(x + 3)(x - 3)}{x - 3} = \frac{(x + 3)\cancel{(x - 3)}}{\cancel{x - 3}} = x + 3$$

6. **(44)** Since this is a trapezoid, the top and bottom sides are parallel to one another. So, you can inscribe a right triangle within the trapezoid to find the length of the unknown side, as seen below.

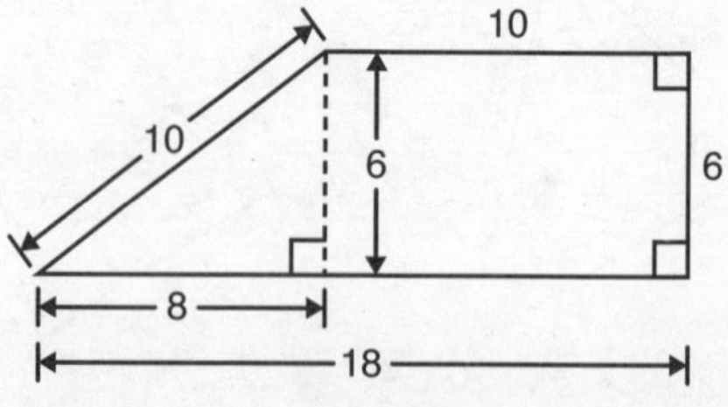


Then, add up the lengths of the sides to find the perimeter of the figure:

$$10 + 6 + 18 + 10 = 44.$$

7. **(B)** The functions are all in slope-intercept form, and they all have different values for the slope. So, find the slope of the function by using the slope formula and plugging in two points. The cost corresponds to the *y* values and the pieces of fruit will be the *x* value. Use the points (6, 13.40) and (12, 25.40) in the slope formula:

$$slope = \frac{y_2 - y_1}{x_2 - x_1} = \frac{25.40 - 13.40}{12 - 6} = \frac{12}{6} = 2$$

The only option that has 2 as its slope is choice (B). Alternatively, you could plug in values to the equations to see which one correctly models the numbers in the table.

8. **(B)** Manipulate the equation to isolate *v*:

$$K = \frac{1}{2}mv^2 \rightarrow$$

$$\frac{2K}{m} = v^2 \rightarrow$$

$$\sqrt{\frac{2K}{m}} = v$$

9. **(B)** The range of the set (difference between the least and greatest terms) will increase by 25, since the smallest member of the set has 5 subtracted from it and the largest member has 20 added to it. The standard deviation (the deviation from the mean) would increase slightly with these changes, but not nearly as much as the range would since the values of the other 13 members of the set will remain constant. So, choice (B) is the correct answer.

10. **(D)** Add the two functions together, combining like terms to put it in a simplified quadratic form:

$$\begin{array}{r} -x^2 + 4x - 3 \\ + \underline{5x^2 - 2x + 8} \\ 4x^2 + 2x + 5 \end{array}$$

In this combined equation, the number 5 corresponds to the constant *k*, making choice (D) correct.

11. **($\frac{5}{3}$, 1.666, 1.667)** First, find the slope of the line comprised of the two points (5, 0) and (0, 3).

$$\text{slope} = \frac{y_2 - y_1}{x_2 - x_1} = \frac{3 - 0}{0 - 5} = -\frac{3}{5}$$

Now, take the negative reciprocal of $-\frac{3}{5}$ to find the slope of a line perpendicular to this one:

$$-\frac{3}{5} \rightarrow \text{Flip the fraction and multiply by } -1 \rightarrow \frac{5}{3}$$

12. **(A)**

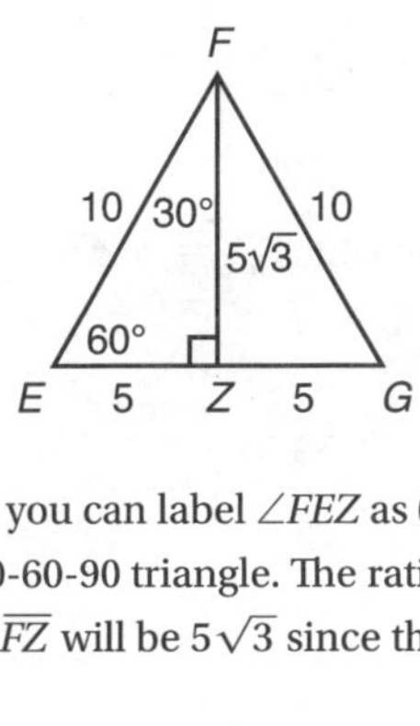


Since triangle *EFG* is equilateral, you can label ∠*FEZ* as 60 degrees. This turns triangle *FEZ* into a special right triangle—a 30-60-90 triangle. The ratios of the sides in a 30-60-90 triangle are $x$, $\sqrt{3x}$, $2x$. So, the length of $\overline{FZ}$ will be $5\sqrt{3}$ since the *x* in this case is 5.

PRACTICE TEST 1

13. **(B)** Since 23% of the recommended daily value of calcium for an adult is 300 mg, calculate the total recommended daily value of calcium for an adult, $x$, using this equation:

$$0.23x = 300 \rightarrow$$
$$x = \frac{300}{0.23} \approx 1{,}304$$

Now, find what percent of 1,304 that 210 is:

$$\frac{210}{1{,}304} \times 100 \approx 16\%$$

14. **(3)** $2\pi$ radians and 360 degrees both represent an entire circle. To see how many angles of the measure of $\frac{2}{3}\pi$ radians are in 360 degrees, divide $2\pi$ by $\frac{2}{3}\pi$:

$$\frac{2\pi}{\left(\frac{2}{3}\pi\right)} = \frac{2}{\left(\frac{2}{3}\right)} = 2 \times \frac{3}{2} = 3$$

So, there are 3 angles of this measure within 360 degrees.



15. **(C)** The greatest possible value for $y$ occurs when $y = x + 2$, since that would maximize its value within the inequality. Set $x + 2$ equal to $-x + 4$, since the value of $y$ would be at its maximum in both inequalities, and then solve for $x$:

$$x + 2 = -x + 4 \rightarrow$$
$$2x = 2 \rightarrow$$
$$x = 1$$

The correct answer is therefore choice (C).

16. **(A)** Try plugging in values from the table to determine which function correctly represents the relationship between the numbers. Before just plugging in numbers to every equation, think about the overall relationship of the numbers. As $x$ increases, $y$ decreases. So, choices (C) and (D) would not work because they would result in increasing functions. Then, you just need to try options (A) and (B). Use the ordered pair (1, 2) to see which of these would work:

$$y = \frac{2}{x^2} \rightarrow 2 = \frac{2}{1^2} \text{ which is true.}$$
$$y = \frac{4}{x^2} \rightarrow 2 \neq \frac{4}{1^2}, \text{ so choice (B) is incorrect.}$$

Therefore, the correct function is in choice (A).

17. **(D)** Use synthetic division to divide. Use 4, $-3$, and 2 as the values in the top of the synthetic division format and use $+3$ to go through the synthetic division steps.

$$\begin{array}{r|rrr} 3 & 4 & -3 & 2 \\ & & 12 & 27 \\ \hline & 4 & 9 & 29 \end{array}$$

This results in $4x + 9 + \frac{29}{(x-3)}$, in which $\frac{29}{(x-3)}$ is the remainder. You could also use long division to solve.

18. **(C)** A selection of the function is graphed below:

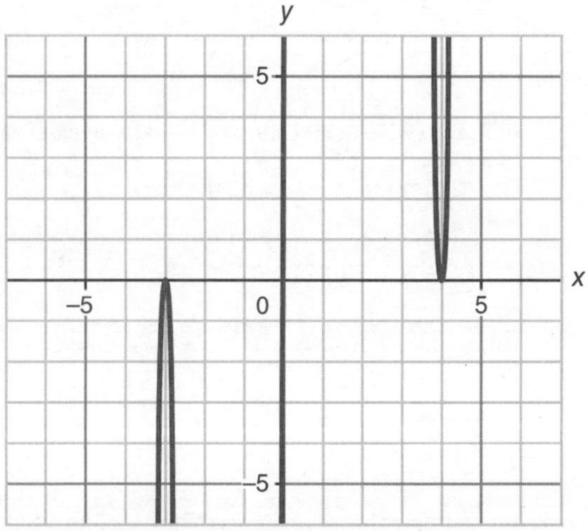


While the function has a high degree, it has only three unique $x$ intercepts: 0, 4, and $-3$. You can see this by examining the equation to see what values of $x$ would cause $y$ to equal zero. If $x = 0$, $x = 4$, or $x = -3$, the value of $y$ will be equal to zero.

19. **(B)**

Since there are twice as many elementary school students as middle school students, $c = 2f$ and $f = \frac{c}{2}$. The number of elementary school students and middle school students is 150, so find the value of $c$:

$$c + f = 150 \rightarrow$$
$$c + \frac{c}{2} = 150 \rightarrow$$
$$1.5c = 150 \rightarrow c = 100$$

So, we know that $c$ is 100.

Since 60% of elementary school students take the bus, find 60% of 100 to find the value for $a$: $0.6 \times 100 = 60$. Since the number of elementary school students is 100 total, subtract 60 from 100 to find the number of elementary school students who walk: $100 - 60 = 40$.

The total number of students who walk to school is 70 based on the table. So, find the number of middle school students who walk by subtracting 40 from 70:

$$70 - 40 = 30$$

To more easily visualize this, all the solved values for the variables are plugged into the spots in the table below:

| | Bus | Walk | Total |
|---|---|---|---|
| **Elementary** | 60 | 40 | 100 |
| **Middle** | 20 | 30 | 50 |
| **Total** | 80 | 70 | 150 |

20. **(C)** The product of these two expressions will be undefined if the denominator on either expression is equal to zero. For $\frac{2}{x}$, if $x = 0$, the expression is undefined. For $\frac{3}{(x-1)}$, if $x = 1$, the expression is undefined since the denominator $x - 1$ would equal zero if $x = 1$. So, the correct answer is choice C.

21. **(7)** The equation will equal zero when $x = 5$ and $x = -2$, as you can see below:

$$y = 7(x - 5)(x + 2) \rightarrow$$
$$y = 7(5 - 5)(5 + 2) \rightarrow$$
$$y = 7(0)(7) = 0$$

and

$$y = 7(-2 - 5)(-2 + 2) \rightarrow$$
$$y = 7(-2 - 5)(-2 + 2) \rightarrow$$
$$y = 7(-7)(0) = 0$$

So, the points (5, 0) and (−2, 0) are the $x$ intercepts of the parabola. Since the $y$ values do not change, simply find the difference between the $x$ values to find the distance between the $x$ intercepts:

$$5 - (-2) = 7$$

22. **(15)**

$$(x + 5)(x + 3) = ax^2 + bx + c \rightarrow$$
$$x^2 + 3x + 5x + 15 = ax^2 + bx + c \rightarrow$$
$$x^2 + 8x + 15 = ax^2 + bx + c$$

Since 15 is the only numerical constant, it will equal $c$ because the $c$ term on the right-hand side does not have an $x$ in it. So, the value of $c$ is 15.

# ANSWER SHEET
## Practice Test 2

### Section 1, Module 1: Reading and Writing

| | | |
|---|---|---|
| 1. ____ | 10. ____ | 19. ____ |
| 2. ____ | 11. ____ | 20. ____ |
| 3. ____ | 12. ____ | 21. ____ |
| 4. ____ | 13. ____ | 22. ____ |
| 5. ____ | 14. ____ | 23. ____ |
| 6. ____ | 15. ____ | 24. ____ |
| 7. ____ | 16. ____ | 25. ____ |
| 8. ____ | 17. ____ | 26. ____ |
| 9. ____ | 18. ____ | 27. ____ |

# ANSWER SHEET
## Practice Test 2

### Section 1, Module 2: Reading and Writing

| | | |
|---|---|---|
| 1. ____ | 10. ____ | 19. ____ |
| 2. ____ | 11. ____ | 20. ____ |
| 3. ____ | 12. ____ | 21. ____ |
| 4. ____ | 13. ____ | 22. ____ |
| 5. ____ | 14. ____ | 23. ____ |
| 6. ____ | 15. ____ | 24. ____ |
| 7. ____ | 16. ____ | 25. ____ |
| 8. ____ | 17. ____ | 26. ____ |
| 9. ____ | 18. ____ | 27. ____ |

# ANSWER SHEET
## Practice Test 2

### Section 2, Module 1: Math

| | | | |
|---|---|---|---|
| 1. | _____ | 12. | _____ |
| 2. | _____ | 13. | _____ |
| 3. | _____ | 14. | _____ |
| 4. | _____ | 15. | _____ |
| 5. | _____ | 16. | _____ |
| 6. | _____ | 17. | _____ |
| 7. | _____ | 18. | _____ |
| 8. | _____ | 19. | _____ |
| 9. | _____ | 20. | _____ |
| 10. | _____ | 21. | _____ |
| 11. | _____ | 22. | _____ |

# ANSWER SHEET
## Practice Test 2

### Section 2, Module 2: Math

| | | | |
|---|---|---|---|
| 1. | ____ | 12. | ____ |
| 2. | ____ | 13. | ____ |
| 3. | ____ | 14. | ____ |
| 4. | ____ | 15. | ____ |
| 5. | ____ | 16. | ____ |
| 6. | ____ | 17. | ____ |
| 7. | ____ | 18. | ____ |
| 8. | ____ | 19. | ____ |
| 9. | ____ | 20. | ____ |
| 10. | ____ | 21. | ____ |
| 11. | ____ | 22. | ____ |

# Practice Test 2

## Section 1, Module 1: Reading and Writing

32 MINUTES, 27 QUESTIONS

**DIRECTIONS**

You will be tested on a variety of important reading and writing skills. Each question has one or more passages, possibly including a graph or table. Carefully read each passage and question and choose the best answer to the question based on the passage(s).

Every question in this section is multiple-choice with four possible answers. Each question has only one best answer.

In science class, the two friends frantically mixed their chemical ingredients together. They had failed to meet over the weekend and their assignment was nowhere close to being finished. When they received a failing grade, the teacher remarked that the _______ to their problem lay in adequate preparation.

**1**

Which choice completes the text with the most logical and precise word or phrase?

Ⓐ solution
Ⓑ mixture
Ⓒ choice
Ⓓ origin

Thad walked through the tunnel to a loud applause. He strolled up to the pitching mound and breathed deeply to calm his nerves. He threw hard and fast but was _______. The catcher had to run and retrieve the wild pitch.

**2**

Which choice completes the text with the most logical and precise word or phrase?

Ⓐ off his mark
Ⓑ highly motivated
Ⓒ not on the mound
Ⓓ serene

The judge decided to __________ on some mistakes as it was his first case. She could remember fumbling through her opening argument the first time she was in court.

**3**

Which choice completes the text with the most logical and precise word or phrase?

Ⓐ provide the prosecutor with consequences
Ⓑ evoke carte blanche
Ⓒ give the prosecutor leeway
Ⓓ grant the prosecutor amnesty

Some bystanders overly concerned about potential litigation have chosen not to help for fear they would make the situation worse, thereby opening themselves up to lawsuits. Some states have passed varying degrees of protection known as "good Samaritan laws" so that people can feel comfortable helping. Some countries have even gone so far as to pass "duty to help" laws that generally require people to assist. While these laws are often criticized as legislating morality, they do help alleviate the negative ________ of the bystander effect.

**4**

Which choice completes the text with the most logical and precise word or phrase?

Ⓐ impacts
Ⓑ collisions
Ⓒ clashes
Ⓓ accomplishments

Poker players are fond of saying that if you look around the table and can't spot the fool, run away as fast as you can; you're it. The same goes for the world of finance, which has quickly become as adversarial as a duel at high noon. Such is the nature of equities, futures, bonds, and derivatives (to name a few): any transaction has both a winner and a loser. Either the buyer has purchased an instrument that is undervalued and will be worth more tomorrow, or the seller has unloaded a <u>bloated</u> instrument that will fall back closer to its "true" market valuation in the near future. Either way, dollars (both unrealized and actual) will flow from one pocket to another.

**5**

As used in the text, what does the word "bloated" most nearly mean?

Ⓐ overvalued
Ⓑ distended
Ⓒ full
Ⓓ waterlogged

# 1 MODULE 1 1

The following text is from Christina Rossetti's 19th-century poem "Who Has Seen the Wind?"

Who has seen the wind?
Neither I nor you.
But when the leaves hang trembling,
The wind is passing through.
Who has seen the wind?
Neither you nor I.
But when the trees bow down their heads,
The wind is passing by.

**6**

Which choice best describes the overall structure of the text?

Ⓐ It analyzes the patterns of weather formation.

Ⓑ It contemplates the meaning of new growth in nature.

Ⓒ It presents different ways that the invisible wind may be seen.

Ⓓ It considers the emotional impact that the wind can have on observers.

The following text is adapted from Daniel Defoe's 1719 novel *The Life and Adventures of Robinson Crusoe.* In it, the title character has left home despite his parents' wishes and sets out to find adventures on the sea.

We were not much more than a quarter of an hour out of our ship till we saw her sink, and then I understood for the first time what was meant by a ship foundering in the sea. I could hardly watch, for from the moment that they rather put me into the boat than that I might be said to go in, my heart was, as it were, dead within me, partly with fright, partly with horror of mind, and the thoughts of what was yet before me.

<u>We got all safe on shore, where, as unfortunate men, we were used with great humanity, as well by the magistrates of the town, who assigned us good quarters, as by particular merchants and owners of ships, and had money given us sufficient to carry us either to London or back to Hull as we thought fit.</u>

**7**

Which choice best describes the function of the underlined sentence in the text as a whole?

Ⓐ To show the scorn with which people treat shipwrecked sailors

Ⓑ To describe how those who experienced shipwrecks are treated with hospitality

Ⓒ To explain the envy that others have of those sailors who have been shipwrecked

Ⓓ To demonstrate how those who experienced shipwrecks are treated with humor

The following text is adapted from W. E. B. Du Bois's 1903 work "Of Sorrow Songs."

> What are these songs, and what do they mean? I know little of music and can say nothing in technical phrase, but I know something of men, and knowing them, I know that these songs are the articulate message of the slave to the world. They tell us in these eager days that life was joyous to the black slave, careless and happy. I can easily believe this of some, of many. But not all the past South, though it rose from the dead, can gainsay the heart touching witness of these songs. They are the music of an unhappy people, of the children of disappointment; they tell of death and suffering and unvoiced longing toward a truer world, of misty wanderings and hidden ways.

**8**

Based on the text, Du Bois's attitude toward those who would suggest that the songs of slaves expressed their happiness and joy is most likely one of

Ⓐ complete agreement.
Ⓑ qualified skepticism.
Ⓒ outright dismissal.
Ⓓ hopeful optimism.

The following text is from Harriet Beecher Stowe's 1852 novel *Uncle Tom's Cabin.* She presents a scene from a time when slavery was widely practiced.

> Late in the afternoon of a chilly day in February two gentlemen were sitting over their wine, in a well-furnished parlour in the town of P________ in Kentucky in the midst of an earnest conversation.
>
> "That is the way I should arrange the matter," said Mr. Shelby, the owner of the place. "The fact is, Tom is an uncommon fellow; he is certainly worth that sum anywhere; steady, honest, capable, manages my farm like a clock. You ought to let him cover the whole of the debt; and you would, Haley, if you'd got any conscience."
>
> "Well, I've got just as much conscience as any man in business can afford to keep," said Haley, "and I'm willing to do anything to 'blige friends; but this yer, ye see, is too hard on a feller, it really is. Haven't you a boy or gal you could throw in with Tom?"

**9**

Based on the text, Haley is best characterized as a/an

Ⓐ humane empathizer.
Ⓑ financial amateur.
Ⓒ aggressive negotiator.
Ⓓ passive mediator.

# 1 MODULE 1 1

| Career Office Service | Percent of Students Who Used Service | Percent of Students Who Found Service Helpful |
|---|---|---|
| **Practice Interviewing** | 31.2% | 69.9% |
| **Resume Assistance** | 74.5% | 68.4% |
| **Workshops** | 37.8% | 63.0% |
| **Job Listings** | 55.4% | 62.1% |
| **Researching Employers** | 32.2% | 60.5% |
| **Career Skills Testing** | 29.4% | 52.4% |

Information adapted from the *Class of 2017 Student Survey*, National Association of Colleges and Employers

The career services office at a college is analyzing the effectiveness of its offerings by evaluating student opinions about the services offered. Some students suggest that the career services office should offer services that students are more likely to find helpful. The administrator of the career services office argues, however, that career services can only be helpful to the extent that students use the services offered.

**10**

Which choice most effectively uses data from the graph to support the office administrator's position?

Ⓐ While 52.4% of surveyed students thought that career services testing would be helpful, only 29.4% of students took advantage of this offering.

Ⓑ Interview practice and resume assistance are among the most sought-out services by college students today.

Ⓒ Although 74.5% of surveyed students used career services resume assistance, only 68.4% of students found this service useful.

Ⓓ Nearly identical percentages of students found that the workshops and job listings provided through career services were helpful.

Physicians claim that broken-heart syndrome often presents symptoms like those of a heart attack but without the defining arterial blockage. Instead of plaque blocking the arteries, scientists believe surrounding muscles constrict the arteries, reducing the flow of blood to the heart and mimicking a heart attack. Unlike a heart attack, broken-heart syndrome is rarely fatal, and can even resolve itself within hours to weeks. Although patients often recover from this condition quickly, the stress that is thought to cause this condition may persist long after their so-called recovery. Unlike broken-heart syndrome, prolonged stress can have consequences on long-term heart health, resulting in heart disease, hypertension, and even stroke. Such consequences exemplify the importance of psychological health, as it can significantly affect one's physical health.

**11**

Which finding, if true, would most directly support the physicians' claim?

Ⓐ Researchers find that they can successfully differentiate between broken-heart syndrome and a heart attack by determining whether plaque is blocking the arteries.

Ⓑ Sociologists report that increasing numbers of people are experiencing a decrease in their mental health due to prolonged stress.

Ⓒ Psychiatrists find that there is a roughly equivalent likelihood of dying of broken-heart syndrome as there is from dying of a heart attack.

Ⓓ A randomly controlled survey of adults between 50 and 70 years of age finds that heart attacks are a greater source of worry than broken-heart syndrome.

# 1 MODULE 1 1

"On the Firing Line of Education" is a 1919 paper by A.J. Ladd, a professor of education at the State University of North Dakota. In the paper, Professor Ladd discusses the future of vocational education in American high schools. He asserts that schools should help guide students into their most appropriate vocational paths.

**12**

Which quotation from "On the Firing Line of Education" most effectively illustrates the assertion?

Ⓐ "Children in these early years are not yet ready to choose their work of life; that they do not yet sufficiently know themselves—their own tastes and capacities for such serious choice."

Ⓑ "To place before children such attractive objective features would result in swerving many from the normal pathway of their development and check it midway. The result has been what might be called a compromise."

Ⓒ "Thru the child-study movement the teacher comes to know child nature so well that direct application can be made to the individual child and an intimate knowledge gained of his tastes, capacities, ambitions, and dominant interests."

Ⓓ "The high school is an institution established by a community for community purposes—to take its young people—all of them—and guide them thru the difficult and transitional period of adolescence, directing, inspiring, shaping, checking, developing for the largest manhood and womanhood possible and providing the community with efficient workmen in various lines."

A student is studying Edmund Burke's 18th-century work *Selections from the Speeches and Writings of Edmund Burke*. The student is specifically analyzing the selection under the title "Colonies and British Constitution." This selection is believed to have been written shortly before the American Revolution and discusses the relationship between the United States and Great Britain. The student argues that Burke asserted that at the time he wrote the text, the recognition of civil rights for the citizens of countries around the world was relatively limited.

**13**

Which quotation from "Colonies and British Constitution" most effectively illustrates the argument?

Ⓐ "These are ties, which, though light as air, are as strong as links of iron."

Ⓑ "Slavery they can have anywhere. It is a weed that grows in every soil."

Ⓒ "Do not entertain so weak an imagination, as that your registers and your bonds . . . are what form the great securities of your commerce."

Ⓓ "Dead instruments, passive tools as they are, it is the spirit of the English communion that gives all their life and efficacy to them."

Microplastics are microscopic particles of plastic that tend to accumulate toxins and are in some cases toxic themselves. Unfortunately, microplastics tend to end up being eaten by various organisms. The primary reason for this problem is that in recent years, approximately 380 million tons of plastic are produced annually. Plastic is not biodegradable, which means that once it enters the environment it can take several hundred years to degrade. Some have proposed plastic-eating microorganisms as a revolutionary solution to this critical issue. Others are skeptical of the claims made about __________

**14**

Which choice most logically completes the text?

Ⓐ whether a bacteria could have any role in harming the environment.

Ⓑ the capacity of microbiologists to analyze bacteria in a laboratory setting.

Ⓒ this bacteria's utility in consuming massive plastic deposits.

Ⓓ the possibility of plastic extending the length it needs to biodegrade.

# 1 MODULE 1 1

According to Florentine records between the end of the fourteenth century and the middle of the fifteenth, the number of women participating in tribunals dropped by 84 percent. The implications of this backslide are significant. By 1450, the power of women to defend themselves in court had suffered a significant blow. And while weakness in the courtroom may not have significantly impacted the elite women of the upper classes, its effects were undoubtedly felt by working women of the lower classes, who were, by the late 1460s, __________

**15**

Which choice most logically completes the text?

Ⓐ essentially at the mercy of their accusers.
Ⓑ able to successfully cite legal precedents in court proceedings.
Ⓒ empowered with a spirit of judicial advocacy.
Ⓓ strong advocates of violent means to obtain justice.

Career websites like LinkedIn, Dice, and Monster make it simple to get started with your job search. ___________ work experience, intern or research positions, and volunteer efforts.

**16**

Which choice completes the text so that it conforms to the conventions of Standard English?

Ⓐ Within your online, profiles it is critical that you include information, about your educational background, previous
Ⓑ Within your online profiles it is critical that you include information about your educational background, previous
Ⓒ Within your online profiles, it is critical that you include information about your educational background, previous
Ⓓ Within your online profiles, it is critical that you include information about: your educational background, previous

Capsaicin, the compound in peppers that makes them spicy, only affects mammals, so ______ effective in driving away squirrels and rodents. Like humans, these animals are often sensitive to spicy foods.

**17**

Which choice completes the text so that it conforms to the conventions of Standard English?

Ⓐ it's
Ⓑ its
Ⓒ their
Ⓓ there

# 1 MODULE 1 1

According to Rognlie, the solution put forth in *Capital in the Twenty-First Century,* since it will do little to limit ________ returns on assets, is no solution at all.

**18**

Which choice completes the text so that it conforms to the conventions of Standard English?

Ⓐ homeowners'
Ⓑ homeowner's
Ⓒ the home owner's
Ⓓ homeowners

The machine shown in Picabia's drawing demonstrated his appreciation for the technology of his time. However, the machine he depicted did not serve any functional purpose, which he used to mock the excessive pride inventors ______ after successfully creating an invention.

**19**

Which choice completes the text so that it conforms to the conventions of Standard English?

Ⓐ feeling
Ⓑ have feeling
Ⓒ will felt
Ⓓ felt

Among the poems that he wrote during his lifetime, Bashō's 1686 haiku "The Old Pond" is his most well known and is, arguably, the best haiku of all time. ________ was inspired by nature: it describes the splashes a frog makes after it jumps into a pond.

**20**

Which choice completes the text so that it conforms to the conventions of Standard English?

Ⓐ Like many other haikus: Bashōs poem
Ⓑ Like many other haikus, Bashōs' poem
Ⓒ Like many other haikus—Bashōs poem
Ⓓ Like many other haikus, Bashō's poem

The Kafala System is a migrant worker system in the Middle East. In 2016, the United Arab Emirates (UAE) implemented reforms that ________ in employment and do not tie the worker to the employer.

**21**

Which choice completes the text so that it conforms to the conventions of Standard English?

Ⓐ allowing flexibility
Ⓑ allow flexibility
Ⓒ has allow flexing
Ⓓ allow flexing

# 1 MODULE 1 1

Around 10,000 years ago, humans started farming in the Fertile Crescent. Farming brought advantages like a more reliable food supply and a less nomadic ______

**22**

Which choice completes the text so that it conforms to the conventions of Standard English?

Ⓐ lifestyle but it also brought a new problem; rodents.
Ⓑ lifestyle; but it also, brought a new problem—rodents.
Ⓒ lifestyle, but it also brought a new problem rodents.
Ⓓ lifestyle, but it also brought a new problem: rodents.

Once a birder has identified the kinds of food they want to put out, the next step is to make sure the environment around the feeder is welcoming and safe. Feeders should be placed either within three feet of or farther than 30 feet away from windows to avoid collisions as birds land and take off. Birds ______ like to have cover as they eat; nearby shrubs and trees can provide safety for birds when they feel threatened. Some birders even like to provide water to go with the food.

**23**

Which choice completes the text with the most logical transition?

Ⓐ also
Ⓑ on the other hand
Ⓒ due to this
Ⓓ as a result

The process of carbon fixation involves combining an enzyme called RuBP oxygenase-carboxylase (rubisco) with carbon dioxide ______ form an organic molecule; however, the rubisco molecule also has the potential to use $O_2$ as a substrate instead of $CO_2$, which contributes to a side reaction called photorespiration.

**24**

Which choice completes the text with the most logical transition?

Ⓐ because
Ⓑ since
Ⓒ while
Ⓓ in order to

While researching a topic, a student has taken the following notes:

- Ibn Battuta was a famous explorer from the 1300s.
- He explored most of the Muslim world in his lifetime.
- He is believed to have travelled as far east as China and the Philippines, and as far west as Morocco.
- Because of his extensive studies in Mecca, Iba Battuta was prized as an Islamic scholar.
- Ibn Battuta successfully used his intellect to obtain influence with rulers and merchants around the world.

**25**

The student wants to underscore the time period during which Ibn Battuta conducted his exploration. Which choice most effectively uses relevant information from the notes to accomplish this goal?

Ⓐ Ibn Battuta traveled as far east as China and as far west as Morocco.

Ⓑ Many rulers and merchants valued Ibn Battuta's impressive academic background.

Ⓒ During his travels, Ibn Battuta used his personal charisma to make connections.

Ⓓ Ibn Battuta travelled through much of the world during the 1300s.

While researching a topic, a student has taken the following notes:

- Pumpkins come in a variety of colors beyond orange, including red, blue, pink, and white.
- Deep reddish orange pumpkins, commonly referred to as Cinderella pumpkins, are a French variety called Rouge Vif d'Etampes that was introduced to the United States in the late 19th century.
- Jarrahdale pumpkins are bluish grey with a golden orange interior and were developed in Australia.
- Porcelain Doll pumpkins were developed in the United States and are pale pink. They also have a wonderful taste, making them a good choice for pumpkin pie.
- Casperita pumpkins are small and white. While they are edible, their size makes them more common for decorations than for food.

**26**

The student wants to highlight two pumpkin varieties that can be consumed as food. Which choice most effectively uses relevant information from the notes to accomplish this goal?

Ⓐ Blue, white, and orange pumpkins will often be found on the dinner table.

Ⓑ Jarrahdale and Cinderella pumpkins are considered delicacies.

Ⓒ Both Porcelain Doll and Casperita pumpkins can be eaten.

Ⓓ Porcelain Doll pumpkins are considered the most delicious pumpkin varietal.

# 1 MODULE 1 1

While researching a topic, a student has taken the following notes:

- The Rice's whale is a unique species of whale discovered in 2021.
- It is named after whale researcher Dale Rice.
- It can grow to a little over 40 feet long and has baleen instead of teeth.
- This whale is found in the Gulf of Mexico.
- The Rice's whale is on the brink of extinction, with fewer than 100 of the whales believed to still be alive.
- Major threats to the Rice's whale include pollution, especially oil spills.

**27**

The student wants to suggest a reason why the Rice's whale is quite difficult to observe. Which choice most effectively uses relevant information from the notes to accomplish this goal?

Ⓐ With so few of the Rice's whales left in the wild, whale spotting opportunities are quite rare.

Ⓑ The Rice's whale is unsurprisingly named for the man who discovered it—Dale Rice.

Ⓒ The geographic vicinity in which the Rice's whale is found is yet to be established.

Ⓓ A potential oil spill poses a major threat to the long-term viability of the Rice's whale.

## Section 1, Module 2, Reading and Writing

32 MINUTES, 27 QUESTIONS

**DIRECTIONS**

You will be tested on a variety of important reading and writing skills. Each question has one or more passages, possibly including a graph or table. Carefully read each passage and question and choose the best answer to the question based on the passage(s).

Every question in this section is multiple-choice, with four possible answers. Each question has only one best answer.

The vestibular system is _______ in the inner ear and is comprised of three tubes on each side of the head. Each tube on the right has a corresponding tube on the left, making up three pairs.

**1**

Which choice completes the text with the most logical and precise word or phrase?

(A) residing
(B) located
(C) lodged
(D) dwelling

Staging can be a win-win situation for both the aspiring chef and the mentor: the mentor receives help in the kitchen, and the aspiring chef acquires new skills that he can apply in a future position. Stages at prestigious restaurants can _______ a chef's resume for future opportunities.

**2**

Which choice completes the text with the most logical and precise word or phrase?

(A) cushion
(B) maintain
(C) bolster
(D) rebuild

Soap is made up of small molecules that have hydrophilic heads and hydrophobic tails; the hydrophilic heads are attracted to water, while the hydrophobic tails are _______ by water. The soap molecules, when dissolved in water, float around and can either act independently or can join with other soap molecules to form bubbles.

**3**

Which choice completes the text with the most logical and precise word or phrase?

(A) repelled
(B) levitated
(C) captivated
(D) narrowed

# 1 MODULE 2 1

Organisms that must consume oxygen to live are known as aerobic organisms, while those that do not need oxygen are considered anaerobic. Aerobic organisms ______ most of their energy from a process known as cellular respiration. This process is oxygen-requiring and cannot be completed by anaerobic organisms. Cellular respiration produces 18 times more energy units per glucose molecule consumed in glycolysis than the anaerobic alternative, fermentation.

**4**

Which choice completes the text with the most logical and precise word or phrase?

Ⓐ discover
Ⓑ inhale
Ⓒ derive
Ⓓ discern

Since its development in 1932 by Soviet engineer Konstantin Khrenov, marine welding has become a highly specialized and ________ career. As the name suggests, marine welders construct or repair infrastructures like oil rigs and bridges underwater. Welding occurs when structures like metals or thermoplastics are heated to high temperatures and melted together, causing the structures to bind.

**5**

Which choice completes the text with the most logical and precise word or phrase?

Ⓐ monetary
Ⓑ exorbitant
Ⓒ budgetary
Ⓓ lucrative

The following text is adapted from the 1918 American Federation of Labor Records. In it, the American Federation of Labor discusses the possible ramifications of labor uprisings and revolts in Europe as the end of World War I approaches.

> The peace then offered would be even worse than that of Haase, namely, . . . adaptation of the status quo ante and "no annexations, no indemnities" formula, with neighboring nations bound by coerced economic treaties and "readjustments of the frontiers."
>
> To aid the German Socialists (positively) and the Bolsheviki (negatively) is not <u>only playing with fire</u>, it is almost certain to end the war before German defeat or American victory—with all the consequences that must inevitably follow such an indecisive outcome.

**6**

Which choice best describes the function of the underlined selection in the text as a whole?

Ⓐ To underscore potentially negative consequences
Ⓑ To predict pending physical harm
Ⓒ To demonstrate possible sources of reconciliation
Ⓓ To forecast a coming perpetual peace

**Text 1**

Sitting at the Art Institute of Chicago is a famous work of art—*A Sunday on La Grande Jatte*. The piece took artist Georges Seurat more than two years to complete. The painting depicts 48 Parisian citizens spending their afternoon along the Seine River. He sought to capture the timelessness seen in historical art using pointillist technique. By positioning dots of contrasting color closely together, the viewers' eyes would naturally blend the pigments when they looked upon it.

**Text 2**

Claude Monet's painting, *Impression: Sunrise*, marked the beginning of the impressionist movement. It was characterized by large, rough brushstrokes that stood out on the canvas. Nature was the preferred muse of its painters, focusing on the shifting light patterns across the environment. Because of the focus on landscapes, most impressionist painters worked outside on small canvases. They wanted to capture the scenery in its fleeting moments, sometimes coming back and repainting the scene in different seasons.

**7**

Based on the texts, the author of Text 2 is more concerned with what objective than is the author of Text 1?

Ⓐ Describing the specific painting technique used in a work

Ⓑ Placing the analysis of a single painting in a larger artistic context

Ⓒ Analyzing the setting in which an artistic scene takes place

Ⓓ Noting the biographical details of a famous artist

"Antigenic drift" and "antigenic shift" are the main ways influenza circumvents our adaptive immunity; they are likely the causes of epidemic and pandemic influenza, respectively. To date, 16 HA and nine NA subtypes have been identified, only a fraction of which are currently infectious to humans. However, because the influenza genome is split into segments, when an animal—a bird, for instance—is co-infected with a strain specific to its species, as well as one capable of infecting humans, the segments may become intermixed during replication in a process called "viral reassortment." When these reassorted genes include either HA or NA, antigenic shift occurs, and the resulting viral particles will express novel proteins to which the entire human race is vulnerable. The aggregation of many point mutations over time is known as antigenic drift, and eventually results in renewed vulnerability to viral strains against which an individual was previously immune.

**8**

Based on the text, would antigenic drift or antigenic shift result in greater fundamental changes to genetic structure?

Ⓐ Antigenic drift because it results in increasing vulnerability to viruses.

Ⓑ Antigenic drift because it can easily spread throughout the body.

Ⓒ Antigenic shift because it entails genetic replication.

Ⓓ Antigenic shift because it involves interspecies genome exchange.

The line between over-sterilization and under-sterilization seems to be a tight rope with falling on either side leading to disaster. However, with common sense and moderation, most healthy people can remain healthy with little effort: Wash your hands when you suspect you may have been exposed to something that could make you ill (raw meat, bathroom germs) and before you eat. The rest of the time, let less harmful germs interact with your immune system to keep you healthy.

**9**

Which of the following, if true, would best support the narrator's position?

Ⓐ A research study finds that those who wash their hands approximately eight times per day have substantially lower incidence of illness than those who wash their hands more than 20 times per day.

Ⓑ Those who only wash their hands before a meal have less illness on average than those who wash their hands only after using the restroom.

Ⓒ The germs that are most affected by hand washing are more prominent in urban areas than in rural areas.

Ⓓ A chemist finds that for the vast majority of germs, hand sanitizer has the same impact on germ reduction as does hand washing.

*The Jungle* is a 1906 novel by Upton Sinclair. In this story, the characters Jurgis, Ona, and Teta find it extremely difficult to plan their budget because of the high likelihood of unpredictable expenses: ______

**10**

Which quotation from *The Jungle* most effectively illustrates the claim?

Ⓐ "She had had to give up all idea of marrying then; the family could not get along without her—though for that matter she was likely soon to become a burden even upon them"

Ⓑ "So Jurgis and Ona and Teta Elzbieta would hold anxious conferences until late at night, trying to figure how they could manage this too without starving.

Ⓒ "This was in truth not living; it was scarcely even existing, and they felt that it was too little for the price they paid."

Ⓓ "There seemed never to be an end to the things they had to buy and to the unforeseen contingencies."

# 1 MODULE 2 1

| | Demographic | Percentage |
|---|---|---|
| **Gender** | Men | 72% |
| | Women | 76% |
| **Ages** | Ages 18-29 | 89% |
| | Ages 30-49 | 82% |
| | Ages 50-64 | 65% |
| | Ages 65+ | 49% |
| **Education Level** | High school graduate or less | 72% |
| | Some college | 78% |
| | College graduate and beyond | 73% |
| **Yearly Salary** | Less than $30,000 per year | 79% |
| | Between $30,000 and $49,000 | 73% |
| | Between $50,000 and $74,000 | 70% |
| | Greater than $75,000 | 78% |

Source: Pew Research Center

A social scientist is researching the general characteristics of people who use social networking websites. The scientist is putting together a presentation and wants to give a concise example of a typical social networking website user. Based on the latest research from the Pew Research Center, the social scientist could best cite this type of person as an example for her presentation: ________________.

**11**

Which choice most effectively uses data from the graph to complete the example?

Ⓐ A 45-year-old man who has an advanced graduate degree

Ⓑ A 35-year-old man who has a master's degree in engineering

Ⓒ A 25-year-old woman who left college without completing her degree

Ⓓ A 15-year-old girl who is a sophomore in high school

The primary electrolytes lost during sweating are Na+ and K+. Water follows Na+ in the body, so when one sweats profusely, a decent number of electrolytes are lost as well. Researchers are looking at electrolyte loss in warm versus hot environments, wondering if there is a difference in performance from the amount of sweat lost. They hypothesize that losing body water would not be as detrimental during exercise in the cold.

**12**

Which observation, if true, would most directly support the researchers' hypothesis?

Ⓐ During the winter months in the Northern Hemisphere, the temperatures in the Southern Hemisphere are generally warmer.

Ⓑ The electrolytes Na+ and K+ can be easily supplemented in the diet through ingestible tablets.

Ⓒ Those who have a relatively high body mass index tend to sweat more than those with a low body mass index.

Ⓓ The average body does not sweat as much in a cold environment compared to a warm environment.

1 MODULE 2 1

Portfolio variance is an estimation of the risk of a portfolio, with a higher number indicating a greater risk and a lower number indicating a lower risk.

| Number of Stocks | Expected Portfolio Variance |
|---|---|
| 1 | 46.6 |
| 2 | 26.8 |
| 4 | 16.9 |
| 6 | 13.7 |
| 8 | 12.0 |
| 10 | 11.0 |
| 20 | 9.0 |
| 50 | 7.8 |
| 100 | 7.5 |
| 1,000 | 7.1 |

Data gathered from Edwin Elton and Martin Gruber in their article "Risk Reduction and Portfolio Size: An Analytical Solution," published in The Journal of Business in 1977.

A stockbroker is trying to recommend the best portfolio construction for a hypothetical client. The stockbroker wants to create a recommended course of action for the hypothetical client to reduce risk but does not know the precise makeup of the client's stock portfolio. The stockbroker anticipates that a significant reduction in portfolio risk would most likely come from the following adjustment: ___________

**13**

Which choice most effectively uses data from the table to complete the statement?

Ⓐ having two stocks instead of just one.
Ⓑ having six stocks instead of four.
Ⓒ having 20 stocks instead of 10.
Ⓓ having 1,000 stocks instead of 100.

Many countries—including the U.S.—have used Keynesian initiatives to varying degrees of success as a jumpstart for their failing economies. It is difficult even for economists to say with any certainty why the policy has worked so well for Sweden. One possible contributor is the remarkable capacity for compromise demonstrated by Swedish politicians, businessmen, labor unions and farmers, even in times of financial turmoil. Although the Social Democrats have remained in power in Sweden for most of the last century, 90% of Swedish industry remains privately owned; labor disputes, in contrast, ________

**14**

Which choice most logically completes the text?

Ⓐ are settled by a governmental bureau trusted by workers and management alike.

Ⓑ are administered by entrepreneurs who seek to maximize profits for shareholders.

Ⓒ look to stimulate the economy through increased governmental spending.

Ⓓ are negotiated by opposing leaders who seek to maximize concessions from the other side.

Guest workers can be subject to abhorrent treatment: they often must pay pre-arrival recruiters exorbitant fees for very minor work, and recruiters may even hold ________ hostage until additional fees are paid.

**15**

Which choice completes the text so that it conforms to the conventions of Standard English?

Ⓐ workers passports' and visas'

Ⓑ workers passports and visas

Ⓒ workers' passports and visas

Ⓓ worker's passports and visas

The scientific method is the process that takes a hypothesis, tests it, and with careful observation, may lead to the discovery of new knowledge. ________

**16**

Which choice completes the text so that it conforms to the conventions of Standard English?

Ⓐ One of the key components of the scientific method is the ability to replicate findings.

Ⓑ To replicate findings is, of the scientific method, one of the key components.

Ⓒ Of the scientific method to replicate findings is one of the key components.

Ⓓ Replicating findings of one of the components is, of the scientific method, key.

# 1 MODULE 2 1

Cats may have been selectively bred by humans for traits like friendliness and tameness, but they may also have developed those traits naturally through generations of coexisting with humans. This is where the phrase "cats domesticated themselves" comes from: no one is certain exactly how we came to have ________ predators in our homes, but we certainly appreciate them.

**17**

Which choice completes the text so that it conforms to the conventions of Standard English?

Ⓐ loveable, fluffy
Ⓑ loveable fluffy
Ⓒ loveable—fluffy—
Ⓓ loveable; fluffy

During the first roller derby event called the Trans-continental Roller Derby, each team consisted of ________ Additionally, female and male pairs would compete against players of their respective gender, and all of the players abided by the same roller derby rules.

**18**

Which choice completes the text so that it conforms to the conventions of Standard English?

Ⓐ two players: one woman; and one man.
Ⓑ two players, one woman, and one man.
Ⓒ two players: one woman and one man.
Ⓓ two players; one woman—and one man.

Comité des Citoyens (the Committee of Citizens) brought *Plessy v. Ferguson* to the Supreme Court, where the Court cemented the separate but equal doctrine into law until it was ________ down in *Brown v. Board of Education.*

**19**

Which choice completes the text so that it conforms to the conventions of Standard English?

Ⓐ striking
Ⓑ strucked
Ⓒ struck
Ⓓ striked

The group of modern artists came up with their movement's name after a knife that was randomly inserted into a dictionary seemed to point to the word "dada." The ____________ to go against conformity and the violence surrounding World War I. Dada was inspired by various art styles like Expressionism, Cubism, Constructivism, and Futurism, although the movement itself was not classified as an art style.

**20**

Which choice completes the text so that it conforms to the conventions of Standard English?

Ⓐ word "dada" means "hobby-horse" in French which suited the premise of the movement,

Ⓑ word "dada" means "hobby-horse" in French which suited the premise of the movement

Ⓒ word "dada" means "hobby-horse" in French; which suited the premise of the movement,

Ⓓ word "dada" means "hobby-horse" in French, which suited the premise of the movement

Many of the greatest battles in history can be simplified to microcosmic struggles between two strong characters. Take Grant and Lee, for instance. Or consider David and Goliath if you prefer an older story. But not often _______ such a struggle occur when both great leaders are on the same side.

**21**

Which choice completes the text so that it conforms to the conventions of Standard English?

Ⓐ do

Ⓑ doing

Ⓒ does

Ⓓ have done

For a casual birder—another name for "birdwatcher"—common backyard birds like house sparrows, European starlings, and American robins can be enough. ___________ want to see all kinds of birds in their backyards.

**22**

Which choice completes the text so that it conforms to the conventions of Standard English?

Ⓐ Some birders however have more ambition they

Ⓑ Some birders, however have more ambition; they

Ⓒ Some birders however have more ambition—they

Ⓓ Some birders, however, have more ambition: they

# 1 MODULE 2 1

Some interpret the pond in the poem as symbolizing subconsciousness—specifically, the subconsciousness of an older person. Just as frogs are motivated to jump into the water by instinct, humans relax and meditate because their biology prompts them to do so. ______ the frog jumping into the water symbolizes the meditative state of the older person.

**23**

Which choice completes the text with the most logical transition?

Ⓐ Also,
Ⓑ Despite this,
Ⓒ Additionally,
Ⓓ Thus,

Creating the closest precursor of the periodic table, Chancourtois—utilizing the invaluable molar mass work of Amedeo Avogadro—graphed 63 known elements in order of increasing atomic weight on his "telluric helix," and observed an element's chemical reactivity. _________ because Chancourtois inexplicably included several polyatomic ions on the helix and published his report using geological rather than chemical terminology, his discovery was largely ignored.

**24**

Which choice completes the text with the most logical transition?

Ⓐ Simultaneously,
Ⓑ Moreover,
Ⓒ Naturally,
Ⓓ Unfortunately,

While researching a topic, a student has taken the following notes:

- The submarine *CCS Hunley* was the first to sink another ship, the *USS Housatonic.*
- The *Hunley* was used by the Confederates during the Civil War and it was human-powered.
- The *Hunley* disappeared after its first and only attack that sank another ship.
- The *Hunley* remained missing until 2000 when it was raised from the sea floor.
- The *Hunley* was in surprisingly good condition, which allowed researchers to learn more about its final battle.

**25**

The student wants to underscore why there was little information to be found about the *Hunley* from the 20th century. Which choice most effectively uses relevant information from the notes to accomplish this goal?

Ⓐ Given the near total destruction of the *Hunley* during a Civil War battle, it makes sense that there was little of historical significance available to analyze.

Ⓑ Because the *Hunley* was preserved in excellent condition, researchers have frequently been able to gather information about it since the Civil War.

Ⓒ Since the *Hunley* was only recently raised from the sea floor, it is understandable that there is little 20th-century research on this vessel.

Ⓓ Lacking a fossil-fuel power source, the *Hunley* did not experience the same type of mechanical decay often observed in Civil War artifacts.

While researching a topic, a student has taken the following notes:

- The increasing digitization of historical records has increased access to those documents and helped increase the popularity of genealogy as a hobby.
- Genealogy is tracing one's family history.
- Knowing a few key kinship terms will help the hobby genealogist get started.
- "Consanguinity" refers to family members you're related to by blood.
- "Affinal" refers to family members you're related to by marriage.

**26**

The student wants to use specialized terminology to emphasize what can be accomplished with digitized genealogical records. Which choice most effectively uses relevant information from the notes to accomplish this goal?

Ⓐ Digitized genealogical records are made using advanced programming languages like Python and Java.

Ⓑ With the aid of digitized genealogical records, hobby genealogists can learn about their family history.

Ⓒ By learning about "family," one can successfully navigate the complex world of digitized genealogy.

Ⓓ Utilizing digitized genealogical records can enable you to determine consanguineous and affinal relations.

While conducting research, a student took these notes:

- Antibiotic resistance has been a growing concern in the medical field for the past decade.
- One pathway taken to resolve this is an adjuvant that targets bacterial translation.
- The gene, *efp*, codes for the elongation factor protein, EF-P, which works to increase the efficiency of polyproline synthesis.
- One study showed that the deletion of *efp* in bacteria increases its susceptibility to beta-lactam antibiotics.
- Another study tried this deletion but tested bacteria's resistance to carbapenem antibiotics instead.

**27**

The student wants to suggest a course of action that would provide comparative analysis of the effectiveness of certain antibiotic medications. Which choice most effectively uses relevant information from the notes to accomplish this goal?

Ⓐ The elongation factor protein and the polyproline synthesis should be examined to see which is more effective in minimizing illness.

Ⓑ The results of the carbapenem study and the beta-lactam study should be compared to evaluate which antibiotic is more helpful.

Ⓒ Studies comparing which bacteria are more susceptible and less susceptible to a particular antibiotic would go quite far in helping doctors skillfully treat patients.

Ⓓ A historical survey of the treatments used prior to the advent of antibiotics would educate practitioners about the evolution of medical interventions.

## Section 2, Module 1: Math

35 MINUTES, 22 QUESTIONS

**DIRECTIONS**

- All expressions and variables use real numbers.
- All figures are drawn to scale.
- Every figure lies in a plane.
- The domain of given functions is the set of all real numbers for which the corresponding value of the function is real.

For **multiple-choice questions,** solve the problem and pick the correct answer from the provided choices. Each multiple-choice question has only one correct answer.

For **student-produced response questions,** solve each problem and enter your answer following these guidelines:

- If you find **more than one correct answer,** enter just one answer.
- You can enter up to five characters for a **positive** answer and up to six characters (this includes the negative sign) for a **negative** answer.
- If your answer is a **fraction** that does not fit in the given space, enter the decimal equivalent instead.
- If your answer is a **decimal** that does not fit in the given space, enter it by stopping at or rounding up at the fourth digit.
- If your answer is a **mixed number** (like $4\frac{1}{2}$), enter it as an improper fraction (9/2) or its decimal equivalent (4.5).
- Do not enter **symbols** like a comma, dollar sign, or percent sign.

### Examples

| Answer | Acceptable Entries | Unacceptable Entries That Will Receive Zero Credit |
|---|---|---|
| 4.5 | 4.5<br>4.50<br>9/2 | $4\frac{1}{2}$<br>41/2 |
| $\frac{8}{9}$ | 8/9<br>.8888<br>.8889<br>0.888<br>0.889 | 0.88<br>.88<br>0.89<br>.89 |
| $-\frac{1}{9}$ | −1/9<br>−.1111<br>−0.111 | −.11<br>−0.11 |

PRACTICE TEST 2

**REFERENCE ∨**

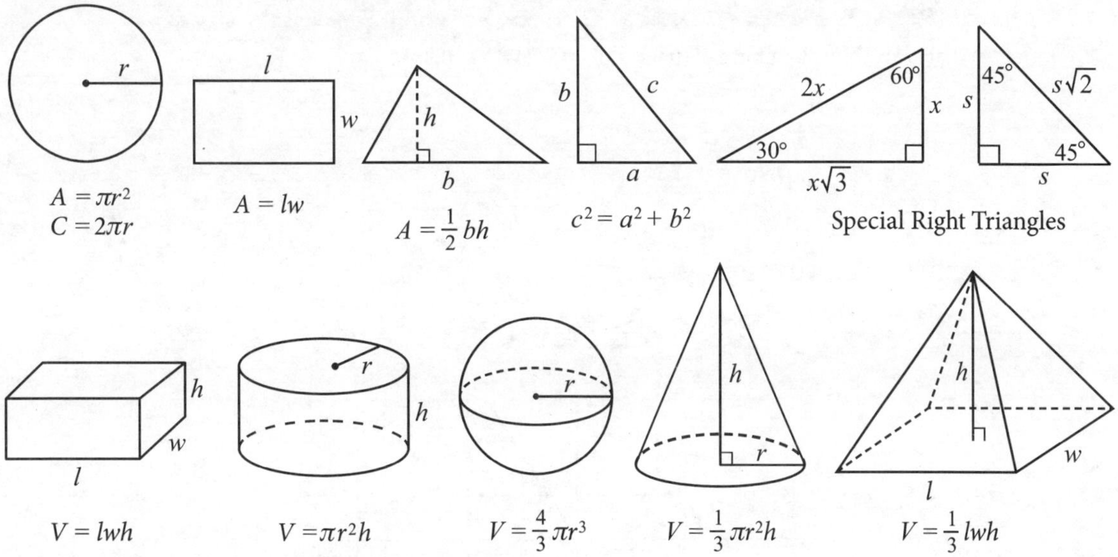


The number of degrees of arc in a circle is 360.
The number of radians of arc in a circle is $2\pi$.
The sum of the measures in degrees of the angles of a triangle is 180.

# 2 MODULE 1 2

**1**

What is an equivalent form of $(0.8a + 0.7b) - (1.4a - 0.3b)$ ?

Ⓐ $2.2a + b$
Ⓑ $-0.6a + b$
Ⓒ $1.12a - .21b$
Ⓓ $-0.6a - 0.4b$

**2**

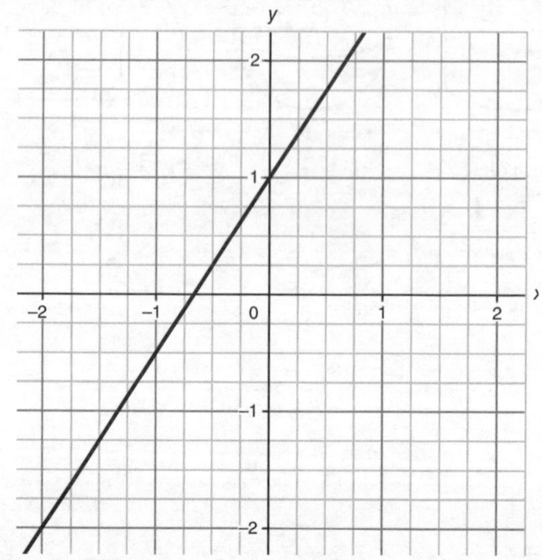


Based on the graph of the line above, what is its slope?

Ⓐ $\frac{2}{3}$
Ⓑ 1
Ⓒ $\frac{3}{2}$
Ⓓ $\frac{4}{3}$

**3**

If $12x - 10 = 4$, what is $-5 + 6x$ ?

2 MODULE 1 2

**4**

The volume of a cylinder, $v$, is given by the equation $v = \pi r^2 h$, in which $r$ is the radius of the cylinder and $h$ is the height of the cylinder. What is the height in terms of the other variables?

Ⓐ $h = \frac{v}{\pi r^2}$

Ⓑ $h = \frac{\pi\sqrt{r}}{v}$

Ⓒ $h = \frac{2\pi v}{r}$

Ⓓ $h = \pi r^2 v$

**5**

Voter turnout rates for different U.S. presidential elections are given in the following graph:

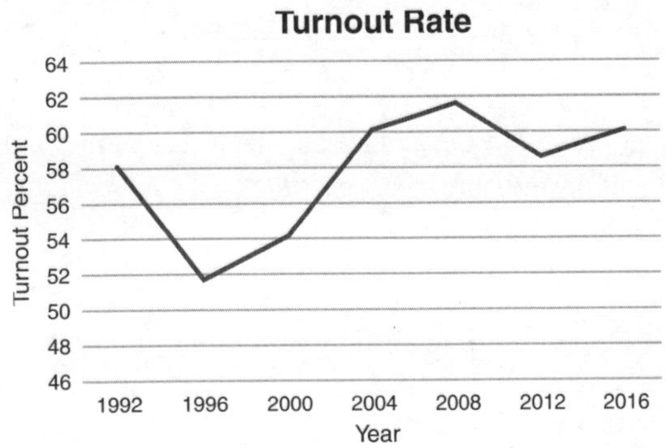


Source: *electionproject.org*

During what year was voter turnout the highest?

Ⓐ 1996

Ⓑ 2004

Ⓒ 2008

Ⓓ 2016

**6**

Which of these options is equivalent to the following expression?

$$(2y^2 - y) - (2y^2 + 2y)$$

Ⓐ $4y^4 - 2y^2$
Ⓑ $4y^2 - 2y$
Ⓒ $-3y$
Ⓓ $6y + 2$

**7**

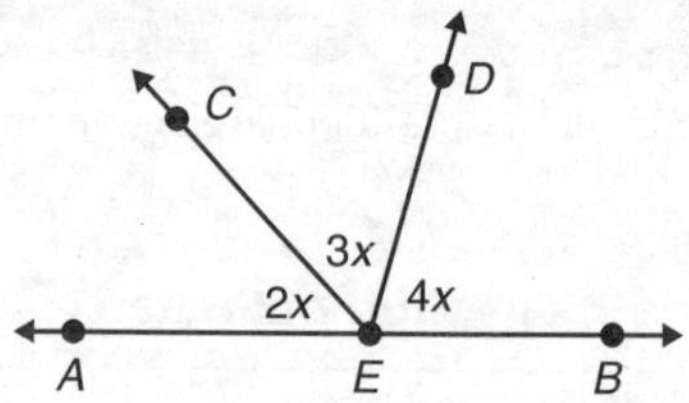


In the figure above, lines $\overline{AEB}$, $\overline{CE}$, and $\overline{DE}$ all intersect at point $E$ and have measures as indicated. What is the measure of angle $\angle CED$?

Ⓐ 20°
Ⓑ 30°
Ⓒ 45°
Ⓓ 60°

**8**

$$(x + 2)^3 = 27$$

What positive value of $x$ would make the above equation true?

2 MODULE 1 2

**9**

| | Appetizer | No Appetizer | Total |
|---|---|---|---|
| **Dessert** | 15 | 35 | 50 |
| **No Dessert** | 25 | 25 | 50 |
| **Total** | 40 | 60 | 100 |

A restaurant tabulated meals from 100 of its diners to record if the diner ordered an appetizer and/or a dessert with a meal. Based on the table above, what is the probability that if a diner ordered dessert, they would also order an appetizer?

Ⓐ $\frac{1}{5}$

Ⓑ $\frac{3}{10}$

Ⓒ $\frac{3}{8}$

Ⓓ $\frac{3}{7}$

**10**

$$y = 2x - 3$$

What is the $x$-coordinate of the $x$-intercept of the line with the above equation?

**11**

The graph of $y = \frac{1}{2}x - 2$ in the $xy$-plane is a line. What is the $y$-intercept of this line?

Ⓐ $-2.5$

Ⓑ $-2$

Ⓒ $\frac{1}{2}$

Ⓓ 2

**12**

If $3 = \frac{3}{2}(4x - 2y)$ and $y = \frac{1}{2}x$, what is the value of $y$?

__________

**13**

Which of the following would be points at which the function $y = (x + 4)(x - 5)x$ intersects the $x$ axis?

I. $(-4, 0)$
II. $(5, 0)$
III. $(0, 0)$

Ⓐ I only
Ⓑ II only
Ⓒ I and III only
Ⓓ I, II, and III

**14**

$$B(h) = 1000 \times 2^h$$

The growth of a population of bacteria is modeled by the above function, in which $B(h)$ represents the number of bacteria after $h$ hours have passed. After how many hours will the population of bacteria be 8 times its initial number?

Ⓐ 1 hour
Ⓑ 2 hours
Ⓒ 3 hours
Ⓓ 4 hours

2 MODULE 1 2

**15**

| Total of Combined Spins | Number of Spins with That Total Value |
|---|---|
| 2 | 1 |
| 3 | 2 |
| 4 | 2 |
| 5 | 4 |
| 6 | 5 |
| 7 | 6 |
| 8 | 7 |
| 9 | 4 |
| 10 | 3 |
| 11 | 4 |
| 12 | 2 |

Pete was playing a children's game that had a spinner with values 1-6; with each turn, he spins the spinner twice and finds the total. He tabulated the combined values of two combined spins from a total of 40 different turns as shown above. What fraction of all his combined spins were 6 or less?

Ⓐ $\frac{1}{40}$

Ⓑ $\frac{9}{40}$

Ⓒ $\frac{13}{40}$

Ⓓ $\frac{7}{20}$

**16**

The population of the greater metropolitan area of Mexico City was estimated to have been 22,000,000 at the end of the year 2020. If the Mexico City area represented 17% of all of Mexico's population at the end of 2020, what would be the closest estimate of Mexico's total population?

Ⓐ 4,000,000

Ⓑ 26,000,000

Ⓒ 104,000,000

Ⓓ 129,000,000

**17**

For the function $f$ as defined below, what is the value of $f(5)$ ?

$$f(x) = (x - 3)(x + 1)$$

________

**18**

The solutions to this set of inequalities are found in which quadrant(s) of the $xy$-coordinate plane?

$$y > x + 1 \quad \text{and} \quad y < -2x - 3$$

Ⓐ Only quadrant 1
Ⓑ Only quadrant 3
Ⓒ Quadrants 1 and 4 only
Ⓓ Quadrants 2 and 3 only

**19**

If a computer costs \$2,000 and depreciates (i.e., the value decreases) by the same amount each year, how much is the annual amount of depreciation if after 6 years the computer is worth \$800?

Ⓐ \$80
Ⓑ \$100
Ⓒ \$200
Ⓓ \$400

**20**

If a circle graphed in the $xy$-coordinate plane has a center at (3, 4) and intersects the origin, what is the equation of the circle?

Ⓐ $(x - 3)^2 + (y - 4)^2 = 25$
Ⓑ $(x + 3)^2 - (y + 4)^2 = 25$
Ⓒ $x^2 + y^2 = 49$
Ⓓ $x^2 + y^2 = 25$

2 MODULE 1 2

**21**

Susan blinks an average of 20 times per minute while awake. In the 16 hours she is awake in a day, how many times will she blink?

Ⓐ 320
Ⓑ 7,680
Ⓒ 12,400
Ⓓ 19,200

**22**

Hugo's $3,000 monthly budget is broken down in this table:

| Rent | $800 |
|---|---|
| Car expenses | $400 |
| Student loans | $300 |
| Savings | $250 |
| Food | $450 |
| Utilities | $250 |
| Clothing | $150 |
| Miscellaneous | $400 |

Hugo is trying to allocate more money into savings. If he cut his allocation towards miscellaneous expenses by half and allocated this amount to savings, by what percentage would his monthly savings increase?

Ⓐ 20%
Ⓑ 50%
Ⓒ 65%
Ⓓ 80%

## Section 2, Module 2: Math

32 MINUTES, 27 QUESTIONS

**DIRECTIONS**

- All expressions and variables use real numbers.
- All figures are drawn to scale.
- Every figure lies in a plane.
- The domain of given functions is the set of all real numbers for which the corresponding value of the function is real.

For **multiple-choice questions,** solve the problem and pick the correct answer from the provided choices. Each multiple-choice question has only one correct answer.

For **student-produced response questions,** solve each problem and enter your answer following these guidelines:

- If you find **more than one correct answer,** enter just one answer.
- You can enter up to five characters for a **positive** answer and up to six characters (this includes the negative sign) for a **negative** answer.
- If your answer is a **fraction** that does not fit in the given space, enter the decimal equivalent instead.
- If your answer is a **decimal** that does not fit in the given space, enter it by stopping at or rounding up at the fourth digit.
- If your answer is a **mixed number** (like $4\frac{1}{2}$), enter it as an improper fraction (9/2) or its decimal equivalent (4.5).
- Do not enter **symbols** like a comma, dollar sign, or percent sign.

## Examples

| Answer | Acceptable Entries | Unacceptable Entries That Will Receive Zero Credit |
|---|---|---|
| 4.5 | 4.5<br>4.50<br>9/2 | $4\frac{1}{2}$<br>41/2 |
| $\frac{8}{9}$ | 8/9<br>.8888<br>.8889<br>0.888<br>0.889 | 0.88<br>.88<br>.89<br>0.89 |
| $-\frac{1}{9}$ | −1/9<br>−.1111<br>−0.111 | −.11<br>−0.11 |

**REFERENCE** ∨

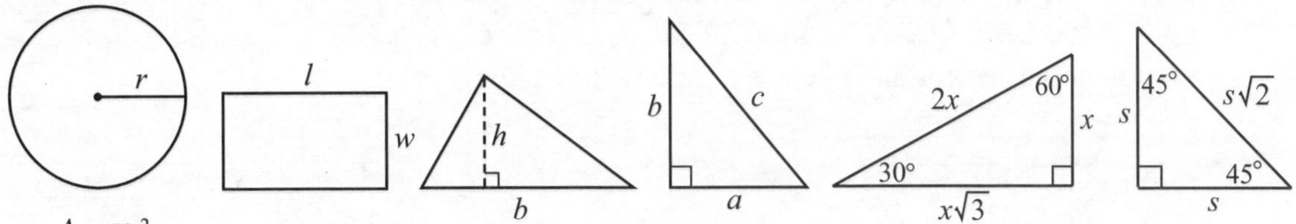


$A = \pi r^2$
$C = 2\pi r$

$A = lw$

$A = \frac{1}{2}bh$

$c^2 = a^2 + b^2$

Special Right Triangles

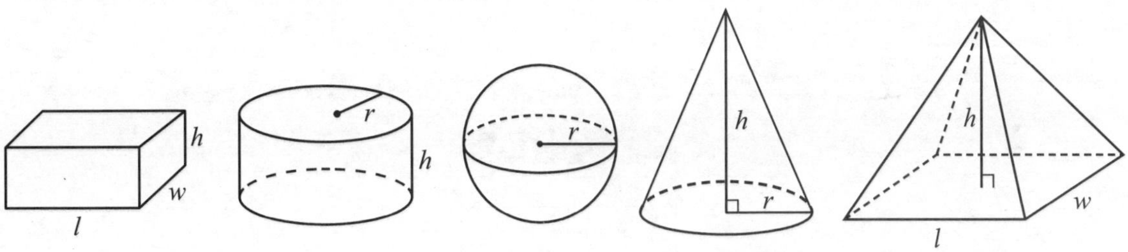


$V = lwh$

$V = \pi r^2 h$

$V = \frac{4}{3}\pi r^3$

$V = \frac{1}{3}\pi r^2 h$

$V = \frac{1}{3}lwh$

The number of degrees of arc in a circle is 360.
The number of radians of arc in a circle is $2\pi$.
The sum of the measures in degrees of the angles of a triangle is 180.

# 2 MODULE 2 2

**1**

The function $g$ is defined by $g(x) = \frac{x^3}{2}$. What is the value of $g(-2)$ ?

Ⓐ $-4$
Ⓑ $-2$
Ⓒ $-1$
Ⓓ $4$

**2**

| $x$ | $f(x)$ |
|---|---|
| 3 | $-1$ |
| 6 | 0 |
| 9 | 1 |

For the linear function $f$, the table above shows some values of $x$ and the corresponding values of $f(x)$. Which of the following equations correctly defines the function?

Ⓐ $f(x) = \frac{1}{3}x - 2$
Ⓑ $f(x) = \frac{2}{3}x - 1$
Ⓒ $f(x) = x - 6$
Ⓓ $f(x) = 3x + 2$

**3**

Which of these is equivalent to $\sqrt[3]{a} \times a^{\frac{5}{3}}$ ?

Ⓐ $a^{\frac{2}{3}}$
Ⓑ $a^{\frac{4}{3}}$
Ⓒ $a^2$
Ⓓ $a^5$

**4**

If $y = ax$ in which $a$ is a constant and $y = 16$ when $x = 8$, what is the value of $x$ when $y$ is $-3$ ?

Ⓐ $-6$
Ⓑ $-1.5$
Ⓒ $1$
Ⓓ $8.5$

# 2 MODULE 2 2

**5**

$$ax^2 + bx + c = 2x^2 + 16x + 32$$

In the equation above, $a$, $b$, and $c$ are all constants. What is the sum of $a$, $b$, and $c$?

Ⓐ 48
Ⓑ 50
Ⓒ 52
Ⓓ 64

**6**

$$S(w) = 500 + 10w$$

Ana receives an allowance of $10 per week. The function above shows how much money she will have in her savings account after $w$ weeks, assuming she saves all her allowance in the account. What does the number 500 represent in the function?

Ⓐ The money in her account at the beginning of the time period
Ⓑ The money in the account at the end of the time period
Ⓒ The weekly increase in money in the account
Ⓓ The net profit she receives after expenses

**7**

On a map, 1 inch represents 3 miles in actual distance. If there is a rectangular plot of land on the map with a width of 2 inches and a length of 3 inches, what would be the actual area of the rectangular plot of land in square miles?

**8**

Samara drove on a 400-mile trip. If the first half of the trip took her 4 hours of driving to complete and the second half took her 6 hours of driving to complete, what was her average driving speed for the whole 400-mile trip?

Ⓐ 20 miles per hour
Ⓑ 35 miles per hour
Ⓒ 40 miles per hour
Ⓓ 80 miles per hour

2 MODULE 2 2

**9**

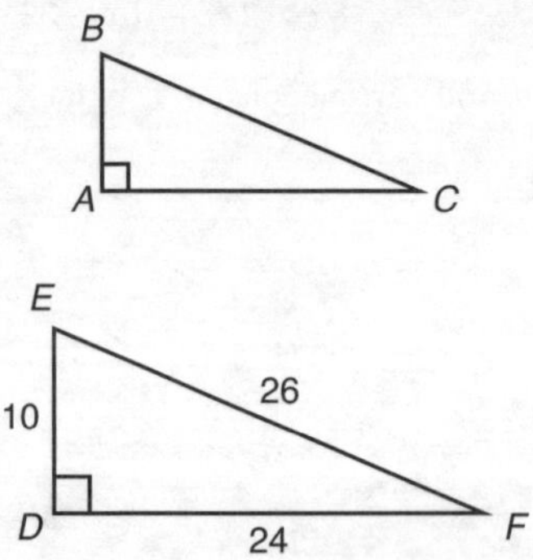


The above triangles *ABC* and *DEF* are similar to one another, with angle *B* corresponding to angle *E*. What is the tangent of angle *C* ?

Ⓐ $\frac{5}{13}$

Ⓑ $\frac{5}{12}$

Ⓒ $\frac{10}{13}$

Ⓓ $\frac{12}{13}$

**10**

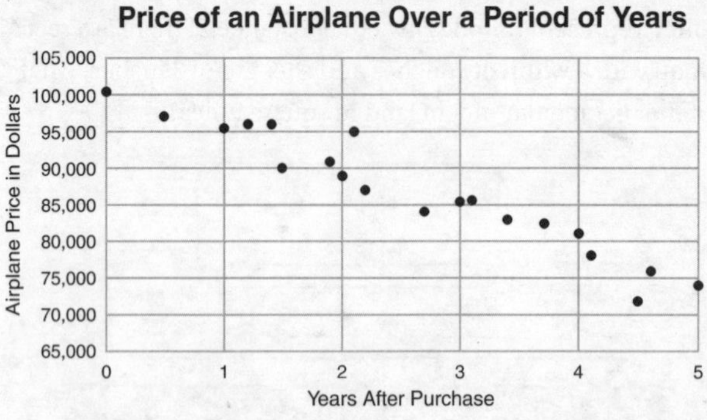


If the airplane continues to decrease in value at a linear rate, at what year after purchase will the plane first closely approximate a value of zero dollars?

Ⓐ 10 years after purchase

Ⓑ 15 years after purchase

Ⓒ 20 years after purchase

Ⓓ 25 years after purchase

# 2 MODULE 2 2

**11**

If $x$ is increased by 400%, what is the result in terms of $x$ ?

Ⓐ z
Ⓑ $2x$
Ⓒ $4x$
Ⓓ $5x$

**12**

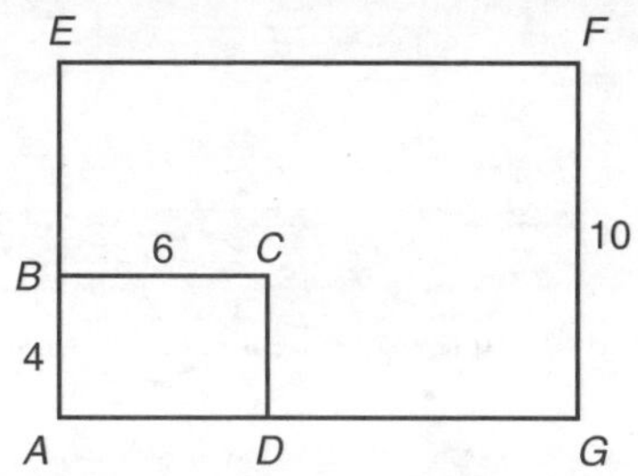


In the figure above, $ABCD$ and $AEFG$ are similar rectangles. If $\overline{AB}$ is 4 units long, $\overline{BC}$ is 6 units long, and $\overline{FG}$ is 10 units long, what is the perimeter of rectangle $AEFG$ ?

Ⓐ 24 units
Ⓑ 48 units
Ⓒ 50 units
Ⓓ 72 units

**13**

How many zeros will a line with the equation $y = k$ have in which $k$ is a constant greater than zero?

Ⓐ Zero
Ⓑ One
Ⓒ Two
Ⓓ Cannot be determined from the given information

**14**

| Quiz Score (Out of 5 Points) | 0 Correct | 1 Correct | 2 Correct | 3 Correct | 4 Correct | 5 Correct |
|---|---|---|---|---|---|---|
| Class 1 Students' Scores | 1 | 2 | 4 | 6 | 4 | 3 |
| Class 2 Students' Scores | 0 | 4 | 7 | 3 | 4 | 2 |

Based on the information in the table, what is the median quiz score of the combined set of both classes?

______

**15**

What would be the value(s) of $x$ that would be a solution or solutions to this equation?

$$\frac{x^2-4}{x-2}=4$$

Ⓐ $-2$
Ⓑ 2
Ⓒ 4
Ⓓ There are no solutions.

**16**

What is the vertex of a parabola with the equation $y=(x-6)^2$?

Ⓐ $(-6, 0)$
Ⓑ $(0, 0)$
Ⓒ $(6, 0)$
Ⓓ $(0, 6)$

# 2 MODULE 2 2

**17**

Out of all the 44 people to serve as president of the United States before the year 2020, 14 of them had previously been U.S. vice president. Which function expresses the relationship between the number of presidents, $P$, and vice presidents who became presidents, $V$?

Ⓐ $V = 14P$

Ⓑ $V = \frac{7}{22}P$

Ⓒ $V = \frac{1}{14}P$

Ⓓ $V = \frac{22}{7}P$

**18**

$$-\frac{1}{4}x + \frac{1}{6}y = 12$$

$$2y = 3x + a$$

If the above set of equations has infinitely many solutions, what is the value of the constant $a$?

**19**

Julian and Maria are budgeting for their upcoming wedding reception. They are inviting people from each side of their families—$J$ people from Julian's side of the family and $M$ people from Maria's side of the family. They are planning on spending \$40 per person invited to the wedding reception. If they want to keep the cost of the wedding reception to less than \$18,000, and have more than 200 people in attendance, which system of inequalities would represent these conditions?

Ⓐ $M + J \leq 200$
$40M + J \geq 18{,}000$

Ⓑ $M + J > 40$
$18{,}000 + M + J > 200$

Ⓒ $M + J > 18{,}000$
$\frac{M + J}{40} < 200$

Ⓓ $M + J > 200$
$40(M + J) < 18{,}000$

**20**

Given that there are 5,280 feet in a mile, which of the following would most closely approximate 30 miles per hour in feet per second?

Ⓐ 28 feet/second
Ⓑ 44 feet/second
Ⓒ 176 feet/second
Ⓓ 158,400 feet/second

2 MODULE 2 2

**21**

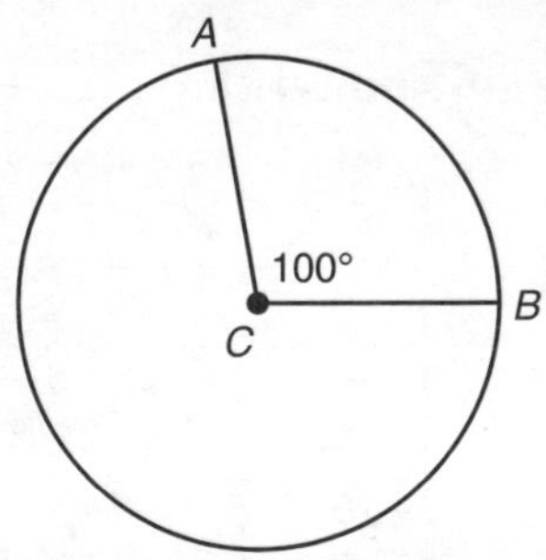


The circle graphed above has a center of $C$, a radius of 7 units, and a central angle $\angle ACB$ with a measure of 100°. What is the area of the sector of the circle designated by $\angle ACB$ to the nearest whole square unit?

**22**

At a café, each cup of coffee has 95 milligrams of caffeine, and each cup of tea has 26 milligrams of caffeine. Shantiel goes to the store and purchases only cups of coffee and tea. If the number of cups of coffee that Shantiel purchased was half the number of cups of tea that she purchased, and the total milligrams of caffeine in all the drinks she purchased was 735, how many cups of coffee did she purchase?

Ⓐ 2
Ⓑ 3
Ⓒ 5
Ⓓ 6

# ANSWER KEY
## Practice Test 2

### Section 1, Module 1: Reading and Writing

| | | |
|---|---|---|
| 1. **A** | 10. **A** | 19. **D** |
| 2. **A** | 11. **A** | 20. **D** |
| 3. **C** | 12. **D** | 21. **B** |
| 4. **A** | 13. **B** | 22. **D** |
| 5. **A** | 14. **C** | 23. **A** |
| 6. **C** | 15. **A** | 24. **D** |
| 7. **B** | 16. **C** | 25. **D** |
| 8. **B** | 17. **A** | 26. **C** |
| 9. **C** | 18. **A** | 27. **A** |

### Section 1, Module 2: Reading and Writing

| | | |
|---|---|---|
| 1. **B** | 10. **D** | 19. **C** |
| 2. **C** | 11. **C** | 20. **D** |
| 3. **A** | 12. **D** | 21. **C** |
| 4. **C** | 13. **A** | 22. **D** |
| 5. **D** | 14. **A** | 23. **D** |
| 6. **A** | 15. **C** | 24. **D** |
| 7. **B** | 16. **A** | 25. **C** |
| 8. **D** | 17. **A** | 26. **D** |
| 9. **A** | 18. **C** | 27. **B** |

# ANSWER KEY
## Practice Test 2

### Section 2, Module 1: Math

1. **B**
2. **C**
3. **2**
4. **A**
5. **C**
6. **C**
7. **D**
8. **1**
9. **B**
10. **1.5 or $\frac{3}{2}$**
11. **B**
12. **.3333 or $\frac{1}{3}$**
13. **D**
14. **C**
15. **D**
16. **D**
17. **12**
18. **D**
19. **C**
20. **A**
21. **D**
22. **D**

### Section 2, Module 2: Math

1. **A**
2. **A**
3. **C**
4. **B**
5. **B**
6. **A**
7. **54**
8. **C**
9. **B**
10. **C**
11. **D**
12. **C**
13. **A**
14. **3**
15. **D**
16. **C**
17. **B**
18. **144**
19. **D**
20. **B**
21. **43**
22. **C**

## Digital SAT Scoring Chart

This will give you an approximation of the score you would earn on the Digital SAT.[1] Tally the number of correct answers from the Reading and Writing section (out of 54) and the Math section (out of 44). Take the total for each of these and find the corresponding section score in the tables below.

| Number of Correct Reading and Writing Questions (Out of 54) | Reading and Writing Test Score (Out of 800) |
|---|---|
| 0 | 200 |
| 1 | 210 |
| 2 | 220 |
| 3 | 230 |
| 4 | 240 |
| 5 | 250 |
| 6 | 260 |
| 7 | 270 |
| 8 | 280 |
| 9 | 290 |
| 10 | 300 |
| 11 | 310 |
| 12 | 330 |
| 13 | 340 |
| 14 | 350 |
| 15 | 360 |
| 16 | 380 |
| 17 | 390 |
| 18 | 400 |
| 19 | 410 |
| 20 | 430 |
| 21 | 440 |
| 22 | 460 |
| 23 | 470 |
| 24 | 490 |
| 25 | 500 |
| 26 | 510 |
| 27 | 520 |

| Number of Correct Reading and Writing Questions (Out of 54) | Reading and Writing Test Score (Out of 800) |
|---|---|
| 28 | 530 |
| 29 | 540 |
| 30 | 550 |
| 31 | 560 |
| 32 | 570 |
| 33 | 580 |
| 34 | 590 |
| 35 | 600 |
| 36 | 610 |
| 37 | 620 |
| 38 | 630 |
| 39 | 640 |
| 40 | 650 |
| 41 | 660 |
| 42 | 670 |
| 43 | 680 |
| 44 | 690 |
| 45 | 700 |
| 46 | 710 |
| 47 | 720 |
| 48 | 730 |
| 49 | 740 |
| 50 | 750 |
| 51 | 760 |
| 52 | 770 |
| 53 | 790 |
| 54 | 800 |



[1] Keep in mind that some of the questions on an actual SAT test will be research questions that will not count towards your actual score. For the sake of simplicity, we are including possible research questions in your calculation.

| Number of Correct Math Questions (Out of 44) | Math Section Score (Out of 800) |
|---|---|
| 0 | 200 |
| 1 | 220 |
| 2 | 230 |
| 3 | 240 |
| 4 | 250 |
| 5 | 280 |
| 6 | 300 |
| 7 | 320 |
| 8 | 340 |
| 9 | 350 |
| 10 | 360 |
| 11 | 380 |
| 12 | 390 |
| 13 | 400 |
| 14 | 410 |
| 15 | 430 |
| 16 | 440 |
| 17 | 450 |
| 18 | 460 |
| 19 | 480 |
| 20 | 490 |
| 21 | 500 |
| 22 | 510 |

| Number of Correct Math Questions (Out of 44) | Math Section Score (Out of 800) |
|---|---|
| 23 | 520 |
| 24 | 530 |
| 25 | 540 |
| 26 | 550 |
| 27 | 560 |
| 28 | 570 |
| 29 | 580 |
| 30 | 590 |
| 31 | 600 |
| 32 | 610 |
| 33 | 620 |
| 34 | 630 |
| 35 | 650 |
| 36 | 660 |
| 37 | 680 |
| 38 | 690 |
| 39 | 700 |
| 40 | 720 |
| 41 | 750 |
| 42 | 770 |
| 43 | 790 |
| 44 | 800 |

Add the Reading and Writing section score and the Math section score to find your total SAT test score:

___________ Reading and Writing Section Score +

___________ Math Section Score =

___________ **Total SAT Test Score (between 400 and 1600)**

Approximate your testing percentiles (1st to 99th) using this chart:[2]

| Total Score | Section Score | Total Percentile | Reading and Writing Percentile | Math Percentile |
|---|---|---|---|---|
| 1600 | 800 | 99+ | 99+ | 99 |
| 1500 | 750 | 98 | 98 | 96 |
| 1400 | 700 | 94 | 94 | 91 |
| 1300 | 650 | 86 | 86 | 84 |
| 1200 | 600 | 74 | 73 | 75 |
| 1100 | 550 | 59 | 57 | 61 |
| 1000 | 500 | 41 | 40 | 42 |
| 900 | 450 | 25 | 24 | 27 |
| 800 | 400 | 11 | 11 | 15 |
| 700 | 350 | 3 | 3 | 5 |
| 600 | 300 | 1 | 1 | 1 |
| 500 | 250 | 1 | 1 | 1 |
| 400 | 200 | 1 | 1 | 1 |

[2]Scoring Data based on information at *collegeboard.org*

# Answer Explanations

## Section 1, Module 1: Reading and Writing

1. **(A)** The teacher is suggesting what the students can do to no longer fail their assignments—therefore, the teacher is providing them with a "solution." Although the assignment relates to mixing chemicals, the teacher is not suggesting a different "mixture." "Choice" and "origin" would not necessarily relate to solving the problem.

2. **(A)** The phrase "off his mark" means that the throw was inaccurate, making choice (A) correct. This can be seen by the fact that the catcher had to run and fetch the wild pitch. It is not choice (B) because there is no question that the pitcher is motivated—he is just not accurate with his throw. It is not (C) because the previous sentence says that he mounted the mound. It is not (D) because the pitcher is nervous, not serene or calm.

3. **(C)** The judge is trying to be patient and understanding with the prosecutor because it was his first case. As such, she will give him "leeway" to make some errors, making choice (C) correct. It is not choice (A) because the judge is being patient with the prosecutor, not giving him consequences. It is not (B) because "carte blanche" means to give someone total freedom—this is too extreme as the judge is only giving the prosecutor leeway on "some mistakes," not all of them. It is not (D) because the prosecutor does not need freedom from punishment, which is what amnesty is; instead, he simply needs the judge to be more patient with his rookie mistakes.

4. **(A)** "Impacts" best fits the meaning needed in this context, since the author is referring to the negative consequences or effects of the bystander effect. Choices (B) and (C) are overly violent, and (D) is overly positive.

5. **(A)** The text refers to a seller ridding himself of a "bloated instrument" which will certainly devalue. Hence, overvalued is a precise word choice. While the other choices are synonyms of bloated, they do not capture the author's meaning as related to inflated value.

6. **(C)** The narrator rhetorically asks "who has seen the wind?," then states that no one has. Instead, we have seen its effects indirectly from the trembling of the leaves and the bending of the trees. So, the overall structure of the text is that it presents different ways that the invisible wind may be seen. It is not choice (A) because it does not examine weather formation in general. It is not (B) because the focus is on the wind, not natural growth. It is not (D) because the emotional impact of the wind is not discussed.

7. **(B)** This sentence explains that the men who were rescued from the sinking ship were given a place to stay and enough money to complete their journey. The citizens of the town were hospitable toward the men when they landed, making choice (B) the best option. There is no evidence within the text that they were treated with scorn (looked down upon), envy, or humor, making the other choices incorrect.

8. **(B)** In reference to some thinkers who might believe that the slave songs expressed joy for a carefree and happy life, Du Bois states that he can believe it of "some, of many." However, Du Bois goes on to state from his viewpoint, the songs of slaves generally express the "music of an unhappy people." Therefore, he ultimately believes that the songs are largely expressions of the extremely difficult lives that slaves led. So, it is reasonable to infer that Du Bois would have an attitude of qualified skepticism toward these claims, since he acknowledges that there may have been some joy expressed in the songs—this is his "qualification" of the claim. He is primarily skeptical, however, believing that the emotional expressions of the songs are mainly ones of sadness. It will not be choices (A) or (D) since they are overly positive. And it is not (C) because he does not completely dismiss those who may think that the songs were happier.

9. **(C)** From the conversation between Haley and Mr. Shelby, it is clear that Haley is first and foremost a businessman. Moreover, he won't be persuaded to just accept Tom as payment for the debt, so choice (C) is an accurate depiction of his character. He is neither empathizing nor passive. In fact, he is nearly uncompromising. Finally, choice (B) won't work because we can infer by his negotiation skills that he is not an amateur.

10. **(A)** The office administrator argues that career services are only useful if students actually take advantage of them. Choice (A) best supports this position because it is the service that the students least used, and it is also the one that students thought would be the least helpful. Perhaps if more students actually tried the career testing, more of them would find it to be helpful. Choices (B) and (D) do not compare the helpfulness and usefulness of services, instead focusing on just one aspect. Choice (C) does not show a large gap between those who used a service and those who thought it would be helpful.

11. **(A)** If we examine the first sentence of the text, we see that broken-heart syndrome often looks like a heart attack with one key difference—there is no arterial blockage. That would mean that if we wished to tell the difference between the two, we could simply look for arterial blockage. If it were absent, we could conclude that the patient is suffering from broken-heart syndrome, not a heart attack. This makes choice (A) the best answer. The other choices do not directly relate to the claim as stated in the first sentence of the text.

12. **(D)** Vocational paths have to do with career choices. Choice (D) best deals with the assertion because it mentions "providing the community with efficient workmen in various lines." Choice (A) asserts that children are not ready to figure out their careers. Choice (B) does not discuss careers at all. Choice (C) is too vague as it would relate to career choices and does not suggest that schools should be in the business of helping guide students in their job options.

13. **(B)** This quotation provides the most direct support to the idea that at the time of the text's composition, the recognition of civil rights for the citizens of countries around the world was relatively limited. It is not choice (A) because this quotation refers to the connection Burke believes that the colonists and the British people share. It is not (A) or (D) because these quotations directly question supposed sources of British governmental authority.

14. **(C)** The previous sentence states that plastic-eating microorganisms could help solve the problem of plastic waste in the environment. The final sentence of the text begins by showing a contrast with the previous sentence—it states that "others are skeptical of the claims." Thus, it makes sense that the insertion should refer to whether bacteria could consume plastic deposits. Choice (A) is too vague. Choice (B) does not make a logical contrast. Choice (D) would make matters worse and so does not make sense.

15. **(A)** The text shows that in 14th- and 15th-century Florence, women were less and less likely to participate in court proceedings. The narrator acknowledges that many upper-class women may not have been affected by this, but that lower-class women were. A way of expressing that lower-class women were negatively affected by not being able to participate in court proceedings would be to state that they were "essentially at the mercy of their accusers," meaning that they could not advocate for themselves while their accusers could make whatever claims they wished. All of the other options would suggest that these women were more powerful than they in fact were in this historical context.

16. **(C)** This choice separates the introductory phrase, "Within your online profiles," from the independent clause that follows. Choice (A) has confused word order, (B) lacks a comma after the introductory phrase, and (D) inserts an unnecessary colon, creating a far too abrupt pause.

17. **(A)** "It's" means "it is," which is correct given the context—this is the only option that has an implicit verb. "Its" and "their" are used to show possession. "There" typically refers to a place.

18. **(A)** "Homeowners'" correctly indicates that there are multiple homeowners who possess returns on assets. Choices (B) and (C) are singular, and (D) does not indicate possession.

19. **(D)** "Felt" is the only option that maintains the past tense verb use in the sentence as seen in the other verbs "depicted" and "used."

20. **(D)** Choice (D) provides a comma after the introductory dependent clause and an apostrophe with "s" after the person's name to signify possession, which is logical since the name is singular. Choices (A) and (C) do not have an apostrophe at all, and choice (B) would be used for plural possession.

21. **(B)** "Allow" is parallel to the next part of the sentence that uses the verb "tie." The other options lack parallel structure. Also, "flexibility" is what it would make sense to permit, not "flexing" as one would do with a muscle.

22. **(D)** This option provides a needed pause between the two independent clauses in the sentence and before the clarification of "rodents." Choice (A) has no pause before "but," choice (B) has an unneeded pause after "also," and choice (C) gives no pause before "rodents."

23. **(A)** "Also" gives the most logical transition, introducing another description of birds in the sentence. The other options are overly wordy and do not provide a logical transition. Choice (B) incorrectly shows a contrast, and choices (C) and (D) incorrectly show cause and effect.

24. **(D)** "In order to" provides a logical transition between combining an enzyme and forming the organic molecule. The other options do not provide a logical transition. Choices (A) and (B) show cause and effect and (C) shows a contrast.

25. **(D)** The student wants to emphasize the time period when Ibn Battuta travelled. Choice (D) is the only option that explicitly refers to the time when he made his explorations—the 1300s. The other options use information from the text but do not mention the time.

26. **(C)** Focus on the specific claim—the student wants to show that there are two pumpkin varieties that can be eaten. Based on the notes, Casperita pumpkins are "edible" and Porcelain Doll pumpkins are a "good choice for pumpkin pie," implying that they too are edible. So, choice (C) is the most logical option. The other options refer to pumpkins in the notes that are not consistently referred to as being edible.

27. **(A)** If there are few of the Rice's whales left, it makes sense that there are fewer opportunities to observe them—thus, choice (A) is the most logical answer. Choice (B) does not have to do with the observability of the whale. Choice (C) is not supported by the notes since the whale is found in the Gulf of Mexico. Choice (D) refers to a potential future event, not to something that presents an issue for observation in the present moment.

## Section 1, Module 2: Reading and Writing

1. **(B)** The sentence shows where in the body the vestibular system is found, so "located" is most appropriate. The other options would be more appropriate in referring to people and where they live instead of where a bodily system is located.
2. **(C)** "Bolster" means "to solidify or build" in this context, making it the most logical option to refer to improving one's resume. "Cushion" and "rebuild" would suggest protecting one's career against a hardship while the emphasis here is on positive growth. And "maintain" does not suggest growth but keeping things as they are.
3. **(A)** The "while" in this sentence indicates a contrast between the attraction that the hydrophilic heads have towards water and the repulsion that the hydrophobic tails have. Thus, "repelled" makes the most sense. Another way you could think about this is to look at the word roots—"phobic" indicates fear or repulsion, making this a logical option. The other options would not provide a logical contrast with "attracted."
4. **(C)** "Derive" means "obtain," making this a logical option to express how aerobic organisms gather their energy. It is not "discover" or "discern," since these are advanced thought processes that are not integral to obtaining energy. It is not "inhale" because while oxygen may be inhaled, the energy is gathered from the process of cellular respiration.
5. **(D)** "Lucrative" suggests that marine welding would be a career that has a high salary. While the other options could be associated with money, they would not be logically applicable to this situation, in which the potential earnings from a career are described.
6. **(A)** In the text, the author summarizes his argument that aiding the German Socialists and recognizing the Bolsheviki would be "playing with fire"—i.e., would lead to potentially negative consequences due to an indecisive outcome to the war. It is not choice (B) because this is too literal an interpretation. And it is not (C) or (D) because this phrase does not refer to making peace or reconciling.
7. **(B)** Text 1 provides a detailed description of the painting *A Sunday on La Grande Jatte*, while Text 2 looks at how Claude Monet's painting *Impression: Sunrise* fits into the overall context of the impressionist movement. This makes choice (B) the most logical option. It is not choice (A) because Text 1 descries the painting technique. It is not (C) because Text 1 describes the setting of the painting. It is not (D) because Text 2 does not provide biographical details about Monet.
8. **(D)** The text describes the genetic changes associated with antigenic shift, stating that via "viral reassortment" the particles will produce completely new proteins "to which the entire human race is vulnerable." While the antigenic drift can also result in renewed vulnerability, it is to viral strains of which one was previously immune. Therefore, the changes would not be as great as those associated with antigenic shift. Likewise, the author uses the example of a genome split in a bird that is capable of infecting humans making (D), rather than (C), the correct choice.

9. **(A)** The narrator argues that balance is key to achieving the best health results with handwashing. If you wash your hands too frequently, it can cause problems; similarly, if you wash your hands infrequently, it can cause problems. Choice (A) is the most logical option because it suggests that those who wash their hands just eight times a day have less illness than those who wash their hands far more frequently. It is not (B) because these are both situations in which the narrator believes handwashing would be warranted. It is not choice (C) because the narrator does not make any comparisons about geography. It is not choice (D) because the narrator does not consider the effects of hand sanitizer.

10. **(D)** The idea that needs support is that the characters in the novel find it quite difficult to plan their budget because of how unpredictable expenses are. Choice (D) provides the best support for this since it mentions how there is no end to the things they had to buy and to unforeseen contingencies, i.e., random expenses that come up. Choice (A) does not focus on budgetary matters. Choices (B) and (C) do not refer to unpredictable expenses.

11. **(C)** The graph indicates that women, those in the age group of 18–29, and those who have completed some college are the most likely categorizations to use social networking sites—choice (C) is the only option that fits all these criteria. Choices (A) and (B) both have males, and (D) uses an age group that is outside the range given by the graph.

12. **(D)** The researchers' hypothesis is that losing body water is not as detrimental if one is losing it while exercising in cold weather. If someone does not sweat as much in a cold environment, there would be less of a need to have water in one's body to produce sweat. Thus, losing body water would not be as detrimental to someone in this situation. It is not (A) because this does not address the specifics of someone exercising in cold conditions. It is not (B) because cold would not affect whether someone could take supplements. It is not (C) because the factor in question is cold, not body mass index.

13. **(A)** We do not know the precise makeup of the client's portfolio, so we can consider the potential impacts of each of the possible switches. If we check the answers against the table, we can see the biggest drop in variance, and thus the biggest drop in risk, occurs as stocks owned go from one to two. This change cuts the variance nearly in half. The other choices still decrease the risk, but not by as much as choice (A).

14. **(A)** The text argues that Sweden has done a great job at political compromise over the years, with stakeholders from a variety of backgrounds in society able to successfully find common ground. This point is emphasized in the last sentence, in which the narrator draws a contrast between the near uniformity of private industry ownership (which would lead one to think that business would have a greater influence than labor on outcomes) and showing how labor disputes can be settled in a way that involves all interested parties. Choice (A) best accomplishes this goal by showing that workers and management both trust in the government managed settlement. It is not choice (B) because this would involve a one-sided deal for business. It is not (C) because that would not necessarily indicate compromise. It is not (D) because such actions would show the failure of compromise.

15. **(C)** This is the only option that correctly uses an apostrophe after "workers" to show that there are plural workers who own passports and visas. Choice (A) incorrectly shows that the visas and passports possess something. Choice (B) does not show possession at all. Choice (D) uses singular possession by putting the apostrophe before the "s."

16. **(A)** Choice (A) puts the words in the most logical sequence, clearly stating the subject of "scientific method" and following with the description of it. The other options all put the words in an illogical order.

17. **(A)** The adjectives "loveable" and "fluffy" can have their order reversed and the sentence would still be logical, so it is appropriate to separate them with a comma, as in choice (A). Choice (B) lacks a comma, choice (C) is too choppy, and choice (D) provides too large of an interruption at this point.

18. **(C)** Choice (C) correctly uses a colon to come before the clarification of who makes up the two players. Choices (A), (B), and (D) have unnecessary punctuation breaking up the two-part clarification.

19. **(C)** "Struck" correctly provides the past tense conjugation of "strike"—this means that the law was overturned. The other options do not provide a proper past tense conjugation of "strike."

20. **(D)** This option provides a comma before the dependent clause that starts with "which." Choices (A) and (B) do not provide this comma, and choice (C) does not have a complete sentence after the semicolon.

21. **(C)** The subject here is "a struggle," which is a singular noun. We need a singular verb to match. "Does" is the correct answer—it is the only singular verb out of the choices. "Do" is a plural verb in this context, "doing" leads to gibberish, and "have done" uses the incorrect tense.

22. **(D)** Choice (D) is the only option to correctly place commas around the transitional word "however." This choice also correctly uses a colon to come before a clarification.

23. **(D)** "Thus" means "therefore," and is logical at this point since the previous sentence discusses how humans follow their instincts in seeking out a meditative state, and the current sentence elaborates on the poem's symbolism. Choices (A) and (C) would introduce new ideas most likely in a list, and choice (B) would be used to show a contrast.

24. **(D)** The text starts by highlighting Chancourtois's important contribution to chemistry. It then goes on to state that because of some minor errors and differences in terminology, his discovery was mainly ignored. Since the author is speaking about Chancourtois's discovery in a positive light, it would make sense to say that it was "unfortunate" that his discovery was ignored. It is not "simultaneously" since the text goes on to talk about the future, which would not be simultaneous to Chancourtois. It is not "moreover" because this is not a continuation of an idea. It is not "naturally" because with all the unusual circumstances surrounding the way Chancourtois set up his table, it would not be logical to describe it as "natural."

25. **(C)** The student's goal is to show why it was difficult to find information about the *Hunley* during the 20th century. Since the ship remained submerged until the beginning of the 21st century, it makes sense that there would be little information about it. It is not choice (A) because the ship was not destroyed. It is not (B) because this would be an accurate assertion about recent discoveries, but not about ones during the 20th century. It is not choice (D) because this is not directly related to the student's goal.

26. **(D)** Choice (D) is the only option that mentions specialized terminology as it relates to genealogical records—"consanguineous" and "affinal." None of the other options mentions specialized terminology.

27. **(B)** The student's goal is to suggest something that could be done to do a comparative analysis of how effective certain antibiotics are. Choice (B) is the only option that provides a direct comparison between two antibiotics and their effectiveness. Choice (A) provides a comparison but not of antibiotics. Choice (C) is rather vague. Choice (D) focuses on history instead of biological analysis.

## Section 2, Module 1: Math

1. **(B)**

$$(0.8a + 0.7b) - (1.4a - 0.3b) \rightarrow$$
$$0.8a + 0.7b - 1.4a + 0.3b \rightarrow$$
$$(0.8a - 1.4a) + (0.7b + 0.3b) \rightarrow$$
$$-0.6a + b$$

2. **(C)** Take two clearly identifiable points from the line: (0, 1) and (−2, −2). The slope is the change in *y* divided by the change in *x*:

$$\frac{y_2 - y_1}{x_2 - x_1} = \frac{-2-1}{-2-0} = \frac{-3}{-2} = \frac{3}{2}$$

3. **(2)** Make things as easy as possible to solve for this expression: simply take half of the equation to find the value of $-5 + 6x$.

$$12x - 10 = 4 \rightarrow$$
$$\frac{12x - 10}{2} = \frac{4}{2} \rightarrow$$
$$6x - 5 = 2 \rightarrow$$
$$-5 + 6x = 2$$

4. **(A)** Manipulate the equation to isolate the height of the cylinder:

$$v = \pi r^2 h \rightarrow$$

Divide both sides by $\pi r^2 \rightarrow$

$$\frac{v}{\pi r^2} = h$$

This corresponds to choice (A).

5. **(C)** The voter turnout in the year 2008 was nearly 62 percent, making it the highest turnout for any of the years presented in the graph.

6. **(C)**

$$(2y^2 - y) - (2y^2 + 2y) \rightarrow$$
$$2y^2 - y - 2y^2 - 2y \rightarrow$$
$$-y - 2y = -3y$$

7. **(D)** All three of the angles will add up to 180, so set up an equation to solve for *x*:

$$2x + 3x + 4x = 180 \rightarrow$$
$$9x = 180 \rightarrow$$
$$x = 20$$

Since $\angle CED$ is equal to $3x$, multiply 3 by 20 to find the measure of the angle:

$$3 \times 20 = 60 \text{ degrees.}$$

8. **(1)** Take the cube root of both sides of the equation, then solve for $x$:

$$(x+2)^3 = 27 \rightarrow$$
$$\sqrt[3]{(x+2)^3} = \sqrt[3]{27} \rightarrow$$
$$x+2 = 3 \rightarrow$$
$$x = 1$$

9. **(B)** The number of diners who ordered a dessert is 50. Out of those 50, there were 15 diners who ordered an appetizer. Solve for the probability that a diner who ordered a dessert also ordered an appetizer by dividing 15 by 50:

$$\frac{15}{50} = \frac{3}{10}$$

10. **(1.5 or $\frac{3}{2}$)** The $x$-intercept of the equation is found when the $y$ value of the point equals 0. So, plug 0 in for $y$ to solve for the $x$-coordinate of the $x$-intercept.

$$y = 2x - 3 \rightarrow$$
$$0 = 2x - 3 \rightarrow$$
$$3 = 2x \rightarrow$$
$$x = \frac{3}{2}$$

11. **(B)** The line is already in slope-intercept form, $y = mx + b$, in which the $b$ represents the $y$-intercept. So, the $y$-intercept is $-2$.

12. **($\frac{1}{3}$ or .3333)** Use substitution to solve for $y$. Since $y = \frac{1}{2}x$, $x = 2y$. Plug $2y$ in for $x$ into the first equation:

$$3 = \frac{3}{2}(4x - 2y) \rightarrow$$
$$3 = \frac{3}{2}(4(2y) - 2y) \rightarrow$$
$$3 = \frac{3}{2}(8y - 2y) \rightarrow$$
$$3 = \frac{3}{2}(6y) \rightarrow$$
$$3 = 9y \rightarrow$$
$$\frac{3}{9} = \frac{1}{3} = y$$

13. **(D)** All of the options have a $y$ value of 0. So, look at what values of $x$ will cause there to be a $y$ value of 0, since a point that intersects the $x$ axis must have a $y$ value of 0. In $y = (x+4)(x-5)x$, if $x$ is 0, $-4$, or 5, the entire right side of the equation would be 0. Therefore, all three options would be points at which the function intersects the $x$ axis.

14. **(C)** The initial number of the bacteria can be found when you plug 0 in for $h$, since when $h = 0$ no time has passed.

$$1000 \times 2^0 = 1000 \times 1 = 1000.$$

Now, determine the value of $h$ that would be needed to find a number of bacteria that is 8 times the initial value of 1,000: $8 \times 1000 = 8000$.

$$B(h) = 1000 \times 2^h \rightarrow$$
$$8000 = 1000 \times 2^h \rightarrow$$
$$8 = 2^h \rightarrow 8 = 2^3$$

Since 8 is equal to 2 cubed, the correct value for $h$ in this situation is 3 hours. If you do not remember that 8 is equal to 2 cubed, you could also plug in the answer choices to solve.

15. **(D)** The spins that had total values of 6 or less are bolded and italicized below:

| Total of Combined Spins | Number of Spins with That Total Value |
|---|---|
| ***2*** | ***1*** |
| ***3*** | ***2*** |
| ***4*** | ***2*** |
| ***5*** | ***4*** |
| ***6*** | ***5*** |
| 7 | 6 |
| 8 | 7 |
| 9 | 4 |
| 10 | 3 |
| 11 | 4 |
| 12 | 2 |

Out of the 40 total turns, there is therefore a total of $1 + 2 + 2 + 4 + 5 = 14$ turns in which Pete has a total of 6 or less. Find the fraction of the combined spins as follows:

$$\frac{14}{40} = \frac{7}{20}$$

16. **(D)** Since the Mexico City area represented 17% of the total population of Mexico, solve for the total population of Mexico, $x$, by using this equation:

$$0.17x = 22{,}000{,}000 \rightarrow$$
$$x = \frac{22{,}000{,}000}{0.17} \approx 129{,}000{,}000$$

17. **(12)** Plug 5 in for $x$ to solve for $f(5)$:

$$f(x) = (x - 3)(x + 1) \rightarrow$$
$$f(5) = (5 - 3)(5 + 1) \rightarrow$$
$$f(5) = 2 \times 6 = 12$$

18. **(D)** The solution set of the two inequalities $y > x + 1$ and $y < -2x - 3$ and the quadrants of the coordinate plane are graphed below:

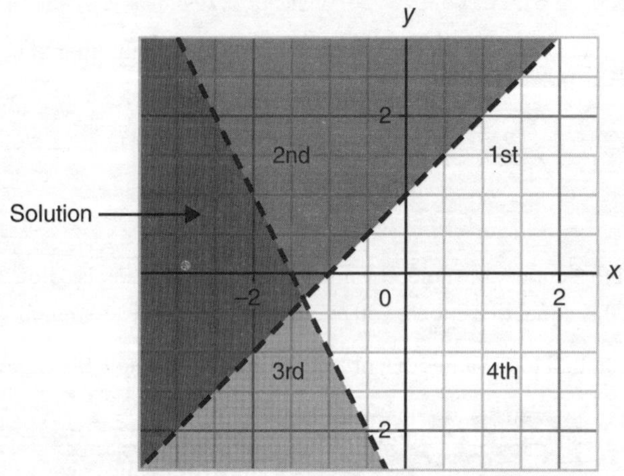


So, the solution set is in quadrants 2 and 3 only.

19. **(C)** The computer costs \$2,000 and goes down by the same amount each year. After 6 years, the total amount of depreciation is $2000 - 800 = 1200$. So, to find the annual amount of depreciation, take 1200 and divide it by 6: $\frac{1200}{6} = 200$.

20. **(A)** A circle with a center at (3, 4) that intersects at the origin, (0, 0) would look like this:

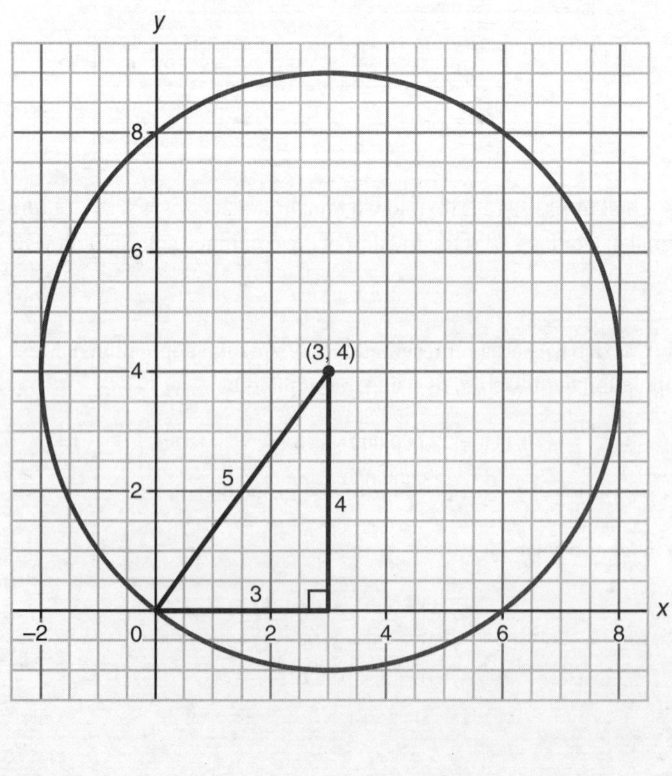


PRACTICE TEST 2

To find the radius, notice that you can inscribe a special 3-4-5 right triangle as shown above. The radius is therefore 5. The equation of a circle is $(x-h)^2+(y-k)^2=r^2$, in which $(h, k)$ represents the center, and $r$ represents the radius. Plug in (3, 4) for the center and 5 for the radius to find the answer:

$$(x-h)^2+(y-k)^2=r^2 \rightarrow$$
$$(x-3)^2+(y-4)^2=5^2 \rightarrow$$
$$(x-3)^2+(y-4)^2=25$$

21. **(D)** Find how many minutes there are in 16 hours:

$$16 \text{ hours} \times \frac{60 \text{ minutes}}{1 \text{ hour}} \rightarrow$$

$$16 \cancel{\text{hours}} \times \frac{60 \text{ minutes}}{1 \cancel{\text{hour}}} = 960 \text{ minutes}$$

Then, since Susan blinks 20 times per minute while awake, multiply 20 by 960 to find the total number of times she will blink:

$$20 \times 960 = 19,200$$

22. **(D)** Hugo spends \$400 a month on miscellaneous expenses. If he cut this expense by half and allocates all that he has cut to his savings, his savings would increase by \$200 a month. Hugo is trying to allocate more money into savings. Now, calculate how large of an increase this additional \$200 would be relative to the \$250 he is currently saving:

$$\frac{200}{250} \times 100 = 80\%$$

So, he would increase his monthly savings by 80% if he were to make this change.

## Section 2, Module 2: Math

1. **(A)** Plug $-2$ in for $x$ and solve:

$$g(x) = \frac{x^3}{2} \rightarrow$$

$$g(-2) = \frac{(-2)^3}{2} = \frac{-8}{2} = -4$$

2. **(A)** The answers are all written in slope-intercept form, and they all have different slopes. So, calculate the slope of the linear function by using two points. We can use (6, 0) and (9, 1) since there is no negative value in the point, which could more easily lead to a careless error:

$$\frac{y_2-y_1}{x_2-x_1} = \frac{1-0}{9-6} = \frac{1}{3}$$

The only option with a slope of $\frac{1}{3}$ is choice (A), $f(x) = \frac{1}{3}x - 2$.

3. **(C)** $\sqrt[3]{a} \times a^{\frac{5}{3}} = a^{\frac{1}{3}} \times a^{\frac{5}{3}} = a^{\left(\frac{1}{3}+\frac{5}{3}\right)} = a^{\frac{6}{3}} = a^{2}$

4. **(B)** First, use the ordered pair (8, 16) to solve for the value of the constant $a$:

$$y = ax \rightarrow$$
$$16 = a8 \rightarrow$$
$$\frac{16}{8} = a \rightarrow a = 2$$

Now, plug $-3$ in for $y$ to the function that has the constant $a$ as 2:

$$y = 2x \rightarrow$$
$$-3 = 2x \rightarrow$$
$$\frac{-3}{2} = x \rightarrow x = -1.5$$

So, the answer is choice (B).

5. **(B)** Match the constants with the corresponding numbers on the other side of the equation. $a$ equals 2, $b$ equals 16, and $c$ equals 32. Add these numbers together to find the sum of $a$, $b$, and $c$:

$$2 + 16 + 32 = 50$$

6. **(A)** In the function $S(w) = 500 + 10w$, when zero weeks have gone by, the value of $w$ will be 0. Plugging 0 into the function for $w$, the amount of money she will have in her savings account will be 500. This represents how much money she has in the account when no weeks have gone by, so it corresponds to choice (A), the money that is in her account at the beginning of the time period. Profit corresponds to revenue minus expenses, and the slope of 10 corresponds to the weekly increase in money in the account.

7. **(54)** The width of 2 inches on the map corresponds to 6 miles in actual distance, and the length of 3 inches on the map corresponds to 9 miles in actual distance. So, multiply 6 by 9 to find the actual area of the rectangular plot of land:

$$6 \times 9 = 54 \text{ square miles.}$$

8. **(C)** The total amount of time that it took Samara to complete the trip is $4 + 6 = 10$ hours. Use the equation Distance $=$ Rate $\times$ Time to work with this problem. The problem asks for the average speed, which corresponds to the rate. Using that equation, the Rate $= \frac{\text{Distance}}{\text{Time}}$. Use 400 for the distance and 10 for the time to solve for the average rate over the entire trip:

$$\text{Rate} = \frac{\text{Distance}}{\text{Time}} \rightarrow$$
$$\text{Rate} = \frac{400 \text{ miles}}{10 \text{ hours}} = 40 \text{ mph}$$

9. **(B)** Since the triangles are similar to one another, the ratios of the sides will be the same. So, the tangent of angle $C$ will be the same as the tangent of angle $F$. The tangent of angle $F$ is the opposite side $ED$ divided by the adjacent side $DF$: $\frac{10}{24} = \frac{5}{12}$. This corresponds to choice (B).

10. **(C)** Based on the best-fit line that could connect the points, the amount that the value of an airplane decreases each year is approximately \$5,000. Since the initial cost of the airplane is approximately \$100,000, divide 100,000 by 5,000 to estimate when the plane value will closely approximate 0 dollars:

$$\frac{100{,}000}{5{,}000} = 20$$

So, 20 years after purchase the plane will closely approximate a value of 0 dollars.

11. **(D)** 400% of $x$ is $4x$. This must be added to the original value of $x$ to find the total value when $x$ is increased by 400%: $4x + x = 5x$.

12. **(C)**

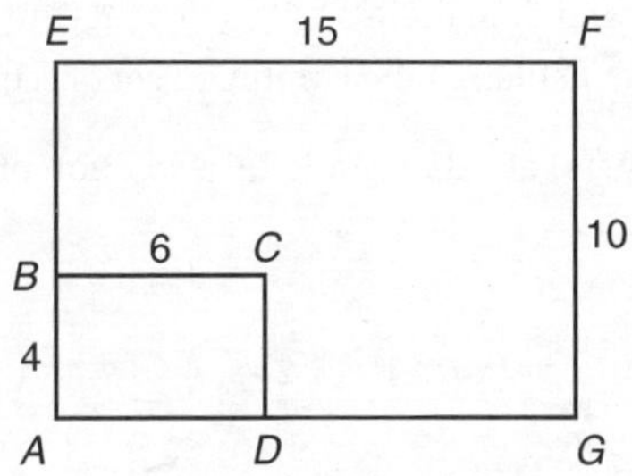


Since the rectangles are similar to one another, the sides are proportional. Therefore, the ratio of $\overline{EF}$ to $\overline{FG}$ will be the same as the ratio of $\overline{BC}$ to $\overline{AB}$. Call $x$ the length of side $\overline{EF}$, and set up a proportion to solve:

$$\frac{x}{10} = \frac{6}{4} \rightarrow$$

$$x = \frac{10 \times 6}{4} = \frac{60}{4} = 15$$

Since *AEFG* is a rectangle, there will be two sides of length 15 and two sides of length 10. Find the perimeter of the rectangle by adding the lengths of all these sides together:

$$15 + 15 + 10 + 10 = 50\,.$$

13. **(A)** A line with the form $y = k$ will simply be a horizontal line. Since the constant $k$ is greater than zero, it will not intersect the x axis at all, and will therefore have no zeros. For example, consider the equation $y = 2$. The graph of this line is given below:

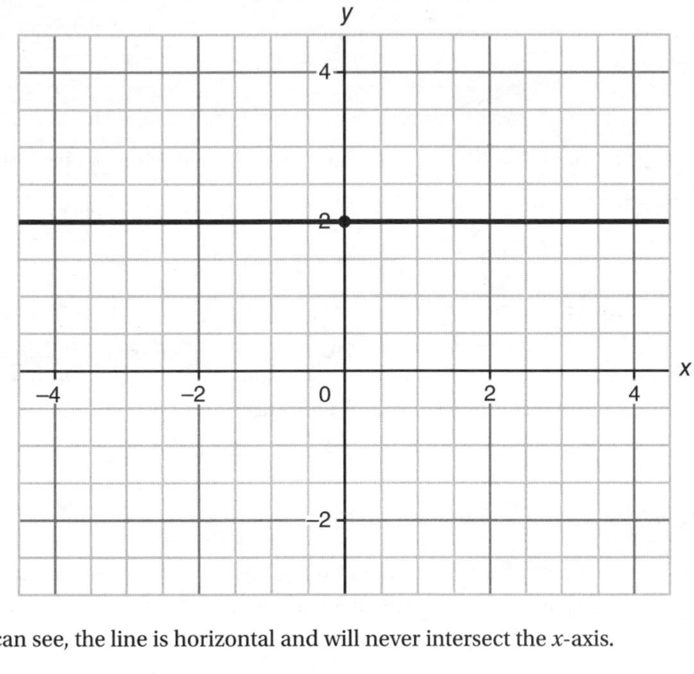


As you can see, the line is horizontal and will never intersect the $x$-axis.

14. **(3)** The combined set of both classes will have a total of 40 students, since there are 20 students in each class. So, the median of the set of both classes will be between the 20th and 21st terms when the numbers are put in order from least to greatest. There are a total of 18 values that are 2 or less, and then there are 9 values that are 3. So, the 20th and 21st terms will both be 3, making 3 the median of the combined set of scores.

15. **(D)** What would be the value(s) of $x$ that would be a solution or solutions to this equation?

$$\frac{x^2-4}{x-2}=4\rightarrow$$

$$\frac{(x-2)(x-2)}{(x-2)}=4\rightarrow$$

$$\frac{(x-2)\cancel{(x-2)}}{\cancel{(x-2)}}=4\rightarrow$$

$$x-2=4\rightarrow$$

$$x=2$$

Now, check to be sure this solution is not extraneous by plugging 2 back into the original equation:

$$\frac{x^2-4}{x-2}=4\rightarrow$$

$$\frac{(2)^2-4}{(2)-2}=4\rightarrow$$

$$\frac{0}{0}$$

This is undefined, so there are no solutions to the equation.

16. **(C)** The vertex in a parabola of the form $y=a(x-h)^2+k$ is $(h, k)$. In the parabola with the equation $y=(x-6)^2$, the value of $h$ is 6 and the value of $k$ is 0. So, the vertex of the parabola is (6, 0).

17. **(B)** 14 out of the 44 people to serve as president of the United States prior to 2020 had previously been vice president. So, $\frac{14}{44}$ of the presidents had been vice presidents. Set up an equation expressing this as follows:

$$V=\frac{14}{44}P\rightarrow V=\frac{7}{22}P.$$

Therefore, the answer is choice (B).

18. **(144)** For the equations to have infinitely many solutions, they must be multiples of one another. Rearrange the equations so that the $x$ and $y$ terms match:

$$-\frac{1}{4}x+\frac{1}{6}y=12$$

$$-3x+2y=a$$

Notice that $-3$ is 12 times $-\frac{1}{4}$ and that 2 is 12 times $\frac{1}{6}$. So, multiply the 12 from the first equation by 12 to find the value of $a$ in the second equation:

$$12\times 12=144$$

So, $a=144$.

19. **(D)** Given that $J$ stands for the number of people from Julian's side of the family and that $M$ stands for the number of people from Maria's side of the family, the first inequality should be $M + J > 200$, since they want to have more than 200 people in attendance. The second inequality represents the costs. The total cost for the reception should be less than $18,000, and the cost for each invited guest is $40. So, the second inequality should be $40(M + J) < 18{,}000$ to model this relationship. These two inequalities correspond to choice (D).

20. **(B)** Use unit analysis to cancel out the necessary terms and convert the value to the required terms:

$$30\frac{\text{Miles}}{\text{Hour}} \times \frac{5{,}280 \text{ Feet}}{1 \text{ Mile}} \times \frac{1 \text{ Hour}}{3{,}600 \text{ Seconds}} \rightarrow$$

$$30\frac{\text{Miles}}{\text{Hour}} \times \frac{5{,}280 \text{ Feet}}{1 \text{ Mile}} \times \frac{1 \text{ Hour}}{3{,}600 \text{ Seconds}} \rightarrow$$

$$\frac{30 \times 5{,}280}{3{,}600} = 44\frac{\text{Feet}}{\text{Second}}$$

21. **(43)** Since there are 360 degrees in a circle, the sector designated by $\angle ACB$ represents $\frac{100}{360}$ of the total area of the circle. The area for this circle is found using the formula $\pi r^2$, and the radius of the circle is 7. So, multiply the area of the circle by the fraction of the area that the sector represents to find the sector's area:

$$\pi 7^2 \times \frac{100}{360} = 42.74$$

This would be rounded to an area of 43, since that is the nearest whole square unit.

22. **(C)** Use $C$ to represent the number of cups of coffee Shantiel purchased, and $T$ to represent the number of cups of tea purchased. Set up a system of equations to solve for $C$. First, since the number of cups of coffee is half the number of cups of tea, one equation would be $C = \frac{1}{2}T$. The second equation represents the milligrams of caffeine. Since there are 95 milligrams in each cup of coffee and 26 milligrams in each cup of tea, the equation would be $95C + 26T = 735$. Solve for $C$ by using substitution from the first equation:

$$C = \frac{1}{2}T \rightarrow$$

$$2C = T$$

Now substitute $2C$ in for $T$ into the second equation, then solve for $C$:

$$95C + 26T = 735 \rightarrow$$

$$95C + 26(2C) = 735 \rightarrow$$

$$95C + 52C = 735 \rightarrow$$

$$147C = 735 \rightarrow$$

$$C = \frac{735}{147} = 5$$

So, she purchased 5 cups of coffee, which corresponds to choice (C).

# PART 7
# Practice Test 3: Adaptive

# Adaptive Test Overview

You are about to take an Adaptive SAT Practice Test. This will simulate the section-adaptive format of the Digital SAT. Depending on your performance on the first module of each section, you will have a more difficult or less difficult second module of each section. (In order to maximize your potential practice material, there are no overlapping questions in any of the modules—i.e., if you do Reading and Writing Module 2B, for example, you can still go back and try Reading and Writing Module 2A for a later practice exercise.) The format of the test is outlined in the table below. You can use a calculator throughout the math section. Good luck!

| SAT Module | Format |
|---|---|
| Reading and Writing Module 1 | 32 Minutes, 27 Questions, Standard Difficulty<br>Score the module after completion to determine whether you do 2A or 2B. |
| Reading and Writing Module 2A or 2B | 32 Minutes, 27 Questions, Adaptive Difficulty<br>If you get 17 or fewer questions correct on the first module, do the less challenging Module 2A.<br>If you get 18 or more questions correct on the first module, do the more challenging Module 2B. |
| **Break—10 Minutes** | |
| Math Module 1 | 35 Minutes, 22 Questions, Standard Difficulty<br>Score the module after completion to determine whether you do 2A or 2B. |
| Math Module 2A or 2B | 35 Minutes, 22 Questions, Adaptive Difficulty<br>If you get 13 or fewer questions correct on the first module, do the less challenging Module 2A.<br>If you get 14 or more questions correct on the first module, do the more challenging Module 2B |

**TEST TIP**

For helpful features the Digital SAT provides while taking the test, please refer to the Introduction at the beginning of this book and the labeled screenshots provided.

# ANSWER SHEET
## Practice Test 3: Adaptive

### Section 1, Module 1: Reading and Writing

| | | |
|---|---|---|
| 1. ____ | 10. ____ | 19. ____ |
| 2. ____ | 11. ____ | 20. ____ |
| 3. ____ | 12. ____ | 21. ____ |
| 4. ____ | 13. ____ | 22. ____ |
| 5. ____ | 14. ____ | 23. ____ |
| 6. ____ | 15. ____ | 24. ____ |
| 7. ____ | 16. ____ | 25. ____ |
| 8. ____ | 17. ____ | 26. ____ |
| 9. ____ | 18. ____ | 27. ____ |

# ANSWER SHEET

## Practice Test 3: Adaptive

### Section 1, Module 2A or 2B: Reading and Writing

| | | |
|---|---|---|
| 1. _____ | 10. _____ | 19. _____ |
| 2. _____ | 11. _____ | 20. _____ |
| 3. _____ | 12. _____ | 21. _____ |
| 4. _____ | 13. _____ | 22. _____ |
| 5. _____ | 14. _____ | 23. _____ |
| 6. _____ | 15. _____ | 24. _____ |
| 7. _____ | 16. _____ | 25. _____ |
| 8. _____ | 17. _____ | 26. _____ |
| 9. _____ | 18. _____ | 27. _____ |

# ANSWER SHEET
## Practice Test 3: Adaptive



### Section 2, Module 1: Math

| | | | |
|---|---|---|---|
| 1. | _____ | 12. | _____ |
| 2. | _____ | 13. | _____ |
| 3. | _____ | 14. | _____ |
| 4. | _____ | 15. | _____ |
| 5. | _____ | 16. | _____ |
| 6. | _____ | 17. | _____ |
| 7. | _____ | 18. | _____ |
| 8. | _____ | 19. | _____ |
| 9. | _____ | 20. | _____ |
| 10. | _____ | 21. | _____ |
| 11. | _____ | 22. | _____ |

# ANSWER SHEET

## Practice Test 3: Adaptive

### Section 2, Module 2A or 2B: Math

| | |
|---|---|
| 1. ____ | 12. ____ |
| 2. ____ | 13. ____ |
| 3. ____ | 14. ____ |
| 4. ____ | 15. ____ |
| 5. ____ | 16. ____ |
| 6. ____ | 17. ____ |
| 7. ____ | 18. ____ |
| 8. ____ | 19. ____ |
| 9. ____ | 20. ____ |
| 10. ____ | 21. ____ |
| 11. ____ | 22. ____ |

# Practice Test 3: Adaptive

## Section 1, Module 1: Reading and Writing

32 MINUTES, 27 QUESTIONS

**DIRECTIONS**

You will be tested on a variety of important reading and writing skills. Each question has one or more passages, possibly including a graph or table. Carefully read each passage and question and choose the best answer to the question based on the passage(s).

Every question in this section is multiple-choice with four possible answers. Each question has only one best answer.

Even if a person does "make it" by creating original content and __________ a viewer base, a career as an influencer is not very stable. Recent changes to an Internet company's monetization algorithm had thousands of short video creators up in arms as they saw profits plummet with no explanation from the platform.

**1**

Which choice completes the text with the most logical and precise word or phrase?

Ⓐ manufacturing
Ⓑ fabricating
Ⓒ escalating
Ⓓ building

Born in 1644 during the Tokugawa period (also known as the Edo period), Matsuo Bashō became interested in poetry and literature after going to Ueno Castle and being in the ________ the lord's son.

**2**

Which choice completes the text with the most logical and precise word or phrase?

Ⓐ company of
Ⓑ incorporation of
Ⓒ commerce of
Ⓓ profession as

## 1 MODULE 1 1

Scientists found a way to avoid the negative impact of chemical selectivity by implementing a more controlled reaction process. Scientists ________ the benzene reaction to produce a product like what they originally intended, but one that did not add multiple sidechains to the benzene ring. This technique came to be known as Friedel-Crafts Acylation, a now widely used technique in the production of benzene-containing products.

**3**

Which choice completes the text with the most logical and precise word or phrase?

Ⓐ modified
Ⓑ expunged
Ⓒ ousted
Ⓓ proposed

In his most recent, *Words Without Music*, Glass discusses his influences, beginning with his Jewish father who ran a record shop in Baltimore. His father's love for Schubert, Shostakovich, and Bartók ______ in Glass a love for music; by the time he was fifteen years old, he had become the classical-music buyer for the record shop.

**4**

Which choice completes the text with the most logical and precise word or phrase?

Ⓐ took
Ⓑ spurred
Ⓒ used
Ⓓ inspire

During transcription, nucleotides are polymerized into a strand of mRNA whose sequence is complementary to that of the template DNA. This "pre-mRNA" typically contains several regions of non-coding material, or "introns," that must be excised prior to translation of the protein-coding regions, which are referred to as "exons." In a complex process known as splicing, the introns are extracted and degraded, while the adjacent ends of exons are adjoined, and trafficked out of the nucleus to the endoplasmic reticulum, where protein synthesis can at last begin.

**5**

As used in the text, what does the word "excised" most nearly mean?

Ⓐ Removed
Ⓑ Translated
Ⓒ Coded
Ⓓ Mutated

# 1 MODULE 1 1



A third of all Fortune 500 CEOs possess liberal arts degrees. LEAP, or Liberal Education & America's Promise, is an initiative launched by the Association of American Colleges & Universities to emphasize the importance of a 21st-century liberal arts education for individuals and a nation "dependent on economic creativity and democratic vitality." According to LEAP's recent national survey, 93% of employers say that "a demonstrated capacity to think critically, communicate clearly, and solve complex problems is more important than undergraduate major." You've guessed it—these three skill sets are the unifying objective of liberal arts programs nationwide.

**6**

Which choice best describes the overall structure of the text?

Ⓐ The writer explains the outline of a liberal arts curriculum.

Ⓑ The writer begins with a historical survey and ends with a financial analysis.

Ⓒ The writer considers expert opinions, then refutes these opinions with statistical evidence.

Ⓓ The writer introduces an initiative, then justifies its economic relevance.

**Text 1**

As online education becomes accredited and archives make it easy for employers to see students' work and achievements, open online education is in position to overtake its predecessor. Digital credentials, reputable degrees, and professional certificates mean that employers cannot only rest assured that employees have extensive training and knowledge, but will also, for the first time, be able to effortlessly glimpse academic accomplishments, rather than try to decipher the meaningless acronyms on standardized transcripts.

**Text 2**

The open educational movement really took off in 2008; and, within just a few short years, providers like Coursera, Udacity, and edX emerged among hundreds of other self-paced, virtual education platforms, including the immensely popular Khan Academy, that offer quality learning at a great price, *free*. Now, students could enjoy learning outside of a formal education environment with asynchronous and unconstrained access to free content.

**7**

Based on the texts, what would the author of Text 1 most likely say about Text 2's characterization of the open educational movement?

Ⓐ It underscores a threat to the quality level of online educational offerings, presaging a loss of recognition for online credentials.

Ⓑ It addresses the major objection to in-person educational programs, given the clear link between free programming and professional certifications.

Ⓒ It demonstrates that while more people have access to free offerings on the Internet, there are fewer opportunities for businesses to profit from these developments.

Ⓓ It shows that barriers to online education have been reduced, likely enhancing the popularity of online certifications.

The following text is from is Walt Whitman's 1881 poem "No Labor-Saving Machine."

No labor-saving machine,

Nor discovery have I made;

Nor will I be able to leave behind me any wealthy bequest to found a hospital or library,

Nor reminiscence of any deed of courage, for America,

Nor literary success, nor intellect—nor book for the book-shelf;

Only a few carols, vibrating through the air,
I leave,

For comrades and lovers.

**8**

What is the main idea of the text?

Ⓐ Practical achievement is inherently better than transcendental creation.
Ⓑ The narrator prioritizes human connection over more visible success.
Ⓒ American success is synonymous with literary accomplishments.
Ⓓ Technology is inherently necessary to musical advancement.

The following text is adapted from James Joyce's 1914 story "An Encounter." A young, unnamed narrator searches for release from the constraints of daily routine.

It was Joe Dillon who introduced the Wild West to us. He had a little library made up of old numbers of *The Union Jack*, *Pluck*, and *The Halfpenny Marvel*. Every evening after school we met in his back garden and arranged [battles]. He and his . . . brother Leo, the idler, held the loft of the stable while we tried to carry it by storm; or we fought a pitched battle on the grass. But, however well we fought, we never won siege or battle and all our bouts ended with Joe Dillon's . . . dance of victory. His parents went to eight-o'clock mass every morning in Gardiner Street and the peaceful odor of Mrs. Dillon was prevalent in the hall of the house. But he played too fiercely for us who were younger and more timid.

**9**

Based on the text, Joe Dillon's personality is mostly

Ⓐ accommodating.
Ⓑ forceful.
Ⓒ compromising.
Ⓓ dishonest.

"How Like a Winter My Absence Hath Been" is a 1609 poem by William Shakespeare. In the poem, the narrator addresses an unseen person, expressing his longing for them. An English teacher claims that the narrator expresses a deep personal feeling of melancholy: ________

**10**

Which quotation from the poem most effectively illustrates the claim?

Ⓐ "What freezings have I felt, what dark days seen! / What old December's bareness everywhere!"

Ⓑ "And yet this time removed was summer's time; / The teeming autumn, big with rich increase,"

Ⓒ "For summer and his pleasures wait on thee, / And, thou away, the very birds are mute:"

Ⓓ And thou away, the very birds are mute: / Or, if they sing, 'tis with so dull a cheer,"

Immobility has many harmful effects on the human body, ranging from bone degradation to cardiac atrophy. This is often seen in astronauts who return from space. Even with workout equipment and hours of exercise completed, astronauts still suffer from cardiac atrophy as a response to immobility. During hibernation, bears do not experience cardiac atrophy—unraveling how bears can combat the harmful effects of long periods of immobilization could provide numerous benefits in human medicine. Therefore, research about bear hibernation will lead to significant applications for human astronauts in the quest to minimize the negative effects of long immobility.

**11**

Which of the following, if true, would most directly undermine the author's hypothesis?

Ⓐ Bears are found to have more success than humans in reducing their muscle atrophy over extended periods of time.

Ⓑ Humans are unable to enter a state of hibernation like bears can.

Ⓒ Astronauts who performed no exercise while travelling in a spacecraft experienced greater muscle atrophy than astronauts who did exercise.

Ⓓ Bears that are placed in orbit in a spacecraft had a similar level of muscle atrophy as did humans in the same spacecraft.

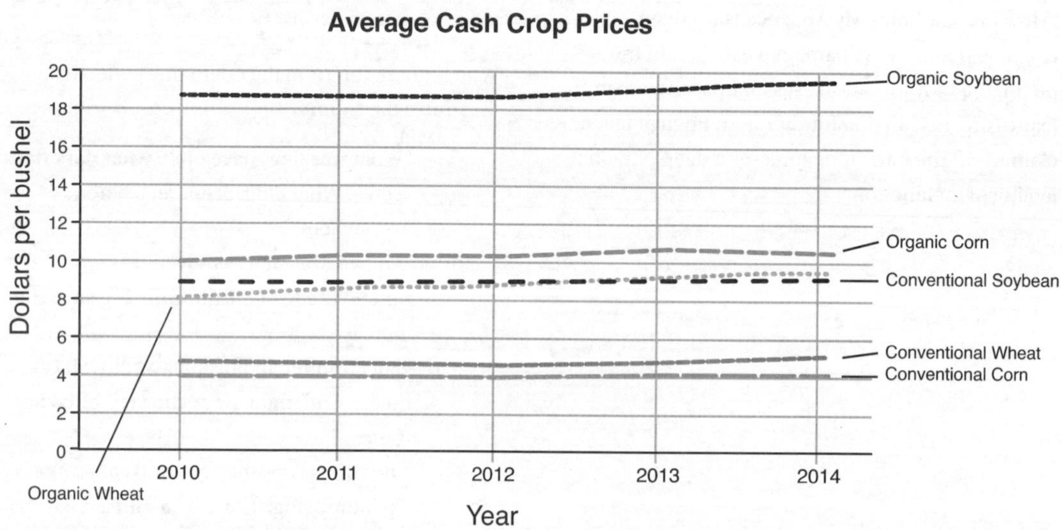


Organic crops have become increasingly popular with consumers who seek out food raised without chemical pesticides. Many consumers, however, are deterred from purchasing organic crops due to the increased costs. A consumer researcher claims that the prices of organic crops can often be substantially higher than those of conventionally raised crops: ________

**12**

Which choice most effectively uses data from the graph to complete the example?

Ⓐ The prices of both conventional wheat and organic corn remained largely constant between 2010 and 2014.

Ⓑ The price of organic soybeans was approximately twice that of conventional soybeans between 2010 and 2014.

Ⓒ While organic soybeans may be rather expensive, organic wheat was only around 9 dollars a bushel throughout the years 2010 to 2014.

Ⓓ Organically grown fruits and vegetables are likely much more expensive than organically grown grains.

# 1 MODULE 1 1



Daisy Bates was the president of the Arkansas State Conference of the NAACP in the 1950s. She wrote a letter to NAACP executive secretary Roy Wilkins on December 17, 1957, about the situation in the Little Rock schools, which had recently been required to comply with the recent decision by the federal government to integrate schools. She wanted to convince school officials that schools should integrate in a safe manner.

**13**

Which selection from the letter from Daisy Bates best indicates that she succeeded in convincing school officials of her point of view?

Ⓐ "We strongly challenged this statement, which he denied making in that fashion."

Ⓑ "We also pointed out that the treatment of the children had been getting steadily worse for the last two weeks in the form of kicking, spitting, and general abuse."

Ⓒ "As a result of our visit, stronger measures are being taken against the white students who are guilty of committing these offenses. For instance, a boy who had been suspended for two weeks, . . . on his return to school, the first day he knocked Gloria Rey into her locker. As a result of our visit, he was given an indefinite suspension."

Ⓓ "[The president] has stated his willingness to come down and address the student body if invited by student leaders of the school. This information was passed on to the principal of the school, but we have not been assured that leadership would be given to children in the school who are willing to organize for law and order."

| Presidential Candidates | Political Party | Number of Votes | Popular Vote Percentage | Number of Electoral Votes | Electoral Vote Percentage |
|---|---|---|---|---|---|
| Woodrow Wilson | Democratic | 6,294,284 | 41.83% | 435 | 81.9% |
| Theodore Roosevelt | Progressive | 4,120,409 | 27.39% | 88 | 16.6% |
| William Taft | Republican | 3,487,937 | 23.18% | 0 | 0.0% |
| Eugene Debs | Socialist | 900,742 | 5.99% | 0 | 0.0% |
| Other | | 33,859 | 0.23% | 0 | 0.0% |
| Total | | 15,045,546 | | 531 | |

The electoral college system in the United States is used to select electors who then select the winner of the U.S. Presidency. A shortcoming of this system is that it is quite difficult for third parties to have their voices heard since it is a "winner-take-all" system. A political scientist claims that a major plus of the electoral college, on the other hand, is that even if a candidate only secures a plurality of the popular vote, they will end up with a majority of the electoral vote, contributing to the country unifying around a single leader.

**14**

Which choice best describes data from the table that support the political scientist's claim?

Ⓐ In the 1912 presidential election, five major candidates participated, together earning nearly 100% of the total votes cast.

Ⓑ The Socialist and Prohibition parties had a strong showing in the 1912 presidential election, together earning over 6% of the popular votes cast.

Ⓒ In the 1912 presidential election, Woodrow Wilson secured only 41.83% of the popular vote but won 81.9% of the electoral vote.

Ⓓ Teddy Roosevelt came up short in his quest for the 1912 presidency, earning only 16.6% of the electoral votes.

## MODULE 1



Motivation is something that drives someone to do something. Intrinsic motivators arise from the individual. Extrinsic motivators are outside forces acting upon an individual. Examples of intrinsic motivators are personal enjoyment, self-fulfillment, and having fun. These examples could be observed in real life as dancing because you like it, reading a book about a topic of personal interest, or journaling because it helps organize thoughts. Examples of extrinsic motivators are money, avoiding consequences, and getting something valued in return for doing something. These examples could be observed in real life as promising a child a toy for taking medicine, going to work to earn money, or ___________

**15**

Which choice most logically completes the text?

Ⓐ contemplating the meaning of a painting for personal enjoyment.
Ⓑ watching movies on a streaming service.
Ⓒ following the law to avoid being arrested.
Ⓓ going on a vacation to a place on your bucket list.

People have different opinions on the key to success. Being successful is not a single-person act. __________ needs others in order to succeed and thrive.

**16**

Which choice completes the text so that it conforms to the conventions of Standard English?

Ⓐ It may, seem unfair, but everyone
Ⓑ It may seem unfair but, everyone
Ⓒ It may seem unfair, but everyone
Ⓓ It may seem unfair but everyone

Cats have woven ______ way throughout much of human history. The earliest evidence of a cat being kept as a pet comes from a grave in Cyprus dated to about 9,500 years ago in which a cat was buried with its owner, likely out of love and respect for the animal.

**17**

Which choice completes the text so that it conforms to the conventions of Standard English?

Ⓐ its
Ⓑ it's
Ⓒ there
Ⓓ their

# 1 MODULE 1 1

The job search can be very frustrating for people who don't realize a key element in most ________ you know, it's whom you know. This old axiom is true in hiring discussions across the United States.

**18**

Which choice completes the text so that it conforms to the conventions of Standard English?

Ⓐ hiring processes, its not what
Ⓑ hiring processes, it's not what
Ⓒ hiring processes; its not, what
Ⓓ hiring processes: it's not what

Hugo Ball, a writer from Zürich, Switzerland, founded the Dada movement in 1916 as a means of expressing his view that the war started due to societal collapse. It is believed that Ball's Dada movement ________ after a meeting with his Cabaret Voltaire: a Zürich-based group of artists and individuals against the war.

**19**

Which choice completes the text so that it conforms to the conventions of Standard English?

Ⓐ taking off
Ⓑ has taken off
Ⓒ took off
Ⓓ taking of

During the process of photorespiration, there is a release of carbon dioxide, a consumption of oxygen, and no chemical energy or food is produced. As a result, photorespiration is considered to be a waste of energy—it does not ________

**20**

Which choice completes the text so that it conforms to the conventions of Standard English?

Ⓐ provide the organism; with the food it needs to thrive.
Ⓑ provide the organism, with the food it needs to thrive.
Ⓒ provide, the organism with the food, it needs to thrive.
Ⓓ provide the organism with the food it needs to thrive.

The crassulacean acid metabolism (CAM) photosynthetic process is an unusual plant adaptation that ________ plants to photosynthesize during the day and perform carbon fixation at night.

**21**

Which choice completes the text so that it conforms to the conventions of Standard English?

Ⓐ enabled
Ⓑ enabling
Ⓒ enables
Ⓓ have enabled

Like with other artistic pursuits, arguably the best training comes from working as an apprentice with a master of the craft. Aspiring chefs may set up ____________ a cook to learn new cooking methods from a highly respected professional.

**22**

Which choice completes the text so that it conforms to the conventions of Standard English?

Ⓐ a "stage" an unpaid internship, with
Ⓑ a "stage"—an unpaid internship—with
Ⓒ a "stage" an unpaid internship with
Ⓓ a "stage"—an unpaid internship: with

While hunting, platypuses store their prey in their cheeks and break down their food using gravel or dirt from the water ________ they have grinding plates in their bills instead of teeth.

**23**

Which choice completes the text with the most logical transition?

Ⓐ while
Ⓑ whenever
Ⓒ but
Ⓓ since

Soap does not kill just bacteria that are fatal to humans. ________ it works as an agent to remove all germs. Therefore, humans who over-wash have much less exposure to relatively harmless germs that their immune systems should be able to fend off.

**24**

Which choice completes the text with the most logical transition?

Ⓐ Also,
Ⓑ Granted,
Ⓒ Instead,
Ⓓ Additionally,

# 1 MODULE 1 1

While researching a topic, a student has taken the following notes:

- Dayton, a city in southwest Ohio, is the birthplace of many inventions.
- Wilbur and Orville Wright, residents of Dayton, conducted aviation research and experiments and developed the first successful motor-powered airplane.
- The self-starter for cars was also invented in Dayton by Charles F. Kettering, allowing motorists to stop hand cranking their vehicles.
- The ice cube tray with a quick release mechanism is another Dayton invention. Before this innovation, ice cubes couldn't be released from the tray without a soak in hot water.
- The Boolean search method and the pop top for soda cans were also invented in Dayton.

**25**

The student wants to present general information about Dayton to an audience unfamiliar with it. Which choice most effectively uses relevant information from the notes to accomplish this goal?

Ⓐ The quick release mechanism on the ice cube tray is a useful invention, since prior to its creation, ice cubes would have to be removed from a tray using hot water.

Ⓑ Charles Kettering, a Dayton resident, was a key figure in the development of automotive technology.

Ⓒ Southwest Ohio city Dayton is the home of many useful inventions in fields ranging from aviation to consumer goods.

Ⓓ Without the contributions of Wilbur and Orville Wright, the famous inventors of the airplane, Dayton would not have the renown it presently does.

While researching a topic, a student has taken the following notes:

- Many people think piranhas are extremely dangerous animals that regularly eat people.
- There are many different types of piranhas and some are vegetarians. The most common type, the red-bellied piranha, is carnivorous.
- Like sharks, piranhas have an excellent sense of small and carnivorous piranhas are attracted by blood.
- Piranhas live in groups and in murky water. When one piranha takes a bite of food, it signals to nearby piranhas that there is food.
- Researchers have found that piranhas exhibit shoaling behavior for their own safety against predators and to protect their nests.

**26**

The student wants to correct a misconception that piranhas exclusively eat animals. Which choice most effectively uses relevant information from the notes to accomplish this goal?

Ⓐ Despite popular understanding, there are in fact some varieties of piranhas that only eat plants.

Ⓑ Piranhas are fiercely protective of their habitats, especially their nests.

Ⓒ While many think that piranhas eat only meat, they also are avid consumers of blood.

Ⓓ Even though piranhas are primarily carnivorous, this is actually not supported by the latest research.

1 MODULE 1 1



While conducting research, a student took these notes:

- Some astronomers have long warned of the dangers of a large asteroid strike on Earth.
- It has long been hypothesized that asteroid impact could lead to the extinction of hundreds if not thousands of species of animals.
- Many scientists have studied the idea of predicting and avoiding asteroid impact, but few definitive strategies have emerged.
- Everything from lasers to bombs have been suggested as possible ways to change the trajectory of a near-impact asteroid.
- In 2022, NASA crashed a spacecraft into small asteroid, succeeding in modifying its orbit.

27

The student wants to suggest a constructive strategy to the "astronomers" as mentioned in the notes. Which choice most effectively uses relevant information from the notes to accomplish this goal?

Ⓐ Since an asteroid will inevitably lead to demise of life on Earth, humans should proceed in earnest to colonize other worlds.

Ⓑ Given the possible threat from a large asteroid strike, researchers should build upon the success of NASA's asteroid orbital modification.

Ⓒ The militarization of space with lasers and bombs is necessary to prevent the extinction of many species of animals.

Ⓓ Concern about an asteroid impact on Earth is unwarranted given the latest scientific predictions about its likelihood.

# ANSWER KEY
## Practice Test 3: Adaptive

### Section 1, Module 1: Reading and Writing

1. **D**
2. **A**
3. **A**
4. **B**
5. **A**
6. **D**
7. **D**
8. **B**
9. **B**
10. **A**
11. **D**
12. **B**
13. **C**
14. **C**
15. **C**
16. **C**
17. **D**
18. **D**
19. **C**
20. **D**
21. **C**
22. **B**
23. **D**
24. **C**
25. **C**
26. **A**
27. **B**

Total Correct Answers: _____ / 27

**Did you get 17 or fewer questions correct? If so, move to Reading and Writing Module 2A on page 759.**

**Did you get 18 or more questions correct? If so, move to Reading and Writing Module 2B on page 769.**

1 MODULE 2 1



# Section 1, Module 2A: Reading and Writing

32 MINUTES, 27 QUESTIONS

**DIRECTIONS**

You will be tested on a variety of important reading and writing skills. Each question has one or more passages, possibly including a graph or table. Carefully read each passage and question and choose the best answer to the question based on the passage(s).

Every question in this section is multiple-choice, with four possible answers. Each question has only one best answer.

Juan was surprised by what he heard but ________ the information as lies. He knew many of his peers were jealous of his success, but he doubted they would stoop so low.

**1**

Which choice completes the text with the most logical and precise word or phrase?

Ⓐ reduced
Ⓑ forgot
Ⓒ conceded
Ⓓ dismissed

Unique markings allow the servals to blend into the waving grasses on the savannahs where they make their homes. Camouflaging into their habitat allows servals to approach their favorite prey without being _______

**2**

Which choice completes the text with the most logical and precise word or phrase?

Ⓐ pictured.
Ⓑ envisioned.
Ⓒ ignored.
Ⓓ detected.

When the speaker was done, the crowd rose and clapped vigorously. Yet, at the question-and-answer session, attentive spectators ______ several points—particularly that the speech's moral lesson came off as condescending and was generally unfounded.

**3**

Which choice completes the text with the most logical and precise word or phrase?

Ⓐ increased
Ⓑ elevated
Ⓒ raised
Ⓓ nourished

# 1 MODULE 2 1

A promising alternative fuel source is biodiesel. Biodiesel is made from animal fats, plant fats, and even used grease from restaurants. The glycerol backbone is removed from the fat, breaking the fat into three different chains, which are then reacted with an alcohol to form the biodiesel. This type of chemical reaction is called a transesterification.

**4**

As used in the text, what does the word "breaking" most nearly mean?

Ⓐ Flouting
Ⓑ Eliminating
Ⓒ Separating
Ⓓ Categorizing

After platypuses first appeared in Australia about 100 million years ago, they took over the country's ______ however, when marsupials appeared in Australia 54 to 71 million years ago, they became the country's dominant species everywhere but in the water.

**5**

Which choice completes the text with the most logical and precise word or phrase?

Ⓐ panorama;
Ⓑ perspective;
Ⓒ landscape;
Ⓓ agriculture;

*Great Expectations* is an 1861 novel by Charles Dickens. In the story, Pip, a poor orphan who is cared for by his sister and her husband, meets the young girl who will become the lifetime object of his affections while simultaneously becoming aware of his lowly position in the British class system.

> For a long time I went once a week to this strange, gloomy house—it was called Satis House—and once Estella told me I might kiss her.
>
> And then Miss Havisham decided I was to be apprenticed to Joe, and gave him £25 for the purpose; and I left off going to see her, and helped Joe in the forge. But I didn't like Joe's trade, and I was afflicted by that most miserable thing—to feel ashamed of home.

**6**

As used in the text, what does the word "afflicted" most nearly mean?

Ⓐ Diseased
Ⓑ Strengthened
Ⓒ Emboldened
Ⓓ Troubled

# 1 MODULE 2 1



Unlike other viruses for which vaccines are available—several of which, through tenacious public health efforts, have been eradicated worldwide—influenza remains a perennial menace, and due to the unique nature of its genome, is unlikely to ever be completely conquered.

**7**

Which choice best states the main purpose of the text?

Ⓐ To express that influenza will continue to be a threat despite scientific advances

Ⓑ To argue that influenza can be fully eradicated with sufficient research funding

Ⓒ To highlight how influenza is unique among diseases in the severity of its symptoms

Ⓓ To celebrate that influenza has been eliminated as a pervasive threat to humanity

The following text is adapted from Elizabeth Cady Stanton's 1867 address to the Judiciary Committees of the legislature of New York. She argued for the right of Black men and all women to vote in the election of delegates to the Constitutional Convention.

> The wheel of progress moves onward, and man must, in the nature of things, throw off old customs, creeds and codes, as the snake sheds its skin in the new growth, and from the dead letters of the past, emerge into higher civilization. History shows that each generation has been marked by some new idea, alike tending to the greater freedom and equality of man; and those who, in their blindness or folly, have tried to block this onward march, have invariably been ground to powder. We see a signal instance of this in the summary manner in which an indignant people have ridden rough-shod over Andrew Johnson and his satellites—showing that even the head of a nation is nothing, but as he represents the leading ideas of his generation. They only are immortal who link the future to the past and roll on the triumphal car of progress to the brighter and the better day.

**8**

Which choice best states the main idea of the text?

Ⓐ Recent events have demonstrated the inability of Andrew Johnson to effectively lead the United States.

Ⓑ The march toward equality is inevitable and leaders should embrace, rather than fight, the coming changes.

Ⓒ Those who stand in the way of social progress should instead redouble their efforts to maintain the status quo.

Ⓓ The examples of harmonious animals in nature should inspire humans to create a more just society.

1 MODULE 2 1

In the 1954 U.S. Supreme Court case *Brown v. Board of Education*, American schools were legally desegregated. In making this decision, the court observed that minority students at segregated schools were usually educationally disadvantaged relative to students at integrated schools.

**9**

Which quotation from the court's decision best illustrates the court's observation?

Ⓐ "In each instance, they had been denied admission to schools attended by white children"

Ⓑ "[In prior cases it was held that] equality of treatment is accorded when the races are provided substantially equal facilities even though these facilities be separate . . ."

Ⓒ "Segregation with the sanction of law, therefore, has a tendency to [slow] the educational and mental development of [minority] children and to deprive them of some of the benefits they would receive in a racially integrated school system . . ."

Ⓓ "This disposition makes unnecessary any discussion whether such segregation also violates the Due Process Clause of the Fourteenth Amendment."

Probiotics are full of millions of bacteria to help create a better digestive system. A popular type of probiotic is one that must be refrigerated. One researcher claimed that the requirement of cold temperatures makes this type of probiotic ill-suited for ingestion in the stomach.

**10**

Which of the following, if true, would most directly support the researcher's hypothesis?

Ⓐ Probiotics that are commonly found in warmer climates are found to have a statistically significant effect on digestive health when used as advised by a doctor.

Ⓑ The effectiveness of probiotics is negatively affected when consumed in conjunction with a lukewarm beverage.

Ⓒ Probiotics that naturally thrive in a colder environment are more likely to be hypersensitive to the high temperatures and acidity of the human stomach.

Ⓓ People who are taking antibiotics for respiratory illnesses typically find that the effectiveness of probiotics is greatly diminished.

**Leading Causes of Traumatic Brain Injuries**

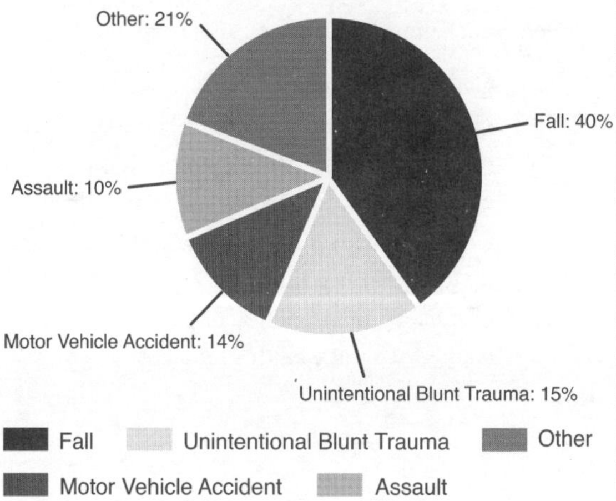


Source: Centers for Disease Control

A researcher is investigating perceptions about the leading causes of traumatic brain injuries. The researcher finds that most Americans believe that violent physical assaults and car crashes are the most significant source of traumatic brain injuries. The researcher would like to educate the American public on the fact that while car crashes and physical assaults are a significant source of traumatic brain injuries, the larger danger is from less dramatic injuries that could take place closer to home: ______________

**11**

Which choice most effectively uses data from the graph to complete the example?

Ⓐ Falls and unintentional blunt trauma cause approximately 55% of traumatic brain injuries.

Ⓑ Further research is needed on the 21% of "other" causes of traumatic brain injuries.

Ⓒ The majority of traumatic brain injuries are caused by a source other than falls.

Ⓓ Motor vehicles are, in fact, more likely to cause traumatic brain injuries than physical assaults.

Because of the antimicrobial properties of soap, a thorough washing will take away almost all bacteria from a surface. Whether a person is washing their hands or wiping down their countertop, soap creates a sterile environment. This is crucial at times when pernicious bacteria are present (like when handling raw food or after using the restroom). However, living in a constantly sterile environment is, for the average person, ________

**12**

Which choice most logically completes the text?

Ⓐ not necessary.

Ⓑ quite advisable.

Ⓒ a highly personal decision.

Ⓓ a viable option.

## 1 MODULE 2 1

Get-rich-quick schemes have probably existed since humans first used money to buy instead of goods to barter. Most have learned to be wary of people and organizations that claim to be an easy path to riches. However, in the 1950s a new type of scheme emerged disguised as a work or career opportunity but was designed to pad the pockets of a select few. This effective setup targeted young women who found life at home to be boring after returning to domesticity after World War II. It allowed a woman to feel like she was contributing financially to her family's well-being while still maintaining her role in the household. This sales system, called multi-level marketing (MLM), still pervades our society today, __________

**13**

Which choice most logically completes the text?

Ⓐ giving ambitious young professionals the opportunity to advance their careers.

Ⓑ inspiring women to break through the glass ceiling to achieve financial windfalls.

Ⓒ with an increased level of interest leading up to military conflicts.

Ⓓ promising unsuspecting targets the chance at great wealth—for a cost.

Throughout Europe, the Age of Enlightenment ushered in a renewed and unprecedented interest in scientific investigation. A devotee to the zeitgeist, 17th-century scientist Robert Boyle redefined the word "element" to describe a substance that cannot be degraded into simpler forms by chemical reaction. His definition not only liberated the word from its erroneous Aristotelian origins, but it survived for a full 300 years—during which it was used in the invention of the periodic table—until __________

**14**

Which choice most logically completes the text?

Ⓐ the theory of biological evolution became quite popular.

Ⓑ the discovery of subatomic particles in the 20th century.

Ⓒ democratic governance attained global prominence.

Ⓓ space exploration changed from a fantasy to reality.

Since the beginning of roller derby, it ____ included players who are often marginalized in society because of their race, which is something that continues to be the case even today.

**15**

Which choice completes the text so that it conforms to the conventions of Standard English?

Ⓐ has

Ⓑ have

Ⓒ had

Ⓓ will have

## 1 MODULE 2 1



March was abnormally __________ the latter part of the month. April, however, was unusually warm for the springtime.

**16**

Which choice completes the text so that it conforms to the conventions of Standard English?

Ⓐ cool; especially so during
Ⓑ cool especially so during
Ⓒ cool, especially so during
Ⓓ cool. Especially so during

Prospective employees see the listings, apply, and wait eagerly by the phone only to never hear anything. No response at all for one job after another—__________

**17**

Which choice completes the text so that it conforms to the conventions of Standard English?

Ⓐ demoralizing quite it can be.
Ⓑ quite demoralizing, it can be.
Ⓒ demoralizing it can be quite.
Ⓓ it can be quite demoralizing.

Some graffiti decreases the value of an area by making it appear abandoned and unkempt. Other graffiti spruces up a blank wall, adds much needed color, and creates art in an otherwise dismal space. __________

**18**

Which choice completes the text so that it conforms to the conventions of Standard English?

Ⓐ How are cities supposed to decide what to leave; and what to paint over?
Ⓑ How are cities supposed to decide, what to leave and what to paint over?
Ⓒ How are cities supposed to decide: what to leave and what to paint over?
Ⓓ How are cities supposed to decide what to leave and what to paint over?

For many students approaching the end of their collegiate studies, the prospect of finding a job is daunting. While some will already have leads based on professor recommendations or internship work, others will look at thousands of posts on online job boards and __________

**19**

Which choice completes the text so that it conforms to the conventions of Standard English?

Ⓐ felt overwhelmed.
Ⓑ felt overwhelming.
Ⓒ feel overwhelming.
Ⓓ feel overwhelmed.

Each discipline has its own focus, but the thought process and science underlying all engineering problems are more similar than different. This empowers ______________

**20**

Which choice completes the text so that it conforms to the conventions of Standard English?

Ⓐ an engineer; to think in an interdisciplinary way.
Ⓑ an engineer—to think in an interdisciplinary way.
Ⓒ an engineer to think in an interdisciplinary way.
Ⓓ an, engineer, to think in an interdisciplinary way.

Whereas a traditional English teacher might assign canonical texts and then assess a ________ understanding of plot, setting, and character analyses, a critical English teacher assigns literature with a goal in mind of what the class will get from that particular text, and then encourages the class to talk about how the social issues reflect their own lives, whose voices weren't heard, and how the story might be told differently from another perspective.

**21**

Which choice completes the text so that it conforms to the conventions of Standard English?

Ⓐ classes
Ⓑ class'es
Ⓒ class's
Ⓓ classes'

Both Truman and MacArthur were American leaders in the late 1940s and early 1950s in the aftermath of the Allied victory during World War II. Naturally, only one of them could emerge victorious from the rubble of ______ power struggle.

**22**

Which choice completes the text so that it conforms to the conventions of Standard English?

Ⓐ there
Ⓑ their
Ⓒ his
Ⓓ one's

# 1 MODULE 2 1



After a year and a half, Wilson's term as president ended and Edith became again just his wife. However, her role in running the country during Wilson's illness should be remembered by history. Whoever ends up being the first woman to take the oath of the office of president will ____________

**23**

Which choice completes the text so that it conforms to the conventions of Standard English?

Ⓐ not be alone she will be standing in Ediths shadow.
Ⓑ not be alone, she will be standing, in Edith's shadow.
Ⓒ not be alone; she will be standing in Edith's shadow.
Ⓓ not be alone, she will be standing in Ediths shadow.

Catering can be a good fit for those who would like to work as a chef on a more part-time basis, ______ they could schedule their catering jobs around their family obligations.

**24**

Which choice completes the text with the most logical transition?

Ⓐ but
Ⓑ which
Ⓒ while
Ⓓ as

The biggest fundamental issue that impacts the fair treatment of guest workers is ensuring that guest workers have a voice. Laws may be in place; ______ they do nothing if the guest workers cannot speak up when something is wrong for fear of retribution.

**25**

Which choice completes the text with the most logical transition?

Ⓐ consequently,
Ⓑ and
Ⓒ however,
Ⓓ because

## 1 MODULE 2 1

While conducting research, a student took these notes:

- The Battle of Gettysburg was a turning point in the American Civil War.
- General Meade commanded the Union forces at the Battle of Gettysburg while General Robert E. Lee commanded the Confederate troops.
- The battle lasted three days.
- Abraham Lincoln visited the site soon thereafter and gave the Gettysburg Address.
- The Battle of Gettysburg was the northernmost battle of the American Civil War.

**26**

The student wants to highlight the leaders of the opposing forces at the Battle of Gettysburg. Which choice most effectively uses relevant information from the notes to accomplish this goal?

Ⓐ Abraham Lincoln's leadership during the Battle of Gettysburg led to the defeat of Robert E. Lee's troops.

Ⓑ Over a three-day period, the armies of the Union and the Confederacy met in furious combat on the battlefield of Gettysburg.

Ⓒ While most of the Civil War was fought in the South, Lee ensured that the Battle of Gettysburg was fought in the North.

Ⓓ The Union commander Meade and the Confederate commander Lee led their armies into combat at Gettysburg.

While researching a topic, a student has taken the following notes:

- Psoriasis is a common skin condition, affecting one out of 100 Americans.
- Psoriasis is an autoimmune condition, caused by an overactive immune system.
- Psoriasis often presents as itchy, silvery plaques, or patches, on the skin, which can become irritated and bleed.
- People with psoriasis can have just the skin changes, just arthritis, or both, called psoriatic arthritis.
- Psoriasis is not contagious, but if the effects or appearance are bothersome, there are many treatment options.

**27**

The student wants to share information about psoriasis to a friend who is extremely concerned about having it to help the friend become less worried. Which choice most effectively uses relevant information from the notes to accomplish this goal?

Ⓐ Psoriasis is caused by an immune system that is not functioning normally.

Ⓑ Psoriasis can lead to arthritic symptoms.

Ⓒ Psoriasis can cause skin irritation and bleeding.

Ⓓ There are many treatment options for psoriasis.

1 MODULE 2 1



## Section 1, Module 2B: Reading and Writing

32 MINUTES, 27 QUESTIONS

**DIRECTIONS**

You will be tested on a variety of important reading and writing skills. Each question has one or more passages, possibly including a graph or table. Carefully read each passage and question and choose the best answer to the question based on the passage(s).

Every question in this section is multiple-choice, with four possible answers. Each question has only one best answer.

Even though it is illegal to do so, some farms and companies do not reimburse guest workers for visa fees and other travel expenses related to obtaining the jobs. Some of the recruiters have even threatened the lives of the families of the guest workers if they did not ________ with the fees.

**1**

Which choice completes the text with the most logical and precise word or phrase?

Ⓐ observe
Ⓑ comply
Ⓒ disobey
Ⓓ ignore

A 1999 article, "The Importance of Music in Early Childhood," advocated for music education in learning of language, mathematics, and social studies. Music—readily available and easily engaged—is a powerful memory ______ that can be approached via "play," beginning in delight but ending in knowledge.

**2**

Which choice completes the text with the most logical and precise word or phrase?

Ⓐ trigger
Ⓑ souvenir
Ⓒ dialect
Ⓓ indoctrination

# 1 MODULE 2 1

When he was in high school at a predominantly white institution, Countee Cullen excelled, despite being one of the few African American students who attended. Additionally, he developed his talents and served as the editor of the high school newspaper and literary magazine and even won a local award for his poetry. Later, he was accepted into New York University, where he received several awards; most notably, he won second place for the Witter Bynner Undergraduate Poetry Contest for his 1923 poem "The Ballad of the Brown Girl." Following his graduation from New York University, Cullen became ________ poet with works like "Copper Sun" and "The Black Christ" and other poems.

**3**

Which choice completes the text with the most logical and precise word or phrase?

Ⓐ a notorious
Ⓑ an imminent
Ⓒ an illustrated
Ⓓ a renowned

Environmentally and cost-conscious planters use more modern solutions only when absolutely necessary. Modern technology allows farmers to test soil in various parts of a field and apply topical treatments as minimally as possible only in areas where it is needed. This process allows crop rotation and soil treatment to work together. However, the drones, testing machines, and high-end equipment for GPS fertilizer applications are very expensive for the average family farm. Consequently, crop rotation remains the ________ choice for everyday soil management.

**4**

Which choice completes the text with the most logical and precise word or phrase?

Ⓐ periodic
Ⓑ staple
Ⓒ subsistent
Ⓓ coarse

The first introduction many students have to the world of investment and the stock market is through their American history class when they learn about the devastating stock market crash that led into the Great Depression, or the market crash that much led us into the more recent Great Recession. However, what is rarely _______ students is the success that the majority of people experience in the stock market when they invest intelligently over a long period of time. Indeed, most of those high school students will (hopefully) go on to have a retirement account that invests in the stock market, allowing them to comfortably cease work between the ages of 65 and 70.

**5**

Which choice completes the text with the most logical and precise word or phrase?

Ⓐ awarded to
Ⓑ produced for
Ⓒ panned out for
Ⓓ impressed upon

The following text is from the Brothers Grimm 1812 fairy tale "The Mouse, the Bird, and the Sausage."

> They therefore drew lots, and it fell to the sausage to bring in the wood, to the mouse to cook, and to the bird to fetch the water.
>
> And now what happened? The sausage started in search of wood, the bird made the fire, and the mouse put on the pot, and then these two waited till the sausage returned with the fuel for the following day. But the sausage remained so long away, that they became uneasy, and the bird flew out to meet him. He had not flown far, however, when he came across a dog who, having met the sausage, had regarded him as his legitimate booty, and so seized and swallowed him. The bird complained to the dog of this bare-faced robbery, but nothing he said was of any avail, <u>for the dog answered that he found false credentials on the sausage, and that was the reason his life had been forfeited.</u>

**6**

Which choice best describes the function of the underlined selection in the text as a whole?

Ⓐ To give a dishonest explanation
Ⓑ To provide a true excuse for the action
Ⓒ To demonstrate the dog's curiosity for the truth
Ⓓ To display an attempt to find common ground

# 1 MODULE 2 1

Though fermentation does not require oxygen consumption, it is not solely limited to anaerobic organisms. Even humans sometimes undergo fermentation when oxygen supplies are low. This often occurs when the organism rapidly needs more energy than can be produced from cellular respiration alone. Some human cells undergo fermentation more often than others, depending on the cell's specific needs. One such example is during strenuous exercise, when oxygen demand for cellular respiration is unable to be met. This results in muscle cells undergoing lactic acid fermentation, which provides additional energy to prevent muscle fatigue.

**7**

Which choice best states the main purpose of the text?

Ⓐ To illustrate that fermentation is the primary process whereby humans obtain energy

Ⓑ To show that humans can use fermentation when extra energy is needed

Ⓒ To explain how vigorous exercise is a way to minimize the amount of fermentation that takes place

Ⓓ To describe how human muscles use fermentation instead of respiration to acquire energy

The following text is adapted from William T. Hamilton, Jr.'s 2020 novel *The Three Stages of Clarinda Thorbald.* In it, young Clarinda is waiting for the day of her wedding to arrive while conversing with her father.

> "Listen, Clarinda, you mustn't weep. Rather you must be filled with joy, for this is a festival. You have come into something new. A great responsibility grasps you in its hand. You are re-born. Nature calls you and you go—it is inexorable—you cannot help. You must not weep; rather you must sing and dance. You must array yourself in gold and in silk and go forth to meet the bridegroom."
>
> "Is there no way?" she asked with pleading in her voice. With terrible finality, he answered "No!"

**8**

Based on the text, Clarinda's father's ultimate attitude toward Clarinda's concerns can best be described as

Ⓐ indulgent and patient.

Ⓑ exasperated and dismissive.

Ⓒ confused and questioning.

Ⓓ friendly and understanding.

The following text is from the 1641 work *Meditations on First Philosophy* by René Descartes in which he muses about the nature of knowledge.

> But, to this end, it will not be necessary for me to show that the whole of these are false—a point, perhaps, which I shall never reach; but as even now my reason convinces me that I ought not the less carefully to withhold belief from what is not entirely certain and indubitable, than from what is manifestly false, it will be sufficient to justify the rejection of the whole if I shall find in each some ground for doubt. Nor for this purpose will it be necessary even to deal with each belief individually, which would be truly an endless labor; but, as the removal from below of the foundation necessarily involves the downfall of the whole edifice, I will at once approach the criticism of the principles on which all my former beliefs rested.

**9**

According to the text, Descartes' minimal threshold for dismissing a knowledge claim is if it is

Ⓐ completely in error.
Ⓑ moderately wrong.
Ⓒ even slightly flawed.
Ⓓ any claim to knowledge.

**Profits Broken Down in a Classic No-Product 8-Ball (1-2-4-8) Pyramid Scheme**

| Order of participants' entry into the scheme | Revenues to each participant at that level | Number of participants at that level |
|---|---|---|
| Initiator | $140,000 | 1 |
| 2nd participants entering the system | $120,000 | 2 |
| 3rd participants entering the system | $112,000 | 4 |
| 4th participants entering the system | $98,000 | 8 |
| 5th participants entering the system | $84,000 | 16 |
| 6th participants entering the system | $70,000 | 32 |
| 7th participants entering the system | $56,000 | 64 |
| 8th participants entering the system | $42,000 | 128 |
| 9th participants entering the system | $28,000 | 256 |
| 10th participants entering the system | $14,000 | 512 |
| Total number of participants who would profit | | 1,023 |
| Number of participants at the lower levels who would lose money | | 7,168 |
| Total of all participants in the scheme | | 8,191 |
| Percent who profit (assuming all those who profit reinvest in new cycles of the pryamid | | 12.49% |
| Percent who lose money at the 10th level | | 87.51% |

* This includes all who participated, regardless of how many times.

** This is the number of participants who have cashed in at least once and some multiple times.

*** This assumes every profiting participant keeps investing in new pyramid cycles. The percentage profiting would be slightly higher or lower depending on how many participants dropped out and when.

Source: Corporate Survey from the Federal Trade Commission at ftc.gov

An economist analyzes the likelihood that someone might make money from participating in a "pyramid scheme," defined as a fraudulent way to make money by recruiting investors into some sort of money-making scheme. Instead of making money from providing a valuable good or service, the people who are the early investors in the pyramid scheme might make money, while the later investors often lose all their investment. The economist claims that over half of those who participate in a typical pyramid scheme are likely to profit, while less than half of participants will lose money.

**10**

Which choice best describes data from the table that weaken the economist's claim?

Ⓐ Over 1,000 participants in a typical pyramid scheme end up profiting.

Ⓑ The initiator of a pyramid scheme can earn more than six figures in revenue.

Ⓒ The latecomers to participate in a classic pyramid scheme might only see about $14,000 in revenue.

Ⓓ In a classic pyramid scheme, only 12.49% of participants profit.

A student is analyzing Robert Louis Stevenson's 1885 poem "My Shadow." The poem shows the playful mindset that a child experiences when learning about how their shadow works. In one instance, the narrator learns about how shadows do not function in the absence of light: __________

**11**

Which quotation from the poem most effectively completes the example?

Ⓐ "I have a little shadow that goes in and out with me, / And what can be the use of him is more than I can see. / He is very, very like me from the heels up to the head; / And I see him jump before me, when I jump into my bed."

Ⓑ "The funniest thing about him is the way he likes to grow— / Not at all like proper children, which is always very slow; / For he sometimes shoots up taller like an India-rubber ball, / And he sometimes gets so little that there's none of him at all."

Ⓒ "He hasn't got a notion of how children ought to play, / And can only make a fool of me in every sort of way. / He stays so close beside me, he's a coward you can see; / I'd think shame to stick to nursie as that shadow sticks to me!"

Ⓓ "One morning, very early, before the sun was up, / I rose and found the shining dew on every buttercup; / But my lazy little shadow, like an arrant sleepy-head, / Had stayed at home behind me and was fast asleep in bed."

The buildings at Chaco Canyon pose a mystery for archeologists who seek to learn their purpose. A vast compound of buildings created by an ancient people, Chaco Canyon does not seem to be a permanent habitation, as there are no significant garbage piles. In addition, it is located in a remote and very harsh environment. It is questionable whether any peoples would have chosen such a place for a settlement. Modern archeologists believe that it could possibly be a spiritual site that is designed to align with astronomical cycles. They have turned to astronomy for answers and have shown how the roads and buildings at Chaco Canyon align not just with the regular cycles of the sun, but, they hypothesize, with the complicated multi-year dance of the moon. Since the moon's rhythm has such a long cycle, however, it will take many more years to confirm this hypothesis.

**12**

Which of the following, if true, would provide the most direct support for the archeologists' hypothesis?

Ⓐ Historical artifacts found in Chaco Canyon that have bright coloration resembling both the daytime sun and full moon at night.

Ⓑ Evidence uncovered of an early road system connecting Chaco Canyon to far-flung territories, confirming the Canyon's important role as a trade hub.

Ⓒ Archeological evidence finding that there were in fact large garbage piles in the Chaco Canyon region and that earlier studies had not sufficiently considered the role of natural decay.

Ⓓ A multi-decade study showing that the south and north walls of Chaco Canyon precisely align with the minimum and maximum moons over a regular 18.6-year interval.

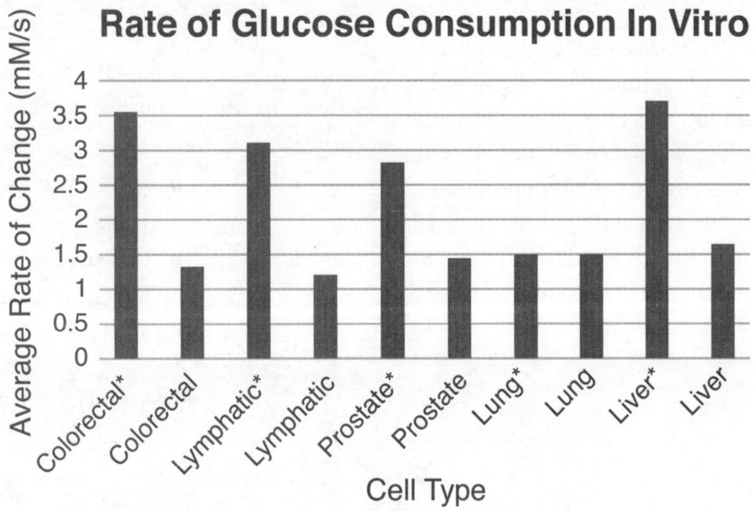


Note: The particular ones with asterisks are cancerous

In a 2014 study on the Warburg Effect, researchers tested the change in glucose concentration over a period of one hour in various cancer cell lines. The average rate of change of glucose concentration in each cell-type is shown in the figure above. (An asterisk (*) denotes the cell tested is cancerous.)

The researchers will use the results from a study on the Warburg Effect to determine what most distinguishes cancerous cells from noncancerous ones. When compared to the noncancerous cells, the cancerous cells ________________

**13**

Which choice most effectively uses data from the figure to complete the text?

Ⓐ have a generally greater average rate of change.

Ⓑ typically have a lower average rate of change.

Ⓒ have approximately the same rate of change.

Ⓓ are more likely to have a rate of change of zero.

"The New York Tenement-House Evil and Its Cure" was written by Ernest Flagg for *Scribner's Magazine* in 1894. In the piece, Flagg discusses the deplorable living conditions in the tenement housing developments, how the tenements came to be, and how the issue might be solved. A historian analyzing Flagg's writing claims that Flagg believed that the primary motivation of those who built the tenement housing developments was to make money.

**14**

Which quotation from "The New York Tenement-House Evil and Its Cure" most effectively illustrates the claim?

Ⓐ "If this desire to cover too much of the land proved objectionable in houses occupied by one family, its results have been simply disastrous in houses occupied by several families."

Ⓑ "Acres upon acres have been covered by them, all constructed on the same general plan based upon the shape of the 25 by 100 foot lot."

Ⓒ "The tenement-house evil is staring us in the face, and the community is daily becoming more and more alive to the imperative necessity for reform."

Ⓓ "It should be made unprofitable to erect the kind of tenements we now have."

Owing to a redundancy in the human genome, there are four copies of the $\alpha$ globin gene, with two $\alpha$-coding regions on each copy of chromosome 16. For this reason, the spectrum of severity in $\alpha$ thalassemia is particularly broad. For instance, deletion of a single gene will result in a carrier state and is unlikely to cause clinically acute symptoms. Deletion of all four, meanwhile, leads to a precipitation during the fetal period of nonfunctional $\gamma$ tetramers, also called Hb Barts, and is universally lethal in utero. Thus, the intensity of thalassemia would be more uniform if there were ______

**15**

Which choice most logically completes the text?

Ⓐ fewer copies of the $\alpha$ globin gene in humans.

Ⓑ the same number of copies of the $\alpha$ globin gene in humans.

Ⓒ more copies of the $\alpha$ globin gene in humans.

Ⓓ less research conducted on the human genome.

Undergraduate degrees in petroleum and nuclear engineering exist. However, both fields could be considered subdisciplines of chemical engineering, and jobs or graduate degree programs can be entered in both fields with a bachelor's in chemical engineering. __________ can be entered with a bachelor's in mechanical engineering. Thus, it may be advisable to earn a bachelor's in mechanical engineering, then specialize in aerospace later.

**16**

Which choice completes the text so that it conforms to the conventions of Standard English?

Ⓐ Similarly aerospace jobs, and graduate degree programs
Ⓑ Similarly aerospace jobs—and graduate degree programs
Ⓒ Similarly, aerospace jobs and graduate degree programs;
Ⓓ Similarly, aerospace jobs and graduate degree programs

After graduating from the program in New Mexico, ______________ before enrolling in the United States Army to fight in Vietnam.

**17**

Which choice completes the text so that it conforms to the conventions of Standard English?

Ⓐ at the San Francisco Arts Institute Cannon briefly studied
Ⓑ at the San Francisco Arts Institute did Cannon study briefly
Ⓒ Cannon briefly studied at the San Francisco Arts Institute
Ⓓ Cannon at the San Francisco Arts Institute studied briefly

Birders pay careful attention to the preferred foods of their favorite birds and make sure to provide the right kinds of snacks for each. This can be done by researching individual birds, reading the packaging on different mixes of birdseed, or consulting an online chart of birds and their ________ foods.

**18**

Which choice completes the text so that it conforms to the conventions of Standard English?

Ⓐ preferring
Ⓑ preferred
Ⓒ prefer
Ⓓ prefers

## 1 MODULE 2 1

Pinckney Benton Stewart (P.B.S.) Pinchback was a successful politician. In 1868, he was elected as a Louisiana state senator. Pinchback was elected president pro tempore, and after the 1871 death of Lieutenant Governor _________ became the lieutenant governor. Then, after an election riddled with accusations of fraud, the governor of Louisiana was impeached. Pinchback became the governor of Louisiana and served the remaining weeks of the term.

**19**

Which choice completes the text so that it conforms to the conventions of Standard English?

- Ⓐ Oscar Dunn, (the first elected African American lieutenant governor), he
- Ⓑ Oscar Dunn (the first, elected, African American lieutenant governor), he
- Ⓒ Oscar Dunn (the first, elected African American lieutenant, governor), he
- Ⓓ Oscar Dunn (the first elected African American lieutenant governor), he

Historians believe that after rye became widely cultivated, the parasitic ergot fungus began to _______ unsuspecting communities. This unfortunate development likely caused strange visions among those affected.

**20**

Which choice completes the text so that it conforms to the conventions of Standard English?

- Ⓐ wreck the havoc of
- Ⓑ wreck havoc with
- Ⓒ wreak havoc on
- Ⓓ wreak havoc toward

In the dry, desert landscape of South America, the CAM (crassulacean acid metabolism) adaptation in pineapples is advantageous. This is ________ pineapple can conserve water despite living in arid conditions.

**21**

Which choice completes the text so that it conforms to the conventions of Standard English?

- Ⓐ because through the CAM adaptation: the
- Ⓑ because, through the CAM adaptation—the
- Ⓒ because; through the CAM adaptation the
- Ⓓ because—through the CAM adaptation—the

Just like in most art forms, traditional Native American art ________ many artists incorporate elements of traditional art into their modern creations.

**22**

Which choice completes the text so that it conforms to the conventions of Standard English?

Ⓐ has, despite many people's efforts to shelter it from outside influences, evolved, and now

Ⓑ has, despite many peoples efforts to shelter it from outside influences evolved and now

Ⓒ has despite many—people's efforts to shelter it from outside influences—evolved and now

Ⓓ has despite many peoples efforts to shelter it from outside influences: evolved and now

While fertilizers and herbicides are very effective at providing nutrients to crops and reducing weeds, they are quite expensive not just to purchase, but also to apply. Farmers who wish to apply herbicides and fertilizers must make extra passes through their fields; this costs the farmer's time as well as wear and tear on equipment that can cost upwards of a million dollars. _______ both fertilizer and herbicides can have negative environmental consequences in the form of runoff. Whereas a good crop rotation will keep weeds down organically and deposit nutrients into the soil, applications of fertilizer and herbicides are merely topical.

**23**

Which choice completes the text with the most logical transition?

Ⓐ In contrast,

Ⓑ In addition,

Ⓒ Due to this,

Ⓓ Accordingly,

When it comes to the biological and biochemical building blocks of organisms, there's no mistaking that humans are special. From our amazing defense mechanisms to our innate ability to adapt to different environments, the human body is quite phenomenal. However, perfection simply does not exist in nature, and thus the human body comes with a variety of flaws. _______ most humans can only dream of being able to filter harmful cholesterol from their blood without having to resort to strenuous exercise or, in more extreme cases, prescription medications. Understanding the mechanisms behind removing cholesterol from our bloodstream remains a relatively unknown mystery.

**24**

Which choice completes the text with the most logical transition?

Ⓐ For example,
Ⓑ In contrast,
Ⓒ Peripherally,
Ⓓ Nevertheless,

While conducting research, a student took these notes:

- Male trees produce pollen and female trees produce a variety of seeds, including pods, nuts, and helicopters.
- To prevent the need to clean up seeds, many cities and homeowners only plant male trees.
- Some homeowners and cities don't plant trees at all so they can avoid dealing with leaves.
- An excess of pollen can greatly exacerbate allergies and other lung complications. People with allergies should avoid pollen heavy environments.
- Female trees absorb pollen out of the air and can help reduce allergy symptoms. Female trees can also produce food such as nuts and fruit.

**25**

The student wants to suggest a type of person who would greatly benefit from planting mainly female trees in their neighborhood. Which choice most effectively uses relevant information from the notes to accomplish this goal?

Ⓐ Someone who suffers from a nut allergy would benefit from being surrounded by female trees.
Ⓑ A person who suffers from pollen allergies would benefit from female tree plantings.
Ⓒ Female tree plantings would be especially good for someone who does not enjoy raking leaves.
Ⓓ If somebody prefers vegetables to fruit, female tree plantings would be particularly helpful.

# 1 MODULE 2 1

While researching a topic, a student has taken the following notes:

- Public domain works are no longer subject to copyright restrictions.
- If something is in the public domain, it can be used without having to seek permission.
- Works that are produced by the U.S. federal government are typically in the public domain.
- If it is 70 years after the death of a work's author, the work typically becomes part of the public domain.
- Works that are privately owned usually require permission from the original creator to use—this permission can sometimes be obtained by paying royalties to the creator.

**26**

The student wants to suggest a work that would most likely not be part of the public domain. Which choice most effectively uses relevant information from the notes to accomplish this goal?

Ⓐ A federal government collection of U.S. presidential speeches is not in the public domain.

Ⓑ A newly created book by a private-sector author who is still alive is not in the public domain.

Ⓒ A novel that was written over 200 years ago is most likely in the public domain.

Ⓓ When a filmmaker pays royalties to the author of a movie screenplay, the final film would be in the public domain.

While researching a topic, a student has taken the following notes:

- Harry Frankfurt is an American philosopher who wrote "Freedom of the Will and the Concept of a Person."
- Frankfurt articulates a theory of what it means for someone to have "free will."
- He breaks human desire into two categories: first-order desires and second-order desires.
- A first-order desire is a want to perform an action; for example, someone could want to eat a meal.
- A second-order desire is a want to have a certain desire; for example, someone could "want" to "want to eat more healthfully."
- Frankfurt argues that someone is acting according to their free will when their actions align with their second-order desires.

**27**

The student wants to present a plausible reason as to why Frankfurt would not consider an animal to possess free will. Which choice most effectively uses relevant information from the notes to accomplish this goal?

Ⓐ Some animals can consider not just what they "want," but what they "want to want."

Ⓑ An animal can only possess second-order desires since it lacks the ability to have first-order desires.

Ⓒ Since an animal most likely only has first-order desires, it cannot be considered as having the capacity for free will.

Ⓓ Only humans can be considered capable of letting their first-order desires govern their actions.

## Section 2, Module 1: Math

35 MINUTES, 22 QUESTIONS

**DIRECTIONS**

- All expressions and variables use real numbers.
- All figures are drawn to scale.
- Every figure lies in a plane.
- The domain of given functions is the set of all real numbers for which the corresponding value of the function is real.

For **multiple-choice questions**, solve the problem and pick the correct answer from the provided choices. Each multiple-choice question has only one correct answer.

For **student-produced response questions,** solve each problem and enter your answer following these guidelines:

- If you find **more than one correct answer,** enter just one answer.
- You can enter up to five characters for a **positive** answer and up to six characters (this includes the negative sign) for a **negative** answer.
- If your answer is a **fraction** that does not fit in the given space, enter the decimal equivalent instead.
- If your answer is a **decimal** that does not fit in the given space, enter it by stopping at or rounding up at the fourth digit.
- If your answer is a **mixed number** (like $4\frac{1}{2}$), enter it as an improper fraction (9/2) or its decimal equivalent (4.5).
- Do not enter **symbols** like a comma, dollar sign, or percent sign.

## Examples

| Answer | Acceptable Entries | Unacceptable Entries That Will Receive Zero Credit |
|---|---|---|
| 4.5 | 4.5<br>4.50<br>9/2 | $4\frac{1}{2}$<br>41/2 |
| $\frac{8}{9}$ | 8/9<br>.8888<br>.8889<br>0.888<br>0.889 | 0.88<br>.88<br>.89<br>0.89 |
| $-\frac{1}{9}$ | −1/9<br>−.1111<br>−0.111 | −.11<br>−0.11 |

## 2 MODULE 1 2



**REFERENCE**

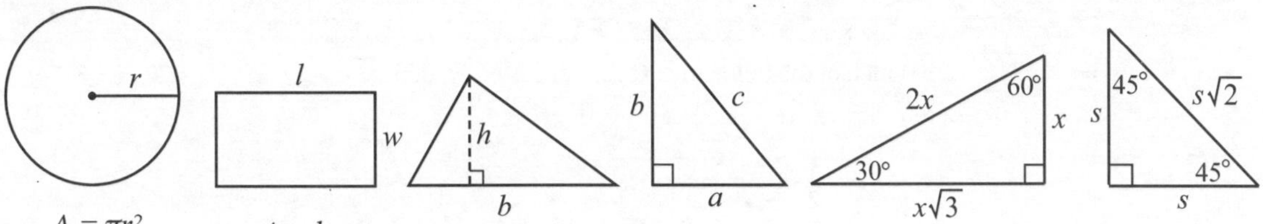


$A = \pi r^2$
$C = 2\pi r$

$A = lw$

$A = \frac{1}{2}bh$

$c^2 = a^2 + b^2$

Special Right Triangles

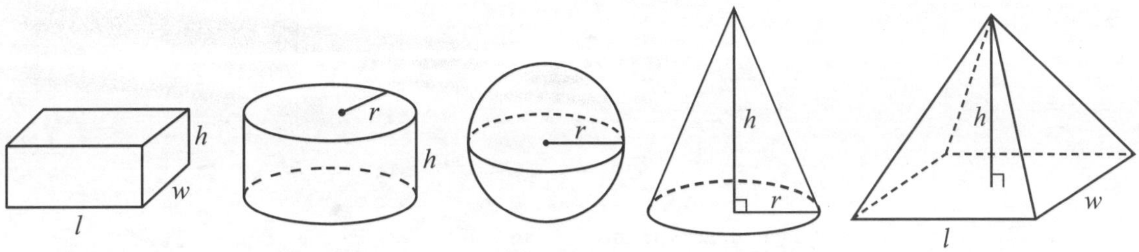


$V = lwh$

$V = \pi r^2 h$

$V = \frac{4}{3}\pi r^3$

$V = \frac{1}{3}\pi r^2 h$

$V = \frac{1}{3}lwh$

The number of degrees of arc in a circle is 360.
The number of radians of arc in a circle is $2\pi$.
The sum of the measures in degrees of the angles of a triangle is 180.

**1**

Which of the following expressions is equivalent to $\frac{1}{2}x^3(x^2-4)$?

Ⓐ $\frac{1}{2}x^6 - 2x^2$

Ⓑ $\frac{1}{2}x^6 - 2$

Ⓒ $\frac{1}{2}x^5 - 2x^3$

Ⓓ $\frac{1}{2}x^5 - 4x^2$

**2**

What number is 5% greater than 200?

**3**

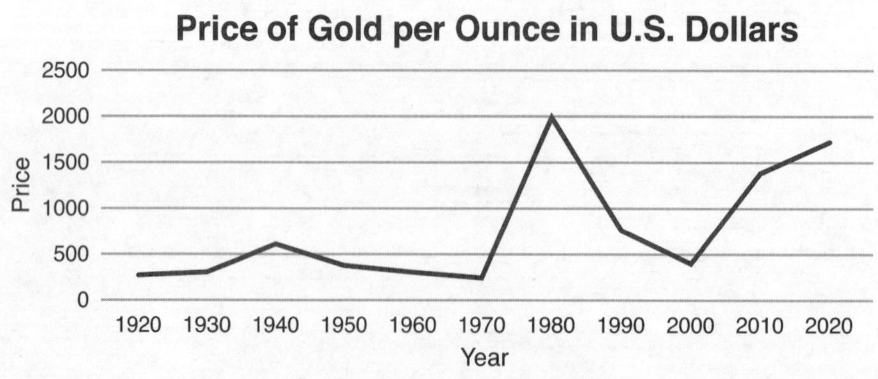


Which of the following is closest to the price in U.S. dollars of an ounce of gold in the year 1970?

Ⓐ $245

Ⓑ $520

Ⓒ $610

Ⓓ $1,225

## 2 MODULE 1 2



**4**

$$2x - 5y = 3$$
$$x + 2y = 6$$

If $(a, b)$ is the solution to the system of equations above, what is the value of $a$?

Ⓐ 1
Ⓑ 2
Ⓒ 3
Ⓓ 4

**5**

A museum gift shop provides a 10% discount for museum members. If a customer who is a museum member purchases a book from the store for $18, what was the original price of the book prior to the discount (ignore sales tax)?

Ⓐ $12
Ⓑ $20
Ⓒ $22
Ⓓ $26

**6**

The Statue of Liberty has a height of 93 meters. A model toy version (done to scale) of the Statue of Liberty is 1/500th the height of the actual statue. Given that there are 100 centimeters in a meter, what is the height of the model in centimeters, calculated to the nearest whole centimeter?

Ⓐ 19 cm
Ⓑ 86 cm
Ⓒ 186 cm
Ⓓ 320 cm

2 MODULE 1 2

**7**

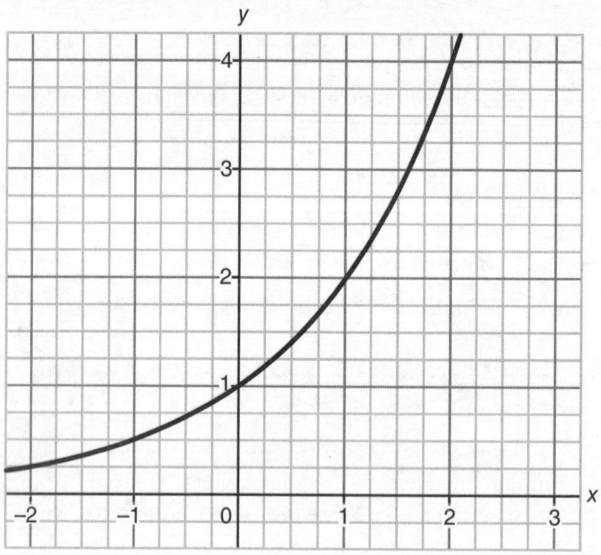


Which of the following models the function as presented in the graph above?

Ⓐ $f(x) = x^2$
Ⓑ $f(x) = x^2 + 1$
Ⓒ $f(x) = 2^x$
Ⓓ $f(x) = 3^x + 1$

**8**

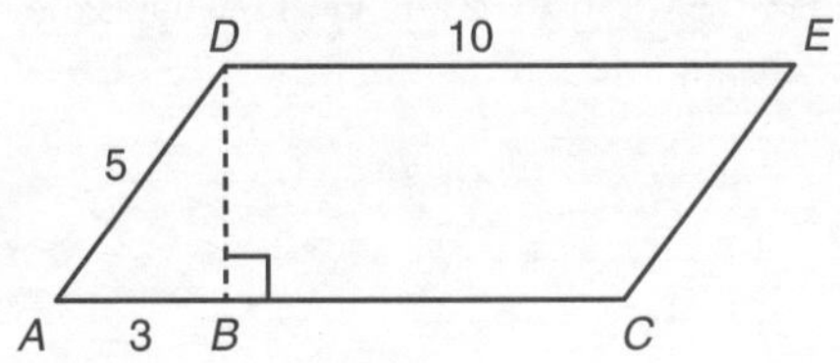


Parallelogram *ADEC* has a side of $\overline{DE}$ of length 10 units, and a side of $\overline{DA}$ of length 5 units. The length from *A* to *B* is 3 units. What is the area of the parallelogram in square units?

**9**

$$A = \frac{v^2}{R}$$

The acceleration of an object moving in a circle is determined by the equation above, in which $v$ is the velocity of the object, $A$ is its acceleration, and $R$ is the radius of the circle. What is the value of the radius in terms of the other variables?

Ⓐ $R = \frac{2v}{A}$

Ⓑ $R = \frac{v^2}{A}$

Ⓒ $R = Av^2$

Ⓓ $R = \frac{1}{Av^2}$

**10**

If $y = bx^2 + 5$ when $x = 2$ and $y = 17$, what is the value of the constant $b$?

Ⓐ $-5$
Ⓑ 3
Ⓒ 4
Ⓓ 12

**11**

An airplane travels 3,000 miles in 10 hours. What is its speed in miles per hour?

________

**12**

$$2x - 3y = 5$$
$$4x + y = 17$$

If $(x, y)$ is a solution to the above system of equations, what is the value of $y$?

________

**13**

Francisco is packing two bags for his trip. The capacity of the small bag is one third that of the larger bag. If the total capacity of the two bags together is 80 liters, what is the capacity of the smaller bag?

Ⓐ 5 liters
Ⓑ 8 liters
Ⓒ 12 liters
Ⓓ 20 liters

2 MODULE 1 2



**14**

| $x$ | $f(x)$ |
|---|---|
| 1 | $1^C$ |
| 2 | $2^C$ |
| 3 | $3^C$ |

In the function with values given above, in which $C$ is a constant, if $f(2) = 8$, what is the value of $f(3)$?

Ⓐ 16
Ⓑ 27
Ⓒ 64
Ⓓ 81

**15**

The height of a certain triangle is twice the width of its base. If the area of the triangle is 25 square units, what is the height of the triangle?

**16**

In the year 1990, approximately 2 million U.S. residents were Internet users. In the year 2000, approximately 115 million U.S. residents were Internet users. Assuming the growth of Internet users was at a steady geometric rate, which function could be used to model the number of Internet users, $I$, in millions of people, $T$ years after 1990?

Ⓐ $I(T) = 2 \times (1.5)^T$
Ⓑ $I(T) = 2 \times (0.5)^T$
Ⓒ $I(T) = 2 \times (1.5)^{-T}$
Ⓓ $I(T) = 2 \times (2.5)^{-T}$

**17**

| Material | Kilograms per Cubic Meter |
|---|---|
| Cement | 1,440 |
| Maplewood | 755 |
| Steel | 7,850 |
| Cedarwood | 380 |
| Glass | 2,580 |
| Gravel | 2,000 |

Based on the information in the table, what is the mass of a solid steel wall that has a volume of 300 cubic meters?

Ⓐ 26 kilograms
Ⓑ 8,150 kilograms
Ⓒ 432,000 kilograms
Ⓓ 2,355,000 kilograms

**18**

The mean height of seven teenage boys is 67 inches. If one of the boys has a height of 74 inches, what is the mean height of the remaining boys to the nearest tenth of an inch?

**19**

$\angle X$ is measured in degrees. If the cosine of $\angle X$ is $\frac{\sqrt{2}}{2}$, what is the sine of $(90 - \angle X)$?

Ⓐ $\frac{1}{2}$
Ⓑ $\frac{\sqrt{2}}{2}$
Ⓒ $\frac{\sqrt{3}}{2}$
Ⓓ $\frac{2}{\sqrt{3}}$

**20**

$$x^3 + x^2 - 20x$$

Which of the following is NOT a factor of the above expression?

Ⓐ $x - 4$
Ⓑ $x - 7$
Ⓒ $x + 5$
Ⓓ $x$

**21**

There are 10 cards, each distinctly numbered from 1 to 10. After a card is selected from the randomly shuffled set, it is returned to the set. If someone first picks a 3 and then picks a 2, what is the probability that on the third selection the person will pick a 9?

Ⓐ $\frac{1}{20}$
Ⓑ $\frac{1}{10}$
Ⓒ $\frac{1}{9}$
Ⓓ $\frac{1}{6}$

**22**

In the equation $3x - 6 = 3(x - a)$, the constant $a$ is greater than 2. Which of the following statements must be true?

Ⓐ The equation has exactly one solution.
Ⓑ The equation has exactly two solutions.
Ⓒ The equation has infinitely many solutions.
Ⓓ The equation has no solution.

# ANSWER KEY
## Practice Test 3: Adaptive

### Section 2, Module 1: Math

1. **C**
2. **210**
3. **A**
4. **D**
5. **B**
6. **A**
7. **C**
8. **40**
9. **B**
10. **B**
11. **300**
12. **1**
13. **D**
14. **B**
15. **10**
16. **A**
17. **D**
18. **65.8**
19. **B**
20. **B**
21. **B**
22. **D**

Total Correct Answers: _____ / 22

**Did you get 13 or fewer questions correct? If so, move to Math Module 2A on page 795.**

**Did you get 14 or more questions correct? If so, move to Math Module 2B on page 808.**

2 MODULE 2 2



## Section 2, Module 2A: Math

35 MINUTES, 22 QUESTIONS

**DIRECTIONS** ∨

- All expressions and variables use real numbers.
- All figures are drawn to scale.
- Every figure lies in a plane.
- The domain of given functions is the set of all real numbers for which the corresponding value of the function is real.

For **multiple-choice questions**, solve the problem and pick the correct answer from the provided choices. Each multiple-choice question has only one correct answer.

For **student-produced response questions,** solve each problem and enter your answer following these guidelines:

- If you find **more than one correct answer,** enter just one answer.
- You can enter up to five characters for a **positive** answer and up to six characters (this includes the negative sign) for a **negative** answer.
- If your answer is a **fraction** that does not fit in the given space, enter the decimal equivalent instead.
- If your answer is a **decimal** that does not fit in the given space, enter it by stopping at or rounding up at the fourth digit.
- If your answer is a **mixed number** (like $4\frac{1}{2}$), enter it as an improper fraction (9/2) or its decimal equivalent (4.5).
- Do not enter **symbols** like a comma, dollar sign, or percent sign.

## Examples

| Answer | Acceptable Entries | Unacceptable Entries That Will Receive Zero Credit |
|---|---|---|
| 4.5 | 4.5<br>4.50<br>9/2 | $4\frac{1}{2}$<br>41/2 |
| $\frac{8}{9}$ | 8/9<br>.8888<br>.8889<br>0.888<br>0.889 | 0.88<br>.88<br>.89<br>0.89 |
| $-\frac{1}{9}$ | −1/9<br>−.1111<br>−0.111 | −.11<br>−0.11 |

# 2 MODULE 2 2

**REFERENCE**

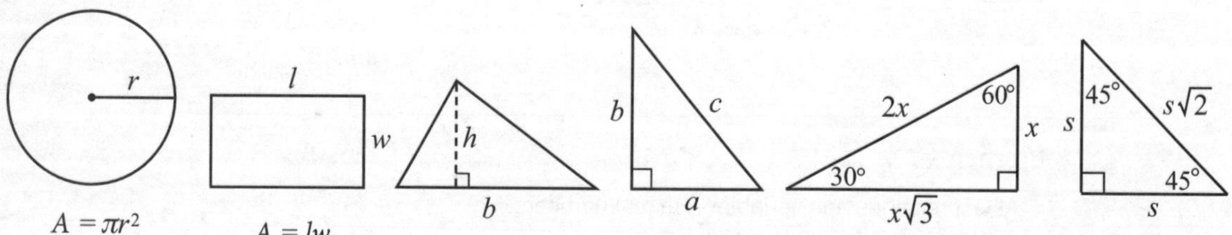


$A = \pi r^2$
$C = 2\pi r$

$A = lw$

$A = \frac{1}{2}bh$

$c^2 = a^2 + b^2$

Special Right Triangles

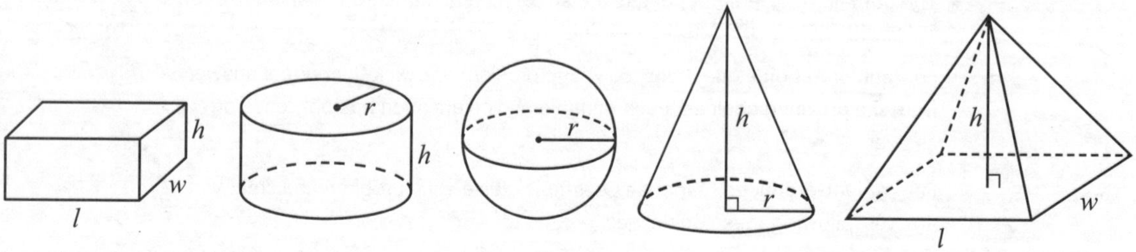


$V = lwh$

$V = \pi r^2 h$

$V = \frac{4}{3}\pi r^3$

$V = \frac{1}{3}\pi r^2 h$

$V = \frac{1}{3}lwh$

The number of degrees of arc in a circle is 360.
The number of radians of arc in a circle is $2\pi$.
The sum of the measures in degrees of the angles of a triangle is 180.

# 2 MODULE 2 2

**1**

In the line formed by the equation $y + 5 = 7x$, what is the value of the $y$-intercept?

Ⓐ $-5$
Ⓑ $-1$
Ⓒ 5
Ⓓ 7

**2**

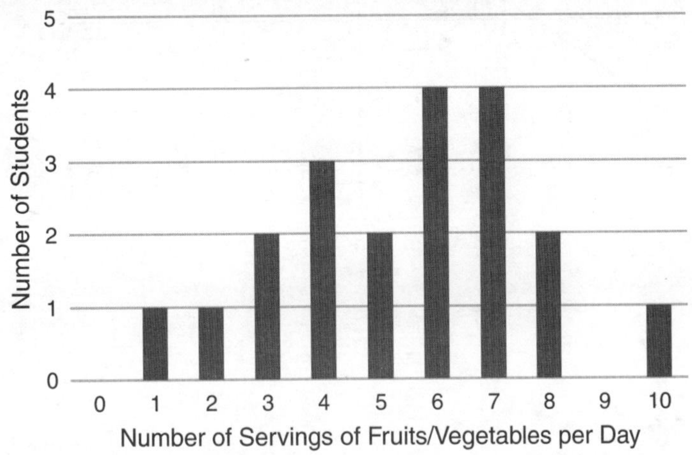


Twenty students were asked the combined total number of servings of fruits and vegetables they have each day. The results are presented in the histogram above. What is the median number of servings of fruits and vegetables consumed each day?

Ⓐ 4
Ⓑ 5
Ⓒ 6
Ⓓ 7

**3**

Which of the following is equivalent to $\frac{x^2 - 81}{x + 9}$?

Ⓐ $x + 9$
Ⓑ $x - 9$
Ⓒ $x^2 - 3$
Ⓓ $x^2 + 3$

**4**

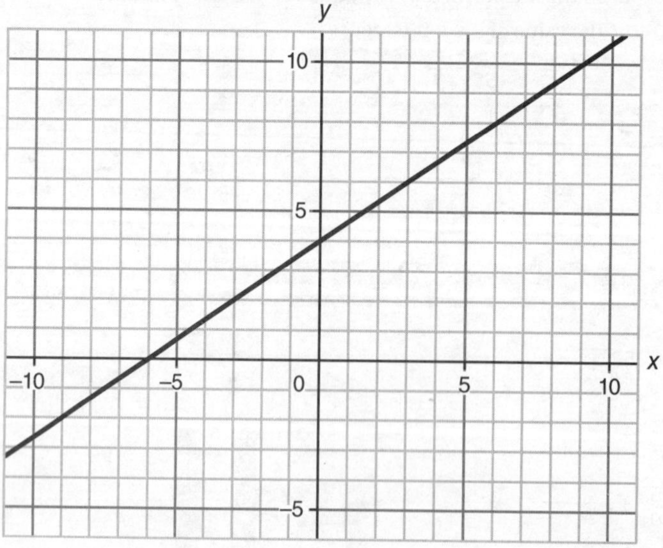


What is the best approximation of the slope of the line graphed above?

Ⓐ $\frac{1}{2}$

Ⓑ $\frac{2}{3}$

Ⓒ $\frac{4}{3}$

Ⓓ 2

**5**

Walter is going backpacking on a trail. The total distance of the trail is 300 miles. If he has already traveled 100 miles on the trail, how many miles per day, $m$, will he need to travel in order to complete his journey in $D$ days?

Ⓐ $m = \frac{200}{D}$

Ⓑ $m = 300D$

Ⓒ $m = \frac{D}{300}$

Ⓓ $m = 200 + D$

# 2 MODULE 2 2



**6**

Which of the following expressions is equivalent to $2(x - 4) + 4$?

Ⓐ $2x - 4$
Ⓑ $2x + 4$
Ⓒ $4x - 4$
Ⓓ $4x + 4$

**7**

The number of dollars, $C$, it costs for Halle to run a restaurant is modeled by the function $C(m) = 10m + 10{,}000$ in which $m$ is the number of meals served. What is the meaning of the 10 in this function?

Ⓐ The total cost for all the meals sold.
Ⓑ The fixed costs for the restaurant to operate.
Ⓒ The profit the restaurant has for each meal sold.
Ⓓ The additional cost to the restaurant for each additional meal.

2 MODULE 2 2

**8**

Which of the following represents the graph of $\frac{1}{2}y + 2 = -x$?

Ⓐ

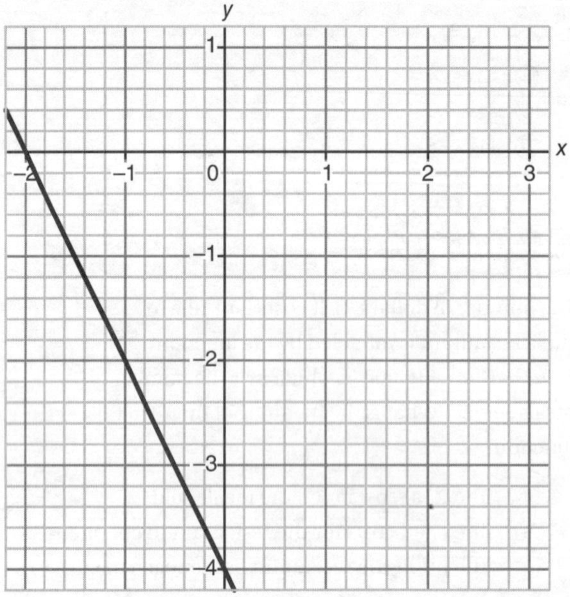


Ⓑ

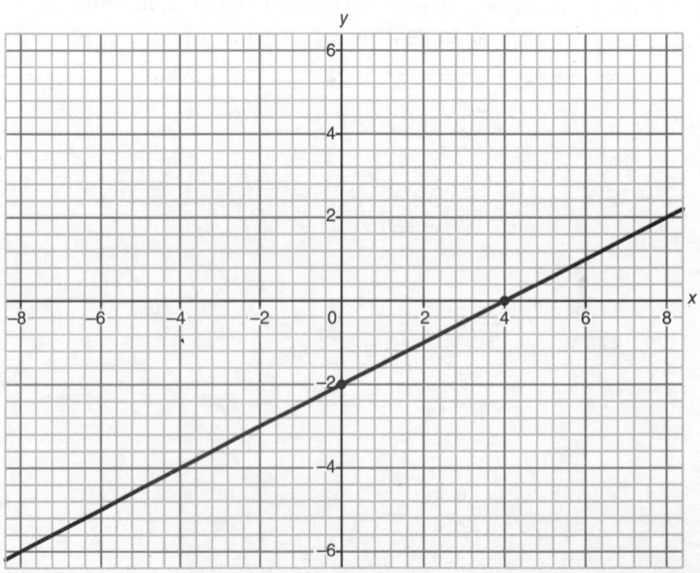

2 MODULE 2 2



Ⓒ
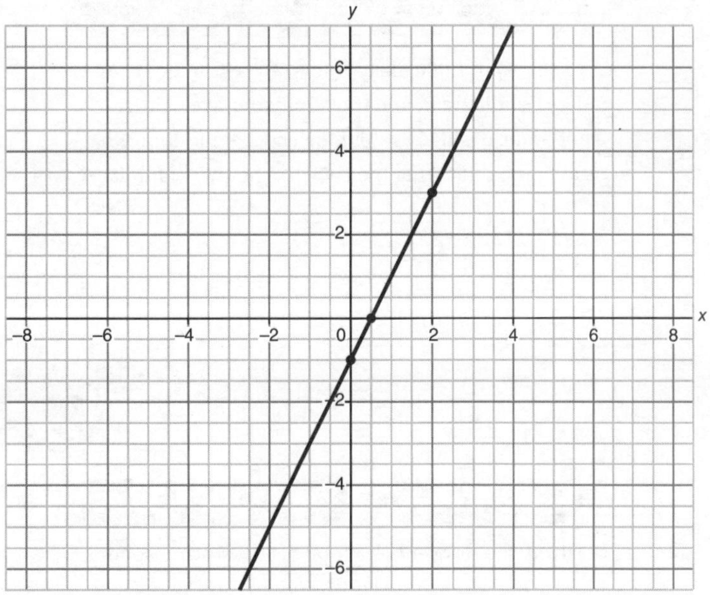


Ⓓ
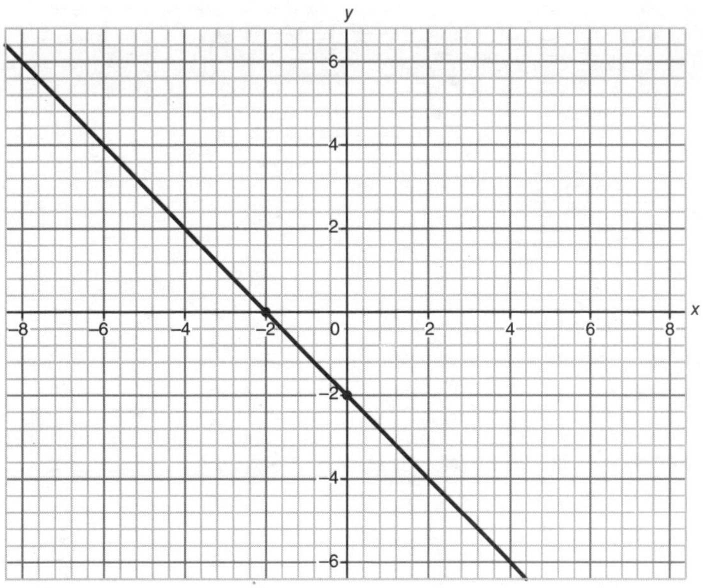

## 2 MODULE 2 2

**9**

In a survey of 1,000 likely voters, $\frac{1}{2}$ like Candidate A, $\frac{1}{3}$ like Candidate B, and the remainder like neither candidate. If a likely voter is selected at random, what is the probability that they will like neither candidate?

Ⓐ $\frac{1}{12}$

Ⓑ $\frac{1}{6}$

Ⓒ $\frac{1}{4}$

Ⓓ $\frac{1}{3}$

**10**

A silverware drawer has a total of 80 forks and spoons. If there are 5 forks for every 3 spoons, how many forks are there in the drawer?

________

# 2 MODULE 2 2



**11**

Traffic density is measured in vehicles/mile/lane. The traffic density in a city is portrayed in the graph below

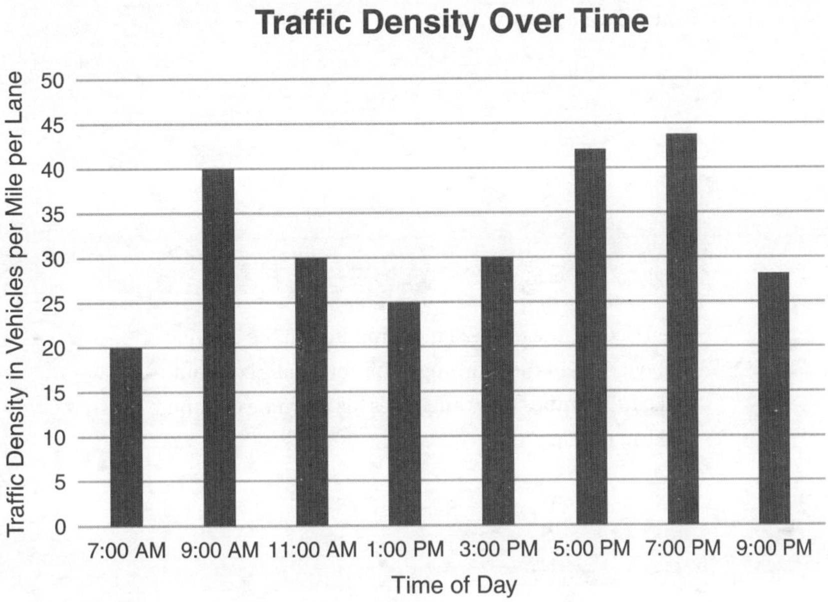


Between what two hours does the traffic density increase the most?

Ⓐ Between 7 a.m. and 9 a.m.

Ⓑ Between 9 a.m. and 11 a.m.

Ⓒ Between 1 p.m. and 3 p.m.

Ⓓ Between 3 p.m. and 5 p.m.

**12**

In the system of inequalities $y + 10 \leq 3x$ and $x \leq -y - 2$, what is the maximum value of $y$?

Ⓐ $-6$

Ⓑ $-4$

Ⓒ $0$

Ⓓ $3$

**13**

A meal costs $x$ dollars. The sales tax on the meal is 7%. If the cashier accidentally subtracted the sales tax from the price of the meal instead of adding it, what would the price be in terms of $x$?

Ⓐ $0.07x$
Ⓑ $0.7x$
Ⓒ $0.93x$
Ⓓ $1.07x$

**14**

Ken's commute takes 25 more minutes in the evening than it does in the morning. If his total daily commute takes 95 minutes, how long does his morning commute take in minutes?

**15**

The function $f$ is determined by $f(x) = \frac{x^3}{4} + 3$. What is the value of $f(2)$?

Ⓐ 1
Ⓑ 5
Ⓒ 6
Ⓓ 9

**16**

If the volume of a right rectangular prism is 90 cubic inches, and the product of the length and width of the prism is 30 square inches, what is the height of the prism?

# 2 MODULE 2 2



**17**

$$x^2 - x - 20 = 0$$

What is the sum of the solutions to the equation above?

**18**

The above circle graph gives the percentages of 800 city residents who voted in favor of a tax levy ("YES") and those who voted against it ("NO"). If the central angle formed by the portion of the circle allocated to "NO" is 45°, how many of the residents voted "NO"?

Ⓐ 90
Ⓑ 100
Ⓒ 110
Ⓓ 120

**19**

Density, mass, and volume are related by this formula:

$$Density = \frac{Mass}{Volume}$$

If the mass of an object is 2 kilograms and its volume is 8 liters, what is the object's density in $\frac{kg}{L}$?

Ⓐ $\frac{1}{8}$
Ⓑ $\frac{1}{4}$
Ⓒ $\frac{1}{2}$
Ⓓ $\frac{3}{4}$

**20**

What percentage of 70 is 35?

Ⓐ 40%
Ⓑ 50%
Ⓒ 75%
Ⓓ 200%

**21**

A line that is perpendicular to the line with the equation $y = -3x + 5$ has a $y$-intercept of 4. What is the $y$ value of a point in this perpendicular line when its $x$ value is 3?

__________

**22**

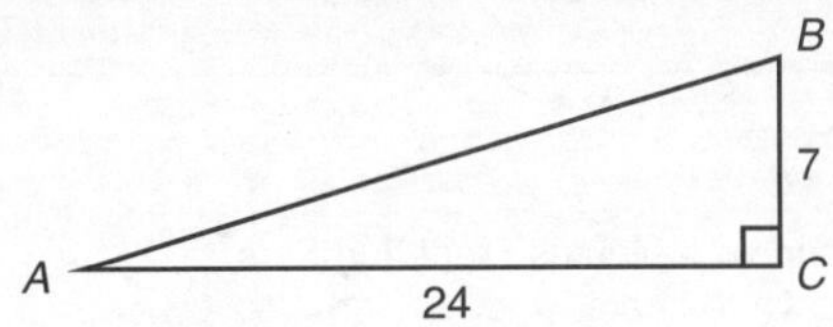


In triangle *ABC* above, $\overline{AC}$ is 24 units long and $\overline{BC}$ is 7 units long. What is the cosine of $\angle ABC$?

Ⓐ $\frac{7}{25}$

Ⓑ $\frac{7}{24}$

Ⓒ $\frac{24}{27}$

Ⓓ $\frac{25}{27}$

2 MODULE 2 2

## Section 2, Module 2B: Math

35 MINUTES, 22 QUESTIONS

**DIRECTIONS**

- All expressions and variables use real numbers.
- All figures are drawn to scale.
- Every figure lies in a plane.
- The domain of given functions is the set of all real numbers for which the corresponding value of the function is real.

For **multiple-choice questions**, solve the problem and pick the correct answer from the provided choices. Each multiple-choice question has only one correct answer.

For **student-produced response questions,** solve each problem and enter your answer following these guidelines:

- If you find **more than one correct answer,** enter just one answer.
- You can enter up to five characters for a **positive** answer and up to six characters (this includes the negative sign) for a **negative** answer.
- If your answer is a **fraction** that does not fit in the given space, enter the decimal equivalent instead.
- If your answer is a **decimal** that does not fit in the given space, enter it by stopping at or rounding up at the fourth digit.
- If your answer is a **mixed number** (like $4\frac{1}{2}$), enter it as an improper fraction (9/2) or its decimal equivalent (4.5).
- Do not enter **symbols** like a comma, dollar sign, or percent sign.

## Examples

| Answer | Acceptable Entries | Unacceptable Entries That Will Receive Zero Credit |
|---|---|---|
| 4.5 | 4.5<br>4.50<br>9/2 | $4\frac{1}{2}$<br>41/2 |
| $\frac{8}{9}$ | 8/9<br>.8888<br>.8889<br>0.888<br>0.889 | 0.88<br>.88<br>.89<br>0.89 |
| $-\frac{1}{9}$ | −1/9<br>−.1111<br>−0.111 | −.11<br>−0.11 |

# 2 MODULE 2 2

**REFERENCE**

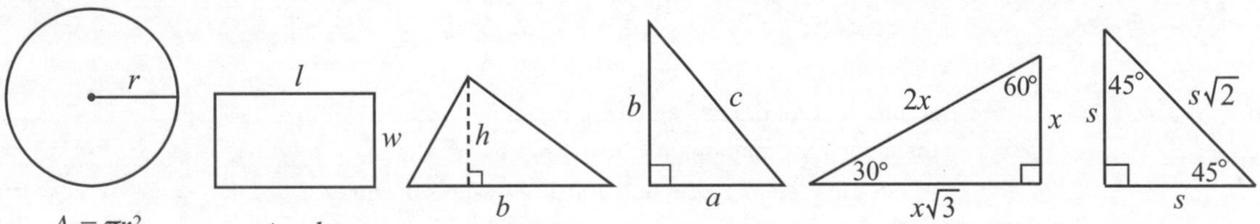


$A = \pi r^2$
$C = 2\pi r$

$A = lw$

$A = \frac{1}{2}bh$

$c^2 = a^2 + b^2$

Special Right Triangles

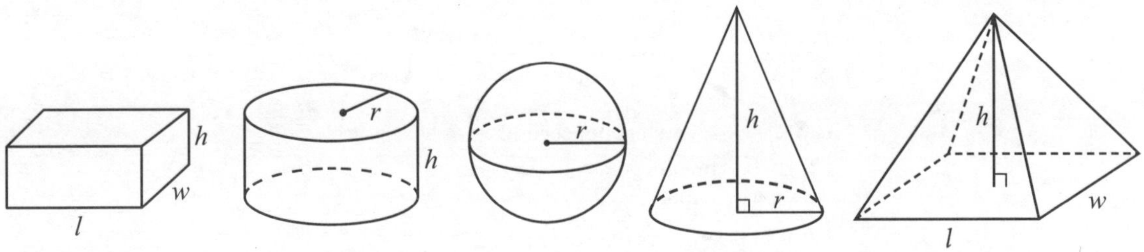


$V = lwh$

$V = \pi r^2 h$

$V = \frac{4}{3}\pi r^3$

$V = \frac{1}{3}\pi r^2 h$

$V = \frac{1}{3}lwh$

The number of degrees of arc in a circle is 360.
The number of radians of arc in a circle is $2\pi$.
The sum of the measures in degrees of the angles of a triangle is 180.

# 2 MODULE 2 2

**1**

In normal atmospheric conditions, the speed of sound through dry air can be approximated with the following equation, in which $V$ represents the velocity in meters per second and $T$ represents the air temperature in degrees Celsius.

$$V = 331.4 + 0.6T$$

What is the speed of sound in air that is 15 degrees Celsius?

Ⓐ −537.3 meters per second
Ⓑ 14.8 meters per second
Ⓒ 340.4 meters per second
Ⓓ 423.5 meters per second

**2**

For the line $l$, $y = ax + n$, where $a$ and $n$ are distinct nonzero constants. Which of these lines must be perpendicular to line $l$?

Ⓐ $y = nx + a$
Ⓑ $y = ax - n$
Ⓒ $y = -\frac{1}{a}x - n$
Ⓓ $y = -ax + n$

**3**

If $\frac{x^{\frac{2}{3}}}{x^{\frac{1}{6}}} = \frac{x^a}{\sqrt{x}}$, what is the value of $a$?

Ⓐ 1
Ⓑ 2
Ⓒ 3
Ⓓ 6

# 2 MODULE 2 2



**4**

Nyla is driving *X* miles per hour. Given that there are 5,280 feet in a mile, what is her speed in feet per second?

Ⓐ $\left(\frac{60}{5,280}\right)X$

Ⓑ $\left(\frac{3,600}{5,280}\right)X$

Ⓒ $\left(\frac{5,280}{60}\right)X$

Ⓓ $\left(\frac{5,280}{3,600}\right)X$

**5**

$$\frac{2x-6}{2}=x+k$$

If the equation above has an infinite number of solutions, what is the value of the constant *k*?

Ⓐ $k=-7$

Ⓑ $k=-3$

Ⓒ $k=0$

Ⓓ $k=2$

**6**

In the equation $3=|x-1|$, how many solutions are there?

Ⓐ Exactly 1

Ⓑ Exactly 2

Ⓒ None

Ⓓ Infinite

**7**

| Heartbeats per Minute | Breaths per Minute |
|---|---|
| 60 | 12 |
| 70 | 15 |
| 80 | 18 |

Assuming Baahir's heartbeats per minute and breaths per minute have a linear relationship with one another, what would Baahir's pulse (heartbeats per minute) be if he is breathing at a rate of 24 breaths per minute?

______

**8**

At exactly how many points will the function $f(x) = x^2 - 3x - 4$ intersect the $x$-axis?

Ⓐ 0
Ⓑ 1
Ⓒ 2
Ⓓ 3

**9**

If $f(x) = 3^x - 1$, for what value of $x$ will $f(x)$ intercept the $y$-axis when graphed in the $xy$-coordinate plane?

______

**10**

A city's population at the beginning of 2010 was 50,000 residents. At the beginning of 2011, its population was 45,000 residents, and at the beginning of 2012, its population was 40,500 residents. If the city's population has continued to change at the same rate each year, which function models the city's population $T$ years after 2010?

Ⓐ $P(T) = 50{,}000 \times (0.9)^T$
Ⓑ $P(T) = 40{,}500 \times (0.09)^T$
Ⓒ $P(T) = 50{,}000 \times (1.1)^T$
Ⓓ $P(T) = 45{,}000 \times (1.09)^T$

**11**

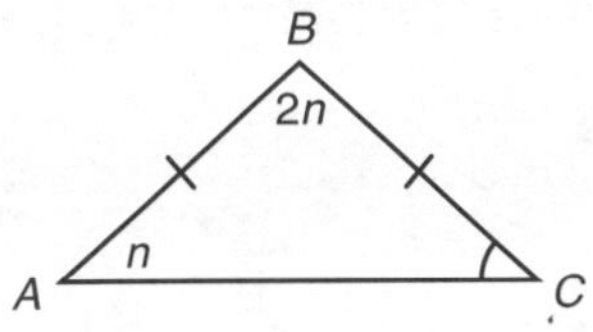


In triangle $ABC$ above, $\overline{AB}$ and $\overline{BC}$ are congruent, and $\angle A$ is $n$ degrees and $\angle B$ is $2n$ degrees. What is the measure of $\angle C$ in degrees?

Ⓐ 20°
Ⓑ 35°
Ⓒ 45°
Ⓓ 70°

**12**

Consider these two histograms showing the frequency of 70 integers between 1–9:

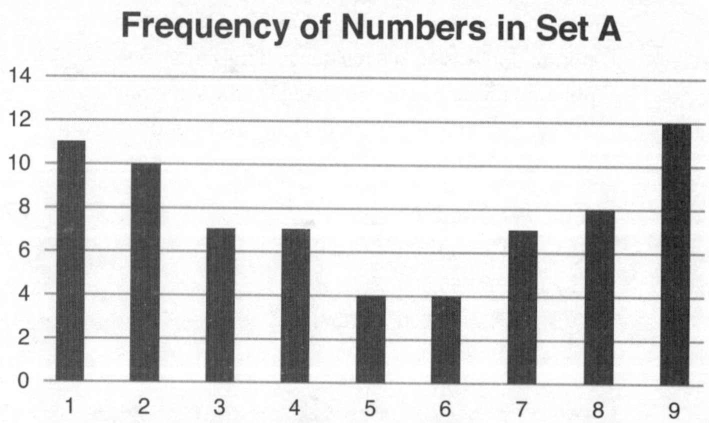


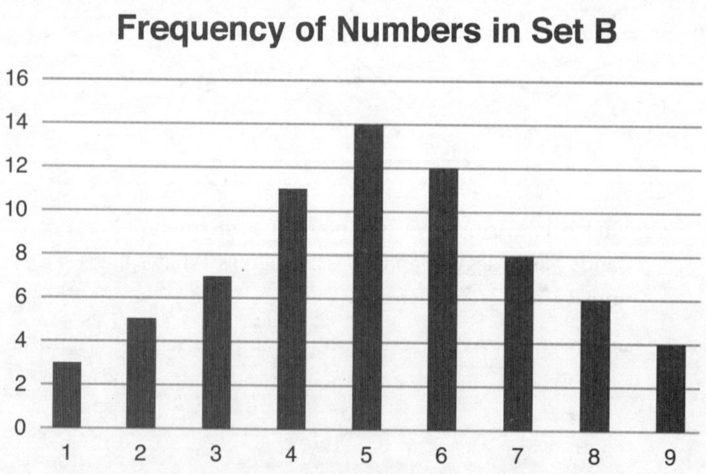


Which of the following quantities would be the largest amount greater for set A than for set B?

Ⓐ Median
Ⓑ Standard Deviation
Ⓒ Range
Ⓓ Mean

# 2 MODULE 2 2



**13**

If a square has a diagonal of $7\sqrt{2}$ units long, how many units would the radius be of the largest possible circle that fits within the square (with the circle tangent to the sides of the square)?

______

**14**

Diana walks at a pace of 100 steps per minute. On Monday, she walks a total of 6,000 steps. If she maintains her pace and wants to increase the total number of steps on Tuesday to 10,000, how many additional hours will she need to walk on Tuesday compared to Monday?

Ⓐ $\frac{1}{6}$ of an hour

Ⓑ $\frac{1}{4}$ of an hour

Ⓒ $\frac{2}{3}$ of an hour

Ⓓ 1 hour

**15**

The linear function $g$ can be written in the form $g(x) = mx + b$, in which $m$ and $b$ are constants. If $g(1) = 7$ and $g(3) = 11$, what is the value of $m$?

Ⓐ $-3$

Ⓑ $-1$

Ⓒ 2

Ⓓ 6

**16**

Two hot air balloons were initially at the same height in the air at 200 feet. After 10 minutes go by, one balloon's height has increased by 30% and the other balloon's height has decreased by 15%. At that point, how many feet apart in height would the two balloons be?

Ⓐ 60 feet
Ⓑ 70 feet
Ⓒ 80 feet
Ⓓ 90 feet

**17**

If $2x^2 + bx + 4 = 0$, for what values of $b$ will there be no real solutions?

Ⓐ $b > \sqrt{2}$
Ⓑ $|b| \leq -\sqrt{2}$
Ⓒ $b \geq 4$
Ⓓ $|b| < 4\sqrt{2}$

**18**

The function $f$ has an equation of $f(x) = -(x + 3)(x - 5)$. For what value of $x$ is the value of $f(x)$ at its maximum?

2 MODULE 2 2



**19**

A pizza parlor has a goal of making at least $10,000 a month in revenue from selling pizzas. The parlor sells small pizzas for $10 each and large pizzas for $20 each. If the total number of pizzas sold in a month must be less than 800, which system of inequalities would represent the number of small pizzas, $S$, and the number of large pizzas, $L$, that would meet the pizza parlor's requirements?

Ⓐ $S + L < 800$
$10S + 20L \geq 10{,}000$

Ⓑ $S + L \geq 800$
$10S + 20L < 10{,}000$

Ⓒ $10S + 20L < 800$
$S + L < 10{,}000$

Ⓓ $10S + 20L \geq 800$
$S + L > 10{,}000$

**20**

The reproduction number, called $R_O$, is used to calculate the spread of disease. If a virus has an $R_O$ of 6, an infected person will likely directly infect six other people. Based on this, if 20 people are infected with a virus that has an $R_O$ of 4.2, how many people will these 20 people most likely directly infect?

Ⓐ 46
Ⓑ 54
Ⓒ 84
Ⓓ 98

## 2 MODULE 2 2

**21**

$$\{2, 3, 6, 6, 7\}$$

Which expression gives the complete set of potential values of a single number $x$ that can be added to the above set of data without changing the median of the set?

Ⓐ $x \geq 7$
Ⓑ $x < 2$
Ⓒ $x < 6$
Ⓓ $x \geq 6$

**22**

How many more units is the diameter of circle $A$ than that of circle $B$?

Circle $A$: $(x - 2)^2 + (y - 7)^2 = 49$

Circle $B$: $(x + 5)^2 + (y - 3)^2 = 25$

__________

# ANSWER KEY
## Practice Test 3: Adaptive

Score whichever module you completed: 2A or 2B.

### Section 1, Module 2A: Reading and Writing

1. **D**
2. **D**
3. **C**
4. **C**
5. **C**
6. **D**
7. **A**
8. **B**
9. **C**
10. **C**
11. **A**
12. **A**
13. **D**
14. **B**
15. **A**
16. **C**
17. **D**
18. **D**
19. **D**
20. **C**
21. **C**
22. **B**
23. **C**
24. **D**
25. **C**
26. **D**
27. **D**

**Total: ____ / 27**

### Section 1, Module 2B: Reading and Writing

1. **B**
2. **A**
3. **D**
4. **B**
5. **D**
6. **A**
7. **B**
8. **B**
9. **C**
10. **D**
11. **D**
12. **D**
13. **A**
14. **D**
15. **A**
16. **D**
17. **C**
18. **B**
19. **D**
20. **C**
21. **D**
22. **A**
23. **B**
24. **A**
25. **B**
26. **B**
27. **C**

**Total: ____ / 27**

# ANSWER KEY
## Practice Test 3: Adaptive

Score whichever module you completed: 2A or 2B.

### Section 2, Module 2A: Math

1. **A**
2. **C**
3. **B**
4. **B**
5. **A**
6. **A**
7. **D**
8. **A**
9. **B**
10. **50**
11. **A**
12. **B**
13. **C**
14. **35**
15. **B**
16. **3**
17. **1**
18. **B**
19. **B**
20. **B**
21. **5**
22. **A**

**Total:** ____ / 22

### Section 2, Module 2B: Math

1. **C**
2. **C**
3. **A**
4. **D**
5. **B**
6. **B**
7. **100**
8. **C**
9. **0**
10. **A**
11. **C**
12. **B**
13. **3.5 or $\frac{7}{2}$**
14. **C**
15. **C**
16. **D**
17. **D**
18. **1**
19. **A**
20. **C**
21. **D**
22. **4**

**Total:** ____ / 22

## Adaptive Digital SAT Score Estimator

This streamlined guide will give you an approximation of the score you would earn on the Digital SAT. On the actual Digital SAT, there will be some small but important differences in how the test will be scored. First, there will be two experimental questions on each module that will be omitted. You will almost certainly be unable to determine which questions are experimental, so just do your best on every single question. In this guide, we are making every question count to simplify your estimation. Second, the Digital SAT will utilize "Item Response Theory" in its scoring. Certain questions may have more weight on your performance than others. More information about the precise scoring guidelines should be available in the fall of 2023—check on *collegeboard.org* for the latest information.

* Be sure you look at the correct chart depending on whether you did Module 2A or 2B for each section. *

### Reading and Writing Scoring Charts

Use this table if you did Reading and Writing **Modules 1 and 2A.**

Tally the number of correct answers from the entire Reading and Writing section (out of 54) to find your Reading and Writing section score. Since you would have to miss at least ten questions to move to Module 2A, the table ends at a maximum of 44 questions correct.

| Number of Correct Reading and Writing Questions (Out of 54) | Reading and Writing Test Score (Out of 800) |
|---|---|
| **0** | 200 |
| **1** | 210 |
| **2** | 220 |
| **3** | 230 |
| **4** | 240 |
| **5** | 250 |
| **6** | 260 |
| **7** | 270 |
| **8** | 280 |
| **9** | 290 |
| **10** | 300 |
| **11** | 310 |
| **12** | 320 |
| **13** | 330 |
| **14** | 340 |
| **15** | 350 |
| **16** | 360 |
| **17** | 370 |
| **18** | 380 |
| **19** | 390 |
| **20** | 400 |
| **21** | 410 |
| **22** | 420 |
| **23** | 430 |

| Number of Correct Reading and Writing Questions (Out of 54) | Reading and Writing Test Score (Out of 800) |
|---|---|
| **24** | 440 |
| **25** | 450 |
| **26** | 460 |
| **27** | 470 |
| **28** | 480 |
| **29** | 490 |
| **30** | 500 |
| **31** | 510 |
| **32** | 520 |
| **33** | 530 |
| **34** | 540 |
| **35** | 550 |
| **36** | 560 |
| **37** | 570 |
| **38** | 580 |
| **39** | 590 |
| **40** | 610 |
| **41** | 620 |
| **42** | 630 |
| **43** | 640 |
| **44** | 650 |

Use this table if you did Reading and Writing **Modules 1 and 2B.**

Tally the number of correct answers from the entire Reading and Writing section (out of 54) to find your Reading and Writing section score. Since you would need to answer at least 18 questions on the first module correctly to do Module 2, the table starts at 18 questions correct as the minimum.

| Number of Correct Reading and Writing Questions (Out of 54) | Reading and Writing Test Score (Out of 800) |
|---|---|
| 18 | 450 |
| 19 | 460 |
| 20 | 470 |
| 21 | 480 |
| 22 | 490 |
| 23 | 500 |
| 24 | 510 |
| 25 | 520 |
| 26 | 530 |
| 27 | 540 |
| 28 | 550 |
| 29 | 560 |
| 30 | 570 |
| 31 | 580 |
| 32 | 590 |
| 33 | 600 |
| 34 | 610 |
| 35 | 620 |
| 36 | 630 |
| 37 | 640 |
| 38 | 650 |
| 39 | 660 |
| 40 | 670 |
| 41 | 680 |
| 42 | 690 |
| 43 | 700 |
| 44 | 710 |
| 45 | 720 |
| 46 | 730 |
| 47 | 740 |
| 48 | 750 |
| 49 | 760 |
| 50 | 770 |
| 51 | 780 |
| 52 | 790 |
| 53 | 800 |
| 54 | 800 |

## Math Scoring Charts

Use this table if you did Math **Modules 1 and 2A.**

Tally the number of correct answers from the entire Math section (out of 44) to find your Math section score. Since you would have to miss at least nine questions to move to Module 2A, the table ends at a maximum of 35 questions correct.

| Number of Correct Math Questions (Out of 44) | Math Section Score (Out of 800) |
|---|---|
| **0** | 200 |
| **1** | 220 |
| **2** | 230 |
| **3** | 240 |
| **4** | 250 |
| **5** | 280 |
| **6** | 300 |
| **7** | 320 |
| **8** | 340 |
| **9** | 350 |
| **10** | 360 |
| **11** | 380 |
| **12** | 390 |
| **13** | 400 |
| **14** | 410 |
| **15** | 430 |
| **16** | 440 |
| **17** | 450 |
| **18** | 460 |
| **19** | 480 |
| **20** | 490 |
| **21** | 500 |
| **22** | 510 |
| **23** | 520 |
| **24** | 530 |
| **25** | 540 |
| **26** | 550 |
| **27** | 560 |
| **28** | 570 |
| **29** | 580 |
| **30** | 590 |
| **31** | 600 |
| **32** | 610 |
| **33** | 620 |
| **34** | 630 |
| **35** | 650 |

Use this table if you did Math **Modules 1 and 2B.**

Tally the number of correct answers from the entire Math section (out of 44) to find your Math section score. Since you would need to answer at least 14 questions on the first module correctly to do Module 2, the table starts at 14 questions correct as the minimum.

| Number of Correct Math Questions (Out of 44) | Math Section Score (Out of 800) |
|---|---|
| 14 | 450 |
| 15 | 460 |
| 16 | 480 |
| 17 | 490 |
| 18 | 510 |
| 19 | 520 |
| 20 | 530 |
| 21 | 550 |
| 22 | 560 |
| 23 | 570 |
| 24 | 580 |
| 25 | 590 |
| 26 | 610 |
| 27 | 620 |
| 28 | 630 |
| 29 | 640 |
| 30 | 650 |
| 31 | 670 |
| 32 | 680 |
| 33 | 690 |
| 34 | 700 |
| 35 | 710 |
| 36 | 720 |
| 37 | 730 |
| 38 | 740 |
| 39 | 750 |
| 40 | 760 |
| 41 | 770 |
| 42 | 780 |
| 43 | 790 |
| 44 | 800 |

Add the Reading and Writing Section Score and the Math Section Score to find your approximate total SAT test score:

___________ Reading and Writing Section Score +

___________ Math Section Score =

___________ **Total Approximate SAT Test Score (between 400 and 1600)**

Approximate your testing percentiles (1st to 99th) using this chart:

| Total Score | Section Score | Total Percentile | Reading and Writing Percentile | Math Percentile |
|---|---|---|---|---|
| 1600 | 800 | 99+ | 99+ | 99 |
| 1500 | 750 | 98 | 98 | 96 |
| 1400 | 700 | 94 | 94 | 91 |
| 1300 | 650 | 86 | 86 | 84 |
| 1200 | 600 | 74 | 73 | 75 |
| 1100 | 550 | 59 | 57 | 61 |
| 1000 | 500 | 41 | 40 | 42 |
| 900 | 450 | 25 | 24 | 27 |
| 800 | 400 | 11 | 11 | 15 |
| 700 | 350 | 3 | 3 | 5 |
| 600 | 300 | 1 | 1 | 1 |
| 500 | 250 | 1 | 1 | 1 |
| 400 | 200 | 1 | 1 | 1 |

# Answer Explanations

## Reading and Writing

### Module 1

1. **(D)** "Building" is the most appropriate of these options to describe growing a group of viewers for social media content. "Manufacturing" and "fabricating" are better used when describing building physical, tangible objects. "Escalating" means to increase, not to necessarily build something.

2. **(A)** "In the company of" means to hang out with someone; that is the most logical meaning to have in this context, since Matsuo was hanging out with the lord's son. The other options all have to do with business practices.

3. **(A)** "Modify" means to "change," which makes the most sense given that the scientists changed the benzene reaction in a way that maintained the original product but did not add the undesired sidechains. "Expunge" and "oust" would be to "eliminate" the reaction, which is not what is expressed. It is not "proposed" because this was actually implemented, not just considered.

4. **(B)** Based on the context, "spurred" is most logical, since it means "inspired." Choice (D) is in the incorrect tense, and (A) and (C) do not convey the precise meaning needed.

5. **(A)** The text describes the transcription process, stating that the introns are "extracted and degraded" so choice (A) is the correct answer. The exons are translated, but the word excised is specifically referring to the introns. The exons are not "coded" into some sort of language, nor are they "mutated" or changed into something else.

6. **(D)** The text starts by introducing the initiative of the LEAP program, then proceeds to give national survey results that show the relevance of the LEAP program's goals to meeting the needs of employers, i.e., demonstrating the economic relevance of the program. It is not (A) because an outline of a liberal arts curriculum would require more details about coursework and timeframes. It is not (B) because a historical survey would look at multiple historical events over a period of time. It is not C because the writer is using statistics to support, not refute, the claim.

7. **(D)** Text 1 focuses on the shift from non-online learning to online learning especially in terms of the growing recognition of online professional certifications, and the information in Text 2 shows how any concerns about costs being a barrier are increasingly negated since there are so many free learning options. Thus, choice (D) makes sense because if the cost barriers to online education are reduced, the popularity of online certifications will likely increase. It is not (A) because having inexpensive learning options would be a plus, not a potential threat. It is not (B) because the focus is on online education, not in-person. It is not (C) because it can reasonably be inferred that if more people have access to free educational opportunities to learn relevant job skills, this would likely help businesses because they would have more access to qualified workers.

8. **(B)** In considering his legacy, the narrator notes that he will not leave a "wealthy bequest" or a "labor-saving machine," but will instead leave "carols" for "comrades and lovers." So, the narrator has apparently prioritized making human connections instead of achievements like wealth and inventions that are more tangible. It is not (A) because the narrator is not suggesting that one of these options is better than another; instead, he is noting what he himself

has done. It is not (C) because this would not represent a main idea of the text. It is not (D) because the narrator has evidently created "carols" "vibrating through the air" and makes no reference to technology being needed to create these.

9. **(B)** Joe Dillon is the character who introduces the narrator to the Wild West stories. He is described as playing fiercely with the other children and consistently winning their war games, making choice (B) correct. He doesn't ever allow the enemy side to win, so choices (A) and (C) can be ruled out. No evidence is provided to support choice (D).

10. **(A)** The teacher claims that the narrator expresses a deep personal feeling of melancholy, which the quotation in choice (A) clearly shows. This selection mentions the "freezings" the narrator has felt, the "dark days" seen, and a sense of "bareness everywhere." The other options use language that is more positive or at least neutral—they do not approach the negativity found in (A).

11. **(D)** A major issue that astronauts have, as described in the text, is that they "suffer from cardiac atrophy as a response to immobility." The author explains that bears do not suffer from cardiac atrophy even after months of hibernation. The author therefore thinks that bears may be the key to solving cardiac atrophy in astronauts. If, however, bears have the same response to time in space that humans have, then this line of scientific inquiry would not be helpful. This makes (D) the best answer. Choice (A) is incorrect as this would be a good reason to further study bears and how they might help astronauts. Choice (B) is incorrect as the author is not a proponent of human hibernation. Choice (C) is incorrect as this does not relate to the study of bears to help astronauts.

12. **(B)** The consumer researcher makes the claim that the prices of organic crops can often be substantially higher than those of conventionally raised crops. Choice (B) best supports this claim, since it accurately notes that between 2010 and 2014, organic soybeans are consistently about twice the price of conventional soybeans. It is not (A) because this doesn't mention a price differential. It is not (C) or (D) because these options only discuss organic crops.

13. **(C)** In choice (C), we learn that because of Daisy's visit to the school, a young man was suspended indefinitely because of his actions against the minority students. This makes choice (C) the best option as it shows that Daisy convinced the administration to make this suspension. Choices (A) and (B) simply show Daisy's beliefs and the facts of the situation, not that she persuaded anyone of them. Choice (D) shows that the president is willing to visit, not that Daisy has convinced him of anything.

14. **(C)** The political scientist wants to show that even if a presidential candidate wins more popular votes than any other candidate, but still has less than an outright majority, the candidate can still win a majority of the electoral votes. Choice (C) demonstrates this because it shows how Wilson won a plurality of the popular vote but a large majority of the electoral vote. Choice (A) does not tell us anything about the election winner. Choice (B) focuses on parties that only won a small percentage of the votes. Choice (D) talks about the second-place candidate instead of the winner.

15. **(C)** The final sentence of the text is elaborating on specific examples of extrinsic motivators. Based on the previous sentence, "avoiding consequences" could be an extrinsic motivator, making "following the law to avoid being arrested" an excellent option. The other options are all examples of intrinsic motivators as described earlier in the text.

16. **(C)** "But" provides a transition between the two independent clauses in the sentence, making a single comma an appropriate way to join these two clauses. Choice (A) is too choppy, choice (B) places the comma after the "but" instead of before, and choice (D) needs a pause partway through the sentence.

17. **(D)** "Their" goes along with "cats" in showing the possession that the cats have for "way." Choices (A) and (B) are used for singular substitutions, and choice (C) is used to show a location.

18. **(D)** The colon provides the best option to give a pause before the clarification is provided. Also, the apostrophe in "it's" is used correctly since this stands for "it is." Choices (A) and (C) incorrectly use the possessive form "its." Choice (B) gives a comma splice—a comma by itself is not sufficient to join two complete sentences.

19. **(C)** "Took off" is the only option that correctly uses the past tense, which is correct given the past tense of other nearby verbs like "founded," "started," and "believed."

20. **(D)** No commas are needed to break up this phrase, making choice (D) correct. Choice (A) uses a semicolon without a complete sentence after it. Choice (B) inappropriately breaks up the phrase "provide . . . with." Choice (C) is far too choppy.

21. **(C)** The subject in the sentence is "process," which is singular. Choice (C) is the only option that provides a singular verb to make this a complete sentence.

22. **(B)** Choice (B) uses dashes to set aside the definition of what a stage is. Choice (A) only punctuates one side of the definition. Choice (C) does not provide any punctuation. Choice (D) inconsistently punctuates the definition.

23. **(D)** "Since" is the only transition that shows a cause-and-effect relationship between the fact that platypuses break down their food using gravel and dirt from the water and the fact that grinding plates in their bills enable this to take place. The other options do not show a cause-and-effect relationship.

24. **(C)** "Instead" is the only option that provides a contrasting transition between the statement that soap does not merely kill lethal bacteria and the statement that it removes all germs. "Also" and "additionally" both transition into continuations of the same idea, while "granted" would transition into an acknowledgement of an objection.

25. **(C)** Since the student wants to present general information about Dayton to an audience that does not know much about Dayton, it makes the most sense for the student to focus on broad facts about the city. Choice (C) accomplishes this goal since it generalizes about how Dayton is home to many useful inventions. The other options are all too specific in focusing on particular Daytonian inventors and inventions instead of on providing a broad introductory overview.

26. **(A)** The student wants to show how a common assumption that people have about piranhas only eating animals is incorrect. Stating that some piranhas do in fact eat only plants would directly address this misconception. Choice (B) does not address the piranha diet. Choice (C) does not make sense because blood would also be an animal product. Choice (D) is inconsistent with the information in the text.

27. **(B)** The astronomers are concerned about the "dangers of a large asteroid strike on Earth." A constructive strategy dealing with this problem would be to have a plan in place to prevent such a strike from happening. Based on the notes, a constructive strategy would be to build upon the success that NASA had in modifying the orbit of a small asteroid. After all, if a small asteroid could be manipulated, it is possible that a larger one could also be manipulated. It is not (A) because this is too extreme in its negativity. It is not (C) because this is more alarmist than constructive. It is not (D) because this would dismiss instead of addressing the concerns of the astronomers.

## Module 2A

1. **(D)** In this sentence, Juan is "ignoring" the jealous comments of his friends; the word "dismissed" would be an excellent substitute. It is not "reduced" or "forgot," because he devotes some thought to what they said. It is not "conceded" because that would mean he would admit the truth of the jealous claims of his peers.
2. **(D)** Camouflage would prevent potential prey from spotting the approaching servals since the prey would not be able to "detect" the servals. "Pictured" and "envision" involve more hypothetical visualization, and "ignored" is the opposite of the intended meaning.
3. **(C)** The spectators are bringing up ideas for consideration—thus "raised" would make sense, since the spectators are sharing ideas, not physical objects. It is not "increased" because someone cannot increase a speaking point. It is not "elevated" because while elevate can be used to refer to raising things in other contexts, it cannot properly be used here to refer to bringing up a point. It is not "nourished" because the spectators are not feeding several points—they are stating them.
4. **(C)** The text refers to "breaking the fat into three different chains," so separating is the closest word meaning. "Flouting" means "defying." "Elimination" would imply that the fat was removed instead of divided. "Categorizing" is a close synonym but indicates a classifying of parts.
5. **(C)** "Landscape" most appropriately describes the land in which the platypuses were prevalent. A panorama is more of a scenic view. A perspective is more of a point of view. Agriculture would not have been associated with the nonhuman activities so long ago.
6. **(D)** "Troubled" is the best choice since the narrator is thinking about a "most miserable thing." Choice (A) is too strong of a word since there is no evidence that the narrator has become physically ill. (B) and (C) inaccurately portray the narrator's shame as a power or strong point.
7. **(A)** The text refers presents that influenza remains a viable threat, and because of its unique disposition, is likely to stay that way. Choices (B) and (D) state the opposite, arguing instead that the virus is likely to be killed off and is essentially harmless. Choice (C) is not correct because influenza's inability to be conquered, not its severity is what makes it unique.
8. **(B)** The text starts with the phrase "The wheel of progress moves onward." This part of the topic sentence sets up the rest of the text to talk about what Stanton sees as inevitable progress and the embrace thereof. This makes choice (B) the best option. Andrew Johnson is only an example, not the main message, so choice (A) is incorrect. Choice (C) is the opposite of her message—she believes that people should embrace change and shift the status quo. Choice (D) is incorrect as she is not discussing animal examples.

9. **(C)** The court observed that if students are in segregated schools, they face an inherent disadvantage when compared to students at integrated schools. Choice (C) directly and specifically illustrates this claim by connecting legal segregation to a delay in educational and mental development. It is not (A) because it is too vague. It is not (B) because this refers to earlier thinking that separate facilities could be equal. It is not (D) because the disposition is not clarified.

10. **(C)** The researcher claims that probiotics that must be refrigerated are ill-suited for stomach digestion. Choice (C) would directly support this claim since it gives specific reasons why the bacteria that prefer a cold environment would be harmed by the stomach conditions. It is not (A) because this option does not relate to probiotics that need to be kept cold. It is not (B) because the warmth from a beverage may not be the same as the warmth in a stomach. It is not (D) because antibiotics are not the same as probiotics, so generalizations about antibiotics would not necessarily be applicable to probiotics.

11. **(A)** To support the idea that traumatic brain injuries are more likely to come from less dramatic, home-based injuries, choice (A) is the best option, as it refers to "falls and unintentional blunt trauma" that cause the majority of traumatic brain injuries. It is not (B) because this does not refer to less dramatic injuries. It is not (C) because it does not consider other sources like unintentional blunt trauma. It is not (D) because both of these sources of injuries are rather violent.

12. **(A)** The final sentence contrasts with the previous sentence, which states that there are times when handwashing is quite necessary. Therefore, acknowledging that living in a constantly sterile environment is "not necessary" makes the most sense. Choices (B) and (D) state the opposite of the needed meaning, and choice (C) is ambivalent.

13. **(D)** The text refers to MLM as a "new type of scheme" that was "designed to pad the pockets of a select few." So, the narrator clearly has a negative opinion of MLM; thus, choice (D) makes sense because it describes MLM quite skeptically. Choices (A) and (B) express a more positive attitude towards MLM, which is not supported by the text. Choice (C) incorrectly connects the present-day MLM to its introduction in the World War II era.

14. **(B)** The text is outlining the evolution of the concept of a chemical element. The final sentence alludes to how Boyle's long-lasting definition was eventually replaced after dominating scientific thinking for 300 years. Referring to "the discovery of subatomic particles in the 20th century" would make the most sense as an option, since it aligns with the chemistry focus of the text and matches the timeline coming 300 years after the 17th century. The other options do not connect to either chemistry or to the timeline.

15. **(A)** "Has" is both consistent with the singular subject of "it" and with the timeframe of the past leading up to the present day, making the present perfect tense correct. Choices (B) and (D) are plural, and choice (C) would use the past perfect, which would not indicate that this sport continues up to the present day.

16. **(C)** Use a comma to separate the complete sentence from the phrase that follows. It is not choices (A) or (D) because what follows is not a complete sentence. It is not (B) because a brief pause is needed.

17. **(D)** "It can be quite demoralizing" is the only option to put the words in a logical sequence. The other options place the subject, "it," later in the phrase, making the phrase confusing to the reader.

18. **(D)** Since just two questions are asked, there is no need for any punctuation to break up the sentence. All the other options inappropriately incorporate extra punctuation.

19. **(D)** "Feel" works along with the future tense to say they will feel; "felt" is in the past tense and would be inconsistent with the other verbs in the sentence. Also, the correct phrase is to "feel overwhelmed," i.e., that one is intimidated by all the work one has to do. "Overwhelming" can be used to describe a situation—my work load is overwhelming—but not to describe how one feels.

20. **(C)** No punctuation is required in this sentence. Choice (A) does not have a complete sentence after the semicolon. Choice (B) uses the dash to provide an unnecessary, awkward pause. And (D) unnecessarily sets aside "engineer" with commas, suggesting a parenthetical that is not needed; without "engineer," the sentence would not make sense.

21. **(C)** The difficult part here is that the correct answer simply looks odd, despite being flawless. A possessive form of understanding of the class is needed: "class's" understanding is the proper way to illustrate this. Choice (A) is both plural and lacking an apostrophe. Choice (B) is an improper way to indicate possession. (D) indicates multiple "classes," whereas there is actually only one class.

22. **(B)** We need a possessive word to serve as a stand-in for Truman and MacArthur. Eliminate choices (C) and (D) for being singular possessives. Eliminate (A) for not being a possessive at all. "Their" is the correct answer.

23. **(C)** The semicolon prevents a run-on sentence or comma splice; there is a complete sentence both before and after the semicolon. In addition to the key error of not breaking up two complete sentences, the other options have different problems: choice (A) has no breaks whatsoever, (B) has an unnecessary comma after "standing," and (D) does not have an apostrophe with "Edith" to show possession.

24. **(D)** "As" provides the needed transition to show cause-and-effect in this situation—the chef wants to work on a part-time basis because they could have more flexible scheduling. The other options do not show a cause-and-effect relationship.

25. **(C)** "However" is the only option that provides a contrast between the idea that laws may be in place and the opposite idea that guest workers can't take action when they experience unfair treatment.

26. **(D)** This option is the only one to specifically mention the leaders of the two armies at Gettysburg: Meade and Lee. Choice (A) is incorrect because Lincoln was not a general in command at the battle—Meade was. Choice (B) does not refer to the leaders. Choice (C) only mentions Lee.

27. **(D)** To calm a friend who is worried about psoriasis, the student would want to give the friend hope that if they had psoriasis, it should not be a cause for concern. Choice (D) correctly incorporates information from the notes, namely that "there are many treatment options." The other options would all highlight negative aspects of psoriasis, contributing to the friend's anxiety.

## Module 2B

1. **(B)** "Comply with" shows that people follow certain rules, which would be the logical choice given that they are agreeing to pay the fees. "Observe" is too passive, and "disobey" and "ignore" are the opposite of the intended meaning.

2. **(A)** The text is arguing that music can help "prompt" or "trigger" memory, thereby helping in learning in a variety of areas. It is not a physical "souvenir." It is not a way of speaking, like a "dialect." It is not trying to brainwash people into a particular way of thinking, like "indoctrination."

3. **(D)** The text as a whole describes Cullen in a positive light, so it makes sense to use "renowned," which means "respected." "Notorious" is too negative. "Imminent" describes something happening quickly. "Illustrated" is not supported by the passage since there is no mention of artwork accompanying his writings.

4. **(B)** The word "staple" takes on one of its less common definitions—it is not the physical staple that holds paper together; instead it signifies that the crop rotation is the "primary" choice for everyday soil management. It is not "periodic" because the text suggests that crop rotation is done consistently instead of occasionally. It is not "subsistent" because while subsistence has to do with food, the text is referring to the importance of crop rotation, not describing basic human nutrition. It is not (D) because this would put crop rotation in a negative light.

5. **(D)** "Impress upon" means to make someone understand something. In this case, the author is stating that students are rarely made to understand that the way to succeed in the stock market is through long-term, thoughtful investing. The students are not being "awarded" anything; nor are they having something "produced" for them. To "pan out" is to "end up" or "conclude," and the author is not suggesting that students will necessarily end up a certain way—instead, they are emphasizing that students need to be made to understand a concept.

6. **(A)** We see earlier in the text that the dog regarded the sausage as "booty" to which he was entitled, and so consumed it. The justification given in this selection is disingenuous, since the true reason the dog behaved as he did was a desire for food. It is not choice (B) because this is not a true excuse. It is not (C) because the dog does not display curiosity for the truth, but rather attempts to hide the truth. It is not (D) because the dog does not seem to care about finding common ground with the bird.

7. **(B)** Throughout this text, the author presents information to support his claim that fermentation is not solely limited to anaerobic organisms. To do this, he extensively explains the reasons why a human cell might use anaerobic fermentation. This best fits with choice (B). Choice (A) is incorrect as the text implies that respiration is the primary process whereby humans obtain energy. Choice (C) is incorrect as the author says that vigorous exercise would increase the chance of fermentation taking place. Choice (D) is incorrect as the text makes clear that when human muscles use fermentation: it is in addition to respiration, not instead of it.

8. **(B)** Although Clarinda continues to plead with her father, he states with a "terrible finality" that there is no other way than to proceed with meeting the bridegroom. Given that he no longer indulges her concerns and that he is rather abrupt, it makes sense to describe his attitude as "exasperated and dismissive." While it is possible that he expressed some of the emotions described in the other options elsewhere in the novel, we do not find evidence of these in the excerpt we see. Ultimately, he does not want to argue with her and simply states what she must do.

9. **(C)** The text states that, at minimum, Descartes can reject a concept if he finds "some ground for doubt." Hence, (C) is his threshold for dismissal. Choices (A) and (B) suggest that Descartes would have to find a more considerable flaw. Finally, dismissing all knowledge as in (D) is not his goal—he wants to have knowledge so long as it is well-justified.

10. **(D)** The economist claims that most people who participate in a pyramid scheme are likely to make money. The table, however, shows that in a classic pyramid scheme, only about 12.49% of participants profit. 12.49% is far less than 50%, showing that the economist's claim is incorrect. Choices (A) and (B) select information from the table that would support, not weaken, the economist's claim. It is not (C) because this gives no information about the proportion of participants who profit.

11. **(D)** The student wants to show that the narrator realizes that light is necessary for shadows to exist. Choice (D) effectively illustrates this because in this selection, there is not sunlight because the sun was not yet up, and the shadow is "fast asleep in bed," showing that it needs the light to come into existence. While the other options all mention shadows, they do not describe the light as a necessary accompaniment to shadows.

12. **(D)** The astronomers hypothesize that the roads and buildings at Chaco Canyon align with both the regular cycles of the sun and the complicated multi-year dance of the moon. The author acknowledges that it will take many years to confirm this hypothesis. Choice (D) would provide the best support for this hypothesis since it would show that there is a clear pattern in the way that the moon appears in the canyon walls. While the other options would provide interesting information about the history of Chaco Canyon, they would not provide evidence in support of there being a regular pattern demonstrating the architectural purpose of the buildings in the canyon.

13. **(A)** In the figure, the cells with an asterisk are cancerous. The reader can learn this by reading the paragraph under the figure. Every cancerous cell has a taller bar than the corresponding noncancerous cell. This shows the reader that cancerous cells have a higher average rate of change and makes choice (A) the best option. Choice (B) is the opposite of the relationship shown in the figure. Choice (C) is not supported by the figure except in the lung cells, which would not provide a sufficiently broad conclusion. Choice (D) is incorrect as no cells on the table have a rate of change of zero.

14. **(D)** Choice (D) is the best option because in this quotation the author shares a solution for ending the building of tenements: making them unprofitable. This leads us to the conclusion that they are only built because they are profitable. Choice (A) is incorrect as it discusses the desire to build tenement style houses, but not why the desire exists. Choice (B) is incorrect as it talks about the unchanging style of the tenements, but again, not about why they don't change. Choice (C) is incorrect because it discusses the public perception of tenement houses, but not why they are built.

15. **(A)** The text contends that the range of effects associated with thalassemia is so broad because there is a redundancy, namely, four copies of the $\alpha$ globin gene. So, we can infer that the disorder would be more uniform, or consistent, if there were fewer copies. The text even suggests that the severity is based on how many copies of the gene are defective—one defective gene produces mild complications, while four defective genes would be lethal. Choice (B) would not change the scope of intensity. Choice (C) would likely increase the variation. Choice (D) does not make sense because the text gives no suggestion that less research on the human genome would relate to a greater uniformity of outcomes.

16. **(D)** A brief pause is needed after the introductory word "similarly." Choices (A) and (B) do not have this needed pause, and both have an unnecessary pause in the middle of the selection. Choice (C) unnecessarily introduces a semicolon when there is not a complete sentence before it.

17. **(C)** This option puts the words in a logical order: "Cannon" should immediately begin the phrase because he was the one who graduated from the program in New Mexico. Choices (A) and (B) put "Cannon" later in the sentence, and choice (D) puts the phrase "studied briefly" later than it should be to maintain a logical flow.

18. **(B)** "Preferred" is correctly used as an adjective in this context, signifying that it is the type of food that the birds most strongly like. The other forms of "prefer" given in the answer options would typically be used as verbs.

19. **(D)** When using parentheses, treat the surrounding punctuation as though the parenthetical phrase were not even there. Choice (D) correctly does this by having a comma after the parenthetical phrase and before a needed clarification. Choice (A) incorrectly places a comma after "Dunn," and choices (B) and (C) add an unnecessary comma after "first."

20. **(C)** "Wreak havoc" means to cause destruction and chaos. The other options use improper phrasing. Choices (A) and (B) use "wreck" instead of "wreak," and (D) uses the incorrect preposition "toward."

21. **(D)** The phrase "through the CAM adaptation" could be removed from the sentence and the sentence would still be logical, so dashes on either side of the phrase would be appropriate in offsetting it. Choice (A) has the colon at an inappropriate spot that would cause the pause to be quite abrupt. Choice (B) uses inconsistent punctuation on either side of the parenthetical phrase. Choice (C) does not have a complete sentence after the semicolon.

22. **(A)** This is the only option that correctly surrounds the clarifying phrase with commas. Choices (B) and (D) do not surround the clarifying phrase with punctuation, and choice (C) places the punctuation after "many," making it come too late to help the flow of the sentence.

23. **(B)** The narrator is arguing that fertilizers and herbicides have negative impacts and thus their use should be minimized. The text first justifies this by stating that herbicide and fertilizer use can be quite expensive. Then the text highlights the negative environmental consequences. Since this is an "additional" shortcoming of using chemicals in farming, "In addition" is the best option. The sentence is not showing a contrast as in choice (A). Choices (C) and (D) would show a cause-and-effect relationship, which is not supported by the context.

24. **(A)** The sentence prior to the needed insertion states that the human body comes with a variety of flaws. The insertion then needs to transition into the example of how humans cannot efficiently filter cholesterol from their blood. Thus, "for example" is the best option. It is not choices (B) or (D) because there is not a contrast. It is not (C) because this is not a "peripheral" or loosely related idea; instead, it provides an example that directly connects to the text.

25. **(B)** The student wants to suggest a type of person who would benefit if female trees were planted in their neighborhood. Based on the notes, female trees "absorb pollen out of the air and can help reduce allergy symptoms." So, someone who had pollen allergies would very likely benefit from having mostly female tree plantings. It is not choice A because female trees produce nuts. It is not (C) because the text implies that all types of trees—both male and female—produce leaves. It is not (D) because female trees would produce fruit and so would not be helpful to someone trying to avoid fruit.

26. **(B)** Be sure to pick up on the "not" in the question—we want something that would not likely be part of the public domain. According to the notes, it will take 70 years after the death of a work's author to be in the public domain. Also, if something is created privately it is not in the public domain. Therefore, a newly created private work would not be in the public domain, as in choice (B). It is not (A) because this is a publicly created work and would be in the public domain. It is not (C) or (D) because these options both suggest things that would be in the public domain. (Choice (C) is correct in terms of such a novel being in the public domain, while choice (D) is incorrect.)

27. **(C)** According to the notes, free will is when someone's first-order desires and second-order desires align. For example, someone may have a first-order desire to eat junk food, but this would not align with a second-order desire to want to eat healthfully. If what the person wants to do aligns with what the person genuinely desires, then the person is acting freely. So, if someone genuinely wanted to eat more healthfully and actually feels like eating healthier foods, the person would be acting freely according to Frankfurt. A plausible reason why Frankfurt would not consider an animal to possess free will is that an animal may only be able to have straightforward wants without the ability to reflect on whether those wants are what it truly desires. So, choice (C) would make sense. It is not (A) because this would support that the animals have free will given their ability to reflect. It is not (B) because first-order desires would be needed to have second-order desires. It is not (D) because this would place humans and animals in the same category as far as having no capacity to reflect on whether certain wants are genuinely desirable.



## Math

### Module 1

1. **(C)** Distribute the $\frac{1}{2}x^3$ to simplify:

$$\frac{1}{2}x^3(x^2 - 4) \rightarrow$$

$$\left(\frac{1}{2}x^3\right)(x^2) + \left(\frac{1}{2}x^3\right)(-4) \rightarrow$$

$$\frac{1}{2}x^5 - 2x^3$$

2. **(210)** 5% of 200 is found as follows:

$$0.05 \times 200 = 10$$

Then, add 10 to 200 to find the number that would be 5% greater than 200:

$$10 + 200 = 210$$

3. **(A)** In 1970, the value of the price is clearly less than \$500. The only option that is less than \$500 is choice (A), \$245.

4. **(D)** Use elimination to solve for $a$, which is the value of $x$ in this series of equations. First, eliminate the $x$ by multiplying the second equation by $-2$ and adding it to the first equation.

$$\begin{aligned} 2x - 5y &= 3 \\ x + 2y &= 6 \rightarrow \\ 2x - 5y &= 3 \\ + -2x - 4y &= -12 \\ \hline 0 - 9y &= -9 \end{aligned}$$

Then, solve for $y$:

$$-9y = -9 \rightarrow$$
$$y = 1$$

Now, plug 1 in for $y$ to one of the equations to solve for $x$. Use the second equation since it is simpler.

$$x + 2y = 6 \rightarrow x + 2(1) = 6 \rightarrow x = 4$$

5. **(B)** Call $x$ the original price of the book prior to the discount. Since there was a 10% discount, the price after the discount is applied is 90% of the original price. So, set up an equation to solve for the original price:

$$0.9x = 18 \rightarrow$$
$$x = \frac{18}{0.9} = 20$$

So, the original price is $20.

6. **(A)** First, find the height of the actual Statue of Liberty in centimeters by multiplying 93 meters by 100 centimeters per meter:

$$93 \times 100 = 9{,}300$$

Then, find 1/500th of 9,300 to find the height of the model in centimeters:

$$9{,}300 \times \frac{1}{500} = 18.6$$

18.6 rounds up to 19 whole centimeters.

7. **(C)** Use easily visible points on the function to plug in values to determine the correct equation. First, try the point (0, 1) into the equations to see what can be eliminated.

(A) $f(x) = x^2 \rightarrow 1 \neq 0^2$ so (A) is incorrect.
(B) $f(x) = x^2 + 1 \rightarrow 1 = 0^2 + 1$ so (B) is a possibility.
(C) $f(x) = 2^x \rightarrow 1 = 2^0$ so (C) is a possibility.
(D) $f(x) = 3^x + 1 \rightarrow 1 = 3^0 + 1 \rightarrow 1 \neq 2$, so (D) is incorrect.

Now, try the point (2, 4) with options (B) and (C):

(B) $f(x) = x^2 + 1 \rightarrow 4 \neq 2^2 + 1$ so (B) is incorrect.
(C) $f(x) = 2^x \rightarrow 4 = 2^2$ so (C) is correct.

Alternatively, you could graph each of the answers using the Desmos calculator embedded in the math test to visualize the different functions.

8. **(40)**

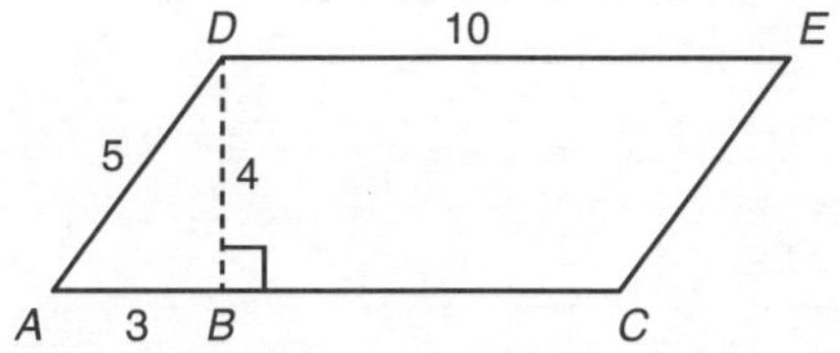


The area of a parallelogram is the base multiplied by the height. The base of the parallelogram is 10, and the height is 4 since it is part of a 3-4-5 special right triangle. Therefore, the area of the parallelogram is $4 \times 10 = 40$ square units.

9. **(B)** Manipulate the equation to get $R$ by itself:

$$A = \frac{v^2}{R} \rightarrow A \times R = \frac{v^2 R}{R} \rightarrow A \times R = v^2 \rightarrow R = \frac{v^2}{A}$$

10. **(B)** Plug in 2 for $x$ and 17 for $y$, then solve for $b$:

$$y = bx^2 + 5 \rightarrow$$
$$17 = b(2)^2 + 5 \rightarrow$$
$$17 = 4b + 5 \rightarrow$$
$$12 = 4b \rightarrow$$
$$b = 3$$

11. **(300)** Divide 3,000 miles by 10 hours to solve for the speed in miles per hour:

$$\frac{3000 \text{ miles}}{10 \text{ hours}} = 300 \text{ miles per hour}$$

12. **(1)** Use elimination to solve for $y$. Multiply the top equation by $-2$ so you can eliminate the $x$ values when you add the equations together:

$$-2 \times (2x - 3y = 5) \rightarrow -4x + 6y = -10$$

Then, add this equation to the second equation to eliminate the $x$ values:

$$-\ 4x + 6y = -10$$
$$+\ \underline{4x + y = 17}$$
$$0 + 7y = 7$$

Then, solve for $y$:

$$7y = 7 \rightarrow y = 1$$

So, the value of $y$ is equal to 1.

13. **(D)** Use $x$ as the capacity for the smaller bag, and $y$ as the capacity for the larger bag. Set up two equations to solve. First, make an equation that expresses the capacities in terms of each other:

$$x = \frac{1}{3}y$$

Then, make an equation expressing the total capacity of the two bags:

$$x + y = 80$$

Then, simplify and use substitution to solve for the capacity of the smaller bag, $x$:

$$x = \frac{1}{3}y \rightarrow 3x = y$$

Plug $3x$ into the second equation to solve:

$$x + y = 80 \rightarrow x + 3x = 80 \rightarrow 4x = 80 \rightarrow x = 20$$

So, the capacity of the smaller bag is 20 liters.

14. **(B)** Use the fact that $f(2) = 8$ to find what the constant $C$ is. According to the table, $f(2) = 2^C$. So, solve for $C$:

$$f(2) = 2^C \rightarrow$$
$$8 = 2^C \rightarrow$$
$$2^3 = 2^C \rightarrow$$
$$C = 3$$

Now that we know that $C = 3$, we can solve for $f(3)$:

$$f(3) = 3^C = 3^3 = 27$$

15. **(10)** Let $h$ represent the height of the triangle and let $b$ represent the width of the base of the triangle. Express the idea that the height of the triangle is twice its width with this equation:

$$h = 2b$$

The formula to calculate the area of a triangle is $A = \frac{1}{2}bh$. Substitute 25 for the area and $\frac{h}{2} = b$ from manipulating the above equation, then solve for the height:

$$A = \frac{1}{2}bh \rightarrow 25 = \frac{1}{2}\left(\frac{h}{2}\right)h \rightarrow 25 = \frac{h^2}{4} \rightarrow 100 = h^2 \rightarrow 10 = h$$

The height is therefore 10 units.

16. **(A)** Look at the differences among the answer choices to save yourself time. We need a function that will show an exponential increase over time. In the function $I(T) = 2 \times (1.5)^T$, as $T$ increases, $I(T)$ would also increase at an exponential rate. With all of the other options, however, as $T$ increases, the value of $I(T)$ would consistently *decrease*. Choice (B) would involve multiplying by an ever-smaller fraction, and choices (C) and (D) would involve dividing by ever-larger numbers. So, the only logical option is choice (A).

17. **(D)** Take the 300 cubic meters and multiply it by the density for steel, 7,850 kilograms per cubic meter, to get the total mass of the wall:

$$300 \times 7{,}850 = 2{,}355{,}000 \text{ kilograms}$$

18. **(65.8)** Calculate the total height of the seven boys by using the mean formula and solving for the sum:

$$\frac{Sum}{7} = 67 \to Sum = 469$$

Now, subtract the height of 74 from the total:

$$469 - 74 = 395$$

Finally, find the mean of the six boys using 395 as the sum:

$$\frac{395}{6} \approx 65.8$$

19. **(B)** $\angle X$ and $(90 - \angle X)$ are complementary angles, since they would add up to 90 degrees. Recall that the sine of one angle is equal to the cosine of the angle that is complementary to it; similarly, the cosine of one angle is equal to the sine of the angle that is complementary to it. Thus, the sine of $(90 - \angle X)$ will simply be the same as the cosine of $\angle X$: $\frac{\sqrt{2}}{2}$.

20. **(B)** Factor the expression to determine what *would* be factors:

$$x^3 + x^2 - 20x \to$$
$$x(x^2 + x - 20) \to$$
$$x(x - 4)(x + 5)$$

So, choices (A), (C), and (D) would all be factors. Choice (B), $x - 7$, would not be, so choice (B) is correct.

$$x^3 + x^2 - 20x$$

21. **(B)** Since the cards are returned to the set after each selection, the total number of choices will remain at 10. So, the probability that someone would pick a 9 on this selection would simply be $\frac{1}{10}$.

22. **(D)** Simplify the equation to visualize what is happening:

$$3x - 6 = 3(x - a) \to$$
$$3x - 6 = 3x - 3a$$

If the constant $a$ is greater than 2, then $3a$ would be greater than 6. This would result in an absurd situation since the equation would no longer express an equivalence. For example, if $a$ were 3 (a value greater than 2), look at what happens to the equation:

$$3x - 6 = 3x - 3a \to$$
$$3x - 6 = 3x - 9 \to$$
$$-6 \neq -9$$

Thus, the equation would have no solutions if the constant $a$ is greater than 2.

## Module 2A

1. **(A)** Put the equation into slope-intercept form, $y = mx + b$ to solve for the value of the $y$-intercept, $b$:

$$y + 5 = 7x \rightarrow$$
$$y = 7x - 5$$

So, the value of the $y$-intercept is $-5$.

2. **(C)** Since there are 20 students, find the number of the servings by the 10th and 11th students to see the median of the set. The values are already in order, so you can see that the 10th and 11th terms are both 6. Therefore, the median of the set is 6.

3. **(B)**

$$\frac{x^2 - 81}{x + 9} \rightarrow$$
$$\frac{(x + 9)(x - 9)}{x + 9} \rightarrow$$
$$\frac{\cancel{(x + 9)}(x - 9)}{\cancel{x + 9}} \rightarrow$$
$$x - 9$$

4. **(B)** Two points that are easy to identify are $(-6, 0)$ and $(0, 4)$. So, take the slope using these two points.

$$slope = \frac{y_2 - y_1}{x_2 - x_1} = \frac{4 - 0}{0 - -6} = \frac{4}{6} = \frac{2}{3}$$

5. **(A)** Since the total distance of the trail is 300 and Walter has already traveled 100 miles, he has $300 - 100 = 200$ miles remaining on his journey. Use the equation Distance $= \frac{\text{Rate}}{\text{Time}}$ to solve.

He has to travel a total of 200 miles in D days, and we are solving for the $m$ miles per day he is travelling. So, the equation will be:

$$\text{Distance} = \frac{\text{Rate}}{\text{Time}} \rightarrow$$
$$m = \frac{200}{D}$$

6. **(A)** Distribute and simplify:

$$2(x - 4) + 4 \rightarrow$$
$$2x - 8 + 4 \rightarrow$$
$$2x - 4$$

7. **(D)** In the function $C(m) = 10m + 10{,}000$, the 10,000 represents the fixed cost to run the restaurant, and the 10 represents the additional cost to the restaurant for each additional meal. If no meals were served, the total cost would be \$10,000. If one meal were served, the total cost would be \$10,010. If two meals were served, the total cost would be \$10,020. So, the cost is going up by \$10 for each additional meal sold.

8. **(A)** Put the equation $\frac{1}{2}y + 2 = -x$ in slope-intercept form, $y = mx + b$:

$$\frac{1}{2}y + 2 = -x \rightarrow$$

$$\frac{1}{2}y = -x - 2 \rightarrow$$

$$y = -2x - 4$$

The equation therefore has a slope of $-2$ and a $y$-intercept of $-4$. This corresponds to choice (A), as graphed below:

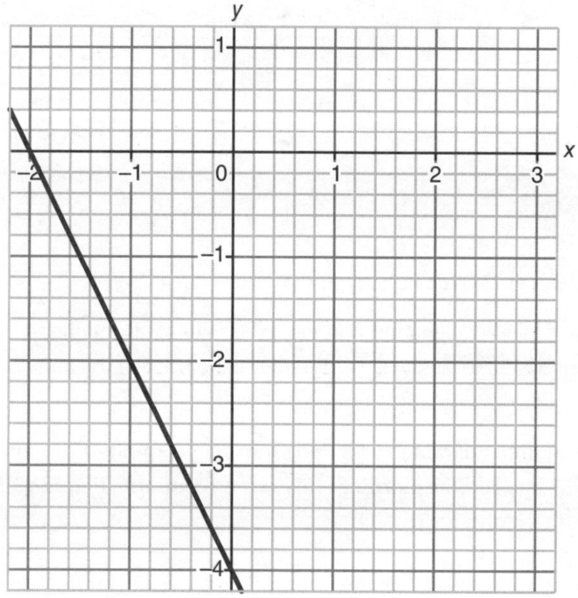


9. **(B)** Subtract the fractions from 1 (which represents the total set of voters) to find the fraction of voters who do not like either candidate:

$$1 - \frac{1}{2} - \frac{1}{3} \rightarrow$$

Put everything in terms of the least common denominator, 6:

$$\frac{6}{6} - \frac{3}{6} - \frac{2}{6} = \frac{1}{6}$$

So, the probability that a randomly selected voter will like neither candidate is $\frac{1}{6}$.

10. **(50)** Let $x$ represent the number of forks, and $y$ represent the number of spoons. The first equation could be for the total number of forks and spoons:

$$x + y = 80$$

The second equation would show the ratio of forks to spoons:

$$\frac{x}{y} = \frac{5}{3}$$

Now, simplify the second equation and substitute into the first equation to solve for $x$.

$$\frac{x}{y} = \frac{5}{3} \rightarrow 3x = 5y \rightarrow y = 0.6x$$

Plug $0.6x$ in for $y$ in the first equation:

$$x + y = 80 \rightarrow x + 0.6x = 80 \rightarrow 1.6x = 80 \rightarrow x = \frac{80}{1.6} = 50$$

So, there are 50 forks in the drawer.

11. **(A)** Between the hours of 7 a.m. and 9 a.m., the traffic density increases from 20 vehicles per mile per lane to 40 vehicles per mile per lane. This is the largest increase in traffic density between any of the intervals.

12. **(B)** Plug the second inequality $x \leq -y - 2$ into $y + 10 \leq 3x$ and simplify:

$$y + 10 \leq 3x \rightarrow$$
$$y + 10 \leq 3(-y - 2) \rightarrow$$
$$y + 10 \leq -3y - 6 \rightarrow$$
$$4y + 10 \leq -6 \rightarrow$$
$$4y \leq -16 \rightarrow$$
$$y \leq -4$$

So, the largest possible value for $y$ is found when $y = -4$.

13. **(C)** Since the cashier accidentally subtracted the sales tax from the price of the meal, the new percentage will be 100% − 7% = 93%. Therefore, the price of the meal in terms of $x$ will be $0.93x$.

14. **(35)** Call $x$ the number of minutes for Ken's morning commute. The commute in the evening would be $x + 25$. So, add the morning and evening commute times together to equal the 95 total minutes, then solve for $x$:

$$x + (x + 25) = 95 \rightarrow$$
$$2x + 25 = 95 \rightarrow$$
$$2x = 70 \rightarrow$$
$$x = 35$$

So, the number of minutes for the morning commute is 35.

15. **(B)** Plug 2 in for $x$ to find the value of $f(2)$:

$$f(x) = \frac{x^3}{4} + 3 \rightarrow$$
$$f(2) = \frac{2^3}{4} + 3 = \frac{8}{4} + 3 = 2 + 3 = 5$$

16. **(3)** The volume formula for a right rectangular prism is $L \times W \times H = V$. Since we already know the volume of the prism and the product of the length and width, we can set up a formula like this to solve for the prism's height:

$$L \times W \times H = V \rightarrow$$
$$30 \times H = 90 \rightarrow$$
$$H = \frac{90}{30} = 3$$

So, the height of the prism is 3 inches.

17. **(1)** Factor the equation to solve for the possible values of $x$:

$$x^2 - x - 20 = 0 \rightarrow$$
$$(x + 4)(x - 5) = 0$$

The possible values of $x$ are therefore $-4$ and 5 since each of these would make the entire left-hand side of the equation equal to zero. Then, add $-4$ and 5 to find the sum:

$$-4 + 5 = 1$$

18. **(B)** Set up a proportion to solve for the number of residents, $x$, who voted no. There are 360 degrees total in a circle, so make the proportion have degrees on one side and residents on the other:

$$\frac{45}{360} = \frac{x}{800} \rightarrow$$
$$x = \frac{45 \times 800}{360} = 100$$

So, there are 100 residents who voted no on the levy.

19. **(B)** Use the density formula $Density = \frac{Mass}{Volume}$, plugging in 2 kilograms for the mass and 8 liters for the volume:

$$Density = \frac{Mass}{Volume} \rightarrow$$
$$Density = \frac{2}{8} = \frac{1}{4}$$

20. **(B)** Take 35, divide it by 70, and multiply the result by 100 to determine what percentage 35 is of 70:

$$\frac{35}{70} \times 100 = 50\%$$

21. **(5)** Find the equation of the new line by calculating is slope—we already know that the $y$-intercept is 4. Take the negative reciprocal of the slope of the first line, $-3$, by flipping it and changing the sign.

$$-3 \rightarrow \frac{1}{3}$$

So, the equation of the new line is $y = \frac{1}{3}x + 4$. Calculate the value of a point on this line when the $x$ value is 3 by plugging 3 in for $x$:

$$y = \frac{1}{3}x + 4 \rightarrow$$
$$y = \frac{1}{3}(3) + 4 \rightarrow$$
$$y = 1 + 4 = 5$$

The $y$ value will thus be 5 for this point.

22. **(A)** While you could solve for the length of $\overline{AB}$ by using the Pythagorean triple, it will be easier if you recognize that this triangle represents a Pythagorean triple: 7, 24, and 25. With the hypotenuse at 25, the cosine of $\angle ABC$ will be:

$$\cos\theta = \frac{\text{Adjacent}}{\text{Hypotenuse}} = \frac{7}{25}$$

## Module 2B

1. **(C)** Plug 15 degrees in for $T$ to solve for the corresponding speed:

$$V = 331.4 + 0.6T \rightarrow$$
$$V = 331.4 + 0.6(15) = 340.4$$

2. **(C)** Since this line is written in slope-intercept form, $y = mx + b$, recognize that the slope is going to be $a$. A line that is perpendicular to this one will have a slope that is the negative reciprocal of $a$: $-\frac{1}{a}$. The only option that has this as its slope is choice (C).

3. **(A)** When dividing exponential expression that have the same base, subtract the exponents from one another:

$$\frac{x^{\frac{2}{3}}}{x^{\frac{1}{6}}} = \frac{x^a}{\sqrt{x}} \rightarrow \frac{x^{\frac{4}{6}}}{x^{\frac{1}{6}}} = \frac{x^a}{\sqrt{x}} \rightarrow x^{\left(\frac{4}{6}-\frac{1}{6}\right)} = \frac{x^a}{\sqrt{x}} \rightarrow x^{\left(\frac{3}{6}\right)} = \frac{x^a}{\sqrt{x}} \rightarrow x^{\left(\frac{1}{2}\right)} = \frac{x^a}{\sqrt{x}}$$

The square root of $x$ is equivalent to $x^{\frac{1}{2}}$. Substitute this in to the equation and simplify:

$$x^{\left(\frac{1}{2}\right)} = \frac{x^a}{\sqrt{x}} \rightarrow x^{\left(\frac{1}{2}\right)} = \frac{x^a}{x^{\left(\frac{1}{2}\right)}} \rightarrow x^{\left(\frac{1}{2}\right)}x^{\left(\frac{1}{2}\right)} = x^a \rightarrow x^1 = x^a$$

So, $x = 1$.

4. **(D)** Convert the miles per hour to feet per second by cancelling out terms:

$$\left(X\frac{\text{miles}}{\text{hour}}\right) \times \frac{5{,}280 \text{ feet}}{1 \text{ mile}} \times \frac{1 \text{ hour}}{3{,}600 \text{ seconds}} \rightarrow$$
$$\left(X\frac{\text{miles}}{\text{hour}}\right) \times \frac{5{,}280 \text{ feet}}{1 \text{ mile}} \times \frac{1 \text{ hour}}{3{,}600 \text{ seconds}} \rightarrow$$
$$= X \times \frac{5{,}280}{3{,}600}$$

This corresponds to choice (D).

5. **(B)** For the equation to have infinitely many solutions, the two sides of the equation should be equivalent. Simplify the left-hand side by dividing everything on that side by 2:

$$\frac{2x - 6}{2} = x + k \rightarrow$$
$$x - 3 = x + k$$

So, for the equation to have equivalent sides, the constant $k$ must equal $-3$.

6. **(B)** For an absolute value equation $3 = |x - 1|$, set up two separate equations to represent both the possible positive and negative values of what is inside the absolute value symbol:

Equation 1:

$$3 = x - 1 \rightarrow x = 4$$

Equation 2:

$$-3 = x - 1 \rightarrow x = -2$$

So, there will be two solutions to the equation, 4 and $-2$.

7. **(100)** Since the heartbeats and breaths have a linear relationship, you can solve for the number of heartbeats per minute by noticing that the breaths go up by 3 for every increase of 10 heartbeats per minute. So, if Baahir breathes 24 breaths per minute, add 10 + 10 to 80 to get 100 heartbeats for minute as his pulse.

8. **(C)** Factor the function to identify its zeros:

$$f(x) = x^2 - 3x - 4 \rightarrow (x - 4)(x + 1)$$

So, the function will intersect the $x$-axis at $x$ values of 4 and $-1$. Therefore, there are two points at which the function will intersect the $x$-axis.

9. **(0)** For the function $f(x)$ to intercept the $y$-axis, it must have a value of 0 for $x$. Here is what the function looks like when graphed:

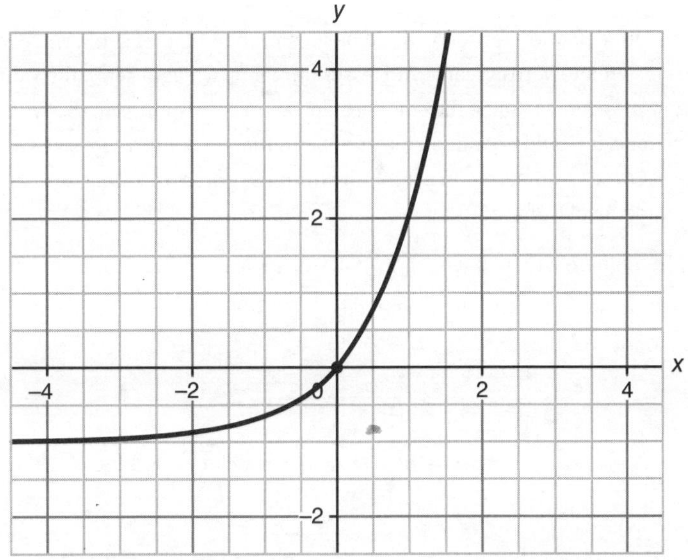


So, do not overthink this question—$x$ simply needs to be 0 for the function to intercept the $y$-axis.

10. **(A)** The population of the city is decreasing exponentially, so choices (C) and (D) can be eliminated since they would model exponential increase. Choice (A) portrays the correct initial population of 50,000 and correctly models a 10% decrease by multiplying by 0.9. Choice (B) has an incorrect initial population and far too great an exponential decrease.

11. **(C)** Since this is an isosceles triangle, the angles that are opposite the congruent sides are equivalent. So, angle $C$ has a measure of $n$.

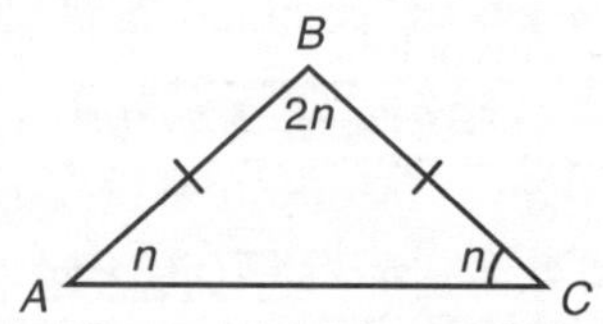


All of the internal angles in a triangle add up to 180 degrees, so solve for $n$ to find the measure of angle $C$:

$$n + n + 2n = 180 \rightarrow 4n = 180 \rightarrow n = 45$$

Thus, the measure of $\angle C$ is 45°.

12. **(B)** The standard deviation for set A would be greater than that for set B, since in set A, the values are clustered towards greater and lesser numbers, while in set B, the values are clustered around the average. Since the standard deviation corresponds to the typical deviation from the average, it would be much greater in Set A than in Set B. The range would be the same from set to set, and based on estimating from the graph, the mean and median would be relatively identical from set to set.

13. **(3.5 or $\frac{7}{2}$)** In a square with a diagonal of $7\sqrt{2}$ units, the sides are 7 units long since the triangle formed by two sides and the diagonal is a 45-45-90 triangle, which would have sides in a ratio of $x$, $x$, $x\sqrt{2}$.

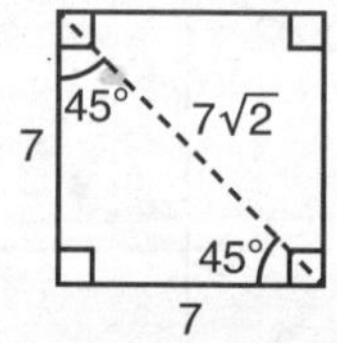


So, the largest possible circle that would fit within the square would have a diameter of 7 units, since it would go from one side to the other. Take half of 7 to find the radius: 3.5.

14. **(C)** Diana will need to walk an additional 4,000 steps since 10,000 − 6,000 = 4,000. Since she walks 100 steps in a minute, determine the number of additional minutes she will need to walk by dividing 4,000 by 100:

$$\frac{4000}{100} = 40$$

Now, convert 40 minutes to hours:

$$40 \text{ minutes} \times \frac{1 \text{ hour}}{60 \text{ minutes}} = \frac{2}{3} \text{ hour}$$

So, Diana will need to walk an additional $\frac{2}{3}$ of an hour on Tuesday.

15. **(C)** The value of $m$ is equivalent to the slope of the function. Since $g(1) = 7$ and $g(3) = 11$, use the ordered pairs (1, 7) and (3, 11) to calculate the slope of the line:

$$slope = \frac{y_2 - y_1}{x_2 - x_1} = \frac{11 - 7}{3 - 1} = \frac{4}{2} = 2$$

So, the value of $m$ is 2.

16. **(D)** The balloons both start at 200 feet in altitude. If one balloon increases its height by 30%, its new height will be $200 \times 1.3 = 260$ feet. If the other balloon decreases its height by 15%, its new height will be $200(1 - 0.15) = 200(.85) = 170$ feet. The different in height between the two balloons will then be $260 - 170 = 90$ feet.

17. **(D)** Use the quadratic formula to approach this problem:

$$x = \frac{-b \pm \sqrt{b^2 - 4ac}}{2a}$$

If the value of $b^2 - 4ac$ is negative, there will be no real solutions to the problem since the equation would require you to take the square root of a negative number. So, see what values of $b$ would make it such that there would be a negative value for $b^2 - 4ac$.

The equation $2x^2 + bx + 4 = 0$ is already in quadratic form, so you can identify that $a = 2$, $b = b$, and $c = 4$ for the purposes of plugging numbers in to the quadratic formula. We can just look at the value of $b^2 - 4ac$ to determine what values of $b$ would cause there to be only a negative value of the expression.

$$b^2 - 4ac < 0 \rightarrow$$
$$b^2 - 4(2)(4) < 0 \rightarrow$$
$$b^2 - 32 < 0 \rightarrow$$
$$b^2 < 32$$

Take the square root of both sides, adjusting for the potentially negative value of $b$:

$$b < +\sqrt{32} \text{ and } b > -\sqrt{32} \rightarrow$$
$$\sqrt{32} = \sqrt{16 \times 2} = 4\sqrt{2} \rightarrow$$
$$b < 4\sqrt{2} \text{ and } b > -4\sqrt{2}$$

The option that expresses this range of possible values is $|b| < 4\sqrt{2}$, since the absolute value would account for both possible negative and positive values for $b$ in this range.

18. **(1)** The function has zeros at $x$ values of $-3$ and 5 based on the equation. Also, the function has a negative coefficient, which means the direction of the function is downwards. So, the maximum of the function will be found at an $x$ value that is halfway between $-3$ and 5: 1. You can see this in the graph of the function below:

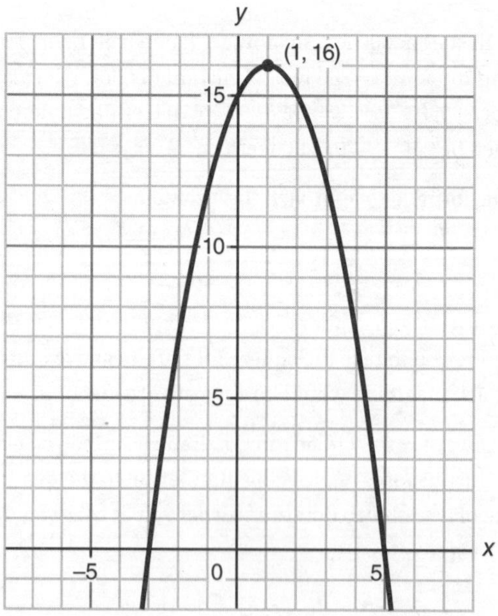


19. **(A)** Use $S$ as the number of small pizzas and $L$ as the number of large pizzas. The total number of pizzas sold in a month must be less than 800, so one inequality will be $S + L < 800$. The parlor needs to make at least \$10,000, so calculate the total revenue from the small pizzas by multiplying each small pizza by 10 and calculate the total revenue from the large pizzas by multiplying each large pizza by 20. This total needs to be greater than or equal to 10,000. So, the second inequality will be $10S + 20L \geq 10{,}000$.

20. **(C)** Based on the definition of $R_O$ as provided in the question, an $R_O$ of 4.2 means that one infected person will infect 4.2 other people. Thus, to determine the number of people that 20 people who are infected with a virus of $R_O$ of 4.2, simply multiply 4.2 by 20:

$$4.2 \times 20 = 84$$

21. **(D)** Since the median of the set is currently 6, adding a number that is 6 or greater would not change the median of the set. For example, if we added 6, the new set would be {2, 3, 6, 6, 6, 7}. This would still have a median of 6. If we add a number greater than 6, that too would be fine. For example, if we added 100 to the set, the set would be {2, 3, 6, 6, 7, 100}. The median of the new set would still be 6. Therefore, the correct answer is $x \geq 6$. It is not Choice (A) because this is not the "complete" set of potential values.

22. **(4)** The equation for a circle is $(x - h)^2 + (y - k)^2 = r^2$, in which $(h, k)$ is the center and $r$ is the radius. Memorize this equation because the SAT does not give it to you. The diameter of a circle is twice that of its radius. Take the square root of 49 to find the radius of circle A: $\sqrt{49} = 7$. The diameter of circle A will be twice seven: 14. Next, take the square root of 25 to find the radius of circle B: $\sqrt{25} = 5$. The diameter of circle B will be twice five: 10. Finally find the difference between the diameters of the two circles to arrive at the solution:

$$14 - 10 = 4$$

# Index